T0378141

The Dragon and the Eagle

This book's companion website (chinaandrome.org) presents the author's richly illustrated comparisons of many cultural and historical features of the Roman and early Chinese empires, as well as the "Silk Road" that linked East and West.

The Dragon and the Eagle

THE RISE AND FALL OF THE CHINESE AND ROMAN EMPIRES

Sunny Y. Auyang

Routledge
Taylor & Francis Group
LONDON AND NEW YORK

First published 2014 by M.E. Sharpe

Published 2015 by Routledge
2 Park Square, Milton Park, Abingdon, Oxon OX14 4RN
711 Third Avenue, New York, NY 10017, USA

Routledge is an imprint of the Taylor & Francis Group, an informa business

——— All maps and figures created by Sunny Y. Auyang ———

Library of Congress Cataloging-in-Publication Data

Auyang, Sunny Y.
The dragon and the eagle : the rise and fall of the Chinese and Roman empires / by Sunny Y. Auyang.
pages cm
Includes bibliographical references and index.
ISBN 978-0-7656-4369-8 (cloth : alk. paper)—ISBN 978-0-7656-4370-4 (pbk. : alk. paper)
1. China—History—Qin dynasty, 221–207 B.C. 2. China—History—Han dynasty, 202 B.C.–220 A.D. 3. Rome—History—Empire, 284–476. I. Title.

DS747.5.A89 2014
931′.04—dc23 2013035418

ISBN 13: 9780765643704 (pbk)
ISBN 13: 9780765643698 (hbk)

記念先父歐陽啓

To my father Auyang Kai
1922–2005

TABLE OF CONTENTS

FOREWORD

The Dragon and the Eagle: The Rise and Fall of the Chinese and Roman Empires is the proverbial exception to the academic historians' rule that only the works of specialists in a particular field deserve serious attention. Author Sunny Y. Auyang—who turned her attention to history after a long and successful career in physics at Massachusetts Institute of Technology—has produced an innovative, lucidly written, thoroughly researched, and illuminating study of the Han and Roman empires that will interest all historians of ancient China and Rome, and World History.

The subject is timely. The contemporary global situation in which the eastern and western extremes of the world are anchored by two superpowers—China and the United States—amazingly replicates conditions that existed two millennia ago. Then also two empires—the Han and Roman empires—occupied the eastern and western extremes of the known world. Both states were comparable, being roughly equal in size to the continental United States, while their populations together amounted to almost half the existing human species.[1] Although contact between these two great empires was minimal, each was vaguely aware of the other's existence. Until the end of antiquity, however, the Romans knew the Chinese only as the Seres, the silk people, who were the source of the fine fabrics the Roman elite valued so much. The Chinese were somewhat better informed about their western double. Their name for the Roman Empire was Da Qin, Greater China. The name itself allows no doubt that they viewed the Roman Empire as a state comparable in character to their own. Unfortunately, extant Chinese descriptions of the Roman Empire are mostly fantasy. It is not surprising, therefore, that the empires' respective histories were essentially unknown to each other.

Modern scholars have endeavored to fill the gap left by the ancient historians. Spurred by the remarkable rise of China as a political and economic power in the last few decades and questions about the contribution of the Confucian tradition to China's success, they have produced numerous comparative studies of China and the West. Most such studies, of course, have concentrated on contemporary issues, but a growing body of scholarship has appeared that compares ancient China with Greece and Rome. Scholars in the humanities have taken the lead in producing such studies, so it is not surprising that most concern cultural issues. The most notable examples of such works are Geoffrey Lloyd's perceptive monographs analyzing the contrasting ancient Chinese and Greek approaches to scientific thought and the audiences for science in both cultures, and their implications for the different developmental trajectories of Chinese and Greek science. Other scholars have worked on broader comparisons, particularly exploring similarities and differences between Confucian and Greek humanism.

Many of the same issues have engaged historians concerned with the comparative study of empires in general and ancient China and Rome in particular. This is particularly true of world historians for whom the comparison of Han China and Rome has become a staple of world history instruction. So far, however, the results have been meager, being limited to general chapters based largely on secondary scholarship in world history textbooks and works on empires. Stanford University recently established a large international collaborative project, the Stanford Ancient Chinese and Mediterranean Empires Comparative History Project, which has sponsored conferences and produced several volumes of scholarly essays. By their nature, however, such conferences and books focus on limited themes and provide at best only a partial view of what is a vast subject. What has hitherto been missing is a comparative history of Han China and the Roman Empire written by a single scholar that is firmly based on the original sources and current scholarship, but still accessible to a broad range of readers. *The Dragon and the Eagle* has filled this gap in scholarship.

Readers in search of a comparative history of the imperial careers of ancient China and Rome certainly will find that and much more in Dr. Auyang's fine book. They also will find illuminating analyses of the sociopolitical, administrative, and economic structures of both empires with often illuminating insights. She shows, for example, that contrary to received opinion, the upper levels of the administration of both empires were roughly the same size. On the other hand, while both empires faced similar frontier problems and adopted similar policies, they sought to achieve them with radically different militaries—the Romans with a larger, long-term professional army and the Chinese with a small standing force supplemented by short-term draftees. Most remarkable, however, is her revisionist account of the Qin dynasty and its legalist policies. She convincingly argues that the Qin dynasty's reputation as an arbitrary tyranny did not reflect historical reality but was the result of propagandistic rewriting of history during the Han Dynasty by Confucian literati, who saw in the legalist emphasis on the rule of law a rejection of the familial and ethical values they associated with the aristocratic traditions of the Zhou dynasty they revered.

Comparative history is hard to do well. The comparisons are often too broad and the conclusions too general to be useful. Dr. Auyang has avoided successfully these common pitfalls of comparative history. By so doing she has produced a valuable contribution to the historiography of world history in general and the history of Han China and Rome in particular. Every scholar interested in ancient empires will profit from reading this excellent work.

Stanley M. Burstein, Professor Emeritus
California State University, Los Angeles

Note

1. The estimate is by Walter Scheidel, "From the 'Great Convergence' to the 'First Great Divergence,'" in Walter Scheidel (ed.), *Rome and China: Comparative Studies on Ancient World Empires* (New York: Oxford University Press, 2009) p. 11.

GUIDE TO PRONUNCIATION OF CHINESE PINYIN

Pronunciation is as in English unless otherwise noted:

c	as in pu*ts*
ch	as in *ch*ow, but with the tip of the tongue curled up
g	as in *g*irl
j	as in *j*ingle
q	as in *ch*eap
sh	as in *sh*out, but with the tip of the tongue curled up
x	as in *sh*e
z	as in nee*ds*
zh	as in *j*aw, but with the tip of the tongue curled up
a	as in m*a*
ai	as in *ai*sle
ao	as in n*ow*
an	as in tr*an*quility
ang	*a* as in m*a* plus *ng* as in wro*ng*
e	as in th*e*
ei	as in h*ei*nous
en	as in chos*en*
eng	as in r*ung*
er	as in f*ur*ther
i	as in sh*ee*p; after c, s, z, as *i* in s*ir; after* ch, sh, zh, as *ir* in s*ir*
ian	(or yan), as in *Yan*cey
ie	as in *ye*t

iong	(or yong), as in German *jüng*en
iu	as in *yo*yo
in	as in d*in*
ing	as in p*ing*
o	as in p*o*t
ou	as in s*ou*l
ong	as in German Acht*ung*
u	as in r*u*le
ua	as in *wa*ter
uai	as in *why*
ue	as in d*ue*t
ui	as in *way*
uo	as in p*oor*
un	as in Spanish j*un*ta

INTRODUCTION

MIRRORS FROM THE DEEP PAST

Time is like a river made up of the events which happen, and a violent stream; for as soon as a thing has been seen, it is carried away, and another comes in its place, and this will be carried away too.

And, to say all in a word, everything which belongs to the body is a stream, and what belongs to the soul is a dream and vapour, and life is a warfare and a stranger's sojourn, and after-fame is oblivion. What then is that which is able to conduct a man?
—Marcus Aurelius, *Meditations*, 4.43, 2.17

Roll after roll, waters of the Yangzi eastward flow,
Away in their waves are all heroes flushed.
Enterprises, merits, gains, and losses turn to naught.
The green mountains forever stand,
How often in the sunset have they blushed?

White haired, I fish and gather wood along the river,
By autumn moons and spring breezes blessed.
Over a flask of old wine we joyously meet.
Things past and present, however numerous,
In talks and laughter we have them assessed.
—Luo Guanzhong, *The Three Kingdoms*

The year 202 BCE (before the Common Era) witnessed two epoch-making battles, one at the western end of the old world of civilization, the other at its eastern end. At Zama in northern Africa, Rome defeated its archenemy Carthage and cleared the roadblock to one of the greatest empires in history. At Gaixia south of the Yellow River, the Han defeated its archrival Chu and reunified China in an empire that matched the Roman Empire in scale, splendor, sophistication, and staying power. Similarities of the two empires have long caught the eyes of world historians, sociologists, and political scientists.[1] Comparative studies surged recently.[2] Some call the two histories "a great convergence."[3] The convergence is far from complete, however. Societies confronting similar problems may adopt similar solutions, but ingrained cultures and changing times foil any panacea or single best model for world history. Institutions and ideologies superb in one condition may flounder in another. Profound differences remained between the Roman and early Chinese Empires. The delineation and critical comparison of their distinctive styles in exercising power and maintaining order, symbolized by the Eagle and the Dragon, are the crux of this book.

Empire has recaptured headlines since the United States–led invasions of Afghanistan and Iraq. Its image tantalizes in the rapidly changing global economic and political orders, especially with the rise of China. A torrent of scholarly and popular publications appeared in the last decade on this form of dominating political regime, which some deem beneficial and durable, others exploitative and unsustainable.[4] Empires differ from small states in many ways. A small state with homogeneous population can achieve domestic consensus rather easily, but its differences with neighboring states often escalate into war. An empire controls or annexes many states, incorporates diverse peoples, suppresses their previous conflicts by coercion or acculturation, and reaps the dividend of prosperity. Peace is precarious, however. Cleavages within an empire's large and heterogeneous population introduce enormous complexity in government. Great distances within its territory, most formidable without modern communication and transportation technologies, increase the difficulty of cohesion.

Empires are rare. A scholar remarks in his book on current American foreign policy: "All told, there have been no more than seventy empires in history. If the *Times Atlas of World History* is to be believed, the American is, by my count, the sixty-eighth. (Communist China is the sixty-ninth; some would claim that the European Union is the seventieth.)"[5] Many of the sixty-seven past empires were ephemeral, regional, or purely predatory. Only a handful attained the status of world empire that contributed to prolonged stability and prosperity over a significant realm. Among the top entries on this short list are the contemporaneous Roman and early Chinese Empires. Each encompassed at its prime about one-quarter of the earth's population and preserved internal peace for centuries.[6] One declared *imperium orbis terrae*, domination over the earth; the other *yitong tianxia*, unity under heaven.[7] Both claimed manifest destiny behind their authority, one in *divinitus adjuncta fortuna*, divine injunction, the other in *tianming*, the mandate of heaven.[8]

This book compares the formative periods of western and eastern political orders beyond tribalism to study their respective style of power. It begins with the births of empire builders, the investiture of the state of Qin in 771 BCE and the foundation of the Roman Republic in 509 BCE. The stories end with the fall of northern China in 316 CE and the fall of the Western Roman Empire in 476 CE, each to a multitude of barbarian peoples that originated from beyond its northern frontier.

Each millennium-long history falls into two roughly equal parts, the rise to empire and the imperial reign. Separating the two is a two-decade pivotal period. The many kingdoms in China that had been warring for centuries were united in 221 BCE under Shihuangdì, the First Emperor of Qin. The prompt collapse of the Qin Dynasty led to a devastating civil war, which ended with the establishment of the durable Han Dynasty by Gaodì after the 202 BCE battle of Gaixia. A similar transition from empire building to civil war to imperial peace occurred later in the West. Julius Caesar crowned centuries of Roman conquests, then violently turned against the Republic in 48 BCE. After assassination ended his dictatorship, the Mediterranean world again suffered wrenching civil wars until Augustus brought stability under the Roman Empire after the 31 BCE battle of Actium. The internal traumas, death knell of the Roman Republic and the birth pang of imperial China, left deep marks on the empires.

Parallel narratives of the rise and fall of empires provide the historical context for the book's central task: a comparative analysis of their relative strengths and weaknesses. Significant similarities in the Chinese and Roman realms alleviate the methodological trap of comparing apples to oranges. Both economies were agrarian but significantly monetized, with land the dominant form of wealth.[9] Both societies were conservative, stratified, and authoritarian, with the patriarchal family their basic unit.[10] Both governments were centralized monarchies, each directly ruling over a vast empire through provinces.[11] Upon this broad background, salient differences are discernible.

Empires flex their muscle, but not all great powers bully in the same way. Culture, especially culture of the political elite, exerts profound influence.[12] An imperial style bespeaks the mentality of its political decision makers: how they judge domestic and international situations with incomplete information, respond to perceived advantages or threats, and allocate limited resources among priorities at home and abroad. The rationales they give for their choices further reflect the worldview of their society. Like a "cultural gene" that continuously adapts to environmental contingencies, the worldview that predisposes behaviors takes a long time to evolve and never entirely forsakes its origin. Empires do not suddenly materialize in full grandeur, and they bear the imprints of their distinct experiences of early strife. The evolution of imperial styles reveals what social scientists call path dependency: an institution's structure partly depends on its genesis. The child is the father of the man.

At the beginnings of our stories, in each case about four centuries before empire formation, Rome and the Chinese states were all city sized. In terms of political organization and economic development, however, the differences between them were as large as that between the West and the East in the nineteenth century.[13] The Chinese world was still in the late Bronze Age, when feudalistic aristocrats basked in courtly elegance. The Mediterranean world was well into the Iron Age, when affordable metal tools and weapons empowered the working people. The ancient worlds did not interact, but put side by side, the two histories of rise to empire make a story of China catching up with the West at high speed.

At its birth, the Roman Republic's economic base was the independent proprietary farmers, who also constituted the citizen infantry. Private property rights were vital to them, who regarded their protection as a major aim of government. The Romans cherished the family, but legally separated it from the state; scions of aristocratic families had to win elections to government offices.[14] The Senate, forum, and judicial court, where various power holders bargained and jostled, fostered a notion of the public, civic virtue, and respect for the law, symbol and guardian of the commonwealth. Reasonable and patient negotiations on power relations facilitated accumulation of political experiences and institutional practices. In two centuries of struggle, backed by effective political organizations and service in the legions, the Roman people won for themselves civil liberties and political rights. The bloodless revolution produced a semidemocratic Republic, which put the bulk of power in the aristocratic Senate but balanced it with the elective and legislative powers of the popular assemblies.[15] The republican constitution enabled Rome to expand and acquire a huge empire. Its structure of checks and balances has become inspirational for modern political thinking, for instance in the framing of the United States Constitution.[16]

When Qin was founded at the western edge of the Chinese world, it joined the company of hundreds of tiny independent states. Their major weapon was the chariot, an aristocratic monopoly. Their main productive organization was communal farming; private land ownership was a notion to come. Their feudalistic state with hereditary ministries was mostly undifferentiated from the ruling family. Cementing this cozy structure were kinship and personal rapport, partially formalized in rituals.[17] Toward the end of the Bronze Age, when the feudalistic establishment began to crumble, Confucius flourished, an impoverished aristocrat attached to the ancient régime. He brought to commoners education previously reserved for his class and provided moral grounding for many of its values, which would persist to sway imperial China. The texts of feudalistic aristocrats, canonized in Confucianism, would mold the mind of imperial literati-officials for two millennia.[18] Nostalgia for sharing in the idealized communal farm partly explained why economic inequality in imperial China, though acute, never approached the stratospherical level in the Roman Empire.[19]

China passed into the Iron Age during the two centuries leading to political unification, traditionally called the Warring States period. Interstate competition and the energy unleashed by technological revolution created the most vibrant ferment in Chinese intellectual history. Diverse ideas flourished. Pragmatic innovators called Legalists promoted equality under the law and led economic development. Their reforms disentangled the state from the ruling family, introduced function-oriented administrative institutions, and opened government offices to diverse talents. The reformed states encouraged small proprietary farms by systematically distributing land to individual families in return for tax and service in the infantry, which replaced chariots in battlefields. The farmer-soldiers were akin to those of the Roman Republic, except Chinese kings bought off the people with land and economic incentives instead of the vote and political incentives offered by the Roman aristocracy. By building up an effective bureaucracy capable of harnessing the prowess of thriving small peasants, Legalists wrested power from feudalistic aristocrats and concentrated it on the monarch. Such was the sociopolitical structure underpinning Qin's unification of China. The First Emperor abolished the hereditary aristocracy and directly ruled the vast realm through a centralized bureaucracy. Its efficiency would have made Augustus envious.[20]

The empire builders have won wars, but military victory is not mission accomplished. Transitioning to stable rule is a hazardous hurdle that has littered history with transient empires. Rome and China survived brutal civil wars and won the peace, but both were scarred. Each lost a precious element that led it to greatness. For satisfaction of the ruling elites, the Roman Empire sacrificed the Republic's democratic ideal, imperial China its nascent rule by law. A sore weakness was left in the heart of the Eagle and the Dragon.

Rome's liberty and empowerment of citizens are adduced by modern historians as factors for the success of its empire.[21] This book argues that these factors worked only in the phase of aggressive expansion, when self-equipped citizens empowered themselves, partly by filling the Republic's legions. The Roman Empire that maintained peace and prosperity stripped citizens of all political rights. Legal rights also eroded. Social privileges shifted from citizenship to wealth. Eventually, poor Roman citizens, legally tied to the land, enjoyed less social freedom than Chinese subjects.[22]

Democratic elections of government officers were passé, but three power bases of the Republic held firm in the Eagle's character: arms, wealth, and the law. A large professional army protected the power of the emperor. Its maintenance in peacetime stimulated trade and the economy, as the military-industrial complex does in the modern world.[23] The Republic had reserved government offices for the rich and correlated a citizen's voting weight with the level of his wealth. The Empire heightened the wealth qualification to bar all but the largest landlords from the Senate, magistracies, and military commands. Across the Empire, native aristocrats sat in city councils and collected taxes for the emperor in return for his support of their local power. Uniting landlords of the world was a key to success that the Empire inherited from the Republic. Cohesion within the ruling class was furthered by the development of closely reasoned civil laws, which resolved disputes among the elites and grew the complex institution behind absolute property rights.[24] Throughout Roman history, militarism and legally backed plutocracy stood clear and unwavering. To keep the army and wealthy aristocrats in check and balanced was the emperor's most onerous and precarious job. When the two ceased to cooperate, dusk gathered in the Empire.[25]

Qin's legal supervision of officer behaviors antagonized the political elite nostalgic for aristocratic privileges untrammeled by accountability.[26] Confucianism, which preaches deference to superiors and family values as political principles, is more favorable to the ruling circle of a dynastic autocracy than is the Legalist rule by law. Politically sidelined for impracticality during demanding times, Confucianism resurged to become the state ideology in the tranquility of the Han Dynasty. Confucian literati colonized the bureaucracy, reduced the notion of law to that of punishment, regarded the state as the family writ large, and proselytized rule by great leaders, hopefully sagacious. Deftly smothering rival ideas by lofty but vague slogans, they gradually evolved into a cultural aristocracy based mainly on ideology and office holding, from which they derived great wealth.[27] The literati-officialdom, a prominent feature of the Dragon, was one of the most long-lived conservative political elites in world history. Its success depended much on the institutional architecture designed by Legalists: a centralized monarchy with bureaucratic administration, another characteristic of imperial China. Nevertheless, literati-officials vilified Legalist rule by law and subverted the bureaucracy's operational principles of efficiency and impersonal regulation by a culture of moralization and personal connection, *guanxi*. The result partly explains the curious bipolar images projected by the Chinese state. Focusing on institution building, a Western scholar remarks with emphasis, "there is good reason for paying closer attention to China than to Greece and Rome in studying the rise of the state, since China alone created a *modern* state." Focusing on government culture, other Western scholars find a weak notion of state: "China is a civilization pretending to be a nation-state."[28]

Sociologists study various sources of power: economic, ideological, and political, the third being analyzable into military and administrative.[29] All sources are necessary, but not necessarily in the same proportions. The Eagle's characteristic emphasis on integrating economic and military powers gave it a tinge of hardness. The Dragon's characteristic emphasis on integrating ideological and administrative powers gave it a tinge of softness. The imperial styles matured during the zeniths of the Roman and early Chinese Empires in their respective second century. How they shaped domestic and foreign policies constitutes a guiding thread through the book's second part, which analyzes and compares their relative efficacies under various conditions.

Both empires realized that superior might, although necessary, is not sufficient to imperial success. Also important is moral authority, the ability to shape perception, attract a following, and galvanize energy. Besides good governance and economic prosperity, authority calls on doctrine and propaganda that support might by right and preach compliance as duty. The hard imperial style featured prominently in Roman panegyric; the soft style in Chinese moralization. However, exalted words could not cover up what the empires had sacrificed. Augustus subverted the Republic but retained a republican facade to disguise his autocracy. The dissimulation fed succession crises and the bloody struggle between the emperor and the aristocrats. Imperial China adopted Legalist institutions but delegitimized them by ideological condemnation. The dissimulation vitiated administrative fairness and arrested rational political development. As the empires aged, harsh laws failed to suppress rampant corruption among Romans, and the morals of personal connections fueled corruption among Han literati-officials. The political elites fragmented into irreconcilable factions. Beneath stale rhetoric, special interests became entrenched, institutions calcified, and governments paralyzed. Weaknesses at the imperial heart grew and spread. As public spirit evaporated, Roman citizens hardly stirred to defend the Empire against barbarian invaders. With the law reviled, moralizing Han literati-officials morphed into brutal warlords. Eventually the empires, each the superpower in its world for centuries, fell to measly enemies. They were so weakened by the cancers in their internal constitutions that minor external infections became lethal.

Characteristic differences of the Chinese and Roman styles may help explain the divergent courses of history after the fall of empires that end our story. A narrow and irresponsible idealism repeatedly caused imperial China to close on itself, stagnate, and fall. The ensuing fire of civil war or foreign conquest burned away deadwood and released the energy of pragmatic ingenuity, just as the violence of warring states did in our stories. After the chaotic catharsis, a resilient institutional architecture and a dogmatic elite were like rhizomes that regenerate a devastated bamboo grove. The moral doctrine and exegetical thinking by which Confucian literati-officials bolstered both autocracy and their own privileged status under it are adaptable to serve new dynasties, even new regimes. The Chinese Empire reconstituted itself after the fall, a feat it would repeat several times in the Dragon's long history. The Roman Empire did not. Its political strength stemmed partly from alignment with the dominant economic class, but landed interests are necessarily regional. A far-flung empire based on the unity of landed wealth was a fluke difficult to repeat. Yet the Eagle would soar again. Rome's unlimited will to power survived like an acorn, which was portable. It would sprout again on more fertile grounds, in alignment with a more formidable dominant economic class, the capitalist. The realistic political thinking and reasonable discourse by which the Romans perfected the republican constitution are adaptable to develop laws and institutions for more complex worlds.

Rome is the paradigmatic empire in Western history. Its influence is so strong that the United States is often called the American Empire as a New Rome.[30] Imperial China lasted until 1911. Many cultural and political traits formed in the period of our study persisted through its history and are still significant in today's New China.[31] Because of their rich legacies, histories of ancient Rome and ancient China are of current relevance. Tang Taizong, eminent seventh-century Chinese emperor, claimed to treasure three mirrors: "The mirror of bronze brings knowledge about attire; the mirror of other people, personal strength and weakness; the mirror of history, the rise and fall of powers." "For it is history alone which without causing us harm enables us to judge what is the best course in any situation or circumstance," explained Polybius, the Greek statesman who in the second century BCE wrote the first history of the rise of Rome's empire.[32] The mirrors of ancient history may be hazy, but juxtaposed images of the Eagle and the Dragon can contribute to a better understanding of twenty-first-century geopolitics.

* * *

In the chapters that follow, the imperial styles outlined above will be substantiated by detailed information on each side. Written for general readers unfamiliar with the history of China or Rome, this book integrates narrative with extensive explanation and analysis. Each chapter—counting Chapters 6 and 7 as one—comprises three parts of comparable lengths. The narrative of China claims one block of text, that of Rome another, both peppered with parallelism and cross-reference. Besides background information, they present the context and serve as a reality check for comparative interpretation—action is more revealing than rhetoric about characters. Investigation of historical forces is reserved for the remaining third of the chapter. The comparative analysis is thematic. Many analytic topics begin with a question and the ideas that frame it. The general explanation is immediately instantiated in particular

Chinese and Roman cases, sometimes within a single paragraph, to accentuate their similarity and contrast, or to create a kind of dialogue. In comparing, my concern is always on the relative, not the absolute; on more or less, not all or none. For instance, the statecraft of both empires utilized all available means from war to psychological manipulation. Difference in styles resides in their relative emphases on one method or another.

The historiographies for China and Rome have each accrued a long tradition and multiple interpretations, Eastern, Western, ancient, modern, postmodern, imperialist, liberal, Marxist, revisionist, and more, often mutually contradictory. Debates are perennial. This book challenges many received views, such as the reasons for Qin's fall and the nature of Rome's grand strategy. The alternative explanations it offers are of course disputable. I try to provide scholarly defense in the space allowed. This book being an introductory attempt that crams too much in too few pages, I am contented if it raises interesting questions without providing definitive answers.

I am indebted to all the modern scholars whose works I cite in the notes, and I apologize for the decision to omit their names in the main text because of the desire to avoid confusion and memory overload in the general reader. The two large historical casts with strange-sounding names are formidable enough.

Notes

Translations from the Chinese-language literature are mine, except otherwise specified in the notes. Chinese classics are cited by title followed by chapter number or chapter title, which is quite standard. Paragraph numbering is not standard. Those provided here are from the editions specified in the bibliography. For the *Standard Histories* (*Shiji*, *Hanshu*, *Houhanshu*, *Sanguozhi*, and *Jinshu*), I use the Zhonghua Shuju edition with notation such as "*Shiji* 6: 235" for chapter 6, page 235. The annals *Zuozhuan* are traditionally cited according to year such as Xi 2, the second year of Lord Xi of Lu (658 BCE). Paragraph numbers of Western classics are almost standard. References to modern works are by page number. All citations of Section x.x refer to sections of this book.

1. McNeill 1963: 324. Mann 1988: 42–51. Finer 1997: 532–536.

2. Scheidel 2009c. Mutschler and Mittag 2009. Kalinowski, Deng, and Bujard 2009. Lloyd 2005: Ch. 35. Burbank and Cooper 2010: Ch. 2. Morris 2010: Chs. 4–5. Fukuyama 2011: Chs. 3–5.

3. Scheidel 2009a: 11, 18–22.

4. Abernethy 2000. Maier 2006. Münkler 2007. Burbank and Cooper 2010. Parsons 2010.

5. Ferguson 2004: 14.
6. Scheidel 2009a: 11.
7. Harris 1979: 129. *Shiji* 6: 235, 243, 247.
8. Brunt 1978: 165. Hsu and Linduff 1988: 101.
9. Section 2.2.
10. Section 2.3.
11. Sections 6.2, 6.6.
12. Taliaferro, Lobell, and Ripsman 2009.
13. Section 2.2.
14. Sections 2.2, 2.3.
15. Sections 2.4, 2.6.
16. Finer 1997: 396. Millar 2002b: 120–134. Sellers 2004.
17. Sections 2.2, 2.3, 2.7.
18. Sections 2.8, 2.9, 5.6, 6.9.
19. Sections 8.3.
20. Sections 2.8, 2.9, 2.10, 4.4.
21. Doyle 1986: 97–99. Burbank and Cooper 2010: 4, 58.
22. Sections 6.2, 6.8, 8.3.
23. Sections 5.1, 6.1.
24. Sections 2.4, 2.6, 6.4, 6.9.
25. Sections 2.10, 6.1, 8.4.
26. Sections 4.4, 4.5.
27. Sections 5.6, 5.7, 6.9, 8.4.
28. Fukuyama 2011: 21. Lucian Pye quoted in Jacques 2009: 374.
29. Mann 1986: 2, 22–28.
30. Nye 2002. James 2006. Maier 2006. Madden 2007. Murphy 2007.
31. Pye 1985. Ropp 1990. Tu 1996. Wong 1997. Hui 2005. Yan 2011.
32. Polybius, 1.35.

PART I

THE ROMAN REPUBLIC AND PRE-IMPERIAL CHINA

CHAPTER 1

NATION FORMATION

1.1 The Old World of Civilization

The names *Asia* and *Europe*—derived from the Assyrian *Asu* and *Ereb* and meaning "land of the rising sun" and "land of the setting sun"—have referred to various places in their long history; Asia was once a Roman province in now western Turkey. Their present referents, as continents, are Eurocentric constructs; Europe is actually a large peninsula of a continent. The physical water-surrounded landmass is Eurasia, which with neighboring Africa constitutes the Old World of human civilization.

Four empires—the Roman, Parthian, Kushan, and Han—spanned the mid-latitude Old World at the beginning of the Common Era (Map 1). In the great Eurasian steppe to their north, the nomadic empire of the Xiongnu was disintegrating under Han pressure. Much of Parthia and Kushan, now the Middle East and Central Asia, fell under Alexander's empire in the late fourth century BCE. The Hellenistic rule was brief, however, especially in the eastern regions. When the first Han envoy reached Central Asia in 128 BCE, the nomads with whom he sought an anti-Xiongnu alliance were on the verge of ousting the Greek remnants in now northern Afghanistan to create the Kushan.[1] By the second century CE, the Greeks and Romans were so starved of information about the east that the travel of one merchant from the Mediterranean to the Parmir, short of China, became the key data for debate between two prominent geographers.[2]

More than 3,000 kilometers of rugged terrain separated the Han and Roman Empires at their peak expansions. The Han sent an emissary to Rome, but the mission was aborted somewhere in Mesopotamia for unclear reasons. Someone claiming to be a herald of the Roman Emperor landed in the part of Han Empire that is now Vietnam, but his authenticity was doubted by historians ancient and modern. Rome, which had no habit of sending diplomats, left no hint for it.[3] After surveying extensive research, a scholar concludes: "In sum, the absence of archeological or textual evidence suggests surprisingly little contact between ancient Rome and the Han dynasty."[4]

Nothing in the world is completely isolated. Imperial peace and consumption encouraged patchworks of long-distance trade, overland and maritime, which would develop over subsequent centuries into the Silk Routes (Map 2).[5] Chinese silk was a coveted luxury in Rome. Magicians, probably Roman slaves, were gifts sent by Parthian kings to perform in the Han court. However, those who traveled the Silk Routes from end to end were rare indeed. Almost all commerce and communication were relay efforts, mediated by the Kushans and Parthians, by peoples of oases and the steppe along the caravan routes, or by inhabitants of ports that hosted voyagers. Goods may survive intact after passing through a hundred hands, but information deteriorated after repeated passages from mouths to ears and translations via many tongues. Consequently, Rome and Han had little knowledge about each other beyond the fact of the other's existence. The action of one may have affected the other, but only indirectly, such as through the movements of nomads in the northern steppe. If the other reacted, it was only to the secondary or tertiary effects, as Rome responded only to the agitation of barbarians at its frontier, heedless of whether the unrest was caused by pressure from nomads used to fighting the Han.[6] Rome and Han China were interrelated but did not interact.

In view of the weak interrelation compared to strong internal dynamics, I am content to relegate mutual perception and trade to Appendices 1 and 2. The main text treats the Roman and early Chinese Empires as essentially isolated entities in a comparative study.

"There are 12,233,062 common households and 59,594,978 mouths. The Han is at peak prosperity"; thus Ban Gu summarized the Han Dynasty's 2 CE census of the imperial realm, after recording analytic census data for 103 province-level jurisdictions.[7] His *Book of Han* is the second of twenty-six *Standard Histories* that continuously cover almost three millennia of Chinese history down to the end of the imperial era, with each dynasty dutifully writing the history of its predecessor.[8] The Han territory was about 4.7 million square kilometers.[9] On today's political map, it occupies parts of China, Korea, Vietnam, and Myanmar. Its sparsely populated Protectorate of Xiyu or Western Territory adds more than 1.3 million square kilometers, which covers China's Xinjiang province and spills into Kazakhstan, Kyrgyzstan, and Uzbekistan.

"In those days a decree went out from Caesar Augustus that all the world should be enrolled," according to Luke's Gospel.[10] "Those days" should be about 1 CE; Jesus was born during Joseph and Mary's journey home for the enrollment. Historians of Rome, however, are skeptical. In no other source can they find a decree for empire-wide enrollment, then or anytime during Augustus's reign.[11] A census in 8 BCE recorded 4,233,000 Roman citizens, privileged conquerors.[12] For the subject populace, the provinces individually registered inhabitants for tax purposes, as Judaea did after it became a province in 6 CE. Few data survive, however. Historians' estimations of the Roman Empire's population vary widely, but a peak value of 54 to 75 million seems reasonable.[13] The Empire's 5 million square kilometers of territory[14] covered, wholly or partly, at least thirty-nine nation-states of today: Albania, Algeria, Andorra, Austria, Belgium, Bosnia Herzegovina, Britain, Bulgaria, Croatia, Cyprus, Egypt, France, Germany, Greece, Hungary, Iraq, Israel, Italy, Jordan, Lebanon, Libya, Liechtenstein, Luxembourg, Macedonia, Malta, Monaco, Morocco, Netherlands, Palestine, Portugal, Romania, San Marino, Serbia, Slovenia, Spain, Switzerland, Syria, Tunisia, and Turkey.

For comparison, the People's Republic of China has a population of 1.35 billion in a territory of 9.6 million square kilometers. The United States of America has a population of 314 million in a territory of 9.4 million square kilometers. Both figures are for 2011.[15]

In terms of latitude, the city of Rome is 7.3 degrees north of Han's capital Changan (today Xian), which is about as far north as Chicago is of Los Angeles. Being north, however, does not necessarily imply being colder; the opposite obtains in this case. The Mediterranean region is under the sway of the Saharan pressure system, which brings it hot dry summers, mild winters, and rains falling mainly in the autumns and winters. The climate of Rome, similar to that of California, favors outdoor activities such as civic gatherings. North China is under the sway of the Siberian pressure system, which gives it a mainly continental climate moderated by the last leg of the monsoon rains. It has warm summers and cold windy winters, not unlike those of Illinois and the Midwest. Its rainfall, mainly in the summer, is plentiful enough to support dry agriculture and scarce enough to put a premium on irrigation.

China is a solid land realm, to which its inhabitants refer as *hainei*, within the seas. "Around the sea" is an apt description for the Roman Empire, whose territories clung to the rim of the Mediterranean. However, the sea at its heart did not make Rome a maritime empire akin to the nineteenth-century British Empire. It enjoyed naval supremacy shortly after it built a war fleet, but its power rested mainly on its marching legions. In the predominance of infantry, Rome was closer to the Han than the Athenian Empire, which dominated the eastern Mediterranean with its ramming galleys in the fifth century BCE. The arduous process of conquering Italy had shaped Rome's character as essentially a land power.

Geography is important in shaping the character of an empire, but so are its history, people, and many other factors that through their interaction amount to more than the sum of their parts. To understand the empires, we start by examining their sprawling roots.

1.2 The Advantage of Openness to Diversity

The people are the foundation of a state. At the beginning of our period of study, not one people but a multitude of diverse peoples inhabited Italy and China. Their amalgamation into a majority people under a united polity was a long process that continued into the era of the Roman and Qin-Han Empire. It revealed the relatively open and absorbent character of the major group in each region, the Romans and the forerunners of the Han-Chinese, then named Huaxia.

A modern historian remarks, "It is thus extraordinarily hard to grasp the enormous diversity in ethnic formation, social and economic structure, political organization, religion, language, and material culture of the different peoples of Italy. Rome succeeded in conquering and assimilating not only peoples like the neighboring and related Latins, but peoples who were as like to herself as chalk to cheese."[16] Greater scale and complexity make the case for China even harder to grasp. From afar, today's Chinese present a homogeneous image, with the ethnic Han-Chinese constituting a 92 percent majority and the remaining populace divided among fifty-five ethnic minorities. Up close, great variations appear among the ethnic Han-Chinese, who got their name after the Han Dynasty. Their apparent homogeneity, hardly existent in the beginning, was the result of a historical process that fused peoples ranging from fur wearers to tattoo wearers, from eaters of raw fish to eaters of no grain.[17]

For some idea of the original diversity, we can crudely divide the peoples of each region into two overlapping groups according to their economy and culture. The first group included in Italy the Romans, Latins, Etruscans, and Greek colonists; in China, the peoples of various Zhou states, who called themselves Huaxia. Mainly agriculturalists settled on plains or in river valleys, they built cities and formed states with relatively complex organizations. The second group of peoples included, among many others, the Sabini, Aequi, Volsci, Samnites, Lucani, and Gauls of Italy and the Rong, Di, Man, Yi, Qiang, and Shu of China. Their political organizations were mainly tribal and their economies various mixtures of farming, herding, hunting, fishing, and raiding. Most lived in villages and built no cities, at least initially. Some had no settled residences but moved with their herds. In Italy, they originated mostly in the hills. Many in China lived in the hills, but others also lived on plains and swamps, exploiting the variegated geography there. Appearing later in history were the steppe nomads excelling in mounted archery, loosely called the Scythians by the Greeks and the Hu by the Chinese. They were a heterogeneous lot. I summarily call them "pastoralists" only for the sake of brevity.

Agriculturalists and pastoralists interacted with each other since prehistory, often peacefully. The Romans formed close relationship with the Sabini, as reflected in the rape of Sabine women in Rome's founding myth. Soon after its birth, the Republic admitted a Sabine group whose head made Roman consul within a decade and founded the powerful Claudian clan that later participated in the Julio-Claudian dynasty of the Empire.[18] The Zhou formed a close relationship with the pastoral Qiang people, especially its Jiang clan. Their myth revered as their first mother a virgin Jiang whose immaculate conception was caused by stepping on a giant footprint. A Jiang commanded their army of conquest and became the ruler of Qi, one of the strongest of Zhou states.[19]

Our stories on either side begin with massive migrations of pastoralists and raids on the relatively prosperous agriculturalists. In response, the plains states put aside their mutual grievances and closed rank, as a Chinese remarked: "Brothers wrangle at home but unite against external threats."[20] The Zhou states formed a federacy under a hegemon "to resist the Yi." Italy, Rome, and other Latin cities ceased squabbling and cooperated to defend against Volsci and Aequi intrusions.[21] Eventually the agriculturists prevailed, their states strengthened by the experience of fighting and the incorporation of the vanquished. The names of many pastoral peoples disappeared from later historical records. Their fates varied. Some were massacred, others subjugated; still others expelled or moved away. Most adopted a sedentary life and after several generations became indistinguishable from neighboring farmers.

Fighting aside, intermarriage, colonization, political integration, and cultural assimilation all contributed to the formation of a unitary people. As the major group in each region, the Romans and the Huaxia were chauvinistic, aggressive, discriminative, and jealous of their own advantages. However, their prejudices were closer to the racism in America after the civil rights movements of the 1960s than to that before the Civil War of the 1860s. Comparing their attitudes with those of contemporaneous Greeks reveals their relative openness to other ethnicities, which enabled them to adapt and absorb others, thus amplifying their own strength.

When Rome began to urbanize, there were some 700 Greek city-states already scattered along the Mediterranean and Black Sea coasts like frogs around a pond, as Plato remarked. Except for a few giants such as Athens and Corinth, most were rather small, with an average population of several thousand. Citizenship in a Greek city-state carried enormous political, social, and economic privileges. Who were qualified for it? Aristotle explained, "In practice it is usual to define a citizen as one born of citizen parents on both sides, and not on the father's or mother's side only; but sometimes this requirement is carried still farther back, to the length of two, three, or more stages of ancestry."[22] Not even distant descendants of marriage to an outsider were safe from expulsion. Double endogamy closed the citizen body upon itself. Its enforcement was so rigorous in democratic Athens that one modern scholar observes, "One gets a distinct sense of siege, of barricades being manned, of determined resistance to constant pressures from outside."[23]

In contrast, intermarriage among peoples with little penalty was common in Italy and China. Rome gradually extended citizenship together with its privileges to the peoples it conquered. Imperial China did not institute formal citizenship but routinely extended uniform duties and privileges to all inhabitants. Furthermore, the Chinese tabooed marriage between persons with the same family name. This precluded intermarriage among most ruling houses, whose members were relatives within the Zhou clan and shared a family name. The necessity of out-marriage compelled many aristocrats to seek unions with locals and commoners, sometimes non-Huaxia in origin.[24]

Criteria of access to authoritative positions are crucial to any power structure. Amid Greek exclusiveness, Alexander was a singularity. The Greco-Roman biographer Plutarch wrote, "Alexander did not do as Aristotle advised—play the part of a leader to the Greeks and of a master to the barbarians, care for the former as friends and kinsmen, and treat the latter as beasts or plants, . . . he behaved alike to all."[25] As soon as he died, his successors reverted to the Greek tradition and expelled from powerful positions all Persians and other natives of the conquered lands. Across the vast Hellenistic world, Greeks and Macedonians became "the new master race," to use the term of modern historians; they formed a closed circle to which very few natives gained access, and then only slowly and painfully.[26] Consequently, the Hellenistic kingdoms never benefited from the talents of subject natives as the Roman and Chinese Empires did. Since the first century BCE, Italians, followed by provincials, crowded the Roman Senate. Later, Roman emperors hailed from Spain, Africa, and Asia. Putting ability and moral quality above kinship and ethnicity as a criteria of governmental appointment was a Chinese ideal since the First Emperor abolished the feudalistic aristocracy. Top ministers came from all across the country, and a surrendered Xiongnu made co-regent to a boy emperor.[27]

Strong exclusiveness prevented the Greek city-states from expansion or unity. Most remained tiny and mired in endless conflicts with neighbors. The Athenian Empire lasted barely fifty years despite Athenian leadership in repelling the Persian invasion. Compared to it and the Hellenistic kingdoms, the Roman and Chinese Empires were far more successful and long-lived.

The Romans and Huaxia did discriminate, but based mainly on behavior, not birth; ethics, not ethnicity; politics, not race.[28] They make good cases for the thesis that credits relative openness and toleration with an empire's ability to expand and endure.[29]

Comparison is intelligible only upon adequate knowledge of individual sides. To provide the requisite information, I will narrate the history of China and Rome separately before further comparative analysis.

1.3 The Mosaic of China

The geographical horizon of ancient Chinese history, which covered only a part of today's People's Republic, centered on two great rivers, the Yellow River and the Yangzi (Map 3). From their sources only 100 kilometers apart in the Tibetan plateau, the two swing widely before running almost parallel across the plains to the seas that bound China on the east. A zone between the two rivers, running from west to east along the Qinling Range and the River Huai, is the traditional divide between north and south China, respectively wheat and rice countries. Imperial China fragmented into north and south regimes for several periods in its long history. The River Huai, accompanied by myriad tributaries, lakes, and swamps, facilitated defense against the cavalries of originally nomadic peoples who ruled north China during disunion.[30]

South China with its hot and humid climate is a land of hills, forests, lakes, and river valleys. Here archeologists recovered remains of cultivated rice from 7,000 years ago.[31] However, its development into a rich land of fishponds and rice paddies began only toward the end of our period of study; clearing jungles and draining swamps required more than primitive technology. The Yangzi delta would become the leader in culture and prosperity. Before its development, the major political theater on the Yangzi was its midsection and tributaries, especially the River Han, which would lend its name to the Han Dynasty.

North China, with just enough rainfall to support dry farming of wheat and millet, is the birthplace of Chinese literacy and the main stage of early Chinese history. Here the Yellow River traverses a loess plateau and erodes its deep layers of yellow soil. Then it rushes down fringe mountains onto the 3,000-square kilometer Central Plain, where the silt it deposits raises its riverbed and causes frequent flooding. At its northern edge, the plain shades into grasslands and deserts, which continue into the Eurasian steppe. Here rainfall is insufficient for agriculture and nomadic pastoralists roamed. Long walls, which run roughly in the zone separating the steppe and the sown, symbolize the historical differences between two cultures. The now-standing Great Wall was built by the Ming Dynasty, founded after expelling the Mongol conquerors in 1369. Remnants of the long walls built in our period of study sit further to the north at places; ecological zones shifted with climate changes.

While on the loess plateau, the Yellow River turns north, then east, south, and east again toward the sea. Where it makes its final abrupt turn, it receives River Wei coming from the west. Together, River Wei and a stretch of the Yellow River form a corridor that opens eastward onto the Central Plain and thrusts westward into the borderland between the sown and the steppe. It harbored two early Chinese capitals: the eastern capital near today's Luoyang on the Yellow River and the western capital near today's Xian on the River Wei. The Qinling Range, which flanks the corridor's south, separates Wei Valley from the strategic Hanzhong on the Han River that flows into the middle Yangzi. On the other bank of the Han River rises the Daba Range, fraught with precipitous canyons, a part of the steep mountains that ring the Sichuan basin in southwestern China. A fertile plain protected by geography, Sichuan has been a haven in many tumultuous times. Through its southern part flows the Yangzi River, which chisels out the Three Gorges on its way east.

China's great rivers generally run from west to east, adding geographical to climatic obstacles to the north-south spread of people and culture. The fragmented terrain depicted in Map 3 should dispel the erroneous impression that the geography of eastern Asia is more conducive to political unity than that of western Europe. The plain of northern China is no bigger than that of northern Europe, and the Qinling and Sichuan mountains not more passable than the Alps or Pyrenees. Scholars have distinguished eight macroregions with natural barriers to interregional trade: the Central Plain, the Wei Valley, the Yangzi delta, the mid-Yangzi drainage, the Sichuan basin, the southeastern seaboard, the southwestern mountains, and the Pearl River basin in the deep south.[32] These do not include the large outlying territories acquired by China later in its history: Manchuria, Inner Mongolia, Xinjiang, and Tibet, each featuring exotic landscapes. The geography of China is easier adduced to explain why this large country had fragmented so many times than why, despite conspicuous regional diversity in terrains, vegetations, economies, dialects, and social customs, the country always reunited. The cohesive forces lie more in its people, history, and culture.

In recent decades, massive digging for infrastructural construction unearthed Neolithic sites in widely dispersed locations with distinctive cultures.[33] China has been a multiethnic and multicultural country from the beginning. Its ancient texts are replete with names of peoples, some of whom have been identified as descendants of particular Neolithic cultures. These peoples would coalesce in history's great melting pot to form the ethnic majority Han-Chinese and many minority Chinese ethnics.

Among the many ancient peoples of China, three of similar cultures—the Xia, Shang, and Zhou—became successive leaders in political organization. Their dominance constituted the Three Eras that would become the Golden Age in Confucian political ideology. The illiterate Xia pioneered state organization near Luoyang. To their east rose their successor, the Shang, who developed writing and chariot warfare, created exquisite bronze art, and practiced human sacrifice. The king of Shang headed a powerful confederation comprising many peoples, among whom was the Zhou clan residing in the Wei Valley. While the Shang were weakened by the rebellious Yi in the east, the Zhou amassed an alliance and conquered the Shang around 1066 BCE. Three more years of campaigning pacified the eastern Yi and pushed Zhou power eastward to the sea.[34]

The Zhou people called their culture Huaxia. Their cities scattered across north China. In the extensive interstitial regions lived peoples whose languages, customs, and economies differed from each other and from that of the Huaxia. So many peoples of diverse ethnicity existed, and they moved and intermixed so frequently, that a clear account is impossible. They are usually summarily called the Rong, Di, Man, or Yi. These convenient names are vague and often used interchangeably, with their referents altering over the centuries. Like the Huaxia, none of the names designates a single homogeneous people; thus, one often reads about the behaviors of the many-Hua or many-Rong. As late as the fifth century BCE, the Central Plain contained uncultivated areas where pastoral peoples thrived. Within sight of the centrally located Wey[35] city tower was a Rong settlement, where the deposed lord of Wey met his end in 478 BCE.[36]

1.4 Zhou Cities Among Pastoralists

A Western historian wrote of the Zhou: "they were conspicuous for their ability to plan far ahead, and for their discipline, even before their conquest of the Shang. They had two virtues that the early Romans held in high esteem: *gravitas* (gravity) and *constantia* (constancy)."[37] The preconquest Zhou had an adult male population of 60,000 to 70,000, as indicated by the scale of excavated settlements. Texts report their army of conquest comprising about 300 war chariots, 3,000 armored warriors, and 45,000 auxiliaries assembled from hundreds of ethnically diverse tribes.[38] China was sparsely populated then, but even so, the Zhou were a small minority. To rule the vast territory they conquered, the Zhou fanned out to maximize their power. The Zhou king invested hereditary lords, the great majority of whom were relatives. He assigned warrior followers to them, sent them to build cities at remote strategic locations, allowed them significant sovereignty in their cities, and demanded certain political and military obligations in return. Unlike Greek colonies that stemmed from population pressure and severed political ties with the mother city, the Zhou colonies were political and strategic in design. Hundreds of widely scattered Zhou cities constituted a loose political federation under the king, a "screen of defense for Zhou."[39] Their functions resembled the colonies that Rome planted in Italy, the "chains of bastions" that tied its peoples together.[40] Originally garrisons, they took root as civilian institutions and spread the Huaxia ways of life in the ensuing peace.[41]

Three centuries of dominance and relative tranquility bred refinement and complacency. Then, in 771 BCE, a great drought scorched the Wei Valley where the Zhou capital sat. Court corruption prevented effective famine relief. Marauding Rong compounded the people's sorrows. The Zhou king was killed in an incursion. His heir, together with great lords in the area, fled east to the Central Plain, never to return. During the royal evacuation, the general from peripheral Qin distinguished himself and was invested as a lord, who alone dared to remain behind in Zhou's original base.[42] By decades of arduous fighting and administration, Qin made itself "the hegemon among the western Rong."[43] The Rong's vitality and resources, tamed and absorbed, would help Qin's empire-building enterprise.

The Zhou court moved to Luo on the Yellow River, where it languished until Qin finished it in 249 BCE. Tradition names the years 722 to 479 BCE after the *Spring and Autumn Annals*, China's first systematic history, written by Confucius toward the end of the period. The subsequent Warring States period ended with Qin's unification of China in 221 BCE. As with most historical periodizations—that between republican and imperial Rome included—no sharp line divides the two Chinese periods. Yet the distinction is significant. One period transitioned into another as a landscape in the movies fades into a portrait. Not a clean break but the unmistakable difference between the earlier and later scenes marks their distinction.

As the Spring and Autumn period dawned, the military colonies that Zhou planted in its early days had grown into hundreds of sovereign city-states, although their rulers retained the title of lord. Wey, Lu, and other states centrally located in the heartland, originally most advanced and prestigious, had stagnated for want of room to expand. Four fringe states—Qi, Jin, Chu, and Qin—rose to hegemonic powers by developing their hinterlands and incorporating neighborhood pastoralists (Map 4). In terms of the seigniorial house, only Jin was certifiably Huaxia, but its lords too married pastoral women. Lord Wen, who first brought it to hegemony, had a Di mother and appointed many Di to high ministries.[44] Chu was a small ally in the Zhou conquest. Unhappy with the low status that it received, its lord spurned Huaxia protocols and declared himself king: "We are Man Yi and do not care for titles of the heartland states."[45]

The Central Plain was no safe haven. The Di peoples descended the northwestern hills, raided the royal domain, attacked many states, and overran a few. The southern Chu gobbled up small states and threatened larger ones in the Huai and Yellow River regions. Compounded by internecine belligerency among Huaxia states and dynastic strife within individual states, the fate of the heartland states hung on a thread. Responses were urgent. Lord Huan of Qi appointed as chief minister Guan Zhong, whose reforms made Qi the strongest of Huaxia states. In the 670s BCE, Lord Huan convened interstate conferences to promote multilateral cooperation. Under the slogan "Honor the king and repel the Yi," he assembled an alliance, rescued besieged cities, restored toppled states, and slowed the advance of Chu and Di peoples. His actions won many allegiances, making him the first *ba* or hegemon.[46]

The Greek *hēgemōn* refers to the supreme commander of a willing alliance. A prime example was the Athenian leadership in the Greek alliance against Persia.[47] Like *hēgemōn*, *ba* originally signifies honor and is interchangeable with *bo*, the eldest brother in the family.[48] A hegemon in the Spring and Autumn period was a leader of lords who, without annexing allies, dominated their foreign policies and intervened in certain domestic affairs, notably against usurpation. It instilled some order among the bellicose states by dispute resolution and diplomacy backed by threat. In the conferences it called, the lords pledged cooperation in many areas. On its demand, allies provided troops and resources for common defense or stability maintenance. Qi, Qin, Jin, and Chu all attained hegemony at various times. Located at the eastern and western ends of a long and narrow political theater, Qi and Qin were geographically off-center. Qi fell prey to internal discord after the death of Lord Huan. Its banner passed to Jin of the northern heartland, which pacified the mountain Di and faced off the southern Chu across a broad front.[49]

Jin under Lord Wen scored a great victory over Chu in the 632 BCE battle of Chengpu, called a well-attended conference, and established hegemony.[50] Chu soon rebounded from its defeat to compete for hegemony and the allegiance of small states. By war and diplomacy, the two engaged in a seesaw balance of power, occasionally disrupted by spikes of Qi. In the process, Chu aristocrats were acculturated. Chu became a regular part of the Huaxia political world when the long-suffering small states caught between the great powers brokered a peace covenant in 546 BCE.[51]

In the power struggle, Jin found a secret weapon in Chu's neighbor, the state of Wu in the Yangzi delta. Jin sent Wu war chariots and trainers, taught it battle formations, and encouraged it to attack Chu. Chu found relief in Yue, Wu's neighbor and enemy. Wars among the southern states Chu, Wu, and Yue at the end of the Spring and Autumn period provided a welcome respite for the northern states.

From the day of the Zhou conquest, political dominance did not blind military colonists to the diverse traditions of subject peoples. Officials from various cities traveled the countryside to collect songs and sayings, which conveyed information about native minds and local elites. Many such "country airs" survive in the *Odes*, the oldest Chinese literature. Singing less of sackers of cities than tillers of fields and seekers of mates, it offers a glimpse into the variegated customs of the vast land. Besides out-marriage, the Zhou principle was "to improve education but not to change traditions, to regiment government but not to change what are appropriate to local situations."[52] Implementations of the policy varied, as did results. The first lord of Qi spent five months simplifying Zhou rituals to suit local customs. Qi grew rich and powerful because people flocked to it, attracted by its straightforward rule. The first lord of neighboring Lu took three years to mold local conventions according to complicated Zhou rituals. Lu became the citadel of Zhou culture and the home of Confucianism.[53]

The Zhou aristocratic culture—rich in rituals, poetry, music, and moral norms—was a cohesive force among Huaxia states and a magnet to non-Huaxia elites. Early Zhou bronze and ceramic vessels of similar design appear in archeological sites more than 1,000 kilometers apart. Regional artifacts show cultural convergence during the following centuries, although it was mainly confined to the upper crust of society.[54] The peoples of Wu and Yue were Man Yi who blackened their teeth, painted their faces, and tattooed their bodies. The ruling classes, like that of Chu, admired Huaxia refinement. Their efforts to develop their realms and enhance their own prestige simultaneously inculcated some Huaxia ways among their peoples, just as the municipal aristocrats of Italy led the Hellenization of Italians.[55] Yet the acculturation did not penetrate deep; much diversity persisted among the lower classes. Furthermore, rulers of various states were also eager to maintain regional identity that bolstered the loyalty of their subjects. Chu, which eventually annexed Wu and Yue, developed a distinctive culture befitting the luxuriant landscape of the southlands. The *Songs of Chu* sing of gods, magic, and love after death. Its ethereal fancy contrasted with the earthy immediacy of the *Odes* from the deep-soiled north.[56] Entrenched regional cultures and identities would play significant roles in Chinese politics, even after imperial unification.

In all regions, the Huaxia and non-Huaxia traded and intermarried. They fought, but also allied against common enemies, concluded truces, pledged friendship, met in conferences, exchanged diplomats, and engaged in other political dealings.[57] The complexity of relationships is apparent in the history of the Jiang Rong, a branch of the Rong people. The Jiang Rong defeated Zhou troops in the Wei Valley in 789 BCE. Later they fled Qin's harassment and took refuge in Jin. Their revenge came in 627 BCE, when they joined Jin to defeat Qin at the battle of Xiao.[58] Ancient annalists spared no word for the battle scenes but poured much ink over an incident between Juzhi, chief of the Jiang Rong, and Fan Xuanzi, executive minister of the hegemonic Jin in charge of an upcoming interstate conference in 559 BCE:

> Intending to arrest Juzhi, a Rong *zi*, Fan Xuanzi personally chided at court: "Come here, Jiang Rong *shih*.[59] . . . Nowadays the lords serve our Lord less diligently than before. Rumors and leaked secrets originate from you. Do not approach tomorrow's conference. If you dare try, I will have you arrested." Juzhi replied: "Previously Qin, strong in arms and greedy for land, expelled us many-Rong. The virtuous late lord of Jin decided that we Rong, being descendants of Siyue, should not be homeless. He granted us southern lands, where foxes dwelled and wolves howled. We Rong cleared the bushes and thorns, drove out the foxes and wolves, and became loyal subjects of the late lord. . . . In the battle of Xiao, the Qin army failed to escape only because of the efforts of us Rong. It is like catching a deer, Jin held the horns, we Rong the legs. Since then we Rong had followed Jin into a hundred battles. Now your negligent ministers alienate the lords and blame it on us Rong. We Rong differ from the Hua in food, drinks, and clothing. We exchange no envoys, and our tongues are mutually incomprehensible. What harm can we cause? We will not regret avoiding the conference." He recited the poem Bluebottle and retired. Xuanzi apologized and invited Juzhi to the conference, preserving his own reputation of venerability.[60]

This narrative comes from *Zuozhuan*, the most reliable and detailed history of the period written in the late fifth century BCE. It does not tell what happened in that conference, but indicates that although second-class, the Rong could have a seat at the political high table. The suffix *shih* was an aristocratic prerogative. Despite the cultural differences Juzhi asserted, some of his people had settled down to farm on cleared land. His own acculturation was apparent in his poem, which survives in the *Odes*. It likens slanderers to buzzing bluebottle flies and appeals: "Oh venerable lord, believe not slanders."[61] Siyue, the grand councilors of a revered ancient king, were believed to be the ancestors to many Jiang clans, among which was the house of Qi. The acknowledgment of related lineages, fictive or not, fashioned a sense of affinity between peoples. Thus the lords of Wu gained acceptance into the Huaxia circle as descendants of an alleged minor branch of the Zhou lineage.[62] Similar practices occurred in the Western world. A prominent example was the alleged Roman ancestry of the Trojan Aeneas, through whom Rome was adopted into the Greek culture.[63] I know of no record of the Jiang Rong after this incident. One may guess that they dissolved into the Jin populace.[64]

As myriad isolated city-states coalesced into a handful of contiguous territorial-states, the heartland populace became more homogenized. Most pastoralists who remained in the Central Plain turned into farmers and merged into the Huaxia. Others who retreated to the peripheral hills and grasslands maintained non-Huaxia identities. Some in the north turned into steppe nomads and perfected mounted archery. These Hu peoples increasingly pressed on the states to their south and would become the nemesis of empire.[65]

1.5 The Mosaic of Italy

Protruding like a boot into the Mediterranean, the Italian peninsula turns its back on the civilized east (Map 5). The Apennine Mountains that run down its spine press close to the Adriatic coast and shield it from excessive intrusions. At its north and south ends, the range turns toward the Tyrrhenian Sea, gathering in its arms the coastal plains of western Italy: Etruria, Latium, and Campania. The River Tiber, whose lower stretch divides the Etrurian and Latin plains, forms the chief route of communication from the coast to the interior. Twenty-five kilometers from its mouth, at the last crossing before it reaches the sea, stand seven hills. On them rises Rome.[66]

North of the Apennines, sandwiched between it and the Alps, lies the plain of the River Po, greater in area than all other Italian plains combined. A marshy floodplain at first, it took Rome the longest time to tame. Once developed, it became a breadbasket of the Roman Empire. The Alps forms a defensive barrier to northern Italy, but one that is penetrable. Through its passes Rome's armies and enemies marched.

The Italian peninsula has almost 3,000 kilometers of coastline. The lack of good ports forced early inhabitants to exploit the land first, but the sea beckoned. Together with the island of Sicily at its toe, the peninsula almost bisects the Mediterranean Sea. Sitting in central Italy, Rome commanded a strategic view of the western Mediterranean basin with its many peoples and undeveloped resources. They would all be its to exploit once it drove out powers that originated in the eastern Mediterranean.

Rome was founded by Romulus in 753 BCE, according to tradition. Archeologists found the date too late for settlement and too early for urbanization. Small villages occupied the hills over the Tiber since around 1000 BCE, but not until the late seventh century BCE, when the low-lying areas later known as the Forum were drained and the hill villages coalesced, would Rome become a city. The mid-eighth century BCE saw no significant event on the Tiber. However, it did see one that would profoundly change Italy: the coming of Phoenicians and Greeks.[67]

Around 1000 BCE, when the Zhou cities were putting down roots all across China, the eastern Mediterranean awoke from its dark age. The Phoenicians invented the alphabet and the Greeks adapted it to an Indo-European language, greatly facilitating the spread of literacy. These two peoples developed a diffused form of government, the autonomous city-states that reproduced themselves like cell division. Overpopulated cities spun off colonies that became independent states. The Phoenicians led the way westward and planted a colony, Carthage, on the strategic African coast opposite to Sicily. The Greeks in their wake scouted western Italy. The mouth of the Tiber was too silted to be inviting. More attractive was the Bay of Naples opening to the Campanian plain. Most popular were the coasts of Sicily and southern Italy, so cluttered with Greek cities they came to be called Magna Graecia (Map 6). Greek exclusiveness incited indigenous hostility and internecine strife, which prevented the initially flourishing Magna Graecia from rooting deep. By the third century BCE, when the Romans came, many cities were withering. Yet the Greeks had already bestowed invaluable gifts on Italy and Rome: arts, culture, and, above all, literacy and the model of city-state.[68]

Greek and Phoenician traders frequented Etruria for its iron, copper, and silver. The Etruscans excelled in engineering and led native Italians in city building. They adapted the Greek alphabets and passed them on to the Latins, together with their own numeral system that we now call "Roman." Many city-states flourished in Latium. Besides language and culture, the Latins shared reciprocal private rights: the rights of citizens from one community to reside, own land, conduct commerce, sign legal contracts, marry partners, and even acquire citizenship in another.[69] These Latin customs were similar to the Etruscan but contrary to the Greek. For the Greeks, ownership of real estate within a city-state was limited to citizens of that state—unless the foreigners were imperial Athenians backed by their powerful navy.[70]

In the central Italian highland lived peoples who spoke a family of Indo-European languages summarily called Italic. They raised livestock and planted crops in upland valleys, but had no city and few towns. Their societies were rustic and their political organizations mainly tribal.[71] The Umbrians imitated their Etruscan neighbors. The Sabini, Aequi, and Volsci had long dealing with the Latins. All Italic peoples eventually succumbed to Roman domination. The ones who fought longest and most vigorously for their freedom were the Samnites.[72]

The many peoples of northwestern Europe, whom the Greeks and Romans summarily called Celts, Gauls, or simply barbarians, began their great migrations in the fifth century BCE. Some crossed the Alps and descended into the Po River valley, the area the Romans later called Cisalpine Gaul, Gaul this side of the Alps. Others lived where France is now, the Gaul that Caesar would conquer.[73]

1.6 Latin Colonies and Hill Peoples

Rome on the Tiber crossing controlled both the river traffic and a vital land route from Etruria to Etruscan cities in Campania. Its location immersed it in the Etruscan cultural zone. Early Rome was ruled by nonhereditary kings. Two of its three last kings, who contributed much to urbanization and institutionalization, were Etruscans. Rome ousted the king but not Etruscan culture. Commerce went on and Etruscan communities continued to thrive in Rome.[74]

At its birth in 509 BCE, the Roman Republic was comparable to large Etruscan city-states. The most powerful of Latin states, it occupied about one-third of Latium and claimed the rest as its protectorate in a treaty with Carthage. The Latins bristled at the arrogance. War ended in 493 BCE with a bilateral treaty between Rome and the Latin League comprising some thirty Latin cities. It came just in time. Alarms were sounding everywhere.[75]

Deep in the overpopulated hills of Italy, tribes stirred. Cities were attacked and overrun as they descended on the plains. The Romans and Latins responded almost every year in the first half of the fifth century BCE. Gradually, the situation turned in favor of the plains peoples. Reports of Aequi and Volsci raids decreased. The Sabini disappeared from the record.[76]

As soon as pressure from the hill peoples eased, Rome turned to settle grievances with the big Etruscan city Veii, its neighbor 15 kilometers away—a morning's walk. Unlike the haphazard forays in the struggle with pastoralists, this was organized warfare between two developed states with similar culture. The war with Veii lasted ten years and assumed epic dimension in traditional narratives. It also revealed several characteristics of Roman conquests. The first two were the perseverance of Rome and the disunity of its enemies. Like Magna Graecia, Etruria was not a political entity but an aggregate of city-states. During the war, twelve Etruscan cities jointly declared neutrality. Even the last desperate appeal from their compatriots brought no help. So fell Veii in 396 BCE.[77]

According to Livy, a Roman historian writing in the late first century BCE, the Senate announced at the eve of victory that anyone who pleased to claim his share in the plunder might go to Camillus, commander of the Roman army before Veii. Thousands happily swarmed into camp. Then dawned "that famous day, of which every hour was spent in the killing of Rome's enemies and the sacking of a wealthy city. Next day, all the free-born townsfolk were sold, by Camillus's order, into slavery. The proceeds of the sale was the only money which went to the treasury."[78] Besides the profit of mass enslavement, the state also gained land that expanded Rome's territory by about 60 percent.[79]

Soon after the annihilation of Veii, some Gauls from the Po valley wandered into central Italy. At Allia, not far from Rome, the armor-clad Romans were shocked by the superb physique that the Gauls nakedly displayed. Even worse, their heavy infantry with spearmen in the inflexible phalanx formation was no match for the Gallic light infantry wielding long slashing swords supported by cavalry. The sack of Rome in 390 BCE left a deep psychological scar. The mention of Allia would invoke fear and justify many occasions of emergency measures that gave officials unlimited authority. However, modern historians aided by archeological data argue that the physical damage to Rome was far less severe than traditional descriptions. Most temples and public buildings on the Capital Hill remained intact. After several months and the exaction of a ransom in gold, the Gauls departed. They were much kinder to Rome than the Romans were to Veii.[80]

Rome's expansionary campaigns suffered a mere hiccup because of the sack. Twelve years later the Romans started to fortify their city with a massive stone wall 10 meters high, which enclosed 4.3 square kilometers, circumscribing the Seven Hills of Rome.[81] Learning from experience, the Romans improved tactics and switched to javelins and short thrusting swords. The Gauls continued marauding, but their tactical advantage was lost against the reformed legions. Their attacks only weakened Etruria and lubricated Rome's eventual conquest.[82]

Capua, the largest city-state in Campania, had been taken over by Samnite immigrants. Then its ruling aristocrats quarreled with cousin Samnites in the hills and asked Rome to intervene in return for its submission. Rome had signed a treaty with the hill Samnites in 354 BCE and treasured its reputation of fidelity, but the temptation was too great. Rome did not conquer Capua. Capuan aristocrats voluntarily submitted to Rome, partly to preserve their domestic control over Capuan plebeians.[83] Ruling elites acting on their immediate self-interests sometimes invite foreign interventions or even negotiate unequal mergers; their possible regret later is another story. Such practice in interstate diplomacy is not limited to the Western world. Three decades later in China, quarrels erupted within the ruling aristocracy of Shu and a faction asked Qin for help.[84] The Chinese have an idiom for such maneuvers: "to invite the wolf into the house."

Rome's First Samnite War of 343–341 BCE for the acquisition of Capua was followed by the Latin War against its former allies. By the settlement of 338 BCE, it was in control of northern Campania, Latium, southern Etruria, and adjacent foothills. Construction of the Appian Way between Rome and Capua commenced in 312 BCE. Crossing marshes on viaducts and cutting an almost straight course for 220 kilometers, it tied the land together. Other roads followed. Infrastructural construction augmented political organization to consolidate a strategic base for Rome in central Italy. With its back protected by the sea, it could assemble its resources, move troops rapidly, and invade both its northern and southern neighbors.[85]

The Samnites waged an ancient version of protracted guerrilla war to defend their hilly homeland against Rome. Finally, fearing for their freedom, the peoples of Italy tried seriously to organize a united front. The Samnites marched north to join the Etruscans, Umbrians, and Gauls. It was too late. Effective cooperation needed practices that they lacked. Their sluggish mobilization gave Rome ample time to respond and their flawed coordination became Rome's luck. In the 295 BCE battle of Sentinum, Rome defeated the combined armies of Samnites and Gauls, an outcome that might have been different had the Etruscan and Umbrian contingents showed up in time. Never again would the four peoples join forces for independence. Rome dissolved the Samnite League and subordinated isolated Samnite tribes by individual unequal treaties.[86]

After the Samnites, rolling up the Greek cities of southern Italy was not difficult. Rome had its first encounter with a Greek professional army in 280 BCE, when King Pyrrhus of Epirus answered the appeal of his compatriots. By then the Roman eagle was fully fledged. Pyrrhus won battles only to lend his name to futile victories.[87]

On the eve of 264 BCE, when Rome decided to venture overseas, it had campaigned almost annually for more than a century and conquered the Italian peninsula south of the Po Valley. After Sentinum, it annexed a broad swath of territory stretching from the Tyrrhenian to the Adriatic Seas, bisecting the peninsula. With it, Rome directly ruled over one-fifth of peninsular Italy and one-third of its population. For the rest, it acted as hegemon of a federation comprising two major types of units, colonies and subordinate allies (Map 6).[88]

Territory was one of the chief spoils of war. To feed the land hunger of its citizens and exert strategic control over conquered peoples, the Roman Republic maintained two kinds of colonies in Italy. Citizen colonies were mainly military garrisons of a few hundred. More important were Latin colonies, where colonists gave up their Roman citizenship for a few hectares of land. A typical Latin colony was a self-governed community comprising 2,000 to 6,000 adult male settlers and their families, plus the natives whom it chose to incorporate. It had the legal status of a Latin city bound to Rome by a specific treaty.[89]

Far-flung colonies generally serve various purposes. As occupied lands, they reduce the productive and resistant capacities of conquered peoples. As a military presence, they deter unrest, provide rapid response to troubles, and serve as springboards to further expansion. Yet they are less costly than garrisons and their effects longer lasting. Colonists are productive folks who support themselves economically. Strings of Latin colonies in strategic locations tied Italy to Rome. Many grew into prospering cities. Looking back from the late Republic, the Roman consul and orator Cicero remarked, "it is worth remembering the care of our ancestors, who sited colonies in such suitable places to ward off danger that they seemed not just towns in Italy, but bastions of empire."[90] Rome's colonies played crucial roles in acculturating native peoples and changing the social landscape, just like the cities in China designed to form a screen of defense for the Zhou.

Divide and rule was a basic principle of Roman policy. Rome destroyed all indigenous organizations among Italian communities and dealt with each individually. A set of bilateral treaties, all converging on Rome like the spokes of a wheel without rim, produced a Roman, not a Latin or an Italian, federation. Dependent Italian communities lost control of their foreign policy but retained significant autonomy in internal affairs, subject to intervention at Rome's pleasure.[91] Their statuses varied greatly. The salient similarity was the necessity to provide troops with their own armaments as Rome demanded. This was not necessarily burdensome; it could be a lucrative investment for the spoils of victory. Despite setbacks, Rome's hegemony held through the dark days of the Hannibalic war.[92]

1.7 War, Policy, and the Melting Pot

Trade and other peaceful contacts are crucial to ethnic integration, but wars overshadow such daily intercourse in the available historical sources. Wars not only divide but also mix peoples. Life-and-death struggles elevate loyalty above birth. Soldiers march afar and refugees disperse, meeting strangers. Violence breaks up local establishments. Peace settlements introduce colonization, relocation, and political integration. The wars in our stories so far, which cover the Roman conquest of Italy and the coalescence of numerous Chinese cities into a handful of territorial states, were small and short. During these periods, the mosaics of Italy and China coagulated but had not yet homogenized. The divide-and-rule arrangement of Rome's confederation strengthened localism. Individual states in China forged strong regional identities such as *Churen*, people of Chu. Much parochialism would fall in two centuries of large wars, and more would disappear in the political integration of the subsequent empire.

The aftermath of war is equally disruptive. To evict old elites and inject new settlers were favorite policies of Chinese conquerors. When Chu annexed states in the more advanced areas, it routinely sent their aristocrats to the deep south, where natives were heterogeneous and economies backward.

After Qin took over Sichuan, home to the Shu, "elder of the Rong and Di," it promptly infused 10,000 households and concluded covenants with natives to smooth conflicts with immigrants. Geographical isolation made Sichuan an ideal place for the dangerous and undesirable. Tens of thousands of political exiles landed there, as did aristocrats and elites from the lands that Qin conquered. Some carried a little money that survived their dislodgement, others nothing except their knowledge, skill, and leadership. The influx "makes us prosperous and our land plentiful," Shu locals said.[93] Yet their distinctive culture submerged.[94]

Similar dislocation and mixing occurred in Italy. About one-third of Italy's free populace was dislodged because of the Hannibalic war, by fighting or Rome's eviction of inhabitants to punish the disloyalty of their cities. The decades of civil wars that destroyed the Republic also tore down entrenched regional traditions. Communities were destroyed and properties confiscated for wrong political alignment. Local farmers were expelled to satisfy the land demand of victorious veterans. From 80 to 8 BCE, about 1.5 million Italians, almost one-half of the free population, were driven from their homes or relocated on government orders. The Gauls were ejected and the Samnites slaughtered. The Etruscan culture disappeared.[95]

Postconquest organization can facilitate acculturation, but its effectiveness varies with the degree of political integration. If the vanquished are incorporated as a political unit with intact institutions, they have more power to resist assimilation. The state within a state may even rebel, especially if it retains its own military command. Later, the Roman and Chinese Empires would both regret admitting integral tribes of foreign warriors into their domains. Incorporation fared better in the early days. As we see in the following chapter, the Romans and Chinese were both building up their state structures as they expanded. Political reforms dissolved the institutions of the vanquished, broke up or modified pockets of regional power, and heated up the melting pots. Individuals absorbed into the victorious state without cohesive organization easily lost their former identity, and their descendants merged into the new environment.

Bitter about the treatment they received despite their contribution to Rome's conquest of the Mediterranean world, Italian allies, *socii*, revolted. Rome prevailed in the Social War of 91–87 BCE only by agreeing to extend citizenship to the free inhabitants of all Italy except Cisalpina. Its centuries of divide and rule finally gave way to a policy of political integration. Later, Octavian launched a propaganda campaign that united all Italians against the wicked East to cover up a power struggle against a noble Roman—Mark Antony. By the time Octavian died as Emperor Augustus, the Italians had become a people of Hellenistic culture.[96]

The unifying efforts of the First Emperor of Qin went further. After Qin annexed six rival states to create China's first imperial dynasty, it registered all inhabitants in individual households of equal status. Thus treated, the eastern Yi peoples quickly blended into the general population. More important, Qin abolished local aristocracies, leveled all barriers of travel and trade, proclaimed uniform codes of law, and standardized measure, coinage, and the Chinese script.[97]

The Han-Chinese spoke many dialects but shared a common written language, and theirs was "the country of caps and belts." Native tongues of Italy gradually disappeared. Italians sharing the Latin language inhabited "the domain of toga-wearers."[98] It took centuries, but the mosaics of Italy and of China each eventually fused into the large and rather homogeneous Italian or Han-Chinese people. Formation of the people—if modern scholars begrudge "nation building" to the ancients—was a consequential and lasting achievement of the period. Furthermore, each people was united under an extensive and centralized state.

Notes

1. McNeill 1963: 316–318. Beckwith 2009: Ch. 3.
2. Ptolemy, *Geography*, Bk. 1, Ch. 9.
3. *Houhanshu* 88: 2918–2920, 2931. Ball 2000: 400.
4. Hansen 2012: 20.
5. Thorley 1971. Elisseeff 2000. Whitefield 2004. Hansen 2012.
6. Gills and Frank 1993: 163–169. Teggart 1939.
7. *Hanshu* 28b: 1640.
8. Wilkinson 1998: 490–497.
9. Taagepera 1979: Table. 3.
10. Luke 2.1.
11. Thorley 1981.
12. Toynbee 1965: 1: 450.
13. Hopkins 1980: 117–118. Potter 2004: 17. Bury 1958: 62.
14. Taagepera 1979: Table 2.
15. Wikipedia. "List of Countries by Population." http://en.wikipedia.org/wiki/List_of_countries_by_population.
16. Crawford 1991: 16.
17. He 1996: 33–34. Weng 2001: part 1.
18. Livy 1.9. Cornell 1995: 157. Scullard 1980: 94–95; 1973: 10.
19. *Shiji* 4: 111. Yang 2003a: 27–28.
20. *Zuozhuan*, Xi 24.
21. Scullard 1980: 93–94. Cornell 1995: 299–300, 304–308.
22. Aristotle, *Politics* 1275b.
23. Davies 2004: 25. See also Whitehead 1989: 140.
24. Liang 1996: 50–52. Yang 2003a: 438–439.
25. Plutarch quoted in Edel 1982: 25. See also Strabo 1.4.9.

26. Walbank 1981: 63–66.
27. *Hanshu* 68: 2962.
28. Cornell 1995: 349. Di Cosmo 2002: Ch. 3.
29. Chua 2006.
30. Huang 1990: 20–24.
31. Chang et al. 2005: 29–31.
32. Skinner 1977: 8–11. Lewis 2009: 10–17. Scheidel 2009a: 12–13.
33. Chang et al. 2005: Chs. 3, 4. Hsu and Linduff 1988: 14, 58.
34. Hsu and Linduff 1988: Chs. 1–3.
35. The standard Pinyin transliteration for 衛 is Wei, which also stands for 魏. To avoid confusion, I reserve Wei for the more important 魏 and use Wey for 衛.
36. *Zuozhuan*, Ai 17. Weng 2001: 62–81.
37. Creel 1970: 203.
38. Hsu and Linduff 1988: 69.
39. *Zuozhuan*, Xi 24.
40. Cicero quoted in Crawford 1993: 37f.
41. Hsu and Linduff 1988: 150–154.
42. Shaughnessy 1999: 320–325, 342–351.
43. *Shiji* 5: 193–194.
44. Hsu 1999: 567–570. Tong 2006a: 141–143.
45. *Shiji* 40: 1692.
46. Hsu 1999: 559–561. Ma 2006a: 2–9. Qian 1940: 55–59.
47. Wickersham 1994: 1–23.
48. Wang R. 2011: 182–183. Pines 2002: 125–126.
49. Hsu 1999: 565–566. Lü 2005a: 351–352.
50. *Zuozhuan* Xi 28.
51. Tong 2006a: Chs. 9–11. Gu and Zhu 2003: 95–101, 114–123.
52. *Liji* 5.
53. *Shiji* 33: 1524; 32: 1480. Hsu and Linduff 1988: 187–188.
54. Rawson 1999: 352–353, 448–449. Falkenhauser 1999: 451–453.
55. *Zhanguoce* 19. Weng 2001: 78–79.
56. Shaughnessy 1999: 295, 332–338. Cook and Major 1999.
57. Di Cosmo 2002: Ch. 3. Ma 2006a: 16–18.
58. *Guoyu* 1. *Zuozhuan*, Xi 33.
59. The standard transliteration for 氏 is *shi*. I use *shih* in order to avoid confusion with *shi* for 士.
60. *Zuozhuan*, Xiang 14.
61. *Shijing* 219, The Bluebottles.
62. *Shangshu*, Yaodian. *Shiji* 32: 1477; 31: 1445.
63. Virgil, *The Aeneid*.
64. Yang 2003b: 291–292. Ma 2006a: 16.
65. Yang 2003b: 283–287.
66. Cornell and Matthews 1990: 10–17.
67. Cornell 1995: §§ 3.1–3.2, 4.3–4.4.
68. Forsythe 2005: 31–36. Scullard 1980: 20–25, 139f. Cornell 1995: 86–87.
69. Cornell 1995: 154–155, 293–297. Scullard 1980: 36–41.
70. Whitehead 1989: 143. Davies 1993: 78.
71. Dench 1995: 117–125, 130–133. David 1997: Ch. 1.
72. David 1997: 22–29. Cornell 1995: 305, 345–346.

73. David 1997: 14–18. Cunliffe 1997: Ch. 4.
74. Cornell 1995: 231, 144–145, 224–225.
75. Forsythe 2005: 116–123, 186–187. Cornell 1995: 205–207, 283, 299–300.
76. Forsythe 2005: 188–190. Scullard 1980: 94–97.
77. Cornell 1995: 310–313. Forsythe 2005: 246–250.
78. Livy 5.20.
79. Forsythe 2005: 246.
80. Livy 5.36. Cornell 1995: 314–315. Forsythe 2005: 251.
81. Cornell 1995: 204, 331. Crawford 1993: 32–33.
82. Forsythe 2005: 252–253. Cornell 1995: 318–319.
83. Cornell 1995: 305, 345–347.
84. *Zhanguoce* 3.
85. Salmon, 1982: Ch. 2. Cornell 1995: 347–351.
86. Cornell 1995: 359–362. Forsythe 2005: 327–334.
87. Cornell 1995: 363–364.
88. Cornell 1995: 380–385. David 1997: 35–36.
89. Salmon 1982: 63–66. Cornell 1995: 301–304, 351–352. Forsythe 2005: 190–191, 308.
90. Cicero quoted in Crawford 1993: 37f.
91. Scullard 1980: 113, 149. Cornell 1995: 348–350. Forsythe 2005: 290–292. Salmon 1982: 71.
92. David 1997: 64–74. Gabba 1987: 221–223. Brunt 1988: 126, 128.
93. *Huayang Guozhi*, Shuzhi.
94. Yang 2003b: 194, 354–356. Gu and Zhu 2003: 262–264.
95. David 1997: 177–181. Gabba 1987: 201–203. Hopkins 1978a: 7, 66.
96. Scullard 1976: 68–70. Syme 1939: 82, 284. Maddison 2007: 57.
97. See Section 4.4.
98. *Shiji* 110: 2902. Virgil, *Aeneid*, 1.282.

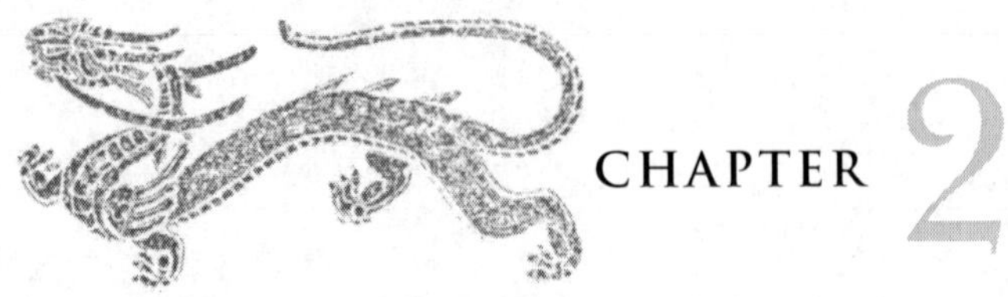

CHAPTER 2

STATE BUILDING

2.1 Blood, Iron, Ideas, and State Building

The Roman Republic and pre-imperial China coincided with the golden ages of classical antiquity. These were the times of Confucius and Socrates, when meritocracy emerged in China and democracy thrived in Greece, when ideas blossomed that are inspirational today. These were also times of exceptional violence, cruelty, and, in the West that extolled freedom, massive slavery. How the humanistic philosophies responded to the realities of their worlds filled abstract theories with concrete meanings. How their times shaped their ethical and political doctrines revealed the genealogy of morals. More important for our purpose, ideas vaguely affect politics. This does not imply that power players follow some overarching ideology. They mostly tackle immediate practical problems or grasp at opportunities. Yet they do not act blindly or arbitrarily. The concepts available to them constrain their thinking. They partake in some tacit customs, preconceptions, preoccupations, and dispositional characters, which the philosophies partially articulate. Even when political elites are mostly self-interested, their decisions are influenced by their community's shared values, which are embedded in their worldview, self-image, and rhetoric. Normative words such as honor and virtue, deployed in innovative ways by philosophers, can help to legitimize or delegitimize a policy or even a regime.

These were also times of economic growth and social transformation. China was advancing into the Iron Age. In Rome, which had completed the technological revolution in prehistory, iron appeared in the form of chains, by which it switched to the slave mode of production. Besides boosting productivity and generating more surpluses for warfare, each change had profound social and political ramifications. Small independent farmers rose in China thanks to improved tools and state land-distribution programs, but declined in Italy under the pressure from large slave-worked plantations. The agrarian version of the middle class, farmers who tilled their own lands, were not only the primary producers and taxpayers but also the reserve for mass infantry. Power emanated from the edge of the plowshare and the edge of the sword. The changing fortunes of small freeholders affected the social composition of the army, the distribution of political power, and the form of government that left lasting imprints on the Dragon and the Eagle.

In these animated milieus rose empire builders. Each conquered a large territory and developed institutions capable of conquest and subsequent government. Besides state building and empire building, it also engaged in nation formation, economic development, and cultural development. Each of these historical processes generally has its own dynamics. They interact and co-evolve, but not with locked steps. Sometimes one acts as an engine pulling the others; other times it lags and drags. Many socioeconomic forces defy the control of government, even modern governments armed with strong institutions and abundant information. Policy makers can at best provide a nudge or some rational guidance. An innovation may fail because relevant factors are not ready for it or are already way ahead. Not only what happens matters, but also when and under what conditions, depending on which an event's effects can be washed away or locked in. The relative *timing* of political actions and rapid changes in socioeconomic forces helps to mold the characters of resultant empires.

Important historical effects are often missed when historical factors are treated statically or processes in isolation. To keep in sight the dynamic interaction between domestic affair and geopolitical pressure, this chapter uses foreign wars as a background and chronological anchor in examining political, socioeconomic, and ideological developments.

The paths to the establishment of the Han Dynasty and Roman Empire each traversed three overlapping phases of war; the first brought city-sized states to territorial states, the second to empires, and the third to peace and stability. The first phase roughly corresponds to the Chinese Spring and Autumn period (722–479 BCE) and the Roman conquest of Italy (509–264 BCE). The second phase of war, the ends of which we can put at Qin's unification of China in 221 BCE and Caesar's march on Rome in 49 BCE, roughly covered the Chinese Warring States period and Roman expansion beyond Italy. The civil wars of the third phase, which ended with the 202 BCE battle of Gaixia and the 31 BCE battle of Actium, were the cruelest.

At the beginning of the first phase of war, lands of the future empires each hosted a constellation of city-sized states amid nebulae of pastoralists. The states came in various sizes and political organizations, but all shared the intimate socioeconomic connection between a city and its environing countryside. The rectangular shape and grid-like layout, which archeologists uncovered in many Zhou cities, were also favorites among Roman cities.[1] I use the clumsy term "city-sized state," because the political structure of the Zhou states was radically different from that of Rome and other classical city-states. The differences had lasting impacts.

As China entered the Spring and Autumn period, more than 1,200 states of various sizes were said to exist. A typical city's jurisdiction ranged between 430 and 1,700 square kilometers. Its inner wall enclosed about 0.5 square kilometer, but many of its roughly 3,000 households spilled into a much larger area surrounded by an outer wall.[2] The states reckoned their strength in terms of war chariots. A four-horse chariot carrying a driver, an archer, and a lancer led about ten foot soldiers, whose number would increase over time. Rarely did the armies of seventh-century BCE states exceed 1,000 chariots.[3] The four largest states—Qi, Jin, Chu, and Qin—were comparable in scale to early Rome. At its foundation, the Roman Republic had a population of between 30,000 and 40,000, which supported 6,000 infantry and 600 cavalry. It ruled over an area of about 900 square kilometers, of which the city itself occupied about 2.8 square kilometers. Although the biggest Latin city, it was unexceptional among Veii, Capua, Tarentum, and other large Etruscan and Greek cities in Italy.[4] In neither realm was the armed force professional. The numbers cited were not of a standing army but of the military reserve, which indicated a state's strength. When not called up for wars, which were often seasonal, reserve soldiers engaged in production, mainly farming. Such were the initial conditions of the minor leagues, whose games we briefly reviewed in the preceding chapter.

Two centuries of merger and acquisition, usually hostile, transformed the geopolitical landscapes. By the tripartition of Jin in 453 BCE, the host of city-sized states in China coalesced into a handful of territorial states. The seven great powers of the Warring States period—Qi, Qin, Chu, Yan, and Jin's three heirs Hann,[5] Zhao, and Wei—each had an approximate area of one or two present-day Chinese provinces. The larger ones matched the size of peninsular Italy. They turned from chariot to infantry, of which political reforms enabled them to field hundreds of thousands in sporadic wars.[6] A similar tenfold escalation occurred in the Mediterranean littoral. When Rome commenced overseas expansion in 264 BCE, Roman Italy excluding the Po Valley had a free population of about 3 million. It persistently fielded more than 100,000 troops in its wars with Carthage, the Hellenistic monarchies, and other Mediterranean powers.[7] Such were the major leagues ready for the second phase of wars, the topic of the following chapter.

Many historians emphasize the critical roles of warfare in state building, foremost in the democratic states of modern Europe, to a lesser extent in the despotic states of the ancient Orient.[8] "War was the great stimulus to state building." "War made the state, and the state made war."[9] Why?

To provide security, conduct foreign affairs, maintain domestic order, and offer essential services, a state needs complex administrative institutions to mobilize and concentrate the resources in its territory for large-scale projects that alter its social and physical conditions. Building organs of government, no easy task by itself, is made more difficult by resistance. Few inhabitants like taxation or conscription, the major burden of the state, even when it is for the common good. Resistance is especially strong if the state infringes on the privileges of preexisting social power, notably aristocrats, tribal chiefs, and parochial elites eager to grab the exaction for themselves. An effective inducement to concession and cooperation is a common enemy, either as a real or imagined foreign threat to security or as a foreign victim at whose expense all can profit. Warfare ruthlessly winnows incompetence. Competitive weaponry spurs technological innovation. Prodigious demand for war material stimulates economic production, the effective aggregation of which calls for financial instruments. External wars foster internal cohesion by offering rally cries, lucrative enterprises, or threats that impose discipline. Besides, they can serve as safety valves by what economists call the externalization of unwanted costs. Just as industries dump pollutants into the environment for others to clean up, a government can assuage domestic grievances by exporting malaise. "Beggar thy neighbor" and "batter thy neighbor" are common strategies. To cooperate in dominating outsiders, citizens compromise among themselves and acknowledge each other's freedom. Thus leading nineteenth-century European philosophers simultaneously promoted liberal democracy at home and imperial colonialism abroad.[10]

Victorious wars often entail territorial expansion. A conqueror must manage the acquired population, which again demands state capacity. Size matters. Expanding city-sized states face the challenge of scaling, which has shattered many imperial aspirants. The designs of most complex systems, physical or social, cannot be arbitrarily scaled up. That is why elephants do not have the skinny legs of insects. The legs break if the insect grows bigger and bigger, unless you make them disproportionally thicker or substitute steel for bone. In either case, you change the design. Tiny states are like insects. Their skeletal administrative structure breaks if scaled up indefinitely without design change. Understanding this, Aristotle argued that the effective government of a city-state obtains only for a citizen body of modest size.[11] His insight on scale and institutional design is not widely shared. The Romans did not heed it, until they learned the painful lesson of civil wars. Chinese Legalist reformers had similar insights, but they would be undermined by literati-officials who extended to a huge empire the political principles of tiny, family-dominated states.

Ancient states initially managed growth by various kinds of reproduction and aggregation. The Greek model of budding off independent colonies was the simplest, but the weak link between the mother city and its colonies prevented political cohesion and expansion.[12] More successful was the Roman organization following a layered hub-and-spokes pattern and the Chinese organization along a fractal configuration, schematically illustrated in Figure 2.1 and separately explained in sections 2.6 and 2.7. The model for each matured during its respective first phase of war. Both eventually failed. Further expansion required radical restructuring of government. When it actually occurred influenced the resultant government's character.

2.2 Technology and the Economy

"Technological progress has been one of the most potent forces in history in that it has provided society with what economists call a 'free lunch,' that is, an increase in output that is not commensurate with the increase in effort and cost necessary to bring it about." Thus remarks an economic historian.[13]

The two great productivity boosters in the preindustrial world are agriculture and iron. Agriculture had already taken root in our period of study. Iron tools spread in the Mediterranean world after the demise of the Mycenaean kingdoms that fought the Trojan War. By the birth of the Roman Republic, the technological revolution was mostly accomplished. Greek art and philosophy continued to soar, but not technology. Inventions such as Roman concrete were evolutionary, not revolutionary, and most benefited public constructions such as monumental buildings. In the private sectors—such as agriculture, textiles, and the use of power and materials—only modest progress was achieved between 500 BCE and 500 CE.[14] Peace induced prosperity by encouraging trade and monetization. Massive slave driving aside, however, economic growth came mainly from spreading known technology and putting more land under cultivation. The Roman economy was not stagnant. Rather, it experienced the maturing of the European Iron Age. As growth matures, it levels off.[15]

The East Asian Iron Age took off when the European one matured. Of the four ancient Old World civilizations, the Chinese was the youngest. Distinguishing features of civilization—writing, stratified society, urban settlement, monumental architecture—appeared in Mesopotamia and Egypt around 3000 BCE. The Hittites used iron before 1200 BCE.[16] In China, the earliest excavated writings, in the form of inscriptions on oracle bones, dated to 1500 BCE. Metallurgical iron appeared shortly before 500 BCE and iron implements spread in the following two centuries, but their quality and prevalence varied regionally. A few specimens were of steel, but many more were of poor quality iron that lay alongside tools of shell and stone in archeological sites. Weapons-grade iron,

Figure 2.1 **Political Structures**

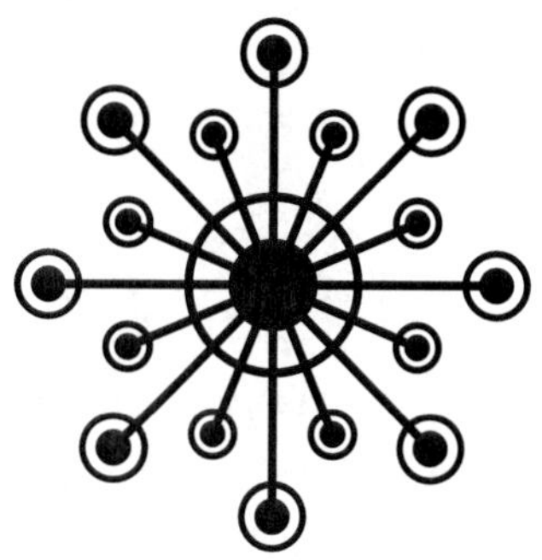

(a) Layered hub-and-spokes

(b) Fractal

which requires reduced brittleness, was rare in the warring states.[17] Near the mausoleum of the First Emperor, who died in 209 BCE, archeologists unearthed iron tools in productions sites. The product, the army of terracotta soldiers, held weapons of bronze, except some arrowheads.[18]

Soon the Chinese iron technology surged, and its radical difference from contemporaneous Western technology indicates indigenous origins. Long iron swords replaced short bronze swords completely in the early Han Dynasty.[19] Along with silk, Chinese iron made its way westward. By the middle of the first century CE, Roman encyclopedist Pliny the Elder wrote: "of all the varieties of iron, the palm goes to the Seric, sent us by the Seres with their fabrics and skins. The second prize goes to Parthian iron."[20] Seres, the Silk People, was the Roman name for the Chinese.

Bronze, being costly, was mostly reserved for weapons and luxuries. Without iron, stone and hard wood were the materials for most working tools. These primitive tools allowed thin margins for survival. To endure illness, famine, and other misfortunes, people pooled their resources in communal living and production, mutual help that we may view as a form of insurance. Scenes of Bronze Age communal farming are depicted on Achilles' shield in Homer's *Iliad* and in several poems in the Chinese *Odes*.[21] Whereas the Homeric age belonged to the mythical past, communal farming was common in China well into the sixth century BCE, when historical memory was well developed. Reverting to it would become a Confucian ideal.

The chariot, the prime weapon of the late Bronze Age in both the West and East, was expensive, demanding operational skill, and monopolized by aristocrats. Archeologists uncovered illustrations of chariots in Mycenaean tombs. By the time Homer wrote about the Trojan War, however, their military function was so remote the poet treated them as glamorous cabs that drove warriors to the battleground, where they alighted to fight on foot. Chariots as shock vehicles or mobile firing platforms dominated the Chinese battlefield in the Spring and Autumn period. In contrast, the Romans used chariots only in races and triumphant parades, not in war.[22]

Iron swords or spears suitable for infantry were more affordable to individual peasants. Moreover, iron tools elevated productivity and enabled family farms to generate enough surpluses not only to weather bad luck but also to buy weapons. Iron spread in the Mediterranean world during the "dark age," about which we know little except that the state structures were weak if existent. By archaic Greece, the small peasant and infantryman were already economically independent and militarily active. A modern scholar observes: "As metallurgy made iron weapons cheaper and more widely available, those who could use such weapons in warfare acquired higher status and with it a new claim on political power. Athenian democracy, especially under the reforms of Cleisthenes, was made possible by the support he could count on from the infantrymen (hoplites) who had become a critical component of Athenian military power."[23] Military service was the paramount criterion for citizenship in Greco-Roman city-states, suggesting their probable military origins. When Rome began to emerge under kings in the sixth century BCE, its social structure already contained widespread iron-using smallholders. Self-equipped farmer-soldiers formed the basis of the Centuriate Assembly, the democratic branch of the Republican government that led Rome to acquire an empire.[24]

Some commoners in feudalistic Chinese states held some political power because of their capacity as chariot warriors. Living in communal farms headed by aristocrats who controlled war gear, they were less powerful than were their Roman counterparts. Contrary to the timing in Rome, here the states already possessed significant political structures before they promoted household farms and mass infantry. Thus the Chinese farmer-infantryman emerged under the aegis of the state. The technological and economic progress that underlay this rise proceeded simultaneously with the formation of centralized monarchies. Both were inimical to aristocrats addicted to traditional privilege and urbanity. They forced the governments to reform. Conversely, a society in socioeconomic flux was more susceptible to state intervention and direction. The interplay between the forces of political, socioeconomic, and technological changes was more complex in China than in Rome.

Agrarian reform and struggle for land were driving forces in the politics of the Roman Republic and pre-imperial China. After sacking Veii, Rome distributed about half of the annexed territory to individual citizens in plots between 4 and 7 *jugera* (1 *jugerum* = 0.25 hectare = 0.625 acre), while keeping the other half as public land. Larger allotments were available later in frontier colonies, where infantrymen received 10 or 20 and cavalry officers 30 or 40 *jugera*. Such generosity was exceptional. Archeology confirmed the general impression that Italian farms smaller than 7 *jugera* were common.[25]

Land in ancient China was initially tied to aristocratic power. Private land ownership emerged only in the fourth-century BCE reforms, when centralizing governments systematically allotted land to individual households in return for tax and military service. The standard plot was 100 *mu*, doubled if the soil was poor. The area of one *mu* varied by more than a factor of two across states. For the most generous states, Qin and Zhao, 100 *mu* = 4.61 hectares = 11.4 acres = 18.2 *jugera*, a standard that persisted into imperial times.[26]

The Romans and Chinese were rational planners who surveyed and divided their lands meticulously. Their standardized tracts for massive distribution left imprints on the landscape still visible today. In many parts of Italy and former Roman provinces, aerial photography reveals grids of 200-*jugera* squares, each embracing a 100 2-*jugera* strip according to the Roman method of "centuriation."[27] In central China and the Wei River valley—the old domains of Qin, Zhao, and Wei, which had the most vigorous distribution programs—large-scale topographical surveys found a rectilinear layout, everywhere oriented north-south and east-west, covering more than 14 million hectares.[28]

Assuming that the average soil fertility was similar and that the Chinese cultivation technologies were catching up with the Roman, comparable typical small farm sizes indicate competitive living standards on the subsistence level. To understand agrarian lives, however, we must go beyond average conditions. Equally important are fluctuations, which often cause irreversible change and terrifying insecurity. Drought, flood, illness, war, irregular exaction, or other mishaps can force a peasant to sell his land and, worse, fall into the hands of usurers. Farmers are further at the mercy of market prices if they have to sell their produce to pay tax in money instead of in kind. Farming is a risky business, especially when irrigation, insurance, and reasonable debt finance are unavailable. Li Kui, reformer of Wei in the late fifth century BCE, calculated incomes and expenses and concluded that a standard 100-*mu* plot allowed a household of five to nine to get by in average years. However, he called for government action because various causes could vary the agricultural yield by up to a factor of twenty, and a few bad years could push a helpless family into inextricable poverty.[29] More memorable than Li's cool argument was the legend of Cincinnatus, Roman patrician and consul of 460 BCE. One of his sons led a gang of young aristocrats to harass proponents of reform, killed someone, and jumped bail awaiting trial on a capital charge. To pay off the bail, Cincinnatus sold everything, left the city, and settled in a deserted hovel. There a senatorial envoy found him laboring on a 5-*jugera* farm. Upon hearing the summons to save Rome from the Aequi, he exclaimed, "My land will not be sown this year, and so we shall run the risk of not having enough to eat!"[30] Farmland was the farmer's livelihood. Because the problem of subsistence was so basic and prevalent, no surprise agrarian reform became a major political concern in both realms.

Li's writing sheds light on another matter; it reckons food in grain but clothing and other expenses in units of coin. Coinage, by which authorities issue standardized pieces of metal marked to guarantee measure and value, is a sign of commercial and political sophistication. Compared to most other ancient agrarian economies, the Roman and Chinese were more monetized. Lydia in Asia Minor invented coinage in the seventh century BCE to receive tributes and pay mercenaries, mostly Greeks. The Greek city-states quickly learned to strike their own coins, discs stamped with elaborate designs that added propaganda to commercial utility. Colonists brought the model to Italy. The earliest Roman currency was bronze ingots. Coin minting was sporadic until the needs of the Pyrrhic War prompted systematic monetization. Rome first issued a series of bronze coins, the basic unit of which was the as, and then in 269 BCE struck the silver didrachma. The silver denarius, first issued in 214 BCE and valued at 10 bronze asses, was widely used for more than four centuries. The Romans often kept accounts in a quarter denarius, the bronze sesterce.[31]

After the king of Zhou started casting coins in 524 BCE, major states and ministerial houses issued their own coins. Bronze coins came in various shapes, but the unit was generally called qian. Large hoards excavated indicate their wide circulation. After unification, imperial China adopted the standard coinage design of a bronze disc with a square hole and inscription of weight. The simple design is utilitarian. The hole facilitates stringing and counting of these small denomination monies, whether or not it also symbolizes a square land under the domed heaven or a straight mind within a rounded personality. Gold was a popular currency among the rich and powerful of the warring states, but not minted as coins.[32]

2.3 Tradition and Social Relations

In many ancient cultures, a person had only one name, with perhaps a patronymic, such as Jesus son of Joseph, which conveys little information about ancestry. In contrast, a Roman or a Chinese had, besides a given name (*praenomen* or *ming*), a family name (*nomen* or *xing*) and, often for aristocrats, a surname (*cognomen* or *shih*) that kept track of clan branches. Married women were known by the family name of their parents, so that all women from the house of Julii were called Julia, as were women from the house of Chen called

Chenshih. The elaborate naming systems helped recognition of marriage alliance and distant relatives, preserved intergenerational memory, and facilitated the endurance of power.[33] They revealed the importance that the Romans and Chinese placed on the family. Both practiced ancestor worship.[34]

Both societies were patriarchic, although with varied customs. As the head of family, the Roman father, *paterfamilias*, had extensive legal power over family members, including all male offspring, married or not. The right to kill adult children became obsolete in the mid-Empire, but authoritarian paternal power spread throughout the Roman Empire and persisted beyond its fall.[35] The power of the Chinese father, *fu*, was no less extensive and enduring. He could punish family members corporally, even when they held high government posts. In Confucian ethics, the son's filial piety cultivated in family life extends into pious loyalty toward his political superior.[36]

The family was a cornerstone of tradition, whose authority ideally maintained sociopolitical stability with minimal coercion. The Romans and Chinese were conservative peoples. A modern historian remarks: "The Romans as a people were possessed by an especial veneration for authority, precedent and tradition, by a rooted distaste of change unless change could be shown to be in harmony with ancestral custom, 'mos maiorum.'"[37] Serving similar functions in China as did *mos maiorum* in Rome was *li*, narrowly ritual, and etiquette, broadly urbane in a status-conscious society.[38] Vaguely, *mos maiorum* or *li* encompasses conventional norms of behavior for various roles in the social hierarchy, so interrelated that ideally harmony prevails when everyone willingly conforms to the norm for his position. Most norms are habitual routines maintained by social pressure. Some acquire extra force from expression in words or formalization in rituals. A few enjoy codification into law. The whole set is supported by moral indoctrination.

Mos maiorum or *li* was embedded in practices, including political practices. A Roman tradition was aristocratic collective rule embodied in the Senate. To foster solidarity among hundreds of ambitious members, the Senate instituted judicial courts to resolve disputes, maintained a status hierarchy, and restricted career opportunities to prevent anyone from outstripping others in achievement and glory.[39] Conformity may encourage mediocrity, but regulated competition and wide distribution of honors created a large body of disciplined aristocrats of high uniform quality, even if less than brilliant. In its consistency and inexhaustibility lay the strength of the Republic.[40]

A Chinese tradition was mutual respect, strongly biased toward those in superior positions: the ruler, father, elder brother, and teacher. Chinese aristocrats did not organize their power in a corporate institution. Nevertheless, numerous rituals and behavioral norms succeeded in maintaining harmony and hierarchical deference among them for a long time. Shortly after the Zhou king fled to Luoyang in 771 BCE, his military power dropped below that of a secondary lord, but morally he was still the unique symbol of authority. No hardcore Huaxia lord who exercised kingly power arrogated the title until the 330s BCE. Such was the force of *li*.[41]

The Romans and Chinese both cherished moral influence through exemplary personality, usually reserved for those in power. The Roman Senate had little *potestas* or official power. Instead, it commanded deference through its *auctoritas* or suasive authority based on excellence and prestige.[42] Cicero deemed the common people imitators, arguing that history shows "the state has taken its character from that of its foremost men. Whatever changes have taken place in the conduct of its leaders have been reproduced in the lives of the people."[43] A similar view occurred in China, where rulers claimed authority through not *quan*, or official power, but *de*, or effective virtue or moral force.[44] *De* appeared often in the *Documents*, a collection of edicts and announcements of ancient kings, for example, "From *de* derives good policies that take care of the people."[45]

Amid similar reverence for moral authority, however, a contrast stood out. The Romans' respect for senatorial *auctoritas* did not diminish their respect for the law. The Confucian orthodoxy deemed the rule by personal *de* sufficient and denigrated the law as nothing but punishment, a coercive instrument.[46] This characteristic difference is detailed in sections 2.9 and 6.9, but we will often encounter its sociopolitical manifestations, which extended well beyond law and order. It stemmed from the two peoples' disparate views of the world order.

Let us crudely divide human relations into personal and social; a spouse engages in the former, a citizen in the latter. As soon as a newborn opens its eyes and sees the smile of its mother, a person-to-person relation is established. Personal relationship engages our private feeling, although its strength varies with the persons related. It is reciprocal, but not always symmetric. Each of us is embedded in a web of personal relations, whose principle virtues are love and loyalty (Figure 2.2a). The primordial bond of humanity, it is the one that holds through hell and high water. However, it is short-ranged and difficult to scale up. A person's direct empathy for another can extend only so far before emotional exhaustion, and personal ties often interfere with each other. Perhaps empathy suffices for tiny simple societies, but cohesive order in a large complex society also calls for common sense. Reasonable negotiation, conflict resolution, and integration of compromises build up social institutions, publicly known "impersonal" rules by which everyone abides, and consensus in which everyone immerses, without specifying the other parties involved (Figure 2.2b). Traffic laws constitute a familiar example of such institutions. Satisfying oneself in it, one simultaneously satisfies the welfare of others.

Social relations, whose principle virtue is justice and fairness, enrich the life of individuals while facilitating order and harmony in large-scale and complex human intercourse. By expanding the intellectual aspect of human activity, they open a public space and create a society akin to a three-dimensional world that incorporates heartfelt two-dimensional personal plans (Figure 2.2c). Personal and social relations can be compatible with each other, but not friction-free. Tragedies as in Sophocles' *Antigone* prompt us constantly to develop rational value judgment and refine our institutions, making them more accommodative to love without breaching justice.

Personal relations are ubiquitous. Patron-client relations, for instance, suffused the Roman and Chinese worlds. More important, familial relations are personal. We saw that both societies similarly cherished the family. Beyond the family, however, contrasts gaped. In feudalistic China, with which our story begins, the state and its ruling family were fused. Lordship and ministries were all hereditary. In Rome, familial prestige conferred such advantage that aristocratic families produced magistrates generation after generation. Nevertheless, magistracies were not hereditary. Everyone had to win elections for them. The Roman Republic made a clear legal distinction between the state and the family, which the Chinese under Confucianism had difficulty achieving.

With its roots in feudalistic China, Confucianism confined politics to asymmetric personal relations, all-pervading *guanxi*. In contrast, social relations were fundamental to the Western classical city-states. Whereas a Chinese was devoted to the ruler as a son was devoted to his father, a Roman citizen pledged allegiance to SPQR, the *Senatus Populusque Romanus* (Senate and the Roman people). Whereas feudalistic Chinese aristocrats were absorbed by family relations, the Romans were also concerned about the politics of living in the *polis* (city-state) and handling public affairs. The Chinese *gong*, now understood as the public, originally meant a lord or pertaining to the seigniorial house.[47] A new dimension shone forth in the name of Rome's *res publica*, the public realm common to the people beyond their family lives in *res privata*, the private realm. Rome had a vibrant public space, embodied in the forum of the popular assemblies and the Senate of aristocrats. There individuals participated in social relationship and developed the idea of a commonwealth. The law and other institutions, impersonal and impartial, represented this public space and introduced the notion of the state distinct from the family. This extra dimension in human life was absent in feudalistic China.

These ingrained traditions and their enduring influences will show up repeatedly in the following discussions. Although Chinese Legalist reformers introduced the public dimension, its growth would be stunted under Confucianism. The public spirit of the Roman Republic mostly collapsed in the Empire, but the institution of law remained firm. As childhoods shape

Figure 2.2 **Human Relations**

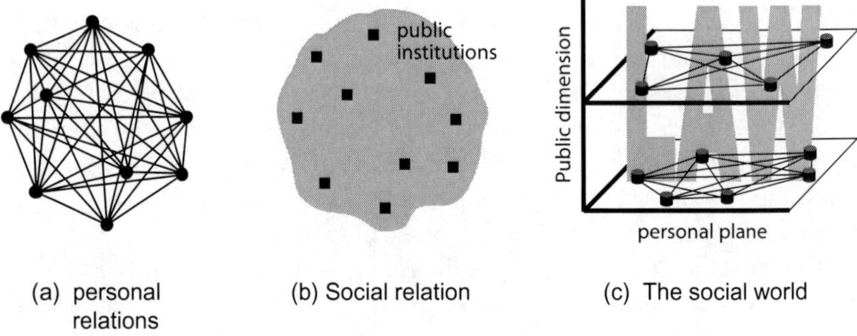

(a) personal relations (b) Social relation (c) The social world

characters, the Chinese would be less respectful of the law and public virtue than the Romans and their heirs.

2.4 Conflict and Merger of the Orders in Rome

The Roman Republic was barely fifteen years old when the *plebs* or commons seceded in 494 BCE. Of the three components of the old regime—the king, the advisory Senate, and the assembly rooted in the citizen militia—the last two changed little. The king was gone but his *imperium*, supreme power, remained and passed on to two consuls annually elected by the assembly. According to Livy, the "first step towards political liberty in Rome consisted in the fact the consuls were annually elected magistrates—in the limitation, that is, not of their powers but of their period of office."[48]

It was only a first step. In some ways, the arbitrary rule of one man merely became that of a few, for all consuls came from a small group of patrician families. Moreover, liberty did not guarantee prosperity. Craft and commerce declined in the infant Republic. Marauding Aequi and other mountain folks threatened security. Hard times forced many small farmers into debt. The plebs demanded debt relief and land allotment. They met coercive responses. Frustration led them to secede when their military service was most needed. In 494 BCE, many commons, including soldiers, left Rome for a nearby hill and disregarded orders to march against the Aequi. The patricians panicked and negotiated. The popular movement created organizations and leaders. More secessions followed, the last occurring in 287 BCE. Events of these two centuries historians call the Conflict of the Orders.[49]

The Conflict of the Orders actually consisted of three intertwining strands: first, the general struggle to build a satisfactory political structure; second, a struggle between two orders of wealthy landowners—the patricians and plebeians—to gain access to high government offices; and third, a struggle between the upper and lower classes on socioeconomic issues. By 287 BCE, the first two struggles were resolved, but the third was only temporarily mitigated. Clashes between the rich and the poor would eventually contribute to the downfall of the Republic.[50]

Many magnates from Latin and Etrurian cities immigrated into the infant Republic. Some joined native elites to constitute the plebeians, who aspired to the consulship and other high magistracies monopolized by the patricians. Their struggle found leverage in the widespread discontent of the plebs. By the Licinio-Sextian laws of 367 BCE, the patrician and plebeian orders reached a power-sharing agreement wherein each reserved one of two annual consulships. The plebeians shared patrician economic interests and promptly adopted patrician attitudes. Together the two formed a new aristocratic ruling circle, the *nobilitas*, notables. For them, the Conflict of the Orders ended in the merger of the orders.[51]

The common plebs demanded protection from arbitrary coercion and reforms in agrarian and debt laws. Their household farms were usually small. To make an adequate living, most needed supplementary income derived from public land. Unfortunately for them, great portions of public land were occupied by the rich and powerful. Access to public land fueled political agitation during the Conflict of the Orders and after. The plebeian elites made much of it, for the common good as well as for their own political ambition and economic encroachment.[52]

Compared to the rebellions of Chinese *guoren* discussed later, the secessions of Roman plebs showed more solidarity, respect for the law, ability at reasonable negotiation, and organizational innovations that accrued social and political gains. Compromises between the plebs and the patricians were not merely private bargains struck between two kin groups, which were local if not ephemeral. Upheld in the strong public spirit characteristic of the Republic, they persisted, accumulated, and were gradually institutionalized. New forms of institutions are central to successful revolutions. Because of them, the Conflict of the Order earned the epithet of "a bloodless revolution."[53]

An expression of solidarity was the citizens' response to the cry for help of a victim coerced by officials. The Chinese had an idiom: "seeing unfairness on the road, one pulls a knife to help," which expresses a personal urge. The Romans raised the aspiration for justice to an institutional level. Their cry for help gradually crystallized into *provocatio*, the citizen's right to appeal to the people for trial in capital cases. This civic freedom that protected citizens from the wantonness of coercive authority was won by the reasonable efforts of the oppressed themselves, not bestowed by the benevolence of sage kings. Repeatedly strengthened by subsequent laws, it became a cornerstone of Roman liberty.[54]

Another crystallization of popular will was the power of the tribunes. Tribunes, elected leaders of the plebs, originally lacked any legal power. Their only shield was their sacrosanctity conferred by the plebs' collective oath to avenge any harm to them. Protected by the lynch threat, a tribune could rescue a pleb from a magistrate by throwing his person between them. Vendettas and collective oaths were common to many cultures. Contemporaneous Chinese clans feuding for political power swore collective oaths, but the oaths died with the clans, leaving only covenant tablets to excite archeologists.[55] In contrast, the persisting organization of the Roman plebs and substantive negotiation with the ruling circle turned the inviolability of their tribunes into an institution, guaranteed by law instead of oath. Gradually, the tribunican ability to check the arbitrary exercise of *imperium* evolved into the legal power to annul an official act, the veto.[56]

Since the first secession, the commons had held their own plebeian meetings, which annually elected tribunes and voted to pass decisions called plebiscites. This "state within a state" was not always at loggerheads with the state. Instead, it cooperated on important issues such as erection of the Twelve Tables, Rome's first code of laws. By the threats of secession and the merits of cooperation, the plebs acquired civic liberty and the freedom from debt bondage. Eventually, their organizations merged into those of the state. The plebeian meeting developed into the Tribal Assembly alongside the original Centuriate Assembly of the Republic. The tribunes it elected became state magistrates. The Hortensian law of 289 BCE made plebiscites laws for the whole Roman people, patricians included.[57]

2.5 Backlash of Closing Imperial Frontiers

Simultaneously with the growth of its political institutions, Rome conquered Italy and, in 264 BCE, expanded overseas against Carthage. Many historians put the golden age of the Republic at the half century between the end of the Hannibalic war in 202 BCE and the destruction of Carthage in 146 BCE. Rome rose to empire and its domestic politics were never so tranquil. Times were good for the people. Distribution of annexed land and foundation of colonies, which assuaged much discontent of the plebs during the Conflict of the Orders, had almost ceased after the conquest of Italy. However, the Mediterranean opened a much wider frontier stretching from Spain to Syria. Legions marched in all directions. They came, they conquered, and they plundered. Victories in the rich and soft Hellenistic world brought abundant spoils and slaves, not to mention patriotic glory. Imperial conquest seemed to offer limitless opportunities that could satisfy everyone at the expense of the vanquished. Social harmony prevailed.[58]

As the law of diminishing returns set in, tensions appeared. The almost simultaneous sack of wealthy Carthage and Corinth on slim pretexts was a turning point not only in the eyes of Sallust, a Roman historian writing in the late Republic.[59] The imperial frontier, though still expanding, was growing at a rate slower than the rate of rising expectations. Wars still raged, but less from choice than from necessity to hold conquered territories and suppress their peoples, especially tough barbarians determined to regain their freedom. After Rome's victory over Macedon in 167 BCE, from pillaging Epirus alone each foot soldier got 200 denarii, almost two years' pay. After the sack of Numantia in Spain in 133 BCE, each soldier received only seven denarii, which probably came from the pocket of the commanding consul. Resistance to the draft appeared, especially to fight where it was easier to spill blood than to extract fat.[60]

Whatever booty legionaries got was a pittance compared to the haul of aristocrats who commanded expeditions and later governed provinces. Immense treasures of the East flowed into the hands of the already rich and powerful. Lacking alternative routes of investment that industrialization would offer, they put the war profit into land, buying or pushing out their poorer neighbors, making easy prey of families whose men were away on campaign. Their investment became more valuable after 167 BCE when Rome, satiated with spoils and indemnities, abolished tax on Italian land. Abundant labor was available to work the large estates. Victorious armies led in their wake strings of slaves. The number of slaves in Italy, which in 225 BCE stood at around 500,000, spiraled in two centuries to between 2 and 3 million. Meanwhile, the free population declined from 4.5 million to 4 million. In rural areas, where most jobs in agrarian economies resided, the free population dropped by 29 percent.[61]

Family farms could not compete. Many disappeared into large slave-worked plantations.[62] Many proud proprietors who marched out in the legions returned to find themselves dispossessed, by foreclosure or forceful seizure. In a way, they had fought for the ruin of their families.[63] Some migrated to Rome to work on public building projects or luxuries that war-enriched aristocrats competed to display. Others stayed as tenants or survived on casual work unprofitable for keeping full-time slaves. Amid the prosperity brought by empire, poverty rose.[64] According to researchers, "The differences between the rich and poor in wealth and style of life widened. The position of the poorest, the urban proletarian and the landless laborer, deteriorated sharply both absolutely and relatively to the rich."[65]

Malaise exported began to return home, bringing dividends that threatened state institutions.[66] Roman legionaries traditionally provided their own arms, for which their wealth had to be above a certain level. As they fell victim to economic polarization, the army reserve dwindled. Tiberius Gracchus, tribune of 133 BCE, piloted a bill to parcel out public land to poor citizens, thus to rejuvenate the middle class and alleviate the army's recruitment difficulty. To make the land available, the bill limited the occupation of public land by any individual to 125 hectares, plus 62.6 hectares for each son, at a time when 2.5 hectares would make a small farm. The bill became law with overwhelming voter support. Most senators regarded it as a gross infringement on their freedom; they had built estates on public land, often without paying rent. When Gracchus sought a second annual term to implement the law properly, opponents accused him of aiming at *regnum*, or one-man rule. They clubbed him and his followers to death, ignoring their civil right to trial.[67]

Ten years later, Gaius Gracchus became tribune and put together a comprehensive reform package that went beyond land allotment. Sharing the fate of his brother Tiberius, he and his followers were slaughtered without trial. His attackers were led by a consul with the explicit blessing of the Senate, which justified extreme actions in the name of national security.[68]

The Gracchi brothers hailed from an illustrious notable family. Their reforms, which addressed widely acknowledged problems, were not revolutionary. However, their method of steering their bills to law was innovative in encouraging the popular assemblies to exercise their legislative and elective power. Its legality was arguable, the laws were ambiguous. The massacres were another matter.[69] The Greco-Roman historian Appian remarked in his history of Roman civil wars that the sword was never carried into the Assembly until the butchery of Tiberius Gracchus and his followers. "And this foul crime, the first perpetrated in the public assembly, was not the last, but from time to time something would always occur."[70]

The disparate outcomes of democratic movements in the early and late Republic reveal the effects of what political scientists call "the circulation of elites," whereby the ruling circle enfeebles the masses by creaming off their potential leaders.[71] In the Conflict of the Orders, the plebeians organized the common people and the plebeian meeting functioned as an opposition party. No such popular organization appeared in the struggles of the late Republic, which Sallust identified as the fatal weakness of the democrats.[72] The plebeians had joined the aristocracy. The tribunes, nominally the people's champions, had become a part of the establishment. Their one-year term and other constitutional rules precluded them from concentrating the diffused power of the masses into a persistent bargaining position. With the best of intentions, they could only stir up temporary popular enthusiasm for individual bills. Such were the Gracchi's achievements. However, they were fragile against concerted aristocratic opposition. The people's power uncovered by the Gracchi soon became a tool for ambitious politicians to advance their own interests without solving basic social problems.

With social reforms withering, the army maintained troop levels by gradually transferring the burden of armament onto the state and lowering the wealth qualification of legionaries. Finally, in 107 BCE, Marius, a new man elected consul seven times on his military merit, openly enlisted proletarians.[73] Conscription continued, but the army increasingly comprised volunteers recruited from the rural poor; urban plebs made lousy soldiers. In return for the blood they risked spilling, soldiers demanded land upon retirement. They found in their generals champions for what their tribunes failed to deliver. Ambitious aristocrats were quick to seize the opportunity. Sulla led the Roman army against Rome in 88 BCE to get his command of a lucrative foreign war. Having won the loyalty of the troops with spoils and the promise of settlement on Italian lands confiscated from political enemies or grabbed by force, he returned to continue the civil war. Pompey and Caesar would follow down the path. Agrarian reform morphed into settlement of veterans. The land problem never went away, but now those who pressed for it had concrete power in their hands, the sword.[74]

2.6 How Democratic Was the Roman Republic?

The Roman Republic had no written constitution. What is now called its constitution, a collection of legislated laws, unwritten rules, and traditional mores, had evolved over the centuries. Throughout all changes, it retained the essential triad of magistracy, Senate, and assembly. Polybius and Cicero regarded it as a mixture of monarchy, aristocracy, and democracy, the three forms of government that Aristotle analyzed.[75] Modern political scientists have another term. One writes, "It is, in brief, the first case in this history of government of '*checks and balances.*' The completest example of this kind in the contemporary world is the government of the United States."[76]

Executive power resided with the magistracy. The Roman Republic had about eighty elected magistrates. Highest in moral authority were two censors responsible for enrolling senators, classifying citizens, managing public land, and granting large contracts for public works. The other senior magistrates, two consuls and eight praetors, held *imperium*, by which they commanded armies, issued edicts, and employed coercion to enforce their will. They convened the Senate and the Centuriate Assembly, proposed bills, and conducted the legislative process. If passed, the resolutions depended on them for execution. However, *imperium* had constraints. Within Rome's city boundary, a magistrate's military command lapsed and his power over citizens met the right to appeal. Outside the city, his *imperium* was kingly, but effective only within the geographical area assigned to his command. He depended on the Senate, which held the purse strings, to provide for his troops. Although immune to prosecution in office, victims of his misconduct abroad could bring charges in Rome after his tenure.[77]

All magistrates except the censors served one-year terms, and severe term limits existed. They served not singly but in colleges, and colleagues could veto the decisions of each other. The ten tribunes held more power than their junior position indicated, not only because they convened and presented bills to the Tribal Assembly, but because they could veto the decisions of any magistrate, even the most powerful. To avoid confusion in an emergency, the people could erect a dictator for a limited term.[78]

The Senate, which met about forty times a year, was the chief deliberative body in the Roman government. Senators numbered about 300 down to 81 BCE, when their number doubled. They sat for life, barring misconduct. Most senators and all the powerful ones were magistrates or former magistrates. As the state's repository of political and military experience, the Senate secured the government's continuity. Revenue and expenditure, the administration of Italy, and details of foreign affairs were its domains. It levied armies, authorized funds for provisions, assigned theaters of command to magistrates, and gave them instructions. When Rome's expanding empire required provincial governors, the Senate arrogated the power to assign proconsuls (*pro*, in place of). On major foreign policies, including wars and peace treaties, its advice required the approval of the assemblies, which usually although not necessarily went along. The Senate lacked formal coercive power. It exerted its will through the consuls and other magistrates, who had the final say if they chose to balk. However, magistrates usually complied with the Senate's wishes, as befitting the aristocratic ethos of collective rule.[79]

The Centuriate Assembly elected the senior magistrates. The Tribal Assembly elected the junior magistrates. Annual election campaigns were fierce. Candidates in shiny white togas diligently canvassed voters, helped by their families, friends, and clients. The popular assemblies also had legislative power. They voted on questions of declaring wars, terminating hostilities, concluding treaties, and making alliances. Their decision to reject or pass a bill into law was final.[80]

The Roman people had ultimate power in their votes. However, the options they could vote on were circumscribed in advance by aristocrats. The popular assemblies could not initiate or amend bills, and voters had no right to speak individually in assembly. When convened by a consul or a tribune and presented with a bill, voters heard arguments pro and con, then returned an up or down vote. The bills that came before them were usually already cleared by the Senate. If mavericks dared to bypass Senate approval, opposing senators could find someone to veto it; there were ten tribunes with the power. A Gracchus may occasionally outmaneuver the Senate, but with a one-year term limit, he could not accomplish much. The assemblies could wrest simple dispensations such as free bread and circuses. On complex social issues and important reforms, however, they were no match for a reluctant Senate.[81]

The assemblies were more capable in electing their own heroes against aristocratic objection. However, candidacy was limited by wealth qualification, a conspicuous feature of the Roman social and political world. Periodic censuses classified citizens into seven orders according to their wealth: the *proletarii* (proletarian), five grades of *assidui* (proprietor), and an upper class of *equites* (equestrian). A proletarian was one with less than 4,400 sesterces; an equestrian, more than 400,000 sesterces, when a day laborer was paid about two sesterces. Only those in the equestrian order could enter the Senate or stand for magistracies. Even in the army, the junior office of military tribune was almost closed to soldiers who were not already equestrians.[82]

Wealth qualifications also determined the voting structure of the Centuriate Assembly that elected senior magistrates. Voters were grouped unevenly into 193 centuries. All proletarians, who constituted about one-half of the citizen body, squeezed into a single century. About 2,000 equestrians occupied eighteen. The highest-grade proprietors shared seventy centuries. Each century returned its majority view in a single vote. The rich centuries voted first and voting stopped as soon as the majority was reached. Thus the poor had no say except on the rare occasions when the rich split evenly among themselves.[83] The Spartan Nabis summarized his observation in his speech to the Romans: "You choose your cavalry and your infantry by assessment of wealth, and you want a few to transcend the others in riches, with the commons subject to these."[84]

In sum, the Roman people reigned and the aristocrats ruled. Formally, the Roman constitution was a direct democracy with popular sovereignty in legislation and election.[85] In practice, wealthy aristocrats, who filled the Senate and magistracies, enjoyed virtually unchallenged control.[86] Legislation gave the people some stake in the government, a way to communicate their desires to the ruling class, and a vent for their grievances. The annual election of magistrates secured smooth transfer of executive power among aristocrats. It made the people legal arbiters and judges in aristocratic competition, so that they acted as a ballast or brake on rampant escalation of rivalry. Scholarly evaluations differ in details, partly because of vagueness in the notion of "democracy" itself. Yet they generally agree that the Roman Republic was essentially an aristocracy, although one with a democratic streak.[87] One summarizes: "Rome was in no sense a democracy; but there was apparently a strong ideological tradition in citizens' rights, backed by the armed force of citizen soldiers, and expressed in popular elections and in legislation by popular assemblies."[88]

In five centuries, the Republic brought Rome from a city to an empire. It eventually failed. Why? To paraphrase a famous answer regarding the fall of the Roman Empire, instead of asking why the Republic fell, perhaps one should rather be surprised that it had lasted so long. A political scientist points out that the formal Republican constitution was self-defeating. Ten senior magistrates and ten tribunes each had the power to pilot bills. The magistrates could veto the resolutions of their colleagues and juniors; the tribunes, the resolutions of everyone. The assemblies had the unlimited power to make into law any bill that came before them. Checking and balancing each other, they could easily produce a do-nothing government. Yet paralysis rarely occurred, until toward the end. The government worked. How? The political scientist answers, "It worked, as the British Constitution does today, very differently from what constitutional law propounded, and by the same device: unwritten rules to supplement and/or circumvent its formal provisions."[89]

The Senate's power, based on aristocratic status and prestige, was mainly traditional. Such power was formidable in conservative Rome. The assemblies held formal rights to legislate, but customarily deferred to aristocratic leadership. Maintaining the balance, on which the Republic thrived, depended on all sides refraining from claiming their respective full legal prerogative. Self-restraint worked when the open imperial frontier served as an outlet for discontent. The true test of a constitution lies in its ability to weather times when social harmony dissipates and interest groups polarize. As the spoils of empire widened the inequality gap and social tension mounted, democratic movements intensified in the late Republic. Unfortunately, under the circumstances they aggravated divisiveness. Tribunes asked the assemblies to exercise their full legislative power. Aristocrats mobilized their whole arsenal to block popular demands.[90] Sallust sighed, "So the whole community was split into parties, and the Republic, which hitherto had been the common interest of all, was torn asunder."[91]

So far, we have discussed Rome's domestic government, where all those involved were Roman citizens. Imperial government was another matter. Rome initially organized Italy in a layered hub-and-spokes configuration, which imposed divide-and-rule vertically and horizontally (Figure 2.1a). Rome annexed central Italy only. Over the remaining four-fifths of the peninsula it exerted hegemonic domination, which required fewer administrative resources. It suppressed previous multilateral political relations among allied cities and subjugated each to itself by a specific unequal bilateral treaty, just like a spoke attached to the hub. On the spokes, the politically isolated subordinate cities were vertically divided from each other and unable to pool resources for opposition. Rome, the hegemon at the hub, had maximum flexibility. It could easily sprout more spokes as it expanded and upgrade or downgrade each spoke as it saw fit. Its colonies also became loyal spokes. Thus Rome expanded by aggregating into a confederacy of small political entities, each with simple and submissive structures.[92]

Two common features stood out among the great variety of Rome's relations with subordinates. First, it always demanded self-equipped troops under its command. The cost of military contingents was an indirect tax on the allies. Nevertheless, active involvement and the prospect of profit made it easier to bear than monetary tribute, which was seldom levied. Victories generated booty, which Rome distributed fairly for a long time. Treaties with major allies formalized the ways of spoil distribution, including the settlement on conquered lands. A profit-sharing military enterprise helped to cement the Roman confederacy.[93]

Another feature of Roman domination was to slice each city horizontally into the wealthy ruling class and the rest. In founding colonies, Rome picked wealthy leaders and exported its own hierarchical social pattern. It dealt with Italian allies in a similar way. Everywhere it suppressed the commons and systematically sought out and strengthened local aristocrats, effectively using them to rule for it. As long as they controlled the commons and submitted totally in foreign affairs, they were allowed significant autonomy in domestic affairs.[94] A historian, describing Rome's conquest of Tarentum, comments, "The episode illustrates a constant feature of Rome's foreign policy, namely her support for the upper classes in the communities of Italy, who regarded Rome as their natural ally, where the masses were normally hostile."[95] Local aristocrats of cities such as Arretium accepted Roman overlordship in return for support against the lower classes. Rome's support was forceful. When the commons of Volsinii seized power in 265 BCE, the Romans occupied the town, destroyed it, and resettled the survivors a few kilometers away.[96] Killing the chicken teaches the monkeys a lesson, as the Chinese say.

Perhaps it is no surprise that the hostility of the oppressed vented itself when Rome's image of invincibility was damaged by Hannibal's invasion. Livy wrote, "All the Italian communities were sick of the same disease—the split between the lower orders and the nobility, the senate supporting Rome, the commons working in the Carthaginian interest."[97] Livy's use of *all* is an exaggeration, and modern scholars warn against attributing class struggle to the ancient world. Nevertheless, Croton and Nola, from which Livy generalized, were less likely accidents than repercussions of characteristic Roman policies. A similar situation occurred later in Greece, where Rome had been propping up the rich for two decades. When Rome lost a battle to King Perseus of Macedon, "the attachment of the people to Perseus, which had been for the most part concealed, burst forth like fire," wrote Polybius.[98] Yet the legions prevailed. Greek democracies were already under oligarchic pressure.

Rome's arrival made their decline final. Henceforth, democracy ceased to be a normal form of government.[99]

The congruence of political and economic interests, which has been identified as a reason for Rome's imperial success, dovetailed on domestic policies. We saw earlier that the Republic classified its citizens according to their wealth and legally concentrated political power in the hands of the wealthy. The rich justified this policy on the ground that they shouldered heavier public burdens in tax and military service. The rationale crumbled in the late Republic, when the Italian land tax was abolished and military service transferred to the poor. Proportional equality morphed into the inequality of a plutocracy, a government of the wealthy.[100]

Plutocracy extended to imperial policies. After the Social War of 91 BCE, Rome's hegemony in Italy turned into direct rule. The vertical or territorial divide-and-rule policy terminated. The hub-and-spokes turned into a cake, but a layered one. The horizontal or economic divide remained a permanent cornerstone of Roman rule. A network of wealthy local oligarchs, the cream of society who shared interests in securing their properties and dominating over the commons, ruled for Rome and extended as its dominion expanded across the Mediterranean. This policy was so successful that the division of the population, citizens and subjects alike, into upper and lower classes, the *honestiores* and *humiliores*, was legally codified in the high Empire.[101]

2.7 Feudalistic Parceling of Sovereignty in China

Lord Yi of Wey was detested for his profligate spending on pet cranes when the pastoralist Di invaded in 660 BCE. The city people grumbled when coming for arms: "Send the cranes. The birds receive stipends. Why ask us to fight?" Lord Yi led the chariots out against the invaders and perished together with the troops. Only 730 persons from the city survived the onslaught.[102] Qi came to the rescue, as befitted its role as hegemon. It sent an army with relief provisions and convened several lords to drive off the Di and build a city in a new location for the Wey. Gathering refugees from two subsidiary towns, Wey was reconstituted as a state with a population of 5,000 and an army of thirty chariots. The new ruler, Lord Wen, reduced levies and promoted agriculture. Instead of accepting his proposal to abdicate in favor of someone more capable in countering renewed Di raids, the city people rallied after him. When the Di sued for peace in 628 BCE, Wey recovered its power as a state with 300 chariots.[103]

Wey's political structure was typical of the states that grew from the Zhou's military colonization four centuries earlier. A state comprised three major groups of people: the aristocracy with the lord at its top, the *guoren* or city people, and the *yeren* or field people. The aristocrats and *guoren*, the descendants of the original conquerors and colonists, mostly lived in the city and its immediate environs. The *yeren* were natives who inhibited the outlying countryside.[104]

The non-aristocrats mostly engaged in communal farming, but the *guoren* organized their communities according to kinship, the *yeren* according to domicile. In the "well-field" arrangement, members of a community collectively worked the lord's demesne. Besides farming, they were obliged to perform corvée labor and submit textile and other goods. For their own subsistence, individual households got allotments of farmland, rotated periodically to give everyone equal access to good and poor fields.[105]

The *guoren* and *yeren* resembled the common Roman citizens and the conquered subjects. The field people were excluded from military service and politics. The city people constituted the army reserve. They paid a military tax but did not provide individual armament as the Roman legionary did; aristocratic houses maintained the equipment for chariot warfare. When not called up, *guoren* mainly farmed, but among them were also artisans, traders, and *shi*, who served as stewards, clerks, and palace guards.[106]

The *guoren* as a group derived considerable power from military service and lineage cohesion. They could conclude covenants with the lord independently of aristocratic ministers, with whom they sometimes disagreed. In aristocratic faction fights, the voices of the *guoren* could be stabilizing, although far less effective than Roman elections stabilizing aristocratic competition. There was no institutionalized forum or consultation channel akin to the Roman assemblies. If a lord chose to ignore them, the *guoren* could only resort to violence. They had deposed many lords and killed many high ministers. Their potential for rebellion or desertion might deter rulers from outrageous transgressions, but at the cost of creating social havoc.[107]

Late Bronze Age aristocrats held the bulk of power and justified their prerogatives by long pedigrees and traditions. Three intertwined principles underwrote their political organization: *zongfa* or lineage rule, *shiguan* or hereditary ministry, and *fengjian* or feudalistic parceled sovereignty. Operating together, they fused familial, economic, and political factors into a feudalistic form of government. Although archaic, they are worth a close look. Together with elaborate rituals and literature, many of their features constitute the Way of ancient kings, the central ideal of Confucianism.

Zhou's *zongfa* was based on patrilineal genealogy. The head of the principal lineage passed his position as the clan's patriarch to the eldest son from his principal wife. His other sons established secondary lineages. They were subordinate to the principal lineage but, as founders, they became heads of their respective lineages and passed their positions to their eldest sons, while their younger sons established tertiary lineages under their authority. The lineages maintained ancestral temples and burial grounds, sponsored schools and ceremonies, and provided hardship relief. The *zongfa* system cemented large kindred groups. Its rigid rules and power hierarchy would decay, but its custom of networking relatives would persist in relaxed forms as a major social bond for millennia.[108]

Fengjian was the political basis of the early Zhou's military colonization. In feudalistic parceling of sovereignty, the Zhou king reigned over all under heaven but actually ruled a limited royal domain. Extra territories he split into parcels, which he apportioned as fiefs to various lords. Within his fief, the lord was suzerain with juridical, fiscal, and military power. His relation with the king changed over time. The strong kings of early Zhou demanded certain services and appointed ministers for the lord's fiefs. By the Spring and Autumn period, the king had lost all ability to interfere, and the lords become sovereigns except in title. A lord organized his state as the king did, albeit on a smaller scale. He directly governed a seigniorial domain and apportioned the remaining territories to his vassals, who acquired titles and managed their own fiefs autonomously. The notion of landlord was undifferentiated from that of lord. The lord exacted corvée labor from his subjects, who worked his demesne in the well-field arrangement.[109]

In Zhou's feudalistic organization, the lords were mostly sons and relatives from secondary lineages of the royal clan. Similarly, tertiary lineages constituted the bulk of vassals. The lineage system and parceled sovereignty worked hand-in-glove. *Qinqin*, the love of relatives, was the chief political virtue. Politics based on familial and personal bonds would become a major component in Confucianism.[110]

State ministers administered the king's royal domain or the lord's seigniorial domain. State ministries were usually hereditary, and the top ones usually claimed by lords to the king or vassals to the lord. Most minister-vassals were relatives, whom the lord found difficult to dismiss without being attacked for vitiating *qinqin*.[111] A minister-vassal attended to both affairs of his lord (*gong*) and affairs of his own fief (*si*). These were the original meanings of the words *gong* and *si*, now understood as meaning "public" and "private."[112]

An ancient text described the feudalistic hierarchy of Zhou government: "The son of heaven founds the state (*guo*). The many lords establish families (*jia*). Ministers set up side houses. Officials start minor lineages. The *shi* have dependent relatives."[113] *Guo* and *jia* originally had similar organizations and functions, differing only in their status and size. While texts on the early Zhou referred to the king's state and the lord's family, those on the Spring and Autumn period referred to the lord's state and the minister's family. *Guojia*, the modern Chinese term for the state, is literally "state-family."

The feudalistic hierarchy created by repeated segmentation of authority resembled what mathematicians call a fractal, which exhibits the same structure at all scale levels. The fractal in Figure 2.1b exhibits at all scales an equilateral triangle composed of three smaller equilateral triangles enclosing an inverted triangular blank. The corresponding basic pattern that occurred at all levels of the Zhou's parceled sovereignty was the family. Imagine that the triangle represents a family, the blank the family's head, and a smaller triangle his subordinate. Within each subordinate family, we find the same pattern of a head and three subordinates. The largest head is the king. The successively smaller heads are lords, vassals, and so on. On each level, the relation of a subordinate to the head is akin to a son's piety to his father, which is natural because of prevalent blood relationship. The notion "to rule the state by filial piety" would persist well into imperial China.[114]

The fractal structure (Figure 2.3a) was hierarchical, but it differed radically from the more familiar hierarchy of the branching structure (Figure 2.3b) characteristic of the army or bureaucracy, where a government comprises many departments, each of which comprises many divisions, and so on. Branching implies a chain of command and a sense of loyalty to the whole. Fractal does not. Segmentation of power and loyalty was the essential characteristic of parceled sovereignty. Direct power relations occurred only within each level. A minister owed loyalty to his lord. A vassal in the minister's family owed loyalty to the minister but not to the lord. This distinction became serious if conflict broke out between the lord and the minister, because one could not serve two masters. When a ministerial family in Lu became too powerful and a vassal of the minister tried to strengthen the lord of Lu, contemporaries censured the vassal for treachery.[115] The loyal vassal was one who declared, "I am the servant of the family, and have no concern for the state."[116] The virtue of segmented loyalty fit well with a power structure based solely on personal relations. It eased the demand on a person by limiting the number of his political relations and the social distance of his relational reach, so that his political thinking was essentially confined to his family or family-like circle. Such thinking would influence Chinese society and politics long after the demise of parceled sovereignty.[117] We will see how it contributed to the demise of the Han Dynasty.

Compared to the hub-and-spokes model of Rome's federation in Italy, the Zhou's fractal model of parceled sovereignty was convoluted. In neither model did the suzerain's power reach down to the local population, except where it ruled directly. Rome divided its subjects into numerous tiny, isolated parcels on a single level, where each subject city faced the resources not only of Rome but also of all the other cities subject to it. Thus Rome's power was everywhere overwhelming. The fractal model organized divisions on several levels, so that on the top level, the Zhou king faced a handful of great lords, whose resources were comparable to his and who could ally against him. His relative power was nowhere as great as that of Rome.

Figure 2.3 **Power Relationship** (solid lines)

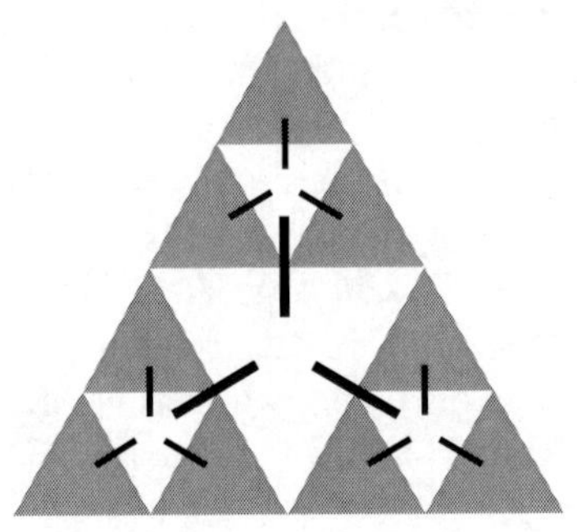

(a) feudalistic (fractal)

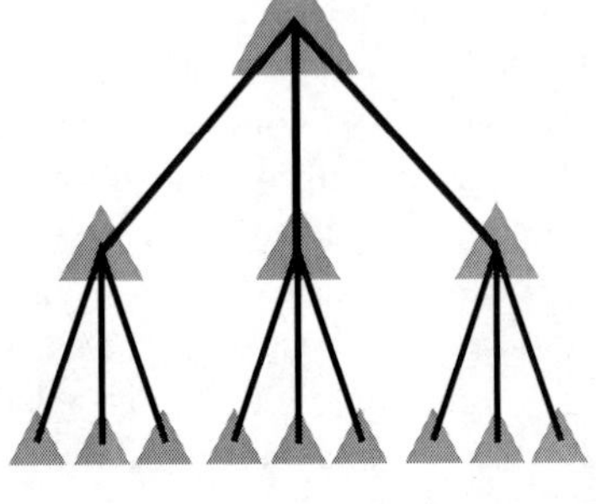

(b) bureaucratic (branching)

The parceling of sovereignty facilitated territorial expansion in the Zhou conquest and again in the early Spring and Autumn period. Large lords annexed small neighbors and invested a host of ministerial houses. These new houses adapted the tested form of government to their variegated environments, experimented with novel administrative techniques, adopted the innovations of rivals, and competed for ascendancy. Like bees swarming to new hives, they encouraged population growth and maximized the effects of fertility. As populations expanded, however, the weakness of parceled authority surfaced. Few new houses appeared in the later Spring and Autumn period. Instead, established ministerial and even seigneurial houses fell as their subordinates turned usurpers. Conditions were ripe for turning from extensive expansion to intensive consolidation of power.[118]

The case of Jin was most illustrative and consequential. More than a dozen new ministerial families were enfeoffed in the mid-seventh century BCE, when Lord Wen conquered large territory, led Jin to hegemony, and rewarded meritorious followers. Besides building up their individual families, these parvenus shared commands of Jin's armies and rotated as the chief executive minister. They were like spirited horses to the chariot that was Jin. Working as a team under the rein of strong lords, they secured Jin's hegemony. Yet the chariot could shatter if the horses went their own ways.

Foreign threats restrained Jin's domestic rivalry for a while. When they subsided after the victory over Chu in the 575 BCE battle of Yanling, internal conflict boiled over. Ministerial houses preyed on each other and encroached on the state. Eventually, only the ministerial houses of Zhao, Wei, and Hann survived. They effectively partitioned Jin in 453 BCE. That year traditionally marked the beginning of the Warring States period.[119]

Besides Jin, usurpation occurred in Qi, Lu, and other states.[120] Viewed within the scheme of parceled sovereignty, power slid from the king to the lords and then to the ministers. Actually, the scheme itself was crumbling. The political structure was slowly transforming from the feudalistic fractal model of Figure 2.3a to the bureaucratic branching model of Figure 2.3b. The feudalistic aristocracy hollowed out, its power gravitating toward the monarch above and the common people below. The old lord of Jin was the big brother among aristocrats. The new lords of Zhao, Wei, and Hann were embryonic monarchs keen on centralizing power. Recognizing aristocratic threats from their own adventures, the usurpers tried to kick away the ladder behind them. Parceling of annexed authority and hereditary ministries were too dangerous. Instead, they experimented with direct rule through salaried officers. They had strived to win hearts and minds on their roads to power. To prevent others from outdoing themselves in the game, they took the initiative in political and socioeconomic reforms, eventually elevating their states to kingdoms. They had big opportunities to seize. Seismic changes were opening up frontiers in several dimensions.

2.8 A New Elite in a Socioeconomic Revolution

In 513 BCE, twenty-three years after Zichan in the state of Zheng published the first code of law in China, Jin followed suit and inscribed its penal code on an iron cauldron.[121] This was the first mention of an iron implement in reliable texts. The temporal proximity of the two firsts was probably not coincidental. New technologies raised productivity and new prosperity stimulated socioeconomic upheaval. In response, governments tried to regulate changes by various reforms, of which the publication of laws was one.

Creeping technological improvement turned into a gallop.[122] As individual households became more confident in producing surpluses to save for hard times, communal farms unraveled. Demesne fields lay in waste. State extraction by corvée labor failing, Lu initiated the land tax in 594 BCE. It diffused to other states as household farms mushroomed on lands previously too difficult to cultivate. The city people's political leverage dissipated. Their communities and lineages decayed. Their charioteering skills approached obsolescence. Infantry increasingly dominated warfare and the field people could fill the ranks equally well. Gradually, *guoren* and *yeren* merged into a single class of commoners.[123]

The states still controlled most bronze works, but private undertakings claimed a large share in the new industry of iron smelting. When not at war, the states tried to keep tariffs low, roads safe, and rivers navigable. Coinage proliferated everywhere. State capitals, originally administrative centers, became consumer cores drawing in specialized products from afar. Commercial cities sprang up near transportation hubs. China's population grew, passing the 10 million mark in the Warring States period.[124]

Alongside people, goods, and money, ideas multiplied and circulated. Sharing the crowded roads with diplomats, soldiers, and merchants were the *shi*: aspiring reformers, egotistic preachers, opportunistic persuaders, and a wide variety of men of various births, eager to tender their services to lords and aristocrats. We have met the *shi* at the bottom of the feudalistic aristocracy and the top of the city people, serving as petty officers. Aristocratic lineages ideally educated their members. The multiplication of lineages piled up excess descendants at the bottom, as did poverty and loss in power struggles. Efforts saved by elevated farming productivity allowed some commoners the leisure for learning. Competition among states and aristocrats made the necessity of talented aides into a creed. Aggressive recruitment and generous patronage opened opportunities. Meritocracy was on the rise. In the sociopolitical upheaval, where aristocrats and commoners met became a conduit of social mobility. From it emerged the transformed *shi*, self-conscious and ambitious. Because of feudalistic segmentation of loyalty, the *shi*, who was rather low on the hierarchy, owed no duty to his native state and could freely serve an enemy state. To kings, foreign officers were often more insightful and less threatening than native aristocrats. The movement of *shi* among various states spread novel ideas and political innovations. They supplied the brainpower for state building.[125]

"The four peoples, *shi*, farmer, artisan, and merchant, are the state's foundation stones."[126] This text, probably written in the Warring States period, was the first articulation of a social division. Set alongside Aristotle's four chief divisions of the masses—farmers, mechanics, shopkeepers, and day laborers[127]—we see three major occupations ranked in the same order. The day laborer may be universal, but the *shi* was not. Educated citizens abounded in Greece, but they did not constitute a politically significant class as they did in China. Born of the decaying aristocracy, the *shi* as a group never severed its umbilical cord to political power. Diverse and intellectually vibrant in its early days, the *shi* would mature into the monocultural and doctrinal *shidafu*, the literati-officials, the signature ruling elite of imperial China.[128]

The preeminent *shi*, Confucius, was an impoverished aristocrat who threw open the door of education by welcoming any student who paid tuition. He styled himself not as an originator but as a transmitter of tradition, especially the Zhou tradition, whose moral underpinning he brought into relief. Acceptable ruling-class customs, interpreted in ethical terms, receive a fresh life rooted in daily practices, especially in family life. The *junzi*, originally meaning the son of the ruler, gradually changes to a superior man, noble in character but not necessarily in birth, clinging to aristocratic values even while slipping in rank and power. Appealing to people's empathy and moral intuition, Confucius expounds the supreme virtue of *ren*, benevolence, which his followers supplement with *yi*, righteousness. Self-cultivation of a virtuous character, firm in moral principle and smooth in maintaining harmonious personal relations, became the ideal of superior men.[129]

Confucius's curriculum comprises the arts standard to aristocratic upbringing, notably music, knowledge of rituals collected in the *Rites*, and the *Odes* and *Documents*, quotation from which was essential for courtier discourse. *The Spring and Autumn Annals*, which he finished just before his death in 479 BCE, record the feudalistic aristocracy through its apex. Accompanied by the *Book of Change* for prognostication, the *Odes*, *Documents*, *Rites*, and *Annals* would become the Five Canons of Confucianism.[130]

Confucius inaugurated the most creative time in Chinese intellectual history, traditionally known as the age of "many masters and a hundred schools." It coincided with the Warring States period, during which technological, socioeconomic, political, and geopolitical conditions all underwent revolutionary changes. Instead of numerous scattered city-sized states led by this hegemon or that, a handful of contiguous territorial states divided a vast land of considerable cultural homogeneity. Seven large states played a volatile balance of power. Neutrality was impossible, security paramount. Lord Wen of Wei, who acceded in 445 BCE, initiated reforms to build Wei into the strongest of the warring states. Qi and other states followed suit to stay competitive. The procrastinating Qin had lost much territory to the reformed Wei and Hann. Knowing that Qin must respond to the geopolitical pressure that forced other states to improve, Lord Xiao called for ideas and attracted Shang Yang from Wei. With the lord's backing, Shang initiated in 356 BCE a series of political and socioeconomic reforms that turned Qin from a straggler to the top dog.[131]

Shang Yang was the most successful of a long line of reformers stretching back through Wu Qi of Chu and Li Kui of Wei to Zichan of Zheng. Further back was Guan Zhong (Guanzi), who helped Lord Huan of Qi to hegemony. After Shang came Hann Fei and Li Si, who contributed to Qin's unification of China. Practicing statesmen rather than proselytizing scholars, they strived to harness the forces unleashed by socioeconomic changes and give them some rational direction with long-term perspectives. To win support for their policies, they articulated their rationale and defended it against aristocratic and conservative critics. Some of their writings survived, although not everything attributed to them is genuine. Despite various details that suited specific political realities, they shared certain principles, which came to be called *fajia*, or Legalist, for their emphasis on government according to *fa*, or law.[132]

Shang Yang shared the fate of Wu Qi in aristocratic backlash. Each was immediately killed upon the death of the lord who backed his reforms and vilified as a mean if not wicked character. Entrenched Chu aristocrats rolled back many of Wu's reforms. The aristocracy was weaker in Qin. Shang was torn to pieces, but his centralizing policies survived to make Qin the winner and, more important, to seed the institutional architecture of imperial China.

When Shang died in 338 BCE, Mengzi, an eloquent third-generation disciple of Confucius, was intensifying his political activity in the east. Three decades of solicitation in various states won him fame, wealth, and a high ministry in Qi, but no rejoinder to the charge of retiring without achievements that actually benefited the people. Lifelong experience and accusations of impracticality did not temper his conviction of being the only man capable of restoring order to the world.[133] His bitterness at his lack of success was comforted posthumously, since he is honored as the sage second only to Confucius. *Mengzi* would become one of the Four Books; the other three being the *Analects* that collects Confucius's sayings, and *The Mean* and *Great Learning*, two short essays extracted from the *Rites*. The Four Books and the Five Canons of Confucianism would mold the mind of Chinese literati-officials until the abolition of imperial civil examinations in 1905.[134]

2.9 The Rule by Law and the Rule by Man

Despite academic categorization into various schools, the contending masters share a common heritage and many ideas. Sima Tan, historian in the early Han Dynasty, rightly observes that Confucians, Legalists, Daoists, and Mohists all aim for good governance and a well-ordered world.[135] None has any inkling of popular sovereignty. However, all realize that the people are fundamental to power. To court them had been common practice in aristocratic power struggles.

Crudely, Confucians and Legalists share the traditional ideal of an authoritarian and paternalistic government as a good shepherd of the people, but split on its form and method.[136] Under the arching doctrines of Confucian rule by men and Legalist rule by law, we can discern at least three major divergences. First, Confucians mainly identify with the aristocratic elite, whereas Legalists aim at building a monarchical state. Second, the Confucian world is essentially confined to personal relations, in which government is based on simple extrapolation of family ethics, whereas Legalists introduce the public dimension with laws and institutions, articulated by what Westerners call "political" concepts such as justice. Resisting these rather abstract concepts in their exegetical mindset, Confucians have difficulty in rational analysis of institutions and often appeal to emotion or grand sloganeering in policy debates. Third, Confucian ethics focuses on subjective motivations, Legalist ethics on objective consequences. Confucian idealism tends to detach from reality, producing lofty doctrines prettier than Legalist pragmatism that addresses ugly problems on the ground.

Mengzi talks much about winning the hearts of the people. The people are heterogeneous, especially in stratified and hierarchical societies such as China and Rome. Thus one has to be careful about the meanings of "the people" in political writings. For instance, analyses of the constitutional writings of Polybius and Cicero have revealed that "the people" who shared power with aristocratic senators and magistrates were often only the equestrians and perhaps rich proprietors who could afford the full panoply of heavy infantry.[137] Similarly, in reading modern writings on Menzi's government "for the people," it is well to ask: for what people foremost?

Mengzi writes, "Those who apply their mind govern others; those who apply their brawn are governed. Those who govern live on provisions produced by others; the governed supply the provisions. This is the righteous principle of all under heaven."[138] He was not the first to divide the people into two tiers. However, he elevated the special power and privilege of an upper class into a universal moral principle, initiating an enduring attitude of intellectuals who deem themselves superior to the masses and alone are entitled to participate in political power and the privileges it entails, a psychological complex visible in today's call for "democracy."[139]

At the time of contending masters, the feudalistic structure was deteriorating. Aristocratic power was declining, but still formidable. Devoted to the Way of ancient kings, Confucians tried to reinvigorate the aristocracy and aspired to join it. Confucius often equated the superior man with the aristocrat. Reinforcement of hereditary ministry was a central plank of Mengzi's "benevolent policy." He also urged plush patronage of superior men, who nudged close to aristocrats with an arrogant posture.[140]

While Mengzi pitied the starving peoples of his time, he everywhere took gold and gifts from aristocrats. His retinue of tens of carriages and hundreds of followers lived off one lord after another, inciting students' scruples about extravagance without contribution or official responsibility.[141] It had been common knowledge that the proliferation of consumers of tax revenue was a reason for the people's poverty. Joining Daoists and Mohists, Legalists deprecated special privileges and unproductive big talkers as "lice" who leeched off peasants and weakened the state. As reformers and state builders, Legalists struggled to replace hereditary ministry with merit-based appointments and to suppress the aristocracy in favor of a centralized monarchy.[142] In historical context, the ideological debate between the two schools was part of a power struggle that was changing China's political structure.[143]

Confucians justify elitist privilege by the doctrine of rule by men: With superior men in ruling positions radiating their personal virtues, world order would be attained effortlessly in one great leap forward.[144] Confucius likens superior men to the wind and the people to grass: "swayed by the wind, grass necessarily bends."[145] The most potent superior man is of course the king. Confucians constructed stories about exemplary sage kings in the Three Eras and prehistoric times: Yao and Shun of the third millennia BCE. References to them fill political discourses. The ruler's personality determines the quality of governance, as Mengzi asserts: "When the ruler is benevolent, all are benevolent. When the ruler is righteous, all are righteous. Once the ruler attains rectitude, the state is well governed."[146] The bottom line is to tie the fate of the entire nation to the ruler's person.[147] "His policy flourishes when he lives. His policy passes away with him."[148] Reaffirmed by neo-Confucians, the unbending faith in ruler determinism was perpetuated with variations through millennia in China as a cult of the great leader.[149]

What virtues do the supreme sage kings exemplify? Mengzi iterates: "The Way of Yao and Shun is nothing more than filial piety and brotherly love." "The love of relatives is benevolence. Deference to seniors is righteousness." "Everyone loves his relatives and obeys his seniors, and the world is well ordered."[150] After becoming king, Shun executed enemies but made his evil brother lord. Mengzi dismisses a student's protest of unfairness by praising the sage king's brotherliness. Fealty, filial piety, and other personal virtues dominate. Substantive political considerations hardly venture beyond the web of unequal personal relations.[151] For those seeking concern for justice and the public good, disappointment waits everywhere in *Mengzi*.

The Confucian political world is mostly confined to the personal plane as depicted in Figure 2.2a. This condition may have seemed natural to feudalistic aristocrats in their tiny, family-like states. However, political and socioeconomic realities had changed radically by Mengzi's time, a fact Mengzi and his disciples stubbornly ignored over the millennia. States and populations had surged tenfold in size, and the expansion would continue. Rulers and ministers have to tend to the welfare of millions of strangers. Can principles such as loving relatives keep them from falling into nepotism and cronyism?

They cannot, Legalists argue. Perhaps a sage king can manage, but sages are rare and hypocrites aplenty. A good and stable government must supplement personal virtue by institutions that function properly even under mediocre kings. It must rule according to the law.[152] While the rule by men relies on the inscrutable virtues of elites, the rule by law relies on the law's publicity, fairness, understandability to the common people, and trustworthiness.[153] With these novel concepts, Legalists introduced in Chinese thinking a new dimension, the social and political dimension. In their writings, the meaning of *gong* turns from the lord to the public.[154] The law, impartial, impersonal, and accessible, opens a public space. The world, enriched by the public dimension, encompasses personal relations and their virtues, but is not shackled by them, as illustrated in Figure 2.2c.

"The ruler makes laws. The officers administer the laws. The people obey the laws. The ruler and the ruled, the superior and the inferior, the noble and the humble all abide by the law. This is great governance."[155] This tenet, quoted from *Guanzi*, is central to Legalists. They explain that lawmakers must take account of current conditions and the people's inclinations. Laws should adapt to evolving social conditions, but only with great care; without persistency and reliability, they cannot win the people's trust. Once laws are published, the ruler himself should abide by them: "The ruler should not change the law to suit his whims; the law is superior to the ruler."[156] Legalist rule *by* law fails to consider legislative procedure and falls short of the rule *of* law as constitutionalism. Nevertheless, it contains the embryonic ideas of the state existing beyond all its constituents and institutional constraints on the ruler. Why these ideas died in embryo is an important question in Chinese history that deserves far more attention than it gets.

Equality under the law was a revolutionary idea, as Hann Fei asserts: "Under the law, clever violators can find no pretext, brave violators dare not fight. Criminal penalties do not excuse high ministers. Rewards do not exclude commoners."[157] Shang Yang did not spare even the crown prince for wrongdoing. Aristocrats and superior men, accustomed to immunity from punishment, denounced the law's impartiality and impersonality as callous and destabilizing. It cut into their prerogatives and self-styled superiority in many ways. Shang Yang refuses to revere the enigmatic sayings of superior men and insists that the common people are capable of understanding the law. Thus he demands that the laws be clear and accessible to them and that the state institute jurists as teachers. Knowing what to avoid, the people would behave themselves. Knowing that the people know the law, the elite would not dare to abuse them.[158] Excavated documents reveal how Qin officials explained the laws by case examples and answers to questions.[159] The law empowers the people. Confucius sensed its threat in his revulsion against Jin's first publication of law: When people can appeal to the law, they would be less deferential to aristocrats. This would undermine the feudalistic world order.[160]

Before Shang Yang published the laws of reform, he put a log in the marketplace and offered ten pieces of gold for its removal. The skeptical people hesitated, so he quintupled the reward. When someone finally removed the log and received the prize, everyone learned that the government meant to keep its word.[161] Public trust is paramount, because the law is a promise the state makes to the people. Trust grows on results, not words. To win the people's trust, Legalists emphasize that law enforcement must be consistent, government administration effective, and state officials responsible. For a government capable of discharging its duties, they introduce two novel concepts to supplement the rule by law. They are *shì*, the institutionalization of authority, and *shu*, techniques to supervise officers.[162]

Confucians and Legalists both bow to kings, but the former revere the person of the monarch, the latter promote the institution of monarchy. Legalists argue that the king's authority emanates not from his person but from his *shì*, the throne's supreme position in a generally respected political institution, which structures the delegation of authority to various offices.[163] Nowadays we all know that to assault a police officer is a serious crime, not because the officer is blue-blooded but because he holds institutional authority, so the offence is not only against his person but also against the institution of justice. At that time, however, the novelty and abstractness of institutional ideas made them difficult to grasp, especially amid the loud denunciations of aristocrats.

Political authority in the feudalistic regime was fused with family relations. Legalist reformers toiled to tease them apart to build a political institution based on rational principles. To maximize cooperation and minimize the chance of power scrambles and duty evasion, they established offices with definite authority and responsibility, a defined position in the chain of command, and specific rank, compensation, and criteria of advancement for its occupants: all characteristics of what moderns call a bureaucracy.[164]

The state institution is a structure of authoritative offices. Its operation depends on officers, who have their own self-interests. A state, be it autocratic or democratic, is responsible for the behaviors of the officers to whom it delegates authority. Delegation expresses trust, but not blind trust. The government should monitor behaviors to prevent officers from abusing their authority. That is why modern police departments institute an internal-affairs section. Legalists were aware of this need. "The sagacious ruler supervises his officers, not the people," writes Hann Fei. The supervisory techniques are *shu*. "The techniques are to appoint an officer suitable for job of the office and demand performance according to the responsibility of his title."[165] As they developed, many supervisory techniques were formalized and integrated into government regulations. Not surprisingly, supervision exasperated aristocrats and superior men, who found accountability insulting to their claimed virtue.[166]

The struggle with feudalistic powers was bloody. Slowly, persistent Legalist reforms took root. Aristocratic power dwindled as birthrights eroded and fiefs came under state laws. Fief holders could not command troops without specific authority from the king. Theirs became "income fiefs," mere sources of revenue that were helpless against the wrath of the state. In ancient versions of modern nomenclature, the reformed states claimed full authority to appoint, promote, and dismiss officers. The form of remuneration was changed from landed income to payment in grain or gold; to stop payment was much easier than to evict landlords. Seals and other insignia, such as that for commanding individual military units, provided clear physical signs for delegation and withdrawal of authority. The central government demanded some kind of annual statistical report from local officers to monitor their performances. To counteract prevalent bribery in such assessments, it prepared checklists and sent circuit inspectors to examine local situations and official behaviors. The standardization of measurements within each state reduced cheating and facilitated accounting. Many practices evolved by trial and error. It took centuries, but a protobureaucratic centralized government (see Figure 2.3b) gradually emerged.[167]

Institutional reforms extended to local government, traditionally the stronghold of aristocrats. Alternatives to aristocratic fiefs appeared in the early Spring and Autumn period, when the lords of Chu, Jin, and Qin retained under their direct control specks of annexed territories called *xian* (county). To these were later added frontier districts called *jun* (province), which had heavier military responsibilities. As populations expanded and tax revenues grew, counties and provinces experimented with ways of management. Shang Yang characteristically systematized effective practices. In the 350s BCE, he consolidated jurisdictions and divided Qin into some thirty large counties, each governed by a centrally appointed superintendent who led a pair of officers dividing civilian and military duties. After Qin unified China, the system of directly ruled provinces and counties would extend to the whole empire, displace all fiefs in local government, and dispense with the feudalistic aristocracy.[168]

Alongside political restructuring went economic development. Confucians and Legalists all wish the people a decent living. In policy evaluation, however, they adopt different stances that respectively emphasize the motivation of the actor or the consequence of action—more specifically, the personal virtue of the ruler or the public utility of his policy. Intention and outcome are correlated, which account for their common wish. Differences mainly stem from how they address the gap created by the possibilities of self-deception, ignorance, inadequate effort, limitation of resources, adverse conditions, and all kinds of realistic contingencies. In complex policies, consequences unexpected or expectable but unintended are frequent and especially ponderous; they can ruin millions of households. Policy makers who ignore the risks of wishful thinking would be irresponsible. Xunzi, a Confucian master whose students included Hann Fei and Li Si, attends to reality and tries to bridge the gap. However, he is excluded from orthodox Confucianism, which exalts idealistic Mengzi.[169] On Mengzi's ideas the following brief comparison with Legalists will focus.

Being certain about the potency of virtuous intentions, Confucians pay little attention to problems of realization. Confucius dismisses questions on agriculture as fit only for the petty man: "The superior man is no instrument."[170] Along this vein, Confucians disdain instrumental reason and technical knowledge, including law, economics, and management.[171] Economics invariably leads one to consider utility, efficiency, interest, cost, and benefit, which aristocrats snub. Confucius says, "The superior man considers righteousness; the inferior man, utility."[172] Mengzi elevates anti-utility into an influential moral doctrine and brands utility chasers as robbers.[173]

Mengzi gained audience with King Hui of Wei. The king asked, "How do you propose to benefit our state?" Mengzi replied: "Why does your majesty attend to benefits? All that matters is benevolence and righteousness." The king was interested in the beneficial consequence expected of Mengzi's proposal. Without any evidence for it, Mengzi attributed a selfish intention to him, sneered at his famine relief as merely a lesser evil, and proceeded to "rectify the ruler's heart" by lecturing on benevolent motivation.[174]

The opposition of righteousness and utility was only one manifestation of Mengzi's idealism that polarized complex matters into simplistic good and evil and declared war between them. Another set kingship against hegemony.[175] *Ba*, like the Greek *hēgemōn*, originally meant an eminent leader, as we saw in section 1.4. Athens changed its behavior after the Persian War; therefore other Greeks changed the epithet, using *polis tyrannos* instead of *hēgemōn*.[176] In contrast, Mengzi degraded *ba* to a despicable tyrant basing not on actual behavior but on an intolerant ideology. The leadership of Lord Huan of Qi and other hegemons had won applause from many, Confucius included. Yet Mengzi dismissed them as beneath discussion simply because they fell short of the ideal king's perfect benevolence.[177] We will see how such airy moral denunciations hamstrung utilitarian officers toiling to achieve something constructive in difficult realistic situations.

Mengzi advocated heavy punishments for "robbers of the people," generals, diplomats, and officers who led land reclamation and distribution.[178] How to maintain national security in the age of warring states? He answered with the mantra "The benevolent ruler is invincible."[179] His benevolent policy called for rejuvenating the well-field system, but never considered the realistic problem of how to obtain the land needed for poor families. The difficulty that bedeviled the Gracchi brothers in Rome was also present in China. In contrast to the Gracchi who took the responsibility of addressing the land problem, Mengzi made it almost impossible by opposing both infringement on great houses and development of new land, which was effortful.[180]

Mengzi's "robbers" were Legalists, statesmen aiming at *fuguo qiangbing*, to enrich the state and strengthen the army. Superior men ignorant of economics and disdainful of production interpreted this as impoverishment of the people, because they imagined the ruler and the people fighting over a pie of fixed size.[181] Those who considered production knew that good policies can create a win-win outcome by enlarging the pie to be divided. To grow the economy, Legalist reformers organized people for water-works and other projects that put land under cultivation. To maximize land and labor productivity, Qin, Wei, Zhao, and other states systematically distributed standard plots to individual households. The land distribution programs helped independent family farms to their feet and became a model for several imperial dynasties.[182]

Because of its equal treatment of households, the Legalist land-distribution program is often confused with Mengzi's well-field system. Actually, it replaced the well-field by a new socioeconomic organization. Dong Zhongshu, leading Confucian scholar of the early Han Dynasty, remarked, "Qin adopted Shang Yang's law, abandoned the Way of ancient kings, abolished the well-field, and allowed people to buy and sell land."[183] He rightly located the innovation as alienable private landed property, although wrongly blamed it all on Shang. The ideas of sovereignty, right of land usage, and ownership of land were on the verge of differentiation in the Spring and Autumn period. Lands changed hands, but justifications for the claims and transactions were murky and inconsistent. Land ownership, which depends on legal definitions of location, occupation, income, transaction, and disposal, is peculiarly complex, even today. Legalist laws and land distribution programs provided clearer formulation and state backing for it. Landed property right, absent under the well-field system, greatly stimulated the economy. Dong's hostility toward it, surprising to us, reflected the anti-utility ideology.

Another difference is the form of government taxation. Corvée levy in the well-field system set the interests of the peasant and the lord against each other. The result was apparent in contemporary reports of peasants working sluggishly on the lord's field in order to save their energy for their individual plots.[184] No wonder Mengzi was eager to purge the people's mind of self-interest and indoctrinate them with righteousness: "No one who is righteous puts the ruler's matters second." Because of his low estimate of petty folks, however, his benevolent ideal ensured that no one "dared" attend to his own affairs before finishing the lord's business.[185]

Instead of futile brainwashing, Legalist policies changed the rules so that while peasants tended to their own interests, they simultaneously suited the state's purpose. Shang Yang stipulated that the government should evaluate taxes according to the harvest and keep rates constant to win the people's trust.[186] Under such "income tax" with fixed rates, a recession would decrease both state revenue and household income, whereas a boom would enrich both the state and the people. Shang argued that economic growth depends on people working hard, and they work most enthusiastically to enrich their own families. To boost their incentives, they should be allowed to enjoy the bulk of their harvests. Therefore tax rates should be low, distribution of tax burdens fair, and tax revenues should not be lavished to reward unproductive parasites and empty talkers, which would undermine work ethics.[187] Qin also imposed tax penalties on loafers and granted tax exemptions to households exemplarily diligent in farming and weaving. The incentive manipulation benefited both the state and the farmer. According to Sima Qian, whose *Records of the Historian* initiated the tradition of *Standard Histories*, a decade after Shang started reforms, taxes were fair, families prospered, and the common people rejoiced. However, most aristocrats seethed.[188] We will see the aristocratic backlash in Chapter 4.

As acting statesmen responsible for the consequences of their policies, Legalists respected empirical knowledge and frankly reckoned with risk, benefit, and utility. They considered the people's aversion to pain and craving for wealth and honor, manipulated their behavior by the "handles" of punishment and reward, and designed ways to align the interests of the people and the state, thus to mobilize their effort for certain political or socioeconomic goals.[189] Such behavioral psychology and risk-benefit calculus are commonplace in modern political science and rational-expectations economics. They fit in with a prominent school in ethics, consequentialism that judges the moral value of an action or a rule for actions by its expected consequences. Its most familiar version is utilitarianism, which opts for outcomes with the greatest happiness of the greatest number. Consequence-based ethics stands its ground in debates with virtue-based ethics and duty-based ethics, especially in substantive matters regarding social justice and public choice.[190] Traditionally, Confucians accuse Legalists of amorality or immorality. Recently, however, scholars have begun to uncover in Legalist writings an ethics based on public utility and responsibility.[191]

2.10 From Aristocracy to Monarchy

From city-sized states to empires, from collective rule to armed struggle in the Roman Republic, from parceling of sovereignty to centralization of power in the Chinese states, these multicentury processes had yet to reach their denouement in imperial monarchies. They converged on the same mountain, but different paths led to its western and eastern slopes.[192] Differences between the Roman and Qin-Han Empires were especially pronounced in their respective first two centuries. First, the prominent element of the Roman government was its large standing army; that of Qin and Han, their civilian bureaucracy. Second, the political elite who ran the government were wealthy aristocrats in Rome and commoners of heterogeneous socioeconomic standings in the early Han. How were these discrepancies obtained, and why?

State building is a complex process with many aspects, so that even a term such as "aristocracy" has several meanings. As a regime, aristocracy stands alongside democracy and monarchy. As a form of government apparatus, aristocracy stands alongside bureaucracy. As a social class, aristocrats stand alongside commoners.

A regime signifies how an institutional arrangement distributes political authority among various groups of constituents. Let us use the Aristotelian categories of the many, the few, and the one.[193] The rule of the many, the few, or the one is theoretically called democracy, aristocracy/oligarchy, or monarchy. In reality, the theoretical types seldom exist in pure form. The Roman Republic is a mixture of the three. The Zhou feudalistic structure fits into none.

At the beginning of our periods of study, all three parties shared in authority, but with different proportions. *The many* who initially had some voice in political decision making, the Chinese city people or Roman proprietors, comprised mainly the middling stratum of society who constituted the army reserve. *The one*, the Chinese king or Roman consul, wielded executive power but was essentially the first among a group of aristocrats, superior but not supreme. The dominant authority resided in Chinese hereditary lords or the Roman Senate, whose constituents were wealthy aristocrats with strong familial ties. It was essentially the rule of *the few*, the haughty few, the band of cousins.

As the stories proceeded, *the one* pulled ahead and co-opted the power of *the many* to subdue *the few*. The redistribution of authority changed the characteristics of all three. In Rome, free proprietors lost ground to the slave-driving rich. The citizen militia they constituted morphed toward a hired army recruited from the poorest stratum of society. Demagogues stirred the popular assemblies, but power traveled with the sword. With money and the promise of land at retirement, ambitious generals bought the loyalty of proletarianized legions and triumphed over the aristocratic Senate. In China, city people lost their identity as their communal farms disintegrated and military service extended to the entire male population. Kings distributed land and promoted small proprietary farmers, who became the reserve of mass infantry armies akin to that in early Rome. With their capacity directly to reach a significant part of the taxation and conscription bases, kings made local aristocrats vulnerable or dispensable. Authority eventually concentrated in *the one*, the imperial heir to the victorious Roman general or the Chinese king.

Absolute monarchies would preside over *Pax Romana* and *Pax Sinica*. The two realms reached this form of government at different stages of imperial expansion. All through its conquest of the Mediterranean littoral, Rome retained its republican government, whose muscle was increasingly inadequate to control the army and the ballooning ambition of aristocrats cum generals. Eventually civil wars would break out, and their horror would prompt the victorious Augustus to reorganize the government. In contrast, the Chinese states had each initiated political reforms to suppress feudalistic aristocrats. Centralization of power, which preceded the large conflicts of the Warring States period, enabled the civilian administration to mobilize resources for war and keep the growing army on a rein. Qin, most thorough in reforms, defeated all other states and extended its centralized government structure over unified China. The disparate timings of political restructure were partly responsible for the character of the coming empires: a military dictatorship for Rome, a bureaucratic autocracy for China.

Whatever its type, a regime needs apparatus to do its administrative jobs. Sociologists distinguish two broad types of apparatus, patrimonial and bureaucratic, which sometimes coexist and compete for similar functions. Patrimonial apparatuses include hereditary office, nepotism, cronyism, tax farming, liturgical system, and fee for service, many of which were privileges of aristocrats and elites. Apparatuses are in one way or another controlled by persons who rank high in social, economic, or honorific terms. As a reward for performing administrative functions, an officer can exploit the administrative office for his own economic benefit or social prestige.[194]

Bureaucratic apparatus rationally separates political and social powers to reduce the potential for official corruption. A bureaucracy is a hierarchical organization of offices, each with clearly defined authority, duty, and qualifications of and compensation for its occupants. An appointed officer derives his authority from the office he occupies, conducts business according to published regulations, and except for the stipulated compensation should not exploit his office for personal gains. Except for the simplest administrations, bureaucratic apparatuses are usually more fair and efficient than patrimonies.

Patrimonial apparatuses served most ancient regimes, including the Roman Republic and pre-reformed China. The administrative apparatus that Legalist reformers built to replace aristocratic functions was ideally bureaucratic.[195] The Roman Empire embarked on a similar enterprise later. These were great achievements. Bureaucracy is such a fixture of modern states we easily forget that after the fall of the Roman Empire, it reappeared in Europe only in the fifteenth century and matured in the nineteenth. It cut into the privileges of patrimonial aristocrats, who resisted every step. We will see that after Confucianism became the state ideology, many patrimonial features would resurge to corrupt the operational culture of the bureaucratic apparatus.

The one holds all authority in a monarchy. However, it is impossible for one person to exercise that awesome power over a large empire. To gather intelligence, make informed decisions, run the administrative apparatus, and rule effectively, the emperor needs the cooperation of *the few*—that is, the tamed few under his rein. The decline and transformation of *the few* is a story line parallel to the rise of *the one* in the formation of the Roman Empire and Qin-Han Dynasties.

Aristocrats of the world come in all stripes, not necessarily hereditary, but are generally jealous of their privileges and licenses, haughtily self-confident in the superiority of their own character and lifestyle, paternalistic and patronizing if not oppressive toward their inferiors, and protective of the status quo.[196] Roman and Chinese aristocrats shared the common traits, but did not lack peculiarities of their own. The Roman Republic being born in a competitive environment, its aristocrats were straightforward and vigorous, clear in political thinking, practical in economic negotiation, and strong in public spirit and corporate organization. In contrast, centuries of dominance in the placid late Bronze Age produced elegant Chinese aristocrats who quoted poetry in political discourses, a habit Roman aristocrats acquired only after they conquered Greece.[197] Enjoying the fusion of hereditary rank, fief, and government office, feudalistic aristocrats cultivated virtues that rolled together familial and political concerns. In the demanding times of socioeconomic progress and geopolitical rivalry, they could not compete with innovative upstarts, especially Legalist reformers. Yet they bequeathed their mentality to Confucian literati-officials who would constitute the "cultural aristocracy" of imperial China.

In the imperial monarchies to come, the Roman senatorial aristocrats and the Chinese ideological aristocrats would constitute the ruling elite, the junior partner in government under the emperor. Their power and privilege over the masses, although still enormous, would pale compared to that of their pre-imperial predecessors. Concession would not come peacefully. In both realms, power struggles between *the few* and *the one* eventually led to bloody civil wars, in which *the many* suffered most.

2.11 Slavery and Freedom

A Marxist historian disputes any suggestion of resemblance between the Chinese and Roman Empires: they were "utterly dissimilar civilizations, founded on distinct modes of production." Rome adopted the slave mode of production; China did not.[198] Did any correlation exist between this difference and another, the absence of a concept of political freedom in imperial China?

Our only concern here is political freedom or liberty, not existential freedom. The latter is a personal state of being marked by uninhibited thinking and imagination. Classical Chinese has notions of *ziyou* or *xiaoyao*, but these notions of existential freedom occur only in literature and the philosophy of life, which are beyond the scope of this book.

We are only concerned with chattel slavery, not subjugation and exploitation in general, which are widespread in all societies. All downtrodden people do not constitute a distinctive social class. Dependent labor takes many forms: war prisoner, serf, client, corvée laborer, debt bondsman, indentured servant, chain gang, and slave. Among them, the chattel slave is peculiar in being a commodity, bought and sold at the pleasure of his owner, whose property right is backed by sophisticated laws. He has lost control over not only his labor but also his person and personality. "The slave is a living tool in the same way that a tool is an inanimate slave," explains Aristotle.[199] Greek and Roman laws meticulously define the thing status of slaves, who are denied kinship, marriage, and all human worth.[200] Slavery is not primitive violence. It is a civilized way to turn a human being, reversibly, into a thing.

Scattered textual evidence indicates that sales of human beings appeared in the Chinese Warring States period simultaneously with the private ownership of land.[201] Slavery as an institution and slaves as a group with distinctive customary or legal status appeared in early imperial times and persisted. Private slaves engaged mainly in handicrafts or household works. Slaves originated mostly from state prison, debt bondage, and the sale of children during famine. Together they constituted less than 1 percent of the total population in the Han Dynasty.[202]

Sociologists distinguish between a society with slaves and a slave-based society. In the former, the slave population is small and the slaves' economic roles obscure. The latter employs the slave mode of production; its slaves constitute a significant portion of the population, play prominent roles in production, and provide the bulk of direct income for the elite.[203]

Evidence exists for hundreds of societies with slaves, among which is imperial China. Only five slave-based societies are known in the whole of world history. Two are ancient: classical Athens and many other Greek cities (but not Sparta); and Roman Italy, Gaul, and Spain (but not all parts of Rome's empire). Three are modern: the antebellum southern United States, the Spanish Caribbean, and Portuguese Brazil. In each of the five, the slave population at its peak exceeded 30 percent of the total population.[204]

A paradox leaps from the short list. Athens and the United States are showcase democracies and champions of freedom. The Roman Republic, although not fully democratic, also advocated liberty. "How is it that we hear the loudest yelps for liberty among the drivers of negroes?" asked a witness of modern slavery.[205] The puzzle began in antiquity, as a scholar remarks: "The cities in which individual freedom reached its highest expression—most obviously Athens—were cities in which chattel slavery flourished."[206] Is it coincidental that the world's first democracy and first slave-based society are identical and emerged simultaneously with the articulation of the concept of political freedom?

The paradox leads to a related question: Why did traditional China lack a robust concept of political freedom? This is usually explained in terms of its stratified and deferential social structure. The explanation carries much truth, but a counterexample reveals its incompleteness. As a modern historian points out, "Roman society was sharply stratified. Divisions of status underlay all social and political life: division between the free man and the slave; the citizen and the non-citizen; the senator and the equestrian; the patrician and plebeian. This point deserves great emphasis. All Romans knew their place."[207] Yet the Romans extolled liberty. Could the social-stratification explanation possibly be supplemented by what was absent in China but conspicuous in Rome and its liberal predecessor Athens—*massive* slavery as an institution vital to the economy and salient in society?

A concept makes a distinction and seldom arises where nothing is outstanding. Today the item "free person" in a census form would be scandalous. When being born free is taken for granted, the freeborn are not considered as a category. Instead of the slave/free man dichotomy in the West, the Chinese traditionally lumped slaves with base people, *jianmin*, in contrast to whom common folks are called good people, *liangmin*. A few slaves attract scant social attention. A historical sociologist explains, "Only when slaves became the main dependent labor force was the concept of personal freedom first articulated (in ancient Greece), and words were then created or adapted to express that idea. It is literally impossible to translate the word 'freedom' directly into Babylonian or classical Chinese."[208] Babylon and China were not slave-based societies.

Rome was the largest of the five slave-based societies.[209] A prominent part of its laws concerned slaves. When talking tools became essential to the economy, they stimulated conceptualization and intellectual reflection, especially the notion of their antithesis, freedom.[210] Classical scholars explain: "The very idea and valuation of freedom was generated by the existence and growth of slavery."[211] "In Rome, as in Greece, freedom is primarily the legal status opposed to slavery."[212] "Agricultural slavery . . . gave peasants the leisure to exercise their political rights and gave aristocrats the means to cut a dash, to live the good life and to hope to control public affairs."[213] The solidarity of democracy "was a powerful means of controlling the growing slave population. . . . The proud, free citizen-farmer, jealous of any alien intruding on the civic community, would happily do that for the slaveholders."[214] "One aspect of Greek history, in short, is the advance, hand in hand, of freedom *and* slavery."[215] The world's first democracy was born when an exclusive circle of citizens succeeded in negotiating significant equality and freedom among themselves. Their magnificent achievements should not blind us to the fact that their success partly depended on exporting inequality and unfreedom to outsiders whom they massively enslaved.

The wretchedness of slaves demanded some moral justification from fellow human beings. The Greek poet Euripides wrote in a tragedy:

> Greeks were born to rule barbarians, mother, not barbarians to rule Greeks. They are slaves by nature; we have freedom in our blood.[216]

Quoting Euripides with approval, Aristotle argued, "It is thus clear that, just as some are by nature free, so others are by nature slaves, and for these latter the condition of slavery is both beneficial and just."[217] Scholars find the idea of natural slavery not Aristotle's idiosyncrasy but a common belief of his time.[218] Adding insult to injury, the masters blamed their victims, whose externally imposed misery was turned into a just desert for alleged intrinsic inferiority. In degrading numerous slaves, one was naturally led to connect freedom with morality: a free man was, or should be, a better kind of man than a slave.[219] Dancing on the back of their slaves, masters proclaimed ever louder the moral superiority of freedom.

The most celebrated notion of political liberty in modern liberal democracy is "negative freedom" as the absence of constraints, with explicit emphasis on political constraints. A leading liberal philosopher explains, "The criterion of oppression is the part that I believe to be played by other human beings, directly or indirectly, with or without intention of doing so, in frustrating my wishes. By being free in this sense I mean not being interfered with by others. The wider the area of non-interference the wider is my freedom."[220]

Liberty as freedom from oppression is an old idea. The broad spectrum of "oppression" helps us understand the many notions of liberty in Roman politics and foreign policies that we will encounter.[221] As a defensive shield that the relatively powerless put up against the arbitrary coercion of the powerful, liberty fostered equality, which was what Roman citizens achieved in the early Republic. As an aggressive justification for the powerful to bulldoze obstacles to their desires, liberty became Rome's battle cry for imperial war and massive slavery. A historian observes, "Most revealing of all is the firm implication in many ancient texts, and often the explicit statement, that one element of freedom was the freedom to enslave others."[222] Between the poles of protective and predatory freedoms are a host of liberties, the rights to which need careful examination. Cries of freedom are exhilarating, but liberal philosophers who have thought deeply about it advocate caution: "It is doubtless well to remember that belief in negative freedom is compatible with, and (in so far as ideas influence conduct) has played its part in, generating great and lasting social evils. . . . Freedom for the wolves has often meant death to the sheep."[223]

Notes

1. Chang et al. 2005: 210–223. Potter 1987: 19–21, 71, 75.
2. Zhao 2006: 43–45. Yang 2006: 35–39.
3. Hsu 1965a: 66–67.
4. Cornell 1995: 204–207, 283. Forsythe 2005: 116–117.
5. The standard transliteration of 韓 is Han. I reserve Han for 漢 and use Hann for 韓.
6. Hsu 1965a: 67–71.
7. Cornell 1995: 380. Scullard 1980: 207.
8. Huntington 1968. Tilly 1975. Lewis 1990. Downing 1992. Rosenstein 2009. Hui 2005.
9. Huntington 1968: 123. Tilly 1975: 42.
10. Tilly 1985. Pitts 2005.
11. Aristotle, *Politics*, 1326a, 1276a.
12. Hopkins 1978a: 74–76.
13. Mokyr 1990: 3.
14. Mokyr 1990: 25.
15. Finley 1983: 108–109. Drews 1993: 75. Cornell 1995: 33. Forsythe 2005: 25. Hopkins 1978b. Greene 2000.
16. Cotterell 1980: 14.
17. Wagner 1993: 95, 206–207. Li, X. 1985: 327–328.
18. Cotterell 1981: 27, 67, 90. Portal 2007: 174–175.
19. Wang, Z., 1982: 122–123. Mokyr 1990: 23–24.
20. Pliny 34.41.
21. Homer, *Iliad*, 18.541–543. *Shijing* 212, 277. Fine 1983: 38–39.
22. Drews 1993: 106–125. Cotterell 2004: 3, 105–107, 128–131.
23. Lakoff 1996: 39. See also Mann 1986: 197–198.
24. Creveld 1999: 26. Crawford 1993: 29f. Cornell 1989.
25. Brunt 1988: 246. Hopkins 1978a: 21. Potter 1987: 106, 113. Kolendo 1993. Cornell 1989.
26. Yang 2003b: 160–161, 166, 176–177. Leeming 1980. *Liji* 5.3.
27. Cornell and Matthews 1990: 49. David 1997: 71.
28. Leeming 1980. Lewis 1990: 63, 273.
29. *Hanshu* 24a: 1124–1125.
30. Dionysius quoted in Hopkins 1978a: 4. See also Livy 3.13, 3.26.
31. Scheidel 2009b: 170–178. Mann 1986: 194–195. Cornell 1995: 288, 394–397.
32. Scheidel 2009b: 139–147. Yang 2003b: 131–142. Hsu 1999: 581–582.
33. Hsu 1965a: 19. Yang 2003b: 436–439. Flower 1996: 209–211.
34. Steadman, Palmer, and Tilley 1996: 68.
35. Hölkeskamp 2004. Arjava 1998.
36. Ch'ü 1972: 20–26. Eastman 1989: Ch. 2. Fairbank 1992: 18.
37. Syme 1939: 314.
38. Schwartz 1985: 67–75.
39. Crawford 1993: 73. Beard and Crawford 1985: 52–53.
40. Astin 1989: 180. Brennan 2004: 43, 56.
41. Shaughnessy 1999: 318–322, 331–332.
42. Brunt 1988: 43, 322.

43. Cicero, *Laws*, 3.31.
44. Hsiao 1979: 108–111. Nivison 1999: 749–750. Pines 2002: 125–129.
45. *Shangshu*, Dayumo.
46. Liang 1996: 95–97. Yan 2011: 28.
47. Qian 1989: 55. Liu Z. 2004: 208–218. Turner 1993: 311.
48. Livy 2.1.
49. Scullard 1980: Ch. 3. Cornell 1995: Chs. 10, 13.
50. Cornell 1995: Chs. 10, 13.
51. Raaflaub 1986a. Ste. Croix 1981: 332–337. Ungern-Sternberg 1986.
52. Cornell 1995: 268–270, 328–330. Scullard 1980: 81–83.
53. Scullard 1980: 84.
54. Brunt 1988: 309. Nicolet 1993: 20–21. Raaflaub 1986a.
55. Chang et al. 2005: 204.
56. Cornell 1995: 258–265. Scullard 1980: 84–86.
57. Raaflaub 1986a. Ungern-Sternberg 1986.
58. Millar 2002a: 98, 168.
59. Sallust, *Jugurthine War*, 41. Scullard 1973: 242. Brunt 1988: 69.
60. Crawford 1993: 75. Astin 1967: 169.
61. Hopkins 1978a: 4, 9, 38, 53–55, 67–68, 102–105. Scheidel 2012a: 90–95.
62. David 1997: 90–95. Rathbone 1981: 11, 19–20.
63. Brunt 1988: 73, 256. Beard and Crawford 1985: 4.
64. Hopkins 1978a: 40, 58–59. Brunt 1988: 73, 256.
65. Hopkins 1978a: 40.
66. Gabba 1976: 5–10. Crawford 1993: 96–98.
67. Astin 1967: 44, 186–225, 306–310. Boren 1968: 46–59, 60–70.
68. Crawford 1993:116–122. Boren 1968: 124–126.
69. Astin 1967: 216. Riddle 1970.
70. Appian 1.17.
71. Finer 1997: 412, 416.
72. Sallust, *Jugurthine War*, 41.
73. Gabba 1976: 3–12. Keppie 1984: 61–63.
74. Brunt 1988: 241, 253–255, 273. Gabba 1976: 17–18, 39–42. Crawford 1993: 125–126.
75. Polybius 6.18. Cicero, *Republic*, 1.69, 2.54–65.
76. Finer 1997: 396. See also Lintott 1999: 1–2, 34.
77. Polybius 5.11, 5.12. Lintott 1999: Ch. 7, 192–195. Finer 1997: 397–407. Beard and Crawford 1985: 32–59.
78. Nicolet 1993: 18. Lintott 1999: 121–129.
79. Polybius 6.13. Lintott 1999: Ch. 6, 196–199. Finer 1997: 408, 414–416.
80. Polybius 6.14. Millar 1998: 46–48.
81. Lintott 1999: Ch. 5, 199–208.
82. Beard and Crawford 1985: 42–45. Hopkins 1983a: 108–111.
83. Brunt 1988: 24–25, 145. Nicolet 1993: 27.
84. Livy 34.31.
85. Crook et al 1994a: 769. Millar 2002a: 111, 165.
86. Cornell 1995: 378. Gruen 1974: xi.
87. Astin 1989.
88. Hopkins 1983a: 114.
89. Finer 1997: 413.

90. Millar 1998: 8–11.
91. Sallust, *Jugurthine War* 41.
92. Cornell 1995: 348–350. Scullard 1980: 111–114. Forsythe 2005: 290–292.
93. Cornell 1995: 271, 301.
94. Crawford 1991: 29.
95. Cornell 1995: 363.
96. Crawford 1993: 21, 35. David 1997: 21. Ste. Croix 1981: 519–521.
97. Livy 24.2; see also 23.14.
98. Polybius, 27.9. See also Livy 35.34, 42.30.
99. Derow 1989: 310–311.
100. Beard and Crawford 1985: 42–45. Hopkins 1983a: 108–111.
101. Wells 1992: 214–215, 246. Harris 2011: 19–20.
102. *Zuozhuan*, Min 2.
103. *Zuozhuan*, Xi 18, Xi 32.
104. Hsu and Linduff 1988: 163. Yang 2003a: 395–397, 423–424. Du 1979: 29–30.
105. Yang 2003a: 185–211.
106. Hsu 1999: 576–577. Du 1979: 64–69.
107. Lewis 1990: 48–49. Yang 2003a: 396–409, 422–424. Tong 2006b: 128–133.
108. Hsu 1999: 566–567. Yang 2003a: 426–436, 441–445.
109. Creel 1970: Ch. 11. Li, F. 2006: 110–116.
110. Hsu 1965a: 2, 78–80. Pines 2002: 138–146. Liang 1996: 9.
111. Hsu 1965a: 3–10, 94–96. Tong, 2006b:147–148. Cai 2004: 58–63.
112. Liu Z. 2004: 208–210, 238–239. Hsu and Linduff 1988: 171.
113. *Zuozhuan*, Huan 2.
114. Pines 2002: 187–199.
115. *Zuozhuan,* Zhao 14. Pines 2002: 154–157. Yang 2003a: 449.
116. *Zuozhuan,* Zhao 25.
117. Liang 1996: 48–49. Tan 2002: 169–175.
118. Hsu 1965a: 31–34, 80–88; 1999: 570–572. Lü 2005a: 194.
119. Hsu 1965a: 82–83, 1999: 558–560. Tong 2006b: 95–97.
120. *Zuozhuan*, Zhao 32.
121. *Zuozhuan*, Zhao 6, Zhao 29.
122. Hsu 1999: 575–589. Wagner 1993: Ch. 4.
123. Hsu 1965a: 107–115. Yang 2003b: 154–159.
124. Hsu 1965a: 116–126; 1999: 580–581. Yang 2003b: 102–144.
125. Hsu 1999: 583–585. Lewis 1999: 641–643.
126. *Guanzi* 20.
127. Aristotle, *Politics*, 1321a.
128. Pines 2009a: 136, 161–162, 168. Schwartz 1985: 58–59.
129. Schwartz 1985: 102–115.
130. Fung 1952: 46–49. Hsiao 1979: 99–101. Qian 1940: 93–101.
131. Lewis 1999: 644–645. Yang 2003b: 188–211.
132. Hsiao 1979: 368–375. Schwartz 1985: 323–335.
133. *Mengzi* 3.9, 6.26, 2.22.
134. Schwartz 1985: 256–257.
135. *Shiji* 130: 3288–3289.
136. Pines 2009a: 188, 198–203. Fu 1996: 23. Song 2010: 70–73, 136–144.
137. Brunt 1988: 148. Wood 1988: 151.

138. *Mengzi* 3.4; see also 3.3, 6.30.
139. *Yantielun* 20. Perry 1992: 148, 151–156. Yü 2003: vi. Bell 2008: 14–18.
140. *Mengzi* 1.12, 3.3, 5.15.
141. *Mengzi* 2.12, 3.9, 7.32. Fung 1952: 51.
142. *Shangjunshu* 2, 3. *Hannfeizi* 13, 50.
143. Hsiao 1979: 33, 36.
144. Hsiao 1979: 116. Schwartz 1985: 102.
145. *Lunyu* 12.19.
146. *Mengzi* 3.2; see also 4.20.
147. Liang 1996: 95–97. Schwartz 1985: 102–103. Hsiao 1979: 122–124.
148. *Zhongyong*.
149. Perry 1992: 149–151. Schirokauer and Hymes 1993: 27–28, 43–44. Liu, S. 1998: 12.
150. *Mengzi* 6.22, 7.15, 4.11, 4.27.
151. *Mengzi* 5.3. Schwartz 1985: 102–103. Pines 2002: 187–199.
152. *Shangjunshu* 1, 8, 14. *Hannfeizi* 40. Liang 1996: 176–180, 258–260.
153. *Shangjunshu* 14, 26. *Hannfeizi* 47.
154. Liu Z. 2004: 208–218, 233–241. Turner 1993: 311.
155. *Guanzi* 45. See also *Shangjunshu* 14.
156. *Guanzi* 16. See also *Shangjunshu* 9.
157. *Hannfeizi* 6. See also *Guanzi* 45.
158. *Shangjunshu* 14, 26. Fung 1952: 321–323.
159. McLeod and Yates 1981: 113.
160. *Zuozhuan*, Zhao 29.
161. *Shiji* 68: 2231.
162. Fung 1952: 316–325. Song 2010: 156–189.
163. *Hannfeizi* 28, 40.
164. Yang 2003b: 221–226.
165. *Hanfeizi* 35, 43.
166. Schwartz 1985: 336–337. Hsiao 1979: 409.
167. Lewis 1999: 601–611. Hsu 1965a: 94–100; 2006: 289–296. Yang 2003b: 213–220.
168. Lewis 1999: 613–614.
169. Liu, S. 1998: 55. Xu 2011.
170. *Lunyu* 2.12, 13.4.
171. Fung 1952: 50.
172. *Lunyu* 4.16.
173. *Mengzi* 7.25. Schwartz 1985: 260–261.
174. *Mengzi* 1.1, 1.3.
175. *Mengzi* 2.3, 7.30. Wang R. 2011: 182–183.
176. Thucydides 2.63, 3.37. Wickersham 1994: 4, 20. Münkler 2007: 43–44.
177. *Mengzi* 1.7.
178. *Mengzi* 4.14, 6.29.
179. *Mengzi* 1.5, 1.18, 2.5, 3.10, 4.7, 7.49, 7.50.
180. *Mengzi* 4.6, 4.14, 6.29.
181. *Yantielun* 7.
182. Hsu 1965a: 82–83, 110–106, 131–133.
183. *Hanshu* 24a: 1126; see also 1137.
184. *Lüshi Chunqiu* 17.

185. *Mengzi* 1.1, 3.3.
186. *Shangjunshu* 2.
187. *Shangjunshu* 2, 8, 23.
188. *Shiji* 68: 2230, 2232–2233.
189. Schwartz 1985: 328–330.
190. Scheffler 1988.
191. Wang 2011: 122–135.
192. Scheidel 2009a: 13–20.
193. Aristotle, *Politics*, 1279a-b.
194. Max Weber, quoted in Bendix 1977: 429.
195. Fukuyama 2011: Ch. 6.
196. Aristotle, *Politics*, 1279a-b, 1294a. Stone 1965: 5–6. Mann 1986: 170.
197. Yü 2003: 18. Hopkins 1978a: 76, 79.
198. Anderson 1974: 419.
199. Aristotle, *Ethics*, 1161b.
200. Finley 1980: 73–77. Wiedemann 1981: 1–13. Gardner 2011.
201. Lü 2005a: 276–278. Pulleyblank 1958: 193.
202. Wilbur 1943: 165f. Chü 1972: 140–164. Hulsewé 1986: 525.
203. Hopkins 1978a: 99–101.
204. Hopkins 1978a: 99–101. Jones 1964: 196–198. Finley 1980: 9, 82. Schiavone 2000: 111–113. Scheidel 2012a.
205. Samuel Johnson, quoted in Brunt 1988: 289.
206. Finley 1983: 114.
207. Crawford 1993: 40.
208. Finley 1968.
209. Scheidel 2012a: 89, 108.
210. Wiedemann 1981: 4–6. Gardner 2011.
211. Patterson 1991: xiv.
212. Brunt, 1988: 283.
213. Davies 1993: 89.
214. Patterson 1991: 80.
215. Finley 1983: 115.
216. Euripides, *Iphigenia in Aulis*, 1400–1401.
217. Aristotle, *Politics*, 1252b, 1254b.
218. Hunt 2011: 41–44. Schiavone 2000: 115.
219. Brunt 1988: 287.
220. Berlin 1969: 123.
221. Brunt 1988: Ch. 6. Crawford 1993: 146. Nicolet 1980: 322–323.
222. Finley 1983: 128.
223. Berlin 1969: xlv.

CHAPTER 3

EMPIRE BUILDING

3.1 The Advantage of the Periphery

In the ages of Chinese warring states and Rome the warrior state, the will to power expressed in collective violence produced carnage unsurpassed in scale until the advent of modern Europe, which coined the word "imperialism."[1] A system of states existed at each end of Eurasia. Rome, Carthage, the Achaean and Aetolian Leagues of Greece, the Hellenistic kingdoms in Macedon, Syria, and Egypt, and myriad city-states jostled in the Mediterranean basin. Qin, Qi, Chu, Yan, Hann, Zhao, Wei, and minor states warred in China. Two centuries of fighting fused each system into a single regime, the Roman Empire and the Qin Dynasty of China.

Traditional historiographies for the two action dramas feature disparate stage settings. On one, a spotlight shines on a single protagonist, Rome; other players appear only in relation to it. The spotlight remains even as larger areas of the stage brighten to reveal Roman expansion. On the other, diffuse stage lights from the beginning illuminate a large portion of China, corresponding more closely to the Mediterranean basin than to the city of Rome. The broad stage shows numerous states growing up together like squabbling siblings. Only belatedly would Qin capture the limelight. The settings stem mainly from disparate interstate power configurations.

Roman expansion has been likened to the growth of the United States of America.[2] The great powers of the eastern Mediterranean were, like European states to America, remote and indifferent. Furthermore, they were not used to alliance. With few exceptions, Rome held military superiority over any one target. It picked its targets, conquered them sequentially, and acquired the habit of giving commands and acting unilaterally. The Chinese arena, which comprised close-knit states of comparable strength as adroit in diplomatic maneuver as in military engagement, has been compared to the balance of power in early modern Europe.[3] Realizing that even the top dog was vulnerable to the coalition of lesser adversaries, the Chinese honed their skills in alliance and multilateral negotiation. These characters in foreign relations would persist into imperial times.

The two empire builders had similar initial conditions. Qin was invested as a Zhou state in 771 BCE. Rome, traditionally founded eighteen years later, became the Republic in 509 BCE. Latecomers, each was born at the western periphery of a magnificent and prosperous civilization. In the eastern Mediterranean, the Greeks held their first Olympic games in 776 BCE. In eastern China, Confucius, who died in 479 BCE, ten years before Socrates was born, taught among commoners. The humanistic intellectuals at either end of Eurasia lived in societies that, although based on agrarian economies, developed significant commerce. Wealth accumulated. Arts and crafts flourished; so did luxuries.

Ensconced in a remote river valley or on a peninsula, Qin and Rome were economically inferior to their respective eastern neighbors. Neither cared much for high learning, nor did they excel in technology. Qin lagged in crossbows and iron swords.[4] Roman weapons were often inferior to those of its enemies.[5] However, they were innovative in organization, and their political institutions were more efficient in resource mobilization. Similarly austere in outlook and pragmatic in thinking, both upheld martial values to augment agrarian ideals. Qin alone among the Chinese states integrated farming and armed service. The Romans blamed Carthage's defeat on its preference to trade over conquest. Each conquered the civilization to its east but submitted to its cultural superiority. Most influential high ministers of Qin came from the east. Few Greeks under Roman rule learned Latin, but the Romans were Hellenized, as the Roman poet Horace wrote: "captive Greece overcame her barbarous conqueror and brought civilization to wild Latins."[6]

The rises of Rome and Qin fit into a well-attested pattern of world history. Repeatedly, epoch-making conquests issued from a marcher power: a state, tribe, or people at the margin of civilization.[7] Countless such marcher entities existed; most passed away unnoticed. Occasionally, however, one soared to change history. Persia surged from the eastern frontier of the Mesopotamian civilization and Macedon from the northern frontier of the Greek. In eastern Eurasia, successive marcher nomads continuously challenged imperial China. The Mongols conquered China and most of eastern Europe. The Manchu conquest of the early seventeenth century founded the last Chinese dynasty. Carthage and Chu, the toughest enemies to Rome and Qin respectively, were themselves marcher powers.[8]

A successful power at the border between high civilization and high barbarism leverages the vitality of the latter by the knowledge of the former. High civilizations with accumulated knowledge are inventive. An invention, however ingenious, may remain a mere curiosity. Sclerotic social conventions may impede innovation, which applies an invention on a large scale to achieve significant social impact. Marcher powers can be more innovative. Unencumbered by indoctrination, their minds are more open to opportunities and agile to catch them. Not enfeebled by decadent culture, their simple lifestyles are more conducive to risk taking and hard work. Unburdened by legacy establishments, their institutions are more flexible to improvement. Unscarred by the mistakes of predecessors, they can benefit from trials and errors, adopt the best model, and leapfrog ahead. The underutilized resources of their hinterlands are freer to move in novel directions, unlike the sunk capital of advanced powers that are tied up in existent structures. All these traits contribute to what historians call "the advantage of backwardness." Furthermore, the marginal locations of marcher societies, although close enough to learn from more advanced states, are distant enough to avoid inciting jealous suspicion and military intervention. They can bid their time, quietly nursing their institutions and developing their hinterlands, until they burst forth as great powers.

The ascent of Rome and Qin seemed abrupt partly because their eastern rivals were in relative decline, just as the moon seems to step out at the zenith because the sunlight that veiled its climb fades at dusk. In the Mediterranean, the Hellenistic kingdoms had lost the infantry-cavalry integration and other innovations that made Alexander's army supreme.[9] In China, the six states had weakened themselves in mutual conflicts. The easterners were aware of the menace. The Greeks saw Rome as storm clouds looming in the west. The six states imagined Qin as a giant eagle perched facing east, its beak hanging over the heartland.[10] Calls for unity against the impending calamity rose in both lands, but in neither did they overcome the temptation of appeasement, which was less effortful. Disunity proved fatal.

The Qin Dynasty and the Roman Empire similarly rose on active conquests. Also similar is the passivity of their ends; both fell without seriously fighting for survival. The spectacular difference lies in their life spans. The Qin Dynasty lasted only fifteen years. In less than a generation it achieved what took the Roman Empire more than four centuries, running down its mighty war machine. Why did Qin demilitarize so quickly that when its existence was threatened by petty rebels, it had to reprieve convicts for self-defense? Why did the early Han Dynasty, which retained most of Qin's institutions, pay tribute to marauding nomads for decades before mustering the will to fight, whereas Augustus launched massive imperial conquests soon after the Roman civil war ended? Did the culture and characteristics of the decision-making elite influence a state's foreign policy? If so, were they observable during the age of imperial conquests?

3.2 Qin in a System of States

The Western name "China" derives from "Qin," also transliterated as "Ch'in" before the People's Republic standardized the Pinyin Romanization of Chinese logograms.[11] For five centuries before it unified China, Qin was the westernmost Chinese state, sitting at the gateway of the only natural corridor to Central Asia, which would become the first leg of the Silk Routes. Thus countries to the west came to know the Chinese world through Qin (Map 2). Strategic geography has been adduced as a cause for Qin's victory over the eastern states. Perhaps the weightiest assessment came from Han statesmen who, although mostly easterners, decided to site the empire's capital in former Qin territory.[12] This area has been called Guanzhong or Within the Passes for good reasons (Maps 4 and 7). It is protected on the northeast by the Yellow River and, south of the river, by the Qinling Range. Piercing the mountains are a few strategic passes that witnessed some of the fiercest battles in Chinese history. Within the natural fortress, a state can safely exploit the rich Wei Valley with access to the fertile Sichuan basin in the south and vast pastureland in the north and west.[13] Guanzhong has been "a land designed for victory." Millennia later, when its comparative advantage was eclipsed by developments elsewhere, its northern periphery would still offer Yanan, destination of the Communists' Long March and the revolutionary base for their eventual triumph. The Han Dynasty forestalled surprises from upstarts by locating its own capital there. It learned history's lessons well. Its predecessor Qin was such an upstart, and before Qin, the Zhou.

The Zhou kept its home base in Guanzhong as a royal domain. At its western edge dwelled the Ying clan, which had for generations mingled with the pastoral Rong. Ying Feizi's expertise in horse breeding impressed the Zhou king, who in the 870s BCE granted him land in Qin to raise horses. In 771 BCE, a large Rong invasion overran Guanzhong and forced the entire Zhou court to take flight. For escorting the royal evacuation, the general from Qin was enfeoffed and allowed to keep whatever land he could recover from the Rong. The first lord of Qin fell fighting. His son pacified the Rong and gathered the remaining Zhou population, whose knowledge enriched the rather primitive skill of his own people. Thus Qin started its career by inheriting Zhou's homeland and people. No one could foresee it would politically succeed Zhou in 249 BCE.[14]

Qin became a great power under Lord Mu, who acceded in 659 BCE and won the honor of "the hegemon of western Rong" by subduing many tribes and opening extensive land. Yet the Rong would remain a security threat for centuries, submitting after military defeat and rebelling after a while, as long as Qin failed to establish effective political control. Not until 272 BCE did Qin succeed to annex Yiqu, its strongest Rong neighbor. In dallying for more than three centuries, Qin seemed less diligent than Rome to eliminate belligerent neighbors.[15]

Lord Mu twice sent massive famine relief to his eastern neighbor Jin and thrice helped to stabilize Jin's dynastic crises. Yet when Qin tried to bypass Jin and project its power to the Central Plain, Jin annihilated its expeditionary army at Xiao. The mountain passes so useful for defending Qin against eastern invaders were also roadblocks to its own eastward advancement, as long as they were in Jin's powerful grip. Bottled up in its western valley, Qin waned after Lord Mu.[16]

Jin's fragmentation into Hann, Wei, and Zhao in 453 BCE changed the strategic picture. Equally significant were the political reforms initiated by the new powers. The upgraded Wei wrested large territories from Qin in a series of offensives. Fortunately for Qin, Wei switched strategy in 361 BCE. It shifted its centers of gravity eastward, as advancing technology made the fertile alluvial soil of the Central Plain cultivable and decrepitude made venerable states there easy prey. Locating closer to the locus of political competition and economic resources was rational for an ambitious state. Hindsight, however, proved Wei's move a fatal mistake. It neglected defense against an opponent whose potential it underestimated. Wei would tire itself fighting Qi and the other eastern powers while leaving its weakened western portion to fatten Qin.[17]

After a string of ineffective lords and domineering aristocrats, Qin finally awoke from its slumber. Lord Xiao supported Shang Yang, who started sweeping reforms in 356 BCE. However, not until 328 BCE did Qin recover all territories previously lost to Wei; so great was the gap it had to close.[18]

In 316 BCE, Qin decided to forgo a prestigious confrontation with Hann in order to take advantage of the discord in the peripheral state of Shu. The military conquest of Shu and the Sichuan Basin was quick and easy. The far more arduous political pacification and integration took decades. All the while, Qin poured tremendous effort into economic development that would turn this fertile basin into a strong base for its eventual campaigns to unify China. Qin's effort illustrates the advantages of a marcher state with room for growth.[19]

In the late fourth century BCE, the warring states emerged from the cocoons of feudalistic parceled sovereignty. Besides domestic restructuring, they constituted a new system of states distinct from the old system of the Spring and Autumn period. A balance of power replaced the competition for hegemony. Great powers fought more over population and territory than over allegiance of allies. The scale of war increased with the states' capacity to deploy resources. Chariots gave way to infantry supported by cavalry. New weapons such as the crossbow appeared. Set-piece battles were augmented by field battles of maneuver and mobility. Fortifications improved, as did siege techniques. Long walls sprang up, both between states and along the northern frontier that confronted the emerging Hu people, steppe nomads excelling in mounted archery.[20]

Before Qin annexed Hann, Chu, Wei, Zhao, Yan, and Qi between 230 and 221 BCE, the seven coexisted with a handful of minor states of shorter life spans. Of the seven, Chu had the largest territory and required Qin's largest army for its final conquest. Despite its vast resources, it was rather lackluster during the Warring States period. Its entrenched aristocrats annulled many of Wu Qi's progressive reforms, and its antiquated political structure failed to organize resources efficiently for interstate competition.

With its capital near today's Beijing, Yan was usually regarded as the weakest of the warring seven, although it left the most iron swords for archeologists.[21] From it came the most famous assassin in Chinese history, Jing Ke, whose song at the sendoff party expressed the spirit of the north: "The wind howls and the River Yi runs cold, the brave embarks on a journey of no return." Jing passed security frisks of the heavily guarded Qin court with a dagger hidden inside the scroll of a map intended for the king's eyes only, but his target was destined to become the First Emperor of China.[22] Yan hated Qin but actually helped it by hurting its two strongest enemies. Its attack eliminated Qi as a major power, and its conflict with Zhao destroyed the last hope of stopping Qin.

Zhao, the northern state sharing the bold and generous spirit of Yan, had a double character. Handan, its capital, was steeped in Huaxia culture, the center of music and dance. It was also favorably located to exploit the resources of the northern frontier. It conquered Zhongshan, a state established by the Hu people, and incorporated its cavalry in 296 BCE. To facilitate riding and shooting, its own people adopted the costumes of steppe nomads. Such measures boosted Zhao strength and made it the last obstacle to Qin's ambition.

The centrally located Hann and Wei were swing states vigorously courted in the balance of power. Hann was the smallest of the seven and the most vulnerable. It sat in the way of Qin's eastward expansion along the Yellow River and was whittled down long before formal annexation. Wei, initially the strongest, continued to play an active role despite its relative decline. It was the nursery of political talents whom it failed to employ. Wu Qi, who won Qin territories for it, was eventually dismissed and went to Chu. Shang Yang, Zhang Yi, and Fan Ju went to Qin, taking Wei's experience with them. These able men working for neighboring states did not bode well for Wei.[23]

Qi and Qin, at the eastern and western ends of the Chinese world, revealed the diversity within a rather homogeneous culture. Agriculture was the economic base in all states. Unlike Qin's single-mindedness, however, Qi on the eastern seaboard also encouraged commerce, fishing, and the salt industry. Contrary to the simplicity of Qin's capital Xianyang, Qi's Linzi, with a population of about 70,000 households, flaunted expensive lifestyles. Adjacent to Lu, the bastion of Zhou tradition and Confucianism, Qi shared the enthusiasm for high culture. Its kings built a Palace of Learning at Jixia, sponsored thousands of students, granted posh stipends to seventy-six masters, and built them big houses.[24]

Such were the warring states. Evolved in competition with each other over centuries, they were trapped in a sibling rivalry run awry. Unilateral disarmament was suicide and a multilateral peace agreement an unrealistic dream. Wearied states that appeased bullying neighbors by ceding land gained not peace but more threats. Victorious states could not afford to relax; the least slackening of their guard would invite challengers. So each was forced to struggle for survival.

Coexisting states are ubiquitous in world history. Systems of states, in which nearby states of equal status share cultural values and maintain close diplomatic ties, are less common. A system of contentious states rarely lasts long. Equilibrium is difficult to maintain: one state—or a neighbor of the system—eventually becomes strong enough to turn the system into a hegemony or an empire. This happened when Rome intruded into the Hellenistic state system in the eastern Mediterranean, and this was the final outcome in China. During the Warring States period, however, the interstate relations in China resembled those in Europe after the Treaty of Westphalia ended the Thirty Years War in 1648. Both presented a multistate system exercising some form of balance of power. Like Britain, France, Austria, Prussia, and Russia, the seven warring states were comparable in strength, neighboring to each other, independent in domestic and foreign affairs, ambitious, and bellicose. Congealed from a more fragmentary Chinese political landscape of long history, they shared values and social norms. Their cultural homogeneity exceeded that of Christendom, although the Zhou royal house was less powerful than the Roman Catholic Church. In the readiness to test military strength and the intensity of diplomacy, they matched the Europeans. Their rulers met frequently and elevated their titles to kings in the 330s BCE not by unilateral proclamation but by mutual acknowledgment. States formed coalitions and switched sides to suit their agendas as readily as "Perfidious Albion," as the continental Europeans called Britain.[25] Each state was as eager to thwart the union of others as Britain was to sabotage attempts at a united continental Europe. However, no extra system great power akin to the United States of America existed to intervene in case of disequilibrium. Finally, Qin succeeded in doing what no European state did.[26]

3.3 From Balance of Power to Unification

The first big clashes among the warring states were the battles of Guiling and Maling between Wei and Qi. Zhao attacked Wey, a client state of Wei. Wei allied with Hann and invested Zhao's capital, Handan. Zhao appealed to Qi for help. Qi ministers figured that if they ignored the appeal, then Wei would take Handan and gain power to Qi's detriment. However, if they helped to raise the siege, then Zhao and Wei would both conserve their strength, again to Qi's detriment. Finally Qi decided to answer Zhao's appeal, but wait until Zhao and Wei fought themselves to exhaustion at Handan, then march straight on Wei's capital, Daliang, thereby forcing Wei to recall from Handan the army that, tired and harried, could be intercepted in a position of Qi's choice. It happened as Qi planned. The Wei army, rushing back to rescue Daliang, was ambushed at Guiling in 354 BCE.

Recovered, Wei returned Handan to make up with Zhao, quashed Qin's opportunistic pestering, and in 342 BCE attacked its former ally Hann. Hann appealed to Qi, which repeated its strategy of waiting and then marching on Daliang. This time Qi lured Wei's main army into a trap at Maling, annihilated it by missiles fired from 10,000 crossbows, killed its general, and captured the crown prince at its head. Qi replaced Wei as the lead power.[27]

Qin was relieved of its greatest pressure by Wei's decline. It set eyes on Hanzhong, a strategic wedge between its home base and its new acquisition Shu. Hanzhong belonged to Chu, then in alliance with Qi. After intensive diplomacy to pry Qi from Chu and form its own alliance with Wei and Hann, Qin wrested Hanzhong from Chu. Then it turned on its allies. When Wei and Hann teamed up with Qi, Qin made up with its previous enemy Chu.[28]

These few examples illustrate the fluidity of interstate relations. When one state became too prominent—first Wei, then Qi, and finally Qin—the others stacked up vertically against it, while it maneuvered to break the alliance by bribing its members with individual horizontal pacts. Alignments changed like the weather. Specialist diplomats called "vertical-horizontalists" crisscrossed the states peddling various schemes of association or divide-and-conquer.[29] No one used the term "balance of power," but the abstract concept is not necessary for factual balance. Many comparable powers, each maneuvering agilely to maximize its immediate interests, can maintain equilibrium, for a while if not indefinitely. Call it the invisible hand working in interstate politics if you please.

Qin's 316 BCE strategic decision disclosed its grasp of balancing power. A minister urged attacking Hann because it was the gateway to Zhou, and by capturing Zhou's emblems of power and controlling the son of heaven, Qin would gain the prestige to command the whole world. Yet the opposition prevailed: "To assault the son of heaven would incur notoriety, not advantage. It brings the name of injustice. It is dangerous to attack what the world is unwilling to see endangered."[30] Qin did lust after Zhou's emblems, but it left Zhou alone until 255 BCE and refrained from destroying Hann or any other major state even longer. It understood the necessity to avoid galvanizing opponents. Swallowing peripheral states such as Shu was fair game; so was robbing major states of some land and population. To extinguish a great power, however, would inflame the fear and loathing of other great powers.

Qin's pragmatic diplomatic insight escaped the scholar-packed Qi. In 314 BCE, Qi's opportunistic intervention in Yan's internal turmoil, approved if not urged by Mengzi, instigated other states to help Yan.[31] All Qi gained by its failed annexation was Yan's hatred. Egged on by the vengeful Yan, Qi annexed Song in 286 BCE and provoked even greater antagonism. Zhao, Wei, and Hann—originally its allies against Qin—switched sides and join Qin against it. Qi lost its army to the Qin-led coalition from its west and almost all of its territory to Yan's surprise attack from the north. Although Yan failed to hold the territory, Qi recovered only to spend its remaining decades sulking in isolationism.[32]

Posterity, with perfect hindsight, blames the six eastern states for failing to combine against Qin. This may be a valid criticism regarding the last two decades. Before that, their strategic priorities were far from clear; other states were no less dangerous. Alliances are always difficult to maintain, especially when the parties are not under immediate existential threat. Complacency blinds the second in line from the menace of a serial aggressor, and the warning "when the lips are gone, the teeth feel the cold" often falls on deaf ears. To forge agreement, several states sometimes appointed a joint minister, but the unity in top command often failed to compensate for the armies' lack of training in joint operations. Free rider psychology, by which one hopes the others will do the hard task, plagued the Wei-Hann coalition in the battle of Yique in 293 BCE. Qin's general Bo Qi routed a coalition force more than twice the size of his own by concentrating his troops to smash the Wei contingent before the Hann army responded, and then turning to finish off the latter.[33]

King Zhao of Qin, who reigned from 306 to 251 BCE, won the throne with the support of the queen dowager and her brother Lord Rang. As premier, Lord Rang seized remote eastern lands as his own lucrative fief and tried to enlarge it, but his repeated attacks on eastern Wei were always foiled by the rescue of Zhao and Yan. In 266 BCE, Fan Ju, a servant from Wei, went to Qin and pointed out to King Zhao that Lord Rang and other aristocrats were wasting the state's troops for their personal gains. He criticized their practice of traversing foreign territories to conquer lands too far to hold. With limited resources, Qin must set priorities. Instead of struggling for prestige and wealth, it should focus on territory and population that it could hold and rule. Succinctly, Fan Ju promoted the policy "to befriend distant states and attack neighbors, so that every inch of land the king wins would be his to keep."[34] This policy of empire building seems obvious to us. The lateness of its articulation and the celebrity it acquired indicate the paucity of grand strategic thinking in the warring states.

Zhao, the last counterweight to Qin, stopped its advances in several major battles. Then the two dug-in armies faced off each other for three years at Changping. The stalemate broke in 260 BCE. Qin's Bo Qi cut Zhao's supply route by a surprise attack at the enemy's rear with 25,000 troops and sliced Zhao's camp into two by 5,000 cavalry. After forty-six days of starvation, the Zhao army of allegedly more than 400,000 was massacred. The disparity in magnitudes, not infrequent in Chinese sources, rouses skepticism about the alleged army size. In any case, the disaster did not destroy Zhao's ability to resist Qin's siege on Handan for three years. Finally, Wei and Chu came to the rescue. In coordination with Zhao and Hann, they routed the Qin army and recovered much occupied territories. Even in the 250s BCE, the balance of power could still work. Unfortunately for the six states, they fell upon each other for quick gains instead of using the breathing space to strengthen their cooperation. Their last anti-Qin coalition of 241 BCE fizzled. For their eventual demise, they had only their own myopia to blame.[35]

An observer of the warring states wrote, "When strong states are many, it is dangerous to be early in fighting and advantageous to be late. When strong states are few, the first to move will gain all power; those that dally will be destroyed."[36] By chance rather than design, Qin built up its strength after the others had tired themselves fighting each other, hence reaping the laggard's advantage. Now, two centuries later, with only six rivals left and none equal to its strength, the young King Zheng, who assumed full royal power in 238 BCE, faced a conscious choice. Qin decision makers were ambitious but not reckless; the history of warring states offered too many lessons of catastrophic reversal of fortune. To soften resistance, gold-laden persuaders infiltrated the courts of the six states, encouraged pro-Qin factions, bribed inept functionaries, and frustrated any attempt at alliance. Qin secured a cozy relation with Qi's pro-appeasement premier, who refused to aid the other five states during Qin's campaigns of annexation and left Qi totally unprepared when Qin finally descended on it. In Qin's carefully prepared campaign, the six states fell like leaves in a gale. United China began in 221 BCE.[37]

That year in the western Mediterranean, news reached Rome that Hannibal had just taken command of the Carthaginian army.

3.4 The Punic Wars

While Rome conquered Italy, Alexander's empire soared like a firework and exploded into several kingdoms destined to crumble in Roman expansion. In resistance capacity, the Greeks and Macedonians in the eastern Mediterranean paled beside Rome's first overseas enemy, the Phoenicians, who had been colonizing the western Mediterranean since the eighth century BCE and coalesced under the hegemony of strategically located Carthage.

The Carthaginians were mainly seafarers and long-distance traders. Their territorial ambition was confined to northern Africa. Elsewhere, they sought to expand and monopolize trade. Peace, the essential prerequisite for trade, was the Carthaginian aim for Spain, Sardinia, and Sicily. In Sicily they maintained a power balance with the Greeks under the leadership of Syracuse.[38]

Aristotle compared the constitution of Carthage favorably with that of Sparta. Polybius said that Carthage and Rome both had "mixed constitutions," although Carthage favored the democratic while Rome the aristocratic element.[39] Cicero remarked, "Carthage would not have held an empire for six hundred years had it not been governed with wisdom and statecraft."[40]

Rome and Carthage had been on good terms for centuries. The two republics signed at least three treaties defining each other's sphere of influence. Modern scholars have advanced strong circumstantial evidence for a treaty term that "the Romans were bound to keep away from the whole of Sicily and the Carthaginians from the whole of Italy."[41] Only the narrow Strait of Messana separated the two realms.

The city of Messana at the northern tip of Sicily was occupied by the Mamertines, Italian mercenaries who pillaged neighboring Greek and Carthaginian cities. When Syracuse intervened, a faction of Mamertines appealed to Carthage, another to Rome. Carthage responded and established a garrison in Messana. The Roman Senate was indecisive for reasons probably beyond the notoriety of the Mamertines. However, with promises of abundant booty and the scary picture of a Carthaginian-controlled Sicily, the consuls persuaded the people to vote war.[42] Thus Rome began its overseas expansion in 264 BCE. Its three Punic Wars, named after the Phoenician origin of the enemy, ended in 146 BCE with the destruction of Carthage. The first two wars, separated by a twenty-three-year lull, can be regarded as a sixty-two-year struggle between two great powers. The relatively short third conflict was the last stand of a disarmed people against a superpower.

"Defensive imperialism dominated Rome's policy." The specific remark of a modern historian refers to Rome's decision to invade Sicily.[43] However, to excuse Roman imperialism generally in terms of defense has been a scholarly fad, now much criticized. Today, most scholars doubt the objectivity of any immanent Carthaginian threat to Rome. For perceived remote risks, Rome did not try diplomacy, alliance with Syracuse, or other unaggressive solutions. This political judgment is confirmed by military behaviors, as a military analyst finds: "The Carthaginians left the strategic and operational initiative almost exclusively to the Romans throughout the First Punic War."[44] Rome's invasion surprised Carthage and Syracuse, which joined ranks to resist but were beaten back. Instead of stopping at Messana as befitting a defensive strategy, Rome doubled its expeditionary army the following year. Syracuse surrendered to become an ally. The Greek city Agrigentum allowed newly recruited Carthaginian reinforcements to assemble. The Romans sacked it and sold the Greek citizens into slavery.[45]

The Romans dominated on land, but failed to take Sicilian coastal cities backed by Carthaginian sea power. Three years into the war, the landlubbers built a fleet of 120 ships in three months and attained naval superiority in a comprehensive victory. In 256 BCE, with a fleet tripled in size, Rome launched a massive invasion of Africa. Its force was defeated by a Greek mercenary commanding the Carthaginian army. The fleet, returning with the remnant troops, sank in a storm, partly because the commander disregarded sea conditions. Undaunted, the Romans built another fleet, only to see it succumb to a similar fate.[46] Polybius remarked, "Now in general the Romans rely upon force in all their undertakings, and consider that having set themselves a task they are bound to carry it through, and similarly that nothing is impossible once they have decided to attempt it. It often happens that this spirit inspires them to success. . . . But when they are contending with the sea and the atmosphere and try to overcome these by force, they meet with crushing defeats."[47]

A stalemate ensued until Rome built a third fleet, which destroyed the Carthaginian fleet supplying Sicilian coastal cities. Thus ended the long First Punic War in 241 BCE. Looking back, Polybius observed that the Romans were superior in individual courage, but the greatest general on both sides was Hamilcar, who threatened Rome's land superiority during the Sicilian stalemate.[48] When he received the Sicilian command in 246 BCE, Hamilcar saw the birth of his first son Hannibal, who would outshine him in generalship

The war exhausted both treasuries. To build its third fleet, Rome raised private loans payable only in the event of victory. To avoid tax hikes, Carthage tried to discount the arrears due its mercenaries. Roman patriotism paid off while Carthaginian greed backfired. The mercenaries rebelled. Worse, Rome took advantage of the turmoil and, disregarding the newly signed treaty, robbed Carthage of rich Sardinia.[49] Polybius wrote, "Concerning Sardinia, it is impossible to discover any reasonable ground or pretext for the Romans' action." Carthage's loss of Sardinia was "contrary to all justice." This, he thought, was the "principal cause of the subsequent war."[50]

With Sicily and Sardinia gone and a heavy indemnity to pay, Hamilcar persuaded the Carthaginians to reestablish and expand their dominance in Spain with its lucrative mines. The 226 BCE treaty with Rome delimited the boundary of Carthaginian dominion at River Ebro in northern Spain. It did not mention Saguntum, a town deep within the Carthaginian realm.[51]

In 221 BCE, the Carthaginian government confirmed the troops' election of Hannibal to the Spanish command. He quickly solidified the realm. Saguntum appealed to Rome. What followed is unclear, but it seems safe to accept the judgment of most modern historians that Rome had no legal ground to restrain Hannibal from attacking Saguntum. Indeed, it did not stir during the eight-month siege of Saguntum, allowing Hannibal to take the city and sack it as brutally as the Romans sacked Agrigentum.[52]

Rome waited three more months before sending an ultimatum to Carthage in 218 BCE. A modern historian writes with emphasis on Rome's typical overseas diplomacy: "The terms were *purposely* set at an unacceptable level, well out of proportion to the nature of the injury reportedly committed."[53] Polybius described the indignant Carthaginian Senate referring to various treatises and arguing for the legality of their action. "The Romans refused definitely to discuss the matter of justification." The negotiation resembled that in the First Punic War, when Carthage sued for peace during Rome's invasion of Africa. The Roman consul "took the attitude that he was already virtually master of the city."[54] The Carthaginians upheld their dignity then. They did the same now.

A war devastates the theater of operations, no matter who wins. Ever since the Romans had beaten off the mountain folks, they took care to fight their wars on other people's territories.[55] This time they immediately dispatched two armies, one for Spain and another for Africa. Unexpectedly, they met an adversary capable of turning the tables on them. Hannibal organized Spanish defense, sent envoys ahead to negotiate passage, assembled a multiethnic army, and set out for Italy through what is now France. Midway, on the River Rhone, he brushed by the Spain-bound Romans. They had sea transport protected by naval supremacy. He marched and lost almost half of his troops to attrition, desertion, casualty in storming through tribal areas, and the elements when crossing the Alps in early winter to reach his chosen theater of war (Map 8).[56]

Polybius wrote, "The number of Romans and their allies able to bear arms totaled more than 700,000 infantry and 70,000 cavalry, whereas Hannibal invaded Italy with an army of less than 20,000 men."[57] Hannibal had 6,000 cavalry besides. His choice of invasion route indicated little expectation for retreat or reinforcement. During his fifteen-year campaign in Italy, he would receive a single reinforcement of 4,000 men from home. Additional troops he had to recruit in Italy, from Rome's subjects and allies. Yet even the sympathetic Gauls in the Po valley, newly conquered by Rome and rebellious, were skeptical of his small army, cruelly punished by the mountains. To inspire confidence and gain support, Hannibal had to win battles, and win with minimal casualties. Losses to his core force would be irreplaceable.

Hannibal came with not suicidal fanaticism but a limited political objective of rolling back Rome's overseas expansion. Polybius recorded his later treaty with Macedon, which envisaged peace terms in which Rome survived but lost control over a list of cities.[58] Rome's conquest of Italy produced a federation. Only one-third of Italians were Roman citizens. The rest belonged to a host of subordinate colonies and allies that provided at least one-half of Rome's military contingents.[59] If they could be induced into uprising, Roman power would be greatly reduced. This Hannibal tried to achieve by wrecking Rome's prestige of invincibility.[60]

At Trebia, Lake Trasimene, and Cannae, Hannibal won against increasingly larger odds as he fought his way through the length of Italy. His tactical ploys in the first two battles made the Romans cry foul, but Cannae in 216 BCE was a set-piece battle fought on grounds of apparent Roman choice. Rome and its allies mustered 80,000 infantry and 6,000 cavalry, intending to overwhelm Hannibal's 40,000 infantry and 10,000 cavalry, about half of whom were Gauls. Rome's largest army yet brought it its largest defeat. Hannibal set a trap in plain sight by weakening the center of his battle line with a convex formation. The fighting retreat of the center slowly drew the Romans into the vise of flanking heavy infantries, giving time for the cavalry to drive off its Roman counterpart, return to attack from the rear, and complete a grand tactical envelopment. Up to 70,000 Romans lay on the battlefield, while Hannibal's casualties amounted to 6,000. Cannae was one of the greatest battles in military history.[61]

The victory set ablaze the Carthaginian enthusiasm to storm Rome immediately. Yet Hannibal rejected the urge, probably for similar military assessments that would prevent Scipio from attacking Carthage after Zama. In accordance with his strategy of breaking Rome's federation, after each victory Hannibal separated prisoners of war into Romans and their allies. He released the allies without ransom, telling them that he had come "to give the Italians back their freedom and to help them recover the cities and the territories which the Romans had taken away."[62] After Cannae, he told Roman prisoners that "he was not engaged in a war to the death with Rome." The same message he sent to Rome together with a proposal for peace.[63]

Hannibal's view of limited war was not idiosyncratic; nationalism was two millennia in the future. Cicero too characterized the struggle between Rome and Carthage as a war for glory and domination, which should be less ferocious than wars of survival.[64] In view of the aftermath of Rome's future victories over Carthage at Zama or over Macedon at Cynoscephalae, Hannibal was not stupid to hope for a reasonable peace settlement after such a crushing defeat, especially when the victor initiated negotiation. The determination of the Romans, however, was exceptional. They turned the Carthaginian envoy back before he approached the city.[65] They wanted no negotiation, not even for ransoming war prisoners. It was victory or a fight to the death. That grim resolve for an ancient version of total war would make Rome the master of the world, but Italians would pay dearly.

The Romans refused battle and allowed Hannibal to pillage the country. They dogged him, scorched the land to deny him provisions, erected ramparts, retook deserter towns, and inflicted severe punishments. The need to defend territories and protect allies cut into one of Hannibal's greatest military assets, mobility. In a protracted war of attrition, the Romans wore down his army by sacrificing the Italian social fabric. Both sides increasingly resorted to terror for control.[66]

Rome's federation cracked, but did not crumble. Hannibal loomed large in southern Italy, but his influence in the north was screened by Roman territories, whose central location was designed to divide Italians. Ports were protected by its navy. Central and northern Italy held. Many common people preferred peace with Hannibal to suffering war's ravages for Rome's glory. However, the local aristocrats mostly remained loyal and managed to keep the commons in check. Rome's divide-and-rule policy worked, as did its militaristic political organization. At its nadir in 212 BCE, when Rome lost about 40 percent of its allies, it was still able to field 240,000 men for its army and navy.[67]

Unlike Rome, where military service was the first duty of citizens and allies, Carthaginian citizens hired mercenaries for foreign wars and loved money above all. Stinginess was enhanced by a strong anti-Hannibal faction in the government. Through the entire war, Carthage dispatched only 82,000 troops overseas. Furthermore, its refusal to rebuild its navy enabled Rome's navy to raid its coasts at will and transport resources between theaters rapidly.[68]

In 210 BCE, the Roman people elected Scipio to command the Spanish war, which was going badly. He launched a surprise attack to capture the capital New Carthage, base of the peninsula and sea link to the outside. Having fought Hannibal at Trebia and Cannae, he adapted the enemy's tactics and trained the Roman legions to fight more flexibly. In five years, he expelled the Carthaginians from Spain. Afterward, he brought the war to Africa, which he laid waste as Hannibal did Italy. The Numidian king tried to broker an honorable peace, but Scipio used the opportunity to capture him by stealth. The Carthaginians recalled Hannibal from Italy for homeland defense.[69]

In 202 BCE, Hannibal and Scipio met between army lines at Zama, where the former made a last, futile bid for peace. Then the battle was joined. Accounts of relative troop strengths varied greatly, but all agreed to Scipio's superior cavalry, partly the fruit of gaining Numidia. A military analyst writes, "It is perhaps strange that two of the most illustrious commanders in history, whose battles had always previously been stamped by originality and subtlety, should have resorted to what was little more than a slogging match when encountering one another at Zama."[70] Perhaps the battle of Zama was symbolic of the two Punic Wars. Brilliant generalship could not mask the basic contest in which two great powers pitted their will and resources against each other. All historians remark on superior Roman manpower.[71] One writes: "In a slogging match, Rome could simply outslog Carthage."[72]

Hannibal and Scipio were both twenty-five when they were popularly elected commander over the reluctance of an old establishment. Born twelve years apart, they would die within months of each other in 183 BCE, both in exile. Their military genius was supplemented by farsighted statesmanship.[73] Hannibal's freedom propaganda among Italian allies and peace offer to Rome after Cannae refuted the image of a vengeful fanatic often attributed to him. He accepted defeat with grace, urging his countrymen to be grateful for Rome's treaty terms and careful in observing them. Elected chief officer to address public crises, he studied the account books and announced that Carthage could pay the indemnity to Rome not by imposing taxes on the people but by recovering embezzled funds from corrupt officials. Livy wrote of his other reforms that curbed the abusive power of judges: "The appreciation this move won for him with the masses was commensurate with the offence he gave to most of the nobility."[74] Aristocrats and aggrieved embezzlers appealed to their natural ally. Rome sent a commission. Hannibal quietly left his homeland and finally drank poison when the Romans closed in.[75]

When he held the power to exact blood, Scipio restrained the Roman desire for retribution and imposed a treaty that was effective to subjugate Carthage but not ruthless enough to incite bitter vengefulness. Carthage retained its African territory and domestic autonomy. However, it was to pay a heavy indemnity and engage in no conflict without Roman permission, not even for self-defense.[76] The arrangement would bring fifty years of peace. Scipio became the darling of the people. Consistent with his rational treatment of Carthage, he argued for liberal policies that respected the rights of Hellenistic states. He too was eventually driven out of public life by narrow-minded politicians. His chief enemy was Cato, the financial officer in his African campaign, who in old age would succeed in swaying the Romans with a mantra, the equivalent of which the allegedly hatred-filled Hannibal never advocated: "Carthage must be destroyed."[77]

Perhaps the Carthaginians were happier after Zama. Like the Romans, they could concentrate on their single love. While Rome triumphed in the eastern Mediterranean, Carthage prospered on commerce and became, in some reckoning, the richest city in the world.[78] Life as a dependent Roman ally was good, except for one thing their money could not buy. Security depended entirely on Roman pleasure. That dependency proved lethal.

Numidia grew powerful with Rome's backing and increasingly encroached on Carthaginian lands and cities. The two sides frequently referred their disputes to Rome. Polybius, a contemporary who had befriended many Romans in high positions, observed that "the Carthaginians always came off second best at Rome, not because they had no right on their side, but because the judges were convinced that it was in their own interest to decide against them."[79]

A deepening sense of injustice and humiliation drove the Carthaginian people to elect assertive democrats. Resistance to a Numidian invasion escalated to a disastrous war in 151 BCE. Far worse than being soundly defeated, Carthage breached the treaty with Rome for the first time, and at a bad time. Ever since Roman inspectors had admired Carthaginian prosperity two years earlier, Cato the censor relentlessly pushed for its destruction.[80] According to Polybius, the Romans "had long ago made up their minds" on a new war with Carthage, "but they were looking for a suitable opportunity and a pretext that would appeal to foreign nations."[81] Now Carthage delivered the desired pretext.

The Carthaginian delegation of atonement reached Rome to find it ready for war. In desperation they agreed to unconditional surrender. Commending the decision, the Senate granted the Carthaginians "freedom and their laws, besides their whole territory," provided they obeyed orders. Meanwhile, a Roman army double the size of a normal expeditionary force set sail for Africa, stuffed with volunteers eager for plunder. Compliantly, the Carthaginians handed over all arms and delivered sons of all leading citizens as hostages. Then the Romans ordered them to yield their city for demolition. They were free to relocate anywhere within their territory, as long as it was ten "miles" inland.[82]

The Carthaginians lived on maritime trade, which required a location within ten "miles" of the coast.[83] Forced inland, banished from their socioeconomic habitat, exposed to the predatory Numidians without their fortified city, and forbidden to fight for self-defense, they would be as free as a grounded whale. Weighing options, they reneged on their unconditional surrender.

All public places in Carthage became workshops for round-the-clock arms production. Men of all classes shared labor; women cut their hair for catapult ropes. For the first time in their struggle with Rome, the Carthaginians united in mortal combat with a determination resembling that of the Romans after Cannae. It was too late, but with their spirit and strong fortification, they defied the legions for three years. Not until 146 BCE did the Romans break into the city. For six days and six nights they fought, furiously resisted in every street. Then they plundered the city thoroughly and burned it to the ground. All cities and towns sympathetic to Carthage shared the same fate. Only about 50,000 persons survived to be sold as slaves. Rome had found the final solution for Carthage.[84]

Scipio Aemilianus, commander of the campaign, was the paragon of culture and *humanitas*. Tears came to his eyes and Homeric lines on the fall of Troy to his lips as he watched Carthage engulfed in the fire set on his order. "A glorious moment, Polybius," he said as he grasped the hands of his tutor, "but I have a dread foreboding that some day the same doom will be pronounced upon my own country."[85]

Did Scipio see in the flames the spirit of Carthage's noble son? Hannibal told his compatriots shortly after Zama, "Peace can never stay for long in a great country. It will find an enemy at home if it lacks one abroad, just as a powerful body appears immune from any external infections but is strained by its own strength."[86] The idea of a counterbalancing force was also familiar to the Romans[87] and the Chinese. Four centuries earlier, a Jin minister argued against war with Chu: "Our ancestors strained their military efforts because Qin, Di, Qi, and Chu were all threatening. . . . Now we have subdued all but Chu. Only sages can avoid both internal and external troubles. Since we are not sages, external peace would foment internal unrest. Why do we not leave Chu as a salutary discipline?" The counsel was unheeded. Jin defeated Chu in the battle of Yanling. Two years later, the assassination of its lord in a civil strife launched Jin on the road to disintegration.[88]

Rome remains the eternal city. The barbarians who sailed from the rebuilt Carthage to receive its unresisted surrender 600 years later were mere vandals. The Roman Republic, however, was more vulnerable and fitting for Scipio's tearful premonition. Thirteen years later, just when Scipio wrapped up another Carthaginian legacy by razing to the ground Numantia in Spain, Tiberius Gracchus was slaughtered in Rome for promoting agrarian reforms. The killing unveiled the Republic's decline, the beginning of which Sallust put at the destruction of Carthage.[89]

3.5 An Empire of Liberty

"It is important to realize that this brutality differed only in degree from what was normal in Roman warfare," writes a modern historian about the destruction of Carthage.[90] Carthage was an old enemy. Corinth was not, but it received similar treatment within months in 146 BCE. It too was razed to the ground and its surviving population enslaved, all for insulting the Roman envoy who came to demand the decimation of the Achaean League. After the Achaean War that left the ruin of Corinth as a reminder of shock and awe at the crossroads of a prostrated Greece, Rome continued to declare all surviving Greek cities free and autonomous. However, illusions must have evaporated about Rome's campaign of "freedom for Greece," declared with so much fanfare five decades earlier at the Isthmus of Corinth.[91]

In the late third century BCE, the eastern Mediterranean basin hosted a system of states anchored by the successors to Alexander's empire: the Antigonid monarchy in Macedonia, the Seleucid in Syria, and the Ptolemaic in Egypt. They coexisted with a host of minor states. The major polities in Greece were the Aetolian and Achaean Leagues, confederations comprising city-states that were independent except in foreign affairs and other agreed matters.[92] As in the system of Chinese warring states a century earlier, a rough balance of power prevailed among the great powers for some time. The balance was tipped, here by an intruder.

Rome turned against King Philip V of Macedon in 200 BCE, as soon as it defeated Hannibal. The war began without negotiation. Polybius narrated the Senate's message to Philip: "he could have peace if he acted thus, but if he did not wish to obey, a war against the Romans would be ready to hand." The ultimatum was so formulated as to be almost impossible for the king to accept under the circumstances.[93] It was characteristic, as a modern historian remarks: "the orders/obedience (or failure to obey) syndrome permeates Rome's dealing with the Hellenistic world."[94] Livy described how the Roman envoy who delivered the Senate's terms to King Antiochus III of Syria drew a circle around the king's feet and bade him give an answer before stepping out of it.[95] The gunboat is the only modern invention in gunboat diplomacy. One by one, the sovereign states of Macedonia, Syria, and Greece refused to take orders. In each instance war followed, Rome won, and the Greeks sank deeper into servitude. Polybius wrote that after the 168 BCE battle of Pydna, in which Rome decisively defeated King Perseus of Macedon, "it was now universally accepted as a necessary fact that henceforth all must submit to the Romans and obey their orders."[96]

Simultaneously as it whipped sovereign states into submission, Rome advertised liberty. No irony was felt in the Greek world, which invented the "liberation" or "restoration of freedom" candy bar for victors to throw to the vanquished, often to sugarcoat the fetters they were imposing. The declaration of small states as "free, autonomous, and democratic" legitimized wars, the overthrow of regimes, and the exercise of suzerainty.[97] Learning quickly, Rome expertly mounted a "freedom for Greece" propaganda campaign to pry allies from Macedon. The theatrical climax occurred after Rome defeated King Philip in 197 BCE. To a large gathering at the Isthmian games, Proconsul Flamininus proclaimed universal freedom for all Greeks, including those in Asia Minor. Rome thus announced the extension of its sphere of interest onto the doorstep of Hellenistic Syria, which it would reduce within a decade.[98]

The Greeks cheered when the Romans withdrew without leaving garrisons. However, whatever freedom a master grants, the master can repeal at whim. The legions returned in three years, then repeatedly, finally to stay. After Pydna, Rome divided Macedonia into four republics, demanded half of their tax revenues as tribute, closed their prospering mines, but did not annex them—that would come two decades later. It was an empire of liberty. The Macedonians "should be free," the Romans declared, "so that nations which enjoyed freedom should feel that their liberty was assured in perpetuity under the protection of the Roman people." They also removed garrisons from Macedon's former ally Epirus, so that the Epirotes "might be free, like the Macedonians." In the same breath, they ordered the Epirotes to produce gold and silver. Systematic plunder followed, and 150,000 Epirotes just assured of freedom found themselves on the auction block for slaves.[99]

A Greek state, democratic or oligarchic, harbored power factions. In 180 BCE, Rome began the policy of active intervention in Greek domestic politics in order to suppress resistance. Officials visited free cities, indicated that they knew who were zealous supporters and who were hanging back, and showed as much displeasure with the latter as with open opponents. Fear spread. Most anti-Romans in Rhodes died, many by their own hands. A thousand leading citizens from the Achaean League were shipped as hostages to Rome, whence fewer than 300 survived to return sixteen years later, among them Polybius. On the other hand, Greek collaborators were plentiful. Politicians soliciting foreign intervention to secure their own position in domestic power struggles had a long tradition in Greek democracies.[100] The Achaean Callicrates insisted that Rome's requests must be obeyed regardless of laws, sworn treaties, or anything else. Their ilk, called "traitors" by Greek schoolchildren in the streets, flourished under Roman wings.[101] "This Roman domination was fastened upon Greek necks by Greek hands," remarks a modern scholar.[102]

Provided they submitted to Rome in all serious matters, the Greeks were free to go their own ways. Their customary squabbles gave Rome ample pretexts to help friends and hurt enemies. The Achaean League tried to dissuade Sparta from seceding. Rome ordered the detachment of not only Sparta but also Corinth and other member states that cherished the League's solidarity. Furious at the demand to reduce their League, the Achaean assembly at Corinth affronted the Roman envoy. Rome sent a second mission to deny any intention of destroying the League and repeat the same order. The Achaeans decided to defend their confederation. Wide popular support was no match for Roman legions. Corinth turned to ruins.[103]

"Words cannot express the hatred, gentlemen, in which we are held in countries overseas because of this scandalous, extortionate behavior of the persons we have sent out to govern them," Cicero told fellow Romans.[104] Perhaps it was no surprise that nearly all free Greek cities in Asia Minor and many in the Balkans welcomed King Mithridates VI of Pontus, a Hellenized kingdom of Persian origin. Even Athens went over. Some 80,000 Italians were massacred around 88 BCE. Rome responded massively despite its internal problems. Sulla perpetrated a civil war to get the command and put Mithridates in his place. Mithridates paused and then retaliated. Finally, after extensive eastern campaigns, Pompey introduced substantial administrative reorganization and established Syria as a Roman province in 64 BCE. By then, a territorial empire was very much in shape (Map 9).[105]

The barbarians of the western Mediterranean were tough foes who dealt Rome several major defeats, but no one could withstand the relentless Roman will to power. Then Rome expanded into today's France in the most famous of its campaigns, Caesar's conquest of Gaul. It presents a telescoped parallel to the Roman enterprise in Greece. Caesar began by parading himself as the liberator of the Gallic peoples from German invaders and ended up depriving them of freedom. He had no grand imperial plan, but seized every opportunity to pick quarrels with allies or foes and subjugate them, justified in terms of providing security for Italy and applauded as the highest service to Rome by Cicero and many Romans. In eight years, at times fighting beyond the Rhine or the English Channel, Caesar added a large province to the Republic's empire and great power to himself. Of Gaul's original population, one-third was killed and another third sold into slavery. These figures given by Plutarch may be inflated, but the exhaustion of the remaining population, mainly the old and the weak, was evident. No big revolt occurred after Caesar left with his army. Gaul was conquered and pacified in one glorious stroke.[106]

3.6 Wars Just and Unjust

"The Gauls fought for freedom, but freedom for what? There is little to suggest that, if left alone, they would have composed their internal rivalries," writes a modern historian on Caesar's conquest. "As it was, a generation bled, suffered and died, but the succeeding one enjoyed peace, thanks to their predecessors' sacrifice and to the wisdom of their conqueror's final settlement."[107]

"To robbery, slaughter, plunder, they give the lying name of empire; they make a solitude and call it peace." This assessment of Rome's settlements was put into the mouth of a resistance leader by Tacitus, senator and great Roman historian writing in the high Empire.[108]

"He who steals a belt hook is a criminal. He who steals a state becomes a lord. To the lord accrue all benevolence and righteousness," remarked a Daoist in the time of the warring states.[109]

Justice is twice infringed when victorious aggressors who write history twist right to embellish might by adding insult to injury. Vilification of the vanquished compounds the injustice perpetrated by violence. Justice itself is tarnished by the victor's arrogation and the cynicism it engenders, like a name brand cheapened by counterfeits.

In a justification of his unification campaigns, the First Emperor of China accused his six victims of breaking covenants, sponsoring assassins, plotting rebellions, colluding against Qin, and other crimes. "Humble as I was, I mobilized the troops to suppress violence and quell unrest. With the blessing of ancestral spirit, the six kings pay for their guilt and the world is in profound order and stability."[110] This claim failed to resonate. The aggressive image of Qin as "tiger and wolf with a heart for swallowing all under heaven," common in late warring states texts, persists. Sima Qian wrote that the political scene of the Warring States period was degenerate. The states, belligerent and faithless, cared only to overpower their enemies by strong armies and shifting coalitions. "Qin seized the world mainly by violence. In an age of volatile changes, it reaped success."[111] Sima was more generous to Qin than most literati, who made Qin into an icon of evil and brutality.

According to the Roman poet Virgil, Roman conquests stemmed from a mandate: to rule, spare the humble and humble the haughty, and supplement peace with law.[112] Thus began a tradition of Roman propaganda similar to that of the First Emperor.[113] It found legions of buyers. In the mid-nineteenth century, when European imperialism dominated the globe, some historians developed the theory of defensive imperialism to justify Roman overseas conquests: "Desiring only the freedom to behave as she wished, Rome was the victim of circumstances."[114] Dominating high scholarship for more than a century, the theory began to retreat in the 1970s. A new crop of scholars exposed Rome's deep-seated militarism and argued that its foreign policy is more appropriately called predatory imperialism.[115] The tide seemed to turn again after the United States–led invasions of Afghanistan and Iraq. Defensive imperialism revived with the glorification of empires.[116] Are interpretations and evaluations as revealing about the interpreters as the history interpreted?

One argument for defensive imperialism is that Rome often did not immediately annex the territories it conquered; and the same applied to the warring states. Qin first reduced the Wei city of Anyi in 352 BCE but did not annex it for sixty-six years. It also waited three decades before putting Shu under direct rule.[117] Its reason was prudential, not moral. So it was with Rome. The aggressors were not reckless. For empire builders ancient and modern, military victory is only the first step in a long process of power consolidation, arduous, perilous, and resource demanding. Occupation of conquered land is risky. Inadequate garrisons provide targets or even arms depots to rebels, who hold the initiative in timing attacks. A strong force may encourage the governor to entertain seditious ideas. Resources are finite, and defending everywhere implies being weak on every point. Instead of being spread thin and tied down in garrisons, troops can be more effective as a mobile force that deters disobedience by its readiness to strike at rebels and inflict terrifying punishment. Besides, it can go on conquering new lands. Not benignity but preference for dynamic offensive over static defense partly explains why after military victories, the warring states often returned some lands seized and Rome granted freedom without garrisons. They would return to tighten control at their own time. Rome's dealing with Carthage was a case in point.

Amid general aggressiveness, some notions of just wars existed in both realms, and not only for rallying and propaganda. Gross injustice incites opposition and may be counterproductive in power struggles. "*Zhi ge wei wu*, to end war is martial," enunciated King Zhuang of Chu. He went beyond the observation that the logogram 武 for *wu* (martial) is composed of two parts, 止 *zhi* (to end) and 戈 *ge* (dagger-axe, extended to mean weapons in general). In a long speech, he expounded seven effective martial virtues: "to suppress violence, demobilize armies, secure greatness, consolidate successes, bring peace to the people, establish concord with other states, and enhance prosperity."[118] Such ideas of righteous war were quite common in Chinese military classics. King Zhuang found himself short on all seven criteria and unworthy of glory, although he had just won hegemony in the 597 BCE battle of Bi. Mengzi's assessment is more sweeping: "None of the wars in the Spring and Autumn period was righteous."[119] Historians generally agree with Sima Qian that morality sank even lower in the Warring States period.

Wars are just under three conditions, according to Aristotle: "first, to prevent us from ever becoming enslaved ourselves; secondly, to put us in a position to exercise leadership [*hēgemōn*]—but leadership directed to the interest of those who are ruled, and not to the establishment of a general system of slavery; and thirdly, to enable us to make ourselves master of those who naturally deserve to be slaves."[120] Cicero justified Rome's imperial conquests on grounds of survival, protection of allies, and interests of empire. He deemed the destruction of Carthage and Numantia certainly just, that of Corinth less so.[121]

Defensive imperialism interprets Rome's overseas ventures as fights for survival or security. How convincing is its arguments? One proponent admits that the Romans "imagined themselves to be threatened when they were not," partly because of "their profound ignorance of eastern affairs."[122] Politicians trumpeted danger to sell wars to the people. Glory-starved aristocrats used scare tactics to get military commands. However, solid scholarship reveals that the Greek world was busy with its own problems and glad to leave barbaric Italy alone.[123] Furthermore, many Roman aristocrats were knowledgeable about eastern affairs through Greek learning, but their expertise was disregarded in most policy decisions.[124] Willful blindness to the conditions of distant targets when launching attacks hardly implies defensiveness.

The distinction between preemption and prevention is as relevant in the interpretation of historical wars as it is in the debate on the recent American-led invasion of Iraq. *Preemption*, a strike launched upon incontrovertible evidence of clear and present danger of an enemy attack, is usually accepted as anticipatory self-defense. The immanence of threat and strength of evidence, which justify preemption, are absent in *preventive* wars, which claim to preclude some vague possibility of unidentified future threat. The threat is hypothetical and evidence of it is dubious. Neither modern international laws nor critical just-war theories recognize any distinction between preventive wars and wars of aggression.[125]

A clear case for prevention, in contradistinction to preemption, is Cato's advocacy that Carthage must be destroyed. Cato stirred sentiment by recounting fifty-year-old atrocities but offered little objective evidence for the possibility of a rerun. Polybius observed that although prosperous, the Carthaginians were enervated and their traditional mercenary recruiting grounds closed since Zama.[126] The loser to puny Numidia could hardly threaten mighty Rome, to which it had been totally submissive. Numerous cases led scholars to conclude that Rome regarded as a threat "the very existence of a truly independent power" or "foreign peoples who might someday be strong enough to attack her."[127] On a scale of 1 to 10 on aggressiveness, how would you rate someone who regards military actions against such threats *defensive*?

To justify war by the defense of allies, one must attend to the condition of alliance. Alliances were ubiquitous among the warring states, but they were usually regarded as expediency for war, not justification of it.[128] A Qin author complained, "Nowadays rescues come regardless of whether the besieged is in the right or not. This is truly unrighteous."[129] Similarly, those worrying about justice must examine the identity of Rome's ally and the ground on which it claimed Roman protection. Rome invaded Sicily to protect its friend. Let us leave aside the wisdom of befriending the Mamertines, who were notorious for atrocities punishable under Roman laws. The crux is that the Mamertines, already at war with Syracuse and Carthage, had no existing treaty that bound Rome to its aid. Rome chose a new friend to defend. A modern historian observes, "The events of 264 [BCE] provide one of the earliest clear instances of what became a standard Roman technique. Rome accepted the Mamertines into alliance quite freely, and in full knowledge that war with new enemies would result. It was an intentional step into a new area. . . . The technique could provide an excuse for an advance in almost any direction under the sanctifying banner of *fides*."[130]

Aristotle's third justification of war is entwined with slavery and freedom: "hunting ought to be practiced, not only against wild animals, but also against human beings who are intended by nature to be ruled by others and refuse to obey that intention, because this sort of war is naturally just."[131] Most Greeks regarded non-Greeks as barbarians and barbarians as slaves by nature.[132] Athenians further extrapolated the notion of political freedom and its antithesis to justify attacking fellow Greeks. The Ionian Greeks, having once submitted to the Persians, would always be considered slaves and unworthy of freedom. Athens, being a thriving democracy and the freest of all cities, deserved to rule them and enjoy limitless possibilities.[133] Modern scholars find that besides democracy and slavery, imperial domination lay at the roots of political freedom in classical antiquity.[134] One writes, "The association of the ideas of love of liberty and love of domination over others is essentially Greek."[135] Another agrees that "freedom became a means of defending its opposite: for the first time in world history, it served to justify oppression and imperial rule."[136] Rome quickly picked up the notion of freedom to dominate. Cicero wrote that other peoples were inferior to the Romans, who alone by divine will had the freedom to rule over them all. To Romans as to Greeks, liberty was the privilege of the imperial people.[137] This justification of war as the freedom of imperialists has no counterpart in China.

The Romans further traced imperial domination to higher authority, as Cicero said: "it was by our scrupulous attention to religion and by our wise grasp of a single truth, that all things are ruled and directed by the will of the gods, that we have overcome all peoples and nations."[138] Believing that their empire was the will of the gods, and a just war was one in which the gods were on their side, the Romans spared nothing to propitiate the gods. However, besides ceremonial correctness, no historical source ever indicated that the priestly laws that sanctioned a war had any concern with the war's moral acceptability. The gods' favor was manifest. A war was finally proved just in the event itself, by a Roman victory. A defeat may imply injustice, but it provided a just cause for the next war: revenge and redemption of honor.[139]

The Romans justified violence in terms of divine will. Aristotle's third criterion of just war appeals to nature's design. Abstracting from the particulars of Roman religion and Aristotelian natural law, a general notion remains: A war's mission is to fulfill some divine command or higher calling that confers the ultimate justification. This general notion, applied to another deity, occurred vividly in the Mediterranean littoral.[140] In the Old Testament, God ordered the Israelites, "in the cities of these peoples that the LORD your God gives you for an inheritance, you shall save alive nothing that breathes, but you shall utterly destroy them, the Hittites and the Amorites, Canaanites, Perizzites, Hivites, and Jebusites, as the LORD your God has commanded."[141] After Christianity became the state religion of the Roman Empire, the historian Sulpicius Severus made God's punishment for the Israelites' laxity in genocide into an object lesson for accommodating barbarians.[142] More famously, Saint Augustine, Bishop of Hippo, combined the Greco-Roman and Judeo-Christian ideas to initiate the Western "just war tradition." Among its doctrines is that of the holy war, a war with divine sanction or higher mission, such as the crusades against Islam that commenced in the eleventh century. Holy wars, whose ends are not tangible goods but absolute ideals, tend to be extraordinarily bloody.[143]

Not all wars with a religious tinge are holy. Holy wars are grounded on divine partisanship: Our action is holy because God wills it. Righteous wars claim moral justification: God helps us because we are good, or our enemies evil. The notion of *tianming*, the mandate of heaven, which the Zhou invented for its attack on Shang, authorizes no holy war.[144] It is based on the allegation that Shang lost the mandate because it mistreated the people. Furthermore, it comes with a warning against future misgovernment: "The mandate of heaven is not constant."[145] After the conquest, Zhou selected virtuous members of the Shang royal house to constitute the lordship of Song. The Chinese notion of the divine aspires to the inclusiveness of the heavenly vault. The notion of a crusade is foreign to it. Western scholars find the notion of righteous war prevalent in the *Seven Military Classics* as well as other Chinese classics on statecraft.[146] One writes, "But in the Chinese texts I have found no parallels with the Old Testament's justification for slaughtering wholesale the people of any enemy in a holy war."[147]

3.7 The Warrior State and the Warring States

The international arena is usually anarchic. Rivalry among states can be palpable. Grievances can accumulate. Information is always woefully deficient. A sense of insecurity prompts each state to increase its own strength, if only for self-defense. Anarchic dynamics can create a whirlpool that sweeps states along in an arms race or escalating war. Even so, there are many ways to assess risks and many responses to address it. One can merely try to do a good job in war or relish in it. Amid the violent whirlpools that enveloped each end of Eurasia for centuries, two attitudes are discernible.

A leading classical scholar writes, "It is notable that there was no internal opposition, among either Athenians or Romans, to empire as such. In Athens I do not know of a single dissenting voice; in Rome there were a tiny number."[148] War to the Romans was a noble and necessary activity for any state desirous of demonstrating its power and virtue. Scarcely any craving for peace appeared in the literature during the height of Roman imperial wars.[149] In contrast, Confucians, Daoists, and Mohists of the Warring States period joined in condemning the raging violence they were unable to stop. Instead of a triumphant parade, a funeral procession was suggested for victory.[150] It was the voice not only of the powerless opposition. Legalists working to strengthen the army and generals expounding the arts of war alike deemed armed conflict less effective than political manipulation in achieving results.[151] Even in essays publicly posted in Qin's capital during the reign of the future First Emperor, we find, "The military is the world's evil-boding tool. Bravery is the world's evil-boding virtue. Only with no option left does one resort to an ominous tool and practice an ominous virtue."[152] This peculiarity struck Western scholars.[153] One writes, "As against . . . Greek and Roman civilization, in traditional Chinese terms warfare was regarded as an activity in which to engage only in the last resort and only when necessity demanded."[154] Another adds, "Herein lies the pacifist bias of the Chinese tradition. War is not easy to glorify because ideally it should never have occurred. The moral absolute is all on the side of peace."[155]

Whatever the ideal, one must deal with reality. Qin was a state of farmer-soldiers who "expand the territory when mobilized, enrich the state when stood down."[156] Rome's own citizen legions had a similar dual purpose. Its confederation of dependent Italian allies, however, was designed mainly for war. From the Italian communities it conquered, it demanded only self-equipped troops. Thus its only way to assert its domination was to lead their troops into war. A year without war meant a year of tax remission for the subordinates.[157] A historian concludes, "War-making was the life-blood of the Roman confederacy in Italy."[158]

The year after the end of the Hannibalic war that devastated Italy, the Roman Senate succeeded in driving the exhausted and reluctant people into a new theater of war, Macedon.[159] After the victory at Changping on foreign soil, Qin's king refused to seize the military opportunity to take Zhao's capital, deciding instead to give his people a nine-month rest. At the height of military conquests, the future First Emperor accepted a proposal to divert manpower to build the massive Zheng Guo Channel that would create farmlands.[160] Such guns-or-butter decisions reveal the relative militarism of the two states.

Impressions of disparate general attitudes toward warfare come with the first reading of classical literature. Historians writing about Republican Rome provided thick descriptions of fierce battles and glorious victories. The exhilaration incited envy in Tacitus, historian of *Pax Romana*: "Their subjects were great wars, cities stormed, kings routed and captured. . . . Mine, on the other hand, is a circumscribed, inglorious field. Peace was scarcely broken—if at all."[161] In contrast, Chinese historians were so disdainful of soldiers and battles they recorded only the thinnest data with occasional mention of grand tactics.[162] Because of the difference in historiographical accent, we know much less about how the Chinese actually fought than we know about the Romans.

The Chinese had nothing remotely resembling Caesar's *The Conquest of Gaul*, but they surpassed the Romans in military theory. Six of seven Chinese military classics originated in the centuries preceding unification.

Sunzi, known for his *Art of War*, was a contemporary of Confucius. Superior theory does not guarantee victory, however. Qin wisely preferred a voluble theoretician to an experienced soldier as adversary. To break the stalemate at Changping, it launched a political operation that caused Zhao to replace the grizzled field commander Lian Po by the learned Zhao Kuo, whose fiasco at the battlefield inspired the idiom "to talk fighting on paper."[163] Hann Fei argued that the vanity of book learning is a bane to a state's military strength; those who can talk like a general scorn fighting as foot soldiers.[164] The Romans would probably nod. Common Roman soldiers enjoyed far higher esteem than did their Chinese counterparts, except perhaps in Qin. The superbly trained legions had their proud identity and initiative. A modern historian observes that the Romans "placed little weight on the tactical and strategic skills of the commanders but instead saw victory as principally won by the soldiers themselves along with the city's god."[165]

The Romans "seem to have been born with weapons in their hands; never do they take a break from training or wait for emergencies to arise," observed the first-century historian Josephus. Modern historians concur: "Roman society can be seen as deeply militaristic from top to bottom, in a way and to an extent that is not true of any Greek state, not even Sparta."[166] Farmer-soldiers constituted the greatest voting weight in the assemblies that decided war or peace. Their readiness to suffer heavy casualties and undertake arduous overseas campaigns continuously for more than a century revealed the depth of Roman militarism.[167] An American historian invokes a Cold War slogan for them: Rome was a "warrior state" whose citizen body was "indeed willing to 'bear any burden, pay any price.'"[168]

A warrior is different from a gladiator or martial artist, as is military valor from individual daring. The latter lacks the public goal that calls for solidarity and discipline. China had no dearth of personal heroism, which was especially vibrant in the Warring States period. Assassins such as Jing Ke willingly defied death to requite friendship or patronage.[169] All warring states tapped into this spirit, but in different ways. Qi employed martial artists in its army and paid them for each enemy killed, regardless of the battle's outcome. Wei maintained highly trained soldiers with generous land grants and tax exemptions. Although effective in combat, the career army drained the state treasury and was limited in size. Xunzi found the military organizations of Qi and Wei inferior to that of Qin, where Shang Yang's integration of peasantry and infantry turned the entire male population into farmer-soldiers or, more exactly, farmer-reserves.[170]

Qin's rule by law tried to forge public solidarity. Xunzi observed that its people were by nature bellicose. Shang Yang's reforms criminalized private feuds and aroused the people's verve by making merit in warfare and farming the only criteria for social honor.[171] The result is visible in the terracotta army stationed near the First Emperor's mausoleum. Even in clay, the roughly 7,000 warriors exude pride worthy of the honor they received. They are not the stereotypical faceless horde. Great effort was taken to give each statue facial individuality. Such respect for common soldiers contrasts with the shameful mistreatment of them in the imperial China of literati-officials.[172]

Peasant conscripts filled the main armies of the reformed Qin and the early and middle Roman Republic. Universal conscription, by which modern nation-states mobilize their human resources, is old hat. Every man of military age is legally liable to be drafted for a specified term. However, many serve only partial terms and many are never called up. When not called up, reservists on the roster engage in normal occupations and contribute to economic production. States reckon their strength in terms of their army reserve. Mistaking the reserve for a standing army exaggerates militarism.

A Qin man was liable to serve two years, not necessarily consecutive, during his military life from age fifteen to sixty. Evidence reveals the two-year term to be an approximation, but not a bad one.[173] When Qin cut the Zhao supply line after a three-year standoff at Changping, the king personally went to the front, called up all men above the age of fifteen in the adjacent county, rewarded them, and sent them to block Zhao reinforcements. This regional full mobilization lasted less than two months.[174] Chinese literati who condemn Qin's levy as draconian should look at the Romans. It was originally thought that after Rome expanded overseas, a qualified citizen served on the average six to seven years during his military life from age seventeen to forty-six. Recent research shows that actual terms were closer to the legal maximum of sixteen years, plus four extra years in case of grave emergency. From 200 to 168 BCE, a yearly average of 16 percent of adult male Roman citizens served abroad. During the wars of the first century BCE, roughly one-third of adult males were engaged for years. Such a prolonged high level of the draft would have ruined the economy if Rome's imperial expansion were not mostly financed by plunder and enslavement.[175]

Qin and Rome both designed elaborate systems of reward and punishment to boost military fervor. Killing 2,000 in a field battle or 8,000 in storming a city qualified the senior officers in a Qin army for elevation in rank and compensation.[176] Killing 5,000 in a single battle against a worthy enemy qualified the Roman commander for a triumph, a military parade through the streets of Rome in his honor. On average, more than one triumph was celebrated every year all through the period of imperial conquests.[177]

In Qin's reward system, a soldier who obtained the head of an armored enemy was elevated one rank in a hierarchy of twenty, entitling him to land and other benefits. Responsibility to provide the awards fell on local officials. Contemporaries observed, "Military merits being the only avenue to profit and rank advancement, people congratulate each other on news of war."[178] The Roman army had established procedures to reward its soldiers by plunder. To despoil surrendered Epirus, it coordinated simultaneous actions in some seventy cities. The Romans collected gold and silver and at the same hour gave signals to commence pillaging.[179] Looting devastated the population but enhanced the solidarity of the army, if executed under discipline. Whereas Qin's reward for individual soldiers sometimes incited internecine scrambles for heads, Roman loot, which was collected in a common pool before being distributed among officers and soldiers, encouraged cooperation.

For those who hesitated to risk their lives for carrots, Qin and Rome wielded physical and psychological sticks. Qin soldiers who shrank back in storming a city had their faces tattooed or noses cut off in public. If one in a five-man squad ran away, the other four received a two-year sentence of hard labor. Ideally, everyone joined in shaming cowardice, so that fathers sent off sons and wives sent off husbands saying: "Do not return without victory."[180] Every Roman legionnaire had a sense of duty drilled into him by strict training and discipline. Anyone found asleep on or absent from night watches was beaten to death in front of the whole camp. Decimation awaited a group that fled the fray; one-tenth of the group was selected at random and clubbed to death, and the rest banished to dangerous disgrace. Polybius reported that many soldiers who could save their skins preferred to escape by death from inevitable disgrace and the taunts of their relations.[181]

3.8 Wars and War Conduct

Pre-imperial China was not a state but an arena with tens or even hundreds of states, comparable not to Rome but to the Mediterranean littoral. To compare with Rome, we have to consider individual Chinese states. Jin, the busiest state in the Spring and Autumn period, went to war about one year in two. During the 232-year period from 453 BCE—when Jin effectively disintegrated into three—to 221 BCE—when Qin united China into one, Qin went to war in at least 114 years.[182]

Rome engaged in war almost annually for nearly three centuries since it expanded beyond its Latin neighborhood. More specifically, it went to war in at least 203 years during the 215-year period from 264 BCE—when the legions invaded Sicily—to 49 BCE, when Caesar marched on Rome. Its regularity was exceptional even in war-prone antiquity. Athens was at war only two years in three during the century and a half since the Persian War.[183] Nevertheless, Athens fought more frequently than Qin, the most militaristic state in China.

The scale of wars is more difficult to compare. Thucydides, who witnessed the Peloponnesian War and wrote the history of it, remarked that "it is impossible to rely on the estimates given, since it is human nature to boast about the size of one's own forces."[184] Roman numbers are more reliable because of standardized legionary organization and detailed historiography. The struggle with Hannibal was the Republic's largest protracted foreign war, at the peak of which it fielded 240,000 men annually. The battle of Philippi in 42 BCE, the largest in the civil war, engaged about 200,000 Romans and a comparable number of auxiliaries for both sides.[185]

The Chinese word *wan*, meaning "ten thousand" or simply "myriad," was especially common in casual usage. In many contexts, "ten *wan* troops" served the same purpose as "a thousand ships" in Homer. Armies in the tens of *wan* were common in the warring states literature. Zhao was said to have lost more than 400,000 troops at Changping, the largest and probably the longest campaign of the period, and still had resources left for stiff resistance. Such an army deployed by one of seven contenders seems incredibly large, considering the population and margin of surplus of the time. After China was united and its economy bloomed, the Han Dynasty mobilized the resources of the whole country against the northern nomads and the literati screamed at the burden of 130,000 to 300,000 troops.[186] Blatant inflations of figures were on record for later periods. For the civil war following the collapse of the Qin Dynasty, Xiang Yu had 400,000 troops, claimed to be 1 million. Later, during the three kingdoms, one side inflated the number of its troops fivefold in propaganda.[187] Probably the warring states similarly puffed up their chests.

Chinese tactics emphasize surprise and psychological manipulation, which is why Sunzi's *Art of War* is reading material in today's business schools. One stratagem is to feign weakness to entice the adversary into complacency and mistake. In the war with Wei in 342 BCE, the Qi commander ordered soldiers to build successively fewer camp stoves each night. In the eye of the Wei general at their heels, the decrease in stoves reinforced his preconception of Qi cowardice and misled him into imagining massive desertion. Encouraged, he went on a reckless cavalry pursuit, only to run into a deadly trap at Maling.[188]

Except Scipio and Caesar, the Romans generally preferred straightforward pitched battles and complained about Hannibal's feints and ambushes.[189] Nevertheless, they did not scorn deception when it was to their advantage. When Hasdrubal, driven out of Spain by Scipio in 207 BCE, went to Italy trying to link up with his brother Hannibal, the Romans concentrated two consular armies to stop him but worried that their overwhelming force might scare the enemy from giving battle. To hide their strength, the consuls ordered the army that arrived second to creep into the camp of the first army after dark. Two armies squeezing into one camp deceived Hasdrubal, until each army routinely sounded its own consular trumpet.[190]

To sabotage the enemy's decision-making capacity is a common idea in Chinese military doctrines.[191] Sunzi writes, "The best offensive is directed against the enemy's deliberation; next, its diplomacy; next, its army; the worst, its fortified cities."[192] Political espionage became an expertise that Qin practiced assiduously, especially during its unification campaigns. Fan Ju explained how it would work:

> Now your majesty decides to attack Hann and invest its city Xing. I suggest your majesty attack not only their territories but also their men. While attacking Hann and investing Xing, your majesty should negotiate with Zhang Yi. If he is smart, he would cede some land to preserve his own position and the remaining of Hann. If he fails to get the point, your majesty should cause his dismissal and negotiate with someone more malleable. Then your majesty can achieve your desire by negotiation.[193]

Just as Rome benefited from Greek traitors, Qin readily found collaborators in enemy courts. Zhao's able generals Lian Po and Li Mu were only two victims of political daggers.

Games of cloak and dagger, although bloody, are no comparison to the battlefield. Fan Ju's phrase quoted above—"attack not only their territories but also their men"—taken by itself, is misinterpreted by a Western historian as the enunciation of a "policy of mass slaughter."[194] Perhaps violence, like beauty, is in the eye of beholders. Language, context, timing, and subsequent action all refute this interpretation. The purpose of attacking decision makers or their deliberation is precisely to reduce military costs and mass casualties. The warring states usually did not aim to annihilate their enemies. Sunzi was only one among many to write, "Leave a gap when encircling an army. Do not press an exhausted invader."[195] The enemy's desperate fight for survival may increase one's own casualties. Such tactics of limited battles may seem insipid in the West. A military historian writes:

> The overall aim of western strategy, whether by battle, siege or attrition, almost always remained the total defeat and destruction of the enemy, and this contrasted starkly with the military practice of many other societies. Many classical writers commented on the utter ruthlessness of hoplites and legionaries, and in the early modern period, the phrase *bellum romanum* acquired the sense of "war without mercy" and became the standard military technique of Europeans abroad.[196]

At the times when people enjoyed gladiator combats or spectacular tortures, war atrocity was no surprise. No one had any qualm in using weapons of mass destruction. Fire and water are weapons that kill indiscriminately. Fire was a favorite ancient weapon everywhere. Geography made water handy in China, where rivers were often diverted and dikes broken to flood cities or degrade their fortification. Such was the fate of fortified Yancheng, where a large Chu army blocked Qin's invasion in 279 BCE. Bo Qi built a channel that directed a torrent to punch a gap in the city wall. Hundreds of thousands inside drowned, their bodies deposited by the current in a depression thereafter called the Stinking Pond.[197] A carpet of floodwater is as devastating as a relentless rain of bombs. Perhaps Bo Qi intended only to eliminate the Chu army. However, the drowned civilians of Yancheng would not be consoled to know that they were only collateral damages and not targets of state-perpetrated terrorism.

Emptying the enemy's palaces and state treasury is one thing; looting homes and destroying the livelihood of ordinary people is another. However, it takes strictly disciplined and well-provisioned armies to observe the difference in practice. In theory, the Chinese thought that a righteous army should not disturb civilians. In practice, contemporaries described how invading armies "slashed crops, chopped down trees, pulled down cities to fill in the ditches and ponds, killed livestock, burned ancestral temples, speared ten thousand inhabitants, and trampled on the old and the weak."[198]

If the line between military and civilian was vague in China, it was almost nonexistent in Greece and Rome. Swords were deliberately used on civilians. In Greece, captives were massacred in about one-quarter of recorded cases; enslavement was as common.[199] After defeating the Melians, fellow Greeks who insisted on neutrality in the Peloponnesian War, Athenians slaughtered all the men and sold the women and children into slavery.[200] Ruthless as they were, the Greeks were terrified by Roman savagery. A Roman law promised massacre for inhabitants of a city that did not surrender before the battering ram first hit its ramparts, but it did not promise safety for cities that did surrender.[201] Polybius described the sacking of New Carthage in 210 BCE:

> When Scipio thought that a sufficient number of troops had entered he sent most of them, as is the Roman custom, against the inhabitants of the city with orders to kill all they encountered, sparing none, and not to start pillaging until the signal was given. They do this, I think, to inspire terror, so that when towns are taken by the Romans one may often see not only the corpses of human beings, but dogs cut in half. On this occasion the amount of such slaughter was very great.[202]

These atrocities were legitimate. According to Greco-Roman laws of war, attested by Plato, Aristotle, Livy, and others, "the victor automatically enjoyed absolute and unconditional rights of property over the fruits of victory . . . the right to destroy them or preserve them for his own profit."[203] Victors who refrained from fully exercising their right earned the praise of clemency. "When foreign peoples could safely be pardoned I have preferred to preserve rather than to exterminate them," wrote Augustus in his *Achievements*.[204] Modern scholars find this attitude chilling, because the merciful smile, which simultaneously asserts the right to exterminate, reveals "the affirmation of a clear conscience, something perhaps more horrifying than the threat itself."[205]

Large round numbers in ancient histories are usually unreliable, large casualty numbers especially so. Aggrandizement and intimidation tactics tend to exaggerate troop numbers, rewards encourage inflation of enemy casualties; and the chaos of battlefields makes collecting statistics particularly difficult.[206] Even with today's computer and intelligence-gathering technology, numbers given for Iraqi deaths in the six years after the 2003 United States–led invasion vary from 98,170 to 1,033,000.[207] With this caveat of inaccuracy in mind, a few oft-cited figures provide a feel for ancient violence. During the last 130 years preceding unification, when the scale of wars peaked, Qin was said to have killed 1.5 million of its enemies. Bo Qi was the most ferocious of the warring states generals. In his four great battles over three decades, including the destruction of Yancheng, total enemy dead exceeded 1 million. At that time, the population of China was estimated at 20 million.[208] Qin's brutality was notorious. Caesar's clemency was famous. Sometimes he did not kill all his prisoners but only chopped off the hands of warriors. For his eight-year Gallic campaign, the number of enemy dead reported ranged from 400,000 to 1 million, when the total population of Gaul was about 3 million. Adding the casualties of his wars in the east, but excluding Romans killed in the civil war, one account credited 1.2 million deaths to his legions.[209] All figures include both soldiers and civilians massacred in all situations. Such colossal casualties were unsurpassed until the Thirty Years War ignited by religious conflicts among Christians in Western Europe, with great-power battle dead of 2.1 million and total casualties topping 5 million. Great-power battle dead for the First and Second World Wars were 7.7 and 13 million respectively, figures that exclude civilian casualties and the battle casualties of minor powers such as China.[210]

Caesar reported that after his victory over the Atuatuci, he auctioned off in a single lot all men, women, and children, totaling 53,000. Altogether, he sold up to 1 million Gauls, the proceeds of which sales gratified his officers and troops.[211] Lacking sophisticated free markets for slaves, Bo Qi had a problem with the horde of prisoners taken in Changping. He figured, "Zhao soldiers are fickle. If we do not kill them all, they may rebel." Three years later, Bo was dismissed for refusing to command the siege of Handan. Upon receiving from the king the sword for suicide, he exclaimed, "What crime against heaven have I committed to come to this?" After a pause he answered his own question: "I deserve to die. After Changping, I tricked and killed hundreds of thousands of surrendered Zhao soldiers. This is enough for the death penalty." He cut his own throat.[212]

Notes

1.Parker 1996: 1–3.
2. Starr 1991: 456–457.
3. Hui 2005.
4. Hui 2005: 95. Li, X. 1985: 327f.
5. Luttwak 1976: 2. Yates 1999: 29.
6. Horace, quoted in Hopkins 1978a: 76, 79.
7. McNeill 1982: 148.
8. Collins 1978. Mann 1986: 161–165. Lü 2005a: 144.
9. Fuller 1965: 88–89.
10. Polybius 5, 104. *Shiji* 40: 1731.
11. Bodde 1986: 20. Pulleyblank 1999: 71.
12. *Shiji* 55: 2043–2044. Bodde 1986: 46.
13. Lewis 2007: 16–17.
14. *Shiji* 5: 177–179. Li, X. 1985: 222–223. Zhu 2004: 166–180.
15. *Zhanguoce* 4. Yang 2003b: 356–357, 407.
16. Hui 2005: 64–66, 93–94. Cotterell 1981: 97–98.
17. Lewis 1999: 618–619, 634. Yang 2003b: 292–303.
18. Yang 2003b: 343–344, 347–348.
19. Lewis 1999: 416–417. Tan 2006: 27–31.
20. Cotterell 1981: 101–117. Lewis 1999: 621–631.
21. Li, X. 1985: 327–328.
22. *Shijii* 86: 2532–2535.
23. Hui 2005: 60–63.
24. *Zhanguoce* 8. *Shiji* 46: 1895; 74: 2346–2348. Lewis 1999: 642–643.
25. Kissinger 1994: 21, 98.
26. Hui 2005.
27. *Shiji* 65: 2163–2164. Sawyer 1993: 14–15. Yang 2003b: 341–346.
28. *Zhanguoce* 14, 30. Lewis 1999: 617–618.
29. Lewis 1999: 632–635. Hui 2005: 67.
30. *Zhanguoce* 3, 2. *Shiji* 70: 2283.
31. *Shiji* 34: 1556–1558. *Mengzi* 1.17–18, 2.17–18.
32. Lewis 1999: 635–638. Yang 2003b: 388–397.
33. *Zhanguoce* 33. Lewis 1999: 532–534.
34. *Zhanguoce* 5. *Shiji* 79: 2409.
35. *Shiji* 73: 2333–2336. Lewis 1999: 633–641. Yang 2003b: 412–419.
36. *Guanzi* 23.
37. Hui 2005: 99–101. Zhang 2003: 139–141.
38. Whittaker 1978: 85. Bagnall 1990: 37–38.
39. Aristotle, *Politics*, 1272b-1273b, 1265b. Polybius 6.51.
40. Cicero, quoted in Scullard 1980: 164.
41. Polybius 3.26. Toynbee 1965: 522, 542–551. Scullard 1989: 534–535.
42. Polybius 1.10–11.

43. Scullard 1980: 167.
44. Bagnall 1990: 104–105. See also Harris 1979: 182–190.
45. Polybius 1.19–20. Bagnall 1990: 49–59.
46. Bagnall 1990: Ch. 4, 5. Scullard 1980: 167–174.
47. Polybius 1.37.
48. Polybius 1.64.
49. Bagnall 1990: Ch. 9. Scullard 1980: 177, 183–186.
50. Polybius 3.28, 3.10.
51. Polybius 3.27.
52. Scullard 1980: 199. Harris 1979: 200–205.
53. Bernstein 1994: 65.
54. Polybius 3.21, 1.31.
55. Cornell 1995: 268.
56. Lancel 1998: 6. Connolly 1981: 147–171. Bagnall 1990: 155–167.
57. Polybius 2.24.
58. Polybius 7.9.
59. Scullard 1980: 151. Brunt 1988: 126, 128.
60. Polybius, 3.77, 3.85, 7.9. Livy, 22.7, 22.58, 22.61. Walbank 1981: 232. Bernstein 1994: 67–68.
61. Polybius 3.112–118. Bagnall 1990: 171–195. Connolly 1981: 166–188.
62. Polybius 3.77, 3.85.
63. Livy 22.58, 61.
64. Cicero, *On Obligation*, 1.38.
65. Livy 22.58, 61.
66. David 1997: Ch. 3.
67. Brunt 1971: 422. Finer 1997: 412f. Lazenby 2004: 87–88.
68. Polybius 2.23. Lazenby 2004: 235, 239.
69. Bagnall 1990: Ch. 6, 7.
70. Bagnall 1990: 295.
71. Connolly 1981: 203–206. Liddell Hart 1926: 164–190. Bernstein 1994: 83–84.
72. Lazenby 2004: 235.
73. Livy 21.3–4, 26.18–9. Liddell Hart 1926.
74. Livy 33.46.
75. Livy 33.46–47, 36.4. Polybius 15.19. Lancel 1998: 180–182.
76. Polybius 15.18.
77. Plutarch, Cato the Elder, 27. Liddell Hart 1926.
78. Polybius 18.35.
79. Polybius 31.21. See also Livy 42.23–24.
80. Harris 1989: 149, 153. Plutarch, Cato the Elder, 27.
81. Polybius 36.2.
82. Polybius 36.4, 36.6. Harris 1979: 234–240. Astin 1967: 270–281.
83. Plato, *Laws*, 704b. Harris 1979: 239.
84. Harris 1989: 156–162. Scullard 1980: 311–317.
85. Polybius 38.21. Astin 1967: 302–303.
86. Livy 30.44.
87. Plutarch, Cato the Elder, 27. Harris 1979: 266–267.
88. *Zuozhuan*, Cheng 16, Cheng 18.
89. Sallust, *Conspiracy of Catiline* 10; *Jugurthine War* 41.

90. Harris 1989: 161.
91. Gruen 1984: 155.
92. Finer 1997: 372–379.
93. Polybius 16.34. Errington 1989: 264.
94. Derow 1979: 5. See also Bernstein 1994: 64–65.
95. Livy 45.12.
96. Polybius 3.4.
97. Walbank 1981: 92–94. Scullard 1980: 288. Gruen 1984: 142.
98. Errington 1989: 270, 266–268. Walbank 1981: 232–233. Gruen 1984: 143–144.
99. Livy 45.18, 34. Polybius 30.15. Derow 1989: 317–319.
100. Rhodes 2007: 37. Gruen 1973. Derow 1989: 316–320.
101. Polybius 24.9, 30.29.
102. Toynbee 1965: 508.
103. Derow 1989: 322–323.
104. Cicero, On the Command of Cnaeus Pompeius, 22.
105. Kallert-Marx 1995.
106. Brunt 1978: 178–183. Sherwin-White 1957. Goldsworthy 2006: 355, 469.
107. Scullard 1976: 138.
108. Tacitus, *Life of Agricola*, 30.
109. *Zhuangzi*, Quqie.
110. *Shiji* 6: 235–236.
111. *Zhanguoce* 14, 24. *Shiji* 15: 685–686.
112. Virgil, *Aeneid* 6.851–853.
113. Brunt 1978: 175–176. Gruen 1984: 275–278.
114. See the critical accounts in Garnsey and Whittaker 1978: 1–3. Gruen 1984: 5–7.
115. Bang 2012: 200–203.
116. Madden 2007.
117. *Hannfeizi* 1.
118. *Zuozhuan*, Xuan 12.
119. *Mengzi* 7.48.
120. Aristotle, *Politics*, 1333b; see also 1333a–1334a.
121. Cicero, *On Obligation*, 1.35, 1.38, 2.26; *Republic*, 3.34–36.
122. Holleaux 1930: 239–240.
123. Gruen 1973. Brunt 1978. Harris 1979. North 1981.
124. Gruen 1984: Ch. 6.
125. Walzer 2006: 74–85.
126. Polybius 31.21.
127. Brunt 1978: 170, 183. See also Gruen 1973: 274.
128. Strobe 1998: 168–170. Yang 2003b: 448.
129. *Lüshi Chunqiu* 7.
130. Harris 1979: 189–190. See also Brunt 1978: 176.
131. Aristotle, *Politics*, 1256b.
132. Aristotle, *Politics*, 1252b. Finley 1983: 104–105. Schiavone 2000: 115.
133. Thucydides 6.76–80; 6.82. Raaflaub 2004: 172–173, 189–192. Rhodes 2007: 28–29, 35.
134. Patterson 1991: Chs. 3–6.
135. Walbank 1970: commentary on Polybius 5.106.

136. Raaflaub 2004: 180.
137. Brunt 1978: 183; 1988: 312, 292–293. Richardson 1991: 4, 8.
138. Cicero, in Brunt 1978: 165.
139. Harris 1979: 170, 119–120, 166–175. Brunt 1978: 178, 165; 1988: 58, 293, 302. Beard and Crawford 1985: 31.
140. Collins 2003.
141. Deuteronomy 20: 16–17. See also 1 Samuel 15:3.
142. Based on Judges 1 and 3. Goffart 1989: 2.
143. Orend 2006: 12–14.
144. Schwartz 1985: 46–53.
145. *Shijin* 235.
146. Johnston 1995: 69. Strobe 1998: 175–178.
147. Turner 1993: 304–305.
148. Finley 1978: 5.
149. Campbell 2002: 12. Garlan 1975: 68–72. Harris 1979: 35. Mattern 1999: 162–166.
150. *Laozi* 31. Turner 1993: 297–298. Liang 1996: 201–204.
151. *Shangjunshu* 10. *Sunzi Bingfa* 3.
152. *Lüshi Chunqiu* 8.
153. Strobe 1998: 168–172. Turner 1993: 297–298.
154. Loewe 1999: 1020.
155. Fairbank 1974: 7.
156. *Zhanguoce* 5.
157. North 1981: 7. Brunt 1978: 173. Beard and Crawford 1985: 74–75.
158. Cornell 1995: 367.
159. Crawford 1993: 56, 61–64.
160. *Shiji* 73: 2336; 29: 1408. *Zhanguoce* 33.
161. Tacitus, *Annals of Imperial Rome*, 4.32.
162. Di Cosmo 2009: 8.
163. *Shiji* 81: 2446–2447. Sawyer 2004: 106–108.
164. *Hannfeizi* 49.
165. Rosenstein 1999: 205. See also Rosenstein 2009: 34–35. Fuller 1965: 74–75.
166. Josephus, quoted in Keppie 1984: 198. Crawford 1993: 46.
167. Hopkins 1978a: 30. Harris 1979: 41–42.
168. Bernstein 1994: 61.
169. *Shiji* 86, 124.
170. *Xunzi* 15.
171. *Xunzi* 15. *Hannfeizi* 1. *Shiji* 68: 2230–2231.
172. Portal 2007: 144–153, 167–170.
173. *Hanshu* 24a: 1137. Hulsewé 1986: 537–538. Yang 2003b: 247–249.
174. *Shiji* 73: 2334–2336.
175. Harris 1979: 44–47. Astin 1967:169–170. Hopkins 1978a: 35. Finley 1978: 4.
176. *Shangjunshu* 19. Yang 2003b: 251.
177. Hopkins 1978a: 26. Sherwin-White 1980: 178.
178. *Shangjunshu* 19, 17.
179. Livy 45.34. Polybius 6.39, 10.15–16. Crawford 1993: 75. Harris 1979: 49–50, 74–75.

180. *Shangjunshu* 19, 18. Lewis 1990: 38. Yang 2003b: 250–251.
181. Polybius 6.35–38. Bernstein 1994: 60–61.
182. My count from Hsu 1965a: 56, 64; Hui 2005: 242–248; Gu and Zhu 2003: 529–564; Yang 2003b: 696–722; and Ye 2007.
183. Harris 1979: 9–10. Bernstein 1994: 57–60.
184. Thucydides 5.68.
185. Brunt 1971: 422. Osgood 2006: 95.
186. Bodde 1986: 99.
187. *Shiji* 8: 364. *Hanshu* 55: 2482. *Sanguozhi* 54: 1262.
188. *Shiji* 65: 2164. Sawyer 1993: 15.
189. Polybius 36.9. Walzer 2006: 225–227.
190. Livy 27.46–47.
191. Sawyer 2004: Chs. 3, 8, 10.
192. *Sunzi Bingfa* 3.
193. *Zhanguoce* 5.
194. Lewis 1999: 639–640; 2007: 38.
195. *Sunzi Bingfa*, 7. See also *Shangjunshu* 10.
196. Parker 2005a: 5.
197. Sawyer 2004: 275–296.
198. *Lüshi Chunqiu*, 7. See also *Mozi* 11. Turner 1993: 300–302.
199. Garlan 1975: 71.
200. Thucydides 5.116.
201. Veyne 1993: 354–355. Harris 1979: 51–53.
202. Polybius 10.15.
203. Garlan 1975: 68–70.
204. Augustus 3.2.
205. Veyne 1993: 354.
206. Brunt 1971: 694. Bodde 1986: 98.
207. http://en.wikipedia.org/wiki/Casualties_of_the_Iraq_War.
208. Yang 2003b: 423, 9. Lin 1992: 534–535. Bodde 1986: 99–100. Lewis 1999: 626–628.
209. Suetonius, Julius Caesar, 74. Gelzer 1968: 284. Goldsworthy 2006: 353, 355.
210. Tilly 1990: 166.
211. Caesar, *Conquest of Gaul*, 2:33. Harris 1979: 74–75.
212. *Shiji* 73: 2335, 2337.

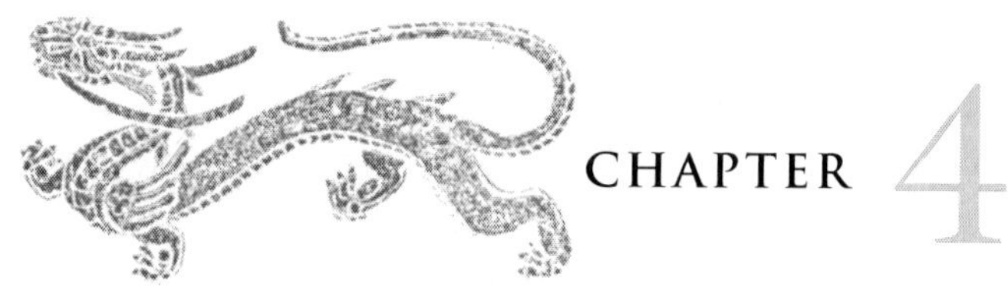

CHAPTER 4

WINNING THE PEACE

4.1 The Empire Strikes Back

The *Book of Change* features sixty-four hexagrams for prognostication. The first hexagram is *qian*, heaven or the creative principle. Its six lines employ the metaphor of the dragon's progress. From the first and bottom line, "The submerged dragon refrains from action," it ascends to the fifth, "The flying dragon holds the sky," the zenith that has come to be identified with emperors. The hexagram does not stop there, however. Its sixth and top line states, "The overstretched dragon has regrets."

To win wars, one needs only to overcome others. To win peace, one must overcome oneself, which is often more difficult and painful. Imperial conquests reached unprecedented heights with Julius Caesar and the First Emperor. Now Rome and Qin faced the most formidable enemy. Internal convulsions, more terrible than external conflicts, have ended many empires with weaker constitutions. Rome and China pulled through. Yet the costs for their peace were dear.

Imperial overreach is common in world history. Its dangers emanate externally and internally. The antagonism of victims persists after defeat and can explode into rebellion if given a chance. Without adequate political institutions to administer and integrate conquered territories, military victories are likely to produce not a stable empire but perpetual turbulence or short-lived occupation. Even worse, the victor's own economy can be strained by military expenditure, its government derailed by the complexity of new populations, and its social equilibrium disrupted by the uneven distribution of spoils. Researchers on modern imperialism call this phenomenon "blowback," the repercussion of conquest feeding back adversely on the conqueror itself.[1] In this view, the ultimate weakness lies in the conqueror's political structure and political elite, which prove inadequate in managing large or rapid imperial expansion.

Blowback was especially threatening to Rome and Qin because of the large scale of their conquests. Who would administer the diverse locals of the vast realm, and how? How would the central government hold peripheral lands together and prevent their governors from evolving into regional kings? To govern a huge empire properly required unprecedented political vision, and new visions trod on old prerogatives. If the eventual successes of the Roman and Qin-Han Empires veil from us the novelty of their initial vision and the baptism by fire through which they executed it, recall the fate of Alexander's empire of conquest.

The word "empire" derives from the Roman *imperium*. We think of empire as a large territorial state under a unified government. To the Romans, however, empire meant power foremost. The *imperium populi Romani* meant the domination of the Romans over other peoples, with or without annexing their territories. Not until the mid-first century BCE did a clear territorial connotation appear and *imperium Romanum* begin to assume the familiar meaning of the Roman Empire.[2] It was then badly governed. Government necessitated numerous officers in provincial administrations. Unlike Chinese states that allowed in talented commoners, the Roman aristocracy jealously guarded the ruling circle and the ambition of its individual members. Instead of draining the circle for provincial governors and risking the danger that individual governors would become too powerful, it preferred to use cronies, collaborators, and private contractors to do the exploitative work. Driven only by self-enrichment and lacking government oversight, these predators were usually harsher on the subject people and less efficient for the state, but they were good enough for the senatorial aristocracy. Farsighted statesmen such as Pompey and Caesar realized that the situation was unsustainable but offered no viable alternative. Not until Augustus did the Romans find a way to enjoy the fruits of victory in a lasting imperial monarchy, but at the heavy price of sacrificing their republican spirit.[3]

The classic verb for Qin's action on other states is *canshi*, literally "to munch like a silkworm." A caterpillar devours a leaf not by swallowing but by relentless shaving. Swallowing implies a notion of the whole; shaving does not. Domination and encroachment seemed to be the major concern of Qin and its fellow warring states. People tired of incessant wars harked nostalgically back at the early Zhou, when concord prevailed under a strong feudalistic king. Anticipation for a unified imperial China was scarce.[4] It was conspicuously absent in *Lü's Annals* under the eponym of Qin's premier Lü Buwei, published one year before the future First Emperor reached adulthood and began to rule. The new political vision crystallized in the young king's court. In the time span that Caesar conquered Gaul, Qin swallowed six rivals whose combined population more than quintupled its own. The First Emperor destroyed not only entrenched kingdoms, but also the traditional regime type by abolishing the feudalistic aristocracy. Reaping the experience of more than a century of Legalist reforms, he instituted a centralized monarchy with bureaucratic apparatuses regulated by law. This vision was so revolutionary that he had to burn books to suppress aristocratic reactionaries. The Qin Dynasty became the martyr to this vision. More consequential victims were the critical thinking of Legalists and the spirit of ruling by law, blamed for Qin's demise and condemned for two millennia by Confucians advocating the rule by men and indoctrination.

Revolts erupted in both empires. Triggered by a mutiny of 900 conscripts, elites and former aristocrats exploded into armed rebellions and brought down the Qin Dynasty. Rome was able to squash local rebellions, but its imperial victims had the satisfaction of seeing the huge spoils extorted from them pay Romans to kill Romans on a large scale. In either realm, the blowback of empire caused violent power struggles among the political elite for a durable government structure—specifically, the struggle between monarchists and aristocrats.

The civil wars and carnage that followed the deaths of Caesar and the First Emperor, more traumatic than imperial conquests, burned away recalcitrant old powers and precipitated a social catharsis that made possible the subsequent imperial peace. Exhaustion and the horror of anarchy created new perspectives on previously unacceptable alternatives. Their residual resistance worn out, the vanquished would settle down as provincials of the empire. Also broken was the backbone of the Roman senatorial aristocracy that assassinated Caesar but would submit, albeit resentfully, to Augustus and subsequent emperors. The Chinese feudalistic aristocracy, which the First Emperor abolished, had a brief revival, and it had bequeathed its spirit to Confucianism. The long power struggle between monarchists and aristocrats climaxed in the three decades studied in this chapter, but it did not end there. Its subdued continuation in the centralized governments would drive much of the politics of the empires.

The tumultuous decades constituted the cusp in both Roman and Chinese history. Standing at the overlap of two eras, a transition can signify emphatically either the end of an old era or the beginning of a new. Caesar marked an end, the First Emperor a beginning. The twilight of the Republic was the major theme of the Roman civil wars, fought partly for want of an alternative vision to the republican constitution made dysfunctional by the demands of empire. Political restructuring that produced a durable alternative—which would come after Augustus's victory—belongs to the story of the Roman Empire, addressed in Part II. Imperial China dawned with Qin's unification and political reforms. Traditional historiography calls the preceding period pre-Qin and treats the four centuries after unification as a group, the Qin-Han

Dynasties. Logically the Qin Dynasty belongs to Part II of this book, and there I leave all institutional analysis. Its events are related here mainly for comparison with the Roman transition to peace.

4.2 Decline of the Roman Republic

Caesar, consul of 59 BCE, presented for Senate approval a bill for distributing land to veterans and poor families. A vote was blocked by Cato the Younger. Undeterred, Caesar summoned the Tribal Assembly and invited Pompey and Crassus to speak. To Caesar's question whether he would lend support against the bill's opponents, Pompey replied, "If anyone dares to draw his sword, I shall take up my shield as well." The crowd cheered, but many senators shuddered. A voting date was set. Pompey's veterans gathered. A majority of senators backed co-consul Bibulus to veto the voting, but a bucket of excrement drove him home. Caesar's bill became law. Further struggle ended in an oath by which senators bound themselves to observe it.[5]

Caesar unveiled his political coalition with Pompey and Crassus, which historians with hindsight consider the beginning of a road that ended in civil war a decade later. At that time, however, it seemed a triumph of the people. The late Republic had become formally more democratic. Secret ballots shielded voters from patronage pressure. The Tribal Assembly, where everyone had an equal vote, dominated legislation. Tribunes and consuls brought bills before it without prior Senate approval. Many common citizens in Rome obtained grain at subsidized prices, later free.[6] Not all was well, however. Electoral bribery distorted voter power. Extended freedom of association encouraged street gangs, whose political impacts were disproportionate because Rome had no police. Physical control of the Forum became a crucial weapon in politics. Violence increasingly came to the fore in a government paralyzed in solving the problems of an expanding empire.[7]

Politicians called *populares* tended to bypass the Senate and use the popular assemblies to push their agenda, thereby promoting both their own political power and the people's sovereignty in legislation. Caesar himself profited from his agrarian bill; tradition made him the political patron of the settlers on distributed land, whom Cicero would call "Caesar's army." Opposing the *populares* were the *optimates*, who insisted on traditional senatorial authority and equality among aristocrats. The line between *populares* and *optimates* was neither sharp nor clear. Some changed colors. Pompey did at least twice.[8] They were all aristocrats with similar vested interests, as a modern historian remarked: "Once in power, the *popularis*, were he Pompeius or were he Caesar, would do his best to curb the dangerous and anachronistic liberties of the People. That was the first duty of every Roman statesman."[9]

Pompey and Crassus each raised a private army on his own initiative to join Sulla, who in 83 BCE returned to Italy and directed the Roman expeditionary army against Roman *popularis* politicians, especially the followers of Marius. Holding the office of dictator, Sulla perpetrated a blood bath, proscribed political enemies, gagged the tribunes, and strengthened the Senate. Reforms completed, he resigned. Some of his measures remained effective in the long term, but his major aim was foiled by his own lieutenants. Jointly elected consuls in 70 BCE, Pompey and Crassus restored full power to the tribunes, thereby gaining the people's gratitude.[10]

The net socioeconomic effect of Roman domination over the Mediterranean had been negative so far. Rome debilitated Rhodes, which had previously policed the sea. As a result, piracy flourished and eventually threatened Rome's own grain supply. In 67 BCE, the people voted an extraordinary command to Pompey, who cleared the Mediterranean of pirates in three months. This demonstration of talent for organizing large-scale operations won him another extraordinary command to deal with Rome's old enemy Mithridates of Pontus. In four years, Pompey left Mithridates dead, the abuses of Roman agents checked, the eastern Mediterranean pacified, and Syria reorganized. His settlement raised Rome's annual revenue from the area by 70 percent, partly by curbing the expenses of middlemen. Local people rejoiced at the order it provided. It showed Rome that sound administration mattered. Pompey himself acquired enormous wealth and many powerful clients.[11]

Pompey returned to Italy and dismissed his army. One wonders if Caesar, who had regarded Sulla's resignation of his dictatorship as politically illiterate, snickered again.[12] Pompey was a great general and greater administrator, but a naive politician. Elsewhere in the empire from Syria to Spain he was highly influential, but not at Rome. From a newly ennobled family, he had pursued an outside track and attained consulship without ever being a senator. Being catapulted to power deprived him of the connections and inside knowledge necessary for successful politicking. Despite his popularity, he fumbled in the Senate and failed in his agenda: ratification for his Eastern settlement and land allotment for his veterans.[13]

The Julii were a patrician family that claimed descent from the gods. Native to the establishment, Julius Caesar pursued the regular track of serving in the Senate and waiting until the legal age of forty-two to stand for consul. The climb to power cultivated associations and a sure touch in politics. Caesar's *popularis* inclination and the marriage of his aunt to Marius incited suspicion from the *optimates*, especially Cato. While Cato rebuffed Pompey's proposal for his niece's hand, Caesar used his only child, Julia, to make a son-in-law of Pompey who was six years his senior. Crassus had long provided financial backing for Caesar, who was chronically in debt to meet the expenditure of a patrician politician. Caesar, Pompey, and Crassus formed what historians call the "first triumvirate" in anticipation of the triumvirate of Caesar's heir. In return for their political support, Consul Caesar arranged relief for Crassus's tax farmers and ratification of Pompey's Eastern settlement. He himself obtained an extraordinary military command with almost complete discretionary power in Cisalpine Gaul for five years, effective immediately. To this was added Transalpine Gaul upon Pompey's proposal, when by luck its proconsul died.[14]

Foreign policy and the annual assignment of provincial commands to proconsuls were traditionally the responsibility of the Senate, whose deliberative capacity was suited for decisions that required expertise and oversight. The democratic turn increasingly put these decisions in the hands of the assemblies, where a demagogue swaying the crowd in the passion of the moment could pass laws with long-term repercussions. Extended military commands with little senatorial supervision were rare and hitherto conferred only on specific missions with clear military needs. Pompey's Mithridatic command was for an ongoing but incompetently conducted war. Caesar's special command was unprecedented for its personal political motivation. Its passage by due legislative process showed how formality could be used to usurp control. The law gave Consul Caesar military backing that enabled him to ride roughshod over the Senate. According to the Roman biographer Suetonius, he openly warned his senatorial opponents that he would "stamp upon their persons." Transalpine Gaul and beyond presented a large territory to invade, and Proconsul Caesar "lost no opportunity of picking quarrels—however unfair and dangerous—with allies as well as hostile and barbarous tribes, and marching against them."[15] He had obtained from the people an almost free hand to pursue war and build up his personal power.[16]

To outmaneuver his political opponents at Rome while he campaigned in Gaul, Caesar strengthened the triumvirate in 56 BCE. He would furlough his soldiers so they could go to Rome to get Crassus and Pompey elected consuls. The consuls would extend Caesar's Gallic command for another five years and ensure him consulship when his command expired in 49 BCE. Also, they would each acquire a five-year command, Crassus in Syria and Pompey in Spain. What Plutarch called "a conspiracy to share the sovereignty and destroy the constitution" worked as planned, except Caesar's final consulate, which precipitated the civil war.[17]

Cicero campaigned for the triumvirs' agenda on the ground of patriotism, so that "the whole of Gaul was to be brought under our sway."[18] Caesar's adroit dispatches from the front, enjoyable to read as *The Conquest of Gaul*, amplified triumphant glory. Pompey stayed near Rome and let his generals take charge in Spain. Crassus decided to emulate Caesar by attacking Parthia from Syria. The invasion of Parthia was on par with the invasion of Gaul, but Crassus lost; therefore his war was unjust. In the 53 BCE battle of Carrhae near the upper Euphrates, the Roman army was annihilated and its eagle standards captured. There the Romans first tasted the ferocity of mounted archery, which gave the Chinese so much pain.[19] Also amazing were Parthian banners that shimmered in the sun. Whether or not the banners were of silk, as some scholars surmised, Chinese silk did reach the Mediterranean around this time.[20]

Back at Rome, the death of Crassus did more to damage the relation between Caesar and Pompey than the death of Julia. A conqueror of Parthia would balance the power between the conqueror of Gaul and the conqueror of Mithridates. Without Crassus's mediation, friend or foe became increasingly a binary choice between Caesar and Pompey. Phenomenal conquests, political support bought with Gallic gold, and a loyal army steeled by victories elevated Caesar's power to unprecedented height. Threatened as never before, the Senate moved toward Pompey, who vacillated but gradually came to think that a new consulship for Caesar would destroy the republican constitution and probably his own dominance. The divided Senate yielded to Cato's insistence and demanded that Caesar disarm before standing for consul, as the law required. To Caesar, this meant political extinction; he would be prosecuted for his previous conduct before election. No one wanted war, but each party had high stakes in intransigence. Propaganda and posturing overwhelmed reasoned judgment. Negotiation collapsed amid mutual distrust.[21]

4.3 Last Flight of the Free Eagle

"The die is cast," said Caesar early in 49 BCE, when he crossed the River Rubicon that divided Gaul and Italy. His march on Rome was a gamble. Italy could rise to defend the Republic. It did not. Pompey evacuated to raise eastern resources, followed by more than 200 senators. However, their divided wills and ambivalence made him an ineffective commander in chief. The die stopped rolling nineteen months later on a Macedonian plain, where the dynasts met. Gazing at the Roman dead at Pharsalus, Caesar said, "They brought it on themselves."[22] Pompey was not among them. He fled, to be murdered on the shore of Egypt.[23]

Pompey "was reluctant to let anyone stand on the same pinnacle of prestige as himself," wrote Caesar. More revealing was Caesar's own confession: "Prestige has always been of prime importance to me, even outweighing life itself."[24] As a contest of rampant ambition, Cicero judged the two equally bad. Yet he joined Pompey, however unenthusiastically. A modern scholar explains, "Pompey was uncomfortable about Caesar's act of violence, since he was still susceptible to certain misgivings raised from the standpoint of the senatorial government."[25] It was simpler for Caesar, who said openly that "the Republic was nothing—a mere name without form or substance."[26] If irresolution was Pompey's bane, underestimation of the Republic was Caesar's.

Securing the allegiance and wealth of the east generated Caesar's famous statement "*Veni, Vidi, Vici*"—"I came, I saw, I conquered." Caesar rebuilt Carthage and Corinth and planted large overseas colonies, which placated the soldiery, quenched land thirst in Italy, and cemented the empire. Cicero and most senators accepted his clemency and returned to public office. Among them were Brutus and Cassius, leaders of his future assassins. Cato alone preferred suicide to bowing to a tyrant, and in death he achieved what he failed to achieve in life. When Caesar read Cicero's *Cato*, which eulogized the martyr of the Republic as the true embodiment of Roman virtue, he understood that just as he valued his *dignitas* above his life, Cato had proved that others valued *libertas*.[27]

The Republic's substance had deviated much from its form, a cause for its impotence in solving pressing problems. Yet the Republic was not yet a mere name. Its traditional hostility to kings as the nemesis of liberty was still alive. As dictator, Caesar held unlimited power and attained near deification, yet it was naked military power sitting atop republican institutions, dysfunctional and antagonistic. He manhandled tribunes, abrogated political associations, manipulated electoral procedures, and issued a torrent of decrees without any consultation.[28] Even common citizens, who adored him for glory, land, gifts, and games, became disgruntled at his political abuses. Caesar often said, "should anything happen to me, Rome will enjoy no peace. A new Civil War will break out under far worse conditions than the last."[29] However, he did little to avert the danger. He ruled supreme in Rome for two years but left no plan for restructuring the government so that its operation would not depend solely on his personal will. Rather than political reforms of necessity, he busily prepared for a war of choice, an invasion of Parthia. Caesar's final official elevation destroyed whatever reconciliation he achieved by clemency. His dictatorship for life ended with him dying, stabbed twenty-three times, at the base of Pompey's statue.

The ancient Chinese recorded their observation of the comet of 44 BCE, which appeared in daylight during Caesar's funeral games, and was hailed as Caesar's spirit ascending into heaven.[30] The official deification of Caesar soon followed. Farmers' almanacs across Italy interpreted the auspice for a golden age, but they were wrong. The age following Caesar's star brought only violence, death, exile, and unprecedented suffering.[31]

That age had begun on the Ides of March. Caesar's assassins spared Antony, Caesar's top general. They considered themselves defenders of the Republic but realized that the republican constitution had not changed to prevent Antony or other aspirants from repeating Caesar's seizure of power, especially with the backing of Caesar's army. Political haggling in Rome proceeded simultaneously with skirmishes, bargains, mutinies, and mobilizations, in Italy and all across the empire. Brutus and Cassius went to the east to raise resources for the ultimate showdown. In their absence, Cicero, senior politician who had shunned Rome during the crucial months of negotiation, returned with a secret weapon, Caesar's heir, then eighteen. "Look at his name and his age," Cicero wrote; he plotted to use "the boy" to fight for Caesar's assassins against Caesar's general, then dispose of him. The old fox would be outfoxed by the cub.[32]

Historians call him Octavian to avoid confusion, but Caesar's grandnephew and adopted son never used his birth name in public life. The name Caesar was his fortune, Antony said; true, but not his only fortune. Octavian inherited three-quarters of Caesar's immense estate, the remaining quarter of which was more than enough to give every Roman citizen seventy-five denarii. Also his was the pious cause to avenge his adoptive father. Perhaps his deepest assets were a cool head, a cold heart, and a burning passion to inherit Caesar's public power. He contacted Caesar's confidants on the one hand, and on the other, stoked Cicero's vanity by flattering letters. With the help of Cicero and his own army, he was elected consul. Having acquired at the expense of Republicans a capacity to negotiate with the Caesareans on equal terms, he logically switched sides and struck a deal with Antony and Lepidus, Caesar's master of horse. The three entered Rome with military pomp in 43 BCE and established the triumvirate with absolute power. Twenty months after disposing of one dictator, Rome acquired three.[33]

Clemency was not on the menu this time. Proscription was, and worse than the nightmare of those who remembered Sulla's reign of terror forty years ago. The triumvirs were determined to root out Republicans and political enemies. A large bounty awaited informants and those who brought in the head of a proscribed person. Addition to the black list awaited anyone who assisted those already on it. Cicero did not escape, the favors he did Octavian notwithstanding.[34]

Many were proscribed simply because they were rich. The triumvirs sorely needed money. Troops were particularly expensive in a civil war where all sides claimed legitimacy but none convincingly. With defection an easy option, troops held their generals hostage. Octavian's first act as consul was to seize the state treasury and gave each of his men 2,500 denarii, more than twenty times the regular annual pay before Caesar. Silver was only the down payment. Land was promised to veterans. For this, territories of eighteen towns, the richest in Italy, were earmarked to be dispossessed. Wielding despotic power, the triumvirate confiscated properties and invented new taxes. They had to work hard; Brutus and Cassius were doing the same in the eastern provinces. Thus the Romans mobilized for war, one side shouting piety, the other liberty. More than one-quarter of free Italian men were under arms.[35]

In 42 BCE at Philippi, the Roman armies facing each other exceeded three times the number of soldiers in the face off between Caesar and Pompey. Antony commanded; Octavian lay ill in his camp. Fighting was fierce. Republicans who flocked to join knew it was their last stand.[36] It was indeed. They brought it on themselves. Marcus Brutus and many others fell upon their own swords. Antony took his richest purple cloak and laid it over the body of Brutus. Octavian had Brutus's head cut off and thrown at the base of Caesar's statue.[37] A modern historian sighs, "The men who fell at Philippi fought for a principle, a tradition and a class—narrow, imperfect and outworn, but for all that the soul and spirit of Rome." This time," he writes, "the decision was final and irrevocable, the last struggle of the Free State. Henceforth nothing but a contest of despots over the corpse of liberty."[38]

"When Rome was first a city, its rulers were kings. Then Lucius Brutus created the consulate and the free Republican institutions in general." Thus Tacitus began his *Annals* and in one paragraph traced five centuries of history to the advent of Augustus's "personal regime." The cycle was closed for the Free State. During its last leg, turmoil inundated all, as Tacitus described: "morality and law were nonexistent, criminality went unpunished, decency was often fatal."[39] Freedom as immunity from arbitrary coercion became an empty word in times of proscription and civil war, when contending armies rolled back and forth, their discipline relaxed to satisfy the soldiers' thirst for pillage. Liberty as "freedom to oppress others," invented by Athens for foreign domination, proved equally efficacious in domestic propaganda.[40] Modern historians confirm Tacitus's observation: "Of course they use specious pretexts and talk about liberty. No one has ever wanted to enslave others and play the tyrant without making use of the very same phrases."[41] Sulla said he led his army against Rome "to free her from her tyrants."[42] Caesar declared war on the government "in order to liberate himself and the Roman People." He was killed by those who called themselves "liberators." His avenging heir wrote in his *Achievements* after becoming emperor: "I restored freedom to the state."[43] That was the freedom under an absolute monarchy.

Since Caesar had marched on Rome to liberate it, some 200,000 Italians were usually in the armies, and busy.[44] The provinces were bled white of resources for wars. Political activists had ruined the people by making the Republic a playground for their free ambitions. As they killed off each other, the tide turned in favor of the common people, who preferred substantive peace to political slogans. Increasingly they realized that what was offered under the freedom propaganda was not worth fighting and dying for.[45]

The third-century Greco-Roman historian Dio divided Rome's history into three phases. The first, democracy, lasted until Philippi in 42 BCE. The third, monarchy, began with Augustus's reign in 27 BCE. Between them was a phase of warlords, which comprised the triumvirate until 33 BCE, followed by Octavian's war against Antony and Cleopatra.[46]

After Philippi, Antony and Octavian ruled the empire as uneasy partners. Antony was initially stronger. Opportunity arose twice for him to suppress Octavian, but he resisted the urge of several advisers. He reestablished order in the east with its complex of provinces, client kingdoms, and dependent allies. Two unsuccessful encounters with Parthia changed his fortune. Antony made many miscalculations and military mistakes, but it seemed unlikely that these included the reason conspicuous in popular stories, that he was bewitched by Cleopatra.[47]

Cleopatra ascended the Egyptian throne at age eighteen in 51 BCE. Egypt was the longest-standing kingdom of Alexander's successors and she was a Macedonian Ptolemy, but she respected the customs and traditions of her subject people. When Caesar marched into Egypt in 48 BCE, she secured her position and bore him a son. Neither Caesar nor Antony annexed Egypt, which remained Rome's wealthiest dependent ally. Antony summoned Cleopatra to Syria in 41 BCE to account for Egypt's neutrality in the war with Republicans. That year he wintered in Alexandria and begot twins with her. Their next meeting four years later in Syria produced another child.[48]

Back in Italy after Philippi, Octavian quickly found land for his soldiers, thereby gaining the good will of recruits and the wrath of people whose properties were confiscated for the purpose. Italy rose against Rome for the last time. Octavian's brutal suppression would make Italians remember what he was capable of, even after he morphed into the benevolent emperor. He was not a good general, but with the help of able Agrippa and Salvidienus, he subdued all opponents. Remittance of debts and taxes won him popular support, as did the repair of public works. Surviving aristocrats trickled back, crestfallen and ready for service. Italy, the home base of empire, began to recover. With Antony overseas, Octavian had a great advantage in appointing senators and magistrates, hence taking control of the government. The balance of power began to tip in his favor.[49]

Octavian took the initiative when the triumvirate legally expired in 32 BCE. Knowing the reluctance of Romans to fight Romans, he declared war not against Antony but against Cleopatra, whom he accused of scheming to become the "queen of Romans." The freedom of speech was traditional to Roman politics. Octavian brought it to a new height by propaganda that demeaned his Egyptian opponents in all possible ways, creating a hatred of them as a people. Thus Octavian led a patriotic Italian crusade against bestial Egyptians, carefully securing its justice and divine sanction by sacred Roman rituals.[50]

Antony stood by Cleopatra. Whether he was passionately in love we cannot be certain, but fidelity was an old-fashioned Roman virtue. Their side of the story did not survive. In hostile portrayals, Antony was reported as henpecked and having "gone native" during his two years' residence in Alexandria.[51]

The adversaries met at Actium in northern Greece in 31 BCE. Octavian won the naval battle but let slip Antony and Cleopatra. As he closed in on Alexandria, Antony ordered a lavish dinner and said farewell to his men. Seeing tears in their eyes, he told them he looked forward to a glorious death in battle. That night, harmonious music and Bacchic chants flew through the city, a portent widely interpreted as the gods deserting Antony. At dawn, the navy and then the army followed the gods to Octavian. Antony stabbed himself upon the erroneous news of Cleopatra's death, but survived long enough to be brought to her and expired in her arms.[52]

Octavian took control of Egypt and posted guards around Cleopatra. Yet nine days after Antony, she died in royal robes on a golden couch. How she managed the escape was unclear. Some pointed to hidden poison because no mark could be found on her body. The snake that clung to her in the image that Octavian paraded in his triumph corroborated his pre-Actium propaganda excoriating "Egyptians who worship reptiles."[53] In any event, the last pharaoh of Egypt denied the first emperor of Rome the glory of herding her in his triumph. Cleopatra was buried beside Antony, her death "fitting for a Princess descended of so many royal kings."[54]

4.4 The Dawn of Imperial China

Ying Zheng, the future First Emperor, was born in Zhao amid intense hostility toward Qin. His father was a neglected Qin prince serving as hostage to Zhao. The merchant Lü Buwei saw in the prince an exotic commodity and, with much gold and political shrewdness, caused him to be inserted into Qin's line of royal succession. The investment paid off handsomely. Lü became premier when the prince became king. To this premiership was added regency when King Zheng inherited the throne at age twelve.[55]

During King Zheng's minority, state matters were controlled by Lü, the queen dowager, and her consort Lao Ai. They did not survive the first encounter with the king when he reached adulthood and began his rule in 238 BCE. The queen dowager was dismissed and Lao executed on conspiracy charges. Lü, in forced retirement, drank poison for fear of further recrimination. Within two years, King Zheng had secured for Qin the internal solidity indispensable for external expansion.[56]

Lü and Lao were both aliens. So were most of Lü's numerous clients. Then it was discovered that Zheng Guo, who masterminded a grand waterworks project, was a Hann agent charged with diverting Qin's resources from pressuring Hann. Urged by native aristocrats, King Zheng expelled all aliens, among whom was Li Si, originally a petty clerk from Chu. However, he rescinded the edict upon reading Li's memorial on the rationale of garnering talents from all under heaven. Recalled, Li became his ablest minister, and he was far from the only foreigner who contributed to Qin's final success. Li argued that Qin had the capacity "to unite the whole world under one government." In the court of the young king emerged a resolve not to squander the historic opportunity.[57]

The annexation of Hann in 230 BCE was Qin's equivalent of crossing the Rubicon. The old system was left behind. Henceforth a new grand strategy reigned supreme: China was to be united. Fighting was fierce, but Qin's diplomatic preparations and lightning attacks preempted attempts at coalition when it extinguished Wei, Chu, Yan, Zhao, and Qi between 225 and 221 BCE.[58]

Peace and stability were the major achievements that the First Emperor claimed: "The kings of six states captured, all under heaven is united. Conflicts and calamities terminated, arms are laid forever to rest."[59] He had the weapons of the former six states destroyed, fortifications and city walls everywhere leveled, and barricades in mountain defiles removed. Even Han literati usually eager to disparage Qin admitted, "The masses rejoiced at relief from the hardship of warfare."[60]

While ramparts came down, roads radiated out from the capital, Xianyang, and canals stretched to link rivers. Only 5 kilometers long but strategic and still in use, the Lingqu connects the Yangzi and the Pearl River drainages by linking the headwaters of two tributaries, creating a navigable network that covers central and southern China. Like the system of roads in the Roman Empire, the roads and canals served not only military purposes but also the flow of goods and people, tying the country together.[61]

The unprecedented territorial and population size challenged political vision. How was the government to be structured? What was to be the relation between central and local authorities? After listening to court debates, the First Emperor decided to abolish feudatories and with them, the feudalistic aristocracy. The bureaucratically organized central government under the emperor would directly rule the entire dominion, which would be organized into provinces with subsidiary counties. The local governments would have uniform structures and centrally appointed governors, who would recruit assistants and clerks from the local residents. This pivotal decision set the lasting political architecture of imperial China. At the time, however, it was hotly contested by ex-aristocrats and their supporters. We will return to the ideological and power struggle when analyzing the fall of the Qin Dynasty.[62]

The Chinese speak many dialects, some mutually incomprehensible and susceptible to evolving into distinct languages, as Latin evolved into the Romance languages. Binding the dialects and cementing the nation is the common written script, a celebrated legacy of Qin. Before unification, several scripts coexisted, similar but with significant variations. Li Si and others worked hard to promote a standard script convenient for writing. Also standardized were administrative and penal laws, weights and measures, coinage and metal currencies, and the gauge of vehicles that could henceforth run in the same ruts. Such standardization "seems conventional today, and it requires a leap of imagination to realize what innovations they were in the third century B.C. Many of these advances did not appear in Europe until the French Revolution, over two millennia later," writes a Western historian.[63]

No military operation was on official record for six years after unification, although scattered actions might have lingered in the mountains. The First Emperor inspected the northern region in 215 BCE. Afterward he ordered Meng Tian, who had been guarding the frontier, to mobilize troops and drive nomads out of the area south of the long wall built by Zhao. A year later, Qin established three new provinces in the south and consolidated them with forced colonization. Thus it expanded to cover roughly the core territory of imperial China (Map 9).[64]

Massive building projects filled the last three years of the First Emperor's reign. The long walls built by various warring states to fortify their northern frontiers were repaired and extended. A straight road connected the frontier to Xianyang. Chinese roads were made of stamped earth, easier to build than Roman roads paved with cut stones but requiring greater diligence for maintenance. More profligate were constructions near Xianyang, which allegedly employed 700,000 convicts. The new Ebang palace with its gigantic audience hall grew but was never completed. Construction of the royal mausoleum reached its final stage.[65] The extravagance of these buildings is undoubted, but they have perished, so we are unable to compare them with the "city of marble" that Augustus left in Rome.

The emperor made five extensive tours of the country to visit the troops and pacify distant peoples, as he announced in the six stone inscriptions erected on sacred mountains that he ascended. Inspection of local conditions resulted in directives such as breaching embankments designed to flood enemy territories in the previously war-torn heartland. As the duty of the supreme ruler demanded, he offered sacrifices to heaven and earth. He also enjoyed the sea and went whale hunting.[66]

During his fifth tour in 210 BCE, the First Emperor died. Loath to mention death in the prime of life, he did not designate an heir until, gravely ill, he wrote a sealed letter to his elder son Fusu, who was with Meng Tian. The letter was in the charge of the imperial secretary Zhao Gao, a eunuch who was a confidant of his youngest son, Huhai. Zhao somehow secured premier Li Si's quiescence as he altered the letter, ordered Fusu and Meng to commit suicide, and erected Huhai as Ershi, the Second Emperor. Li would pay for his treachery.[67]

Irregular succession is an easy way to political discord. World history is replete with accounts of an illegitimate heir who, feeling insecure, lashed out against potential opponents and ruined both himself and the state. The Second Emperor's three-year reign surpassed the combined malice of Emperor Claudius, manipulated by freedmen, and Emperor Nero, who fiddled while Rome burned. A puppet of Zhao Gao, he wantonly stepped up the excesses of the First Emperor and perpetrated a bloodbath of royal kin and high ministers.

Ten months into his reign, heavy rains held 900 conscripts heading for the northern frontier at Dazexiang in former Chu territory. They had no way to report for duty on time. The officers in charge expected punishment for being late. Chen Sheng, a locally selected section chief, conferred with another, Wu Guang: "Escape or revolt, we risk death. It is death anyway; why not die for a kingdom?" After psychological manipulation, the pair killed the Qin officers and swayed the conscripts by a grim picture of garrison.[68] In the words of early Han scholar Jia Yi, Chen "stepped from the common rank, rose among centurions, led poor wearied soldiers in the hundreds, and revolted against Qin. They cut trees to make weapons and raised flags on utility poles. All under heaven gathered like clouds and reverberated like echoes."[69] Attracting followers on the way, they seized the provincial capital from which Chu previously ruled. There Chen declared himself king and dispatched lieutenant Zhou Wen to attack Xianyang. Thus began the first large-scale rebellion in the history of imperial China.

News of rebellions reached the Qin capital quickly, but no one dared to suggest deploying troops for suppression after the Second Emperor penalized messengers who told the truth. Finally, when Zhou Wen's troops walked through the unguarded mountain passes, he agreed to reprieve and arm the convicts working on the royal mausoleum. Led by Zhang Han, the hastily assembled army smashed the approaching rebels and proceeded to rout Chen's main army, already intoxicated by power and weakened by internal conflicts. The victories were too late for Qin. Former royal houses and elites had reasserted themselves, and opportunists mushroomed in the eastern countries. They killed many Qin governors and declared allegiance to Chen. Qin garrisons, if present, were ineffective. Xiang Yu took over Huiqi Province in the Yangzi Delta, and Liu Bang the Pei County to its north. While the rebels strengthened, Qin's army of ex-convicts received meager reinforcement from its supposedly mighty war machine. Zhang surrendered at Julu, defeated by

Xiang's small army of soldiers who showed their determination by sinking their boats after crossing the Yellow River, smashing all cooking utensils, and carrying only three days' rations. While Xiang engaged the Qin force, Liu reached Xianyang with little opposition and received Qin's surrender in 206 BCE, but it would be years before he could defeat Xiang and become Gaodì, the founding emperor of the Han Dynasty.[70]

The footprints of nova-like empires such as Alexander's are usually large but shallow, delights for archeologists after a few centuries. Qin was exceptional for being a progenitor. By inculcating an indelible sense of political unity that made it not a brief empire but the brief first dynasty of perdurable imperial China, it caused a "genetic mutation" that revolutionized the significance of Zhongguo, hitherto geographical and cultural, henceforth a political entity, the Middle Kingdom. Inherited and passed on with modifications by the Han Dynasty, the new political gene in Qin institutions evolved through the changing environments of two millennia, many of its expressions still functioning today.[71]

4.5 Regret of the Overextended Dragon

Why did the Qin Dynasty collapse? Why were its institutions adopted by subsequent dynasties despite its notoriety in traditional propaganda? These questions are important. Interpretations of this turning point in Chinese history reflect perennial tensions in power and ideology.

Luck and human errors played their parts. In some ways, the First Emperor resembled Julius Caesar. Each possessed the energy befitting his enormous ego, and a sense of duty commensurate with the huge realm that he ruled. Caesar would not stop writing his correspondence even while watching circus games. The First Emperor measured documents by weight and refused to retire at night before finishing the daily quota he assigned himself.[72] Their diligence was denounced as power greed by sidelined senators or ministers. The grumblers may have been most concerned with their own power, but their criticism had a point. By taking as much matter in their own hands as possible, Caesar and the First Emperor weakened the decision-making capacity of institutions and made government over dependent on their person. Neither was prepared for death. Caesar was fifty-six when he died, the First Emperor only forty-nine. Failure to plan for the succession of power was one of their biggest mistakes.

Peace is sweet, but massive demobilization can create social problems bitter to many, as was seen in the aftermath of World War I. The Romans retained large armies after the civil war, created overseas colonies, and still incited an Italian uprising in their efforts to settle veterans.[73] Qin's demobilization problem was far greater, because it was coupled with conquest and pacification. The warring states had been armed to the teeth. Prolonged rivalry among them had bred many able men, and meritocracy had spread ambition into wide social strata. Armies of martial artists had thrived in Qi and military households in Wei. Corps of officers high and low had enjoyed status unavailable in the civilian world. Persuaders offering stratagems had reaped rewards in one state or another. Hordes of literati had prospered under the patronage and employment of rival aristocrats, using the threat of defection to leverage their privileges. All these and war profiteers found their opportunities dried up by the unification of seven warring states into one China. Their frustration fueled the malice of the vanquished. Many constituted the "youths of the east" who echoed the Dazexiang uprising. Some, such as Zhou Wen, left their names in history.

If the momentum of violent history was like an avalanche that Qin tried to stop, then feudalistic and parochial entrenchment was like a mountain that it tried to level. Qi, Chu, and other states that Qin annexed had eight centuries of history, each with its peculiar and sophisticated culture. Qiren or Churen (*ren* means "man" or "people") sounded as natural as "Englishman" or "Frenchman" does to us. Their native dialects were probably mutually incomprehensible. Look at a political map and imagine that, within several years, eastern Asia had changed from a patchwork of color, as in Western Europe today, into a single color, and then you may appreciate what Qin had done. Of course the Qiren or Churen hated the old enemy turned new master, to whom many had lost loved ones in previous wars. In the rebels' efforts to win popular support, Chen Sheng invoked the memory of a Chu hero who died defending the homeland, and Xiang Yu erected a king from the former Chu royal house, to whom Liu Bang also pledged allegiance.[74] Their actions revealed the hearts of people lying with their old kings. The main target of their uprising was not a brutal ruler but a foreign occupier. That explains why lands of the old Qin state remained quiet.

Han literati depicted Qin's collapse as a great surprise to suit their allegation of singular evil and blame Legalist rule by law. They ignored history. Gleaning the rich experiences of the warring states, Wu Qi had observed, "To be victorious is easy, to preserve the fruits of victory difficult," and Xunzi, "To annex land is easy; the difficulty lies in the consolidation of rule."[75] This wisdom is universally valid. The vanquished may hunker down for a decade or a generation to recoup strength, but volcanic eruptions of simmering resistance have caught many conquerors off guard. Mengzi's tutelage and his buddy's command did not avert the disastrous end of Qi's occupation of Yan. A German monument in the Teutoburg Forest commemorates the revolt that rolled back Roman expansion beyond the Rhine.[76]

Speed increases the hazard of consolidation. To overcome entrenched customs and win the loyalty of conquered peoples require patience as well as good governance. A world historian summarizes the experiences of the Qin Dynasty, Roman Empire, and British Raj: "Victorious empire-builders have most reason to fear a violent undoing of their work when they established their rule at one stroke, and when they have imposed it on a world of parochial states long accustomed to enjoy and abuse a status of sovereign independence."[77] Qin was precisely in such a condition. History would prove the superiority of its vision. Had it implemented its policies gradually, as the Han did later, it might have succeeded in softening the resistance of feudalistic customs. In pushing numerous reforms at once, however, it bent a resilient bar too rapidly and fell victim to its backlash.

Far more surprising than the outbreak of revolt is Qin's failure to quash it. I reject the received view that blames the failure on tyranny; Qin would have done much more to suppress the revolt if the government were as brutal as alleged. The aftershocks of conquest aside, little evidence points to deteriorating material conditions for the masses. I will argue that those most aggrieved were the political elites who lost privileges in Qin's abolition of the feudalistic aristocracy and resented legal supervision of officers. Qin's failure to mollify the elites, including those working in its government, intensified the peril of imperial overreach and rapid demobilization. Later, the literati fabricated stories about Qin brutality, blamed Qin's demise on its abandonment of the Way of ancient kings that favored aristocrats, and deployed Confucian ethics to warn emperors against following Qin in putting the law above elitist privileges.

To study the causes of rebellion is not to pass moral judgment by our standards. Qin was certainly brutal, but it existed in a savage age. To understand why Qin fell, we should set its behavior not against ideals but against practices common to its time. Was Qin exceptionally exploitative? If so, why did it succeed in defeating formidable rivals?

Xunzi, Confucian master, native of Zhao, and longtime resident of Qi and Chu, visited Qin a few decades before it unified China and reported that its people were straightforward and submissive to the authority. Local clerks were somber, astute, trustworthy, and not abusive. Ministers in the capital focused on public business and formed no private clique. The royal court allowed no case to sit undecided but administered unhurriedly, as if there was no government. Such observations led Xunzi to conclude that Qin had been victorious for four generations not because of luck but because of policy. Qin approximated the ideal of governance: to maintain order with ease, attend to details with simplicity, and achieve results without exertion. Despite its achievements, however, it still feared the coalition of other lords. Why?

Xunzi answered that Qin still fell short when measured according to the Way of kings because it had few Confucians, which was its grave weakness.[78] Unfortunately, he did not compare the social and administrative conditions of Qin to those of Qi or Lu, where Confucians teemed.

Xunzi saw in Qin a state of law and order. What he missed was not ethics and culture, which are not Confucian monopolies, but an ideology. Confucianism, which demanded absolute deference to elders and the upper class, bristled at the little leverage Legalist policies gave to youths and the lower class. Equality under the law aside, Qin discouraged large households and distributed land to nuclear families. Financial independence boosted the dignity of young couples, so that sons showed pride in lending tools to their fathers and daughters dared to argue with their mothers-in-law. Han Confucians condemned such behaviors as beastly immoral.[79] However, Legalists did not set to destroy filial piety as charged. Primary sources recorded Qin laws that granted special treatments to sick and elderly persons. One law stipulated the state's refusal to accept accusation of parents by their offspring, thus leaving certain authority to the head of family.[80] Other excavated documents taught honesty, uprightness, diligence, and other traditional virtues. *Lü's Annals*, a broadminded anthology not lacking criticism of the government, was publicly posted in Xianyang's marketplace. The First Emperor instituted the office of Erudites for scholars, including Confucians, and listened to them before making his own decisions.[81]

Sima Qian observed that as soon as Qin fell, some Erudites spread lies about it.[82] Western historians warn readers that Han writers, "because they are so often marked by evident anti-Qin bias, should be approached only with extreme caution."[83] Vilification of Qin served the interest of the Han, rebels eager to justify themselves and prevent others from following their rebellious example. The *Book of Han* records many cases of Han literati "borrowing Qin as an analogy," ascribing to it whatever they thought bad, and using its dire fate as an object lesson to push their own agenda.[84] Qin became identified with evil, just as Yao, Shun, and the Three Eras were identified with virtue. In either case, the ascriptions mix history with fiction. One politician told contradictory stories when advocating different policies.[85] Where scholarship meant quoting each other, repetition generated a false air of truth. A modern researcher outside the echo chamber observes that "the archeological and textual evidence exposes these criticisms as self-serving Han propaganda with little relation to Qin policy or its failure."[86]

Take, for instance, the increasingly dramatic descriptions of monstrous Qin taxation. Taxes in the warring states were not light; Mengzi was not the only one who complained. Were the people worse off after the Qin conquest? Sima Qian did not mention tax increases in his list of Qin Dynasty policies.

Rebels and critics who experienced the period barely cited heavy taxes as grievances. Early Han politician Wu Bei tried to dissuade the king of Huainan from rebelling against the Han, arguing that Qin was terrible, therefore the revolt against it succeeded; Han was much better, therefore revolts would fail.[87] His polemic is studded with metaphors and plain fabrications. Several disparaging sentences appear verbatim, and without corroboration, in the Food and Money chapter of Ban Gu's *Book of Han*, written two centuries later.[88] Among these is the claim that Qin "collected more than one half of the produce in taxes," which annotators construe to be two-thirds. It became probably the most widely cited "authoritative source" on Qin's crushing taxation. However, its credibility was destroyed by modern scholars seeking corroboration and substantiating evidence.[89]

The tax rate at the beginning of the Han Dynasty was one-fifteenth.[90] How it got to that level should be familiar to Han historians. The annals of emperors, which collect many official documents, are the most reliable part of the *Standard Histories*. Ban's lengthy Annals of Gaodì details his fiscal measures and efforts to win hearts. Conspicuously absent is any mention of general tax reduction, which would be the most benevolent and popular act worth trumpeting. Historians concur that the Han generally adopted Qin institutions.[91] Dong Zhongshu, the leading Confucian scholar of early Han, specifically asserted continuity in tax rates.[92] The most cogent evidence comes from excavated bamboo strips: documents interred about 217 BCE, four years into the Qin Dynasty, and fragments of the Han law published about 187 BCE, fifteen years into the Han. Fragments of "land laws" indicate that both dynasties collected the land tax in the form of grain and fodder. Both stipulated the same amount for the latter, and in the same words.[93] If the same applied to grain, then the Han's initial land tax rate of one-fifteenth was inherited from the Qin Dynasty. For comparison, Lu collected one-fifth in taxes at the time of Confucius, and Mengzi's ideal demanded one-ninth.[94]

Corvée labor was, besides the land tax, the heaviest government exaction. The rule for both Qin and Han Dynasties was one month per year, and little complaint was heard in the Han. Excavated primary sources reveal that Qin used convicts for chores whenever possible; several years of hard labor was the most frequent punishment for theft.[95] These sources corroborate textual sources stating that attempted fugitives, bondservants, and other social undesirables filled colonies of the south. Ordinary people often received tax exemption or other incentives for relocation. No levy was on record for the mausoleum when the First Emperor died. Instead, convicts building the Ebang palace were diverted to work on it.[96]

The largest mobilization in the Qin Dynasty was 300,000 troops for Meng Tian's campaign against northern nomads.[97] The seven warring states had each fielded hundreds of thousand troops. All numbers are probably exaggerated, but even as stated, the dynasty's empire-wide call-up was hardly outrageous—the Roman Empire kept a standing army of 300,000. Furthermore, a Qin army consisted of conscripts serving short tours as needs arose, such as the eight- and eleven-month tours recorded in an excavated autobiography.[98] To maintain troop level for an extended period, the government had to continuously call up replacements. There are reasons to believe that the dynasty's large draft did not last long. Active fighting was over in two years. Peacetime frontier garrisons usually involved few troops, as we will see in later Han practice. The 900 draftees who mutinied at Dazexiang came from at least three counties, judging from the origins of known leaders, and their call was answered by civilians, not larger mutinies.[99] How long did Meng's army, initially called up in 215 BCE, keep its high troop level? It was responsible for building the long wall, which, like taxation, has been trumped up to become a myth of Qin cruelty. Recent research has found that although laborious, wall building was not as appalling as it appears in traditional propaganda.[100] Considering various factors in Appendix 3, I estimate that long-wall construction under the First Emperor required roughly 238,000 man-years of labor. If this is correct, then Meng Tian's 300,000 troops could have accomplished the mission in a year and then been discharged. It would explain why they were never mentioned in 209 BCE when the government desperately needed troops to suppress rebels. Those condemning Qin for unremitting militarism fail to answer a crucial empirical question: Where was the Qin army in time of dire need?

In sum, if we look past propaganda at available facts, Qin's tax and levy were not harsh by contemporary standards. However, that obtained only for ordinary people. For those in the powerful and previously privileged class, conditions worsened. Many warring states built long walls, but only Qin's wall building inspired horrible stories. The First Emperor sentenced corrupt officials to the labor, which outraged the articulate officialdom. The conflict between the state and the unruly political elite was Qin's greatest worry. It began with the state's fundamental architecture.

In the Zhou system that Confucians extolled, power was held by feudalistic aristocrats, who remained powerful in the late warring states. Three princes, each patronizing thousands of *shi*, led the coalition that defeated Qin and rescued Zhao after the battle of Changping. Legalists strived to curb aristocrats in favor of monarchy, with varying degrees of success in various states. The struggle came to a head in the crucial decision: What would be the institutional architecture for the united China? Venerated ministers led by the premier advocated the Way of ancient kings, in which territories of the former six states would be divided into subordinate feudatories ruled by kings chosen from the emperor's sons. Li Si alone objected. Pointing to the endless fighting among descendants of relatives enfeoffed by the Zhou, he argued that long-term peace and stability required the emperor to rule the whole country directly. The First Emperor agreed: "To re-establish feudatories would be to encourage the use of arms."[101]

In 213 BCE, eight years after the abolition of feudalistic aristocracy, Chun yu Yue, an Erudite from former Qi, urged restoring the Zhou model: "Your majesty possesses all under heaven, but your sons and brothers are mere commoners. . . . I have never heard of any undertaking that endures without imitating antiquity." The emperor, as usual, referred the matter to court discussion. Li Si argued that times had changed, so why should the emperor imitate the Zhou? To stop bigots from using the authority of books to mislead the people, he proposed limiting the access of most books to official scholars. The First Emperor ordered many books burned, except the copies at the imperial library. His purpose was mainly political, to protect the new institutions of centralized government and pacify conquered peoples. Spared were books on medicine, agriculture, and other practical topics.[102] The prime targets were histories of the former six states, followed by the *Odes* and *Documents*, the authority for the Zhou model. The books of "a hundred masters" suffered little damage. Intellectual creativity continued. Many classical texts attributed to pre-imperial masters, including *The Mean*, were actually written during the Qin and early Han Dynasties.[103]

One year after the book burning came "the massacre of Confucians," although not all victims fit the name. Many literati made huge fortunes by pitching ideas of the supernatural to the First Emperor. Among them, Lu and Hou promised the elixir of immortality. Unable to deliver and fearing the law for fraud, the pair fled and denounced the emperor as a tyrant unworthy of it. The enraged emperor ordered an investigation. Literati incriminated each other. The emperor executed almost 500, ignoring Fusu's warning: "The world is newly pacified. The allegiance of distant peoples is not yet solidified. The literati all follow Confucian teachings. Your majesty punishes them according to the law. I fear it may cause instability."[104] Fusu was prescient. Three years later, many Confucians, including a direct descendant of Confucius, hastened to join Chen Sheng's rebellion.[105] Contrary to subsequent propaganda, the First Emperor did not intend to root out Confucians. The massacre was limited. Erudites continued to attend court. One, Shusun Tong, a Confucian master with more than 100 students, misrepresented intelligence to ingratiate himself with the Second Emperor, then deserted, served one warlord after another, and finally landed a plush post by designing court rituals for the Han Dynasty.[106]

Book burning responded to the subversive agitation to reinstate the feudalistic aristocracy. Swindling lit the fuse for the massacre. However, the two events are often rolled together as Qin's gravest crime. They exposed deep-rooted tensions. Most apparent was the struggle between two parties of officers, as Lu and Hou reproached the emperor: "He trusts only law officers and works closely with them. The seventy Erudites he only appoints but does not heed."[107] Underlying this power struggle was an ideological conflict of lasting impact. "The Faults of Qin," an essay by Jia Yi, was widely quoted and influential.[108] Its gist was summarized by a Confucian historian in late imperial China: "Qin enshrined the law, sidelined benevolence and righteousness, so that the rebellion of a few commoners led to a landslide in the world."[109]

Westerners would be puzzled: Why is the law incompatible with benevolence and righteousness? Answers to this question are important, because they shed light on the strong headwind facing the rule of law in China. Here are a few thoughts; more clues are offered in section 6.9.

The Legalist separation of state and family, which the First Emperor endorsed, seemed immoral to Confucians, who upheld the primacy of family values in government. The love of relatives was the crux of the feudalistic power structure. Confucians, who advocated benevolent governments, added a moral halo that turned the love of relatives into the crux of benevolence and hence a universal political doctrine. Confucius regarded good government as an extension of filial piety and brotherliness. To set an example, the sagacious ruler should "elevate his relatives to high positions, grant posh provisions, and share their desires."[110] Mengzi similarly preached, "The love of relatives is the substance of benevolence." As an exemplar, he argued that the sage king Shun must have enfeoffed his wicked brother: "Being the son of heaven but allowing his brother to be a mere commoner, how can that be love?"[111] Chunyu Yue used almost identical words in attacking the Qin institution. The ruler's exemplary effect was paramount in Confucian rule by men. By making his relatives mere commoners, the First Emperor set a bad example that deserved denunciations of "malevolence" and "ingratitude," staples in anti-Qin propaganda.[112]

More ponderous than morality was the self-interest of political elites. For the ruler to split land and enfeoff lords was the hope of the ruling circle. Aristocratic titles were the common desire of rebels; many promptly declared themselves kings and lords.[113] Enmity to Qin's centralized government oozed from the words carved on a meteorite that fell ten years after unification: "The First Emperor dies and the land is parceled."[114] Learning the lesson, the Han Dynasty started by reinstituting feudatories.

In the eyes of Han literati, "repudiation of the Way of ancient kings" was Qin's foremost fault.[115] It goes beyond the abolition of venerated aristocracy. Qin's bureaucratic government entailed a new type of officers who ran it. As mere state employees, the new political elite lost the aristocratic prerogatives of the old governing class. They could no longer do as they pleased but were held accountable for their behavior. The law was no longer merely punishments that superior men wielded to control inferiors; it applied equally to themselves. Faced with such a step down, the bitterness of superior men was palpable beneath their self-righteousness. A bureaucratic government requires competent and responsible officers strong in public virtue. To produce a reliable pool of such talents is difficult even today. Qin's attempt to regulate official behavior by impartial laws induced dangerous hostility.

"Persistent reliance on punishment and law" as the chief reason for Qin's demise, enunciated by the Confucian scholar Lu Jia in early Han, was widely espoused by traditional literati. Today, some scholars still argue that Qin fell because of its Legalist policies.[116] All critics of Qin complained about harsh punishments, but few were frank about the specific harshness that infuriated them most. Being tough on crime for deterrence was a Legalist tenet, and enforcing uniform laws in conquered lands did increase the number of offenders. However, the difference with prevailing conditions of that time was not great. Literati promulgated an image of convicts in red uniforms filling half of the street in Qin, but never compared it to the image in Qi: prosthetic feet outselling shoes because of widespread penal mutilation.[117] Nor did they mention that many of Qin's tortures were already prevalent in Zhou.[118] For failure in reporting punctually for military duty, Qin laws on excavated bamboo strips imposed monetary fines on officers, a penalty that later might have been raised to death. According to the *Documents*, the son of the great sage Duke of Zhou threatened death to all laggards: officers, soldiers, and suppliers of provisions. Death was also decreed for civilian drunkenness.[119] A modern scholar summarizes the condition of Zhou as depicted in the classics: "awe of ruthless power is more evident than the virtue of leniency and generosity."[120] As far as the common people were concerned, the trope of benevolent Zhou and cruel Qin was a blatant double standard.

It was another matter with the privileged elites. Sentimental talk of bloody punishment hid the elite's chief grievance, which was not penalties per se but the law that stipulated them: specifically, legal impartiality. Early Han historian Sima Tan expressed the elitist assessment: "Legalists make no distinction between relatives and strangers, aristocrats and lowly people. They apply the law uniformly to all, ignoring the love of relatives and deference to high statuses. This can serve temporary expediency, but should not be adopted in the long term."[121] Fairness and equality under the law were to the literati not virtues but necessary evils akin to war, perhaps useful in conquests, but to be discarded in peacetime in order to maintain harmony within the ruling circle. "Punishment does not reach up to ministers" was the Zhou tradition. Against it Qin insisted, "Criminal penalties do not excuse high ministers."[122] Jia Yi compared the two, praised Zhou's heartfelt indulgence for cementing the ruling circle, and blamed callous legal equality for Qin's quick demise. In Jai's view, privileges ensured the loyalty of ministers, and stability of rule depended on aligning with the powerful. By putting impartial law above elitist prerogative, Qin imperiled the ruler's vital asset, a friendly ruling class.[123]

Holding officers accountable for fair adjudication protected the common people. However, to sentence crooked officials to long-wall building was, in Jia Yi's simile, to try to stop a rat from stealing from a precious vessel by throwing a stone at it. The stone endangered the vessel—that is, the throne. Excavated documents show most Qin laws to be administrative regulations applied to officers.[124] Chen Sheng was not the only officer to rebel. As a village sheriff responsible for escorting a gang of convicts to work in the capital, Liu Bang expected fines for losing some of his charges; so he released the remaining convicts, led some into banditry, and was later called to rebellion by his county superintendent. Several other superintendents and provincial governors were on record as betraying their posts as soon as they smelled opportunity. Qin had ignored Mengzi's tenet: "Government is not difficult, do not antagonize the great houses." "If the ruler regards ministers as dust and grass seed, then ministers regard the ruler as bandit and foe."[125] Qin antagonized the political elite who thought they should be above the law. Disloyalty and inaptitude are the impressions one gets from the few records of local responses to uprising. The weakness of the imperial government allowed a spark to spread into a lethal conflagration.[126]

"Qin lets slip its deer, and the world joins in a hunt" has become a Chinese adage for grand-scale political opportunism and the consequent chaotic carnage, the recurrence of which we will see at least twice in this book. The hunters had heterogeneous social backgrounds. Chen Sheng, once a hired farm hand, was the humblest, but he was literate and politically informed. Liu Bang, village sheriff turned brigand chief, was a step up the social ladder. Closer to the upper end of the spectrum, the Xiang family had produced generations of top Chu generals. Such pre-imperial elites constituted the bulk of warlords after Chen's uprising. Descendants of the six former royal houses all reclaimed kingship.[127]

Xiang Yu was the strongest of warlords after Qin's demise. Reverting to the Zhou model, he divided the country into nineteen autonomous kingdoms that formed a confederation under himself as hegemonic king of Chu. Liu Bang was accorded the kingship of Han, but quickly subdued other kings to take over Qin's old home. Thus he secured a superior economic base for the five-year struggle between Chu and Han.

The struggle between Xiang and Liu somehow resembled that between Antony and Octavian. Like Antony, Xiang was a better general and more steeped in the aristocratic tradition. Like Antony, he was initially stronger, dominated the wealthier eastern region, had opportunities to eliminate his archrival, but could not bring himself to it.[128] Liu was a "rogue" fond of snatching caps from literati and pissing into them; Octavian "a young thug who was reputedly capable of tearing out a man's eyes with his bare hands."[129] These upstarts were more comfortable in tapping the rigorous energy and fresh thinking of lower social classes. As Octavian gained advantages by controlling Italy, Liu established himself in the former Qin state. Liu lost many battles but learned to avoid them. Instead, he harassed Xiang's flanks and supply lines, thus whittled down the Chu army by attrition. With promises of rich rewards, he secured allies for the final encirclement.[130]

At Gaixia, Han soldiers surrounding the remnant of the Chu army followed orders to learn and sing Chu folk songs. The music demoralized homesick Chu soldiers, who dispersed into the gaps the siege left for them. In his tent, Xiang Yu exclaimed, "Has the Han taken Chu? How have they recruited so many Chu men?" Ordering wine for his lieutenants and his consort, Yu Ji, he improvised a song:

> My might can topple mountains, hey, my will cover the world,
> Fortune is against me, hey, Zhui loses his flight.
> Without Zhui's fight, hey, what can I do?
> My Yu, hey, Yu, what is your plight?

She replied in refrain:

> The Han has captured our land; Chu songs on four sides rise.
> At the end of my king's path, I will not steal a life.

All wept. Mounting Zhui, his favorite horse during the five-year campaign, Xiang led 800 cavalry to breach the siege. Most fell to Han pursuit, but fleet-footed Zhui brought Xiang to River Wu, where loyalists had a boat waiting. They assured him that Chu remained intact and its people devoted. Xiang entrusted faithful Zhui to their care but refused to cross himself, saying he could not face the elders back home after leading 8,000 of their sons to war and bringing none back. On foot, he rejoined the melee, received many wounds but delivered many more lethal blows. Then he met an old friend among his enemies. "Ah, take my head for the prize gold," he said, and used his sword on himself.[131]

4.6 Rupture and Continuity

In three decades, the political and imperial scene at each end of Eurasia changed fundamentally. *The Roman Revolution* is perhaps the most influential modern book on what transpired from the triumvirate of Caesar, Pompey, and Crassus through the reign of Augustus.[132] A Western historian remarks that Qin achieved "a transformation of the face of China so great both quantitatively and qualitatively that it deserves the name 'revolution.'"[133]

Both the Roman and Chinese revolutions substituted monarchy for republicanism or feudalism. Henceforth the emperor ruled supreme over a large territory directly through provinces. His triumph came at the expense of aristocrats who dominated the old regimes, republican senators or Chinese feudalistic lords. Resistance was fierce, especially in Rome, where the hatred of kings was instinctive. The Chinese were accustomed to hereditary kings, yet political elites seethed at Qin's abolition of feudalistic aristocracy. Caesar was assassinated. The First Emperor survived three close-call attempts; it is little surprise he became secretive about his movements.[134] Many of Caesar's assassins and the third assassin of the First Emperor had received clemency from their respective future target. More often, however, ruthlessness prevailed. Caesar banned all political clubs, and his heir's proscription list contained the names of about 130 senators and up to 2,000 equestrians.[135] The First Emperor burned books to suppress advocacy of the feudalistic aristocracy and slaughtered more than 460 "Confucians."[136] This bloodletting paled beside the carnage on the battlefields of Pharsalus and Philippi and the devastation wreaked by post-Qin warlords.

The defense of liberty was a piercing battle cry among Roman aristocrats, as was the defense of the Way of ancient kings among Confucians and ex-aristocrats. However, intoxicating rhetoric often detached these elites from reality and blinded them to their own selfishness and inaptitude. The liberators who slew Caesar brought mayhem partly because they never planned for the ramifications of their action. Verbose Confucian masters failed to suggest anything workable when the First Emperor consulted their expertise on offering sacrifice to heaven or when the second Han premier consulted them on government.[137]

Nevertheless, the elites held a trump card besides the strength of tradition. The emperor needed their cooperation to rule effectively. When peace returned under the Roman Empire and the Han Dynasty, many of their old values would resurface to constitute links with the past despite the break in the form of government. The successor to Caesar and the First Emperor would succeed where they failed, to strike a bargain with the political elite. Roman senators cured of political activism would share in the rule of wealth.

Chinese literati-officials serving in the government bureaucracy would subvert its regulatory impartiality by personal connections glossed by moralization. These rehabilitated elites would dampen the effects of the revolutions.

In their struggle with aristocrats, monarchists had reached out to a wider circle of people. Caesar had accepted many Italians and the less-than-well born into his government. Many of the First Emperor's chief officers were foreigners or lowly born. Their successors went further. Followers of Octavian had been called "enemies of society" and those of Liu Bang, "fugitives and scoundrels."[138] These descriptions, although exaggerated, are not all lies. Ascending fortune gradually attracted men with lustrous backgrounds, as Octavian was joined by the Etruscan magnate Maecenas, and Liu by the former Hann aristocrat Zhang Liang. However, vitality mainly resided in their early companions, fresh and unburdened by old dogmas, loyal and able despite humble birth. Octavian's coeval Agrippa was "a man closer to rusticity than to elegance." Yet he "embodied the military and peasant virtues of old Rome" and had longer vision than many polished aristocrats. Victorious in Spain, he gave up the honor of a triumph that would have thrown into sharp relief Octavian's disastrous defeat in Sicily.[139] Xiao He, friend of sheriff Liu and the first premier of the Han Dynasty, was a clerk in Qin's county government. The tramp Hann Xin became a guard under Liu and rose by merit to top commander.[140] Society abounds with such "crouching tigers and hidden dragons," whose potential is too often sadly stifled. For their willingness and ability to tap into a wide talent pool, would-be monarchs were highly rewarded.

At the expense and to the bitterness of old aristocrats and smug literati, the revolutions cracked open the doors to government from two directions. Horizontally, the imperial monarchy reached beyond the imperial center to include elites in the periphery and gradually erased regional discrimination. Vertically, it reached a step down the social strata, thickened the crust of political elites, and made it more porous to upward mobility. A historian of Rome remarks, "In the Revolution the power of the old governing class was broken, its composition transformed. Italy and the non-political orders in society triumphed over Rome and the Roman aristocracy."[141] A similar transformation occurred around the time of Qin and early Han. Chinese historians are struck by the millennium-old regime of hereditary ministers yielding to "a regime of homespun-clothed generals and premiers at the beginning of Han."[142] *Buyi*, denoting homespun cloth devoid of silk or embroidery, is the term for commoners in classical Chinese. It had intellectual as well as social significance at the dawn of imperial China, when the stair of advancement was accessible to people with diverse learning and abilities, unlike in later times when it was limited to Confucians narrowly versed in embroidered literature.[143]

Among the talent tapped was that of women. The First Emperor bestowed high honor on a provincial widow for astute management and generosity with her earned wealth. While a village sheriff, Liu Bang married Lü from a local family. Liu later had more wives, but none could replace Lü, who participated in decision making and became effective ruler after Gaodì's death.[144] While a triumvir juggling for power, Octavian divorced the wife who bore him his only offspring to marry Livia, who by birth and first marriage belonged to the Livii and Claudii, two of the most venerable Roman families. The marriage won him much aristocratic support, and Livia was increasingly involved in imperial politics.[145] Lü and Livia were among the most powerful imperial women.

Caesar wrestled with resilient republican institutions and eventually lost. The First Emperor suppressed feudatories only as long as he lived. Augustus and the Han Dynasty succeeded to establish stable imperial monarchies. Looking back at Caesar from a post-Napoleonic vantage, a German philosopher wrote, "in all periods of the world a political revolution is sanctioned in men's opinion, when it repeats itself. . . . By repetition that which at first appeared merely a matter of chance and contingency, becomes a real and ratified existence."[146] A tragedy in the first round, a drama in the second: perhaps the repeat also benefits from insight and maturity, so it avoids the mistakes of its predecessor and mellows the intensity that singed the first attempt. Learning the lessons of their predecessors, Augustus and Gaodì were more willing to bargain with the old establishments. Augustus paid lip service to republican institutions and Gaodì enfeoffed feudalistic kings.

If the destruction of the Roman Republic or the six sovereign states was a crime, it fell on the shoulder of Caesar or the First Emperor. Augustus and Gaodì could claim absolution from the wrongdoing, the former in legitimate inheritance of power, and the latter in rising against evil. They also benefited from violence and time. The carnage of civil wars decimated intransigent forces, taught submission to survivors, and created exhaustion conducive to peace. Most stubborn Republicans who frustrated Caesar fell at Philippi and the remnants joined Antony, another loser. Loyalists of the former six states rallied at Qin's collapse, only to be quashed again. Symbolically, the civil war ended when the last king of Qi and his 500 followers all chose suicide rather than bowing to the Han.[147] Death was irreversible. Time erased memories. When peace returned, the younger generation had only dim recollections of lives in the Roman Republic or independent states, and even those soon faded. The present reality of empire seemed not only legitimate but also natural.

Civil wars divulged an option so terrible it made all others bearable: anarchy and chaos. "War, fire, and great slaughter," the ways Sulla dealt with political enemies, were adopted by other dynasts. By some accounts, Italy suffered more from Rome's wars with itself than from Hannibal's invasion. Caesar cared to restrain pillage, as did Liu Bang, but military discipline was hazardous when rivals recruited deserters. Caesar's troops were often uncontrollable without his personal presence.[148] The eight years of tumult that followed the Dazexiang uprising wreaked far more havoc on the common people than decades of Qin campaigns. At the beginning of the Han Dynasty, even the emperor's carriage lacked four horses of the same color. In 200 BCE, ten years after the death of the First Emperor, Gaodì passed through Quni and admired its big houses. The mayor informed him that the city had had 30,000 households under the First Emperor; most died or fled, leaving only 5,000 on the register.[149] Quni was not the worst; located on the northern plain, it escaped the heaviest fighting. Not surprisingly, *luan* or chaos and instability terrified the Chinese, as the thought of it still does. They are not alone. "He attracted everybody's goodwill by the enjoyable gift of peace": thus Tacitus explained Augustus's success.[150]

Roman citizens, who had regularly elected their magistrates for centuries, came to decide that election may not be the best method under some circumstances and accepted monarchy. As for the "aristocratic and parliamentarian" freedom lost under the Empire, that had concerned at most a few thousand political elites, for whose ideals the mass of common people had shed enough blood. While activists agitated for *libertas* or *dignitas*, the ordinary people desired peace, order, security, and tranquility.[151] "The only things they care about at all are their fields, their houses, their money," rebuked Cicero.[152] He had underestimated the strength of these simple desires. From the ranks of those he scorned, Octavian recruited most of his initial adjutants, and on them the trust of Augustus and subsequent emperors remained. The Empire meant the victory of the nonpolitical classes.[153]

As a service to the people, a government justifies itself by its long-term function of satisfying the demands of the community with its peculiar cultural and socioeconomic conditions. The community chooses its own priorities. Life has many dimensions, of which political activism and participation constitute only one. Each dimension has its values that often defy comparison with others on a single scale. When times are favorable, people tolerate incommensurate values, as modern democracies sometimes choose to sacrifice some civil liberty for the sake of a little more security. Under hard times, choices can be painful. "Right colliding with right" is the stuff of high tragedy.[154] Not that the Romans loved republicanism less, but that they loved stability more. The author of *The Roman Revolution* summarizes: "There is something more important than political liberty; and political rights are a means, not an end in themselves. That end is security of life and property: it could not be guaranteed by the constitution of the Republican Rome. Worn and broken by civil war and disorder, the Roman People was ready to surrender the ruinous privilege of freedom and submit to strict government."[155]

The Roman Republic has been inspiring in political thoughts, for example in the American and French Revolutions.[156] Some of its principles, notably liberty, checks and balances in the government, and the regular election of magistrates, are self-evidently good in the eye of many moderns. However, the man who spoiled these principles won admiration. The Germans and Russians honored him with their titles *Kaiser* and *Czar*. The fashion of styling American presidents as Caesars echoes a remark from a founding father of the United States: "The greatest man who ever lived was Julius Caesar."[157]

Diametrically opposite appraisals befall the man who destroyed the Roman Republic and the man who created a unified China. The First Emperor was demonized. Literati who became the new political elite developed tropes in which "brutal Qin" is synonymous with evil.[158]

Gross dissimulations eased the transitions to imperial peace. Augustus ostensibly preserved the form of a republic but radically subverted its functions in his absolute monarchy. The Han Dynasty loudly condemned Qin but quietly adopted most of its centralist institutions. Did false consciousness come with a price?

Notes

1. Johnson 2000.
2. Kallet-Marx 1995: 25–27. Richardson 1991: 1, 6–7.
3. Brunt 1978: 174–175. North 1981: 2–3. Sherwin-White 1980: 179.
4. Pines 2009b: 82–87.
5. Gelzer 1968: 72–74, 78. Millar 1998: 126–127.
6. Nicolet 1980: 386–387. Millar 2002a: Ch. 6.
7. Brunt 1988: 54, 306. Millar 1998: 125.
8. Lintott 1999: 173–175. Brunt 1988: 32–33, 61–64, 329–330.
9. Syme 1939: 154, see also 51.
10. Ward 1977: 60–64, 69–70. Seager 2002: 26–37.
11. Millar 2002a: 223. Seager 2002: 44–50, 60–62.
12. Suetonius, Julius Caesar, 77.
13. Seager 2002: 76, 79–81. Syme 1939: 30–33.
14. Gelzer 1968: 19–21, 31–32, 69. Goldsworthy 2006: 164–167, 174–181.
15. Suetonius, Julius Caesar, 22, 24.
16. Crawford 1993: 84. Gelzer 1968: 86–87, 95–96, 103, 108.
17. Gelzer 1968: 119–123.
18. Cicero, quoted in Crawford 1993: 157.
19. Mattern-Parks 2003: 387. Bivar 1983b: 48–56.
20. Boulnois 2005: 2.
21. Scullard 1976:124–127. Gruen 1974: xix, 449–497.
22. Suetonius, Julius Caesar, 32, 30.
23. Seager 2002: 162, 165–168. Gelzer 1968: 238, 240.

24. Caesar, *Civil War*, 1.4, 1.9.
25. Gelzer 1968: 79.
26. Suetonius, Julius Caesar, 77.
27. Gelzer 1968: 243, 287–320.
28. Gelzer 1968: 287–288, 290, 298–299, 310–312, 317, 319–320.
29. Suetonius, Julius Caesar, 80, 86.
30. Ramsey and Licht 1997: 61–94. Syme 1939: 117.
31. Osgood 2006: 136.
32. Syme 1939: 113, 142–143; 163–167. Rawson 1975: 278–279, 288–289.
33. Southern 1998: Ch. 2.
34. Syme 1939: 190–192. Osgood 2006: 62–64. Rawson 1975: 296.
35. Syme 1939: 187, 192–196. Osgood 2006: 45, 48–49, 51, 82–83, 88–89.
36. Osgood 2006: 95. Huzar 1978: 124–127.
37. Plutarch, Brutus, 53. Suetonius, Augustus, 13.
38. Syme 1939: 205.
39. Tacitus, *Annals*, 1.1, 3.27.
40. Nicolet 1980: 322–323. Crawford 1993: 146. Brunt 1988: 263–265, 308. Raaflaub 2004: 179–180, 192.
41. Tacitus, *Histories*, 4,73. Syme 1939: 155.
42. Tacitus, *Histories*, 4.74. Appian 1.57.
43. Caesar, *Civil War*, 1.22. Augustus, *Achievements*, 1.
44. Nicolet 1980: 322–323. Brunt 1988: 255, 327–330. Wirszubski 1960: 88–91.
45. Wirszubski 1960: 95.
46. Dio Cassius 52.1. Eder 1990: 74.
47. Syme 1939: 216, 220, 226, 263–266. Huzar 1978: 139, 176–183.
48. Syme 1939: 260–261, Huzar 1978: 153–154, 167–168.
49. Southern 1998: 65–77.
50. Osgood 2006: 338–339, 353–356, 368–369. Huzar 1978: 200–201.
51. Huzar 1978: 208, 215–216. Syme 1939: 274–275.
52. Plutarch, Antony, 75–77. Huzar 1978: 219–226.
53. Osgood 2006: 355. Huzar 1978: 227–278.
54. Shakespeare, *Antony and Cleopatra*, V.ii.326–327, after Plutarch, Antony, 85.
55. *Shiji* 85: 2505–2509.
56. *Shiji* 6: 227. Bodde 1986: 44–45.
57. *Shiji* 6: 230; 87: 2540. Bodde 1986: 43–44, 48.
58. Yang 2003b: 429–433. Lewis 1999: 640–641.
59. *Shiji* 6: 250.
60. *Shiji* 6: 239; 112: 2958.
61. Bodde 1986: 56, 67–68.
62. *Shiji* 6: 239. Bodde 1986: 54–55.
63. Loewe 2007: 70–79. Lewis 2007: 55.
64. *Shiji* 6: 252–253, 256. Bodde 1986: 64–66.
65. Cotterell 1981: 55–81. Hiromi 2007: 92–93.
66. *Shiji* 6: 243, 245, 252, 262–263. Kern 2007.
67. *Shiji* 6: 264. Bodde 1986: 81–82.
68. *Shiji* 48: 1950–1952.
69. Jia Yi, Critique of Qin, in *Shiji* 6: 281–282.
70. *Shiji* 6: 269–273; 7: 297–310; 8: 349–358. Bodde 1986: 82–84.

71. Fu 2002: 103. Zhang F. 2003: 686–694.
72. Millar 2004: 8–9. *Shiji* 6: 258.
73. Syme 1939: 207–211.
74. *Shiji* 48: 1952 ; 7: 300.
75. *Wuzi* 1. *Xunzi* 15.
76. *Shiji:* 34: 1557. Todd 1992: 265–267.
77. Toynbee 1957: 6.xxv.3.
78. *Xunzi* 16, Qiangguo.
79. *Shiji* 48: 2244; 56: 2504, 2510.
80. Xu and Hu 2000: 79, 87. Liu H. 2006: 69, 84–86, 364–377. Wang Z. 2006: 102–103.
81. Hulsewé 1978: 182–184. Kern 2000: 183–196. *Shiji* 85: 2510.
82. *Shiji* 28: 1371; 15: 686.
83. Bodde 1986: 59.
84. *Hanshu* 51: 2327, 2338; 36: 1954; 45: 2171, 2174; 51: 2369; 56: 2504; 64a: 2783, 2800; 64b: 2811; 67: 2918.
85. *Shiji* 112: 2954, 2961.
86. Lewis 2007: 71. See also Bodde 1986: 85–86; 95–102. Dull 1983: 285–286. Zhang F. 2003: 708–709.
87. *Shiji* 118: 3090, 3086.
88. *Hanshu* 24a: 1126.
89. Dull 1983: 286–294.
90. *Hanshu* 2: 83, 87.
91. *Shiji* 23: 1159–1160. *Hanshu* 19a: 722; 100a: 4207. Lewis 2007: 71.
92. *Hanshu* 24a: 1137.
93. Hulsewé 1985: 215. Cao 2005: 130. Gao 2008: 134.
94. *Lunyu* 12.9. *Mengzi* 1.12, 3.3.
95. Hulsewé 1978: 216; 1986: 533–534. Li X. 2004: 71.
96. *Shiji* 6: 253, 256, 259, 270. Dull 1983: 289–290.
97. *Shiji* 6: 252; 110: 2886.
98. *Hanshu* 24a: 1137. Hulsewé 1986: 537–538.
99. *Shiji* 18: 1949, 1952.
100. Waldron 1990: 16–18.
101. *Shiji* 6: 239.
102. *Shiji* 6: 254–255.
103. Bodde 1986: 69–71. Qian 1957: 20–21, 26–27.
104. *Shiji* 6: 258. Bodde 1986: 71–72.
105. *Shiji* 121: 3116; 89: 2573. *Hanshu* 88: 3592. Pines 2009a: 216–217.
106. *Shiji* 99: 2720–2724. *Hanshu* 43: 2124.
107. *Shiji* 6: 258.
108. Collected in *Shiji* 6: 276–284.
109. *Ershiershi* 1.
110. *Zhongyong* 31. *Lunyu* 2.21.
111. *Mengzi* 7.15, 5.3.
112. *Hanshu* 48: 2244; 63: 2754; 64a: 2796.
113. *Shiji* 7: 298; 55: 2040–2041; 56: 2055; 89: 2574; 91: 2601. Dull 1983: 300–317.
114. *Shiji* 6: 236, 259. Pines 2009a: 82–84.
115. *Shiji* 6: 280, 283; *Hanshu* 14: 393; 56: 2504; 64a: 2796.

116. *Shiji* 97: 2699. *Hanshu* 56: 2510–2511; 63: 2754; 64a: 2796. Li 2002: 48. Wang 2010: 117.
117. *Hanshu* 23: 1096. *Zuozhuan* Zhao 3.
118. *Shangshu*, Lüxing. *Hanshu* 23: 1079, 1091. McLeod and Yates 1981: 122. Xu and Hu 2000: 25–26.
119. Dull 1983: 301–313. *Shangshu* Bishi, Jiugao.
120. Hsiao 1979: 116.
121. *Shiji* 130: 3290–3291.
122. *Liji. Hannfeizi* 6.
123. *Shiji* 6: 282–283. *Hanshu* 48: 2252–2258.
124. Bodde 1986: 49–54.
125. *Mengzi* 4.6, 4.31.
126. Dull 1983: 309, 311, 315.
127. *Shiji* 48: 8, 7. Loewe 1986b: 111–114.
128. Qian 1957: 32–33. Suetonius, Augustus, 27.
129. *Shiji* 97: 2692. Beard 2007: 53.
130. Loewe 1986b: 116–118.
131. *Shiji* 7: 333–336, Yu's song in annotation.
132. Syme 1939.
133. Bodde 1986: 90.
134. *Shiji* 6: 249, 55: 2034; 86: 2534–2537.
135. Gelzer 1968: 287. Osgood 2006: 63.
136. *Shiji* 6: 255, 258.
137. *Shiji* 6: 242; 28: 1356; 54: 2029.
138. Syme 1939: 130, 201. *Ershiershi* 2.
139. Pliny 35.26. Syme 1939: 341, 231.
140. Hulsewé 1989: 75–76.
141. Syme 1939: 8.
142. *Ershiershi* 2.
143. Hulsewé 1989: 51–52.
144. *Shiji* 129: 3260; 8: 346; 9, 395–396.
145. Syme 1939: 368.
146. Hegel 1965: 313.
147. *Shiji* 94: 2648–2649.
148. Brunt 1971: 285, 287, 289.
149. *Shiji* 56: 2058; 30, 1418. Qian 1957: 39–40.
150. Tacitus, *Annals*, 1.2.
151. Wirszubski 1960: 92. See also Lintott 1999: 40, 199–200.
152. Cicero, quoted in Crawford 1993: 189.
153. Syme 1939: 513.
154. Bradley 1962.
155. Syme 1939: 513.
156. Sellers 2004. Millar 2002b.
157. Alexander Hamilton, quoted in Freeman 2008: 362.
158. Lewis 2007: 70, 72.

PART II

THE ROMAN AND EARLY CHINESE EMPIRES

CHAPTER 5

COURSES OF EMPIRE

5.1 *Pax Romana* and *Pax Sinica*

They lived happily ever after. This familiar ending for stories of strife and toil is not limited to fairy tales. "The end of history" has been proclaimed by twentieth-century triumphalists at the end of the Cold War.[1] Such euphoria, even if not delusory, is short-lived. Like a river emerging from a gorge into a basin, history shorn of turbulent events induces complacency. Yet undercurrents lurk beneath a placid surface and white water may be waiting behind the next bend.

A great reign stood out in the course of the Roman Empire or Han Dynasty. Augustus reigned for forty-one years, not counting the time he wielded dictatorial power as Octavian. Wudì's fifty-three-year reign was even longer. They were the greatest imperial conquerors, but their most influential legacies were in political institutions. Augustus inherited Caesar's mighty war machine and succeeded in compromising with the wealthy senatorial aristocracy that filled top offices. The Han had adopted the Legalist bureaucracy—which the First Emperor instituted over all China—and Wudì enshrined Confucianism as the criterion for officer selection, thereby initiating arguably the most enduring secular indoctrination machine in world history. Caesar and Augustus are often mentioned together as the shapers of the Roman Empire, as Qin's First Emperor and Han's Wudì were the shapers of imperial China. After them, the characters of the Eagle and the Dragon gradually matured.

The grandeur of the empires is dazzling. Yet the sun casts shadows, even at high noon. For peace and compromise with the ruling elites, each empire sacrificed a certain vibrancy of the preceding challenging age. In the void, easy and luxurious imperial life bred decadence. The effects were most apparent when hard times revealed the true worth of empire.

The liberty of common Roman citizens dropped precipitously with the destruction of the Republic and continued to erode in the Empire. Political rights were the first to go. Legal protection and social privilege gradually migrated from the citizen to the rich, exposing poor citizens to the treatment allotted to slaves. More than two centuries into the Empire, Roman citizenship was granted to all its free inhabitants. However, the title devoid of substance met with apathy. When barbarians came, the resistance of Roman citizens was weaker than that of Chinese subjects under similar circumstances. Even in Rome, citizens once unsurpassed in public spirit did not defend the city symbolic of honor. Twice they opened the city gate and surrendered.

Equality under the law and other political concepts, with which Legalists achieved an institutional revolution, were blamed for causing Qin's demise, branded as immoral, and banished to disgrace with no opportunity for development. Literati-officials spurned the public dimension, effectively confining government principles to family values, personal relations, and the claimed personal virtues of the ruling circle. Certain that ancient canonical texts contained the perfect solution for all times, they drained intellectual energy into exegesis. Crises found them faltering in solving social problems and in conducting themselves. Twice in our story, moralizing literati-officials turned into predatory warlords.

Some risk factors were visible early, but the cancers that eventually ailed the empires took a long time to develop. Fallibility is human. The brief previews of old age should not distract us from the glories of the Eagle and the Dragon at their prime.

Of the five centuries of the Roman and early Chinese Empires covered in Part II, *Pax Romana* and *Pax Sinica* lasted less than three, and with interruptions. Even so, it was an achievement to maintain relative stability and security for a period so long and over a territory so huge it seemed to fill the civilized world.

At its peak, the Roman Empire embraced the Mediterranean littoral and a large chunk of Europe, bounded by the Atlantic on the west, the Rhine and Danube on the north, the Euphrates and upper Tigris on the east, and the Sahara on the south. Diagonally, it stretched more than 4,000 kilometers from Britain to Egypt (Map 11). The Han Empire extended from today's North Korea to northern Vietnam, embracing the vast "core" of China bounded by seas on the east and south, mountains on the southwest, and deserts and the steppe on the north. Without an internal sea, it was more compact than the Roman Empire, stretching about 3,000 kilometers from the northwestern Yumenguan (Jade Gate) to Jiaozhi (Vietnam). West of the Jade Gate, its Protectorate of Xiyue (Western Territory) extended more than 1,000 kilometers further (Map 12).

To appreciate the challenges that territorial size posed to government, it is more useful to reckon distance according to the conditions of premodern communication and transportation technology. A signaling system of the fire and smoke type was the fastest. The Han built a long-distance signal communications system more advanced than that featured in the Greek tragedy *Agamemnon*. Signals covered in thirteen hours what took the standard post six days: the 547 kilometers between the frontier outpost Juyan and the provincial capital Zhangye. In thirty-six hours, signals from Juyan reached the Han capital Changan.[2] The high cost and limited complexity of messages confined signal communication to military purposes.

Both empires were avid road builders. Estimates put the principal network in the Roman Empire at 78,000 kilometers, that of the Latter Han, excluding the Western Territory, at 35,000 kilometers. Roughly one-tenth of these were trunk routes.[3] Along main roads in both realms, imperial officials had the rights to commandeer local animals and vehicles. Permanent government post services, first established in China by the Qin Dynasty, appeared in the Roman Empire in the third century. Relays galloping more than 200 kilometers a day could bring frontier messages to the capital in days, but exorbitant costs restricted employment. Sea travel, faster if available, was hostage to weather and season. Normally, dispatches from Syria took weeks, perhaps up to two months, to reach Rome. Realities on the ground compelled significant local decision making, whatever centralization of control may have existed on paper.[4]

As detrimental to political unity as slow communication were high transportation costs, which encouraged regional economic isolation. The imperial government at Rome or Changan could hardly survive without grain shipped from afar. Provision for the capital always received top administrative priority, followed by that for frontier troops. Emperor Diocletian once set prices for various modes of transportation in his efforts to fight inflation. Modern researchers compared costs in the Roman Empire to costs in eighteen-century England, for which detailed figures on transport costs were available.

Ratio of Costs of Transport by Sea, River, and Land[5]

	Sea	River	Land
Diocletian's price edict	1	6	55
Roman Empire data	1	5	28
Eighteen-century England data	1	5	23

Similar reliance on muscle and wind power justifies the assumption of similar ratios for China. Land transport, which required fodder for pack animals, was five to nine times more expensive than river transport, depending on terrain. It is therefore no surprise that the Romans stationed legions along great rivers and the Chinese eagerly developed navigable networks. The lack of river access to China's northern frontier magnified its remoteness. The ability to ship over the Mediterranean Sea, five times cheaper than river delivery, compensated for the larger distances in the Roman Empire.

Sitting near the geometrical center of its empire was Rome, the glorious master that consumed most profits of empire. With a population estimated to exceed 1 million, it dwarfed other big cities, Alexandria and Carthage's second incarnation, each home to roughly half a million.[6] Not until the seventh century would Rome's record be surpassed by Changan, resurging as the capital of the Tang Dynasty with a population approaching 2 million in some accounts. As capital of the Former Han Dynasty, Changan was more modest. Estimations based on archeological excavations put its population close to 800,000. The metropolis was attended by "suburbia," nearby imperial mausoleums around which more than 100,000 wealthy provincial households had been forcibly relocated.[7]

Pulsating with the vitality of a marcher state that had conquered the world, Rome and Changan each garnered the resources of advanced regions at the eastern part of its empire and pumped them to the less developed areas in the west and north. Strategically, Rome watched over the frontier to northern Europe and Changan the gateway to the western regions and central Asia. As the empires aged, however, the imperial center of gravity gradually retreated eastward. Rome's political influence waned when emperors ruled from imperial residences away from it. The transformation of the classical city of Byzantium into Constantinople near the fulcrum of the Danubian and Persian frontiers signified not only a new strategic reality, but also the revival of the deep-rooted economic and cultural bases of the East. Founded in 330 CE, Constantinople would grow into the eastern capital, its estimated population of half a million resembling that of Luoyang, capital of the Latter Han Dynasty.[8] The Han's decision in 25 CE to move its capital away from the frontier onto the Central Plain was not only strategic retrenchment but also recognition of the economic potential of the Yangzi delta, which would become the heart of China's economy. Even at the most conspicuous level, the site of the capital, the empires evolved.

Major hostility ceased in China with the death of Xiang Yu in 202 BCE and in the Mediterranean world with the death of Antony in 30 BCE. The victors became emperors with theatrical flourish. Liu Bang thrice refused the imperial title offered by seven kings, only to accept it "for the sake of the people" two months after the battle of Gaixia. Octavian waited until 27 BCE, when he ostensibly gave up all his power and restored the Republic, only to grab under different guises what he had relinquished, and more. Octavian was only thirty-five when he turned Augustus, twenty years younger than Liu when he turned Gaodì or Emperor Gao. Yet this was not the reason for his leisurely pace. His dallying did not signify that he was less confident than the hasty Liu or that his situation was less secure. The contrary obtained.

Liu grasped the supreme title at the moment of victory, thus capturing some sense of legitimacy from the consent of other kings, who were inferior only in military might. The new emperor had not even fixed a capital city. His core supporters preferred East Zhou's capital, Luoyang. A cart-pushing soldier gained audience to argue for the strategic superiority of Qin's capital, Xianyang, to be renamed Changan. The flip-flop on such an important matter indicated the inexperience of the decision-making circle. In contrast to the First Emperor, who ordered city fortifications demolished in the peace of a unified realm, Gaodì ordered the walling of county capitals. The fear of unrest was rational. Gaodì would spend much of his reign on horseback to consolidate his shaky dynasty, but his hasty accession enabled him to conduct it as a sovereign quelling rebels.[9]

As triumvir, Octavian had already held dictatorial power for more than a decade. He was a long way from the young terrorist who proscribed senators and burned the Italian city of Perusia. Italian reconciliation had begun even before Actium. Victory brought him the allegiance of Antony's oriental clients. He completely controlled affairs in the empire and had developed the finesse and patience requisite for co-opting Republican constitutions to serve one-man rule. Power firmly in hand, he could afford to "make haste slowly," as he said.[10]

5.2 Augustus and His Dynasty

Two years after he defeated Antony at the 31 BCE battle of Actium, Octavian returned to Rome and celebrated three days of triumphant parade. Amid the jubilant crowd was a man with a raven that cried, "Hail Caesar, victorious *imperator*!" Delighted, Octavian awarded a large sum to the trainer of the "dutiful bird." Then the man's partner, denied his share of the profit, revealed the existence of a second raven, which when produced dutifully cried, "Hail Antony, victorious *imperator*!"[11]

Such neutrality was not limited to the common people, but neither was it universal. Several hundred senators sided with Antony. The antagonists differed in worldview and policy. Antony inherited Caesar's cosmopolitan outlook. Had he won, the Latin and Greek halves of the Empire might have become equitable partners in government, better integrating the realm. To combat him, Octavian championed "Romans, masters of the world."[12] His victory secured Latin domination. Despite cultural and economic superiority, the Greek provinces would have to wait centuries before gaining political parity.[13]

Caesar's heir never let slip his military power and maintained a large standing army that swore loyalty to him personally. Shortly after returning to Rome, he administered the first of several purges of the Senate, replaced undesirable elements by his own clients, and raised its qualification to exclude all but the extremely rich. With everything under control by 27 BCE, he summoned the dramatic meeting of the Senate to "restore the Republic."[14] Augustus claimed to transfer his power to the Senate and the Roman people. Dio, who wrote the fullest existent account of the Augustan period, put it the other way around: "Through this process the power both of the people and of the Senate was wholly transferred into the hands of Augustus, and it was from this time that a monarchy, strictly speaking, was established."[15]

Without holding the office of consul, Augustus held the consular *imperium* for life, in Rome itself supreme and in the provinces, superior to the power of any proconsul. Without holding the office of the tribune, he acquired tribunican power as the protector of the people. He controlled the provinces where most of the legions were stationed, leaving the Senate to appoint governors for provinces without military might.[16] "He gradually pushed ahead and absorbed the functions of the senate, the officials, and even the law," wrote Tacitus.[17]

The result was "an absolute monarchy disguised by the forms of a commonwealth," in the words of a leading early modern historian of the Roman Empire.[18] What was Augustus? In view of his function, people consider him Rome's first emperor. Formally, he made *Imperator* his personal name, but the military acclamation did not become the official title "emperor" until his dynasty was over. He called himself *princeps* or first citizen, but it was only a republican honorary term; many dynasts of the late Republic were *principes*. By giving the impression of an officer, *princeps* covers up the peculiarity of Augustan rule: power without office.[19] In 22 BCE, Augustus theatrically rent his clothes to quiet the people who wanted him to take the office of dictator. "He knew that the authority and the honour he already possessed raised him above the position of past dictators, and he was rightly on his guard against the jealousy and hatred which the title would provoke," Dio explained.[20] Constitutional formalists are theoretically correct that his regime was not a monarchy; there was no throne. All power was vested in the person of Augustus, legally a private citizen, effectively the dictator and commander in chief of the army, honored as Father of the Fatherland. To him by personal name senators, soldiers, and the whole populace swore the oath of allegiance.[21] The contemporary Roman poet Ovid portrayed his personal rule best: "Caesar Augustus *is* the state."[22]

In rhetoric, emperors received their power from the Senate. In practice, senators owed their positions to the emperor. They handled routine business but never stood up to the emperor on important policies. The discrepancy between the Senate's form of sovereignty and its function as a rubber stamp bred resentment and conspiracy.[23] Finding German bodyguards insufficient for his peace of mind, Augustus created the elite Praetorian Guard, the model for future storm troopers.[24] "That crafty tyrant, sensible that laws might colour, but that arms alone could maintain, his usurped dominion, had gradually formed this powerful body of guards in constant readiness to protect his person, to awe the senate," writes the leading early modern historian.[25] Yet swords cut both ways. The time would come when the Praetorian Guard became a maker of emperors.

A republican facade covered a powerful but insecure emperor, an impotent Senate with restive senators, and an armed force slowly growing its own mind. Adding to the complexity were palace intrigue and dynastic manipulation, as political marriages involved many powerful aristocratic clans. Had Augustus succumbed to sickness in 23 BCE, civil war would probably have broken out again, but fortune was kind to Rome. He lived long enough to congeal power and see a generation maturing knowing only one-man rule. Even so, he had to step up repression in his old age. Politically incorrect literature fueled public bonfires. Written libel became liable to treason charges.[26]

Hereditary power was antithetic to republican form but crucial to monarchical function. Augustus, totally identified with the house of Julius Caesar, killed Caesar's son with Cleopatra at first opportunity. He had only two direct blood relatives, his sister Octavia and his daughter Julia. His callous manipulation of them and their children for an heir of the blood exposed the price of incongruous form and function. However, even the power of the Roman emperor could not contest fate. His nephew and grandsons died prematurely. Without hiding his bitter disappointment, he made an heir of his stepson Tiberius Claudius, with the stipulation that Tiberius pass the power to Germanicus, Augustus's grandnephew by blood. His manipulations planted the seed for the grim tragedy of the Julio-Claudian Dynasty.[27]

Aged fifty-five when he acceded in 14 CE, Tiberius professed reluctance to bear all the burden of empire and proposed to share responsibility with the Senate. Tacitus treated the exercise as the farce of an arch-hypocrite. However, modern historians tend to believe its sincerity: "The accession of Tiberius marked a restoration of the Republic more genuine in many respects than that proclaimed and enacted by his predecessor—if behaviors be valued higher than legal formula."[28] It did not work out. Tiberius governed the Empire decently, but his moderation in games and festivities disgruntled Rome's populace accustomed to imperial beneficence. Imitating Augustus, he tried to win senators and achieved some success in the first part of his twenty-three year reign. Unfortunately, Germanicus died in 19, followed shortly by Tiberius's biological son. The lack of an heir apparent ignited frantic jostling among aspirants that saturated Rome with factious intrigues. Tiberius entrusted Sejanus, prefect of the Praetorian Guard, and in 26 retired to the island of Capri, whence he governed by letters and agents. Left as the imperial representative in Rome, Sejanus took advantage of the emperor's sense of insecurity and initiated deadly treason proceedings against prominent senators and imperial relatives. Tiberius eliminated him, but treason proceedings continued. Tiberius died in 37, hated by senators.[29]

Germanicus had married Julia's daughter. Thus their son inherited Augustus's blood on both sides. Since boyhood, he had been a darling to the troops, who bestowed the nickname Caligula, Little Boot, for the miniature uniform he wore in camp. Now he was twenty-five. Caligula's accession seemed to the Roman people like a dream come true. Disregarding Tiberius's will for a co-emperor, the Senate unanimously conferred absolute power solely on him.[30] Formal constitutional legitimacy, however, did not alleviate the danger of rule by man. Contrary to his predecessors, Caligula detested administrative duties but loved self-aggrandizement. He quickly exhausted the large surplus that Tiberius had left in the state treasury and went on to extract money by arbitrary taxation, confiscation, and execution. His four-year reign of terror ended in assassination.[31]

The immediate aftermath of the assassination revealed two competing ideas of government. Senators talked liberty. Praetorian guards searched the palace for an imperial relative, found Caligula's uncle Claudius trembling behind a curtain, and hailed him *imperator*. They got rich rewards and henceforth regarded as their legal right large donatives from each new emperor. Thus was supreme power of the Empire thrust on Claudius, aged fifty but hitherto excluded from politics because of his apparent mental illness. A novice oblivious of the danger of thin ice and less threatening to seasoned politicians, his accession eased the tension between the emperor and senators. He opened up the Senate to more provincials. Successful foreign wars conducted by his generals brought prestige. The staff of freedmen who managed the imperial household began its growth into a government apparatus with specialized departments for finance and other functions. Fear of plots increased the emperor's vulnerability to manipulation. Poisoned mushrooms supplied by his niece/wife Agrippina ended Claudius's thirteen-year reign. Of the Julio-Claudian emperors after Augustus, he alone received the honor of posthumous deification.[32]

Nero's minority was the occasion of a struggle for the power of the regency. The dominance of the empress dowager Agrippina was checked by praetorian prefect Burrus in alliance with Seneca, eminent poet and Nero's tutor. The struggle lasted five years before the will of the adolescent broke through. Nero caused the murder of his mother in 59, then replaced Burrus and Seneca by toadies talented in flattery and venality. He wiped out all influential members of the imperial family and the old aristocracy by treason accusations, doing to the Julio-Claudian Dynasty what the Second Emperor did to the Qin. Rome's great fire of 64 ignited popular wrath. Generous relief measures did not assuage the rage of seeing a grandiose imperial palace rising on the burned grounds. Nero's life, memorable for its monstrosity in ancient annals, received a new modern portrait: "It remains so vivid because it was created by an artist."[33] Genuine in his passion for music and drama, Nero sang in Greek theaters and won 1,808 trophies while trouble flared up around the Roman Empire. Riots in Judaea intensified. Britain rose up. Armenia almost slipped out of control. Far worse, the army, bulwark of the Empire, became restless, partly because of the unjustifiable death of respected generals. By 68, all had deserted the emperor, leaving only a few freedmen to help him slit his throat. The artist as a young tyrant dropped the curtain on the dynasty designed by the artful tyrant.[34]

5.3 Militarism in the Roman Peace

Domestic and foreign affairs were more entwined in Rome than in China, where a precocious bureaucracy gave civilians better control of the military. Augustus established a large professional army and engaged the legions in incessant foreign wars, thus keeping their sinews exercised and their minds too busy for seditious thoughts. Imperial expansion slowed after Tiberius. Nevertheless, the legions were dispersed at the frontiers of the Rhine, the Danube, and the East, too remote to threaten Italy. Emperors resolutely kept the army under their personal control, monopolizing glory, dispensation of benefaction to the troops, and, increasingly, military decisions. These arrangements suspended for two centuries the danger of military ascendancy in politics.[35]

An early warning did occur, however. Roused from their political stupor by Nero, the legions revolted. A short but sharp civil war erected four successive emperors within the single year of 69. The troops in Gaul hailed Galba emperor, promptly confirmed by the Senate. Yet Galba's attitude—"I do not buy my soldiers, I select them"—ran afoul of the grain of the time.[36] After his murder, Otho became emperor, backed by the Praetorian Guard and the Danube legions. The Rhine troops chose Vitellius as their own emperor, marched south, and defeated Otho. The legions of the Danube and the East jointly declared for Vespasian, who had recently suppressed the great Jewish revolt of 66–70 CE. While his younger son Domitian represented the Flavian family in Rome and his supporters deposed Vitellius, Vespasian stayed in Alexandria to control the grain supply for fifteen months.[37]

"At Rome the Senate decreed to Vespasian all the usual powers," Tacitus wrote curtly.[38] It had decreed the same powers to Galba, Otho, and Vitellius, immediately upon the deaths of their respective predecessors, on the same day if the news arrived early. Vespasian dated his reign from the time of his acclamation by the troops, six months before the enactment of a law that legitimized the emperor's absolute power. The backdating of the law to accommodate the fact effectively annulled even the formal need for senatorial consultation.[39]

The year of four emperors exposed two trends, the rivalry of the army to the Senate as the context of the emperor's operation, and the slippage of power out of Rome and Italy. Changes were slow, but their results would be unmistakable in the third century, not to mention the military despotism of the later Empire centered in Constantinople.[40]

Galba's accession in Spain "divulged a secret of state: an emperor could be made elsewhere than at Rome," wrote Tacitus.[41] Vespasian came from a small Italian town. Emperors after the Flavian Dynasty hailed from Spain, Gaul, Africa, Syria, and the Balkans. While enthusiastic about traditional Italian values that made Rome great, these emperors were more responsive to the needs of the Empire at large and receptive of provincials in the central government. Italians became the minority in the Senate by the end of the second century. The proportion of Italian soldiers in the legions dropped even faster. Already the minority under Vespasian, they almost vanished a century later.[42]

Like all emperors before 235, Vespasian was a senator. Although draped in the purple by the army, he knew he could rule only with the Senate's cooperation and tried to reduce tension with it by formal courtesy and operational distance. A usurper and an upstart, he faced resistance but felt secure because of an advantage enviable to most Roman emperors: Vespasian had mature sons, and he frankly founded the hereditary Flavian Dynasty by making his elder son, Titus, his partner in empire. Provisions for the continuity of rule deterred thoughts of rebellion. Spared such fear, he tolerated some opposition and relaxed irritating security measures. During their reigns, totaling twelve years, Vespasian and Titus repaired the damages of civil war and introduced reforms that would reach systematic fruition under the Antonines. The confidence of the Empire scintillated in the Colosseum and other large building projects.[43]

Domitian, last of the Flavians, ascended in 81 and continued many policies. He dispensed justice meticulously and suppressed corruption vigorously. As one modern historian notes, "The people of the Empire had much to thank him for, even though the Senate feared and hated him."[44] Aristocrats hated his ostentation of power, his attempt to rid the Senate of inept members, and his promotion of nonsenators. His crackdown on vociferous criticism bred conspiracy. Terrified by the military rebellion of 89, he encouraged informants and prosecuted alleged treason. Treachery and faction fights added fuel to three years of terror, which did not end with his assassination in 96. Many who survived him perished in mutual vengeance.[45]

Senators joyfully smashed images of Domitian and declared as successor Nerva, whose involvement in the assassination was whispered. To assuage the fury of the army and the Praetorian Guard, the sonless Nerva adopted as successor Trajan, governor of Upper Germany and commander of two Rhine legions. The choice was the top achievement of his fifteen-month reign.[46]

Trajan was reputed to be the best emperor after Augustus. Alone among pagan emperors, he escaped the Christian Hell through the prayer of Pope Gregory. However, modern historians uncovered remarkable continuity in power and policy from Domitian to Trajan, akin to that from the Qin to the Han Dynasties: "Trajan's rule was no less and perhaps more autocratic than that espoused by the detested Domitian, and some of the procedures and programmes Trajan assiduously pursued, and brought to fruition, were not noticeably different from those initiated by his predecessors."[47] Trajan benefited from the dirty work of Domitian, who decimated recalcitrant opponents. Leniency toward corruption and tact in dealing with senators also helped. A century after the fact, the veil was finally worn out. Tacitus and Pliny the Younger, contemporary senators full of praise, expressed the pliancy of aristocrats coming to term with autocracy. Augustus and Tiberius had rebuked those who addressed them as *dominus*, master. Pliny routinely addressed Trajan as master in his letters, while publicly proclaiming the address fitting only for tyrants.[48]

Trajan's reign of 98–117 inaugurated the "age of gold" of the Roman Empire. He died sonless. The troops acclaimed Hadrian, his nephew married to his niece. The prompt execution of four leading senators indicated possible hitches in the accession. Hadrian also had no son. Shortly before his death in 138, he arranged succession for two generations. He adopted sonless Antoninus Pius, then fifty-five, on the condition that Antoninus adopted Marcus Aurelius, Hadrian's prime choice, then seventeen. Aurelius reigned from 161 to 180 and passed the throne to his son Commodus, who began the "age of iron and rust."[49] These reigns were loosely called the Antonine age, when the Empire enjoyed the "the immeasurable majesty of the Roman peace." The only blemish was Hadrian's suppression of the Jewish Bar-Kochba revolt of 132–135, which left 580,000 persons massacred, the slave market flooded, and Judaea a desert.[50]

To the Roman, the word "pax" can seldom be divorced from notions of conquest or at least compulsion.[51] Trajan revived the Augustan verve for imperial expansion. The Nabataean Kingdom was turned into the Roman province of Arabia. More consequential were his two large wars of choice, against Dacia and Parthia. His practice of campaigning in person won glory for himself but had long-term repercussions. Away on military campaigns for years, he undercut Rome's importance by demonstrating that the Roman Empire need not be ruled from Rome. Furthermore, his precedent obliged subsequent emperors to conduct major campaigns in person, so that the center of power increasingly shifted to the army camp. Worse, when conflicts erupted in several places, the impossibility of one emperor commanding everywhere tempted usurpers, a source of instability from the third century on.[52]

Dacia, north of the Danube, was rich in gold and silver. Plunder from Trajan's Dacian wars financed most of his extravagant building projects. For his second triumph alone, he staged 148 days of games, in which 11,483 gladiators and innumerable beasts were killed. "Trajan, more than any of the emperors, recognized the expectations of the common people of Rome. He knew that his unchallenged authority was effectively based on two things above all, the *annona et spectacula*, the corn supply and shows—and more especially the 'amusements'—rather than the more serious matter of state." Thus remarked Fronto, tutor to young Marcus Aurelius.[53] Whatever Aurelius learned, he could not afford to emulate the extravaganza. Trajan's Parthian campaign strained the empire's resources. When Aurelius realized he must defend Trajan's Dacia against barbarians, he raised military funds by auctioning palace treasures in Trajan's Forum.[54]

Aurelius had a son, and the heir of blood always enjoyed the loyalty of troops. Sole emperor at age eighteen, Commodus seemed to be a second-rate Nero. A failed assassination attempt by high aristocrats, his own sister probably complicit, ignited the spiral of retaliation and terror. Like Nero, Commodus left governing to sleazy favorites and disgusted aristocrats by appearing in public shows, although he preferred the gladiatorial ring to Nero's Greek theater. His domestics and the praetorian prefect got rid of him.[55]

The year 193 was a replay of 69, except in this round the civil war dragged on. The Praetorian Guard offered the purple to the highest bidder in public auction. While two senators haggled over prices in Rome, armies in three regions each acclaimed its own emperor. The Danubian army was closest to Rome. On its approach, the Senate quickly abandoned its choice and transferred the purple to Septimius Severus. The Severan Dynasty lasted from 193 to 235. Its first four years were spent in fighting the legions of Britain and the East.[56]

The decline of Italy accelerated during the Severan Dynasty. Previous Roman emperors, even those born in the provinces, were of Latin stock. Severus was the first non-Latin emperor, a descendant of Punic notables in Africa with roots traceable to Carthaginian times. By his time, the army was recruited almost exclusively from the provinces, but the Praetorian Guard was still predominantly Italian. One of his first acts was to disband the old guard and replace it with an enlarged version with men drawn from his own legions. Henceforth, Italian youths, spared military chores and deprived of the power associated with them, could concentrate on bread and circuses, if not the freedom of banditry. Their formal distinction vanished in 212, when Caracalla, Severus's son and successor, conferred Roman citizenship on all free inhabitants of the Empire.[57]

5.4 Roman Anarchy and Revival

Civil war is the cruelest of conflicts. For the brief wars in 69 following Nero's demise, Vespasian fixed damages at 40 billion sesterces, equivalent to almost five decades of normal state revenue. Although inflated, the amount indicated the scale of devastation.[58] The wars following Commodus's death in 193 were lengthier and more widespread. Severus and his two contenders had supporters all around the Empire. Retribution against political enemies affected many cities.[59]

Civil war was not among the army's normal duties but, once erupted, often became its first priority. Troops diverted to internal conflicts weakened frontier defense. Troubles had already occurred during the wars of 69 and 193–197.[60] However, they were mild compared to the almost deadly correlation between civil and foreign wars of the third century, which began in 235 with the assassination of Severus Alexander. The troops acclaimed Maximinus, the first soldier-emperor who rose from the ranks and had never been a senator. The Senate conspired with two other emperors and outlawed him. Civil wars ensued and did not end with his death or the deaths of many subsequent emperors. In five decades until the accession of Diocletian, the Empire ran through at least twenty-four emperors and as many pretenders, who differed from emperors only in their failure to control the city of Rome, and not for lack of desire. Domestic convulsion encouraged enemies beyond the Rhine, Danube, and Euphrates. The necessity to campaign in person further strained the emperor. The Roman Empire fragmented into three from 260 to 274, which coincided with the lengthier fragmentation of China into three kingdoms.[61]

The Persians pierced the eastern frontier, the Germans the northern. Troops were required to fight them and, even more urgently, pretending Romans. To fund additional armies, the government raised taxes and reduced the silver content in its coinage. The currency collapsed. Prices skyrocketed. The economy tottered. The Senate continued to wane. By the 260s, senators withdrew from military commands. More soldiers rose to the purple from the ranks. Rome, although retaining titular and psychological significance, lost political relevance as emperors routinely resided elsewhere.

Historians call the five decades after 235 "the third-century crisis," but Romans were nothing if not resilient. The eclipse of the conservative aristocracy opened opportunities for innovative new men to shine in these dark days. Gallienus reorganized the army and defeated the barbarians in 268. His successor Claudius II pacified the Danube frontier. Aurelian, brilliant commander nicknamed "hand on hilt," reunited the Empire in 274, although Dacia was lost forever. These energetic but short-reigned soldier-emperors had no luxury for long-term planning. They met pressing emergencies by improvising piecemeal remedies. However, their practical measures became building blocks in the comprehensive reforms by which Diocletian and Constantine laid the foundation of the Later Roman Empire.[62]

Diocletian, a soldier of humble origin from Illyricum, was acclaimed emperor in 284. Realizing that the empire was large enough to accommodate, in fact to demand, more than one supreme executive, he instituted power sharing to stabilize power transition. The emperor, entitled Augustus, appointed a Caesar as his colleague and intended successor. Later each post was doubled to create the Tetrarchy, the rule of four. One Augustus-Caesar pair was responsible for the eastern and the other the western part of the Empire. At the cost of quadrupling bureaucracy, the four kept close contacts with their respective troops, forestalled divisive ambitions, and repelled incursions. After they returned the Empire to a sound footing in 305, Diocletian and his fellow Augustus became the only emperors to retire voluntarily and peacefully. They were committed to orderly succession, but they underestimated the hereditary principle and power lust.

Constantine, son to an Augustus but not officially a Caesar, brushed aside the law and had himself proclaimed Augustus by his father's troops. His six-year scheme and war for the mastery of the western Empire culminated in the 312 battle of the Milvian Bridge outside Rome, which he fought under the sign of the Christian God. For the next twelve years, Constantine split the Empire with the eastern Augustus, whom he eventually defeated in a decisive land-sea engagement near the Strait of Bosporus. Until his death in 337, the Empire was at peace under a sole ruler.

Constantine completed many reforms that Diocletian started. A new stable currency based on gold blunted inflation. Subdivision of provinces and military commands reduced the risk of usurpation. The army expanded, as did the civilian bureaucracy with increasing administrative efficiency. Taxes rose. Social stratification calcified. Details we leave to comparative analyses.[63]

Constantine oversaw the triumph of the Orient over the Occident. The Empire's center of gravity moved to the east. The ancient city of Byzantium became a magnificent New Rome, Constantinople, today Istanbul. Constantine adopted all the pomp of an oriental despot. More important was the triumph of an oriental cult, Christianity. Now members of the state religion, Christians turned from the persecuted to persecutors. The Christian church, backed by state power, acquired numerous privileges to become, after the emperor, the largest landlord in the Empire.[64]

Constantine's bloody grab of power set the example for his heirs. As soon as he expired, his son Constantius II engineered the murder of all adult male members of his house, except his own two brothers. Then the brothers fell on each other. Pretenders and civil wars followed, until Constantius II solely held the crown in 353. He was succeeded by Julian, a half cousin who had escaped his bloodbath by being a child. A scholar, capable administrator, and brilliant general, Julian was also known for his attempt to revive paganism. His reign lasted only twenty months, cut short by a spear wound of unknown origin during his campaign against Persia. The status of Christianity as the state religion was secured.[65]

Julian's death in 364 ended the house of Constantine and unitary imperial rule. Except during a few months in 394, when Theodosius was sole emperor, two emperors henceforth ruled the Roman Empire simultaneously, each the head of his own government and army. The first pair was Valentinian I in the west and Valens in the east. The two soldier-emperors kept the barbarians at bay until their deaths. The arrogance of a Quadi envoy exasperated Valentinian I into a stroke. Three years later, in 378, Valens died at Hadrianople fighting the Visigoths. The balance of power between Rome and the barbarians was shifting.[66]

Domestic government, too, underwent significant changes. Only sixteen when his father Valentinian I died, Gratian heralded the age of child emperors. Wealthy senatorial aristocrats, effete and inept, resurged in power. After Hadrianople, emperors ceased to campaign in person in foreign wars and hence gave up direct control of the army. Crucial decisions began to pass from the emperor to generals and high aristocrats, who struggled for power behind the scene. Dusk gathered on the Western Roman Empire.

5.5 United China Takes Root

Ten months before he defeated Xiang Yu in the battle of Gaixia in 202 BCE, Liu Bang received a letter from Hann Xin, who reported victory over the king of Qi and requested the title of effective king for himself to administer the acquired territory. Liu was about to let loose a tirade but changed his words upon a little kick from his counselor. Hann got the title of real king and ample incentives to fight against Xiang. He also got a surprise immediately after the victory. Liu barged into his camp and relieved him of military command.[67]

Hann was one of seven kings who urged the title of emperor on Liu Bang. Unlike him, the other kings had independent power bases and could have sided with Xiang. Liu secured their alliance by the promise of sharing sovereignty in the feudalistic way. None expected all seven to be executed or exiled for treason during Gaodì's seven-year reign. Hann, whose generalship had been indispensable to Liu's success, was the first but not the last to be falsely accused. His remark has become a Chinese idiom: "When the hare is dead, the hound is boiled. When the birds are eliminated, good bows are buried."[68]

Gaodì was spared the blame of malevolent ingratitude that rained on the First Emperor who did not slaughter supporters after success. The Han emperor reverted to the Way of ancient kings. Instead of allowing his sons and brother to remain mere commoners, he enfeoffed them to replace the slain meritorious kings. Ten kingdoms, each with significant fiscal, personnel, and military autonomy, ruled over about two-thirds of the country in the populous east, where the six former warring states had been located. The kingdoms were subordinate to the imperial government, which ruled the territory of the old Qin state directly through provinces. The arrangement consolidated the dynasty of the Liu family.[69]

The vassal kings maximized native advantages and revived regional economies. Some helped to suppress a coup in the imperial center. These early achievements proved not the superiority of the feudalistic way, however, but only the wisdom of shedding an invidious habit gradually to avoid painful withdrawal symptoms. As society recovered from the devastations of civil war, the increasingly restive kings became destabilizing. Ominous signs presaged a rerun of the warring states, as the First Emperor and Li Si had warned. It did not happen. Qin bequeathed political insight and a precedent. Early Han officers of diverse learning and real-life experience were pragmatic and open-minded. The Legalist Chao Cuo urged reducing the feudatories while the central government still held the edge. Jingdì, the fifth emperor, listened. Seven powerful kings rebelled at the edict of 154 BCE. They were quashed within three months, although not before Chao Cuo was executed for vitiating the love among imperial relatives.[70] The central government, having grown in confidence and administrative capacity, directly controlled ever-expanding territories. Feudalistic aristocrats resisted, but their last great conspiracy in 122 BCE failed to get off the ground. A century after the first unification under Qin in 221 BCE, provinces directly under a centralized bureaucratic government again covered almost the whole realm.[71]

Tending to the craving for calm in a society traumatized by civil war, the first five reigns of the Han Dynasty adopted *wuwei* or a hands-off stance, a mixture of Daoist and Legalist ideas asserting that the people would be happy and well behaved if the ruler sets simple and strict regulations; then live and let live. Excavated documents of the Qin and early Han Dynasties confirm the traditional view that Xiao He, the first Han premier, adopted most of Qin's legal codes. His successor Cao Can embraced the Daoist stance of refraining from active involvement. A folk song expressed contemporary appraisal: "Xiao He made laws as plain as a straight line. Cao Can followed and adhered without deviation. Rules pure and tranquil united the people in peace."[72] Wendì and Jingdì favored Legalist ideas and simplified administration. Many rules obstructing commerce and industry were repealed, but promotion of agriculture continued. Urged by Chao Cuo, the land tax was reduced by steps from one-fifteenth to one-thirtieth.[73]

After six decades, population registration rebounded sharply, the treasury was full, and families spared by natural disasters were well off.[74] However, the austere government had deferred addressing many serious problems. Jingdì began to deal with the potential insubordination of feudalistic kings. Internal consolidation enabled his successor to tackle nomad marauders of the northern frontier.[75]

Wudì acceded in 140 BCE at age fifteen and ruled until 87 BCE. Were he a Western emperor, he would be called "the Great," but the Chinese were ambivalent about his accomplishments. His offensive against the nomadic Xiongnu led to imperial expansion beyond the Pamir and diplomacy as far as Parthia. To find quality officers, he regularized channels of recruitment to give the small men all across the country a standardized route for advancement. Attracted to aristocratic culture and the aura of sage-kings, he made Confucianism the state ideology. To mobilize production and extract resources for military and cultural expenses, he enlarged the administrative apparatus and built up an "inner court" of imperial attendants to help the emperor make decisions. We will discuss his policies in comparison with Roman achievements. Suffice here to note that he transformed the utilitarian "small government" he inherited into a flamboyant and more autocratic "big government."[76]

Foreign wars, cultural extravaganza, and court profligacy strained the economy. Social unrest appeared. Finally, shaken by the death of Crown Prince Wei in a conspiracy and the annihilation of an expeditionary army, the aged emperor reversed course and directed efforts away from imperial expansion to agricultural production.[77]

Two days before his death, Wudì named the eight-year-old son who would succeed him as Zhaodì. To assist the boy emperor, he appointed a quartet of senior officers, including Huo Guang and Sang Hongyang. Huo eventually grabbed all power and managed the succession crisis after Zhaodì died sonless in 74. Xuandì, a grandson of Crown Prince Wei, was born in prison, smuggled out of the palace, and raised as a commoner. With special attention to the dispensation of justice and the selection of officers, his twenty-four-year reign earned the reputation of good governance.[78]

Zhaodì and Xuandì reverted to the policies of Wendì and Jingdì "to lighten levies and reduce taxes, let the people rest." Government loans helped distressed peasants. The economy recovered and prospered. In foreign affairs, they negotiated, distributed subsidies, but maintained military readiness. Peace prevailed on the northern frontier for more than half a century. The Han reached its apogee during the reigns of Zhaodì and Xuandì.[79]

5.6 Confucianism Ascending

Confucians enjoyed prestige and patronage in the feudatories. However, except as masters of ceremony, they held few offices in the early Han government toiling to get concrete socioeconomic results. As the ruling circle became increasingly comfortable and complacent, the masters of aristocratic culture climbed up the political ladder, first by "adorning laws and policies with literature and the Canons," then by advocating the restoration of ancient ways. They flattered the emperor by images of the sage king and bombarded rival ideas with moral rhetoric. Daoism was dismissed as fit only for servants. Legalists were condemned for poisoning the world's morality and posing the gravest danger to stability.[80] Urged by Dong Zhongshu and other Confucians, Wudì closed the government recruitment channel to scholars of other persuasions and established an imperial academy devoted exclusively to the Confucian Canons. Wudì's "dismissal of the hundred schools and enshrinement of Confucianism" has been hailed as his most benevolent achievement by some, deplored alongside the First Emperor's book burning by others.[81] Anyway, it is his most influential legacy. It ended the age of intellectual vitality and inaugurated Confucian literati-officials as the imperial ruling elite.

Confucians triumphed over Legalists, but not completely. The centralized and bureaucratized institutions that Legalists designed had passed the trial by fire to become the lasting architecture of imperial China. Their rule by law would be replaced by the Confucian rule by men. The law's impartiality, substantiality, and understandability by the common people would be eclipsed by the privileges and inscrutable virtues claimed by superior men in powerful positions. The bureaucratic rationality of organization by function and evaluation according to performance would be corrupted by patrimonial and feudalistic practices, especially the preponderance of personal connections. Institutional spirit would falter. However, institutional structures would stand to impose some restraint on arbitrary claims of moral superiority.

Anti-utilitarian idealism, exemplified in Dong Zhongshu's echo of Mengzi—"To illuminate the Way and not to reckon with utility"—suffused literati indoctrination.[82] Exegesis of the Canons, which convey the lofty Way, became a political principle. However, reality is unforgiving. To be effective or simply to continue existing, a government must tend to mundane matters and produce results, for which rational value judgment and instrumental reason are indispensable. Responsible officers quietly acquired empirical knowledge, developed an analytic faculty, and worked to benefit the people in fact, not merely in words. Those abiding by Confucius's teaching that "the superior man is no instrument" employed pragmatic subordinates to get things done. The rational and utilitarian thinking of Legalists was forced underground but not extinguished.[83] Denounced in Confucian moralization through millennia, it received little credit from traditional interpretations.[84] Many modern historians have another view. Penetrating rhetoric and analyzing effective policies, many find Legalist substance beneath Confucian varnish: "Such economic policies, for example, as the 'ever-normal granary,' various government efforts to equalize private holdings of land, or governmental monopolies of salt, iron, and other products, all probably owe as much or more to Legalism than they do to early Confucianism. Recent study shows that the same may even be true of what has traditionally been thought to be a peculiar Confucian institution: the civil service examination system used in imperial times to recruit government personnel on the basis of intellect rather than birth."[85] Perhaps the imperial civil service examination is a miniature reflection of the government: The open, fair, and meritocratic recruitment process is Legalist; its exclusive examination content that limits "merit" to mastery of the Four Books and Five Canons, Confucian.

The ascent of Confucians was neither quick nor easy. Early Han officers were capable and farsighted. Wendì preferred Legalist ideas and deemed sophisticated rituals irrelevant to government. Jindì did not appoint Confucians.[86] The achievements of their reigns, reputed to be among the best in Chinese history, disprove the Confucian pretention that canonical learning is necessary for moderation, low taxation, and good governance. Wudì himself was renowned for employing all kinds of talent, which he needed for solving pressing problems.[87] Despite preferential treatment, the bookish literati had a difficult time elbowing out officers with practical acumen, administrative experience, and moral rectitude in actions. Xuandì insisted on balancing Legalist and Confucian ideas. Only in the reign of his heir Yuandì did Confucians succeed in dominating the bureaucracy.

On top of Wudì's agenda were the fierce nomads of the northern steppe, a perennial threat to imperial China more severe that the Germanic threat to the Roman Empire. The Han had paid increasingly heavy annual tribute to the Xiongnu for almost seven decades. Appeasement decreased but did not stop the raids that devastated frontier populations. Wudì, taking the offensive, initiated a century-long struggle with the Xiongnu. To meet war expenditures, he appointed Sang Hongyang and other men with mercantile backgrounds to high offices, thus gaining the benefit of financial expertise that was crucial to sound fiscal administration but usually scarce in government because of traditional prejudice against merchants.

To raise revenue for national projects is a chore for all governments ancient and modern. How should the tax burden be distributed among various groups of people? The main revenue of agrarian economies comes from land. The Han's land tax rate of one-thirtieth was about one-quarter of Rome's and one-third of Mengzi's ideal.[88] Wudì chose to keep it at that low level and put the extra burden on speculators and the commercial rich, who made huge profits but had hitherto paid no tax. Sang Hongyang and others also tried to design fiscal policies that would increase efficiency and cut waste. They reformed the currency and streamlined government procurement procedures to coordinate demand and supply and reduce speculation and transportation costs. The state monopolized the salt and iron industries, employing as managers industrialists who forfeited private profits. These innovations stabilized prices and enabled the state to finance the large anti-Xiongnu war without raising taxes on the common people.[89]

The Han's fiscal policies are called "modernist" by a Western historian.[90] Their architects were denigrated as "promoters of utility" by Han literati who followed Mengzi in opposing utility to righteousness.[91] Of course, no fiscal policy can satisfy everyone. Complicated novel methods such as these inevitably have flawed details, even without counting deficiencies in implementation. In 81 BCE, Zhaodì called a conference "to inquire about the people's grievances and discuss the abolition of state monopoly on salt and iron." With the premier presiding, Sang Hongyang and other high officials met with more than sixty literati from all across the country. The lengthy conference records were liberally edited by the Confucian Huan Kuan as *Discourses on Salt and Iron*.[92] The conference was a hopeful experiment on open policy debate. Unfortunately, it produced no result and was not repeated. A wide range of political and social problems were broached, but Huan Kuan and Ban Gu both noticed that all the discussion came down to the ideological contention of "benevolence and righteousness" versus "power and utility."[93]

"Competing for profit with the people," the opening salvo on current policies from the literati at the conference, was a standard accusatory slogan of Han Confucians.[94] It sounded righteous, but only in its vagueness. One of its victims would be the policy of the ever-normal granary, designed to smooth grain price fluctuation, a major cause of economic insecurity for the masses. The policy called for the government to buy grain at above market prices during bumper crops, store it in local granaries, and sell it at below market prices during poor harvests, thus helping both farmers and consumers. The ever-normal granary proved a great success and would flourish in later dynasties, but it lasted only eleven years in the Han under Xuandì. Moralists ignored its social benefits and convinced Yuandì that the policy was unrighteous because the government thereby competed for profit with the people.[95] The people whose profit they protected were grain speculators and big landlords capable of stocking grain. The common folks whose distress in famines they portrayed in tearful words, their action hurt. Instead of deliberate duplicity, as often charged, I think more culpable was the self-deception of an irresponsible literati culture addicted to feel-good slogans and too lazy to investigate the causes of problems.

The fiscal policies denounced by the literati in the Salt and Iron Conference served the vital purposes of national security and protection of the frontier populace. For the problem of nomadic incursions, which had worried policy makers since the beginning of the Han, the literati offered a breezy doctrine, iterated endlessly to counter all arguments: "Confucius says, 'When aliens are defiant, attract them by cultivating urbane virtue.'" "Yao performed the shield-dance ritual and the barbaric Miao submitted." "Disband the army and promote civility, abandon force and practice virtue, demolish gates and passes, dismantle border fortification and defense, and preach benevolence and righteousness, then invasive threats on the northern frontier will disappear and the Middle Kingdom will be free of war worries." "The *Spring and Autumn Annals* says: The benevolent king is invincible." "The ruler who adopts benevolent policies is indomitable in the world, where is the need for defense expenditure?"[96] It was not the illusion of a few. No sooner did a part of the Xiongnu surrender than calls for complete disarmament became so loud in the government that Yuandì had to order in 33 BCE, "Stop advocating the abandonment of border defense." By the Latter Han, "promotion of urbane virtue and dismissal of military merits" was so successful it encouraged domestic rebels and foreign raids.[97]

The argument fits into a pattern. Perfect order will prevail under sage kings, so where is the need for laws? Harmony flourished in antiquity when people bartered goods, so why should the state waste effort to mint coins?[98] Losing touch with reality and talking with their heads in the clouds with no thought for consequences are recurrent critiques of the literati.

The imagined perfect world of antiquity is the major premise of literati idealism. Instead of respecting history, however, it reveals dogmatic disrespect for historical facts. The most reliable textual sources on the ancient history of China, the *Odes* and *Documents*, depict an ancient world with much oppression and cruelty.[99] When critics refer to a bloody war account of the Zhou's conquest, Mengzi says it must be false, because the Zhou king, being benevolent and thus invincible, must have won without resistance. "To believe wholly in the *Documents* is worse than to have no *Documents*."[100] Exegetes who tear the sentence out of context and rave at its "critical thinking" confuse two traits. Ideas and evidence are often both multifarious and flawed, calling for judgment. The critical mind weighs all evidence to challenge its own ideas. The dogmatic mind dismisses evidence that contradicts its doctrines and cherry-picks agreeable facets to decorate them.[101] Willful blindness to Xiongnu raids bolstered the literati's unshakable faith in the invincibility of benevolent kings.

Disdain for empirical evidence is characteristic of the exegetical mode of thought common to traditions based on scriptural commentary, be the scripture the *Bible*, the *Koran*, the *Analects*, or the *Quotations of Chairman Mao*.[102] To the faithful, the scripture encompasses the complete truth and ultimate good, admitting nothing false or trivial, missing nothing profound or edifying. Doubts and dissents are to be purged. All problems of the world are to be answered by citing chapter and verse. Fortified against all disagreeable facts and reasoning, the faithful gain a self-flattering sense of righteous superiority. Their attacks on alternatives are zealous and relentless. In this vein, the Han literati treated the Confucian Canons as the Holy Bible and made their cases by quotations, even in adjudication and policy debate.[103]

The exegetical mindset nurtures dogmatism rather than deliberation. Policy planning requires respect for facts, rational value judgment, and prudential assessment of expected consequences. Successful political discourse in any regime, be it monarchic or democratic, demands reasonableness: respect for reality and evidence; recognition that one's knowledge is limited and one's ideas are fallible; awareness that the best is often unfeasible and an imperfect solution may be acceptable; appreciation of diverse claims and multiple options; willingness to compromise in making difficult choices for concerted action. To exegetes devoted to the scripture's absolute moral authority, however, compromise is intolerable, because it means yielding to evil. Such was the case in the Salt and Iron Conference. While pragmatic statesmen sought feasible improvements, the literati opted to destroy the existing system and remake the world in one great leap. Their perfect ideal backed by the authority of sages was nonnegotiable. Alternatives to wishing away practical problems required effort and cost, which they condemned with moral zeal.[104] Many chapters of the proceedings end with the sigh of pragmatic ministers. Instead of conceding the debate as the editor implies, the wordlessness indicates the collapse of reasonable discourse. The bombastic literati at the conference promptly received government appointments, but none was known for any merit afterward.[105]

Xuandì was diligent in Legalist supervision of official behavior, having learned from social experience that corrupt officials in collusion with abusive magnates prey on the people. As crown prince, Yuandì deemed the impartial regulations harsh and proposed employing Confucians instead. Xuandì rebuked him: "The Han statecraft should be a blend of the kingly way and the hegemonic way, how can it rely purely on virtue and imitation of the Zhou?"[106]

Yuandì discarded the hegemonic way and relied purely on virtue. From his reign onward, almost all Han premiers were Confucians, and high offices became uncomfortable to anyone lacking literary refinement. The ruling elite of imperial China finally came of age. Like the ruling class of many other regimes, literati-officials derived wealth, polished leisure, and social prestige from their hold on government privileges. Literati clans formed marriage alliances and increased their socioeconomic power. To this was added the moral authority of an exclusive ideology. Elevating Confucius to a "king without crown," literati-officials constituted the core of a status group, which some modern scholars call the cultural or ideological aristocracy of imperial China.[107]

Disciples of the sage occupied the throne and top ministries. However, the kingdom of benevolence did not come. Contrary to rosy promises, administrative quality and social condition both declined. Spurning utilitarian thinking, literati-officials turned their attention from the consequences of policies to the intentions of proponents. Objective analysis gave way to *ad hominem* attacks. Inability to negotiate a workable consensus left policy decisions dependent on personal connections, faction fights, or sheer power struggles. Frequent infighting among literati-officials caused irresolution even in matters of their core competence and concern. Take, for example, the rituals for imperial ancestral temples, which employed some 12,000 musicians and masters of ceremony, four times as many guards, and countless laborers to tend sacrificial animals. Successive factions in power all implemented their own ideal. Changes back and forth caused enormous waste.[108] The gain in ideal and rhetoric failed to compensate for the loss in competence and substance. Ban Gu lamented, "Xuandì's achievements were ruined." Yuandì agreed with contemporary critics: "most officials are not up to their jobs."[109] His reign marked the beginning of the Han's long decline.[110]

Concentration of land and economic inequality intensified. The poor in desperation sold themselves or their children. The swelling ranks of slaves aroused much concern, although their proportion in the population was minuscule compared to that in Roman Italy. Yuandì's loving indulgence of relatives and high officials encouraged abuses, made worse by his ineffective successors. In four reigns that lasted from 48 BCE to 5 CE, controlling power resided with affine families, which were related to the imperial house by marriage. Perhaps this was a logical conclusion of politics dominated by family ethics. Even if the love of relatives excluded in-laws, filial piety sanctified the authority of the empress dowager. Logic is of little concern in the exegetical mindset, however. Literati-officials blamed affine families and saw the mandate of heaven shifting. Calls went up for emperors to emulate the ancient sage kings Yao and Shun, who practiced *chanrang*, abdication in favor of someone worthy. Many supported the eminent litterateur Wang Mang.[111]

In the kaleidoscopic struggle of affine families, the Wang family, anchored on Yuandì's empress and long-living widow, held its own. Becoming regent in 1 BCE, Wang Mang built a granary in the capital for the poor and expanded the imperial academy to more than 10,000 students. His popularity was greatest among the literati, whose ideals he exemplified, but not confined to them; 487,572 persons around the country petitioned to honor him in 5 CE. Four years later, Wang Mang ascended the throne as the first and last emperor of the Xin Dynasty. His rise and fall marked the climax of Han Confucian idealism and exposed its vacuity.[112]

Rebellions from the Liu house were suppressed easily. Almost all officials accepted the new dynasty, as did most literati clans. The mandate of heaven had shifted—until Wang Mang tried to justify the change by enacting many benevolent policies. The sale of slaves was prohibited. An edict excoriated magnates for land encroachment, capped land possession, and ordered families that exceeded the cap to distribute the surplus to poor relatives and neighbors in the manner of well-fields.[113]

The literati got what they ardently advocated, but discovered a consequence that would have been obvious had they paid attention to reality. The first Han literati premiers had bought or encroached on large tracts of land.[114] In their wake, literati clans amassed wealth, bought slaves, infiltrated the upper echelon of society, and grew into powerful local magnates. They themselves were a significant part of the social problem. Their self-interests would be hurt by Wang's implementation of their ideal policy.[115] A true moral choice confronted them.

Their reaction was unambiguous. Literati turned warlords, setting a precedent for history. Extensive research on historical sources reveals that those who took up arms against Wang Mang were mainly literati clans and powerful families. Significantly, before the implementation of Wang's policies on land distribution and slave-sale prohibition, these clans mostly supported him. After the implementation, literati clans and powerful families everywhere rose in armed rebellions. Why? After digging into the evolution of literati clans, the researcher answers, "Although Wang Mang courted literati-officials, he also cracked down on moguls who abused the small people. This conflicted with the interests of the majority of the powerful literati clans."[116]

Talk of interests was beneath political intellectuals, who deftly changed their righteous rhetoric. Instead of denouncing inequality, they condemned usurpation. Under the virtue of fealty, the mandate of heaven snapped back to the Han. Abdication as an alternative to hereditary power succession was discredited forever. Historians discern a great change in Chinese political culture that occurred between the two Han Dynasties. In the Former Han, most debates on government attended to social problems and criticized social policies. Such critique died out in the Latter Han. Henceforth gross economic inequality and the magnates' oppression of the poor became accepted norms.[117]

Wang pushed a spate of reforms to revive the Way of ancient kings. They collapsed. Heaven itself frowned. The Yellow River broke its banks and, in 11 CE, made one of its nine great course changes that earned it the epithet of "China's sorrow." Government relief efforts were woefully inadequate. Hungry refugees and displaced peasants merged into large but loosely organized forces. Rebellious elites and literati clans jumped in to reap advantages. By 23, the Xin Dynasty was over, its fourteen years a brief interlude in the Han.[118]

Writing early in the Latter Han, founded by a rebel, Ban Gu started the mainstream judgment of Wang Mang's reform as the ploy of an arch-hypocrite.[119] Other historians see hypocrisy on the other side. Wang's major measures had been previously proposed by Mengzi and Han literati-officials whom his detractors admired.[120] He failed, partly because he shared the literati's inflexibility and nonchalance regarding reality, and partly because he was betrayed by comrades necessary for successful execution. Demonizing him covers up the debilitating attitude of which he was an exemplar.

Decades earlier, Xuandì had observed, "The pedantic literati, having no understanding of current affairs, are addicted to praising the ancient and condemning the present. They confuse name and substance, mislead the people, and leave all in bewilderment."[121] This common criticism predated him and would last long after. Ban Gu applied it to Wang Mang. Wang's detractors were even worse.[122]

Disregard of evidence, escape into metaphysics, intransigence in negotiation, and refusal to face realistic problems may not matter much for hermits, who at most hurt themselves. However, the literati scrambled for powerful government offices, where policies affected the lives of millions, where unexamined ideals and the indifference to consequential risks can hurt or even kill massively. Intellectual indolence that shirks critical thinking and basks in exegetical dogmatism is among the worse legacies of the imperial ruling elite.[123] Their Way is so vague and scarce in substantive content that it can be replaced by any "-ism" or "-cracy" without changing mindless self-righteousness. Grand slogans and gilded hyperboles intoxicate. Heroic dreams of saving the world gratify the ego. Impractical zealots pushing their ideals detached from reality, however, can be ruinous. Xuandì worried that his doctrinaire crown prince would bring chaos to the world. Wang Mang was not the last to vindicate the worry about irresponsible idealism. Doctrines change; the messianic vanity of ideologues does not.

5.7 The Han's Descent into Anarchy

Guangwudì, who won the post-Xin civil war to found the Latter Han Dynasty, claimed descent from a surplus son of Jingdì, although six generations had eroded royal privileges. He and many associates were wealthy landlords versed in the Confucian Canons, as were many rivals whom he crushed.[124] Learning and moralization did not prevent their fighting from pulverizing the people. Household registration plummeted by two-thirds and for centuries failed to regain the Former Han level.[125]

Guangwudì repealed many pedantic edicts of Wang Mang with fanfare. On socially beneficial issues, he continued Wang's policies halfheartedly. The civil war eased his tasks by creating room for reconstruction. Some lands laid waste by chaotic violence were distributed to the poor or rented to the needy. Many slaves were freed and debt bondages annulled. Further progress stalled, however. The social force that resisted Wang's agrarian reforms had not diminished but grown. Landlords capitalized on their merit in founding the new dynasty and forced Guangwudì to abandon a resurvey of farmland for fair tax assessment.[126] Despite economic progress, taxable land in the Latter Han never exceeded 90 percent of that registered at the end of the Former Han. Graced by imperial benevolence, the elites evaded taxes and grew richer.[127] Inequality spiraled. In the contests between the state and landed wealth and between rhetorical ideal and self-interest, the second of each pair won.

Farsightedness seemed not to be Guangwudì's strength. Intending to secure his dynasty, he transferred much authority from the bureaucracy to the palace, but it created havoc when his weak progeny failed to control the imperial household. Foreign defense was another example. His abolition of military training to cut expenditures ruined the fighting capacity of the militia. Provincial governors and local magnates who hired volunteer soldiers eventually developed into warlords who tore apart the empire. Modern historians see in his proclivity to shirk immediate efforts the roots of major problems that blighted the Latter Han and beyond.[128]

Nevertheless, as a founding emperor, Guangwudì was more utilitarian than his successors, as illustrated in the following episode. A princess's servant killed in broad daylight. Dong Xuan, prefect of the capital, had no authority to enter royal residences. So he waited for the killer to come outside in order to drive the princess, arrested him, tried him, and executed him on the spot. Summoned before Guangwudì upon the princess's complaint, the prefect preferred death to apologizing for doing the duty of his office. To the emperor's fulmination he retorted, "On what would your majesty rule the world if you indulge your servant in killing decent people?" Guangwudì released him with a reward and a head broken by attempted suicide. The disappointed princess asked, "When a commoner, you sheltered fugitives and officials dared not approach your door. Now you are the son of heaven, how come you cannot bend a puny officer?" The emperor laughed, "That is the difference between a commoner and the son of heaven."[129] Guangwudì and his followers had been local magnates whose mentality the princess expressed best. As emperor, he acquired new interests, which caused him to put Legalist principles above the love of relatives. Dong Xuan made bigwigs tremble and died penniless. His consignment to the derogatory category of "brutal official" in the *Book of Latter Han* indicates the prevalent attitude of literati-officials. That attitude would win out when Zhangdì emulated Yuandì's rule of pure virtue and resumed indulging the ruling elite.

Guangwudì promoted urbane virtue as a policy. His successors Mingdì and Zhangdì were Confucian scholars.[130] The social criticism of the Former Han gave way to a century of exegetical indoctrination. Since Yuandì, mastery of one of the Five Canons gained tax exemption. Latter Han emperors showered more gold on canonical learning.[131] The imperial academy crested at more than 30,000 adult students; many stayed for years, establishing close ties with officials. In addition, masters of the Canons recruited disciples, each in the thousands. Wealthy literati clans patronized students, inculcated the duty of reciprocity, and engaged in high politics.[132]

The literati ethos of Latter Han was outstanding, rivaled only by that of the Song Dynasty, when neo-Confucianism emerged. Guangwudì extolled the integrity of officials who had refused to serve Wang Mang and rewarded them with high offices, thus training officers to devote themselves to the imperial family instead of to the state or the common good. Seeking personal connections became the overriding concern of officials. Ministers who appointed junior officers regarded this action as a personal favor for which the appointees were morally obligated to reciprocate. Many accrued tremendous personal power by accumulating protégés and former protégés, which enabled them to turn warlords later.[133] The ethics of personal ties in government had become a deep-rooted source of corruption, which continues to hurt today.[134]

State sponsorship and private patronage produced far more literati than the government could employ. Competition for office was fierce, but administrative quality did not improve, for the chief criterion of placement shifted from job competence to personal fame. After a century of pampering, the literati were called to contribute ideas for addressing the nascent Qiang uprising. Emperor Andì was disappointed: "The responses were all trite and superficial words without insight and freshness."[135] Official abuse and ineptitude caused the rebellion to spread and recur. In six decades, it left innumerable people dead, homes destroyed, and the Han Dynasty exhausted. The cultural aristocrats in the capital were indifferent. They were too busy building connections in *qinyi* or pure evaluation, by which they threw perfume on friends and mud on rivals.[136]

The propensity for factions in government, which had picked up under Yuandì, became ponderous in the Latter Han. Wealthy clans that helped found the dynasty competed for imperial influence. The personality evaluation movement fanned factiousness. Besides bickering among themselves, literati-officials who controlled the bureaucracy struggled for power with the inner court, especially eunuchs, who came to dominance after helping young Huandì consolidate power in 159.[137] Unlike the great eunuchs of the Later Roman Empire who wielded power individually, eunuchs of the Latter Han formed a clique around the emperor, gaining power from proximity to him.

Some eunuchs were undoubtedly corrupt, but others were upright and creative. Cai Lun, for example, improved the technology of paper making so much he was traditionally credited with inventing paper.[138] Coming from downtrodden families, eunuchs might have injected some diversity into the bookish monoculture. Instead, they earned the spleen of cultural aristocrats, who loathed the "foul" mutilated creatures who competed for available jobs and diverted emperors away from the path of "purity." Anti-eunuch movements precipitated three nasty faction fights in the successive reigns of Huandì, Lingdì, and Shaodì. Both sides abused power and employed illegal violence, increasingly bloody. The emperor sided with literati-officials when they prosecuted eunuchs legally. When they killed eunuch associates indiscriminately, Huandì and Lingdì listened to eunuchs and proscribed partisans. More than 100 partisans were killed and 1,000 imprisoned or banished, many for sheltering fugitives. They gained huge sympathy. The banished became such celebrities that a jealous officer petitioned to join the proscription list.[139] Literati-officials had their revenge under Shaodì. All eunuchs and many men unlucky enough to lack facial hair were massacred, totaling more than 2,000.[140]

The mainstream Chinese historiography blames the decline of the Han on eunuchs, the "force of darkness," and applauds as heroic martyrs anti-eunuch partisans who vowed to "purify the world."[141] However, maverick historians who analyzed the composition of proscribed partisans present another picture: "This heterogeneous lot defied a single judgment. They acted impulsively, often overstepping the bounds, and might not be good administrators if appointed to office. Mutual eulogy for gaining influence is not laudable. Contemporary literati rallied to them for fame; in the Han's nomination system, a short cut to office was to form cliques to advertise celebrity."[142]

Many literati were upright and many partisans exhibited great personal heroism. However, their movement generally confused the war on eunuchs with the war on corruption. Corruption suffused the government. Many literati-officials were deep into it too. When a master in the Canons was convicted of gross venality, more than 1,000 literati gathered before the palace to clamor for his release.[143] When two provincial governors abused the law to massacre eunuch affiliates not convicted of crime, the literati applauded them as heroes against corruption.[144] The double standard revealed that corruption was secondary to elimination of enemies in a faction fight.[145]

After the accession of the child emperor Shaodì in 189, many anti-eunuch partisans gathered around the new regent He Jin and their long-time collaborator, the renowned litterateur Yuan Shao. Yuan persuaded He to summon the general Dong Zhuo, ignoring warnings of insubordination of frontier troops in the capital. All eunuchs perished in a bloodbath. Literati-officials realized their ideal of purifying the world. The masses once again suffered for irresponsible idealism. The army summoned burned the capital city, Luoyang, and did not stop at that. Dong deposed Shaodì and erected the puppet Xiandì. Yuan and regional officials allied to fight Dong, then turned on each other. The Han Dynasty lingered for three more decades, but only in name. The warlords dismembering the state and devastating the people were not eunuchs but mostly famed literati-officials.[146]

5.8 Colored Glasses of Historiography

Without conquests and big events, histories of empires tend to morph into serial biographies of emperors. A corollary of focusing on personal behavior instead of institutional and social conditions was the propensity of ancient historians, both Roman and Chinese, to explain events in moral terms. Vice was a favorite explanation for the demise of the Roman Republic and Empire, the Qin and Han Dynasties. On a smaller scale, historians tended to explain the working of a policy by the personality of its framer, for example attributing a tax policy to the emperor's liberality or avarice.[147] Tacitus treated the degeneration of Tiberius's reign as an unveiling of hypocrisy; Ban Gu treated Wang Mang's reign similarly.

Even in politics, a narrow focus on the emperor misses larger factors. To rule instead of merely to reign, an emperor had to work and perhaps struggle with his governing circle, which had its own dispositions. Tiberius was grim and rancorous, Wang arrogant and inclement, but these traits were not exceptional among powerful men. The warped personality with which each ended his life resulted not only from the corruption of power. Also important was reaction to his corrupt environment, the ring of aristocrats and officials full of intrigue, self-interest, and self-righteousness, exerting psychological pressure if not physical threat. Han literati regarded regulation of officials as malevolence. The major problem for an early Roman emperor was his relation with senators: as a modern historian remarks, "Whatever the acts and policy of a ruler at the outset, each reign went wrong soon or late. It is not easy to apportion the blame."[148] It is tempting to blame everything on the despot, who is safely dead. More illuminative of history is the politics of a dissolute ruling circle, where plots and counterplots, insecurity and preemptive strikes constitute a vicious spiral into calamity. Such political cultures, if not long-lived, can recur.

Tradition censures the last emperors of the Former Han Dynasty before Wang Mang's usurpation in 9 CE. Intrigues and sexual licentiousness corrupted the court, but how did the empire fare? The literati painted grim pictures, which page after page Marxist historians collated with the conclusion, "the oppressed masses struggled on the edge of hunger and death, and history entered a dark period."[149] However, Ban Gu chose the 2 CE census as the sample of political geography in the *Book of Han*, adding, "The Han is at peak prosperity."[150] The cold statistics undoubtedly left out numerous instances of human suffering. Social and administrative deterioration did occur. Nevertheless, household registration was a sensitive measure of order and stability. A far darker period would come when desperate people fled their homes, seeking food or safety. The 65 percent drop in census figures half a century later indicates the significance of the big picture.[151] Ban Biao, a historian who lived through the post-Wang civil war, explained why similar bedlam spared the Former Han during its last decades under bad emperors: "The danger started from the top, and the damages did not penetrate into the populace below."[152]

Such phenomena were also pronounced under Tiberius and Domitian. Tradition condemns them for ending in reigns of terror that decimated great aristocratic families. From provincial perspectives, however, a different assessment obtained. Both rulers managed the Empire well, choosing their governors carefully, repressing abuses, and protecting the subject population.[153] The provinces became increasingly prosperous under Tiberius, and many of Domitian's policies continued into the golden reign of Trajan. The posthumous condemnation of Domitian, enthusiastically pursued by senators, excited only tepid responses from the provinces.[154] The atrocities of Tiberius and Domitian apparently fell mainly on the imperial entourage and the political circle closest to it, sparing most of the populace. Tacitus, who lived through the reign of Domitian and condemned Tiberius in the *Annals*, observed elsewhere, "the tyrant only oppresses his nearest neighbours."[155] That neighborhood was the home of traditional historians, including Tacitus and Ban Gu. Had it put colored glasses on historiography?

Without excusing bad emperors, a historian can ask what the badness entailed. Fascinating narratives can lead us to mistake politics for policy, the imperial court for the empire, personality for institution. Court politics and state policies are correlated, but correlation is not deterministic causation. Under favorable conditions, a government with a convulsed top can persist for a while in executing set policies, operating on inertia or the automatic pilot of its strong institutions. If lucky, it can get through the turbulence with little damage to the population, as in the dynastic crises of the early Han or early Roman Empire. When institutions weaken, however, things are different. Without capable leadership, a government would fail to respond to natural disaster, foreign invasion, or other external shocks. We will see it happen in the decline and fall of empires.

If ugly politics does not necessarily precipitate disastrous policies, does a cozy court necessarily preside over a happy populace? Is it possible that some good emperors got their reputation from their indulgent politics, the effects of which had limited range? Were the common people better off under the flattered emperors of early Latter Han than the benighted emperors of late Former Han? Was the apparent contentment an impression created by a changed literati fashion, which had turned from social criticism to adulation of state patronage of literary culture?

The golden age from Trajan to Marcus Aurelius was better served by panegyrics than historical accounts. Panegyrists, literati whose job was to praise those in power, flourished. In contrast, Tacitus and Suetonius did not choose to write about the reigns they professed to admire, nor did Plutarch add to his biographies. Poetry and other literary creativity also shriveled, heedless of blooming wealth. Even the rosiest panegyric appeared stultified and futureless.[156] Is happiness an image seen through eulogies without narrative?

Perhaps the most often quoted assessment is that of a leading eighteenth-century British historian: "If a man were called to fix the period in the history of the world, during which the condition of the human race was most happy and prosperous, he would, without hesitation, name that which elapsed from the death of Domitian to the accession of Commodus." The same historian estimates the Empire's slaves to outnumber its free population.[157] What is the humanity of a human race that nominates as its happiest a period when it enslaves a large portion of its own?

The second-century physician Galen described various kinds of ulcers that Roman country folks got in early summers from eating grass and twigs, because the city dwellers left them insufficient grain to last until the next crop. He was conducting a scientific study on foods.[158] A modern historian of the Antonine age remarks, "Many of the people in the rural areas lived a miserable life of continual or sporadic destitution and starvation, in contrast to many of the 'city-dwellers.' . . .

It is strange that so little is heard about this."[159] Only recently has the question of poverty and destitution in the Empire attracted scholarly attention.[160] Traditional Chinese elites were shepherds closer to the flock. They may be condescending and lethargic on practical solutions, but they protested for the people.

Historical writing invariably reflects the historian's own culture. The most important histories of the early Roman Empire are Tacitus's *Annals* for the Julio-Claudians and *Histories* for the subsequent civil war and the Flavian Dynasty. Cassius Dio's *Histories* fills in the reign of Augustus and much more. Tacitus and Dio were senators of consular rank, as was the younger Pliny, whose letters and panegyric provide much information on the early Antonine period. Suetonius, who wrote biographies of the first twelve Roman emperors, was an equestrian in charge of imperial correspondence under Hadrian. To these members of the upper class, perhaps the foremost quality of an emperor was his respect for and treatment of senatorial aristocrats.[161]

Chinese historians were elites but of lower ranks. The grand annalist, an office "responsible for recording all actions of the ruler, to keep them careful in words and deeds," was common in many pre-imperial states. The post was dangerous when reality was ugly. A Qi minister who murdered his lord in 548 BCE also killed the grand annalist who insisted on recording the regicide. The annalist's two brothers inherited the office successively and refused to cover up the truth. The minister killed them both but relented when the youngest brother proved equally stubborn. Had he kept on killing, he would not have prevailed. The junior annalist was already en route to the office.[162]

The tradition had degenerated in imperial times, but not completely. The office of the grand historian continued, but only with the lowest grade allowed to attend court. As grand historian, Sima Qian fulfilled his father Sima Tan's vision in the *Records of the Historian*, which covers Chinese history from its mythical beginning to his own time in the reign of Wudì. He was undeterred when, seven years into the project, he was found guilty of vouching for a general who surrendered to the Xiongnu and castrated because he could not afford the fine for commutation. Ban Gu also continued the aspiration of his father Ban Biao. He embarked on a history of the Former Han Dynasty but was arrested by the local governor for making a private enterprise of state history. His younger brother Ban Chao saved him and got him a job by appealing to the emperor. The Ban family had produced middling officers for three generations, but it was not rich. After they moved to the capital for Ban Gu's new job as an imperial librarian, Ban Chao toiled as a hired scribe to support their mother before throwing down the ink brush to join the army. Twenty years later, indiscreet politics landed Ban Gu in prison, where he died in 92, five years before Ban Chao, as protector general of the Western Territory, dispatched a deputy in quest of the Roman Empire. His lifetime work *Book of Han* was completed by his sister Ban Zhao, independently renowned for her literary accomplishments.[163] Another historian, Fan Ye, author of the *Book of Latter Han*, was from a great family. Like Chen Shou, author of *Records of the Three Kingdoms*, he drew on writings of other historians and official materials, but he did not receive an official post for historical writing. The initiatives of these historians developed into a tradition. Their books became the most cherished of twenty-six *Standard Histories*.[164]

Major Roman historians tended to be aristocrats working at their own leisure; their Chinese counterparts, junior officers working with state sponsorship. It would be interesting to assess their relative independence of judgment and freedom of expression by comparing their critiques, not of condemned reigns such as those of Tiberius or the Qin, but of sanctified or current reigns such as those of Augustus or the Han.

Notes

1. Fukuyama 1992.
2. Jing 2002: 360. Chang 2007: 2:169–171. Tian and An 2008: 366.
3. Starr 1982: 117. Needham et al 1971: 26–29. Bodde 1986: 61.
4. Hopkins 1978b: 42–47. Wells 1992: 138–139. Gao 1998: 196–223. Loewe 2005a: 158–162.
5. Hopkins 1983b: 104. Greene 1986: 40.
6. Wells 1992: 194–195. Hopkins 1978b: 38.
7. Benn 2002: 46. Nishijima 1986: 574–575.
8. Cameron 1993: 42–43, 62–63. Nishijima 1986: 574.
9. *Hanshu* 1b: 58–9; 43: 2119–2121.
10. Augustus 34. Syme 1939: 299–301.
11. Millar 2002a: 294.
12. Virgil, *Aeneid*, 1.282.
13. Wells 1992: 30. Rostovtzeff 1960: 162–163. Grant 1978: 202.
14. Syme 1939: 311, 323–324. Millar 2002a: 270.
15. Dio Cassius 53.17.
16. Wells 1992: 50–52. Syme 1939: 340, 353, 414. Gruen 2005.
17. Tacitus, *Annals*, 1.1.
18. Gibbon 1994: 93.
19. Syme 1939: 323, 311–312. Gruen 2005: 33–35.
20. Dio Cassius 54.1.
21. Lewis and Reinhold 1990: 1:588–590.
22. Ovid, quoted in Gruen 2005: 34.
23. Jones, A. 1964: 6. Wells 1992: 107. Raaflaub and Samons 1990.
24. Le Bohec 1989: 20–21. Keppie 1984: 153–154.
25. Gibbon 1994: 128–129.
26. Wells 1992: 59–60. Rostovtzeff 1960: 194–198. Syme 1939: 426, 486–487; 1959: 427, 432.
27. Wells 1992: 64–67. Syme 1939: 507.
28. Syme 1958: 427.
29. Wells 1992: 98–99. Seager 1972.

30. Suetonius, Gaius (Caligula), 13–14.
31. Scullard 1976: 292–297.
32. Suetonius, Claudius, 10. Scullard 1976: 298–314. Wells 1992: 110–116.
33. Champlin 2003: 237.
34. Tacitus, *Annals*, 15.39. Champlin 2003. Scullard 1976: 315–329.
35. Keppie 1984: 149. Syme 1939: 352–353.
36. Tacitus, *Histories*, 1.5.
37. Mattern 1999: 205–206. Isaac 1992: 2–3, 51, 372–377. Gibbon 1994: Ch. 3: 97–98.
38. Tacitus, *Histories*, 4.3. Wellesley 1975.
39. Lewis and Reinhold 1990: 2:11–13. Wells 1992: 158–159. Wellesley 1975: 216–217.
40. Millar 1981: 3.
41. Tacitus, *Histories*, 1.4.
42. Grant 1994: 156. Starr 1982: 59–60. Lintott 1981: 125.
43. Wells 1992: 157–165.
44. Wells 1992: 167.
45. Suetonius, Domitian, 8. Jones, B. 1979: 4–7. Alston 1998: 178–190.
46. Wells 1992: 167–168. Alston 1998: 191–196.
47. Bennett 1997: 208.
48. Longden 1954: 203–204, 221. Stockton 1991: 157. Wells 1992: 173–174. Alston 1998: 198–200.
49. Wells 1992: 202–203, 207–208.
50. Mattern 1999: 100, 120, 191–194.
51. Syme 1939: 304.
52. Millar 1993: 105; 2004: 26, 175–179. Southern 2001: 250–253, 282.
53. Fronto, quoted in Bennett 1997: 102–103.
54. Birley 1987: 160.
55. Birley 1987: 116–117, 184–189, 199.
56. Potter 2004: 85–114. Southern 2001: 20–37.
57. Dio Cassius 74.2.5. Potter 2004: 99, 102–103, 138. Wells 1992: 258–259, 265–266.
58. Suetonius, Vespasian, 16. Bennett 1997: 126.
59. Potter 2004: 106, 112–113. Jones, A. 1964: 25.
60. Southern 2001: 36. Mattern 1999: 96–97.
61. Southern 2001: 63–65, 97–102, 115–119.
62. Southern 2001: Ch. 3.
63. Cameron 1993: 32–42.
64. Southern 2001: 177. Mitchell 2007: 62–70.
65. Mitchell 2007: 70–79.
66. Jones, A. 1964: 139–142.
67. *Shiji* 92: 2621, 2626.
68. *Shiji* 92: 2627.
69. Loewe 1986b: 123–126.
70. *Shiji* 6: 283–284. *Hanshu* 48: 2239; 35: 1906. Chang 2007: 70–71.
71. Loewe 1986b: 139–144.
72. *Shiji* 54: 2031.
73. *Hanshu* 88: 3592; 24a: 1135. Loewe 1986b:140–150. Qian 1957: 41–42, 59–61.

74. *Shiji* 30: 1418–1420.
75. Chang 2007: 142–144. Hsu 1980: 22–23.
76. Chang 2007: 71–72, 78–88. Loewe 1986b: 156–157.
77. Loewe 1986b: 176–178.
78. Loewe 1986b: 179–187. Zhang X. 2007: 64–71.
79. *Hanshu* 7: 233. Loewe 1986b: 178–190. Yü 1986: 391–400.
80. *Shiji* 112: 2950; 121: 3123. *Hanshu* 84: 3421; 89: 3623; 56: 2504, 2510.
81. Shryock 1966: 34, 45, 70–72. Qian 1957: 73–74. Lü 2005b: 641–659.
82. *Hanshu* 56: 2524.
83. Hsiao 1979: 21, 467–468. Yan 1996: 283, 437.
84. *Hanshu* 48: 2244; 56: 2510. Liu, S-H. 1998: 9, 11.
85. Bodde 1981: 183.
86. *Shiji* 23: 1160; 121: 3117. *Hanshu* 88: 3592.
87. *Hanshu* 58: 2633–2634; 6: 197.
88. See Chapter 7.
89. *Hanshu* 24b: 3261. Chang 2007: 71–88.
90. Loewe 1986b: 104–106.
91. See Section 2.9.
92. Loewe 1986b: 187–190.
93. *Yantielun* 60. *Hanshu* 66: 2886, 2903.
94. *Yantielun* 1. *Hanshu* 56: 2520–2521.
95. *Hanshu* 24a: 1141–1142.
96. *Yantielun* 1, 42, 47, 49.
97. *Hanshu* 94b: 3805. *Houhanshu* 60a: 1954.
98. *Yantielun* 3, 4, 56.
99. Hsiao 1979: 116.
100. *Mengzi* 7.49.
101. Nivison 1996, 283–284.
102. Henderson 1991: 89–129.
103. Bell 2008: 107–127. *Ershiershi* 2: 26. Qian 1957: 187–188.
104. Hsiao 1979: 467.
105. *Yantielun* 42, 60.
106. *Hanshu* 9: 277.
107. Loewe 1986a: 292–297. Yan 1996: 494. Qian 1957: 74–76. Yü 2003: 195–198.
108. *Hanshu* 73: 3115–3130.
109. *Hanshu* 71: 3043; 9: 288, 299.
110. Nishijima 1986: 557–559. Qian 1957: 187–192.
111. Chen 1986: 772–773.
112. Bielenstein 1986b: 224–230. Chen 1986: 773.
113. Bielenstein 1986b: 232.
114. *Hanshu* 88: 3596, 3620; 81: 3346, 3349.
115. Yan 1996: 494. Qian 1957: 74–76. Yü 2003: 195–201.
116. Yü 2003: 202, 204.
117. Lü 2005b: 174. Qian 1957: 294.
118. Bielenstein 1986b: 232–250. Lewis 2007: 23–24.
119. *Hanshu* 99c: 4194.
120. Bielenstein 1986b: 223, 232–233, 239. Yan 1996: 388.
121. *Hanshu* 9: 277.

122. *Hanshu* 24a: 1143. Waldron 1990: 172–174. Schirokauer and Hymes 1993: 27–28, 43–44.

123. Pye 1985: 42. Fairbank 1987: 92, 152. Schwartz 1996: 50–51, 59. Dunstan 2004: 329.

124. *Houhanshu* 1a: 21; 35: 1125.

125. See Table 1 in Chapter 8.

126. Hsu 1980: 55, 210–211. Ch'ü 1972: 203–204.

127. Nishijima 1986: 558–559, 597. Ebrey 1986: 615–625.

128. Bielenstein 1986b: 268. Lewis 2007: 259–262.

129. *Houhanshu* 77: 2489–2490.

130. *Houhanshu* 1b: 69; 17: 666.

131. *Hanshu* 88, 3594, 3620; 73: 3107; 81: 3346, 3349.

132. *Houhanshu* 79a: 2545–2546. Lewis 2009: 28–31.

133. Ebrey 1983: 535–541. De Crespigny 1980: 52–53. Qian 1940: 175, 216–218.

134. Hao and Johnston 2002: 594–595. Harris 2003: 66–67.

135. *Houhanshu* 5: 210.

136. De Crespigny 2009: 106.

137. Bielenstein 1986b: 274–278, 287–290. Ch'ü 1972: 99–100.

138. *Houhanshu* 78: 2513.

139. *Ershiershi* 5. Yü 2000: 498–499.

140. Crespigny 1980: 45–51. Beck 1986: 324, 327–330.

141. Tian and An 2008: 405–409. Yü 2003: 259.

142. Lü 2005b: 291. See also Crespigny 1980: 57. Beck 1986: 367.

143. *Hanshu* 83: 3389. *Houhanshu* 79a: 2556.

144. *Houhanshu* 62, 2050; 67: 2212, 2214.

145. Crespigny 1980: 47–49, 51. Chen 1975: 23, 27.

146. Beck 1986: 334–336. Liu C. 2006: 6–7.

147. Bodde 1986: 85–86. Wiedemann 2000: 524–525. Lendon 1997: 16–17. Syme 1958: 254, 421.

148. Syme 1958: 440.

149. Lin 2003: 571–580.

150. *Hanshu* 24a: 1143, 28: 1640.

151. *Hanshu* 28b: 1640. *Houhanshu*, Zhi 23: 3533.

152. *Houhanshu* 40: 1323.

153. Syme 1958: 422, 439.

154. Wells 1992: 101–102, 167, 183. Jones, B. 1979: 4, 87.

155. Tacitus, *Histories*, 4.74.

156. Schiavone 2000: 13.

157. Gibbon 1994: 103, 69.

158. Galen, quoted in Grant 1994: 151. MacMullen 1974: 33–37. Brunt 1961: 221, 223.

159. Grant 1994: 151.

160. Harris 2011: Ch. 2.

161. Rutledge 2001: 177–178. Ste. Croix 1981: 381–382.

162. *Hanshu* 30: 1715. *Zuozhuan*, Xiang 25, Wen 2. Bodde 1981: 179.

163. *Houhanshu* 84: 2784–2792.

164. Wilkinson 1998: 490–497.

CHAPTER 6

ARTS OF GOVERNMENT

6.1 Imperial Characters

High officers meritorious for founding the Former Han Dynasty gathered to brag, drink, and, when high-spirited, shout and bang their drawn swords on pillars. Annoyed by his former comrades, Gaodì appointed Confucians to design protocols. Watching hundreds of officers perform a perfect ceremony in 200 BCE, he remarked, "Now I know the dignity of being emperor."[1]

Augustus often wore a breastplate beneath his toga, even when attending the Senate, but believed it provided only slight protection. In 18 BCE, when he decided to downsize the Senate, he added a sword to his steel corselet, surrounded himself by burly friends, and allowed senators to approach only singly and after a thorough frisk.[2]

An emperor tamed his elite subordinates, although elites of different kinds, the Chinese uncouth, the Romans aristocratic. How much the characters of the ruling elite changed was revealed in the new victors of civil wars about two centuries later.

Guangwudì and the generals who helped him found the Latter Han Dynasty in 25 CE were mostly wealthy landlords who discussed Confucian Canons when dismounted.[3] To his crown prince's questions on strategy, the emperor quoted Confucius: "Military affairs I have not studied."[4]

Septimius Severus, the emperor newly acclaimed by the troops in 139 CE, addressed the Senate surrounded by armed guards. At his deathbed, he advised his sons whom he made joint heirs, "Get along, make the soldiers rich, and don't give a damn for anyone else."[5]

A contrast between the Dragon and the Eagle is apparent. The emperor was at the zenith of his power, having built up the indoctrination or war machinery and concentrated power in his hands. However, his lopsided civil or martial bias was ominous. Fast-forward another two centuries, and dusk closed on him.

Xiandì abdicated in 220. Romulus Augustulus was deposed in 476. Amid the commotion of crumbling empires, the formal ends of the Han Dynasty and the Western Roman Empire generated hardly a ripple in history. Instead of perishing in a palace fire or on the executioner's block, both ex-emperors were allowed to live out their lives as privileged lords. They had long been puppets, so their continued existence posed no threat to the new rulers.[6]

Hopefully the preceding snapshots will remind the reader that government institutions and power distributions are always evolving, although dynamics tend to be crowded out in cross-sectional comparative analyses, the tasks of this chapter.

The tempora overlapping Qin-Han Dynasty and Roman Empire were comparable in population and territorial size. An absolute monarchy presided over each and divided its vast realm into provinces ruled directly through centrally appointed governors. The two governments were similar in many ways, but characteristic differences were also salient.

Military organization was a pronounced difference between the Roman and Qin-Han style of imperial power. Divergence began with demobilization. After defeating Antony, Augustus discharged about half of the armies on both sides. Loyal legionaries he pensioned off or settled in colonies. The soldiers he retained he organized into twenty-eight legions plus a comparable force of auxiliaries, totaling about 300,000 troops. This army dwarfed the ten to fourteen legions with which the Republic conquered an empire; Caesar had opened his Gallic campaign with six legions and won the climactic siege of Alesia with 30,000 to 40,000 legionaries plus auxiliaries.[7] Augustus faced no foreign threat but needed an army to secure his own monarchical power. Breaking with Republican tradition, the new imperial army comprised professional soldiers serving sixteen years or more, all having sworn loyalty to the emperor's person and family. A large peacetime standing army organized as a strike force was a peculiarity of the Roman Empire. Besides foreign exploits, it played increasingly significant roles in domestic politics, culminating as a maker of emperors.[8]

The Han also maintained a standing army core in peacetime, but it numbered only in the thousands, except during the decades of imperial expansion that required skilled cavalry to combat nomads. Four months after becoming emperor, Gaodì sent most of his soldiers home with the promise of tax exemption for six years. Following Qin, the main Han army comprised rotating conscripts called up for yearlong tours as needed. Also, the early Han promoted small peasantry by allotting standard plots to commoners, as recorded in excavated legal documents. Small peasants constituted the army reserve in the Former Han.[9] Unlike a standing army, an army reserve engages in normal production and consumes little when not called up for war. The disparate army organizations are suggestive of two imperial grand strategies discussed in the following chapter.

Besides the army, both empires had imperial guards. The Roman Praetorian Guard became an emperor maker before the army surpassed it in this role. The Han also had security forces near the capital. One, the North Unit, was active in the first dynastic crisis but was disbanded one year after the accession of Wendì, whom it helped enthrone.[10] In China, armed forces were far less influential in imperial succession than dowager empresses backed by the ideology of filial piety.

The type of regime was a major decision confronting founding rulers. The Romans were familiar with two political models. The Republic, although dysfunctional, still commanded nostalgia among aristocrats. Alexander's empire was admirable, but one-man rule so antagonized aristocratic collective rule that Caesar grafted it onto the Roman polity only by military force. Wary of Caesar's fate, Augustus held the army tight and deftly hid the barb of monarchy behind a republican facade. Residual resistance was ground down by the Julio-Claudian emperors. One-man rule was naturalized by the time of the Antonines.

The Han also had two models of government: Qin's centralized bureaucracy promoted by Legalists and Zhou's feudalistic aristocracy dear to Confucians. Wary of Qin's collapse, Gaodì enfeoffed subordinate kings to rule a major part of the realm. The atavistic arrangement bred instability. The kings rebelled and were suppressed. By Wudì's reign, a centralized monarchy again ruled the whole empire directly. This time it lasted and won the allegiance of Confucian literati.

The functionally organized administrative structure designed by Legalists also lasted. The Roman Empire developed its bureaucratic apparatus only slowly, and its efficiency seemed to lag behind that of the Han. At their respective high noon, each empire employed about 240 high officials, from top magistrates to provincial governors. Roman officers were organized along aristocratic lines; Chinese officers, bureaucratic. Roman aristocrats had fewer chores than Chinese bureaucrats, who were also expected to lead in education and economic development. Yet their compensation was almost ten times higher. This, together with the large standing army, partly explained substantially heavier Roman taxation.

Below the emperor were the political elite who participated in making decisions and executed policies. Unlike the ruling circle of many monarchies dominated by a handful of great hereditary lords, those of the Roman and

Han Empires were relatively fluid and porous. The positions of Han literati-officials were not hereditary. Few houses in the Roman senatorial aristocracy entrenched and grew. New men continuously replenished the ruling circle in both empires, creaming off leaders from society to reinvigorate the top. Deft circulation of elites was similarly crucial to the success of imperial Rome and China. The big difference lay in the criterion of recruitment: wealth for Rome and ideology for China. The disparate mentality and socioeconomic composition of the two ruling elites colored the characteristics of the Eagle and the Dragon.

6.2 The Ruler and the Ruled

The Chinese had no notion of democracy, which the Greco-Roman world knew but had forsaken. Even as Roman *imperators* called themselves *princeps* or first citizen, the Greeks realistically translated *imperator* as *autocrator*, the ruler answerable to none.[11] The corresponding Chinese title is *huangdì*.[12] The Roman Empire was more plutocratic and militaristic, the Chinese more dynastic and bureaucratic, but the emperor of each was the autocrat on whom all authority of the vast realm devolved. Both empires were absolute monarchies.

A Western historian writes, "The Principate, though absolute, was not arbitrary. It derived from consent and delegation; it was founded upon the laws. This was something different from the monarchies of the East. The Romans had not sunk as low as that."[13] What was different besides stereotyping? The law enjoyed high esteem not only in Rome. Legalist doctrines prevailed in the Qin and early Han dynasties. Regrettably, they declined with the rise of the Confucian ruling elite, who relegated the law to mere punishment. Respect for the law was indeed an outstanding Roman virtue, as we see in section 6.9. To say the Roman monarchy was founded on the law, however, one must first ensure that the requisite laws existed.

Substantive laws roughly fall into three classes. *Public* laws include penal laws, by which the state defines as crime certain behaviors, such as robbery, that warrant its efforts of prevention and punishment; and administrative laws, by which the state regulates its officers and constrains conduct such as extortion. *Private* or *civil* laws address the claims and duties that individuals have toward each other—such as marriage, ownership of property, sale of slaves, and compensation for injury. *Constitutional* laws set out the principles underlying the structure and limits of the state's authority—such as the division of power and the process of legislation.

"The rule of law" means different things in different contexts. In everyday life, it may simply mean law and order, the success of public law enforcement in deterring crime and civil law adjudication in resolving disputes. Concerning political structure, the rule *of* law implies constitutionalism and limited government. It prevails in a state equipped with constitutional laws delimiting sovereign authority and independent judiciary institutions strong enough to enforce these laws on wielders of power. A state that falls short of the rule *of* law can still be ruled *by* law or rule *according to* law, if the rulers voluntarily abide by existing laws.[14]

Penal laws were harsh and punishments cruel in both empires. The ideal of equality under the law also eroded in both. The Han Dynasty gradually codified most social stratifications fundamental to Confucian ethics. The circle enjoying legal privileges expanded from royalty and officials to almost the whole stratum of literati and wealthy landlords.[15] Already in Republican Rome, upper-class convicts under the death sentence were routinely allowed to escape into exile, while poor convicts were immediately executed. Under the Empire, laws defined a person's status. The lower class was susceptible to torture; the upper class was not.[16]

In civil law, the crown jewel of their jurisprudence, the Romans far outshone the Chinese, who had a few laws but preferred reconciliation or arbitration to litigation. However, the difference weighs little for the issue at hand. Crucial to the foundation of states are constitutional laws. These were undeveloped for both the Roman and Chinese Empires.[17]

No law functioned to delimit the authority of the Roman emperor. According to one modern scholar, the "entire period does not present a single instance where the emperor's right or power to take any particular action was specifically tested or challenged." If he pleased, an emperor might refer matters to the Senate, just as the First Emperor of China referred matters to court debate. However, "it is never implied that their actions or pronouncements would lack validity unless confirmed by the senate."[18]

"What has pleased the emperor has the force of law." This assertion of the Roman jurist Ulpian applied equally to imperial China, where Minister of Fairness Du Zhou said, "What the earlier rulers decided became statutes. What the later rulers decided became laws."[19] Furthermore, how emperors arrived at their decisions was opaque in both empires. "Most events began to be kept secret and were denied to common knowledge," Dio complained.[20]

The power of a Roman emperor was as arbitrary as that of an oriental monarch, but neither was merely capricious. Tradition, morality, religion, and established institutions exerted some restraining force, although they failed as ultimate limitation. Inertia of the administrative apparatus and power politics within the ruling circle added more constraints.

The Roman and Chinese Empires lacked the rule *of* law, but both aspired to the rule *by* law and hoped their emperors would voluntarily submit to existent laws. The younger Pliny praised Trajan, Rome's thirteenth *princeps-imperator*: "You have spontaneously subjected yourself to the laws. . . . What I hear for the first time, now learn for the first time, is not 'The *princeps* is above the laws,' but 'The laws are above the *princeps*.'"[21] What was news to Pliny is the central Legalist tenet, as Shang Yang insists: "The law is what the ruler and ruled all uphold."[22] The idea was still influential in early Han. Wendì just missed being injured when a man rushing from underneath a bridge upset the horses in the imperial procession. Minister of Fairness Zhang Shizhi, having ascertained the transgression unintentional, imposed monetary fines. To the furious emperor who demanded a heavier penalty he replied, "The law is common to the son of heaven and all under heaven. Now the law stipulates this penalty. To change it would betray the people's trust in the law." Wendì paused for a long time but finally agreed.[23] Nevertheless, the rule by law rested on the grace of emperors. Even Trajan turned several provinces from public territory into imperial patrimony almost overnight, without consulting the Senate. Empress Lü got her way by simply replacing the remonstrating premier with someone more compliant.[24] Subjects in both empires learned to live according to the statement Tacitus put in the mouth of a senator: "I pray for good emperors, but I take them as they come."[25]

Did Roman emperors rule by the consent of their subjects in a way that oriental monarchs did not? What counts as consent is always a stumbling block in political theories. Rebels against Qin lay down their arms under the Han. Antony's forces deserted to Octavian. Few insurrections disturbed the *Pax Sinica* or *Pax Romana*. Such "tacit consent" to rule aside, in neither empire did the people regularly vote their preferences. However, the Romans did have an explicit expression. Since Augustus, the Empire's entire population swore allegiance to a new emperor upon his accession and renewed the oath on each anniversary. An early pledge, unencumbered by later flatteries, began thus: "I swear by Jupiter, Earth, Sun, by all the gods and goddesses, and by Augustus himself, that I will be loyal to Caesar Augustus and to his children and descendants all my life in word, in deed, and in thought, regarding as friends whomever they so regard, and considering as enemies whomever . . ."[26] The Chinese would learn in modern times the collective ritual of pledging their hearts and mind to their great leader, but it would be interpreted not as the citizen's consent to rule but as the despot's control of his subjects.

Some scholars commend the empowering effect of citizenship, prominent in Rome but absent in China.[27] "Citizen" usually implies political rights and perhaps participation in political activities. This implication held only in the Roman Republic, not in the Empire, as scholars point out: "Under the Empire the people lost all effective constitutional rights—in legislation or elections."[28] Shorn of political rights, the Roman citizen became a privileged subject, and citizenship became the badge by which conquerors discriminated against the vanquished. Such discrimination faded fast in China. As soon as Qin annexed the six states, it granted the same status to all inhabitants in its realm. Conquerors and the conquered all became *bianhu qimin*, equal peoples in registered households with similar duties and benefits. All men with ability in the Empire were eligible for government offices, an important privilege that in Rome was reserved for citizens only. Subsequent dynasties adopted the same policy. Furthermore, Chinese subjects enjoyed one thing that Roman citizens lacked. The Han government urged converting swords into plowshares but did not legally disarm civilians.[29] In contrast, the Roman Empire deprived all nonmilitary persons, citizens and subjects alike, of the right to bear arms.[30]

Citizens constituted only about 10 percent of the Roman Empire's population for more than two centuries. Initially they retained some social and legal privileges, but these too gradually became attributes of wealth, not citizenship. "I bought this citizenship for a large sum," a Jerusalem tribune brags in the Bible.[31] By the Antonine age, poor citizens classified as *humiliores* lost their right to appeal, immunity to torture, and other legal protections, so that they became liable to cruel penalties previously reserved for slaves.[32] Perhaps it was not ironic that Caracalla, who in 212 granted Roman citizenship to all free inhabitants of the Empire, was known not for liberality but for rapacity. The name "citizen" offered little benefit to tenants without legal freedom to leave the land or artisans forbidden to leave their fathers' occupations. Caracalla's edict excited far less enthusiasm from contemporaries than from moderns. It was not even mentioned on the coinage, the usual propaganda machine. A historian explains, "The upper classes already knew where their interests lay, and to the lower classes it no longer made much difference."[33]

Constantine paid oriental despotism the highest compliment of imitation. *Despotes* became the usual term for addressing the emperor, to whom Roman citizens spoke of themselves as "your slaves."[34] "But this orientalism was a superficial etiquette," a Western scholar notes; "the autocrat seldom forgot that his subjects were freemen."[35] The proportion of slaves in the Greco-Roman world far exceeded that in any oriental society. Sociologists also found that ordinary Persians enjoyed more factual freedom from state intervention in their daily lives than did the Greeks, because the Persian Empire left significant domestic autonomy to localities.[36] What the Greeks and Romans scorned as abjectness was mainly the ceremonial homage that oriental peoples rendered their rulers, including prostration. Such homage was precisely what they themselves later adopted toward their emperors. Nevertheless, the change may be superficial after all. Centuries before they physically prostrated, the Greeks had spiritually prostrated as the Chinese never did. They worshipped their living kings and emperors as gods, and the Romans later followed this example.[37] At the beginning of imperial Rome's golden age, Senator Pliny addressed Emperor Trajan: "You order us to be free, and we will be free."[38] Such was the height to which the proudest of Roman citizens had risen under the lord of free men.

6.3 The *Imperator* and the *Huangdì*

At the end of a civil war, even ravens learned to hail "victorious *imperator*." Who should succeed to the throne in peace? A Western scholar constructs an enlightened "doctrine of adoption" for the Roman Empire: "The emperor was not a monarch of the Oriental type; . . . the power was not transmitted from father to son merely in virtue of blood relationship. The emperor adopted the best man among the best men."[39] A closer examination does uncover evidence for an ancient doctrine of nonhereditary imperial succession, but in China, not Rome.

This may be surprising in view of the Darwinian evolutionary edge that the Chinese upper class had over its Roman counterpart. More than 100,000 persons were descended from Gaodì and his two brothers in two centuries.[40] In contrast, the Roman aristocracy could not replenish itself by natural birth. The phenomenon was conspicuous enough to induce speculations about sterility caused by frequent hot baths. Or it may be simply because aristocrats preferred pleasure to child rearing, as Tacitus remarked. Anyway, despite policies that encouraged childbearing and censured celibacy, many Roman aristocratic families were empty nests.[41]

The Antonine emperors who adopted their successors had no biological son of their own. Acts out of necessity prove no principle. Where choice was available, the results were unambiguous. Vespasian declared, "My son shall succeed me, or no one." Between the rule of his family and anarchy, the Senate took no time to decide.[42] While aristocrats resigned themselves to the dynastic principle, the troops and the common people embraced it. The Praetorian Guard promptly hailed Claudius, apparently retarded as he was. The crowd supported the choice, and legionaries balked at the rebellious conspiracy of their officers. Elagabalus was acclaimed emperor on physical resemblance to Caracalla; even a bastard son had advantages. A historian summarizes his extensive research: "No Emperor who had a son living was ever peacefully succeeded by anyone else."[43]

Even on paper, evidence is lacking for the alleged adoptive principle. Stoicism demands a good king, but is generally silent on any principle of succession. Marcus Aurelius, the Stoic philosopher-emperor, happily passed the purple to his son. Most scholars doubt that a principle of adoption ever existed in the Roman Empire.[44]

Proof of existence is easier than proof of nonexistence. Since the warring states, the Chinese developed a doctrine of abdication, *chanrang*, and constructed exemplars out of the sage kings Yao and Shun.[45] Ideally, Wendì remarked, a king should "search the world for a worthy and virtuous man and pass the throne to him."[46] In the nonideal world, abdication offers not a substitution but an escape clause from the dynastic principle under limited conditions; the mandate of heaven is not permanent. In 78 BCE, Sui Hong petitioned the emperor to emulate Yao and Shun. Eighteen years later, Gai Kuanrao wrote in a memorial to the emperor, "He who regards the world as belonging to all men passes it to the worthy. He who regards the world as belonging to his family passes it to his son."[47] The doctrine of abdication played a prominent role in the rise of Wang Mang and the succession of the Former Han by the Xin Dynasty. Discredited by the Xin's failure, *chanrang* henceforth becomes a euphemism that usurpers use for their purposes. The dynastic principle dominated in China as it did in Rome.[48]

The image of the ruler as a good shepherd was common to both realms.[49] Augustus's *Achievements* and the First Emperor's stone inscriptions both valued moral authority above mighty power. Augustus wrote, "I excelled all in authority (*auctoritas*), although I possessed no more official power (*potestas*) than others who were my colleagues in each office."[50] Corresponding to *auctoritas* in the Chinese tradition was *de* or effective virtue, in contradistinction to *wei* or intimidating capability. The word w*ei* appeared only four times in the First Emperor's six inscriptions, all in connection with conquest of the six states. In the context of subsequent rule, *de* appeared eleven times; for instance, "The Emperor's *de* preserves and calms the four extremes."[51] Augustus and the First Emperor each projected into his self-image an autocrat, paternalistic but not tyrannical. Similar ideals were elaborated by the Stoics and Confucians. True kingship is not a license to pleasure but a duty that demands toil for the welfare of the people and the solidity of the kingdom.

Emperors discharged their duty as the final decision maker with various degrees of enthusiasm. Caesar, Marcus Aurelius, and the First Emperor worked into the night.[52] Most emperors delegated more responsibilities to the government apparatus. Lax ones indulged favorites. Tiberius left matters to the praetorian prefect while ensconced in Capri, as Yuandì did to the director of secretariat while engrossed in music.[53] Worse delinquency occurred. When the likes of Nero or the Second Emperor came, their subjects could only groan or resort to violence. Such was autocracy.

Generosity in bestowing rewards for merit and beneficence to the masses was a paramount kingly characteristic in both empires. Promotion to the Senate was a coveted reward in Rome, as was a lordship in China. Money and material gifts were more common. Roman emperors dispensed cash to citizens and much larger amounts to the troops. Most spectacular were the free bread and circuses for inhabitants of the City Rome.[54] Serving similar functions as Roman games, emperor-sponsored Chinese festivities helped to bind the people to the ruler. Han emperors frequently showered on every man in the empire ranks that carried tradable social and material benefits. Besides, each hundred households received an allotment of food and wine, presumably for a communal party.[55]

Religion was a part of imperial control in both empires. As the supreme head of his state cult, each emperor had irreducible ritual roles. The Roman emperor was also the high priest who performed public rites and decided on matters ranging from sacred laws to temple restoration. In China, the emperor alone could offer a sacrifice to heaven, but not all emperors cared for this task. Wudì was the first Han emperor to perform the grand ritual, nine decades into the dynasty.[56]

In secular ceremonies, the triumphant parade was the most pompous for Roman emperors. Many Han emperors followed the ancient ritual of leading the court in the annual plowing of a sacred field, a symbol of dedication to agriculture.[57] These rites, in which the emperor shared with the people the glory of victory or the virtue of work, publicized the disparate ideologies of the two empires.

As supreme heads of state, the emperors manifested the values of their realms. Except for the First Emperor, who diligently inspected the country, the Chinese emperor was attached to family and seldom stirred from the dragon throne in the capital. Most people never saw his face or image. They knew him simply as "the emperor" or "the current ruler." His personal name was not to be mentioned and his official name came posthumously.[58] In contrast, Roman emperors were public celebrities who often marched ahead of the legionary eagle standard. They frequented parades and games, where the people could express their sentiments by clamoring. Keen to advertise themselves, the emperors erected statues everywhere. Their images on coins constantly reminded their subjects to render to Caesar what was Caesar's.[59]

Han emperors never took the field in a foreign war after Gaodì's debacle with the Xiongnu. They participated in strategic decisions and assigned generals to fight. In contrast, the almost supreme value that the Romans put on military conquest and victory made it dangerous for an emperor to allow expeditionary generals too much glory. Augustus with his overwhelming prestige could send legates and arrogate their honor. Lesser emperors tried to monopolize command. After Trajan, emperors were obliged to campaign in person.[60] Despite the powerful image of leading an army, a head of state who dared not delegate field command was politically weak. He was becoming hostage to the military.

The dispensation of justice was a duty of emperors in both realms. The Chinese emperor was the ultimate judge whose permission was required for the prosecution of high officials. Some emperors adjudicated personally, but more often they passed on responsibility to the ministry of fairness with the instruction to report indecision.[61] In contrast, Roman emperors spent considerable time hearing cases and resolving disputes. The city-state tradition of referring minute matters to the top persisted into the Empire. Consequently, the emperor often decided trivial local and personal affairs. In one council, Trajan judged on the demagoguery of the leading man in a Greek city, the misconduct of a military tribune's wife, and a forged will.[62]

Moderns used to the division between legislative, executive, and judiciary jobs may wonder: An emperor's energy is finite. Overwhelmed by mundane issues, how did he initiate reforms and frame state policies? He usually did not. Augustus had inaugurated almost three centuries of relatively passive and inert government. The central government pursued few policies and was largely content to respond to pressures and demands from below. The people's general expectations of an emperor were listening to requests and hearing disputes. These roles required rather limited and simple administrative apparatus. This explains why emperors could spend so much time on the warpath, where it was impractical to take along the records, experts, and information necessary for complex socioeconomic decisions.[63]

Minor issues also gained the attention of Chinese emperors, but what appears routine to historians of Rome surprises historians of China.[64] Effective administrative institutions enabled Chinese emperors to assign routine chores to appropriate ministries and save attention for larger problems. Perhaps in response to complaints, Jingdì decided certain regulations unfair and instructed the premier and the minister of fairness to change them. They drew up new rules regarding subtle forms of bribery. The deliberation was theirs; the assignment and final approval belonged to the emperor.[65] Because such power delegation was routine, to appoint able ministers and solicit worthy counsel had become almost the top expectations of a good Chinese emperor. This does not imply imperial quiescence, as is sometimes suggested.[66] The selection, coordination, and supervision of deputies are always activities crucial to the person in the top office, for modern as for ancient institutions.

6.4 The Government and the Elite

All authority in both the Chinese and Roman Empires devolved on the emperor. A person has authority if it follows from his saying "let it be done" that it *ought* to be done. A person has power if it follows from his saying "let it be done" that it *is* done.[67] To translate his formal authority into tangible power, an emperor needs aides to whom he delegates authority for information gathering, decision making, and policy execution. Government institutions structure the delegation of authority. Officers who run the government constitute the ruling elite, the junior partner in empire.

The elites, those who possess independent social power based mainly on birth, wealth, education, or admired social traits, have diverse backgrounds and interests. Many are local leaders, including local strongmen. Many have no political ambition. Others are eager to enter government, for their own aspirations or for the privileges that political power entails. On the other side, emperors are eager to siphon talents from society, first to secure their service in the government, second to prevent them from nurturing seditious ideas and organizations. In their own ways, Chinese and Roman rulers were equally skillful and successful in the circulation of elites.

The ruling elite's worldview and social composition influence a state's capacity to attend to the welfare of all people. When policy makers and executives all come from the dominant socioeconomic group, state actions tend to reflect the demands of that group.[68] The alliance of political and socioeconomic powers can strengthen a state, provided the dominant socioeconomic group itself is united. The caveat is especially important when land is the dominant form of wealth and the state is territorially large. Land being regional, landed interests exert a centrifugal force that an imperial government must somehow counteract. Both empires would suffer from regionalism.

In terms of political and socioeconomic alliance, the Roman Empire was stronger than the Qin and Former Han Dynasties. The Romans always had a clear idea, as Cicero declared: "The chief motivation behind the establishment of states and city structures was to ensure the maintenance of private property."[69] Alignment of political power with landed wealth was strengthened in the Empire. To secure his own monarchical power, Augustus stripped political power from the Senate, the corporate body of the landed aristocracy. Having thus defanged the senatorial order, he increased its stranglehold on the populace by tripling the Senate's minimum wealth qualification to between 1 million and 1.2 million sesterces. The equestrians retained their republican qualification of 400,000 sesterces. Below them were the decurions or town councilors with at least 100,000 sesterces. In short, Augustus reorganized the empire's social structure, molding it into a stratified system with legal distinctions between statuses. A scholar concludes, "The new order was patently, though not frankly, plutocratic."[70]

The Senate had 600 members. Equestrians numbered in the thousands. Roughly the top hundred families in a city made councilors, on the average. The three orders of the socioeconomic elite with shared interests in landed wealth monopolized the door to the ruling elite. By backing the local power of town councilors and absorbing them into the lower echelon of government, the emperor undercut the common people's ability to organize resistance to his domination.[71] High posts of the central government were the exclusive domain of senators and equestrians. For more than a century, senators filled almost all top political and military posts, cementing the twin pillars of the Roman Empire, wealth and arms.[72]

Birth and the emperor's favor were tickets to the Senate. A senator's privileges passed on to his descendants up to three generations. Nevertheless, many senatorial families failed to entrench because of imperial persecution, low fertility, high expenditure, and the withdrawal of sons who inherited senatorial privileges but refused the burden of service. Rich provincials were eager to take their places. Non-Italian senators, who constituted 2 percent of the Senate under Augustus, became the majority by the time of Septimius Severus.[73] The fluidity of members did not erode the wealth threshold for membership. The Senate had changed from an elite Italian club to a club of empire-wide elites, but the criterion of elitism endured. Similar conditions obtained for the two lower elite orders.[74]

Wealth bias also permeated the army, where few not in the equestrian order made commissioned officers. Nevertheless, military merit was apparent and an army in wartime was a hotbed of opportunity. Trajan chose magistrates from his friends in the military oligarchy. During the third-century crisis, soldier-emperors rose through the ranks. Senators accustomed to refined living withdrew from military commands. The equestrians who replaced them similarly tended to plutocratic interests, but the divergent outlooks of disciplined professional soldiers and leisured senatorial aristocrats created a crack in the ruling elite. It would widen to lethal proportions toward the end of the Western Roman Empire.[75]

The wealth-qualified ruling circle looked after its interests and grew its power. By the reigns of Trajan and Hadrian, a legal line separated the upper class, *honestiores*, from the masses, *humiliores*. The rich enjoyed political and legal privileges while the poor, citizen or not, lost much freedom and were susceptible to be treated like slaves. Civil law, the gem of Roman jurisprudence, mainly addressed issues of property rights and protected the interests of wealthy property owners. Agrarian reforms that drove republican politics disappeared. Concentration of land in the hands of a few skyrocketed. The plutocratic character of the Roman Empire penetrated deep into society.[76]

In China, the abolition of the feudalistic aristocracy opened doors in the government. Officers in the early Han government were diverse in socioeconomic background and intellectual persuasion. Previous occupations of farmer, swineherd, or firewood gatherer seemed not to stain their official career.[77] To recruit talented officers, Wendì ordered provincial governors to recommend men with integrity and intelligence. Wudì established a regular procedure for this purpose. Each provincial governor was to nominate two candidates annually and be held accountable for their quality. The quota changed in the Latter Han to one nominee from a fixed number of people, which attenuated voices from sparsely populated frontier provinces. The nomination system produced about 200 recruits a year. It garnered regional knowledge, pumped fresh minds to the central government, and became a unifying force by opening a channel for people all over the empire to become involved in administration and identify with the regime.[78]

"To appoint worthy ministers" has always been a Chinese ideal. What are the criteria of worthiness? How are they assessed? Meritocracy is fruitful only if what counts as merit is relevant to the jobs and promotions available. When merit meant vision, ability, and performance among the warring states, intellectual vibrancy espoused a wide range of knowledge and skills. What they lacked was cohesiveness. When the empire settled down, the monarchy needed a steady pool of men coherent enough to render reliable service but not strong enough to pose a threat. Legalist equality under the law was unpalatable to the emperor and the elites alike, a cause of Qin's fall that the Han literati turned into an object lesson.[79] Confucianism was better positioned. It clung to the texts of the ancient aristocracy that conferred prestige and forged ideological cohesion. Its faith in the ruler's omnipotent personal virtue was easily adapted to serve autocracy. Its ethics of asymmetric mutual deference benefited everyone in power. Elites rendered personal loyalty to the emperor, whose personal benevolence protected their status and privileges. Together they lorded over commoners, whom they indoctrinated to obey superiors and be content with their lot.

Wudì banished scholars other than Confucians from the regular recruitment channel. Confucian literati multiplied among provincial nominees, who were joined by graduates of the imperial academy devoted to the Confucian Canons. After a few generations, they permeated high offices, nominated friends, attacked rivals, and constituted a self-promoting class that made doctrinal correctness and literary polish the overriding merits for government offices. Already in early Han, Sima Tan had observed, "Confucianism is massive in corpus but sparse in essential substance, laborious in effort but meager in achievement, and seldom thorough in affairs."[80] This characteristic was amplified by a century in power. Exegesis of one Canon exceeded a million words and was fast rising. The expertise of expressing one drop of idea in an ocean of words created a peculiar language full of jargons, which restricted the range of discussable topics and excluded those not familiar with canonical allusions from political discourse. Learning the language required more and more effort, but entrance into government and the profits it entailed made the effort worthwhile. "Bequeathing to your son one Canon is better than bequeathing a basketful of gold," so went a contemporary saying.[81] The prospect of office fueled enthusiasm for education, but one sadly narrow and rigid. Empirical knowledge and objective reasoning were snubbed. Ideologically incorrect concepts, especially political concepts that went beyond the state as a big family, were condemned as immoral. Brainpower was drained into memorization and exegetical indoctrination, smothering creative thinking, shackling rational value judgment, and starving productive areas of talent. Stunted potential for competitors ensured the longevity of the Confucian ideological aristocracy. It also destroyed the capacity for political reforms and encouraged emperors to be increasingly despotic.[82]

Despite their lofty rhetoric, literati clans were thirsty for fame and gold, which always bestowed actual advantages by enabling officials to acquire higher education, maintain refined leisure, and cultivate social connections. Cliques of wealthy literati clans gradually usurped the nomination system to exclude candidates from humble families. After producing warlords that destroyed the Han Dynasty, the ideological aristocracy would grow into a bona fide aristocracy that eclipsed the throne in the subsequent period of disunity.[83]

The emperor and the elite needed and benefited each other, although their relation was always tense. Confucianism served well the Chinese Empire and the literati, as did plutocracy the Roman Empire and the landlords. In comparison, the ideology-based Chinese elite were more dependent on the throne than was the wealth-based Roman elite. Wealth constituted an independent powerbase, but early Han experiences divulged the difficulty for Confucian masters to retain disciples without the promise of government jobs or aristocratic patronage.[84] Dependency on the state made the Chinese elite more submissive. On the other hand, softness imparted a certain tenacity. Virtue rhetoric was pliable to please new masters, whereas regionalism made the hard power based on landed wealth brittle.

The imperial ruling elites enjoyed tremendous power and privilege over the common people. Yet they were pale images of the haughty pre-imperial aristocracies. Nostalgia bred discontent and perhaps agitation, against which ever-vigilant emperors did not hesitate to take preventive measures, justified or not. In China, cursing the living emperor or slandering the court was treasonous, and the laws of impiety penalized acts such as leaving any object belonging to the emperor on the ground. Since Augustus had criminalized libel, treason in the Roman Empire covered anything from taking into a brothel a coin bearing the emperor's image to consulting the horoscope about the emperor's death.[85] It is difficult to tell which records more deaths of officers on sedition charges, Ban Gu's *Book of Han* or Tacitus's *Annals*. Condemnations of imperial repression fill historiography. Less noticed is the elites' complicity in the game. Some officers gained advantage by false accusations or used legitimate regulations to settle private feuds. Such practices became tools for faction fights. Roman senators were as adept at them as Han literati. Mutual incrimination escalated, if it did not precipitate, many imperial persecutions.[86]

The throne and the ruling elite evolved together amid tension and power struggle. An effective bureaucracy without which emperors could not get things done could develop into a countervailing force, as happened in eighteenth-century Europe. Failing active influence in policy making, the elite could passively upset policy execution by uncooperative dawdling. Competent elites had some capacity to constrain autocratic power and to increase the constraints by improving political and legal institutes. Incompetence also frustrated, but it risked encouraging despotism at the elite's own expense. Power came with responsibility as well as privilege and must be earned with effort and patience.

Exertion gradually became distasteful to the pampered elites of both empires. Overproduction of literati created social problems in the Latter Han Dynasty. Instead of applying their minds constructively, jobless literati busily socialized. They "seek connections and form cliques for mutual advantage, steal fame and cheat the world for profits," as the contemporary scholar Wang Fu described.[87] When Tiberius, reluctant to bear all the burdens of empire, tried to share part of the responsibility with the Senate, senators merely asked "Which part?" Talking emptily of regaining liberty but balking at substantial duty, they let the emperor reign supreme and evoked the disparaging comment from Tiberius, "Men fit to be slaves!"[88]

6.5 The Emperor and the Government

The civilian governments of the Chinese and Roman Empires alike evolved from the management of royal households, but at different times and along different paths. The feudalistic state of the Zhou was undifferentiated from the ruling family. Legalist reformers introduced function-oriented offices, experimented with organizations, and rationalized practices to cope with the complex problems of expansion. Through practice and experience, the royal household gradually calved off an administrative institution that, although retaining vestiges of household management, acquired independent dignity and identity. By imperial times, the central government featured a duality: a dominant emperor with his household and a subordinate "establishment," in which a premier led a bureaucratic hierarchy.[89]

A similar emperor-establishment duality existed in the Roman Empire, although theirs was a shotgun marriage stormy at the beginning. The establishment was the Senate, the republican governing body that lost its power but not all its dignity. Alongside it, the emperor sprang up in a huge empire and faced the task of effective administration based on mainly city-state experience. Besides directing senators, the emperor also managed the provinces by his personal slaves and freedmen, who executed his commands and reported only to him as head of the imperial household.[90]

A manifestation of duality was the existence of two treasuries each in the Roman Empire and Han Dynasty. One was the state treasury, the Roman *aerarium* and the Han *dasinong*. The other was the imperial treasury for the emperor's household expenses, the Roman *fiscus* or moneybag and the Han *shaofu* or minor treasury. The Romans divided revenue mainly according to properties managed by the Senate or the emperor. The Han mainly differentiated various kinds of tax. Which treasury had the larger share of revenue? Think twice before placing your bet. Emperors were enormously rich and often subsidized public expenditure out of their private pocket, munificence that earned them gratitude. With the maturation of monarchical government, the lines between the state and imperial treasuries gradually blurred. Eventually the *fiscus* absorbed the *aerarium*, and the *dasinong* absorbed the *shaofu*.[91]

A government has offices and officers. Some organizations emphasize the function of various posts; others, the status of persons. Let us loosely call the former bureaucratic and the latter aristocratic. The Han establishment was formally more bureaucratic, although its operation was increasingly biased by personal connections among literati-officials. Roman senators were aristocratic. It would take more than two centuries for them to yield to a Roman bureaucracy staffed by equestrians appointed to task-oriented offices.

According to republican tradition, Roman senators followed structured advancement paths in government: quaestor, praetor, and consul. Regulations specified the minimum age for holding an office and the waiting time before advancing to the next stage. The offices, such as the consulate invested with *imperium*, were vague in function except as baptism to the exclusive high officialdom. Only senators of consular or praetorian rank were qualified for legionary commands and provincial governorships. Appointments came from the emperor.[92]

The Senate as an institution declined irreversibly in policy making. By Trajan's time, it was reduced to cheering imperial decisions and debating such questions as whether to allow a senator to hold a market on his private estate. It continued to conduct routine business and resolve disputes that became precedents in civil laws. However, issues coming before it were increasingly trivial; petitioners preferred to go to the emperor.[93]

The Han Dynasty inherited Qin's rudimentary bureaucracy. Below the premier were a deputy who functioned as imperial censor and a supreme commander for military affairs, the post of which was often unfilled. The pyramid was flattened into the "triumvirate" in the Latter Han to reduce the power of the premier. The premier transmitted imperial decrees, evaluated official performance, and shared the emperor's authority of appointment and dismissal. On major issues, the premier led court conferences, where officers each presented his opinion. The First Emperor had listened to debates before his decisions to abolish the feudatory aristocracy and, to prevent its revival, burn books. Among issues deliberated in Han court conferences were the selection of a new emperor, the recruitment of officials, and a curb on slavery and land concentration.[94]

The premier led nine ministries of the central government. In serving the populace, justice and the economy came first. The ministry of fairness conducted important trials, heard appeals, and resolved difficult cases submitted by provincial governors. The state treasury divided into five departments. Besides collecting taxes and remitting state expenditures, they managed the money supply, stabilized price levels, constructed roads and waterworks, facilitated transportation, maintained granaries across the empire, prepared for famine relief, and regulated the economy in various ways. Its twin, the minor treasury, financed the emperor's court and entourage, including the imperial secretariat. The prestigious ministry of rites oversaw all cultural matters, including temples of the royal house and the imperial academy. Two ministries shared the jobs of imperial guard and palace security. The seventh ministry received foreign emissaries. The remaining two ministries, which handled the imperial clan and transportation, retained characteristics of imperial domestics.[95]

Like the Roman Senate, the Han bureaucracy gradually declined in influence, although less steeply. Competition came from developments in the imperial household. Wudì's ambitious policies required extensive planning and deep mobilization of resources. To muster the officialdom, he took personal control with the aid of close confidants. Thus began the Han's "inner court" supervised by the chief secretary, in distinction to which the establishment under the premier came to be called the "outer court."[96] Similar to the inner court, an administration of advisory friends and equestrians gradually developed around the Roman emperor. The phenomenon should not be strange to Americans familiar with the growth of the presidential advisory and the White House staff alongside formal departments and agencies of the federal government.

Augustus introduced the powerful offices of prefects for the Praetorian Guard, the city of Rome, and the fire brigade. To collect taxes and provision troops in imperial provinces, emperors increasingly replaced domestic servants by procurators with equestrian rank. Equestrians lacked a parallel to the senatorial career ladder, but advanced through service in hierarchical offices. A bureaucracy grew and eventually calved off to displace the Senate.[97] More ponderous in the emperor's entourage were his close advisers, *amici* or friends, who acquired the structure of a *consilium* or imperial council by the second century. Its most regular member was the praetorian prefect, who commanded the imperial headquarters. Many high-ranking senators and equestrians found admission. In the Later Empire, the *consilium* developed into the formal consistory, an active council of state with regular members who debated matters of moment and advised the emperor.[98]

As their structures became more formal and their membership more ponderous, the Roman consistory and the Han inner court became new establishments, drifted away from the emperor, and retraced the footsteps of the old establishments. After the Senate, the consistory became an assembly of notables summoned to hear and cheer imperial decisions. After the Han premier, the chief secretary lost to those closer to the source of authority.[99] The emperor was surrounded by generals in the camp, by women and eunuchs in the harem. Imperial women and their relatives held influence only strong emperors could contain. When the emperor was a child, the regency belonged to them, not the consistory, not the imperial secretariat.[100] Faction fights among Han literati-officials, affine families, and eunuchs ended with all three losing to warlords. Since partition, the Eastern Roman Empire accommodated powerful women and eunuchs while the Western Roman emperor fell under the thumbs of great generals.[101] With political institutions decaying, eventually naked force dominated.

6.6 State and Society

At its most elaborate, each empire had, below its central government, three layers of administration that respectively emphasized supervisory, structural, and operational functions: the Roman *diocese*, *provincia*, and *municipium*; the Han *zhou* or circuit, *jun* or province, and *xian* or county.

Individual attention from the emperor is possible only for a few, but corrupt officials are the hatred of all. Both empires had supervisory institutions to check the potential of officers to mistreat the people or, worse, to become too powerful and mutinous. Wudì divided the Chinese empire into thirteen inspectional circuits. Inspectors were empowered to investigate provincial governors for embezzlement, brutality, indulgence of delinquent relatives, and collusion with local magnates. Originally junior officers, the inspectors gradually grew in power and eventually transformed into plenipotentiary viceroys.[102]

The Romans usually preferred judiciary to administrative channels. Mistreated provincials could bring charges against ex-governors at Rome. To avoid stiff defense, most plaintiffs simply sought restitution for illegal extortion without penalty for the accused, who were senators, as were the judges.[103] Superstructural jurisdictions appeared in the Later Empire, which grouped the provinces into twelve dioceses for better supervision and administration.[104]

Provincia and *jun* both originated as military commands and transformed into civilian administration. At its peak, the Qin Dynasty had forty-six provinces. By expansion, splitting domains, and retaining some kingdoms as income fiefs, the Han had 103 provincial-level units, abbreviated as provinces.[105] The Roman Empire had forty-six provinces at the end of the Antonine age. After Diocletian and Constantine split large provinces to prevent overpowerful governors, Roman provinces numbered 116.[106]

Provinces constituted the empire's major administrative structure. For a long time, provincial governors with the power of life and death were the highest administrators and judges outside the central government. Roman governors spent most of their time in assize tours among litigious cities. Only later would they intrude more into internal municipal affairs.[107] They deferred to the emperor in important matters, as the Greek panegyrist Aristides described: "If they feel the slightest doubt about their subject's lawsuits, public or private, or whether petitions should be granted, they immediately send to him [the emperor] and ask what to do, and they wait for a signal from him, as a chorus from its director."[108]

Han governors had more initiative. They toured the counties annually, and not only for hearing cases. They were responsible for directing county management and writing annual reports to the premier. They appointed officers for counties and other local units, evaluated performance, and nominated candidates for the central government. Besides, governors were expected to be upright exemplars, providing leadership in advancing agriculture, public works, and perhaps education.[109]

The estimated peak population of each empire exceeded 50 million. Thus an average province had more than half a million inhabitants. They generated heavy administrative workloads: law and order; census and survey; construction and maintenance of roads and other public facilities; maintenance of lodging and transports for imperial travelers; delivery of military recruits and provisions; and above all, the assessment, collection, and forwarding of taxes. The governor with his small headquarters staff could only plan, coordinate, and supervise. Substantive operations belonged to local units, Roman cities and Chinese counties. These constituted the fundamental layer in which the state penetrated society and impinged on the lives of its constituents. Here the Roman plutocratic and Han bureaucratic characters were more pronounced than they were in the central or provincial governments.

The classical city of the Greco-Roman world was one for consumption based on rent from agriculture, radically different from the medieval city, which was a production center based on trade and industry. The great majority of Roman cities were essentially rural; crafts and services existed but were minor. The urban area was the administrative and consumption center, where absentee landlords who constituted the city's governing circle resided and spent their income.[110]

Democracy in domestic organization and belligerency in foreign relations were characteristic of many ancient city-states. Rome suppressed both when converting them into subject cities. Forbidden to fight, cities found two vents for their rivalry. Trivial litigation kept Roman governors busy. Competitive display of magnificence bankrupted many cities but left beautiful ruins for posterity to admire. Democracy was already in decline before Roman conquest. Cities democratic in form, such as Athens, had in substance morphed into oligarchies. Rome made it final. It controlled the cities by backing rich and powerful locals. Gone were the republican days when Italian commoners resisted Rome. The Empire had squashed the lower class's hope for agrarian reform.[111] Aristides praised Rome in the days of Antoninus: "You have divided into two parts all the men in your empire. . . . The men of greatest standing and influence in every city guard their own fatherlands for you."[112] Many scholars regard the co-option of the local rich a key to successful Roman rule.[113] It ensured "satisfaction for all those who were, even potentially, powerful, and powerlessness for the potentially dissatisfied."[114]

Rome fixed a tax quota for each city. Councilors failing to collect enough had to make up the shortfall themselves. On the other hand, they had the liberty to decide who should pay what and the power to flog and imprison protesters. Being the richest in the locality, they had the most to gain from misdistribution of the tax burden. The expenses of collection were high, so that much more came out of taxpayers than went into the imperial treasury. Councilors customarily allotted public lands at low lease rates to themselves. Furthermore, emperors often granted lavish fiscal immunities to them, and many made their way into the imperial government. On balance, service in the city council was a good deal initially. When the job became unprofitable in the Later Empire, many councilors wanted to quit. Rome forced it on them and their descendants, partly because of the privilege they previously enjoyed. At the same time, imperial procurators increasingly intervened into municipal affairs.[115]

Many councilors deserved the honor and gratitude bestowed by the locals for their services. Abuses were also common, however, as a historian observes: "In town or country there was poverty and social unrest—but Rome could not be held directly responsible for the transgressions of the wealthy. Rome seldom intervened against the local dynasts."[116] Rome's nonintervention is often lauded as respect for the freedom of self-governed cities. This simple assessment overlooks the complex relations among the central power, local power, and common people. Consider the case of Jesus. Powerful Jewish groups accused him of some crime and wanted him dead. Roman governor Pilate examined him and judged him innocent. Nonetheless, he yielded to local pressure and washed his hands of the blood of Jesus.[117] Condoning injustice affected a few. Government policies could affect millions. If transgressions of local dynasts were rampant, could the nonintervening Rome as easily disavow the blood of the local masses?

While the Greco-Roman city passed with classical antiquity, of which it was a hallmark, the county has been the most enduring administrative organization in China since its unification. In the Han bureaucracy, county officials collected taxes and managed routine matters of justice, finance, and culture. The county superintendent, nicknamed "the parent official," was the imperial officer most familiar to the common people. To get things done, he had to obtain information on local conditions and establish good relations with local magnates. Hence he relied heavily on local subofficials, who constituted more than 90 percent of his staff. Despite lowly status and stipends, local subofficials undertook significant responsibilities and often wielded more substantive power than did their superiors appointed from outside, who came and went while the locals stayed on. Given their familiarity with the job, knowledge of all customs, and tricks for graft, they provided invaluable service but also became an inveterate source of corruption.[118]

Unlike Roman patronage, the Han government was wary of local magnates; many had roots traced to pre-imperial times. The rich acted like "lords without titles." Gangs proliferated.[119] Gross abuses by powerful magnates became the first mission of circuit inspectors. Emperors selected "brutal officers" capable of standing up to the powerful and spurning the bribes of the rich, but also capable of massacring innocents together with wrongdoers when targeting an intransigent clan with hundreds of households.[120] These effects were only temporary. Increasingly, literati-officials joined the rank of wealthy magnates. Many policies designed to reduce abuse and assuage inequality, such as the ever-normal granary and Guangwudì's land survey for fair tax assessment, fell under elite pressure cloaked in virtue rhetoric. As literati clans grew, the Latter Han government climbed into bed with local landlords and its policy converged with that of Rome.

6.7 The Myth of "Big Government"

The contrast between bloated Han bureaucracy and skeletal Roman government is a common stereotype. Some say the Han employed twenty-five times more functionaries than did the Roman Empire.[121] Does the difference reflect actual employment or the comprehensiveness of employment statistics? Let us compare the governments at the ends of the Former Han Dynasty and the Antonine age, when each empire was near its zenith.

The Roman top government was staffed by senators and equestrians. As in the Republic, senatorial magistracies were honorary but came with generous expense accounts. From the expense account for his year as governor of Cilicia, Cicero, who was exceptionally clean in office, was able to beg a surplus of 2.2 million sesterces. In imperial times, senatorial governors annually drew about 1 million sesterces.[122] Officers with the equestrian's rank were salaried. High-ranking procurators, the *trecenarius*, *ducenarius*, *centenarius*, and *sexagenarius*, respectively carried annual stipends of 300,000, 200,000, 100,000, and 60,000 sesterces.[123] At the opposite end of the pay spectrum were subofficials such as clerk and messenger. The official stipends of these ranged from 1,200 to 300 sesterces, but unofficial profitability induced candidates to purchase available posts. As a baseline for comparison, the average wage of a day laborer was about 3 sesterces and the annual pay of a legionary was 300 denarii or 1,200 sesterces, of which about one third or 400 sesterces was deducted for rations and additional amounts for clothing and equipment.[124] Thus a *ducenarius* received the pay of 167 legionaries or the ration of 500.

More than twenty senatorial magistrates managed the state treasury, sat as judges, administered the city of Rome, and granted contracts for various civic projects as needs arose. Many more served in the provinces as governors and commanders. All told, about ninety-five high-ranking senators held active posts each year. The number of high-grade equestrians grew over time. By the end of the Antonine age, some thirty-six *ducenarius*, forty-eight *centenarius*, and fifty-one *sexagenarius* were active annually.[125] Together with the senators, about 230 high officials were active administering the Empire.

Governors did not descend on the provinces alone. A Roman governor was accompanied by a financial officer of junior rank and probably a senior senator as deputy. Attached to him was a military contingent consisting of a centurion, a handful of lesser officers, and about fifty soldiers; more if the province had a legionary base. He was also equipped with a staff comprising scribes, heralds, lictors, messengers, and an omen reader. All these gave the governor's headquarters the appearance of a minor court. In total, one estimate counted up to 10,000 functionaries operating in the forty-six provinces at the time of Trajan.[126]

The *Standard Histories* provide long lists of Han offices, complete with their jobs, grades, stipends, subordinates, and histories of evolution. Whereas the names of Roman grades such as *ducenarius* derived from their salaries, the names of Chinese grades such as *erqianshi*, literally "two-kilo bushels," are only of ordinal significance. Their corresponding salaries were stipulated in amounts of grain measured in *hu* (1 *hu* = 19.7 liters). The Former Han Dynasty differentiated eighteen grades of functionaries roughly divided into three categories. Four grades belonged to high officialdom: the ten-kilo, with a monthly stipend of 350 *hu*; supra-two-kilo, 180 *hu*; mid-two-kilo, 120 *hu*, and sub-two-kilo, 100 *hu*. Junior officialdom encompassed eleven grades, three of which were the one-kilo, with a monthly stipend of 80 *hu*; six-hundred, 70 *hu*; and two-hundred, 30 *hu*. A gap in the promotion ladder separated them and the three grades of subofficials: the one-hundred, with a monthly stipend of 16 *hu*; clerk, 11 *hu*; and aide, 8 *hu*.[127] As a baseline, the monthly ration of a foot soldier was around 2.6 *hu*.[128] Thus a mid-two-kilo received the ration of 46 soldiers.

In the ten-kilo grade were the triumvirs and a couple of honorary posts such as the emperor's tutor. The three grades of two-kilo constituted the bulk of high officialdom. There were ten supra-two-kilos: the heads of nine ministries plus the prefect of the capital. Twenty-seven lesser two-kilos served in the central government; more than half were commanders of guard units. The bulk of their grade, totaling about 200, served as circuit inspectors, provincial governors, and commanders in charge of army reserves. Together with their colleagues in the capital, the total number of active high officials was not much more than 240.[129]

Besides active officers, the Han government also maintained dozens of sinecure two-kilos with titles and stipends but no definite responsibility. They undertook special imperial missions but usually served as advisers, creating a pool of reserves akin to high-ranking Roman senators not on active duty. The small number of top jobs compared to the large number of aspirants generated tremendous pressure from below, which the Chinese sinecure posts, like the Roman Senate, mitigated.[130]

About 100 junior officers worked in the central government. Archeologists have recovered a copy of Donghai's annual report for 13 BCE, which provides details of provincial government. Donghai was a large province with population over 1 million. Its provincial headquarters employed thirty-nine functionaries: the governor and commander plus two junior officers and thirty-five subofficials.[131] Taking this as the average without neglecting the slight difference in two types of provincial units, that is about 186 high officers, 186 junior officers, and 3,405 subofficials—a total of 3,777 functionaries—on the provincial level. The Han court alone could appoint high officials, but some junior officials could receive assignment from their superiors. Subofficials on government payroll were always chosen by their direct superiors.[132]

Juxtaposing the Roman and Han governments down to the provincial level, they are comparable in personnel size. Each central government employed a few dozen high officers and appointed a couple of hundred more to govern the provinces. Supplementing them were hundreds of junior officers and thousands of subofficials. However, the expenditure of the Roman government was larger because of higher salaries at the top. Together, the compensations of 230 high Roman officials amounted to the ration of 275,150 soldiers; that of 241 Han high officials, 10,965.

As compared, the Han government was near at its maximum size, the result of rapid expansions under Wudì. Many posts would be cut by Guanwudì.[133] In contrast, expansion of the Roman government, which had been mild hitherto, would soon accelerate under Diocletian. Two centuries after the dates of our comparison, the Han high officialdom had not changed much, but the number of senior Roman officers had jumped to about 6,000. Not the entire jump is attributable to different definitions of "high official." Except for brief periods, the Later Roman Empire had two or more simultaneous emperors, hence a duplication of central headquarters and officers. Further expansion occurred in the provinces, which engaged most officers. The number of Han provinces remained constant, but the number of Roman provinces more than doubled. Also, Rome increasingly appointed procurators to keep city councilors in line. All these additions increased the size of government.[134] Finally, the prize of Big Government goes to Rome.

Below the provincial level, different government structures make comparison more difficult. Each Han province had jurisdiction over ten or more counties, each of which oversaw several districts. Depending on a county's size, its administration comprised two to four junior officers of grades between one-kilo and two-hundred, supplemented by locally hired subofficials. Excavated records show 120 junior officers and 2,044 subofficials working in Donghai's thirty-eight counties.[135] Donghai was larger than most provinces. Extrapolation of its figures falls within the ballpark of the empire-wide figure in the *Book of Han*'s list of official posts: "From aides to the premier, the total was 120,285."[136] According to this proportion, less than 300 were high officials, 7,000 were junior officials, and the remaining were subofficials.

With a population of about 50 million, the entire Han bureaucracy engaged about one functionary per 416 inhabitants. For comparison, in 2002 the U.S. federal government alone had 1.7 million civilian employees, or about one per 176 inhabitants. These do not include the large numbers of civil servants in the state, county, and local governments.[137]

Roman cities were self-governed, but self-government did not mean no government. Although locals, municipal magistrates were imperial agents in an important sense: they collected taxes for Rome and relied on Rome to back their local power. The cities varied greatly in size. A typical city had about six magistrates, selected from councilors. Their service was honorary, but the city paid for constables and subofficials.[138] Detailed numbers are not available, but one can guess that the size of Roman city administration was not incomparable to that of the Han county.

6.8 Taxation and the Economy

Imperial peace and road systems enhanced trade. Conspicuous consumption stimulated crafts. Sima Qian admired the large volume of trade but added that although commerce was efficient in profit making, merchants preserved their wealth in land and farming.[139] A similar picture obtained in the Roman world, where craft and trade were low-status jobs often relegated to slaves and freedmen working for aristocrats.[140] Although eye-catching, craft and commerce lacked social respect and constituted only a tiny portion of the Chinese and Roman economy, which were mainly agrarian.

The great majority of peasants lived mainly on what they produced themselves. Unlike most subsistence economies, however, both empires were highly monetized, Rome more so. Coin circulations were large. Significant portions of prices were quoted and taxes collected in money. For more than two centuries, the Roman Empire maintained the republican system anchored by the silver denarius and the sesterce or quarter denarius. The system collapsed in the third century crisis. The army levied provisions and officials received stipends in kind for many decades, until Constantine stabilized the currency with the gold solidus.[141]

Qin's basic design of the bronze coin qian had become the norm throughout imperial China, supplemented by gold and later gold and silver ingots. The early Han changed the weight of its qian ten times and allowed private parties to flood the market with underweight coins. Not until 113 BCE did Wudì ban private mints and introduce the qian weighing five *zhu*, which was mainly stable through the Han and beyond. Official stipends, although quoted in amounts of grain, were at least partly commuted to money.[142]

The land tax and head tax were the two major regular sources of imperial revenue. Tithes, sevenths, and fifths being attested in various parts of the Roman Empire, scholars estimate an average land tax hovering around 15 percent. Surtaxes came in the Later Empire as military provision.[143] The rate of land tax was one-fifteenth at the beginning of the Han, but was often halved. From 156 BCE onward, it stayed at 3.3 percent through the Han Dynasty, except during the brief civil war, when the tithe was collected.[144] Although cited in rates, the usual practice in both empires was to fix an annual tax amount for each taxpayer according to the acreage and quality of land owned.[145] It made tax collection easier but peasant life harder. Fair taxation became dependent on fair land assessment, the difficulty of which was evident from the fierce resistance to Guangwudì's land survey. Fraudulent tax assessment in the Roman Empire also fueled spiraling inequality.[146]

The annual head tax fell on Romans aged twelve or fourteen to sixty-five, for males only in some places, for both genders in others. Rates varied;

details I do not know.[147] The Han settled on an annual rate of 120 qian for everyone aged fifteen to fifty-six, and twenty qian for a child. After the currency stabilized under Wudì, the commutation rate for corvée labor was 2,000 qian per month. At this rate, the 120 qian head tax amounted to 1.8 days of labor.[148]

The levy on labor, as conscription or corvée, was the other direct burden on the people. The Roman Empire had a professional army. Legionaries, who served sixteen to twenty-five years, got pay and pension plus imperial donatives. Noncitizen auxiliaries were treated less well but could look forward to bonuses and Roman citizenship upon honorary discharge. Most soldiers were volunteers. However, the draft never vanished, and it resurged in the Later Empire. Laws forcibly drafted all sons of soldiers and veterans. Other conscripts were levied on the same assessment as the land tax. When some selected men cut off their own thumbs, Theodosius ordered cities to produce two self-mutilators for one sound soldier. Despite recruitment difficulties, Rome excluded from its army slaves and people of base occupations such as innkeepers or cooks. The honor and pride of the military admitted no compromise.[149]

To fight the nomadic Xiongnu, the Former Han maintained a professional cavalry with orphans of fallen soldiers and quality volunteers from six frontier provinces. Nevertheless, the Han's standing army was minuscule compared to Rome's. The bulk of its army consisted of conscripts. A man between the ages of twenty-three and fifty-six was liable to serve for two years, one of which was essentially for training. The frequency of call-ups varied. Having to serve two full years was among the bitterest indictments the literati hurled against Wudì's anti-Xiongnu war.[150] Men of mean occupations were frequent targets of the Han's levy for remote campaigns, but reprieved convicts had become the favorite.[151]

An empire needed large labor forces for public works. Soldiers, state slaves, and paid laborers did some work, but a large burden rested on corvée, state exaction in the form of unpaid labor. Roman soldiers and traveling officials had the right to extract irregular services. Routine chores were for the cities to organize, with denizens rotating, usually in one-year terms.[152] According to Han law, a man between twenty-three and fifty-six was liable for one month of corvée per year. Service for local jobs could start as early as age fifteen.[153]

Tax policies distribute the burdens of state among various groups of people. Their design is a powerful tool for government to influence society. Surveying policies of the Roman Empire, scholars observe that its regular taxes were regressive.[154] The same applied to Han taxation. A pauper and a millionaire paid the same amount of head tax. A subsistence farmer and a large landlord paid the same rate of land tax. Subtracting necessary living expenses, a disproportionate amount of the poor's surplus went into tax, although the rich derived most benefit from the public security and facilities bought by tax revenues. Modern progressive taxation mitigates the problem by hiking the tax rates for higher incomes. This idea had occurred to Legalists. Hann Fei proposed using tax policies to reduce economic inequality.[155] Several measures that Sang Hongyang designed for Wudì to defray the huge costs of the anti-Xiongnu war were progressive. One example was a tax of 6 percent on commercial properties, mainly vehicles and wholesale inventories. Large merchants had hitherto paid no tax despite windfall profits on war speculation. Sima Qian observed that they tripled or quintupled their capital and sneered at annual returns less than 20 percent. At 20 percent capital gain, the 6 percent commercial property tax was equivalent to a 30 percent "capital gains tax." It was abandoned in nine years under fierce opposition. An experiment on progressive taxation failed.[156]

Tenant farmers pay rent to landlords. Landlords pay tax to the government. Landlords tend to squeeze the most from their tenants. The rate of rent varied across regions, but hovered above 50 percent of produce in both empires.[157] A scholar argues that the Roman land tax, which was relatively low by ancient standards, provided a carapace for magnates to siphon most profits from a fixed amount of surplus.[158] The Chinese land tax was much lighter than the Roman. It was benevolent in the Qin and early Former Han Dynasty with its economy of small peasants tilling their own lands. As time went on, land concentration increased, and many peasants became tenants.[159] Xun Yue of the Latter Han wrote: "The ancients taxed one part in ten and thought it fair. Now some Han people pay one part in a hundred for land tax, the burden is light indeed. However, increasingly more land passes into the hands of the rich and powerful, who appropriate more than half of the crop for rent. The government taxes one part in a hundred, the people pay in excess of one part in two. . . . Dispensations from the top fail to trickle down and advantages flow to the powerful moguls."[160] These moguls were increasingly dominated by literati clans.

Hann Fei had argued that tax policies should vary according to circumstances and spending needs. Ignoring current conditions, insisting on light taxation, and condemning as immoral brutality any suggestion of raising revenues actually frustrate rational planning and may hurt society.[161] The Latter Han kept land tax low despite acute land concentration, thus fueling inequality. Even worse, dwindling revenues undermined the government's capacity for famine relief and other public responsibilities. When emergencies such as the Qiang rebellion came, desperate officials resorted to arbitrary means to raise funds, causing great harm.

Perhaps the heaviest burden on the people was not legal taxation but an indirect tax, government-condoned corruption. Corruption had been chronic but escalated as the empires aged. Its consequences we will see in section 8.4.

6.9 Law and Order

Aristotle distinguishes "two senses of good government—one which means obedience to such laws as have been enacted and another which means that the laws obeyed have also been well enacted."[162] Here we consider the first sense, bracketing legislation to concentrate on the operation of law—the rule by law as law and order. Some literati slight the rule by law because it falls short of the rule of law as constitutionalism. They follow Confucianism in confusing law abidance with shameless submission. Actually, respect for the law is a civic virtue based on reason and understanding. Without it or with an elitist mentality that self-righteousness overrides the law, a high-sounding constitution that formally limits the government's authority is a piece of paper that cannot effectively maintain the rule of law.

Our focus is not the contents but the conceptions of law. Contents invoke such questions as whether a specific law is good or bad, tough on crime or lenient. Conceptions address general questions such as what law is, what it contributes to society, how it relates to ethics, and how law abidance is justified.[163] Contents can change under a constant conception, as specific laws can be repealed without vitiating the institution of law. Therefore having some bad laws, such as laws enforcing slavery, does not entail a derogatory conception of law.

Disparate conceptions of law constituted a characteristic difference between the Eagle and the Dragon.[164] Generally, the Romans esteemed the law, which featured proudly in panegyrics. Chinese Legalists also respected the law, but they were blamed for Qin's demise and gagged shortly after the rise of literati-officials. Confucians, who preferred the rule by men, tolerated the law as punishment, which shared a chapter in the *Standard Histories* with war as necessary evils.

Different conceptions were apparent in the polar reactions to the first publication of law in each realm. Rome published its first code, the Twelve Tables, in 451 BCE, during the Conflict of the Orders. The event was celebrated from the beginning. Roman annalists regarded it as a plebeian triumph over patricians. Modern historians also credit patrician self-regulation.[165] Codification of law, which selects, articulates, rationalizes, or modifies certain customary practices, increases the predictability of social intercourse. The common people win; clear explanations of rules elucidate available options, and written laws curb arbitrary interpretation of tradition by those in power. The ruling class need not lose; the codes solidify the status quo, especially existing property rights, by arresting surprising changes in customs.[166]

Animosity greeted China's first code of laws, published by the state of Zheng in 536 BCE amid the decline of feudalistic power. Shu Xiang, a celebrity Jin aristocrat, wrote a long letter of denunciation: "When people know what to avoid, they lose fear of the authority and acquire contentiousness, because they can appeal to the written codes and hope to get away with what they do." Confucius chimed in when Jin inscribed its laws on a cauldron in 513 BCE: "Jin is about to perish; it is out of bounds. . . . Now that people can appeal to the cauldron, why should they defer to the nobility? By what can nobilities keep their status? Without hierarchical difference between the noble and the humble, how can a state survive?"[167]

Significantly, neither man opposed punishment or its cruelty, which had long been routine. Fifteen years before Jin's laws, Shu handled a land dispute and imposed three death sentences respectively for murder, bribery, and corruption. His ruling won praise from Confucius. Besides harshness, the case revealed the arbitrariness of judgment. Bribery with immunity was prevalent. Shu himself was on record to abet it.[168] However, as Shu wrote in his letter, rulers decided cases as they arose and did not set rules in advance to encourage contentiousness. Inscrutability and unpredictability enhanced the noble's power in the eye of the humble. In short, the Confucian target was not coercion but the publicity and consistency of the law that regulates its use.[169]

According to a Western scholar, what is uniquely Chinese about Shu Xiang's letter "is its insistence upon the moral and political dangers involved in the public promulgation of the legal norms. This view of law seems to have no real parallel in any other civilization."[170] More peculiar is that after Legalists propounded the notion of public laws to be upheld by the ruler and the ruled alike, the Confucian distaste for the law has persisted, although in a subdued form, for more than two millennia and still contributes to the headwind to the rule of law today.

The complex reasons for it are beyond the scope of this book, which broaches only a few points in various places. First, as is apparent in the reactions of Shu and Confucius, was the determination of the ruling elite, the feudalistic aristocrats and later the literati-officials, to protect their own privileged status and power.[171] The same self-serving determination obtained in the Roman ruling elite, but different worldviews and intellectual temperaments led them on different paths of development. As seen in sections 2.7 and 2.8, the Confucian Canons—having originated in the feudalistic time when the state was undifferentiated from the ruling family—promote a moral and political order consisting entirely of asymmetric personal relations whose virtues are benevolence and righteousness, the latter being essentially fealty and loyalty. To this small cozy world of personal bonds, the impersonal and impartial law seems a cold intruder, as captured by Confucius's image of a cauldron. Actually, justice does modify private relations but does not crush them, as the Romans demonstrated; even Qin laws refused to accept cases on certain family affairs. The law opens up a public dimension, introduces new venues for human intercourse, provides alternatives to deference to superiors, and broadens the human horizon by expanding the moral and political order (Figure 2.2c). To be fair in a huge public world with heterogeneous strangers and diverse interests, justice is in a way severe, as expressed in its image of a blindfolded goddess holding a balance and a sword. Unlike the Confucian ethic that appeals mainly to warm feelings, concepts of justice appeal more to cool reasoning. Being more abstract and complex, they took a long time to develop in the Western world by accumulation of experience and integration of reasons. Trying to explain them in terms of the notions in the Confucian Canons is like trying to explain a sphere to two-dimensional beings living on a flat surface. Legalists have introduced many new concepts, notably equality under the law. However, they are denounced as callous and discredited in the exegetical mindset, which insists that the Canons have encompassed all wisdoms under heaven. Since literati-officials became the ruling elite and their exegetical mindset entrenched to protect their special privileges, the public dimension has withered.

The Confucian conception of law is encapsulated in the endlessly quoted teaching of the master: "Lead by regulation and guide by punishment, the people will avoid transgression and lose their sense of shame. Lead by virtue and guide by rituals, the people will develop self-respect and good character."[172] Confucians insist that people can become good only by internalizing rituals and imitating virtuous superiors, the environment for which comes only in the rule of men. The law, identified with penalty and detached from morality, can only produce shamelessness.[173]

Proponents of the rule by law agree that ethical education is necessary for a healthy society. In contrast to proponents of the rule by men, however, they regard the law and law abidance as an essential component of education. Aristotle explains why people can become good through knowing and respecting the law. Laws clearly spell out various rules of conduct and the consequences for their compliance or violation. Habituated to behave according to legal norms, people internalize instructions, not different from their internalizing customary practices. Moreover, because laws are explicit, detailed, and often attended by their underlying rationale, people develop not only habit but also understanding, hence good characters with not only a sense of shame but also a reasoned sense of right and wrong.[174] Hann Fei advances similar explanations. Shang Yang argues that laws appropriate to their time can transform and improve social customs, and where the rule by law succeeds, legal penalties lie idle.[175] In short, reasonable and widely accessible laws are essential to building society's moral fabric. According to this view, Legalists toiled to spread legal knowledge and Roman schoolchildren recited the Twelve Tables by heart.[176]

The rule by law could have complemented Confucian ethics in three ways to nurture more rounded personalities. First, it promotes justice and public virtue, scarce in an ethics of unequal personal relations. Second, it encourages rational thinking, weak in exegesis. Third, it teaches people to step beyond wishful thinking and consider the consequences of their actions, for which they must bear responsibility. Not surprisingly, the rule by law was unwelcome to impractical literati-officials.

Consider Mengzi's answer to the question of what would happen if the sage king Shun's father committed murder: "Shun regards discarding his kingdom as discarding a worn sandal, stealthily bears his father and escapes to the coast, where he lives happily, never giving a thought about the world."[177] The king's hypothetical action was lauded by neo-Confucians as a revelation of the highest of heaven's principles. Shun was not a private person but the king, whose action affected the well-being of the world's people. His responsibility was especially heavy in the Confucian doctrine that hinged government on the ruler's personal example. By parading the paradigmatic sage king's disregard of justice, desertion of his people, and indifference to the danger of the country plunging into chaos because of his flight, Mengzi's thought experiment exposed a blind spot in the ruling elite's public responsibility. The lack of public virtue and a sense of responsibility were revealed in numerous other examples.[178] Utopian ideals were simply the unlimited extrapolation of personal feeling and private concern: "Everyone loves his relatives and obeys his seniors, and the world is well ordered."[179] This doctrine seems plausible—until we remember that the murdered victim of Shun's father had loving relatives too.

To avenge one's relatives was a Confucian moral code.[180] However, the Qin state, looking beyond personal relations to the public good, realized that blood feuds vitiated social tranquility. Therefore the state took over the responsibility of prosecuting wrongdoers and legally suppressed private vendettas. The Han government preserved the law, but the literati flouted it in the name of morality. Avenging wrongs on relatives and friends became a fashion in which avengers won personal fame. Revenge led to further revenge, condoned by many officials despite the law.[181] The exegetical mindset prevented the ruling elite from recognizing its selfish disdain for the common good.[182]

Personal revenge arouses emotion. Its replacement by retributive justice calls for rational value judgment. Reason, a universal human faculty, is the fount of law. Aristotle writes, "He who commends that law should rule may thus be regarded as commending that God and reason alone should rule. . . . Law is thus 'reason without desire.'" Cicero writes, "When reason is fully developed, it is law."[183] Western cultures emphasize that laws are rational and that ordinary people are capable of using their own minds to understand the rationale for the conduct that laws demand. That is why laws are edifying and law abidance is not shameless but dignified.

Reason, both in choosing ends and in choosing means to achieve a given end, is necessary although insufficient to resolve many difficulties in situations of any complexity. Being susceptible to public articulation, reason is crucial to maintaining public order. In many practical issues, rationality is simply common sense. Because laws are general rules that should fairly apply to particular cases, legal common sense emphasizes respect for truth, empirical evidence, and the consistency of ideas. In different intellectual inclinations we encounter a significant basis for disparate Greco-Roman and Confucian discourses on the law. Comparative philosophers highlight a basic intellectual difference between Aristotelian and Confucian ethics: the former tends to analyze specific factors; the latter tends to draw vague analogies.[184] By considering alternative ends and breaking processes into steps, Aristotelian reasoning attends to details of actions, crucial to legal common sense. Confucian analogies, such as that between serving the ruler and serving one's father, are mostly holistic, short on substantive details but strong in stirring sentiments, more suitable for preaching than legal reasoning.

In theory, Rome and China both upheld the principle of fairness that similar cases should receive similar treatments, as revealed in their honor of precedents. However, to judge concrete cases fairly requires efforts far beyond sloganeering. Citing precedence in legal arguments is a form of analogy, but not trivial analogy. Cases are rarely if ever exactly identical; human affairs have too many particularities. Critical analysis is indispensable. Only one aspect of a precedent may be relevant to a complex case. Several relevant precedents or laws may be contradictory in various aspects. Worse, laws may be ambivalent for a specific case, and what in fact happened is often unknown. Fair adjudication depends on laborious effort to analyze a case and tease out its aspects, with attention to evidence and specifics. Here practices diverged.

Roman history illustrates the development of laws through prolonged sociopolitical intercourse that exercised analytic reason and weighed evidence. Professional Roman jurists in the Empire taught and wrote law books but mostly refrained from advocacy in order to maintain impartiality. Magistrates and judges sought their advice to resolve difficulties. They reckoned with claims, interpreted laws, and reconciled differences. In explaining their specific judgments, they partially made explicit their intuition gained through long experience. Their solution of a difficult case could expose previous errors, smooth out kinks in the law, or illustrate a general principle applicable to a class of cases. The cases they helped to settle became precedents and their clarification of ambiguities was often incorporated into new edicts or revised laws. In this way, step by small step over the centuries, Roman jurists built up a huge corpus so carefully reasoned and intricately connected as to defy significant alteration by an emperor. The history of Roman law presents persistent application of organized common sense to a whole range of problems, increasingly separating them from the exercise of arbitrary authority. The laws capable of restraining brute power are not handed out of burning bushes but are the fruit of generations of intellectual toil.[185]

One political elite analyzed; the other moralized. While Roman jurists sweated out the details of complex cases and accumulated their experience by clear articulation, Han literati-officials sang of the Way, lofty and vague. Their doctrine, which persisted through imperial China, was *dezhu xingfu*, the rule of virtue augmented by punishment. Legal codes, being detailed and to the point, were deemed tedious and fit only for clerks. Superior men prided themselves on inscrutable virtue derived from memorizing the grand principles in the Confucian Canons. Dong Zhongshu, an early promoter of *dezhu xingfu*, also pioneered *Chunqiu duanyu*, judging cases by citing the Canons, which became widely practiced by literati-officials through the Han Dynasty.[186] Confucian ethics always focused on a person's intentions: "The doctrine of *Chunqiu duanyu* is to judge by intentions. Spare those with good intentions, even if they acted against the law. Condemn those with evil intentions, even if they acted within the law."[187] People's intentions are usually very complex and obscure. Lack of reliable evidence let in more arbitrariness. Judges claiming to be virtuous tended to rely on their own subjective feelings. Ban Gu observed that as literati-officials applied canonical principles, judges for political cases attributed hidden intentions to those suspected of disloyalty or treason. An accusation of "calumniation in the belly" could take a life.[188] In the charge of subversion against the king of Huainan, Wudì appointed Dong Zhongshu's disciple Lü Bushu to judge according to the Canons. The case resulted in tens of thousands dead.[189] By the end of the Han Dynasty, Ying Shao criticized judgment by subjective feelings and canonical citations for "vitiating the law, confusing policies, and generating regrets."[190] Bloodbaths added fuel to denunciations of the law's cruelty. However, the literati did not realize that the real culprit was not Legalist rule by law, but the law as mere punishment in the rule of men.

The canonical principles, being vague and scarce in substantive contents, left large room for exegetical license. Kind-hearted literati-officials did mitigate legal harshness in many cases, leaving valuable precedents. However, additions to the contents of law failed to compensate for the harm done to the institution of law. Their doctrine undermined the law's transparency, specificity, and consistency.[191]

Upright and insightful officers individually brought justice to many, but their acumen died with them. The admiration they won in folk legends bespeaks their rarity. More often, literati-officials scorned mundane law and order.[192] Only some acquired judiciary ability befitting their public duty. Many remained legally illiterate, judged cases by reciting the Confucian Canons, and gained fame thereby. By the Jin Dynasty, contemporaries complained that officers high and low knew no law. Precedents filled more than 900 volumes. Unlike the Roman jurists who strived to resolve contradictions and build up a legal system, Han officials merely swept together arbitrary opinions, which required far less intellectual effort. For similar cases, sentences varied greatly and judgments contradicted each other.[193] The irregularity provided more food for literati deprecation of the law and more excuse for adjudicating by virtuous whim. The practice of passing verdicts without citing the law or giving adequate reasons persisted in imperial China.[194] To show off their benevolence, Latter Han emperors regularly granted universal amnesty, which so undermined the law that criminals planned murder ahead of expected pardon.[195] The principle of fairness had gone with the wind.

As mere punishment, the law was reduced to the coercive arm of the rule of men. The change in conception was visible in the name of the government office. Qin's *tingwei*, which I translate as "the minister of fairness," connotes the senses of "public" and "level as water." Its image of a balance invoked by Zhang Shizhi should be familiar to moderns.[196] After the Han and up to the end of imperial China, law and order fell under *xingbu*, the department of punishment.

Notes

1. *Hanshu* 43: 2126–2128.
2. Dio Cassius, 54.12. Suetonius, Augustus, 35.
3. *Ershiershi* 4. Yü 2003: 231–232.
4. *Houhanshu* 1: 85; 32: 1125.
5. Wells 1992: 258, 260. Potter 2004: 124.
6. Loewe 2006: 179. Jones 1964: 182–187, 341–342.
7. Goldsworthy 2006: 213, 324, 335.
8. Wells 1992: 123–124. Syme 1939: 304, 352. Southern 1998: 156.
9. *Hanshu* 1b, 54–55. Loewe 2006: 61–64, 138. De Crespigny 2009: 93.
10. He and Wang 1997: 55. Li Y. 2002: 298–299.

11. Polybius, 40. Wells 1992: 7. Purcell 1991: 193.
12. Bodde 1986: 53–54. Zhang F. 2003: 198–203.
13. Syme 1939: 516.
14. Honoré 1995: 7–8. Lucas 1985: 106–108. Peerenboom 2002: 3, 8–9.
15. Hulsewé 1986: 524.
16. Kunkel 1973: 68–69, 73.
17. Finer 1997: 536–537. Nicolet 1993: 9. Lawson 1965: 104–105. Hulsewé 1986: 536–541.
18. Millar 1992: 616.
19. Ulpian, quoted in Wells 1992: 212, 263. *Hanshu* 60: 2659.
20. Dio Cassius 53.19. Compare Loewe 2006: 171–178.
21. Pliny, *Panegyric*, in Lewis and Reinhold 1990: 2:21.
22. *Shangjunshu* 14.
23. *Hanshu* 50: 2310.
24. Bennett 1997: 209. *Hanshu* 40: 2047.
25. Tacitus, *Histories*, 4.8.
26. Lewis and Reinhold 1990: 1:589, 2:7.
27. Loewe 2006: 171. Burbank and Cooper 2010: 4, 58–59.
28. Millar 1981: 13. See also Jones 1964: 3–4.
29. Loewe 1986b: 120. *Hanshu* 89: 3640.
30. Ward-Perkins 2005: 48.
31. Acts 22: 28.
32. Bennett 1997: 120. Ste Croix 1981: 455–462. Wells 1992: 214, 246. Garnsey and Saller 1987: 111, 116–118.
33. Wells 1992: 265–266.
34. Cameron 1993: 42.
35. Bury 1958: 16.
36. Mann 1986: 246.
37. Walbank 1981: 215–217. Lewis and Reinhold 1990: 1:620–623. Millar 2004: 298–301.
38. Pliny, *Panegyric*, in Lewis and Reinhold 1990: 2:22, 21.
39. Rostovtzeff 1957: 116, 121–122.
40. Lü 2005b: 439.
41. Ward-Perkins 2005: 39. Tacitus, *Annals*, 3.25.
42. Suetonius, Vespasian, 25. Dio Cassius 65.12.
43. Millar 1981: 34.
44. Wells 1992: 218. Starr 1982: 110–112. Bennett 1997: 67–70.
45. Schwartz 1985: 282–286. Pines 2009b: 63–71. Qian 1957: 215–219.
46. *Shiji* 10: 419.
47. *Hanshu* 75: 3154; 77: 3247.
48. Qian 1957: 284. Tian and An 2008: 258–259.
49. Dio Chrysostom, First Discourse on Kingship, 12. *Zuozhuan*, Xiang 14.
50. Augustus 34.
51. *Shiji* 6: 245.
52. Millar 2004: 8–9. *Shiji* 6: 258.
53. Wells 1992: 104–107. *Hanshu* 93: 3726.
54. Millar 1981: 18–19. Garnsey and Saller 1987: 149–150.
55. Loewe 2006: 9, 13. Lewis 2009: 122–131.
56. Millar 1992: 59–60. Qian 1957: 98–99. Loewe 2005b: 128–131.

57. Beard 2009. *Hanshu* 4: 125; 56: 2512.
58. Wang, Z. 1982: 4–5. Liao 2003: 158–167. Ch'ü 1972: 70–71.
59. Millar 1992: 209, 211.
60. Campbell 2002: 12–13. Mattern 1999: 12–13, 200–202. Millar 2004: 26, 176–177.
61. Ch'ü 1972: 69–70, 97.
62. Millar 1981: 12. Purcell 1991: 197–198. Syme 1958: 224.
63. Millar 1992: 6, 10, 266–267, 271, 617; 2002a: 298; 2004: 21–26.
64. Loewe 2006: 92.
65. *Hanshu* 5: 140.
66. Finer 1997: 482–483, 535.
67. Lucas 1985: 16.
68. Skocpol 1985: 9–12.
69. Cicero, *On Obligation*, 2.73, 2.83–84.
70. Syme 1939: 351.
71. Finer 1997: 412, 416. Gabba 1987: 210–211.
72. Garnsey and Saller 1987: 112–115. Millar 1981: 28–31. Bennett 1997: 6–9.
73. Hopkins 1983a: 120–127, 194–197. Garnsey and Saller 1987: 123–125.
74. Millar 1992: 283–285. Starr 1982: 59.
75. Harris 1979: 13. Syme 1958: 230–231. Southern 2001: 254–256.
76. Brunt 1988: 9, 54, 62. Rostovtzeff 1957: 63. Wells 1992: 214–215, 246. Crook 1967: 282–283.
77. Loewe 2006: 76. Ch'ü 1972: 104–106. Qian 1957: 50–51.
78. Loewe 2006: 40, 74–75. Qian 1957: 50–51, 74–76, 90–93. Liao 2003: 50.
79. *Hanshu* 48: 2252–2253. *Yantielun* 55–57. See section 4.5.
80. *Shiji* 130: 3290.
81. *Hanshu* 73: 3107; 88, 3620. Ch'ü 1972: 102–103.
82. Huang 1990: 57. Fung 1952: 50–51. Hsiao 1979: 79–80.
83. Lewis 2007: 116–122. Ch'ü 1972: 104–106, 206–207. Qian 1957: 50–51.
84. *Hanshu* 43: 2125–2126.
85. Chü 1972: 69. Millar 1981: 27–28. Rutledge 2001: 87–89.
86. *Hanshu* 72: 3081–3082; 76: 3215–3216. Yu 2000: 251–253, 278. Rutledge 2001: 87–89. Millar 1981: 27–28.
87. *Qianfulün* 2.
88. Tacitus, *Annals*, 1.11, 3.65.
89. Loewe 2006: 17–21. Qian 1957: 256–258.
90. Purcell 1991: 197–203.
91. Wells 1992: 115–116. Millar 2004: 47–88. Su 2001: 159–187. Loewe 2006: 29–31.
92. Millar 1981: 28–31. Bennett 1997: 6–9.
93. Millar 1981: 21–27. Syme 1958: 224. Starr 1982: 56–59.
94. Loewe 2006: 17–18, 20, 87. Su 2001: 62–65. Liao 2003: 183–197.
95. Loewe 2006: 25–33. Su 2001: 69–75.
96. Loewe 2006: 31. Huang 2002: 439–447.
97. Millar 1981: 55–58. Eck 2000b: 241.
98. Millar 1992: 110–122. Starr 1982: 69, 83. Syme 1958: 50. Jones 1964: 333–337.
99. Jones 1964: 338–341. Lao 2006: 57, 61. Huang 2002: 445–446.
100. Hopkins 1978a: 173–177. Eck 2000a: 211. Ch'ü 1972: 97–101, 168–174.

101. Loewe 2006: 185. Jones 1964: 341–344.
102. Loewe 2006: 54–55. Yang and Ouyang 2005: 281–285.
103. Garnsey and Saller 1987: 113.
104. Jones 1964: 373–375. Potter 2004: 368–371.
105. Bielenstein 1986a: 507. Yang and Ouyang 2005: 286–289.
106. Adkins and Adkins 1994: 111–112. Gibbon 1994: 1:614.
107. Millar 1981: 64–66. Lintott 1981: 65–69.
108. Aristides, *To Rome*.
109. Loewe 2006: 40–42. Su 2001: 208–210.
110. Jones 1964: 714–715; 1940: 268–269. Garnsey and Saller 1987: 28–30. Hopkins 1978b: 67–75.
111. Jones 1940: 166–170. Rostovtzeff 1957: 63.
112. Aristides, *To Rome*, 59, 64.
113. Wells 1992: 214, 238. Starr 1982: 95–96. Lintott 1981: 20–21.
114. Meier 1990: 57.
115. Jones 1964: 467–469, 724–734, 1049–1051. Potter 2004: 40–49.
116. Syme 1939: 476.
117. Matthew 27.24.
118. Loewe 2006: 47.
119. *Shiji* 30: 1420; 122, 3133, 3154. Chen, C-Y, 1984: 144–145. Lewis 2007: 85–86.
120. *Hanshu* 19a: 742; 90. *Houhanshu* 77.
121. Hopkins 1980: 121. Garnsey and Saller 1987: 20.
122. Potter 2004: 69–72. Jones 1964: 31. Lintott 1981: 48–49.
123. Millar 2004: 132, 156. Eck 2000b: 251.
124. MacMullen 1988: 124. Lewis and Reinhold 1990: 2:469–471.
125. Millar 2004: 132, 156. Eck 2000b: 251. Lewis and Reinhold 1990: 2:470.
126. Millar 1981: 61–62. Lendon 1997: 3–5. Lintott 1981: 50–52. MacMullen 1988: 145.
127. *Hanshu* 19a: 721, annotation. *Houhanshu* 24: 3558–3559. Su 2001: 116–117. Ch'ü 1972: 84–92.
128. Loewe 2006: 64–65; 2009: 74. Hsu 1980: 68–69.
129. Loewe 2006: 78. Su 2001: 75–78, 119–121.
130. Liao 2003: 218–225. Loewe 2006: 18.
131. Bu 2002: 286–288, 293, 316. Loewe 2006: 38–39.
132. *Houhanshu* 24: 3558–3559. Hsu 1965b: 368–369.
133. *Houhanshu* 24: 3555.
134. Heather 2005: 28. Kelly 2004: 111. MacMullen 1988: 144–145. Cameron 1993: 39–41.
135. Su 2001: 78–80. Liao 2003: 280.
136. *Hanshu* 19a: 743.
137. Light 2003.
138. Jones 1964: 725–726.
139. *Shiji* 129: 3261, 3274, 3281.
140. Wiedemann 1981: 8. Garnsey and Saller 1987: 43–51. Rostovtzeff 1957: 192, 343, 346.
141. Scheidel 2009b: 170–178. Greene 1986: 48–50, 59–62. Jones 1974: 69, 75–76.
142. Scheidel 2009b: 143–155. Nishijima 1986: 585–590.

143. Brunt 1981: 161–162. Potter 2004: 55. Jones 1974: 132–135.
144. *Hanshu* 24a: 1135. Nishijima 1986: 597.
145. Millar 1981: 93. Nishijima 1986: 597.
146. Jones 1974: 86–88, 129.
147. Jones 1974: 164–165. Potter 2004: 56–57.
148. Nishijima 1986: 598. *Hanshu* 1b: 46; 7: 230.
149. Millar 1981: 99, 120–122. Mattern 1999: 83–86. Jones 1964: 614–619.
150. De Crespigny 2009: 93.
151. Loewe 2006: 61–64. Hulsewé 1986: 538. Lin 2007: 481–491.
152. Millar 1981: 81, 97–98. Jones 1964: 724.
153. Nishijima 1986: 599. Hulsewé 1986: 537.
154. Jones 1974: 172–173. Potter 2004: 59.
155. *Hanfeizi* 46.
156. *Shiji* 129: 3274. *Hanshu* 72: 3075. Nishijima 1986: 599. Lin 2007: 456–457.
157. Jones 1974: 116; 1964: 1043. *Hanshu* 24a: 1137.
158. Hopkins 1980: 104–105, 122.
159. Nishijima 1986: 597–598.
160. Xün Yue, *Hanji*, quoted in Tian and An 2008: 247.
161. *Hanfeizi* 46.
162. Aristotle, *Politics*, 1294a.
163. Hart 1961: 2–3, 6–11.
164. Turner 2009: 58–59.
165. Cornell 1995: Ch. 11. Borkowski 1997: 28–30.
166. Eder 1986. Turner 1993: 314–315; 2009: 62–63.
167. *Zuozhuan*, Zhao 6; Zhao 29.
168. *Zuozhuan*, Zhao 14.
169. Bodde 1981: 178. Schwartz 1985: 324–328. Peerenboom 2002: 29–30.
170. Bodde and Morris 1967: 17.
171. See sections 4.5 and 5.6.
172. *Lunyu* 2.3, 13.3.
173. Bodde and Morris 1967: 20–23. Peerenboom 2002: 28–33. Fu 1996.
174. Aristotle, *Ethics*, 1180b; *Politics*, 1332b-1333a. Swanson 1992: 144–149.
175. *Shangjunshu* 8, 17. *Hannfeizi* 26. Bodde and Morris 1967: 23–26.
176. *Shangjunshu* 26. Cicero, *Laws*, 2.59.
177. *Mengzi* 7.35.
178. *Mengzi* 4.52, 4.59, 5.2, 5.3, 7.69.
179. *Mengzi* 7.15, 4.11, 4.27, 6.22.
180. *Liji* 1.53, 3.53.
181. *Houhanshu* 28a: 958. De Crespigny 1980: 49–59. Qian 1940: 186–190.
182. Song 2010: 374, 326–327.
183. Aristotle, *Politics*, 1287a. Cicero, *Laws*, 2.11; *The Republic*, 3.33.
184. Yu 2007: 157–158.
185. Lawson 1965: 105–108.
186. *Ershiershi* 2. Xu and Hu 2000: 116–118.
187. *Yantielun* 55.
188. *Hanshu* 24b: 1160, 1168.
189. *Shiji* 118: 3094; 121: 3129. *Hanshu* 24b: 1160; 44: 2152; 27a: 1334.
190. *Houhanshu* 48: 1611.

191. Xu 1985: 2:305, 339. Li Y. 2002: 22–35.
192. Chang 1996: 82–83.
193. *Jinshu* 30: 923. Yu 2000: 348–351.
194. Bodde and Morris 1967: 6. Peerenboom 2002: 39.
195. Turner 1993: 315.
196. *Hanshu* 50: 2310; 19a: 730, annotation.

CHAPTER 7

STRATEGIES OF SUPERPOWER

7.1 Eurasian Geopolitics

"The Huns fell upon the Alans, the Alans upon the Goths and Taifali, the Goths and Taifali upon the Romans, and this is not yet the end."[1] Thus Bishop Ambrose remarked on the domino effect that opened what would become the final act of the Western Roman Empire. Did the Huns have some pressure at their back further east?

In an interconnected world, a state's capacity to maintain peace and security depends much on the power and attitudes of its neighbors, which have other neighbors of their own. The web of interstate relations across Eurasia was exceptionally broad and dynamic in our period of study.[2] Eventually it would entangle the empires. Let us take a clockwise tour of Eurasia, beginning at the Roman Empire's north border and ending at its east (Map 13).

At the northwestern corner of the continent was Germania, northern European lands east of the River Rhine and north of the Danube, covering much of today's Germany, Poland, Czech Republic, and Slovakia. Most of it was a forested plain, swampy at the northern part, but not as forbidding as ancient Mediterranean writers had it. The peoples of Germania shared languages and cultures of certain family similarities. They divided into many tribes and identified themselves not as Germans but, for example, as Langobards or Saxons. Even these tribal names were generic and lacking in fixed referents. As bands merged and split, often the name of a small tribe became the appellation of a larger federation comprising many groups.

The Romans first encountered the Germans in the 120s BCE. Two tribes migrated south, defeated the republican army in two great battles, and vexed the Romans for more than a decade before they succumbed to Marius's reformed legions.[3] Caesar had a brush with the Germans and distinguished them from the more civilized Gauls, whom he conquered. Under Augustus, the imperial army advanced beyond the Rhine but was pushed back by a revolt. The exclusion of Germania from the Roman Empire left a rough boundary discernible today, with speakers of the Germanic languages on one side and, on the other, speakers of Romance languages descended from Latin.[4]

The Germans were mainly farmers who fought on foot. Archeological excavations revealed many communities that dwelled in the same sites for decades and even centuries. However, they migrated occasionally. By the third century, the Saxons and Franks pressed on the lower Rhine and the Alamanni on Raetia, the Roman frontier between the upper Rhine and upper Danube. The Goths, originally from what is now northern Poland, had slowly moved to what is now Romania and western Hungary, north of the Danube. Scattered German groups gradually coalesced into larger federations—for example, the Vandals.[5]

The Germans lived in punctuated peace with the Empire during its first two centuries, mingling with Romans along the borders. Trade penetrated further. As a relatively poor region, Germania's major exports to the Empire were people, and not merely slaves. Beginning as bodyguards, soldiers, and then generals in the imperial army, the Germans would climb to become kings who tore out limbs of the Western Roman Empire even before it officially expired.[6]

Lack of cohesion was a German weakness apparent to Tacitus. After describing a German tribe wiped out by a coalition of others, he remarked, "More than sixty thousand fell, not by the arms and weapons of the Romans, but, more magnificent still, to delight our eyes. Let there continue and endure, I pray, among foreign peoples, if not affection for us, at least hatred for one another, since, as the destiny of empire drives us on, fortune can furnish us nothing greater than the discord of the enemy."[7] In this respect, the Roman Empire was more fortunate than the Han.

Where trees thinned out on the Hungarian and Ukrainian plains, the Germans met nomads, the Sarmatians, Alans, and the newcomers, the Huns, who emerged from eastern mists in 376. Nomads, too, divided into many tribes and bands, but they were more capable of coalescing for aggressive exploitation of opportunities. The Huns were small in number. Their ability to integrate the Germans they defeated was what made Attila the Scourge of God when he turned against the Empire.[8]

Under a big sky unobstructed by trees, an ocean of grass sweeps from the Hungarian plain in the west through Ukraine, southern Russia, Kazakhstan, western China north of the Tianshan Range, Mongolia, to the Manchurian plain in northeastern China. This was the home of steppe nomads, whom the ancient Greeks generically called Scythians and the Chinese called Hu. They produced many empire builders, the most successful being the thirteenth-century Mongols. In our period of study came the Xiongnu and the Huns.

Pastoral nomads specialized in animal husbandry with free-range grazing and without stables. Besides herding, they also hunted for subsistence. Sima Qian wrote of the Xiongnu: "Little boys ride sheep and shoot birds and rabbits, older boys ride horses and shoot foxes and hare, for food." Ammianus Marcellinus, fourth-century Roman historian, wrote that the Huns "are almost glued to their horses."[9] The union of man, horse, and bow in everyday life nurtured supreme horsemanship and marksmanship, readily converted into military prowess most formidable before the advent of firearms.

Nomads planted crops under favorable conditions, but their mobile lifestyle precluded substantial industry. They were eager to obtain goods from sedentary folks, by trade or other means.[10] Sima Qian wrote of the Xiongnu, "Customarily, they get their living from herding flocks and hunting animals in good times, but resort to armed raids and pillages in crises." According to Ammianus, the Huns, "without encumbrances, aflame with an inhuman desire for plundering others' property, made their violent way amid the rapine and slaughter of the neighbouring peoples."[11] To spare all sides trouble, some nomads extracted regular payment from villagers for protection against other nomads and themselves. Such was the conflict-punctuated symbiosis of nomadic and sedentary peoples, who sometimes crossed over from one culture to the other.[12]

The emergence of sophisticated political organizations brought significant changes. Strong sedentary empires felt responsible to protect their frontier populations from nomadic raids, sometimes taking offence as the best defense. On the nomadic side, social differentiation increased the capacity for war and the aristocratic craving for luxury goods produced in sedentary empires. Trade and petty raids were possible. Large-scale extortion was more profitable. The nomads were happy to leave the chore of collecting revenue to the sedentary government and then wring the lump sum from it. Intimidation required force sufficient to defeat the imperial army, even if insufficient to conquer the empire. By conquest or coalition, nomadic tribes sometimes formed a confederacy, in which the supreme leader appointed governors to oversee component tribes that retained much autonomy under their own chiefs. The tribal chiefs ceded decisions on foreign matters to the supreme leader and expected from him gifts derived from foreign ventures. The nomadic confederacy concentrated military force and diplomatic bargaining power. By threats of invasion, the steppe leader extorted huge amounts from the sedentary emperor, until the latter retaliated.[13]

Lying between herding and farming cultures was not a thin line but a broad ecological zone where conditions were tolerable to both but optimal for neither.

It could serve as a buffer or, under favorable conditions, a breeding ground for marcher superpowers. More often, it acted as a double-edged sword that, in the hand of one side, cut close to the core of the other. Thus each side regarded it as necessary to control but difficult to defend. Constrained by ecology, a conqueror could not hold the spoils for more than a few generations without the help of industry and technology unavailable to the ancients. Grass and sand covered abandoned farming colonies in borderlands. Descendants of occupying nomads dissolved into the subject peasantry. No good solution existed. Unilateral inaction certainly was not one. Thus persisted what may be called a clash of civilizations, were the term "civilized" not defined by sedentary peoples in their own images.[14]

Nomads were famous for mounted archery in field battles. Diverse accounts described similar showering missiles, lightning attacks, unexpected dispersals that drew out enemies, and even more unexpected regroupings that netted the pursuers.[15] In the 53 BCE battle of Carrhae, the Parthian light cavalry of nomadic style avoided close combat, in which the Roman heavy infantry excelled. The Parthians maneuvered at a safe distance, retreated when the legions advanced, and twisted their bodies at full gallop to shoot backward at the unwary pursuers, the "Parthian shot" that was also familiar in Chinese drawings. After breaking up the Roman line, they rode circles around scattered groups, their arrows penetrating shields and armor. Legionaries who hoped for exhaustion of missiles despaired to see camel trains continuously bringing up munitions.[16]

Although terrifying at first encounter, nomadic tactics were not unbeatable against disciplined and innovative troops. The Romans lost at Carrhae, but regained confidence and turned the tide against Parthia. Chao Cuo analyzed the relative tactical advantages of the Han and the Xiongnu. The Xiongnu were superior in the quality of horses, the hardiness and martial skill of warriors, and advantages amplifiable by rough terrain. However, where battle formations did not suffer from broken terrain, Han infantry could overcome Xiongnu cavalry. The infantry's sturdy armor and sharp swords outclassed the Xiongnu's wooden shields. Its crossbows with mechanical triggers had superior aim and range, enabling the Han soldiers to inflict casualties before the nomadic archers could return fire. Crossbows required less skill and thus allowed mass deployment to compensate for their relatively low rate of fire.[17]

The Han's military weakness was not tactical but strategic. The major problem was not battling nomads but pinning them down for battle. Nomads in the steppe had the strategic advantage of fish in the ocean. The vastness of their habitat maximized the effects of their speed and mobility. By changing mounts and sleeping while on the gallop, nomads excelled in surprise maneuvers and strategic encirclement, as the Huns showed in their conquest of the eastern Goths. More important, great distance and ecological inhospitality to their sedentary enemies offered them the best protection. Many Chinese ministers argued similarly about the steppe nomads as did the Greek historian Herodotus: "A people without fortified towns, living as the Scythians do, in wagons which they take with them wherever they go, accustomed, one and all, to fight on horseback with bows and arrows, and dependent for their food not upon agriculture but upon their cattle: how can such a people fail to defeat the attempt of an invader not only to subdue them, but even to make contact with them?"[18] Marching attrition alone would destroy ill-prepared invaders. No single Han expedition against the Xiongnu lasted more than 100 days because of logistical constraints.[19] The Romans were spared the difficulty. By leaving the open steppe, the Huns lost most of their strategic advantage in the close quarters of European terrains. Even the Hungarian plain was too confining for nomadic strategies.

With static defense foiled by enemy mobility and offensives frustrated by logistics, sedentary empires were militarily inferior in their wars against nomads. On the economic and ideological fronts, however, they held the cards, provided they had the political will to use them. The Han won several battles against the Xiongnu, but its final victory also depended on economic strangulation, diplomatic isolation, and patient accumulation of advantageous potentials. In modern terms, economic sanctions, foreign aid, and manipulation of interstate relations were as important as punitive strikes and defensive fortifications in the Han grand strategy and, to a lesser extent, the Roman.

The Xiongnu grew strong during the post–Qin civil wars and defeated many nomadic tribes to forge a confederacy.[20] Among its victims was the Yuezhi, who originally dwelled on the rich pastures north of the Qilian Range, which would become the Han's Hexi Corridor. Evicted by the Xiongnu, the Yuezhi rode into Western history. There they were known as the Tokhari, the nomads who took Bactria from the Greeks who followed Alexander, according to the Greco-Roman political geographer Strabo.[21] They overran Bactria in what is now northern Afghanistan in the 120s. The Kushan Empire they founded lasted until 225. To the north, its arts influenced the Scythians beyond the Roman frontier north of the Black Sea. To the south, its realm stretched beyond the Indus River. Roman merchants sailing from the Red Sea and Persian Gulf to buy Chinese silk at the ports of what are now Pakistan and northwestern India called the hinterland Scythia.[22]

The Han pursued the Yuezhi as an anti-Xiongnu ally. The Han envoy Zhang Qian reached the Yuezhi in 128 BCE, only to find them about to overrun Greek Bactria, with no intention to cooperate with the distant Han and settle their grudge against their former enemy. Instead of an ally, Zhang brought back a trove of information about western countries, which fostered the Han's strategy to wrest them from Xiongnu hegemony and hence deprive it of economic resources. Gift-bearing diplomats led the way, followed by armies, then merchants and military colonists.[23]

Like a billiard ball scattering others, a migrating people displaced other peoples, who set even more peoples in motion. The Yuezhi's movement dispersed the Sakas, some of whom rode southwest into eastern Iran, then under Parthian rule. Little is known about them and other central Asian nomads. However, several Parthian and later Persian kings fighting the Romans had to abandon a siege or accept unfavorable peace terms in order to deal with nomadic disruptions in their north or Kushan threats in their east. As enemies to the enemy, the nomads were unknown friends to the Romans.[24]

Parthia was founded by a seminomadic people who in the mid-third century BCE moved into northeastern Iran. Slowly but steadily, the Parthians drove the Seleucids from Iran until, in 141 BCE, they captured Mesopotamia. Their empire stretched from the Euphrates to the Oxus, from the Caspian Sea to the Persian Gulf, encompassing today's Iraq, Iran, and part of Turkmenistan.[25] Parthia received an emissary from Han Wudì and returned an embassy in 113 BCE. A few years later, the first silk-bearing caravan arrived from the east via Bactria.[26]

Parthia offered friendly alliance to the Roman Republic in 92 BCE. Sulla treated its envoy with contempt and allowed only vassal status. The Parthians demonstrated their capacity for self-defense by defeating Crassus's invasion and their capacity for peace by holding a truce after Augustus. Trajan renewed hostilities. Parthia's losses angered its peoples and led to its overthrow in 224 by the Persians from what is now southern Iran. Descendants of the empire that Alexander destroyed, the Persians were more assertive and better organized.[27] Nevertheless, Persia shared Parthia's greatest disadvantage in Roman eyes: it had no standing army and had to assemble warrior aristocrats and hire mercenaries for each war. Also like Parthia, the enemies who claimed its first priority were not the Romans but the nomadic tribes in central Asia. The Huns, for example, attacked Persia first before menacing the Roman Empire.[28]

Parthia was neighbor to the Roman Empire but remote from the Han, yet the Han established friendly relations with it ahead of Rome. Militarily supreme for centuries, the Romans generally showed little curiosity about peoples beyond striking distance and rarely deigned to send diplomats. Their preference for military confrontation with Parthia/Persia would be a lasting drain of strength on both sides. Military superiority usually belonged to the nomadic enemies of imperial China. To compensate for it, the Han were more diligent than Rome in diplomacy, demonstrating their capacity to coexist with other states as equals. Deficient as ancient intelligence was, the Han knew more about Rome than Rome knew about the country that produced the silk it imported (Appendix 1).

7.2 China's Loose Rein

"The son of heaven engages the Rong and Di by keeping them on a loose rein without severing relationship."[29] Writing early in the reign of Han Wudì, the prose-poet Sima Xiangru could not have expected that the metaphor "loose rein and continuous relationship," *jimi wujue*, would become the name of a major foreign-relations stance of imperial China. Its underlying idea is to control the periphery not by brute force but by perceived power and effective virtue, often expressed in generous subsidies.[30] Of course, it works only if the center possesses enough might to back up its soft influence. That condition was unattained in the early Han Dynasty, which was inferior to the nomadic Xiongnu in political will and military might.

The Xiongnu at their apex claimed 300,000 bow drawers or adult males. From that figure we can estimate that the Xiongnu population was about 1 million, which fits with the usual comment of Han officials that the Xiongnu had only the population of a large Han province. Below the Xiongnu supreme leader, titled *chanyu*, were the left and right wise kings. They presided over the ruling council comprising six pairs of hereditary aristocrats. Twenty-four generals each commanded between a few thousand to 10,000 cavalry, which together constituted an active army of roughly 150,000 warriors, about one-half of the army reserve.[31]

The Xiongnu confronted the Han on the north and northwest. From the eastern seaboard, the frontier ran westward to the big bend of the Yellow River, cut diagonally across it, and reached Hexi. Long walls did not prevent Shuofang at the northern leg of the Yellow River from falling to the Xiongnu after Qin's demise. Shuofang and Hexi were economic bases that produced grain to supplement the Xiongnu's pastoral economy and surplus to sustain its prolonged campaigns. Beyond Hexi the Xiongnu abutted the Qiang people, whose range extended into the Tibetan Plateau. An alliance of the two peoples would threaten the Han's capital region on three sides (Map 12).[32]

One year after the foundation of the Han Dynasty, Chanyu Maodun led the Xiongnu to attack Mayi, a trading city 200 kilometers south of the long wall. Gaodì led a relief force in person and was soundly defeated at Pingcheng. The fiasco forced the Han to accept the *heqin* or amity treaty, which provided that the Xiongnu should refrain from incursion and the Han should annually render a fixed amount of silk, wine, and grain. Whenever a new emperor acceded on either side, the treaty was renewed, usually with an increase in the annual payment and the presentation of a Han princess to become the *chanyu*'s consort.[33]

First struck in 198 BCE, the amity treaty held for more than six decades. The Xiongnu reduced their raids and flocked to border markets sponsored by the Han, but peace was far from complete. Thirteen major incursions were on record, minor infiltrations innumerable. The Xiongnu attacked cities and killed provincial governors. In 166 BCE, they burned the old capital of the Qin state. Eight years later, they invaded so deeply that alarm beacons were visible at Changan. The Han drove them out, but not in time to save frontier dwellers from despoliation. After the invasions, the Han delivered annual tribute to the Xiongnu as usual.[34]

Amity degenerated into appeasement. Large tributes further strengthened the Xiongnu. Han emperors and ministers agonized whenever the treaty was up for renewal, but political and military realities constrained their options. Restive vassal kingdoms weakened the central government. As long as they were powerful, a foreign war would fail to muster requisite resources and, worse, would tempt civil discords. Such a rebellion during the Xiongnu incursion of 177 BCE had forced Wendì to forgo pursuit after driving off the intruders. Not until after Jingdì reduced the vassal kingdoms did the Han achieve sufficient internal security to address foreign threats.[35]

Farsighted, pragmatic officers did not sit idle. Chao Cuo and others advanced multiprong plans to build up what we may call, in anticipation of comparison with Roman strategy, defense-in-depth. For effective defense, the enemy must be pushed back from the border to allow early warning of potential raids. Also, a minister pointed out, "The Xiongnu repeatedly invaded only because they have no fear of the Han."[36] The perception that they could strike with impunity at a weakling must be reversed if they were to be deterred from invasions. To create the requisite physical and psychological distance, an offensive demonstration of power was necessary. Realizing that cavalry was essential to military confrontation, Wendì encouraged private horse ranging and Jingdì set up state stud forms. Thus they strengthened themselves while placating the Xiongnu.[37]

Inherited a booming economy and ample state capacity, Wudì promptly dispatched Zhang Qian to seek allies in western lands. In 133 BCE, the young emperor summoned his court: "The Xiongnu never cease their raids and our frontier populations are repeatedly terrorized. We are concerned and contemplate military offensive. Let us hear your opinions." Many points mooted over the decades had lost weight in new realities. Nevertheless, policy makers were cautious and picked a tried strategy.[38]

Back in the warring states, Li Mu of Zhao had trained a cavalry but hid it and feigned weakness in countering minor raids. After several years, the emboldened Xiongnu launched a major invasion. Li drew them in and threw out both flanks with his cavalry for a double envelopment. Thereafter no Xiongnu dared approach the Zhao border for more than a decade. Now that the Xiongnu had been emboldened by prolonged appeasement, the Han tried to lure them to attack Mayi and ambush them. The Xiongnu discovered the plot and withdrew in time. Nevertheless, the Han had found the political will to stand up to the bully.[39]

The century-long struggle between the Han and the Xiongnu would rage on military, diplomatic, and economic fronts. Han troops would march north into the Mongolian steppe and west across the Pamir. Han diplomats would venture further, bringing in their wake traders who eventually developed the silk-routes commerce. The economy of the Han would be stretched to its limit; that of the Xiongnu, beyond the breaking point. When the Xiongnu split, with one *chanyu* surrendered and the other killed fifteen years later in 36 BCE, the Han would be honing their skill on an effective "loose rein." Their patiently developed defense-in-depth would work for centuries to minimize infiltrations and provide everyday security for the frontier population.

The Han geared up slowly. Its first offensive in 129 BCE ended badly, except for the rise of a young talent, Wei Qing. Wei and, later, the even younger Huo Qubing would become the greatest generals in the war against the Xiongnu. Both were humble in origin, obtained their first post thanks to relations to the empress, and climbed on merit. Neither would have achieved much without thoroughly planned logistics and the Han cavalry, nurtured over the decades and proving themselves the match of born nomads in field battles.

In five campaigns over eight years starting in 127 BCE, the Han turned the table on the Xiongnu. In most cases, they simultaneously attacked at several points on the extended front. Not all thrusts were victorious, but they blunted the nomadic edge in mobility and prevented the enemy from reinforcing the main target or encircling the main thrust. The Han's speed and operational boldness surprised the Xiongnu, who lost Shuofang and Hexi. The *chanyu* withdrew to the north of the Gobi Desert, confident that the desert would exhaust Han troops if they dared to penetrate it. Undeterred, Wudì fattened his warhorses on grain, divided 100,000 cavalry between two prongs, and organized a baggage train of 140,000 private horses. Wei defeated the *chanyu* amid a sandstorm. Huo routed the left wise king and pursued deep into Mongolia, living off enemy supplies. The Xiongnu suffered more than 80,000 casualties and retreated further northwest. However, they remained politically strong and continued to mount minor raids. The Han were unable to exploit their victory, having lost more than 10,000 soldiers and three-quarters of their horses, which were not hardy enough for steppe campaigns. The northern front fell mostly quiet for over a decade after the cross-desert campaign of 119 BCE. Wei and Huo died during the lull.[40]

Wudì sent his infantry in other directions. Restive peoples in the southwestern mountains were pacified. The Han Empire acquired territories in what are now North Korea and northern Vietnam. Nevertheless, its chief attention never left the northern frontier. It set up special administrations for surrendered Xiongnu and handsomely rewarded their aristocrats to entice more defection. Into the Xiongnu-vacated northeastern area it moved the nomadic Wuhuan and instituted a dedicated supervisor to ensure that the buffer worked in the Empire's interest. The Xiongnu desired renewal of the amity treaty. The Han demanded political submission in return for economic subsidy. The decade of cold war was like a game of go, wherein each side maneuvered to trim the other's options, degrade its potential, and thus to amplify the disintegrative effects of domestic discord or natural disaster, which would happen eventually.[41]

Both sides saw Shuofang and Hexi as the locus of future conflicts. The Xiongnu shifted their forces westward and allied with the Qiang for a two-prong attack in 112 BCE. The Han recruited settlers from the interior, built fortifications, and planted military-farming colonies to mitigate the logistics of supplying remote garrisons. Most significant was the establishment of a row of four provinces that constituted the thousand-kilometer-long Hexi Corridor, protected by the desert on its north and nourished by streams from the Qilian Range that flanked its south. Like an arm thrusting west, the Hexi Corridor strategically separated the Xiongnu from the Qiang and protected east-west traffic for the Han. Guarding the corridor's western terminus was the massive Jade Gate. It opened onto the Western Territory.[42]

Zhang Qian, who had been captured by the Xiongnu and detained for ten years before escaping to reach the Yuezhi, returned from the west in 126 BCE. Based on the intelligence he gathered, he proposed befriending western states "to sever the right arm of the Xiongnu" and deprive it of much needed resources. Especially important was Wusun, a major nomadic state with a population about half a million in the Ili Valley near the border between today's China and Kazakhstan. The enthusiastic Wudì sent Zhang on a second imperial embassy, laden with gifts. Wusun's old king feared the Xiongnu but sent an envoy to return with Zhang. Zhang's deputies to Parthia and elsewhere also returned accompanied by state representatives. Upon seeing the Han's wealth and strength, they were happy to develop the relationship. Henceforth, western roads were busy with envoys traveling both ways. Private merchants followed.[43]

The Western Territory, over which the Han would establish a protectorate, extended from the Jade Gate to a little beyond the Pamir, mainly the Ili and Ferghana Valleys. East of the Pamir, the Western Territory comprised many oasis states. Except for a few giants, most had population in the thousands. Watered by glacier-fed streams from the surrounding mountains, they formed a ring in the Tarim Basin, encircling a desert. Xiongnu was the hegemon of the Western Territory, whose importance was elevated by the loss of Shuofang and Hexi. Not surprisingly, the Xiongnu were furious about Han activities there.[44]

The Xiongnu resumed raids around 107 BCE. Wudì's northwestern campaigns, partly for the hegemony of the Western Territory, were less successful than his northern campaigns. The Xiongnu had learned to maximize their strategic advantage by avoiding battle. The Han supply line had extended tremendously, all through arid terrains. If the oasis states en route closed their gates, a Han expeditionary force could fall to the elements, as it almost did once. Some campaigns, especially crossing the Pamir to invade Ferghana, fit the worldview of an Alexander or a Caesar better than the Chinese temperament. The Han won the allegiance of most oasis states and expelled the Xiongnu from significant parts of the Western Territory. However, casualties were high and setbacks aplenty. A heavy loss, together with the tragic death of the crown prince and social unrest, changed Wudì's mind. When officials in 89 BCE proposed military colonization to consolidate newly won territories around Luntai near the mid Tarim, he issued an edict saying, essentially, enough. Two years later he died.[45]

Wudì's Luntai edict halted vainglorious expansion but not military readiness. Although often failing to engage the enemy in battle, his expeditions penetrated deep into the steppe, sent people and herds fleeing good pastures, and caused many calves to abort. The stress, plus losing the resources of Shuofang, Hexi, and the Western Territory, strained the Xiongnu economy, and discontent fomented discord. The Han's favorable power balance enabled Wudì's successors to reduce military activity without releasing pressure on the enemy. Zhaodì implemented the Luntai colony that Wudì had rejected. Xuandì capitalized on Wudì's investment in a marriage alliance with the Wusun and grasped an opportunity to negotiate a joint military operation in 72 BCE. A distant ally neutralized the Xiongnu's advantage of withdrawing beyond the Han's capacity of pursuit. The news of a Han mobilization sent the Xiongnu fleeing en masse, so that the Han army captured only strayed enemies, as happened before. This time, however, it was augmented by the long second arm of a strategic pincer. Slammed into the Wusun army, the withdrawing Xiongnu forces suffered great losses. The Xiongnu sent a large army against Wusun for revenge, only to have it decimated by a killer snowstorm. Afterward the Xiongnu declined precipitously.[46]

In 60 BCE, the Han established its Protectorate of the Western Territory, which ruled over thirty-six statelets and lasted on and off for more than a century.[47] Thus China marched to control what is now its Xinjiang Province for the first time. It would repeat the feat twice, the first time in the seventh century and the second in the early eighteenth century, less than a century before the United States expanded across western America in pursuit of its own manifest destiny.

Starting in 57 BCE, civil conflicts wrecked the Xiongnu. Xuandì intensified divisive diplomacy. Chanyu Huhanye, defeated by his brother Zhizhi, surrendered. After eliminating Zhizhi, the Han escorted Huhanye home north of the Gobi desert as *chanyu* of the united Xiongnu. The loose-rein policy worked. Alarm beacons for invasion lay unlit for three generations. Frontier provinces prospered.[48]

Huhanye revisited Changan in 33 BCE and married an imperial lady-in-waiting, Wang Zhaojun. Numerous Han princesses had been married to the Xiongnu and other minority peoples. None achieved the legendary status of the commoner Wang, who by her beauty and volunteerism inspired endless poems through two millennia.[49] In retrospect, the Han woman riding beside her Xiongnu husband into the great steppe was a fitting image for the Han Dynasty at its height. Their descendants are Chinese.

7.3 Isolationism Ascendant

All allies and subordinate states broke loose during the post-Xin civil war. The Xiongnu, Xianbei, and Wuhuan all resumed incursions. Two decades into Guangwudì's reign, the north no longer had a quiet year. Yet the security of frontier populations took a back seat to urbane virtue in the Latter Han, whose ruling circle comprised mainly landlords and literati clans from the interior. When eighteen states of the Western Territory sent hostage princes to request restoration of the Han's protectorate, without which they said they had no choice but to ally with the Xiongnu, Guangwudì bade them do what they pleased. He extolled the virtue of letting things be without bothering to investigate reports of heavy frontier casualties.[50]

Luck smiled. A once-a-century disaster of drought and locusts ravaged the Xiongnu and caused it to split. In 48 CE, the South Xiongnu pledged allegiance to the Han, followed by the Wuhuan and Xianbei, all attracted by generous subsidies. The North Xiongnu remained hostile. Leading the states of the Western Territory deserted by Guangwudì, it attacked the Hexi Corridor and kept cities there in a constant state of siege. Over the objection of most literati-officials, the affine family in power decided to fight in 73 and again in 89–91. The North Xiongnu were routed. Their remnants molested the Western Territory until 151, after which they moved west and disappeared from Chinese records. Whether they later appeared in the west as the Huns remains controversial.[51]

The Latter Han followed the loose-rein policies developed since Wudì, but characteristically cut corners to save effort. Having absorbed many surrendered kinsmen in 91, the South Xiongnu proposed returning to the steppe, in line with the mutually beneficial settlement of Huhanye by the Former Han. Literati-officials objected to the cost of supporting an ally. Consequently, the Latter Han squandered the final victory of the Xiongnu war by allowing the

Xianbei to step into the vacuum, take over the northern steppe, and become the new menace. The South Xiongnu stayed as a heavily subsidized and threatening émigré state close to the imperial center. In 317, it would sack Luoyang and take over north China.[52]

After the anti-Xiongnu campaign of 73, the Han reinstituted its Protectorate of the Western Territory, which in earlier days had blocked Xiongnu influence and kept roads open for trade and diplomacy. However, trade, foreign relations, and frontier security meant nothing to isolationist literati-officials, who denounced the protectorate for incurring such a heavy burden on the interior that "the people's miseries move heaven and earth to pity." Zhangdì listened to them after the Xiongnu counterattacked and killed the protector general in 76. When the literati denied relief to the remnant troops, however, a pragmatic argument prevailed: "Who would your majesty send to fight the next Xiongnu invasion?" While literati pontificated, the besieged soldiers boiled their leather harness, squeezed liquid from horse droppings, and moved the earth to yield water by a well thirty-five meters deep. When rescue came months later, only thirteen made their way back to the Jade Gate.[53]

The Latter Han would have abandoned the Western Territory but for the will of one man. Ban Chao had set off in 74 as ambassador with thirty-six followers. With daring, politics, and the backing of Han promise, he persuaded many states to switch allegiance. At Shule just east of the Pamir, news came that the Han had reneged on its protectorate. The allies Ban had just won were terrified at the prospect of Xiongnu reprisal. They beseeched him to stay. Consequences could be dire, and not only if he failed at the mission impossible. The initiative and ability of officers who got practical results were targets of jealousy for venerated literati-officials. Under circumstances similar to that confronting Ban, two junior officers in the field had seized an opportunity to eliminate Chanyu Zhizhi. Instead of reward, however, their great achievement invited only censure from high court officials.[54] Regardless of such precedents, Ban decided to maintain trust with the new allies.[55]

Ban mustered native troops, scored a victory, and stabilized the situation. Then he wrote to ask for state support, arguing that the Han could control the Western Territory by employing local resources and using aliens to fight aliens, so that few troops needed to come from the interior and they could be self-sufficient in provision. Years passed. Reckoning that the Han refused involvement, mutineers appeared along the communication route. Finally, a Han detachment of 1,000 troops arrived, with a reinforcement of 800 coming four years later in 84. The tiny contingent of mostly reprieved convicts signaled the Han's willingness to be hegemon again. It gave Ban the key to unlock the value of perceived power and trustworthy reputation, the legacy for which people of the Former Han had sacrificed so much blood and gold.

Ban was able to negotiate better deals with allies, mobilize more native troops, and subdue tougher foes. The Western Territory was pacified in 94. Traffic to the west flowed again.[56]

After Ban Chao's death in 102, the Latter Han again abolished its protectorate and again the North Xiongnu moved in to threaten Liangzhou, which comprised provinces in and near the Hexi Corridor.[57] Literati-officials clamored for closing the Jade Gate. In 119, Ban Chao's son Ban Yong persuaded the government to grant 300 soldiers for active defense, with 500 added four years later when security deteriorated as he predicted. By leveraging Han commitment and rallying local states, he kept the Xiongnu away. Western trade flourished.[58]

In his debate with literati-officials, Ban Yong argued that the obsession with instant savings would only encourage invaders and escalate long-term risks.[59] The consequences of myopia were apparent in the bungled responses to the Qiang revolts, which started in 107 and flared up intermittently for six decades, decimating frontier folks and draining the state treasury.

The seminomadic Qiang divided into numerous bands without large political organization. Population pressure drove them into Liangzhou and surrounding areas. Many dispersed among the Han population under regular provincial administration. Others formed autonomous groups, which were usually exempted from taxes but not from corvée and military levy. The Han instituted supervisory agents to address their concerns and often mustered Qiang cavalry alongside Hu cavalry of the Xiongnu and other nomads.[60]

The Qiang presented a perfect minority people upon whom literati-officials could practice the benevolent ideology they preached. Military intervention was unnecessary. Sound local governance sufficed. The literati filled most provincial posts, where they could make a real difference. Some officers obviously did, and where they worked, they won over even rebels. Unfortunately, they appeared to be the exceptions. Their practical achievements were often ignored if not mocked.[61] Inept provincial officers, predatory local magnates, and discriminating Han-Chinese neighbors were the major causes of Qiang unrest, identified by contemporaries and historians alike.[62]

The uprising began small, but official responses were dismal, as contemporary Wang Fu described: "Too cowardly to fight, they sit and write reports. . . . They misstate the size of banditry, twist facts, and lie under literary elegance. . . . After egregious waste emptied official coffers, they force loans from the people and seize properties."[63] Literati-officials promptly called for pitying the people of the interior and sparing them the burden of pacifying Liangzhou. Central ministers, busy struggling for power with eunuchs, complained of costs. Provincial governors, who mostly came from the interior, were eager to shirk responsibility. Immediate evacuation of five Liangzhou provinces was permitted. When Han residents refused to abandon their homes, officials had their crops mowed and houses burned. Qiang rebellions spread. The corpses of refugees strewed the roads.[64]

Effective objection came from Yu Xu, a junior officer. Like Ban Yong, he argued that the defense of the interior would be far more costly once the frontier was in enemy hands. The disregard of frontier folks was not only callous but also myopic. Han residents of Liangzhou were high in martial spirit, and their loyalty constrained Hu and Qiang aggressiveness. If they felt betrayed by the government and revolted, the Han would have an enemy far more dangerous than the Qiang.[65]

Yu Xu's reasoning prompted top ministers to reverse their decision of abandoning Liangzhou and adopt the pragmatic policy of promoting frontier leaders to address local issues. Yet problems were widespread. Faction fights in the central government inhibited policy consistency. Violence flared up after temporary calm. When Qiang uprisings were finally suppressed in 168, the Han Dynasty was exhausted.[66]

Ideological monoculture, which vitiated the state's brain and brawn, was partly responsible for the Han's poor responses. Virtue rhetoric clouded assessments of realistic situations, and exegetical thinking numbed the intellectual faculty to tackle problems. The pedant tried to quell unrest by distributing the *Canon of Filial Piety*.[67] Lack of training wrecked the army. Conscripts could not fight. More and more, the Han had to depend on Hu and Qiang warriors.[68] By cultural snobbishness and administrative incompetence, the Middle Kingdom alienated the peoples of its periphery, on whose military prowess the imperial center increasingly relied. The days of reckoning neared.

7.4 Rome's Empire Without End

> For these I set no limits, world or time,
> But make the gift of empire without end.

Thus Jupiter ordained these "Lords of the world, the toga-bearing Romans" in Virgil's *Aeneid*, written early in Augustus's reign.[69] Virgil's *imperium sine fine*, empire without end, expressed an enduring Roman worldview. The Empire preserved intact the republican élan enunciated by Cicero: "That the Roman people should be subject to other people is contrary to divine law; the immortal gods have willed it to rule all nations."[70] Four centuries after Virgil, Rutlilius Namatianus sang of the Roman Empire:

> Your power is felt wherever the sun's light shines,
> Even to the farthest edge of the world.[71]

At that time, the City Rome had already surrendered to the Visigoths. "Empire without end" became mere rhetoric very late. Rome backed it by a professional army, well trained, supplied, and organized as an offensive force. Founded by Augustus, the imperial army fluctuated around the 300,000-man level for more than two centuries, trending upward.[72] Imperial expansion began soon after Augustus settled political scores with the Senate in 27 BCE. Pacification of Spain and Africa pushed the Empire west to the ocean and south to the desert. Only two frontiers remained interesting. Neither was exhaustible, and they were one too many. Augustus decided to reduce hostility on the eastern front and concentrate on the north.[73]

In the east, the province of Syria anchored Rome's confrontation with Parthia, its only organized neighbor and an affront to its freedom to expand beyond the River Euphrates. Rome claimed suzerainty over Armenia, which shared culture with Parthia and often took a Parthian prince as its king. Armenian succession offered many excuses for Rome and Parthia to quarrel or shove. Crassus's invading army was annihilated. Caesar's plan for revenge was foiled by assassins. Antony's incursion hurt himself foremost. Augustus's intimidating diplomacy was more successful. In 20 BCE, Parthia returned the legionary eagle standards that it had captured from Crassus and Antony.[74] Augustus displayed this event, symbolic of Roman honor redeemed, on his armor in his most popular statue. "He received them as if he had conquered the Parthians in a war," remarked Dio.[75]

Imperial attention concentrated on the northern frontier for the remaining three decades of Augustus's reign. Logistical planning of Augustan campaigns dwarfed that of the Gallic campaign, when shortage of provisions constantly dogged Caesar. Archeologists found the beginning of a systematically organized flow of goods from the Mediterranean to the northern frontier, partly to supply its numerous forts and fortresses. The emperor personally stayed in Gaul from 16 to 13 BCE to supervise the campaign wherein his stepsons proved their military talent. In coordinated attacks, Tiberius marched west from Gaul and Drusus north from the Alps, adding to the Roman Empire today's Switzerland, Austria, and a part of southern Germany (Map 11).[76]

The brothers received separate commands in 12 BCE. Tiberius campaigned in the wild country of Pannonia, today's Slovenia, Croatia, and eastern Hungary. Controlling the land route from Italy to the Balkans, Pannonia was the fulcrum between the eastern and western parts of the Empire. Tiberius's victories, coupled with actions in the Balkans, extended Roman territory to the Danube along its whole length. Drusus crossed the Rhine and invaded Germania via three routes. In 9 BCE, Roman troops reached the Elbe, at whose mouth now stands Hamburg. They did not venture beyond it, however. Shortly afterward Drusus died, Tiberius retired, and Augustus turned his attention to dynastic manipulation.[77]

Like the First Emperor of China, they rested too early. Pannonia revolted in 6 CE, and the rebellion spread all across Illyricum. Augustus assembled the largest force since the civil war by drastic measures amid bitter protests. With it and three years of hard fighting, the recalled Tiberius suppressed the great rebellion in the land he had conquered two decades earlier.[78]

The exhausted imperial house had five days to savor its triumph before disastrous news arrived from Germania. The Romans had enlisted many subdued Germans into their auxiliary units and made citizens and junior officers of their leaders. Among these was Arminius, the twenty-five-year-old chief of the Cherusci. Notice his Latin name, which nationalists struggling for German unification discarded in favor of Hermann when they erected a giant monument for him in 1841.[79] Augustus had considered Germania pacified and ordered the governor Varus to establish normal taxation.[80] It was a mistake. Varus was ambushed by a German alliance led by Arminius. Three legions—half the total force in the Rhine area—perished in the Teutoberg Forest. Augustus rent his clothes in grief and repeatedly banged his head on the door, crying, "Varus, give me back my legions!"[81] The Elbe was lost, but Tiberius's quick action saved the Rhine. Arminius failed to expand his alliance and exploit the victory. Troops transferred from other theaters rebuilt the Rhine army, which Augustus put under the command of young Germanicus, Drusus's son and next in the line of intended succession after Tiberius.[82]

Augustus claimed to have pacified Germania "to the mouth of the Elbe" in his *Achievements*, finished months before his death in 14. Contrary to this ebullience, however, he advised in his will against extending the Empire beyond its current boundaries.[83]

The Romans returned to Teutoberg Forest in 15 and regained honor with massive slaughtering. Germanicus offered the prospect of final victory in one more year, despite heavy casualties from combat and marching attrition. However, Tiberius called off the German campaign. With his experience of nine commands in Germania, the new emperor knew the peoples and conditions on the ground. Military victories were futile without adequate organization for occupation, the requisite resources for which were unwarranted for such poor and intransigent folks.[84]

Tiberius's successors were more active. Caligula directed a German campaign, which he turned into a farce. Claudius conquered Britain, a significant addition to the Empire. Nero planned a grandiose eastern campaign. After winning the civil war, Vespasian cleared Raetia and expanded the adjacent province to create a smooth northern frontier.[85]

The endless empire crested under Trajan. Augustus left the imperial army at twenty-five legions, its low point. Trajan built it up to thirty legions, each enlarged in size. With it, he expanded the Empire beyond the Danube and

Euphrates. Dacia in today's Romania sat across the Danube, facing Roman provinces in what is now Bulgaria and Serbia. Trajan's Dacian campaigns ended in 106 with most Dacian men killed or enslaved and the surviving native population expelled. The state treasury was filled with the last great haul from Roman imperial conquests. A salient protruding beyond the Danube became a new Roman province, populated by settlers recruited from the Empire and greatly extending its defense line.[86]

Parthia had only minor frictions with Rome since it made peace with Augustus. Trajan launched a war of conquest and annexation in 113. His huge invasion force included soldiers from seventeen legions and auxiliaries. The Parthians cooperated by quarreling among themselves. After three years of fighting, Trajan captured their winter capital Ctesiphon near Babylon (south of Baghdad), made two Roman provinces out of their territory, and sailed with his fleet down the Euphrates to become the only Roman emperor to wash his sword in the Persian Gulf and dream of Alexander the Great. The wake-up bell rang promptly. The loss of Ctesiphon induced the Parthians to unite in harassing his supply line. Unrest flared up around the empire strained for the war effort. Trajan retreated in 117 and wrote to the Senate: "So vast and infinite is this domain, and so immeasurable the distance that separates it from Rome, that we do not have the compass to administer it."[87] He died within the year and received the posthumous honor of *optimus princeps*. All eastern territories he conquered were relinquished by Hadrian within a few days of accession.[88] "Thus it was that the Romans, in conquering Armenia, most of Mesopotamia, and the Parthians, had undergone severe hardship and dangers for naught," wrote Dio.[89]

Not all was naught. Unlike Augustus's futile venture beyond the Rhine, Trajan's campaigns beyond the Danube and Euphrates were pregnant with consequences, and not only because Dacia and Parthia yielded more loot than Germania. The actions pulled the Empire's center of gravity away from Italy and the Rhine. The Danube frontier would become preponderant in foreign affairs and domestic politics, and its legions would produce the best soldiers and many able emperors. Trajan had also shattered the image of Parthian invincibility in homeland defense. Henceforth his war replaced Augustus's diplomacy as the paradigm of Roman grand strategy. It elevated the risk for the Empire to face two hot fronts. Increasingly more troops tied down on the Euphrates would weaken the northern frontier. At the hinge of the Danube and Euphrates frontiers would rise Constantinople. The collapse of the Rhine frontier would be the fatal blow to Rome.

All fronts were quiet for more than four decades after Trajan. Upon the accession of Marcus Aurelius in 161, Parthia regained enough strength to resume its usual pestering and get the usual swat, now upgraded by Trajan's exploit. Aurelius sent his co-emperor Verus, who sacked Ctesiphon and destroyed Seleucia across the Tigris, although the Greeks in this last Hellenistic outpost had received Roman troops as friends. The expedition had two unintended consequences. The returning army brought back the plague, which would kill about one-tenth of the Empire's population. The second consequence may be less unexpected. Drawing off troops to fight the Parthians gave opportunities to the Germans.[90]

An incursion of about 6,000 barbarians across the Danube was repelled by local legions in 166. Four years later, the Marcomanni and Quadi crossed the Alps into northern Italy while other tribes on the lower Danube burst into the Balkans. The panic in Rome was short-lived. Aurelius swept them out. However, he realized something new was afoot. Over the centuries, German agricultural productivity had been creeping upward. Populations grew. Slowly, pressure mounted. Unrest simmered all along the Danube front. Aurelius launched an offensive to stem it.[91]

The so-called Marcomannic War actually involved some twenty-five tribes, mostly Germanic. It dragged on for a decade. Aurelius imposed harsh treaties that impeded assembly, curbed trade, and extracted troops for the Roman army. The piecemeal victories were hard won. Subdued tribes revolted again in collusion with other tribes. The enemies had to be defeated group by group, repeatedly and patiently. Although distressful to his temperament, Aurelius bore the Roman emperor's duty to campaign in person; Verus had died prematurely. There, in the snowy mud and gloomy forest of the Danube frontier, his health failing, he wrote his diary we know as the *Meditation*, in which he summoned the inner strength of a Stoic philosopher to overcome the grim reality in a protracted test of will with the Germans. He died in camp near today's Vienna in 180.[92]

7.5 Defense Resources Strained

What Rome conquered was by divine right Rome's. Trajan's ephemeral annexation of Parthian territory bequeathed a duty, which Septimius Severus fulfilled. His 195 invasion established the lasting Roman province of Mesopotamia in today's northern Iraq. Rome's victories weakened the Parthian royal house, which fell in 224. The Persians who replaced it began to reclaim the territories it lost. To meet the challenge, Severus Alexander left for Syria in 231, taking with him troops from the Rhine and the Danube. The Romans won, but as they nursed their own casualties bad news arrived. The Alamanni overran Raetia. Soldiers worrying about their homes became restive. Alexander took five months to march from the Euphrates to the upper Rhine, where he defeated the Alamanni in 234. Instead of pursuing deep into Germania, however, he negotiated peace and earned the wrath of soldiers who had lost their families. His murder precipitated five decades of political anarchy. The Romans began to pay for the legacies of the *optimus princeps*: two far-apart fronts and the obligation for the emperor to campaign in person.[93]

Persia was quiescent until the accession of its second and most aggressive king, Shapur I. Taking advantage of Rome's internal discord, Shapur I waged three campaigns and defeated three emperors. Gordian III was killed and Valerian captured. Philip escaped by paying a large sum. The Persian victories were not repeated, however. Rome recovered to score a decisive victory in 298, by which it regained all its former territory and then some.[94]

The boundary of Roman Mesopotamia cut through territory traditionally under Parthian hegemony and separated peoples who shared common language and culture. Rome had to hold down an alien population in the face of a tenacious rival fortified by a sense of justice. Parthia/Persia wanted Mesopotamia back, which was reason enough for Rome to launch preventive strikes. Scholars who survey Rome's Persian wars find that Rome was usually the attacker.[95] Shapur I's invasions in 253 and 260 were the only occasions in which Persians crossed into Syria before the sixth century, and they did not stay. Roman troops were in Ctesiphon far more often. Dio, who served as provincial governor under Septimius Severus, predicted that Mesopotamia would be a source of constant, costly, and futile wars, because as the occupier Rome would be fighting other peoples' wars.[96] History confirmed his insight. Constantine, Constantius, and Julian invaded in vain. The potentially lucrative Visigothic immigration in 376 turned into the Hadrianople calamity partly because engagement with Persia left the Danube front with insufficient troops to handle the influx. Augustus's premonition came to bear: Those who overextend themselves risk losing their possessions.[97]

Tacitus, who had considered German tribes more dangerous than Parthian kings but for their disunity, would dislike the increase in German cohesiveness, but would not be too alarmed. Names such as Alamanni, Franks, and Goths—which respectively meant "all men," "the fierce or free," and "human beings"—designated not mere tribes but federations. However, their organizations were still loose.[98] German operations of the third century were raids by small bands aiming at plunder of movable goods. Their scale and intensity seem comparable if not smaller than those of the Xiongnu raids into the Former Han Dynasty under the amity treaty. The decisive battle of 271, by which Aurelian halted the Goths, claimed less than 5,000 Gothic deaths. Most other barbarian bands were much smaller. Inferior in discipline, weaponry, and supply, they were subdued as soon as the Romans took time out from fighting each other. The Goths settled into treaty relations with the Romans, who paid subsidies for Gothic troops.[99]

Although not cataclysmic to imperial security, the hit-and-run raids devastated local populations and posed a dilemma to imperial grand strategy. The imperial army was designed foremost to secure the position of the emperor, but protection of provincial populations demanded different military organization and strategies. The difference may not have mattered when the army had ample capacities for both. Such happy times were passing, however. Increased taxation could support an army of up to 645,000 by some estimates, but how to deploy it still presented difficult choices for emperors.[100]

Diocletian secured internal stability by sharing political power. Using Roman troops released from civil conflicts, he reinforced the frontier. Repaired fortifications, new roads, and logistic bases restored the empire, battered by five decades of anarchy, as a fortress with a defense ring of significant depth. It was austere, but as a modern strategist concludes his analysis, "In the stern rule of Diocletian lay the key to a difficult salvation for the empire and its civilization, while in the seemingly happier age of Constantine were the beginnings of the final disaster."[101]

Constantine had spent the larger part of his political life in civil wars to become the sole emperor. He created large field armies, the *comitatenses*, which enjoyed more privileges than ordinary legions on the frontier. The best *comitatenses* were central armies stationed close to the emperor. As mobile reserve, they were useful against usurpers or massive invasions. However, most actual foreign threats were small-scale incursions scattered along a long frontier, against which the central strike force was like a catapult against flies.[102] Furthermore, the *comitatenses* creamed off powerful mobile elements from the frontier. The remaining frontier troops, the *limitanei*, were slighted and often short on supplies and imperial donatives. Constantine repaired frontier fortifications, but with less zeal than the lavish construction of Constantinople. No systematic effort for fortifying the Rhine frontier occurred in the fourth century, although the need for it skyrocketed.[103]

In 376, seven years after Emperor Valens and Gothic leader Athanaric sealed a treaty both sides could claim to have won, the balance of power was upset by an unexpected factor—the Huns. Throngs of Visigoths appeared across the Danube and begged for asylum from these terrible nomads. They obtained legal entry into the Empire, warriors, women, and children, numbered in six figures. Corrupt officials disregarded the order to disarm and allowed through many weapons. Inept administration incited the starving refugees to rebel. Local forces were overwhelmed. Valens, far away confronting the Persians, hastily concluded a deal to disengage his field army. Troops promised by his western co-emperor Gratian did not arrive. Valens met the Visigoths at Hadrianople in 378, only to perish with two-thirds of his army.[104]

Up to 20,000 Romans fell at Hadrianople. Ammianus regarded it as the greatest disaster since the battle of Cannae, where Roman casualties approached 70,000. The Republic bounced back with only the resources of peninsular Italy. Now, the Empire boasted a population of 70 million, marshaled against an enemy puny compared to Carthage. Hadrianople was a historic turning point not because of the size of the loss but because of the Empire's weakness in recovery. Cracks appeared in Roman resiliency.[105]

The Visigoths defeated the new army assembled by Valens's successor, Theodosius. The Romans were unable—or unwilling to exert themselves—to expel or eliminate the intruders. Neither side could win, but Theodosius claimed victory in the peace treaty of 382. An émigré state as an ally, the Visigoths received land inside the Empire, where they retained their arms and autonomy without supervision. In return they contributed troops, who fought under their own commanders alongside Roman legions. The Visigoths had destroyed one emperor, two armies, and countless Roman homes, but got reward instead of punishment, a lesson not lost on other barbarians. Theodosius was unforgiving by nature; at least 7,000 Roman citizens in Thessalonica were indiscriminately massacred to assuage his wrath over the lynching of its governor in 390. In conceding to the Goths, he might just have had higher priorities on his agenda, such as purging pagans and dissidents within the Christian Church.[106]

Theodosius twice summoned the Visigothic immigrants to fight civil wars, the second of which doubled as a holy war because his western rival solicited pagan support. In the 394 battle of River Frigidus, the Visigoths helped Theodosius to become sole emperor for a few months. The Christian historian Orosius praised Frigidus for two Roman victories, one over pagans, the other over barbarians, because the Visigoths suffered heavy casualties at the front line of Theodosius's deployment. Perhaps the barbarians had the last laugh. Exasperated by Roman callousness to their losses, the Visigoths rebelled in 395 and became the strongest of the barbarian groups that would carve up the Empire. Furthermore, Frigidus decimated the western field army. To reinforce it, border garrisons were stripped of troops. Then, at the end of December 406, the Rhine froze. Vandals, Alans, Suevi, and other Germanic groups walked across the river and spread over Gaul, Spain, and Africa to repeat the adventure of the Visigoths. The emperors were protected by the central field armies, but the loss of the provinces sealed the fate of the Western Roman Empire.[107]

7.6 Imperial Grand Strategies

Our comparative analysis of imperial foreign policy proceeds from broad horizons to local situations. The Roman and Han Empires expressed certain worldviews interpretable as imperial grand strategies. To realize their overarching objectives and maintain asymmetric power relations with their neighbors, their hegemonic statecraft utilized psychological, diplomatic, economic, and military means. The empires also tried to secure the everyday safety of their frontier populations from incursions. Such frontier defense can be compatible with an aggressive grand strategy.

Grand strategy, which aims to preserve and enhance a state's overall, long-term interests in peace and war, is the result of foreign policy making at the highest level; for example, in the national security council chaired by the president and attended by the heads of the state department, defense department, treasury, intelligence agencies, and relevant political leaders.[108] It is much more than military strategy, which is the job of the defense department. Writings such as Sunzi's *Art of War* concern military strategy. Attempts to lift a grand strategy from them produce misleading pictures of a nation obsessed with war.[109]

Ancient governments lacked the capacity to draw up systematic plans, but they did not lack visions. By "grand strategy" I mean not a blueprint but a stabilizing "gyroscope," not a grand decision but a rough coherence in myriad smaller decisions, some disposition or general understanding that fosters some consistency in response to erratic challenges. Rome's persistency in conquests and resiliency in setbacks bespoke a gyroscope in operation. So did the Han's long struggle with the Xiongnu. A gyroscope is susceptible to resetting or malfunction, especially over several centuries. This we see in the grand strategic shifts from the high to late empires.

A realistic foreign policy responds to geopolitical conditions but is not solely determined by them. Policy makers must act despite the dearth of information and the scarcity of resources. Under these constraints, the characteristics of the ruling elite affect how they assess foreign threats and mobilize for action.[110] The elite are heterogeneous. Empire and emperor, prosperity and security, interior and frontier, present and future—each has its claims. Assembling diverse desirables and setting some priority for concerted action are among the most difficult of grand strategic chores.

Historians who study them face further difficulties. The intentions of historical actors are often hidden or disguised in propaganda, which led Polybius to distinguish between reasons and pretexts for Roman wars. Sources are scarce and historians often resort to revealed preferences. Just as economists try to discover what consumers want by observing where they spend their money, historians try to elicit tendencies from patterns of behavior.

When Parthia meddled in the Armenian succession, Nero summoned his council and asked, "Was it to be a hazardous war or a humiliating peace?" The council decided on war without hesitation.[111] When Gaodì died, Chanyu Maodun asked for Empress Lü's hand, saying he had always desired to reside in the Middle Kingdom. The empress rejected the insolence but sent gifts and begged him not to invade. In the subsequent decades, Han emperors repeatedly asked their courts whether to renew the amity treaty. They preferred paying tribute and offering princesses to a hazardous war.[112]

Emperors are the focus in textual sources. Combing through what emperors did and how they were appraised by contemporaries and close posterity, scholars discern two widespread patterns. High praise for conquest and empire was the all-pervasive judgment of Augustus's contemporaries. The ideology of an empire without limit remained central to the Roman stereotype of a good emperor. Later ages prayed for an emperor "braver than Augustus and better than Trajan." The two were the greatest imperial conquerors.[113] The appreciation they received from the Romans contrasted with the Chinese appraisal of Wudì, the greatest Han conqueror who expanded territories in all directions. Wudì's offensive against the Xiongnu was closer to a war of necessity than were the wars of Augustus and Trajan; the Xiongnu had frequently invaded and were gaining strength from Han tributes. Yet his military achievement became a black spot of his reign. Literati-officials objected to posthumous honor because of it. Ban Gu obliterated it in the short praise that concludes Wudì's annals in the *Book of Han*.[114]

The three martial emperors each suffered a significant setback shortly before his death. Wudì lost an army in the Western Territory. Augustus lost three legions in the Teutoberg Forest. Trajan was forced to withdraw from Mesopotamia. The defeats prompted the first two to rethink their policies. Wudì issued the Luntai Edict, which blamed others for the defeat, halted foreign expansion, and limited military activities to maintaining readiness, so that the people could rest and devote themselves to farming and enrichment.[115] Augustus saved his thoughts for an advice appended to his will, read posthumously. Unlike Wudì's edict, its text has not survived. According to Tacitus, he counseled that the Empire be kept within its present frontiers. Dio included his warning that further expansion would be difficult to defend and might cause the Empire to lose what it had already acquired.[116]

The similar admonitions from Wudì and Augustus elicited different responses. Wudì's edict came to be called the Luntai Contrition. Ban Gu exaggeratedly said that the emperor "deeply regretted his previous policies."[117] Subsequent arguments often referred to it. Overall, Wudì's retrenchment won applause and exerted constraint. Contrast Tacitus' remark on Augustus's advice: "Either he feared danger ahead, or he was jealous." Germanicus campaigned as if it did not exist. Hadrian did not invoke it to justify his controversial decision of abandoning Trajan's conquests.[118] Nor did Commodus mention it when he ended his father's war. The rate of Roman expansion subsided after Augustus, but none of his successors won admiration for restraint.[119] Indeed, Tacitus indicted Tiberius for dereliction: "Rome was plunged in gloom, the ruler uninterested in expanding the empire."[120]

The integration of political and military considerations is a cornerstone of grand strategies. Failure in integration manifests itself in the weakness of political will. Diverse self-interests coexist within the decision-making elite. What counts as cost or gain depends on who does the reckoning. Topmost is the emperor's concern for self-preservation. Claudius invaded Britain mainly because he needed the military glory to firm up his shaky accession. After his conquest, no emperor could afford to be the one who lost Britain, regardless of the resources it drained from the Empire.[121] Guangwudì refused to lift a finger to prevent western states from joining the Xiongnu to despoil frontier populations. Having gained the throne by insurrection, he was eager to please his supporters, landlords of the interior unwilling to pay for frontier security.[122] In these cases, the emperor's self-interest could take partial cover in characteristic values, Roman glory or Han urbane virtue. The worst detriment to imperial grand strategy was rivalry to the throne and civil war, which became rampant in the twilight of empires.

Regionalism is a curse of empires. A foreign policy has various impacts on various regions of a large empire, whose responses vary accordingly. Han literati decried expenditures to justify their reluctance in resisting Xiongnu incursions and their eagerness for abandoning Liangzhou to Qiang rebels. Selfishness, not virtue, led them to refuse help to frontier kin who fought for the safety of all, countered Sang Hongyang, who compared the interior and frontier to a person's trunk and limbs. Chao Cuo wrote that frontier people yearned for protection and would desert if they felt ignored by their government.[123] Their arguments were equally cogent against parochialism in the late Roman Empire. Themistius, mid-fourth-century senator and a favorite of three emperors, opposed defending Syria or rebuilding the cities ruined by German raids: "even if we succeeded in doing so, the only ones to notice would be the Syrians, Thracians, and Gauls, and the victory in each case would belong only to the neighboring territory. But if a moderate fiscal policy were conducted, it would be for the common benefit of all those inhabiting the world."[124] To paraphrase Yu Xu's retort to a similar argument, if Gaul fell to barbarians, Rome would not enjoy low taxes for long. This reasoning history would soon validate.

Future generations have few champions in the present, but intergenerational trade-offs are no less vital to imperial grand strategies that must reckon long-term consequences. How should present decisions account for future costs and benefits? How would mortgaging the future affect imperial longevity? The German or Xiongnu problem was perennial, and fortunes fluctuated. Some emperors realized that if the empire did not address the problem when its capacity was ample, its people would suffer more when the balance of power shifted. For durable security, Marcus Aurelius wore himself out on campaign to punish the Marcomanni who invaded the Empire. Wudì decided to apply the present generation to fight the Xiongnu, as he told his crown prince: "I take on the chore, so you can inherit leisure."[125] In contrast, Theodosius rewarded the Goths who ravaged several provinces, contented with levying troops from them. Guangwudì preached, "Those who sacrifice the near in pursuit of the distant labor in futility. Those who sacrifice the distant in pursuit of the near enjoy fruits in leisure."[126] Their minimization of effort won contemporary flattery. For Theodosius's complacency, his son's generation paid with the ruins of Greece and Italy. The consequences of Guangwudì's myopic foreign policy were longer coming, but modern scholars blame it partly for the loss of northern China and the subsequent three centuries of bloody disunity.[127]

7.7 Hegemonic Statecraft

Ancient peoples at either end of Eurasia had notions of "the world"—the Chinese *tianxia*, Roman *orbis terrarum*, and Greek *oikumenē*. The First Emperor of Qin repeatedly claimed in stele inscriptions that he united "all under heaven" for the first time.[128] Since then, political unity has become the persistent ideal that helped China to regenerate itself after periods of fragmentation. The West experienced a series of empires: Assyria, Media, Persia, Macedonia, and Rome. Adapting the idea of imperial succession, Rome claimed domination over the globe.[129] Coins and sculptures depicted the globe under the feet or on the palm of goddess Roma, Augustus, or other emperors. These images inspired a recent interpretation of Romanization as "globalizing Roman culture."[130]

Despite the rhetoric of world mastery, contemporary writings all acknowledged the reality of territories beyond the imperial boundary.[131] They distinguished between *imperium* as power and *imperium* as territorial empire.[132] The Roman and Han aspired to endless hegemonic power with a large territorial core, which had some kind of boundary. The Roman Empire was bounded by desert, the ocean, and great rivers. Heads of state sometimes met on bridges or vessels, as Valens and Athanaric met on boats midstream on the Danube.[133] Lacking natural landmarks on their northern frontier, the Chinese built long walls. Wendì wrote Chanyu Laoshang to complain about Xiongnu incursions that violated amity: "The country of bow drawers north of the long wall *chanyu* rules. The country of cap and girdle wearers south of the long wall is our jurisdiction."[134]

Neither empire considered its boundary fixed or a barrier to its power and influence. The Zhou kings imagined five degrees of rule that spread out like attenuating ripples from a royal center. Stripped of archaic details, this view distinguished the royal zone ruled directly by the king, the lords' zone ruled indirectly by the king, and the less civilized zone where the king reigned but did not rule.[135] The power structure was illustrated as three concentric circles in the Chinese literature. It resembles the schematic for Rome's hegemonic empire offered by a modern strategist.[136] In their early days, the Han and Roman Empire each contained significant subordinate kingdoms in its geographical interior, so that the middle ring of indirect rule appears thick on the power schematic. These kingdoms were mostly eliminated during a century of consolidation that turned the interior into a huge, directly ruled territorial state. New client kings appeared, however, especially beyond the respective northern imperial boundary. Instead of disappearing, the zone of indirect rule was squeezed into a thin crust.

The matured imperial world order comprised three zones with fuzzy boundaries: an interior core, a frontier zone, and the outland. The large core was organized into provinces, whose governors were appointed by the central government. So was a part of the frontier, which stretched extensively on both sides of the empire's political boundary and accommodated many subordinate kings and chiefs. Beyond the frontier were more peoples, whom the empire tried to influence. How did the empire maintain relations with peoples of the outland? How did it tighten the rein on the frontier kings and pull them toward the core? These were the goals of its hegemonic statecraft.

Asymmetry was characteristic of the relations. A superpower extolling its order and wealth and civilization faced a bunch of peoples, warlike but poor, with small populations, inferior tools, and motley organization, illiterate, barbaric. Because of the disparity in power, these peoples posed no lethal threat to the empires for centuries. However, they were more than nuisances. Their raids drew blood and instilled fear along the frontier. Disparate cultures made them difficult to assimilate. With these enemies, which the empires could defeat but could not eliminate or govern with reasonable costs, the empires maintained asymmetric relations augmented by asymmetric warfare, which only rarely escalated into symmetric battles. Their hegemonic statecraft involved many operations other than war: political manipulation, diplomatic suasion, economic control, and, not least, psychological pressure.

Targeting the mind of adversarial decision makers is a preferred strategy in classical Chinese arts of war. Strategic planning should aim "to leave one's force unscathed while winning the benefit intact," wrote Sunzi.[137] One way to achieve this goal is to demonstrate one's *de*, effective virtue, and *wei*, puissance, prestige, or intimidating strength. When Minyue, a minor kingdom in southwest China, attacked its neighbor in 135 BCE, Wudì ignored pacifist counsel and called up an army. The show of force cowed Minyue. "Puissance intimidated the brutal king" without losing a single soldier: that was the message Wudì sent his pacifist uncle.[138] Evident power to hurt and self-restraint in using it awe perceivers. "Deterrence" is the modern strategic term.

"The Romans understood all the subtleties of deterrence," wrote a modern strategist.[139] Their practices were characteristically more forceful. A historian, having compiled pages of examples from the Republic through the Empire, concludes: "The strategy of deterrence by terror was not a policy invented by a particular emperor and his council. It was traditional; it was the Roman way."[140] The Roman response to resistance, although not always swift, was certain and, when it came, ruthless, relentless, and loudly advertised. "To inspire terror" was Polybius's explanation for the ferocity of republican massacres. Tacitus described how imperial Romans "terrified the surrounding population" by denying surrender to a city and exterminating its inhabitants.[141] The strategy extended to barbarians beyond the Rhine and Danube. The legions invaded this hinterland roughly four times every century, wiping out all who did not submit to them. Slaughtering of unarmed villagers, as reported by Ammianus, was deliberately planned to terrorize civilian populations. Treaties that the invading emperors imposed on barbarian kings immediately after the state-perpetrated terrorism often kept barbarians subdued for a generation, thus achieving an economy of force.[142]

China and Rome was each convinced of its own moral and cultural superiority, which it envisioned as a beacon that attracted voluntary Sinicization or Romanization. "To shine forth in virtue, not to display military force" was a Zhou tenet cherished by Confucians.[143] The conjunctive invocation of virtue and puissance was more congenial to pragmatists. Ban Yong proposed supervisory officers "to promulgate puissance and spread virtue, win allegiance, and frustrate the Xiongnu."[144] Skillful deployment of Janus-faced psychology enabled him to maintain order in the vast Western Territory with only hundreds of soldiers. The Chinese claimed the mandate of heaven. The Romans crowned their city on the hills with a divine halo. They regarded their Empire with its law, government, and Graeco-Roman culture as a package instituted by the gods or God to bring human beings to the highest possible state of existence.[145]

Ideological propaganda of civilizing missions is likely more effective in fanning domestic jingoism than persuading foreign compliance. The empires did attract many, but most people probably admired something other than their vaunted morality and political institutions. A Latter Han officer remarked of the Xianbei nomads who flocked to border markets, "They come in greed for the Middle Kingdom's riches and goods, not in awe of our puissance or respect of our virtue."[146] Tacitus wrote of the Romanization of conquered Britons, "they were led to things which dispose to vice, the lounge, the bath, the elegant banquet. All this in their ignorance, they called civilization, when it was but a part of their servitude."[147]

Economic superiority and material control are imperial trump cards. The barbarians or nomads wanted, or even needed, trade with the empire. Both empires controlled trade to maximize their own advantage and made trading rights a privilege for political friends. The Romans restricted trade with barbarians to designated cities, but might relax restrictions as a reward. Large border markets held periodically at fixed locations under military supervision were a major favor that the Han granted northern nomads. Trade goods reached peoples far from the borders, increased their economic dependency, and drew them closer to the imperial orbit. To prevent them from gaining military prowess, both empires banned export of strategic goods and materials, especially iron. However, the embargos were no match for smuggling and corruption as soon as imperial vigilance slackened.[148]

Using wealth and material culture to entice greed and inspire awe is another form of psychological statecraft. Athanaric came to Constantinople two weeks before his death. Stunned by the sight of vast walls and bustling streets, he cried, "Surely the emperor is a god upon earth, and whoever lifts up his hand against him is committing suicide."[149] He had fought the Empire all his life and his Gothic people had killed Valens at Hadrianople three years earlier, yet he saw the futility of fluke victories against a power so deep and colossal. Partly to cultivate such realization, Wudì dispatched embassies to the west and invited return envoys, so that they could "inspect the Han and learn of its greatness."[150]

Ancient diplomacy exchanged envoys without establishing embassy in residence. Both empires played good hosts and raved about the large volume of incoming emissaries, which they interpreted as foreign deference. Augustus's long list included envoys from as far as India.[151] The Han term *chongyi*, "multiple translations," referred to missions from lands with a vast linguistic gap to bridge. The emperor regarded foreign presents as tributes, in return for which he bestowed gifts. A gift with a value at least equal to that of the tribute, often much higher, was an element of the Han loose-rein policy. The huge amounts involved constituted a form of government-conducted economic exchange.[152]

If diplomatic reciprocity signifies relations between equals or near equals, then Rome seemed more chauvinistic than Han China, because it seldom initiated embassies. Roman emperors campaigned in person and negotiated face-to-face with foreign kings. However, little evidence exists for Rome conducting diplomacy at a distance, except military officers delivering chastisements.[153] In contrast, the Former Han actively dispatched missions to seek relations with western states. To maintain some dialogue even in a hostile standstill was a part of Han foreign policy when it was strong, expressed by *wujue*, "not severing connections." Obduracy in terms did not kill talks with the Xiongnu during the decade-long "cold war" after the 119 BCE campaign. When the Latter Han degenerated, it cut its foreign contacts and turned to navel gazing.[154]

The northern neighbors of the Han and Roman Empires had variegated identities, cultures, and political organizations. Even the Xiongnu *chanyu* or a German super-king had to placate numerous subordinate tribal chiefs and warrior leaders. Besides, they faced many external rivals, peoples of their kind. With such neighbors, the favorite strategy of both empires was divide-and-conquer. Three common methods were alliance with some states in conquering others, subversion of a state by backing a sympathetic faction, and enlistment of foreign soldiers in the imperial army, either individually or as contingents. All three featured the magic of money.

Encouraging internal discord played a major part in the Han's reduction of the Xiongnu. It subsidized the South Xiongnu, Wuhuan, and Xianbei and used them to fight the North Xiongnu and other nomadic tribes.[155] Drusus excelled in bribing the Germans to fight among themselves. The Marcomanni were probably Rome's most powerful neighbor on the Danube in Augustan times. Their king Maroboduus refused to take advantage of Rome during the Teutoberg disaster, but Rome subverted him by fomenting conflict among his subordinate tribes. By Trajan's reign, the Marcomanni king was reduced to a Roman client.[156]

On either side of the border, the empire settled subordinate groups and bestowed formal status on their kings. Chosen kings received their diadem from the Roman emperor. Seals and sashes of various colors were the emblems of Han patronage. These insignia advertised imperial backing that gave the bearer an edge in nasty native politics. The subordinate kings served two imperial purposes: first, to rule their own peoples in sympathy with imperial interests and, second, to screen the empire from the disturbance of tribes further away. By putting some military and administrative burden on their shoulders and paying for the services, the empires realized certain economy of force. Trust, however, was not atop their menu. Both empires demanded royal hostages. Young hostages were seduced by civilized luxuries, which increased their tendency to pursue pro-imperial policies when they later returned home to assume leadership.[157]

Manpower, especially for troops, was the major imperial extraction from subordinate tribes.[158] Germans had long served in the Roman army, as did Hu peoples in the Han army, many as hired volunteers. The empires stepped up the levy as they tightened their grip on the tribes and their own subjects increasingly spurned military service. Marcus Aurelius extracted 5,500 cavalry from the defeated Sarmatians on the Danube and sent them to Britain. The Han drafted 3,000 cavalry from Wuhuan in the northeast to fight in the northwest. The levy for distant campaigns was especially oppressive on the tribes and sometimes caused rebellions.[159]

Subordinate kingdoms maintained a ring of relative stability along the imperial frontier. The empire paid for this benefit. When it was comfortably the hegemon, its subsidies were economic aids, compensations for troops, or fees for security services. When hegemonic dominance was marginal, the imperial payment often smelled of bribes for respite. Such was the spiraling amount of gifts that the Latter Han gave the resident South Xiongnu. Many Later Roman emperors granted German tribes gifts that were denounced as shameful tributes by their successors who felt strong enough to discontinue payment. Worse was the protection money that the Han paid the Xiongnu in the second century BCE or that the Romans paid the Huns and Goths in the fifth century, for which the flabby empires received nothing in return except the mercy of their militant payees.[160]

Subordinate kingdoms retained significant autonomy in internal affairs. This was especially consequential for émigré states. The Han differentiated between subordinates who lived outside its defense belt and those who settled inside, imposing tighter control over the latter.[161] The Former Han had instituted special administrations to supervise large groups of surrendered nomads. The Latter Han adopted the model to administer the South Xiongnu émigré state. A dedicated general on par with a provincial governor assigned 2,000 cavalry and 500 soldiers to "protect" the *chanyu*. Ideally, control strengthened as assimilation proceeded, eventually integrating the minorities into regular provincial administration. It was a slow process, however, partly because émigré states retained their customs and tribal organizations under the Han's loose-rein policy of "refraining from deep rule" and "letting aliens rule aliens." Thus many Xiongnu continued their nomadic lifestyle and were able to rally as an independent kingdom after three centuries of residence in Han territory.[162]

For a long time, the Roman Empire admitted barbarians only in relatively small numbers, enlisting them under Roman commanders or keeping them as semi-slaves bound to the land, with no hesitation to slaughter troublemakers. The immigration policy was radically changed in 376 with the Visigothic émigré state. In substance, the restrictions that Theodosius imposed on the Visigothic federation in 382 were similar to those imposed by Valens in 369. However, that the Visigoths were no longer beyond the Danube but physically inside Roman provinces made Theodosius's restrictions far weaker. His measure breached all precedents. The Visigothic federation had about 20,000 warriors capable of reproducing themselves from accompanying families. It had rebelled once but was still allowed to remain armed, semiautonomous, free to move among an unarmed Roman population, and unencumbered by any "Gothic agent" of the Roman government. Not surprisingly, it rebelled again in a dozen years.[163]

By patiently cultivating friendly tribes, undercutting their independence, and strengthening control over subdued enemies, each empire built up client states that constituted a part of their frontier defense. However, using barbarians to fight and control barbarians, in which some barbarians gained strength from the use, was a dangerous game of knife juggling. The empires at their primes played with ease, but the day would come when falling knives would get the better of the aged jugglers.

7.8 Frontier Defenses

Amid desolation and the graves of fallen soldiers the new recruit trekked. "Just when you think you are at the world's end, you see the smoke from east to west as far as the eye can turn, and then under it, also as far as the eye can stretch . . . one long, low, rising and falling, and hiding and showing line of towers. And that is the wall!" Hadrian's wall. The passage comes from an English storybook about Roman garrison troops, written at the beginning of the twentieth century.[164]

In the early eighth century, when the Tang Dynasty repeated the imperial exploits of the Han, a Chinese poet wrote about the Liangzhou frontier:

> The Yellow River seems to distant white clouds climb,
> A lone city in ten thousand mountains sits.
> Why are parting tunes so sad on flutes of the Qiang?
> The spring breeze never through the Jade Gate seeps.[165]

Romantic or bleak, the frontier invoked a spectrum of images. To inhabitants, life went on, often monotonous, but that might have been preferable to too much excitement. The frontier was an extended zone. Inside the zone ran a defense belt with variable depth that stretched on both sides of the demarcated border, the Roman *limes* or Chinese *sai*.[166] It signified state presence at the limit of formal administration but not of imperial power.

The defense belt need not imply a defensive strategy. Fortifications can serve as staging areas for invasion or garrisons for occupation. Aggressiveness is not recklessness, and defense is mandatory in all conflicts. The Chinese and Romans were both security-minded even in imperial expansion. "First deprive the enemy of conditions to win, then search for conditions to triumph over it," wrote Sunzi.[167] The Roman marching camp exemplified such thinking. After each day's tiring march, the legions spent more than three hours building a camp with perimeter ditches and obstacles that precluded surprise night attacks and allowed soldiers to sleep soundly in hostile territory. The camp defense was a tactic in offensive operations. In seeing the Roman Empire as a marching camp writ large, strategists may not be too far from scholars who regard frontier fortifications as constituents of a mainly aggressive Roman grand strategy.[168]

In one aspect, however, frontier fortification is essentially defensive: the everyday protection of the local population from minor infiltrations. It is not a "Maginot defense" against major invasions. Static defense of a long border is generally futile against large-scale attacks, for which a preemptive strike, a reserve field army, diplomacy, and other tools in hegemonic statecraft are more appropriate. Preventing large invasions, however, is not enough for folks living near the border. Raids by a few thousand devastate frontier towns, although they may sound trivial to smug inhabitants of the interior. Small incursions came frequently from the disorganized Germans or the loose Xiongnu confederation. To prevent them or minimize their damages were the major aims of imperial frontier defense.[169]

An effective frontier defense needs significant depth on both sides of the border. In front, the Roman or Han Empire projected its power physically and psychologically. A belt of subordinate allies or client states created physical distance from unfriendly peoples. Deterrence, attained by whatever means, made the rashest chiefs think twice before mischief.

Behind the border, the empire consolidated its frontier provinces. Lying between the developed interior and the undeveloped outland, the frontier was relatively poor and sparsely populated, often unable to support large garrisons without help from the interior. Many frontier regions were also politically marginal, their provinces being newly conquered and pacified, home to tribes prone to rebellion or sympathetic to external barbarians or nomads. The stabilization and consolidation of such regions was a priority in imperial strategy.

The Roman Empire gave the job to the military. The imperial army consisted of 300,000 to 645,000 soldiers who, serving almost lifelong terms, lived segregated from the civilian world. When Roman expansion slowed, troops settled down in permanent bases, up to two-thirds of which were located along the Rhine and Danube. To provision them, large amounts of goods flowed from the Mediterranean. Well-paid soldiers were good consumers. Their bases became magnets to civilian settlements. Although professional soldiers were forbidden to marry until Septimius Severus, many lived with women and raised children anyway. Veterans received land. Many settled near the area of their service, and their sons became new recruits. The imperial army became an agent for developing the frontier provinces over the generations. Military bases seeded major European cities: Cologne, Bonn, Mainz, Vienna, Budapest, and Belgrade.[170]

The Roman Empire had little worry of barbarian infiltration during its first two centuries. Barbarians had far more to fear from Roman deterrence by terror. When the tide began to turn in the third century, linear ramparts such as the Raetia palisade proved inadequate. Points being easier to defend than lines, walls rose around many frontier towns. Initiatives in most regions fell on local inhabitants, and efforts varied widely. Only in Gaul did relatively uniform constructions indicate an imperial program. Cooperating with mobile strategic reserves for counterattack, these self-contained strongholds constituted effective defense-in-depth against incursions, especially by barbarians incapable of siege.[171]

The Former Han army comprised mainly conscripts serving yearlong terms, except the skilled cavalry for anti-Xiongnu wars. After Wudì's victories, regular troops on the entire frontier from the sea to the Jade Gate numbered only in the thousands. Xuandì reduced the number further by 20 percent. These figures from textual sources are confirmed by excavated documents, a tally of which shows 3,250 soldiers guarding the sensitive northwestern frontier. In the Latter Han, when abandonment of training rendered conscripts ineffective, volunteers filled the rank for campaigns. Temporary mobilizations aside, the Han had a standing army core of barely 10,000.[172] When the most powerful frontier viceroy Dong Zhuo entered Luoyang toward the end of the Han period, his cavalry and infantry totaled 3,000 and were ordered to sneak out every night and reenter the city in the morning as if they were new troops in order to intimidate political rivals.[173] Such skeletal forces were able to maintain some tranquility in the frontier, partly because civilian frontier populations shouldered more responsibilities in the Han Empire than they did in the Roman. Different defense organizations in the two empires manifested the social-oriented and military-oriented characters of the Dragon and the Eagle.

To strengthen its frontier, the Former Han government continuously moved civilian settlers from the interior—the poor, the landless, petty crooks, ex-convicts—by incentive or coercion. According to Chao Cuo's plan early in the dynasty, the state allotted settlers free land and housing, subsidized the cost of tools and clothing until they became self-sufficient, granted tax exemptions, and even arranged mates for single people. It organized civilian settlers into communities, provided military training, selected able leaders, and posed rewards for expelling Xiongnu raiders. At strategic points it built fortified cities of at least 1,000 households, linked by roads. The settler militia, naturally motivated to protect their families, became an integral part of frontier defense. Although they were unable to counter incursions when the Xiongnu camped on their doorsteps, they supplemented regular troops to constitute a system of defense-in-depth after Wudì's offensive pushed the Xiongnu away from the border. Aided by efficient intelligence and systems of early warning signals, the settlers deprived raiders of much spoil. Left empty-handed, raiders seldom returned.[174]

Frontier populations remained relatively low. In 2 CE, when they enjoyed peak prosperity after decades of peace, the nineteen provinces along the northern border and in Liangzhou were home to only 8 percent of the empire's population. Yet they produced a significant portion of the officer corps in the central government, because the Former Han's recruitment system assigned an equal quota to every province. Frontier populations declined sharply in the Latter Han and were almost excluded from the central government by the new population-based recruitment quota system.[175] Polished literati-officials neither understood nor cared about the rough frontier. Despite government neglect, frontier folks helped themselves and developed their own identity and culture. Women joined men in military activities to defend their homes. They put up the strongest resistance when north China fell to minorities in the early fourth century. Even after evacuation into the interior, their resistance movements persisted for a century—a persistence for which no Roman veteran group was known.[176]

Constantine's creation of the central field army depressed the status of frontier *limitanei*. Some changed from professionals to farmer-soldiers. The denigration of farmer-soldiers is unwarranted. They won the empire for the Republic and, if properly organized and provisioned, could protect provincials from low-intensity infiltrations in the Later Empire.[177] *Tianzu* (farmer-soldiers) and *tuntian* (military-farming colonies) were outstanding in Han frontier defense. Soon after Wudì wrested the Hexi Corridor from the Xiongnu, 50,000 to 60,000 farmer-soldiers began to dig canals there for farms. A significant troop level was required to counter raids, but raids came only occasionally. During quiet times, soldiers had ample work capacity left after training and patrolling, which could contribute to self-support and economic development. Colonization increased the staying power of troops, and its advertisement added psychological pressure. Logistic difficulties often limited the duration of Han campaigns in remote regions. By settling on part-time farming, an army showed its determination for protracted engagement, which could persuade the enemy to give up. Guerrilla-type rebels who failed to get the message faced economic blockade by the colonists. Military colonization was not as glorious as assault, but by argument and performance, General Zhao Chongguo proved its superiority in subduing the rebellious Qiang.[178]

The frontiers were lands of mixed populations, hosting Romans and barbarians, Han-Chinese and minorities. Peoples interacted and infiltrated across the boundaries. When Trajan invaded Dacia, he met an army whose best soldiers were recruited from the Roman Empire and whose siege machines were built by Roman artisans. After his first victory, he demanded the return of all Roman deserters and forbade the Dacian king to accept the service of any Roman. This was not the first time that Roman flight to barbarians posed a problem for the Empire, nor the last.[179] A similar need to close the door on its own people also occurred in the Han Empire. In 33 BCE, when literati-officials advocated unilateral disarmament, Hou Ying advanced ten reasons for the necessity of border control. Common-sense security arguments aside, five of his reasons pertained to political functions. Criminal fugitives desired escape. Surrendered nomads wanted to link up with their kin. Slaves and poor peasants yearned for better living in the steppe. Families of captured soldiers forsaken by the dynasty preferred reunion on the other side. The Qiang, encroached by local magnates and cheated by corrupt officials, were always restive. Besides keeping enemies out, border garrisons helped to preserve order within the border by pacifying these groups.[180]

Already in their golden ages, the empires failed to command full allegiance. Conditions worsened as imperial power declined and social harmony deteriorated. Many Han-Chinese lived among nomads and many Romans among barbarians, serving their chiefs.[181] Han envoys to the Xiongnu court encountered renegade Zhongxing Shuo, who extolled the natural simplicity of nomads over the tedious artificiality of the Han. The diplomat and historian Priscus met in Attila's camp a fellow Greek who preferred his new freedom under the Huns to the old life in the corrupt Roman Empire.[182] Some critiques of these upper-class deserters were self-serving, but the ideological cliché mustered to counter them were even further from reality. Desertion was more frequent among the lower classes. When the Xiongnu émigré state rebelled and declared an independent kingdom in 304, it won the support of many Han-Chinese until its atrocity turned them away.[183] Orosius wrote that after the barbarians crossed the Rhine in 406, some Romans in Gaul preferred to live among them, "poor but in liberty."[184] People voted with their feet for a better life. The empires, chauvinistic about their cultural superiority and civilizing mission, often failed to realize that the beacons of their vaunted virtues did not shine on the bottom strata of their own societies.

Where a great power confronts and infiltrates diffuse forces with different cultures, the frontier is like the tidal zone between the land and the sea. Daily influences from the two sides produce a peculiar ecology with its own life-forms. The tidal zone shifts slowly as shoreline erodes or silt builds up. As the sea level of the Han or Roman Empire dropped, the gradually drying areas in the old zone exposed the consequences of the empire's worst enemies: oppression, discrimination, and misgovernment.

Notes

1. Bishop Ambrose, quoted in Heather 2005: 190.
2. Gills and Frank 1993: 163–169. Teggart 1939.
3. Scullard 1976: 53–56.
4. Southern 2001: 195–198. Todd 1992: 19, 47–52.
5. Todd 1992: 9–10, 17–19. Southern 2001: 207–208.

6. Heather 2005: 46–55. Southern 2001: 195–198, 207–208.
7. Tacitus, *Germania*, 33.
8. Thompson 1996: 33, 235–237.
9. *Shiji* 110: 2879. Ammianus 31.2.6.
10. Khazanov 1994: 16. Di Cosmo 2002: 24–27, 35. Beckwith 2009: 320–321.
11. *Shiji* 110: 2879. Ammianus 31.2.12.
12. Di Cosmo 1994: 1101–1103, 1114–1115. Khazanov 1994: 202–206, 222–223.
13. Barfield 1989: 8. Khazanov 1994: 254.
14. Lattimore 1940: 472–475. Beckwith 2009: 320–324.
15. Sinor 1981. Thompson 1996: 58–60.
16. Plutarch, Crassus, 24–25. Dien 1986: 36. Needham and Yates 1994: 278.
17. *Hanshu* 49: 2281. Needham and Yates 1994: 121–123.
18. Herodotus 4.46. Compare *Shiji* 112: 2954.
19. Yü 1986: 390–391.
20. *Hanshu* 94: 3756–3757; 96a: 3890–3891. Beckwith 2009: 70–73, 86–89.
21. Strabo 9:8.2. Liu, X. 2001.
22. Narain 1990: 155–161. Millar 1981: 283–284. Beckwith 2009: 84–85.
23. *Hanshu* 61: 2687–2692. Millward 2007: 20–21.
24. Bivar 1983a: 191–193. Millward 2007: 13–15. Katouzian 2009: 42–44.
25. Bivar 1983a: 189–191. Katouzian 2009: 41–42.
26. *Shiji* 123: 3162. *Hanshu* 96a: 3890.
27. Katouzian 2009: 46–48. Millar 1981: Ch. 14.
28. Ball 2000: 8–9, 12–18. Heather 2005: 202–203.
29. *Hanshu* 57b: 2583.
30. Peng 2004. Yang, L-S. 1968: 31–33.
31. *Shiji* 110: 2890–2891. Di Cosmo 2002: 176–178.
32. Di Cosmo 2002: 163, 174–179. Barfield 1989: 8, 32–41.
33. Chang 2007: 136–141. *Hanshu* 94a: 3753–3754, 3762.
34. Chang 2007: 142–144. *Hanshu* 94a: 3761–3764.
35. *Hanshu* 4: 119–120. Loewe 2009: 68.
36. *Hanshu* 52: 2399.
37. Chang 2007: 146–151.
38. *Hanshu* 52: 2399–2403. Loewe 2009: 67–70.
39. *Shiji* 81: 2450. *Hanshu* 94a: 3765.
40. Chang 2007: 161–187.
41. Yü 1967: 16–19, 72–78; 1986: 446–460. Chang 2007: 86–88. Loewe 2009: 71.
42. Chang 2007: 201–213. Loewe 2009: 80–82.
43. *Shiji* 123: 3168–3173. Yü 1986: 164, 405–409.
44. Chang 2007: 220–223.
45. *Hanshu* 96b, 3913–3914. Millward 2007: 21–22. Chang 2007: 218–225.
46. Yü 1986: 405–411. Millward 2007: 24–25. Chen 2007: 286–292.
47. Yü 1986: 405–411.
48. Yü 1986: 394–398. Loewe 1986b: 211–212.
49. Yü 1986: 398. Chen 2007: 309–317.
50. *Houhanshu* 18: 695–696; 88: 2924; 89: 2940; 90: 2982. Lewis 2009: 238–239.
51. Yü 1986: 400–402. De Crespigny 2009: 95–97.
52. Yü 1967: 67–77. *Houhanshu* 89: 2943–2946, 2953–2954; 41: 1415–1416. *Jinshu* 97: 2548.
53. *Houhanshu* 19: 720–723; 48, 1598.

54. *Hanshu* 70: 3010–3021. Loewe 1986b: 211–212.
55. *Houhanshu* 47: 1571–1575. Yü 1986: 415–416.
56. *Houhanshu* 47: 1576–1582; 88, 2910; 4: 168. De Crespigny 2009: 99.
57. *Houhanshu* 47: 1583–1586.
58. *Houhanshu* 47: 587–590; 88, 2911–2912. Yü 1986: 415–416.
59. *Houhanshu* 47: 1587–1589.
60. *Houhanshu* 87: 2878. Yü 1986: 422–430. Zhang C. 2008: 90–118.
61. *Houhanshu* 58: 1880.
62. De Crespigny 2009: 103–105. *Houhanshu* 87: 2878, 2886–2887.
63. *Qianfulün* 24.2.
64. De Crespigny 2009: 103–105, 109. Lewis 2007: 258–259.
65. *Houhanshu* 58: 1866. Loewe 1986a: 302–303.
66. Yü 1986: 433–434. De Crespigny 2009: 105.
67. *Houhanshu* 58: 1880.
68. *Houhanshu* 28: 3621–3622; 87: 2889–2890. De Crespigny 2009: 109.
69. Virgil, *The Aeneid*, 1. 374–375, 379.
70. Cicero, *Philippic*, 6.19. See Yang and Mutschler 2009: 110–111.
71. Rutilius Namatianus, quoted in Grant 1990: 184.
72. Keppie 1984: 146, 150–151, 173–174. Mattern 1999: 83–85, 205–206.
73. Dio Cassius 54.11. Wells 1992: 69–70, 124–125.
74. Isaac 1992: 20–29, 52–53.
75. Dio Cassius 54.8.
76. Fulford 1992: 295–296. Wells 1992: 71–72.
77. Seager 1972: 18–23. Wells 1992: 70–73.
78. Seager 1972: 32–35. Keppie 1984: 160–168.
79. Todd 1992: 265–267. Heather 2005: 46–48, 55.
80. Dyson 1971: 256–257. Isaac 1992: 54, 56–57.
81. Suetonius, Augustus, 23. Dio Cassius 56.18–23.
82. Wells 1992: 75–76.
83. Augustus 26. Tacitus, *Annals*, 1.11. Gruen 1990: 407–408.
84. Tacitus, *Annals*, 2.17–18, 20, 25. Seager 1972: 61–74.
85. Mattern 1999: 90–93.
86. Bennett 1997: 85–89, 94–95, 99–101. Southern 2001: 120–121.
87. Isaac 1992: 28–30.
88. Rostovtzeff 1957: 355–358. Bennett 1997: 200. Lightfoot 1990.
89. Dio Cassius, in Bennett 1997: 204.
90. Birley 1987: 140–141, 149. Millar 1981: 117–118.
91. Birley 1987: 149, 163–166. Todd 1992: 55–56. Heather 2005: 86–88.
92. Birley 1987: 176–179, 208–210.
93. Southern 2001: 33–34, 41–42, 53–54, 59–63.
94. Southern 2001: 227–244. Luttwak 1976: 154.
95. Isaac 1992: 5–6, 15–16, 52. Millar 2004: 193; 1993: 99, 102.
96. Dio Cassius 75.3, 56.33.
97. Lightfoot 1990: 124. Mann 1979: 183. Heather 2005: 160–162.
98. Todd 1992: 56–59. Southern 2001: 205–208. Heather 2005: 84–86.
99. Todd 1992: 152. Cameron 1993: 4. Southern 2001: 211, 215.
100. Heather 2005: 63. Luttwak 1976: 188–190.
101. Luttwak 1976: 130.
102. Luttwak 1976: 178–179, 186–188. Shaw 1999: 149.

103. Jones 1964: 97–99. Potter 2004: 451. Whittaker 1994: 208.

104. Todd 1992: 249–283. Heather 2005: 72–73, 145–146, 158–181.

105. Heather 2005: 63, 181–189.

106. Jones 1964: 156–157, 169. Gibbon 1994: 2:57.

107. Heather 2005: 193–195, 198–199, 212–213. Mitchell 2007: 89, 250.

108. Murray and Grimsley 1994: 2–3. Wheeler 1993: 12, 35. Kennedy 1983: ix, 5. Kagen 2006: 348–349.

109. Johnston 1995.

110. Taliaferro, Lobell, and Ripsman 2009: 23–32. Murray and Grimsley 1994: 17.

111. Tacitus, *Annals*, 15.25.

112. *Hanshu* 94a: 3754–3755. Mittag and Mutschler 2009: 424.

113. Gruen 1990: 395–396, 406, 411–412. Whittaker 1994: 36. Wells 1992: 76–78.

114. *Hanshu* 6: 212, 75: 3156. *Ershiershi* 2. Loewe 2009: 86–87.

115. *Hanshu* 96b: 3912–3914.

116. Tacitus, *Annals*, 1.11. Dio Cassius 56.33.

117. *Hanshu* 96b: 3912–3914.

118. Tacitus, *Annals*, 1.11. Birley 1997: 78. Bennett 1997: 203.

119. Ober 1982. Whittaker 1994: 29–30, 35–36.

120. Tacitus, *Annals*, 4.32.

121. Strabo 2.5.8. Mattern 1999: 158–161.

122. *Houhanshu* 88: 2924. Yü 1986: 413–414.

123. *Yantielün* 12, 16. *Hanshu* 49: 2278, 2285, 51: 1688. Yü 1986: 431–432.

124. Themistius, quoted in Goffart 1989: 290.

125. *Zizhi Tongjian* 22: 727.

126. *Houhanshu* 18: 696.

127. Bielenstein 1986b: 268.

128. *Shiji* 6: 246, 243. Kern 2007: 110.

129. Brunt 1978: 162, 168. Gruen 1984: 274, 281, 329.

130. Hingley 2005: 2, 9, 44–45.

131. Yü 1986: 377–379. Mattern 1999: Ch. 2.

132. Kallet-Marx 1995: 25–27. Richardson 1991: 1, 6–7.

133. Mattern 1999: 110. Tacitus, *Annals*, 1.9. Heather 2005: 72.

134. *Hanshu* 94a: 3762. Waldron 1990: 42–43.

135. Yü 1986: 379–381. Yan 2011: 58–59.

136. Li D. 2006: 19. Luttwak 1976: 22.

137. *Sunzi* 3. Graff 2002: 23–24.

138. *Hanshu* 64a: 2788.

139. Luttwak 1976: 3.

140. Mattern 1999: 119, 115–117.

141. Polybius 10.15. Tacitus, *Annals*, 12.17.

142. Heather 2005: 457, 81. Shaw 1999: 133.

143. *Guoyu* 1.

144. *Houhanshu* 47: 1589.

145. Heather 1997: 73.

146. *Houhanshu* 48: 1609.

147. Tacitus, *Agricola*, 21.

148. Thompson 1982: 15. Southern 2001: 196–198. Yü 1967: 95–100, 119–120. Huang 2005: 186–203.

149. Quoted in Thompson 1982: 5. See also Gibbon 1994: Ch. 26, 1078.
150. *Shiji* 123: 3169.
151. Augustus 26, 31.
152. *Houhanshu* 89: 2946.
153. Millar 2004: 220, 222, 224–225.
154. *Hanshu* 94b: 3834. *Houhanshu* 89: 2946–2948. Peng 2004: 17–21.
155. *Houhanshu* 86: 2838. Yü 1967: 14–16.
156. Tacitus, *Annals*, 2.60; *Germania*, 42. Pitts 1989: 46–53.
157. Braund 1984: 9–17, 23–29. Yü 1967: 68–70, 141–142. Peng 2004: 21–34. Pitts 1989.
158. Southern 2001: 201–203. *Committee on Chinese Military History* 2006: 110, 134.
159. Dio Cassius 72.16. *Houhanshu* 73: 2353. Mattern 1999: 86–87. Yü 1967: 83–84.
160. Yü 1967: 41–48. Southern 2001: 192–193. Heather 1997: 69–71.
161. Yü 1967: 65–77. Li D. 2006: 57–71.
162. Peng 2004: 4–6. Li D. 2006: 86–91, 127, 135–136, 150–152, 209–211.
163. Heather 1997: 62–65; 2005: 159–161, 184–188. Southern 2001: 188–190, 198–200.
164. Rudyard Kipling, *Puck of Pook's Hill*, quoted in Whittaker 1994: 1.
165. Wang Zhihuan on Liangzhou.
166. Jing 2002: 193–194. Isaac 1992: 408–409.
167. *Sunzi* 4.
168. Luttwak 1976: 55–57, 66. Isaac 1992: Ch. 9. Whittaker 1994: Ch. 1.
169. Luttwak 1976: 69, 74–78.
170. Fulford 1992: 296–299. Millar 1981: 119–125. Wells 1992: 125–128.
171. Luttwak 1976: 131–137. Southern 2001: 114, 155, 214, 252.
172. *Hanshu* 69: 2989; 94b: 3810; 8: 249, 268. Di Crespigny 2009: 93.
173. *Houhanshu* 72: 2323.
174. *Hanshu* 49: 2286–2289. Chang 2007: 18–20.
175. *Hanshu* 28b. *Houhanshu* Zhi 19–23. See Map 16.
176. *Houhanshu* 70: 2258. Di Crespigny 2009: 103–109. Zhou 1997: 15–26.
177. Jones 1964: 649–653. Luttwak 1976: 171–173.
178. *Hanshu* 69: 2984–2992; 94a: 3770. Chang 2007: 17–18. Millward 2007: 22.
179. Dio Cassius 69.14. Whittaker 1994: 188, 228–229. Ste. Croix 1981: 476.
180. *Hanshu* 94b: 3803–3804.
181. Weng 2001: 180. Mitchell 2007: 202.
182. *Shiji* 110: 2899–2900. Thompson 1996: 205–207.
183. *Jinshu* 101: 2645–2649.
184. MacMullen 1966: 231–232. Mitchell 2007: 202.

CHAPTER 8

DECLINE AND FALL

8.1 Glorious Sunset Clouds

The "culmination of human history" was the reign of Constantine to contemporaneous historian Eusebius.[1] The Later Roman Empire recovered from anarchy and civil wars. A civilian bureaucracy came of age and effectively collected elevated taxes from the lower classes. The enlarged military organized the best troops into mobile field armies, the cream of which attached to the emperor. The currency was stabilized with a new gold coin partly financed by the systematic despoliation of pagan temples. Christianity triumphed as the state religion and its church soared in power and wealth. Constantinople sprang up with dizzying speed, crowded with magnificent palaces and churches and endowed with a Senate of its own. Barbarians were defeated and captured kings fed to wild beasts.[2] A panegyric sang of Constantine, "you defy the remnants of the defeated tribe and compel them never to abandon their fears but to be in constant terror, and to keep outstretched their hands in submission."[3] Persia came to bid for peace, but was rebuffed. Constantine "proposed to wage the war as a Christian crusade," a modern historian writes.[4] He died while embarking on the campaign. That was 337 CE. Rome would be sacked by the Visigoths seventy-three years later and, in sixty-six more years, the Western Roman Empire would disintegrate into barbarian kingdoms.

"Neither too hard nor too soft" was the significance of *he* in the posthumously accorded imperial title Hedì.[5] Flood, drought, and earthquake jam the annals for the Latter Han's fourth emperor, as do government actions in opening state granaries, extending loans, forgiving arrears, and encouraging refugees to return home. The state's capacity to organize relief in far-flung areas of the empire indicated general prosperity.[6] The Han finally defeated the North Xiongnu. The South Xiongnu settled down as an émigré state. Ban Chao restored the protectorate in the Western Territory. Parthian embassies brought lions and other gifts. Yet traditional appraisals of Hedì's reign are usually unenthusiastic.[7] The emperor was only ten at his accession. The family of the empress dowager initially held power, and Hedì appointed eunuchs after taking personal control. Literati who indiscriminately condemned eunuchs and affine families regarded Hedì's reign as the beginning of decline. Based on chronology, they have a point. Hedì died in 106 CE. The Han Dynasty would degenerate into anarchy in eighty-four years, and in 125 more years, the resident Xiongnu would lead Hu minorities to carve up northern China.

The demise of the Han does not astound scholars. Four centuries make a dynasty boring. In a comparable period, the Roman Empire had gone through at least five dynasties, many unrelated successions, frequent duplication of emperors, and five decades of anarchy. It was China's turn for six decades of fragmentation into three kingdoms. Even the brevity of renewed unity under the Jin Dynasty and the loss of the imperial heartland to nomads attract little inquiry. Historians write narratives; the events are as messy as the fall of Rome. For culprits, it seems sufficient to round up the usual suspects.[8]

"The strange death of Roman Europe," by contrast, is hailed as "one of history's greatest mysteries," attended by a huge investigative literature with inconclusive results.[9] With German thoroughness, a scholar compiles 210 causes that have been proposed over the centuries: anarchy, barbarism, Christianity, decadence, economic stagnation, poison from lead pipes, and so on.[10] Then the whole postmortem is declared wrongheaded by the fashionable school that denies the death of the Roman Empire and propounds its peaceful transformation.[11]

Peaceful it certainly was not, but neither was there a titanic clash. The mighty empires went out with a whimper. The Germans who carved up Roman Europe were, like the nomads who took over north China, small in number and disunited. The fall of Rome was antithetic to the fall of Troy or Carthage. Instead of heroic defense and honorable defeat, dreary attrition and sobbing surrender prevailed. Resistance was even weaker than that of the Han-Chinese. It was so out of the Roman character. What happened?

The empires aged, but not all conditions worsened—far from it. Centuries of Romanization or Sinicization had created significant bonds within the elites. By the end of the Antonine age, a traveler from Britain to Syria could pass through cities of substantially uniform design.[12] Imperial homogeneity is testified by the similarity of Roman ruins in Europe, Asia, and Africa. Chinese buildings, mostly of timber and other perishable materials, had long vanished, but underground tombs tell a similar story. Excavations in sites as far apart as Korea and the Jade Gate uncovered luxury goods styled after the fashions of the capital.[13]

The flourishing upper classes of the two empires converged in stylishness. An aristocracy of amazingly uniform ethos and language ruled the Roman Empire.

An African landlord would feel at home among the oligarchs who held local power in Greek cities, or a Greek litterateur among senators in Gaul. All were linked by their education, whose bedrock was the intense study of a small set of texts under the guidance of a master of language and literary interpretation.[14] A similar education with a different set of texts shaped the Chinese Confucian literati. Led by the imperial academy, private schools mushroomed around the country, producing large crops of sophisticates wedded to the ruling class.[15] Literati self-identity that burgeoned in the waning Latter Han won posterior acclaim, as did the achievement of Latin literature in the waning Later Roman Empire.[16] The crimson clouds of elegance reflected on something else rosy, economies robust enough to support the leisure and luxury.

Monetization had regained footing. The third-century crisis wiped out the Roman silver coin, but the currency stabilized around the gold solidus, into which many taxes and levies were commuted.[17] After the Wang Mang interregnum, the bronze qian again dominated transactions and served as the unit of account even for huge fortunes in the Latter Han.[18] The growth of giant estates, self-sufficient because of their diversified production, reduced the need of trade within both empires. If a decline in commercial activities occurred, however, it was not sharp. More important, agriculture, the base of both economies, stood firm.

Archeologists uncovered evidence of thriving rural communities in many parts of the late Roman Empire. Except for the most heavily raided frontier regions along the Rhine, most areas recovered fully. Syria prospered, as did the African provinces, a breadbasket to the Western Empire. Production and settlement density crested in many places during the fourth century. Evidence suggests that agriculture was not depressed, despite elevated taxes to support the enlarged army and bureaucracy. Scholars explain that suitably higher taxes can stimulate increased productivity when peasant labor capacity is underutilized. The necessity to pay taxes drives peasants to work more, hence increasing production and growing the economy.[19]

The economy was similarly healthy toward the end of the Latter Han. The government kept taxes low. Many of its policies, including the abolition of state monopolies on salt and iron, would warm the hearts of free-market advocates as it did Confucian literati. Numerous inscriptions attested to the extensive construction and maintenance of roads and bridges. Productivity rose. Fertile lands in south China increasingly yielded to the plow. Crafts of great variety thrived, buoyed by new technologies including papermaking, the wind-powered bellows, and an early form of porcelain. Conspicuous luxury consumption soared.[20]

With the exculpation of economic depression, another usual suspect comes to the fore, depopulation. Here we can catch a culprit of continental impact.

Plagues broke out almost simultaneously at the two ends of Eurasia and raged during their chronologically overlapping "third-century crises." Epidemics are civilized diseases; germs need a sufficiently large population density to spread infections effectively. Egypt and Mesopotamia reached the threshold first. India joined the club via Alexander's invasion. China and Europe, thanks to their belated development and geographical isolation, had relatively little experience of the scourge of civilization. Imperial expeditions and long-distance trade brought them into contact with more established disease pools.[21]

Smallpox is suggested, but no one is certain; several diseases could be involved. Some kind of pestilence ravaged the Kushans and then enervated the Parthians in the early second century.[22] Roman troops returning from their 167 Mesopotamian campaign brought the disease with them and spread it around the Empire. For fifteen years it raged, killing more than 10 percent of the population and inserting a sad note into the happy Antonine age. It recurred during the height of the third-century crisis. The 251 outbreak in Egypt infected the whole empire and depleted the ranks of the army. Another flare-up in 270 killed Emperor Claudius II, together with a large number of the Goths fighting against him.[23]

Previous Chinese records of diseases were mainly mass illness following natural disasters and afflictions in the army or subtropical heat. Most occurrences were local. Rarely did one make the list of ominous signs interpreted as divine warnings, with a dedicated chapter in the *Standard Histories*. Luoyang suffered in 125 and 151. Then a string of widespread epidemics popped up on the ominous list, in the years 161, 171, 173, 179, 182, 185, and 217, leaving the country in consternation. The imperial annals also recorded big epidemics in 224, 234, 292, and 311.[24] The 217 flare-up claimed many in the imperial family and all four of the leading poets. Contemporaries wrote of deaths in every family and funerals held for whole clans. "Three or four in ten died" at the peak of the 320–322 outbreak in Guanzhong.[25] Significantly, during the early period of pestilence, the millenarian cult that culminated in the 184 Yellow Turban rebellion gained popularity through magical healing. In the 208 battle of the Red Cliff, the imperial army was weakened by pestilence. It lost. Had it won, China would not have fragmented into three kingdoms.[26]

Plagues weakened the empires, but by how much? The Roman Empire seemed to weather the ordeal well. No census data survived. Estimates for the peak population range from 50 to 120 million, but the high numbers seem incredible. Whether the peak occurred under Marcus Aurelius or Constantine is not clear. The interim years saw wars and recurrent plagues, but remains of settlements reveal that the population in most areas had recovered by the fourth century, and some even reached new heights. With archeologists likely to uncover more settlements, many scholars believe that the Empire had at least 70 million inhabitants on the eve of the barbarian invasion.[27]

The Roman army had been expanded and reorganized. A list of all civilian and military offices dated at the end of the fourth century indicates an army of 645,000, if all units were in full strength. However, most historians think full strength usually unlikely. Barbarians increasingly filled the ranks.[28]

Some Han census data survived. A comprehensive census is not easy even with today's information technology. Ancient efforts were unavoidably inaccurate and tended to undercount; census fraud and tax evasion were twins. The figures in the table below are more informative on the trend than on absolute magnitudes.

Population and Arable Land in the Censuses Specified by Dates and Reigns[29]

Year	Reign	Household	Population	Arable land*
2	Former Han Pingdì	12,233,062	59,594,987	8,270,536
57	Latter Han Guangwudì	4,279,634	21,007,820	
75	Latter Han Mingdì	5,860,573	34,125,021	
88	Latter Han Zhangdì	7,456,784	43,356,367	
105	Latter Han Hedì	9,237,112	53,256,229	7,320,170
125	Latter Han Andì	9,647,838	48,690,789	6,942,892
144	Latter Han Shundì	9,946,919	49,730,550	6,896,271
156	Latter Han Huandì**	16,070,906	50,066,856	
280	Jin Wudì	2,459,840	16,163,863	
283	Jin Wudì	3,770,000		

* Land area quoted in *qing*; 1 *qing* = 100 *mu* ≈ 11.39 acres = 4.61 hectares.
** The figures seem to contain a mistake.

The two periods of sharp population decline both saw civil wars that accompanied dynastic change. Plagues, which reached peak ferocity during the second period, added to the number of casualties. Crueler than microbes were warlords who turned population centers into battlegrounds. Fighting killed many people and displaced far more. Dynasty change damaged administrative machineries.

Unlike archeological sites, which shed light on physical demography, household registers reveal "political population," a combination of physical demography and the state's capacity to reach the population. After the Jin reunified China in 280 and initiated a program to settle refugees, the number of households jumped by 50 percent in three years.[30] "Arable land" in the table reads "taxable land." By abandoning an honest land survey, Guangwudì allowed big clans to screen resources from the state. As land continued to concentrate in their hands, tax evasion spiraled upward, which explains why acreage declined through the Latter Han despite massive development in south China. Many dispossessed peasants dropped from the household register and became drifting laborers. Others became tenants or dependents of big landlords, who were more effective in resisting state levies.[31] Considering these social trends, we can surmise that a larger population existed, but it was invisible to the government and could not be mobilized to solve urgent social problems. Could a similar problem have caused recruitment and other difficulties for Rome, which also depended on peasant registries?

After the post–Qin civil war, only three out of ten households remained on the register. After the post–Wang Mang civil war, the 57 CE census registered about one-third of the Former Han population. If we estimate that the 280 CE census figure registered only one-third of the people who survived the plagues and post–Han civil war, then China's population would be 54 million. A generation of peace and prosperity followed the reunification.[32] Had it continued, the Jin would be in a decent position to deal with nomadic minorities.

The military system had changed much since the Former Han. Conscripts gave way to temporary volunteers and minority troops. The three post-Han kingdoms instituted military households to ensure a constant supply of trained troops. From them the Jin Dynasty developed a hereditary military caste. In contrast to the Later Roman Empire, where similar measures failed to fill recruitment quotas, hereditary soldiery and minority troops mostly met Jin's military demand. Conscription was rare.[33]

Such were the economic, demographic, and military conditions of the late empires. Although far from pristine, they hardly suggested impending calamity. Yet power is relative to the strength of rivals. Had the Germanic barbarians and Hu minorities advanced disproportionately?

8.2 Barbarians and Nomads

Exposure to enemies on two sides was a strategic weakness of the Roman Empire. Fortunately, actual behavior belied Persian aggressiveness in hostile propaganda. Persian kings were usually honorable enough to keep treaties and strong enough to control their subjects. They did not bother the Roman Empire during most of the fourth century and almost all of the fifth. The eastern frontier, heavily fortified, still tied down some troops, but the Romans could concentrate on the Germans in these critical times. Significantly, the Eastern Empire, which alone was vulnerable to Persia, survived.[34]

To the north, the Roman Empire faced barbarians across the Rhine and Danube. Most were familiar neighbors. The major exception was the nomadic

Huns, unknown before 376. Refuting the popular depiction of hordes, a scholar who pored over the evidence writes, "we may safely conclude that the enormous conquests of the Huns were carried out by 'a ridiculously small band of horsemen.'" That band probably totaled not much more than 15,000 Hunnic warriors.[35] They usually divided into groups of a few thousand for raiding. Their larger achievements depended on their ability to captivate and unite the Germans. The Huns' impact on the fall of Rome was large but indirect; their empire collapsed before Rome's did.

The barbarians who dismembered the Western Roman Empire were mostly Germans, with a pinch of nomads, notably the Iranian-speaking Alans. They entered the Empire in three bouts (Map 14). In 376, the Visigoths crossed the lower Danube by permission, rebelled under mistreatment, and won the battle of Hadrianople two years later. The second bout consisted of several waves between 405 and 410. A group of Goths invaded Italy under Radagaisus, whose defeat was followed closely by the breach of the Rhine frontier. After that, most Germans came under the control of the Hunnic Empire, whose collapse in 455 unleashed the third bout of invaders, chief among whom were the Ostrogoths.[36]

The Visigoths could field some 20,000 soldiers. They and their families constituted the first émigré state within the Empire. Radagaisus led about 20,000 warriors; many later joined force with the Visigoths. The Vandals, Suevi, Alans, and others who crossed the Rhine in 406 totaled more than 30,000 warriors; the Burgundians who followed in 410, at most 15,000. About 10,000 warriors invaded the Empire after Attila's hold on them collapsed. The Franks had at most 15,000 men fighting before the end of the Western Empire, although afterward they would become a power rivaling the Visigoths. In sum, between 110,000 and 120,000 armed invaders took part in toppling the Western Empire. The last of these invaders came eight decades after the first.[37]

Against intruders spread out in time was a standing Roman army up to 645,000 strong, better trained and equipped, with more available replacements for casualties than the barbarians trapped within the Empire. Allowing for severe under-strength and excluding garrison troops tied down along the frontier, the mobile field armies probably comprised some 150,000 men, numerically superior to the invaders at any one time.[38]

If only fighting men intruded, biology would have taken care of them in a few decades. They brought along their families. Among the some 80,000 Vandals and Alans who crossed from Spain to Africa in 429 were 15,000 to 20,000 warriors. This implies one warrior out of four or five persons. Extrapolating this warrior-to-population ratio, we estimate at most 0.6 million barbarians broke into the Roman Empire, which had a population of up to 70 million.

They came in three bouts. If distributed evenly, all the intruders in each bout could have fit into Rome's Circus Maximus to enjoy a chariot race.[39]

Barbarians invaded all along the Rhine-Danube frontier but somehow all ended up devouring the Western Empire. Suppose the Eastern Empire contributed nothing to defense, and suppose only 40 percent of the Empire's population resided in the West. Even so, we still see 0.6 million barbarians intruding into the Western Empire of 28 million over eight decades. It was more like a glassful into the bucket than a flood. No wonder historians who research deeply into it puzzle about the strange death of Roman Europe.

The barbarians who toppled the Western Empire were recent intruders. The nomads who initially took over north China were long-term residents. In both cases, many more foreigners would enter later; the northern forest and steppe were nurseries of inexhaustible peoples. However, those are beyond the scope of our story of the fall of empires.

The frontier of imperial China was more porous than that of the Roman Empire, not only because of the lack of great rivers as natural boundaries. Even when strong, the imperial practice was to settle defeated tribes rather than killing them off, as the Romans often did. Five groups of Hu minorities carved north China into more than sixteen kingdoms, not all simultaneous, between 308 and 431. They were the Xiongnu, Jie, Xianbei, Qiang, and Di. The Jie was a branch of the Xiongnu (Map 15).

In 91, four decades after it became an émigré state, the (South) Xiongnu registered 34,000 tents, 237,300 heads, and 50,170 warriors. Thus, on the average, each tent sheltered seven persons and more than one warrior.[40] Natural disasters in the steppe and accommodative policy encouraged more immigration, boosting the Xiongnu population to about 400,000 in early Jin.[41] The first to rebel, the Xiongnu were the counterpart of the Visigoths, but more numerous and politically sophisticated.

The Xianbei divided into many branches. The first to set up courts in China were small branches with populations below 200,000 and troops below 50,000. Only later would the largest branch drain the steppe population into north China to unify it. They were like the Franks and Lombards who surged late but became durable heirs of the Roman Empire.[42]

Some scholars estimate up to 700,000 Qiang immigrated during the Han Dynasty, but brutal suppression of their rebellions left them decimated.[43] The Di, their neighbors and relatives, were closer to the Han-Chinese and more quiescent. Two records of their resettlement within the empire after military operations of the early third century amounted to 53,000 tents.[44]

After the Xiongnu sacked Luoyang, their kingdom registered about 200,000 tents of Hu and 430,000 households of Han.[45] Notice the large size of the minority, especially if we accept the available data of seven persons per Hu tent and five persons per Han household. The Xiongnu kingdom had a Hu population of 1.4 million. Considering the Xianbei hostile to it and the Qiang beyond its jurisdiction, it seems reasonable to assume that at least 1.4 million minorities were already in north China at the beginning of the takeover.

Accompanying minority immigration was the exodus of Han-Chinese from north China (Map 16).[46] Fighting and the flooding of the Yellow River scattered the inhabitants of the Central Plain. Insecurity depopulated many frontier regions. Southern kingdoms diligently developed their realms. By 280, only 57 percent of the population was registered in north China. With an estimated 54 million total, this puts the population of north Chinese at 31 million.[47]

In sum, I roughly estimate that at least 1.4 million minorities took over north China with a population of about 31 million, and at least 0.6 million barbarians conquered the Western Roman Empire of about 28 million. These numbers do not include the 23 million inhabitants of south China or the 42 million of the Eastern Roman Empire. Nor do they include the influx of nomads or barbarians after the fall of north China in 316 or the Western Empire in 476.

Besides sheer numbers, the political organization, military technology, and strategic situation are also crucial to conflicts. For all four factors, barbarians in the Roman world seemed worse off than minorities in the Chinese world. Antagonists of each empire divided into many groups, which more often fought each other than united against imperial forces. The Germans had evolved larger political units since Tacitus relished their disunity, but their organizations were still weak. What we conveniently call the Visigoths or Vandals were supergroups nonexistent prior to invasion, formed only under the pressure of survival within the Roman Empire. In comparison, the Xiongnu, although divided into many branches, had a tradition of organization and a precious memory. Once they had been great, the head of a powerful federal empire that made the Han Dynasty pay tribute. Revival was their desire. Historical prestige brought them rallying value to which no German group could aspire.

The Xiongnu were mounted archers of the same caliber as the Huns, who defeated the Germans. With experience gained from long residency, they named their kingdom the Han to tap the prestige of the great Han Dynasty in propaganda. Fine iron and sharp weapons were abundant to them, obtained directly or indirectly through imperial subsidy.[48] In contrast, poverty of metal persisted among the Germans. Tacitus remarked on their lack of helmets and iron tipping for wooden spears. Comparing the battles of Hadrianople and Teutoberg Forest, a historian writes, "There is no reason to think that Fritigern's men had appreciably greater quantities of metal at their disposal than Arminius' warriors had had 350 years earlier."[49]

The Germans were probably more similar to the Qiang; both were aggregates of ill-organized groups. A group, say the Vandals, constantly split into many small raiding parties. Against them, the Romans preferred blockade and harassment by small detachments. Sharpshooters were brought in from the east to pick them off one by one. General Sebastian organized a troop of 2,000 specially trained soldiers that successfully eliminated many raiders.[50] Similar tactics helped the Chinese to deal with Qiang marauders. General Ma Lung selected and equipped 3,500 volunteers with special archery skills, infiltrated rebel homelands without maintaining contact with the government, and pacified Liangzhou.[51] Against enemies sharing certain characteristics, both empires found regular armies less effective than what Ammianus called "undercover piecemeal action."[52] The modest numbers of special operations troops involved indicate that the enemies were much weaker than they appeared when left to run amok.

A strategic difference existed between the two unconventional wars. As rebels, the Qiang played on their home turf. Scattered in remote regions of the empire, they were familiar with the rugged terrain and had access to sympathetic kin with economic capacity. The Han imperial army pursuing elusive rebels had more worries about supply and shared the predicament of Marcus Aurelius trying to subdue the Marcomanni on their home turf. The reverse situation occurred for fifth-century barbarian invaders, who had left the wild forests of Germania and ventured into the cultivated fields of Greece, Gaul, Spain, and Italy. A common resistance to such invaders is what the Chinese call "to strengthen fortifications and clear all fields." The incapacity of mounting sieges made the Germans more vulnerable to the Romans' ability to secure all sources of food and supply behind walls. Starvation often forced barbarians to surrender or risk calamitous battle. Populations of intruders fared far worse, because warriors must also feed noncombatant dependents and the draft animals for their wagons. Rapid exhaustion of foraging grounds drove them to plod on in hostile territory, unable to stop and farm, their wagon train the only defense for the women and children. With all the information from deserters, they knew less about the country than the Romans who governed the local population. It was as if the Vietcong had left Vietnam and come to play guerrilla in California. Odds were against them on all counts.[53]

The minorities had resided in China for generations, mostly peacefully, their occasional agitations quelled. Why did they revolt all at once and why did they succeed this time? The barbarian invaders were relatively few in number, inferior in weaponry, short on provisions, and dragged down by noncombatant dependents. The Roman Empire had defeated much stronger enemies before.[54] This round, a scholar remarks, "barbarian attack constituted an insurmountable threat not because the barbarians were so many or so strong, but because the defense was so weak."[55] Why was it so weak?

8.3 Social Coagulation

A state's capacity to marshal resources and direct them to bear on pressing problems depends on political institution and social structure. Mobilization flounders if taxpayers resist or if corrupt officials siphon revenue into private pockets. To allocate the expenditure of limited revenue, the government must identify problems, reconcile claims, and set priorities. Reconciliation is never perfect, and friction engenders waste even in good times. Social bifurcation and entrenchment of local powers increase tax evasion, especially by the rich. Extreme ideologies and stubborn factions paralyze decision making and policy execution. Civil wars are worse. As revenues drain into infighting or dissipate in mismanagement, problems dangerous to all, such as rebellion or invasion, sit on the back burner, where they can grow to lethal proportions. Among such factors are some more likely explanations proposed for the decline and fall of empires.

Social coagulation and political polarization are in some ways similar to the progression of cancer. Individuals and families in an empire are like cells in a body. Their regulated division and multiplication is vital to the organism's growth. Occasionally, a genetic mutation confers a survival edge on a cell, which proliferates, happily passing the advantageous gene to its progeny. If a second beneficial mutation renders one of the offspring even better at elbowing out competitors, then it would multiply and amplify the mutated gene. Several mutations later, these special cells form tumors. If more mutations enable them to beat the body's regulatory mechanisms and multiply untrammeled, they become cancerous. Cancer cells are the fittest that survive in Darwinian evolution. For the organism of which they are a part, however, they are lethal.[56] The entrenchment of special interests is like the progressive development of cancer cells. As they become more efficient in encroaching on others, they prosper to the detriment of the state and community. Like cancer progression, power roots slowly. Just as cancer afflicts mostly elderly persons, predatory elite groups come to dominance in aging empires.

The rosy pictures presented in section 8.1 pertain to the overall Roman or Han economy. The aggregate masks many problems. Imagine an economy in which 1 percent of the population is rich and 99 percent poor, the income of each rich person being 100 times that of each poor person. Now imagine that the economy grows by 25 percent, the income of the rich doubles, and luxury booms. Celebration is in order, but only if one neglects the 99 percent whose income is halved. Inequality quadruples and the poor sink into destitution. Gaping inequality was a cancer in both empires.

"Fewer have more."[57] These three words, into which a modern scholar compresses the socioeconomic evolution of the Roman Empire, apply equally to the early Chinese Empire. They differed only in degree. The socioeconomic configurations of both empires were pyramidal, but the Roman pyramid was steeper than the Chinese. This is apparent in the pay schedule of government officials. The stipend of a Han provincial governor was fifteen times that of the aide, the lowest person in the official ladder, with compensation comparable to that of a foot soldier. The pay for each of the ten senior centurions in a legion was thirty-three times that of a soldier, and they were below tribunes and commanders, who were below provincial governors.[58]

The Chinese literature brims with denunciation of the filthy rich.[59] A substantive case was Prince Kang, Guangwudì's son, who amassed 1,400 slaves, 1,200 stabled horses, and 3,688 hectares of land. This was near the top of Han wealth. Princes also enjoyed the tax revenue of their income fiefs, but these were county sizes at best and rather lean on the 3.3 percent land tax. Private estates larger than 5,000 hectares were almost unheard of; divided inheritance was more effective than legal caps on hoarding.[60] The Romans operated on a different order of magnitude. Six men owned one-half of the province of Africa before Nero confiscated their estates. Senatorial heiress Melania's fertile estate near Rome contained, besides a magnificent villa, 62 hamlets, each with about 400 slave cultivators. Together with her other properties in Italy, Sicily, Africa, Spain, and Gaul, her estimated income rivaled the tax revenues of two African provinces, where the land tax exceeded 15 percent. This would put her among the wealthiest in Constantinople, but in Rome, she made only the middle range. A top western senator needed several hundred thousand hectares to generate his reported incomes. Wealthy Romans dwarfed the grandees of Victorian England enriched by the industrial revolution.[61]

"The basic economic weakness of the empire was that too few producers supported too many idle mouths," a modern scholar writes of the late Roman Empire.[62] "Idle mouth" is a perfect translation for *fushizhe*, literally those who eat without ground, as a late Han minister wrote: "The treasury is depleted, *fushizhe* aplenty."[63] The elite clubs contained more than royalties, aristocrats, and large landlords. The Christian Church expanded its estates from imperial grants and the faithful who followed Jesus's advice to invest their treasures in heaven, safe from moths, rust, and thieves. By the sixth century, bishops and the clergy far outnumbered administrative officers in the Roman Empire and were better paid.[64] Similarly, leisurely literati swarmed the Latter Han. The imperial academy aside, wealthy clans each patronized thousands of students. Enthusiasts traveled wide to seek connections. On occasion, thousands of literati gathered to chat.[65] Although not completely parasitic, their contributions were dwarfed beside their voracious compensation.

Many idle mouths shirked taxes legally or illegally and grew fat thereby. Feeding them and paying taxes were peasants, whose burden became crushing. The concentration of wealth in the hands of a few dispossessed many. The small freeholder became an endangered species. Tenant farmers, Chinese *dianhu* and Roman *coloni*, constituted the majority in many parts of the late empires. In the vast estates of big landlords, they toiled alongside hired hands, slaves, and workers of various forms of dependency. Rents were oppressive, upward of half of the crop.[66] Nevertheless, many tenants and their landlords developed some kind of patron-client relationship. Large landlords were usually local magnates who could offer protection in exchange for submission. Those powerful enough concealed some tenants and the lands they cultivated from state levy, thus increasing both their own income and the dependency of sheltered tenants. Standing between the government and the small folks, the magnates truncated state power by promoting mutual interests in evading tax, always easy to condemn. Many Chinese tenants were relatives of their landlords, and some families stayed for generations. Nevertheless, tenants were legally free to leave at the end of their lease.[67] The freedom to seek better deals was denied to most Roman tenants by the time of Constantine. Developing the plutocratic tradition, laws tied tenants and their descendants to the land and gave landlords the right to chain and punish escapee suspects. Theodosius decreed that tenants were "slaves to the land itself to which they are born."[68] The different degrees to which the government backed wealthy landlords to squeeze poor peasants may contribute to explaining a puzzle about the Roman army.

The Chinese and Roman armies of the later empires similarly comprised a mixture of conscripts, volunteers, and nomads or barbarians. Han officials and later warlords seemed to have little recruitment problem, provided they offered good terms. Sun Ce, who founded the Wu Kingdom, declared amnesty to defeated troops and tax exemption for the families of volunteers, and in ten days enlisted 20,000 quality troops.[69] This should not be surprising; the army offered poor peasants an alternative way to make a living. The pay and pension for Roman legionaries were generous, but the army faced chronic recruitment difficulties. In vain did emperors issue harsh draft laws, reduce qualifications, and create a military caste by making service compulsory for sons of soldiers and veterans. The almost lifelong service deterred many. The law that bound tenants to the land deprived many of essential free choices and created a barrier to recruitment. Instead of enticing individual peasants, the army had to pry lucrative tenants from powerful landlords. The largest landlord, the emperor, legally put his tenants off-limits. Lesser landlords did their best to scare their tenants, resist the army, and let go only the least fit men. The shortage of soldiers would grow into a cancer in the Empire.[70]

Although generally docile, peasants are capable of revolts when pressed to the wall. Ancient texts lump social unrest under the rubric of "bandits," Chinese *zei* or Roman *latro*.[71] Between the poles of ordinary criminals and usurpers were various agitators boiled up from the lower strata. Armed bands began to disturb *Pax Romana* in the mid-second century, when the army had to detach more troops for internal policing. The 187 "deserters' war" in Gaul engaged large forces. By the end of the fourth century, even the prefect of Rome dared not venture beyond the city wall because brigands infested Italian roads. Throngs of travelers followed the regular tours of a governor, hoping to rub safety from his military escort. Thunderous laws were toothless against bandit collaborators, who were none other than the rich and powerful of local communities.[72] Unrest was also prevalent in China since the second century. Starting with riots involving hundreds or thousands of people, it escalated in scale and climaxed in the countrywide Yellow Turban uprising, to which we will return.[73]

The rich grew richer partly by evading taxes and pushing the burden onto the poor, who grew poorer. Economic bifurcation destabilized society as the poor in desperation joined the predatory rich or rose in protest. Local magnates offered protection in return for loyalty and gained the ability to evade more taxes. Armed bands grew, in some cases penetrated by elites who exploited peasant discontents for their own political ambitions. Like tumors in a body, the bottom-up coagulation of society created centrifugal forces that impeded the state's effort to mobilize resources for ballooning problems. Furthermore, many local magnates were political elites who also held high offices in the central government, where power corruption stimulated tumors to mutate into cancers.

8.4 Political Corruption

The final century of the Western Roman Empire and Han Dynasty shared one bane. By luck or human design, their emperors all ascended to the throne as children and were at best mediocre when grown up, in times that demanded strong leaders for addressing mounting problems. Honorius, safe at Ravenna, did nothing to relieve Rome during its three blockades by the Visigoths. When news came that Rome had perished—sacked—he exclaimed, "And yet it had just eaten from my hands!" The emperor had given the name of the city to his favorite pet chicken.[74] Famine was common during the tumultuous reign of Huidì of the Jin Dynasty. When informed that folks were dying for lack of grain, the emperor replied, "Let them eat meat."[75] A healthy government could compensate for weak emperors, as the early Roman Empire weathered the novice Claudius and the early Han Dynasty its feeble Huidì. Unfortunately, the late imperial governments were themselves dysfunctional.

When the empires were young and energetic, their greatness inspired broad visions that encouraged loyalty and public service. Horizons narrowed as they aged. Rome had relinquished much of its public spirit under the Empire, and the remnants expired under Christian otherworldliness. The rule by impartial law introduced by Chinese Legalists withered under Confucian literati. As aristocratic or feudalistic ideas revived, family and faction dominated government. The militaristic-plutocratic character of the Eagle and the bureaucratic-moralistic character of the Dragon revealed their dark faces. The army and the bureaucracy, the more practical parts of the government, deteriorated. The political elites from the emperor down cared foremost about their own interests and commandeered pretentious slogans for self-preening.

The proverbial debate between guns and butter is common to many societies. The shrillness of the protests from those soaked with butter against a few guns desperately needed for public security was peculiar to the late empires. While Ban Yong begged for 300 soldiers to defend the Jade Gate, some 30,000 state-sponsored career students joined the chorus of officials to denounce military extravagance and advocate abandoning the beleaguered frontier populace.[76] When Stilicho bought the services of Visigothic troops for 4,000 Roman pounds of gold, senators cried, "This is not a treaty, but a pact of slavery." Rome and Constantinople each had about 2,000 senators; the richest senators each had an annual income of 4,000 Roman pounds of gold and 160,000 Roman pounds of silver, plus one-third as much in produce. They routinely spent 2,000 Roman pounds of gold on a single program of seven games but stripped public artwork to pay for public security.[77] We will see that the Han literati turned into brutal warlords and the Romans massacred the families of barbarian soldiers enlisted in the Roman army. Thus urbane virtue or religious love, which featured prominently in propaganda, was not the essential ground for their opposition to defense spending. As they pushed their own agendas, imperial armies were starved of adequate provisions, just when foreign enemies threatened the survival of the empires. Generals unsure of replacements avoided battles because they could not risk casualties. A modern scholar observes, "Perhaps the most basic reason for the failure of the imperial government . . . was that the two main groups in the Latin world—the senatorial aristocracy and the Catholic Church—dissociated themselves from the fate of the Roman army that defended them. Both groups unwittingly sapped the strength of the army and of the imperial administration."[78] The ultimate beneficiary was barbarian invaders.

Roman militarism and plutocracy had been congruous through the high Empire, when emperors and top civilian and military officers all came from the senatorial order. Since the 260s, senators dropped from military command and their political influence waned. Soldier-emperors rose from the ranks. Diocletian, Constantine, Valentinian I, and Valens all hailed from provinces known for army recruitment rather than cultural elegance. Yet these energetic men did not lack brains. They were the ones to develop a civilian bureaucracy separated from the military, for it better met practical needs of the empire.

The death of Valentinian I in 375, which almost coincided with the immigration of the Visigoths, inaugurated a new age. A child was left on the Western throne. The blue-blooded and demilitarized aristocracy revived and by the fifth century grabbed all top positions in the civilian government.[79] The Han government followed the same path. By the second half of the Latter Han, Confucian masters occupied about 47 percent of the top offices. Pragmatic administrators bent on bureaucratic efficiency sank lower and lower, their critical voices smothered by powerful cultural aristocrats.

The Roman and Chinese aristocrats of the late empires both loved high office but scorned the responsibility that came with it. Their book learning imparted a taste for refined leisure coupled with contempt for administrative technicalities. A modern scholar describes what the Romans called *otium*: "The aristocratic ideal of leisure, inherited from the Greeks, led by an easy decline to the disdain of serious effort, to the advertising of elegant accomplishments as a pretext for sloth or emptiness."[80] The aristocrats controlled high government.[81] In office, "they simply annexed the governmental machine to their own style of life, which had regarded politics with studied hesitation, and administration as an opportunity to look after one's friends." Writing letters of recommendation for their friends and clients was their most assiduous job. "These were as accomplished and as jejune as the visiting cards of the mandarins of imperial China."[82] Latter Han literati provided a paradigm of such mandarins. Versed in the Canons that preach the sufficiency of exemplary personality, they swanked of *qinggao*, lofty purity, and made administrative incompetence into a virtue.[83] Their ardent pursuits were fame and connections, the shortest route to advancement. Contemporaries complained, "High officials devote themselves to socializing and commend themselves pure for being aloof of administrative work."[84] "From triumvirs to provincial governors, all ignore state affairs and concentrate on receiving visitors whose Confucian robes clog the street. . . . They leave documents to clerks and detainees of unheard cases to rot in prison, too busy in their private affairs of seeking influence and chasing advantages."[85] These do-nothing Roman and Chinese officials were not merely sophisticated idle mouths. Waltzing on the bridge of the *Titanic* on a collision course with an iceberg, they constituted brain tumors of the late empires.

Corruption among the ruling elites, which predated the foundation of the empires, became cancerous as the empires aged. Its scale skyrocketed and the imperial government gave up regulatory efforts to join in grasping. Sales of government offices grew into a big business in both realms. Everyone knew that official salaries were insufficient to recoup the costs of purchase.

Officers raised funds by illegal means, for which more opportunities existed in the provinces, hence the especially high prices for governorships. By selling offices, emperors gave a tacit green light to fraud. Han Andì and Huandì sold middling posts in the central government. Lingdì extended sales to top ministries and actively solicited takers. To rebuild fire-destroyed palaces, for a few years he demanded money for all appointments. Officers without ready cash were allowed credit but not resignation. Some committed suicide to preserve their integrity.[86] Sale of provincial governorships was a regular Roman institution for two centuries, so that "borrowing on the security of an office" became a normal practice and governors descended on the provinces with creditors in train.[87] Ammianus remarked, "it was Constantine who first of all opened the throats of his friends, but Constantius who stuffed them with the marrows of the provinces."[88]

Corruption became such a routine that minor offences were taken for granted. Illicit exactions marked as "customary form of old" were legalized in the late Roman Empire.[89] A provincial governor in the late Han, responsible for recommending six persons, found himself inundated by letters from illustrious connections. Yet he resolved to reserve one position for meritorious candidates to thank the state's trust in him. He was noted for his conscientiousness, not corruption. Immunity to bribery was the only virtue relevant to public office among the traits praised by Latter Han literati.[90] It was also extolled in Rome, where some officers earned high reputation for abstention from the common vice of avarice. Remarks of modern scholars on them apply equally to the Han officialdom: "It showed exceptional merit merely to be honest," behind which, unspoken, was "the unhappy acknowledgment that corruption was rather the rule than the exception."[91]

Corruption deprives the people without benefiting the state. The Roman army in the fifth century was a mystery. Official lists gave its strength at 645,000—powerful indeed. Accounts of barbarians running almost unchecked within the Empire, however, raise the question of just where the Roman army was.[92] Many scholars argue that up to one-half of the official army existed only on paper. A soldier absent without leave remained on the official roster for four years.[93] The depleted army delighted barbarian invaders but not Roman taxpayers, as a historian explains: "whether they were alive or dead or totally imaginary, pay and allowance were issued for 645,000 men."[94]

Stealing public authority for private ends, although no less corruptive than stealing money, acquired some moral justification from the ethics of reciprocity and personal loyalty. Latter Han literati extrapolated filial piety to Confucian masters and official patrons. Being master for one day entails being father for life, as they said. Many masters were also high officials who looked after the career of their students. Instead of the state's recruiting agent, officials postured as benefactors to whom appointees owed lifelong gratitude. They selected youths with long prospects for fulfilling their moral obligations. Protégés and former protégés who went out of their way to repay their patrons won wide acclaim.[95] Reciprocating favors cemented personal networks within government. For example, an emblematic literati family, the Yuans, maintained hereditary mastery in a Confucian Canon and produced five triumvirs in four generations. Through generations of teaching, government office, and generous patronage, the family had accumulated students and former protégés all over the empire. Some 30,000 attended the funeral of Yuan Shao's mother. When the empire began to disintegrate, a viceroy of the northern provinces yielded his army and authority to Yuan Shao, partly because he was Yuan's former protégé.[96]

Feudalistic ethics, which lacks the notions of civic virtue and the state separated from the family, demands one owe loyalty not to the state but only to one's direct superior, as we saw in section 2.7. Embedded in the indoctrinating Canons, it revived and thrived among the literati. Provincial governors acquired power far exceeding their official authority, because they appointed local officers, including county superintendents. Those serving long terms usurped sufficient authority over current and former appointees to screen out the central government; as a contemporary saying went, "Orders from the region or province are received like thunderbolts. Imperial edicts arrive only to decorate the wall."[97] The preponderance of personal connections in government lubricated the transformation of provincial governors into warlords.[98] "That was the morality of the time," modern Confucian scholars explain.[99] Their appreciative evaluations of the Latter Han literati ethos indicate that the morality is not limited to that time. The underlying ethics of *guanxi*, personal connections, always extolled for their warm feeling, contributes to the cultural background of today's political corruption.[100]

8.5 Internal Discords and Civil Wars

Power struggles precipitated usurpation and civil war, the threat of which absorbed imperial attention and drained state capacity from problems such as frontier defense. Civil discords became cancerous in the late Roman and Han Empires. The large professional Roman army was the major actor in internal conflicts. The more diffused Han political elite bred chaotic fragmentation. It is difficult to tell which was more ruinous to the common people.

Dissimulation has its price. The republican facade that Augustus installed prevented the throne from developing full legitimacy and created intrinsic instability at the imperial center. To secure it, he instituted the professional army, which soon grew a will of its own. Army cabals acclaimed their own emperors first in 69. It set a precedent. Almost 100 mutinies occurred in the five decades after 230. The fourth century was better than the third, and even it saw civil wars in more than thirty years.[101] Emperors eager for self-preservation cut foreign defense to save troops for dealing with potential pretenders. Constantine restructured the government according to his long experience in civil wars. The fifth-century Greek historian Zosimus complained that Constantine's military reorganization weakened the frontier.[102] His heirs followed suit, as Ammianus wrote: "Constantius, though he suffered grievous defeats in foreign wars, prided himself on his successes in civil conflicts, and bathed in the blood which poured in a fearful stream from the internal wounds of the state."[103] Similarly, Theodosius swallowed defeat by the Visigoths but vaunted victory over rival Romans.[104]

While the military establishment bred warlords in Rome, the lack of it contributed to the Han's problem. The Latter Han abolished military training to save effort, effectively ruining the militia. Later, social unrest forced the government to allow civilian governors to recruit volunteers, build up their private forces, and eventually tear the empire apart.

Here we come upon an interesting phenomenon. Local riots, cults, banditry, and various forms of protest are common everywhere in the world.[105] Many agitators, such as the initial Red Eyebrows in Wang Mang's reign, were desperate refugees of disasters eager to return to normal life. Unrest not mollified is usually contained if not suppressed, shackled by the insurgents' provincialism or lack of organization, as were the Jewish revolts in the Roman Empire. Chinese history is peculiar in its propensity for local fluctuations to amplify into empire-wide turmoil that ravaged the population and weakened if it did not topple the imperial government.[106] A spark spreading into a prairie fire happened thrice during the five centuries under our study. At least five more dynasty-change-related uprisings would occur in subsequent imperial history. Why was the Chinese society so prone to large-scale instability? Why did repeated rebellions change only dynasty but not regime? Why did the political elite who prided themselves as intellectuals fail to generate even any idea of alternatives to the monarchical or feudalistic form of government?

Popular uprisings that vented mass grievances started the great rebellions in our period but did not end them. The Dazexiang mutiny against the Qin and the Yellow Turban cult against the Latter Han were suppressed. However, in each case, elites and adventurers capitalized on the commotion and turned the uprising into a ruinous anarchy of warlords. Literati clans also commandeered the forces of the Green Foresters uprising against Wang Mang. They escalated unrest and reaped its ultimate benefits.

Elite reaction to Qin is not surprising. Rebellions in newly annexed states, wherein the people drive out a foreign occupier, are common in world history.

More specifically, the rapid demobilization of six warring states and the abolition of feudalistic aristocracy created a huge pool of able men with frustrated ambitions. Liu Bang saw the First Emperor in the capital and sighed, "This is what a real man should be." Xiang Yu saw the First Emperor on a tour and blurted, "His position can be grasped and him replaced."[107] More memorable was Chen Sheng's rallying cry, "Kings, lords, generals, and ministers are made, not born."[108] Their words substantiated Jia Yi's assessment of the warlords who materialized after Dazexiang: "They shouted anti-Qin slogans but actually fought for their own gains."[109] Their bloody game of "deer hunt" resulted in a commoner on the throne, setting an inspirational precedent for the ambitious.

The first emulators were the elites who rebelled against Wang Mang. Their intention for joining the deer hunt was apparent in a plea to Liu Xiu to take the throne: "Literati-officials of the world leave their families and follow you into battles, because they hope to fulfill their aspirations by clinging on to the dragon's scales."[110] Latter Han literati also articulated their opportunistic mentality frankly. Taking advantage of the Yellow Turban turmoil, Yuan Shu claimed the title of emperor and later presented it to his cousin Yuan Shao, saying: "The Han has long lost the world. The son of heaven is in the minister's hands. Political power resides in the family. Magnates fight each other and carve up the realm, just like the seven states warring at the end of the Zhou, waiting for the strongest to take all."[111]

After Han Wudì banished the one-hundred schools, the imperial elite mostly embraced Confucianism. How does an ideology of morality and stability accommodate unabashed opportunism? I think it has partly to do with a simplistic doctrine of rule by men and an exegetical mindset that brandishes catchy phrases instead of analyzing rights and wrongs.

King Wu of Zhou militarily rebelled against his liege Shang. Fealty to the ruler is paramount in Confucian ethics, but King Wu is extolled as a sage. Mengzi tried to resolve the contradiction by accusing the last king of Shang of being a tyrant for his alleged abuse of benevolence and righteousness. In killing a tyrant, King Wu was no disloyal rebel.[112] "Benevolence and righteousness" is so vague and encompassing that anyone can be accused of abuse. A student of Confucius had already pointed out that much of Shang's alleged wickedness stemmed from the victor's propaganda.[113] A responsible theory of civil disobedience would at least substantiate the criteria of wrong that warrants violent opposition, so that it would not become an excuse for opportunistic armed rebellion, which invariably leads to massive chaos and bloodshed. Mengzi did not care to do so. Neither did millennia of exegetes. Their accounts of King Wu's rebellion in ways resemble the Roman attitude that justifies a war by its eventual victory. Mengzi's two-sentence rationalization of rebellion is more like a slogan, and an influential one. The chief imperial general responsible for suppressing the Yellow Turban was solicited to emulate King Wu. He refused, but others rallied to the slogan. A viceroy conspired with anti-eunuch partisans to assassinate the unrighteous emperor.[114]

The word *yi*, "righteousness," appears everywhere in *Mengzi*. What is right? What principles help us to decide whether an action or a type of action is right or wrong? Why should we adopt these principles? One can find few answers beyond obeying superiors and deferring to elders. Literati moralization deploys black and white images of Good versus Evil, the Sage King versus the Tyrant, with scant substantive description and little analysis of decision and action. It is fine for propaganda or denunciation of enemies but provides little guidance for moral choice in the complex, gray world of reality. In difficult times, literati following this dogma or that can behave erratically. Their flip-flop contributions to the rise and fall of Wang Mang's reign, which brought enormous harm to the people, we saw in section 5.6. Similarly, at the end of the Han, literati-officials with the slogan to save the world by fighting eunuchs turned into warlords with the slogan to save the world by fighting a corrupt emperor, unaware that they were actually ruining the world while fighting for their own power.

The imperial bureaucracy's hold on local societies was tenuous. Local elites built up power through wealth, prestige, and coercion. Many acquired political power through their relationships to literati-officials. They shared everyone's desire for stable social harmony and contributed much to its maintenance. However, their encroachment on land exacerbated inequality and created social tension. The literati's penchant to repress civil disputes in the name of harmony instead of resolving them according to the law encouraged predation and built up grievances. Personal loyalty cemented gangs, often with connection to local elites. According to a historian, "Behind the façade of imperial authority, there was frequent conflict between local bullies and their gangs of retainers, so that, regardless of banditry, the provinces of China had a high level of lawlessness."[115] Self-righteous elites thought themselves above the law. They blamed the emperor, although their own self-interest made many problems insolvable. Incompetent literati-officials reluctant to exert effort allowed ailments to grow, like underbrush piling up in a bone-dry forest, waiting for a lightning strike.

Grassroot riots that signaled imperial weakness ignited elite opportunism. Bandit gangs and local bullies jumped into action. Literati clans, each with hundreds of households, rallied. Warlords called "heroes" mushroomed; the final winner would become the founding emperor of a new dynasty. Years or even decades of bloodletting winnowed incompetence, cultivated pragmatism, and left horrible experiences no one wanted to repeat. The carnage destroyed recalcitrant powers, taught flexibility to survivors, and opened the possibility for some social consensus. Like forest fires that burn away underbrush and clear the ground for new growth, the chaos created conditions for a period of stability. Thus the political elite boasting of intellectual civility resorted to naked violence to solve real-world problems.

Geming, into which "revolution" is translated in modern times, means in the Confucian Canons a radical shift of heaven's mandate from one family to someone unrelated.[116] The insurgents fought to capture the mandate in the "deer hunt." The literati were ready to serve as officials under the winner, using their propaganda machine to sanctify the new emperor and demonize the losers. However, radical changes in the political institution, essential to modern revolutions, were unthinkable; the literati lacked the concepts for it. The Confucian Canons, written in the pre-reform feudalistic age when the prime principle of power was loving relatives, hardly contain concepts that Westerners call "political," such as law, justice, rights, and power structures, by which people can analyze the political situation and negotiate changes. The political concepts introduced by Legalists, which could open the door to deliberation, are rejected as immoral in canonical exegesis. Without conceptual tools to think about alternative institutions, a new dynastic cycle began, more benevolent than its predecessor in words but more despotic in fact. In the rule of men upheld by literati-officials, a good emperor is all that the people can hope for. If he is bad, opportunists are waiting to emulate the sage King Wu.

8.6 End of the Han Dynasty

The eighth emperor in a row to begin his reign as a child, Lingdì ascended in 168 to a throne surrounded by eunuchs and a government infested by incompetence, corruption, and factions. His proscription of anti-eunuch partisans alienated the literati. Many carried their grudge to the provinces and reinforced centrifugal regional powers.[117]

Ominous signs of heaven's displeasure multiplied. Most portentous was widespread disease. The plague struck in 171, then recurred. Early in the epidemic appeared Zhang Jiao, who preached a millennium of grand peace and attracted multitudes by healing with magic water. His disciples set up secret cells all around the country, penetrating the palace guard itself. In 181, a minister warned of potential unrest and suggested dispersion of cult members. The government preferred toleration, not knowing the plan for armed uprising. Early in 184, within ten days of Zhang's order, eight of the empire's thirteen circuits were aflame, all in the prosperous interior. Called the Yellow Turban for their headdresses and Moth Bandits for their large numbers, the rebels plundered communities and battered local governments. The central government hastily elevated generals, recruited volunteers, and pardoned proscribed partisans. Local elites, official and private, rallied against the rebels. Many personages of subsequent history made their debut in the fighting. The Yellow Turban was quashed in nine months, but imitators and sympathizers continued to flare up around the empire. The Han Dynasty was changed irreversibly.[118]

The devolution of power from the central to the local government, ongoing for decades, became precipitous. Many governors retained the armies they recruited for suppressing the Yellow Turban, which augmented local loyalty and gave them the power of independent lords. More formidable were circuit viceroys, each overseeing eight provinces on the average. The wary Han government used to grant them only supervisory power. Now it appointed reputed potentates with full military, financial, and personnel authority. Moral fame acquired in socialization notwithstanding, the new plenipotentiary viceroys promptly diverted tax revenue to arm their own turfs. Tigers joined wolves in local governments, ready to devour the empire and its people.[119]

The literati's zeal to purify the world of eunuchs boiled over when the boy Shaodì succeeded Lingdì's in 189. Surrounded by pardoned partisans, the famed literati-official Yuan Shao brushed aside warnings of dire consequences and urged the new regent to summon frontier generals. Dong Zhuo was a military careerist whose potential insubordination had long worried the government. To him, the anti-eunuch summons came as a godsend. Leading 3,000 seasoned troops into Luoyang, Dong swiftly absorbed other military forces, took control of the court, and deposed Shaodì to install his puppet, the nine-year-old Xiandì. Yuan Shao fled to the east and gathered three viceroys, seven governors, and other officials under an anti-Dong banner. In response, Dong moved the capital west to Changan and torched Luoyang to deny it to the enemy. Hundreds of thousands of Luoyang inhabitants were forced on the road, where myriads perished. More starved in Changan, which was unprepared for the influx. The world rejoiced at Dong's assassination in 192. Unfortunately, the ministers who plotted it had no plan to manage his generals, who mutinied, sacked Changan, kidnapped the emperor, fought each other, and laid waste the western part of the country.[120]

Eastern China fared no better. Leaders of the anti-Dong coalition failed to agree on a course of action. While they vied in banqueting and rhetoric, their pillaging troops killed almost half the population in the staging counties. After the coalition disbanded, every local officer recruited troops to protect and expand his turf. Literati clans and local magnates raised arms to bet on winners. Anarchic fighting reigned.[121]

Xiandì and his court had passed through many brutal hands west of the mountain passes since their abduction by Dong Zhuo. In 196, they escaped and returned to the scorched Luoyang. To support the emperor, even in formality only, required much resource and restraint. The presence of the Han emperor within their sphere of influence challenged the loyalty of literati-official-cum-warlords. What should they do? Han literati divided elites into the "pure stream" and "turbid stream." Famous big shots in the pure stream did nothing, leaving the opportunity to a middling fry in the turbid stream.

Cao Cao's father was the adopted son of a eunuch, but Cao Cao had befriended the literati. He alone greeted the refugee Han emperor and escorted him to safety in Xu, his own turf, where he reinstated court institutions and installed himself as the dictatorial regent. The remaining prestige of the Han court and Cao's own statecraft attracted capable lieutenants, enabling him to join the major league of warlords. Successes accrued. The upset victory over Yuan Shao in 200 was followed by subjugation of all northern warlords. In 208, one of the four southern circuits, Jingzhou, astride the Yangzi River, surrendered. Only two southern rivals to Cao remained, Sun Quan and Liu Bei, who formed an alliance.[122]

Yangzi, the third largest river on earth after the Amazon and the Congo, has a discharge volume more than twenty times that of the Yellow River. Its strong eastward current would repeatedly block northern invaders in Chinese history. The 208 battle of Red Cliff set the precedent. Sun's general Zhou Yu disguised as grain transports ten ships loaded with flammable material soaked in fish oil and, taking advantage of a favorable wind, set them afire and launched them into Cao's fleet. The fire at Red Cliff shaped a tripartite geopolitics: Cao in the north, Sun in the south, and Liu in the southwest Sichuan Basin. Cao Cao died in 220. His son Cao Pi immediately became emperor of the Wei Dynasty by forcing Xiandì of the Han to abdicate. Liu Bei and Sun Quan also claimed the imperial title. Historians call them respectively rulers of the kingdoms of Wei, Shu, and Wu.[123]

The end-of-Han chaos stirred up new men who administered a dose of chemotherapy to the tumorous government culture that put the family before the state and personal connections before public responsibilities. Cao Cao had promoted elementary education but offended the literati by appointing officers based on ability and performance instead of moral posture. After Liu Bei's death, Zhuge Liang as the premier of Shu refused to indulge local elites and adopted Legalist policies of ruling by laws that were strict but clear and fair. His dedication to service and good governance won him the enduring love of the local people, who maintained shrines for ages.[124] However, they were unable to reverse a stubborn social trend. The growth of the great literati families, which began in the Latter Han, would persist through the centuries of disunity. Their estates would expand and their grip on high government offices would become effectively hereditary. Combining birth, culture, power, and wealth, the network of literati clans would culminate in a new aristocracy, *menfa shizu*.

The three kingdoms were effectively a fragile southern alliance against the powerful north. The first to end was Shu, annexed by Wei in 263. Wei yielded to Jin in a coup two years later. In 280, Jin conquered Wu and reunified China. The unity proved to be a brief interlude, however. The Jin Dynasty lost north China to rebellious minorities in 316. In a long historical perspective, the 208 battle of Red Cliff inaugurated protracted north-south fragmentation and separate development, ended only when the Sui Dynasty reunified China in 589.

The Cao house picked up an effectively defunct Han court, reunited northern China, and then replaced Han by the Wei Dynasty upon merit. The Sima house that usurped the Wei throne to found the Jin Dynasty had no merit, only conspiratorial ambition. As a Wei minister, Sima Yi built up a faction and grabbed dictatorial power by a bloody coup. His grandson forced the abdication of the emperor and became Jin Wudì in 265. The Simas had been a literati family for generations. Wudì promoted filial piety and demonstrated his love of relatives by enfeoffing many as plenipotentiary kings in strategic and populous regions.[125]

For the second time, imperial China reverted to the Way of ancient kings. The Han's atavism lasted for three generations before vindicating the First Emperor's judgment, "To re-establish feudatories would be to encourage the use of arms." This time around, the retribution for ignoring history's lesson promptly descended on Wudì's successor. In the "catastrophe of the eight kings," which lasted from 300 to 307, imperial family members led hundreds of thousands of troops against each other. At its end, the lone survivor, Sima Yue, became the dictatorial regent to Huaidì. Power struggles continued to simmer. Physical damages to the country were great. Equally ruinous was moral bankruptcy; the intrafamilial killing shattered the virtuous mask fashionable since the Latter Han. Thus the Jin Dynasty committed hara-kiri. Ethnic minorities were ready to deliver the coup de grâce.[126]

8.7 Revenge of the Xiongnu

In Chinese as in Roman civil wars, factions enlisted immigrants and sought foreign allies. These moves were not necessarily disastrous, however. Minority and hired troops could be loyal under proper discipline and leadership. In foreign and minority relations, the pragmatism of the three kingdoms produced better results than did virtue rhetoric. The Latter Han treated frontier peoples as troublesome burdens and nudged local elites to rebel by its eagerness to abandon Liangzhou. In contrast, the kingdoms Wei and Shu treated frontier peoples as valuable assets and provided better government by courting elites who had won the trust of minority peoples. A similar story happened in the north. Wary about the Xiongnu's large population, Cao Cao dispersed them into five groups and appointed frontier viceroys capable of winning over local elites and enlisting their warriors.[127] Jin ministers would look back with nostalgia: "During Cao's rule, many nomads immigrated, but bullying and conflict were rare."[128]

A string of natural disasters in the steppe drove many Hu nomads to seek refuge between 265 and 287. Jin rulers catered to the landlords' demand for cheap labor and encouraged immigration to replenish the population reduced by war and plague. However, they shirked efforts to beef up administration. Soon the prevalence of warlike minorities and disgruntled immigrants in the northern provinces alarmed experienced officers. Their temporary submission in no way guaranteed durable tranquility. From where they were, their cavalry could sweep across major centers on the northern plain in three days. Seeing disasters looming behind a policy that tried "to constrain a feisty horse with a weak rein," officers proposed deporting some Hu folks, or moving in more Han-Chinese, or at least strengthening management. Before any measure was adopted, the strife within the imperial house exploded, and the immigrant problem took a sharp turn.[129]

The Xiongnu royal house, which in its heyday had taken many Han princesses, adopted Liu as family name after it settled as an émigré state. Versed in Confucian Canons and proficient in mounted archery, Liu Yuan served as a hostage to the Jin court, where he had risen to high positions. The government was so cagey about his ability it had denied him the command to suppress a Qiang riot. The war of the eight kings gave him an opportunity. Two frontier viceroys who supported Sima Yue had secured help from Xianbei tribes, the fiercest of nomads after they took over the steppe. This situation worried Sima Ying, then regent. Taking advantage of Sima Ying's crisis, Liu Yuan secured permission to rally Xiongnu troops to counter the Xianbei. Home in 304, he immediately won acclaim as the great *chanyu* of all Xiongnu groups and in twenty days assembled 50,000 warriors. He founded the kingdom of Han and in 308 declared himself emperor, with a capital less than 200 kilometers northwest of Luoyang.[130]

Xiongnu immigrants comprised nineteen ethnically heterogeneous branches, of which the Jie with high nose and lush facial hair would found a kingdom of their own. Shi Le the Jie was illiterate but fond of listening to readings. A captive sold into slavery, he escaped to join Liu Yuan and rose rapidly to become his most successful general. Xiongnu forces knocked out dozens of walled towns in the Central Plain. Without the strategic protection of the steppe, however, they were vulnerable. Three futile assaults on Luoyang cost them heavy casualties. Even Shi Le suffered severe defeats from Jin forces. On the other hand, the Jin were unable to eliminate or contain the Xiongnu.[131]

The escalating Xiongnu challenge had not taught cohesion to the Jin imperial house. Huaidì resented the dictatorial control of Sima Yue, who in turn begrudged the emperor's interference. Ignoring all objections, Sima Yue decided on an offensive and took with him almost all troops and the best officers, leaving Luoyang defenseless. The stultifying weight of filial ritual became apparent when he died five months later and his officers dropped everything to escort his body home for burial. The news set Shi Le on a pursuit. His cavalry caught up with the funeral procession, circled it, and shot the whole lot dead. Thus was the central Jin army annihilated in 311. Shortly after, other Xiongnu forces attacked Luoyang. Thirty thousand perished in the flames that consumed the Jin capital. Huaidì was captured and later killed.[132]

Exploiting his victory, Shi Le marched to attack Jianye on the southern bank of the Yangzi, where many refugees from the Central Plain gathered. Rain, determined resistance, and shortage of supply foiled his offensive. A new surprise greeted him on his retreat north. The central government had collapsed, but coordinated local resistance sprang up. Everywhere, he met cleared fields and staunchly defended towns. Unable to forage, his starving troops almost disintegrated. This near disaster prompted him to heed his Han-Chinese advisers and invest in a base equipped with civilian administration. Stable taxes were levied and deals reached with fortified towns, which were left alone if they paid up. Only then did Shi Le turn from an effective bandit living on plunder to a territorial ruler. In 319, he proclaimed an independent kingdom in eastern China called the Latter Zhao.[133]

The main Xiongnu force that sacked Luoyang in 311 proceeded directly to take Changan. Guanzhong was already bleak and depopulated, its economy ruined by rebellions and civil wars. Yet locals and Liangzhou forces rallied to a successful counterattack. At Changan, they erected Mindì to succeed Huaidì and fought off repeated assaults for four years. Finally Mindì surrendered, ending the West Jin Dynasty in 316.[134] After five centuries of imperial unity, north China reverted to a land of warring states. This time, ethnic minorities were kings (Map 17).

8.8 Coming of the Huns

Around 313, while the Xiongnu wreaked havoc in northern China, some Sogdian merchants in the relatively quiet western territory wrote home to today's Uzbekistan. They bewailed the loss of profitability in China because of the pillaging *Xwn* or Hun. The unsent letters, written in Sogdian, were recovered in a ruin near the Jade Gate. Their translator comments on the name *Xwn*: "here we find a name that is indistinguishable from that of the *Hūna, Oὔννοι, Hunni*, Arm *Honk*,' Saka *Huna*, Khwarezmian *Hūn*, employed not of nomads of vague definition, but actually of genuine Far-Eastern Hsiung-nu [Xiongnu]. And, what is more remarkable still, this name . . . was in use well before the time when . . . the European Huns . . . made their first appearance in history."[135] The Xiongnu had built a kingdom near Sogdia in the first century BCE. Thus their name would have been familiar to the Sogdians.[136]

Ammianus, who gave the best Roman account of the Huns, never dreamed of the possibility that the nomads who "exceed every degree of savagery" were once repelled by the Silk People "forever unacquainted with arms and warfare." He simply located their origin "near the ice-bound oceans" beyond the Black Sea.[137] Nineteenth-century scholars, mostly German, identified the Huns as descendants of the Xiongnu, based mainly on linguistics and textual scraps.[138] Since the 1930s, other scholars, again led by Germans, doubted any relation between the two, based mainly on comparing art form of archeological finds.[139] Evidence for either thesis is slim.

The Xiongnu split in 48. The South Xiongnu who surrendered to the Han were the ancestors of the *Xwn* about whom the Sogdians wrote. The North Xiongnu rode west and disappeared from Chinese records after 151. Between then and the appearance of the Huns beyond the Roman frontier in 376, the vast Eurasian steppe hid countless secrets, about which scholars can at best speculate. One thing is almost certain. Nomadic groups mixed and split. Neither the Xiongnu nor the Huns was homogeneous. Each comprised a miscellany of tribes, some transient, others of different ethnicity. Let us suppose that an aristocratic core of the North Xiongnu managed to maintain its identity under its old name, *Xwn* as known to the Sogdians. Even so, the group the *Xwn* led must have collected various tribes as it wandered about the steppe and may have adopted many of their customs. Is it possible that such a group later appeared as the Huns? Decide for yourself.

For our study of power, possible causal links between the Huns and Xiongnu are less important than their comparable traits. Harsh steppe environments being prohibitive of dense population, a nomadic people usually disperse into small bands to maximize available grass and water for their herds. The bands' leaders enjoy significant autonomy, although they gather in council and sometimes acknowledge a super leader. Such power diffusion was the political state of the Huns when they first approached the Roman Empire, or the state of the Xiongnu when imperial China first crystallized under the Qin Dynasty. Unlike many other barbarians, however, these two nomadic peoples were endowed with imperial instinct, an ability to unite themselves and integrate others to confront a powerful enemy. Hunnic warriors did not exceed 15,000 by much, but they skillfully incorporated the peoples they defeated into their confederation to build "an empire of many colors," akin to the Xiongnu's "great state of a hundred fierce peoples," *baiman daguo*. Their Germanic subjects were so numerous that a Germanic dialect became a major language in their realm. The Huns realized Tacitus's nightmare by uniting a large number of Rome's poor northern neighbors into something akin to a rival imperial power. If they had had a poetic virtuoso like Virgil, they might have sung the glory of raising the lowly and humbling the haughty.[140]

The Huns fought for the Romans as often as against them. The relationship between the two fell into three phases. Contacts were indirect in the first phase; the Huns pushed the Visigoths across the Danube in 376. For the following decades, the Huns served mainly as a Roman ally, albeit one costly and irritating. Finally, the era of Attila, which lasted from 441–452, was notorious for its hostility and brevity. The Hunnic Empire fell with Attila. Unlike the Xiongnu, it had not solved the problem of power transition.

The Huns' debut was barely within Rome's eastern horizon. A Gothic group built a defensive wall on the northern shore of the Black Sea. In a lightning strategic maneuver characteristic of steppe warfare, the Huns rode a large arc to attack it from the rear. The terrified Visigoths sought asylum in the Roman Empire. The pressure was psychological. The Huns did not pursue. For decades, their mass remained some 1,700 kilometers to the east, close to the Caucasus, whence they launched a futile attack on Persia.[141] Scattered bands fought for whoever employed them, the Romans included. In 409, Emperor Honorius summoned 10,000 Huns against the Visigoths. As the Huns gradually moved west, unity emerged. By the 420s, they began to build up a formidable empire on the Hungarian plain across the Danube from the Roman Empire.[142]

For the 409 deal, the Romans sent as hostage young Aetius, whose sojourn created a bond with the Huns. As friend and later foe, the Huns helped bolster Aetius's fame as "the last true Roman," who dominated the Western Empire after 433. Attila joined Aetius to attack the Burgundians on the middle Rhine. Their victory of 437 inspired the epic *Nibelungen* and a great opera cycle. Sustained Hunnic support also enabled Aetius to subdue the Visigoths and regain control over Gaul.[143]

Attila attacked the Eastern Roman Empire in 441–442, while its main force was away dealing with the Vandal conquest of Carthage. The Huns took Naissus and Viminacium, top-rank fortresses astride military trunk roads in the Balkans. The loss shocked the Romans; strongholds hitherto impregnable to barbarians had been a cornerstone of their imperial strategy.[144] Successful siege required not only heavy machinery but also effective leadership to organize concentrated troops and supply them for a significant period. Probably the Huns had learned from the Romans, but they had been in the same school for a much shorter time than the Germans, who remained "at peace with walls." Constantinople signed an unfavorable truce but broke it as soon as its African-bound troops returned. Attila made the preemptive strike in 447. The Huns routed the imperial field army at Chersonesus and devastated the Balkans as much as the Visigoths did earlier.[145]

Constantinople agreed to elevate the annual tribute in addition to paying up the arrears. With his eastern front thus secured, Attila opened his western campaign in 451, taking an imperial marriage as pretext. Besides Huns, his army contained large numbers of Goths and assorted tribes of the Hungarian plain. It surged from the mid Danube, overran the mid-Rhine, and plunged into Gaul, where Attila met his erstwhile friend Aetius. Anticipating the attack, Aetius augmented the Roman army by a coalition of Visigoths, Franks, and other barbarians residing in the Empire. The "battle of nations" on the Catalaunian Plain ended with Attila hiding behind a defensive wagon circle and ready for suicide. Aetius did not press his success; he had to conserve his force. The Visigoths lost their king and were eager to withdraw. Thus the victorious Roman coalition disbanded and the crestfallen Attila returned home safely.[146]

The western campaign took the Huns about 1,200 kilometers from home base, more than twice the distance covered in their Balkan campaign. It was not a steppe expedition where ubiquitous grass fed rides and self-propelled food supplies for warriors. This does not imply that the Huns had given up horses and fought on foot, as some scholars suggest.[147] They were still superb in the tactics of mounted archers. However, geography had deprived them of the strategic advantage of steppe warfare and forced them to organize their own logistics through the forests of Germania. Their commissariat fell short, and foraging reduced military speed.

The next year Attila chose a closer target, northern Italy. He again miscalculated. The cities that he had to storm were more heavily fortified and closely spaced. Protracted siege exhausted northern Italy. Supply ran out for the Hunnic army. Plague thinned out its contingents. The Eastern Empire under a new emperor took advantage to attack the Huns' home base in Hungary. These realistic factors recalled the Scourge of God, not the sweet talk of the pope as in Christian propaganda. That winter Attila died and his empire fell apart.[148]

"Attila, it has been said, was only the Scourge of God for the Roman priests and administrators interested in keeping the nations under the domination of Rome," comments a modern historian.[149] His invasions, although serious, posed no existential threat. The Huns were a major player in the demise of Rome, but not the prime villain. In a way, they actually retarded the whole process of the German dismemberment of the Empire.[150] They reined in the Germans, so major barbarian invasions stopped for three decades after 411. Furthermore, they provided military support for Rome to check those barbarians who had intruded. Hostility concentrated in the dozen years after 441. The Hunnic Empire was a foreign enemy to the Roman Empire, as the Xiongnu was to the Han. Neither nomadic empire aimed for conquest and occupation. Their goals were mainly plunder and extortion. They provoked great wars and wreaked vast damage, but each disintegrated before its enemy. They were barbarians at the gate, ferocious but easier for the sedentary empires to address than barbarians within the gate, such as the Visigoths or the South Xiongnu in the Jin, who aimed for settlement and a piece of the political pie. For the adverse behaviors of these internal enemies, the imperial elites themselves must share responsibility. Most lethal were barbarians in the heart.

In a way, the Hunnic Empire served the late Roman Empire as Carthage once did the Roman Republic. The threat of a strong enemy disciplined the ruling class and prevented factious conflicts from becoming barbaric. The Romans celebrated the death of Attila as the dawn of a new era. A rival superpower had fallen, but it was not necessarily a boon. The new world of myriad small powers and regional conflicts proved to be more complex and dangerous. German tribes released from Hunnic control quickly reverted to their habit of mutual antagonism, and violence spilled into the tired Roman Empire. Worse, internal conflicts intensified among the Romans relieved of Hunnic threat. Aetius survived Attila by only one year. He had been the stabilizing force of the Western Empire for twenty years and the only general capable of stopping the Huns. When the second function expired, the first became expendable. Domestic turmoil boiled over after his murder in 454. The Western Empire had only two decades left.[151]

8.9 The Fall of Rome

Gratian's solo reign, which began when his father and co-emperor Valentinian I died in 375, saw the breach of a tradition as old as Rome. Soldiers lost the protection of helmets and cuirasses.[152] This breach was remedied by Gratian's successor, but other changes proved more enduring. Unlike Valentinian I, who gained experience as a soldier, Gratian received the best classical education. He promptly replaced the rough and tough appointees of his father by men of letters. His tutor, a great poet, became praetorian prefect. Senatorial aristocrats from venerable and immensely rich families monopolized all high offices in the civilian government. They had long converted from militarism to cultural elegance as dainty as that of the Han literati. Many jumped to top positions without any experience in administration, for which they had neither interest nor respect.[153]

Catholic bishops were another group that crowded Gratian's court. They shared the delicate sensitivity of aristocrats and disdained the vulgarity of soldiers. Furthermore, they had no tolerance for barbarians. Although most barbarians were Christians, they were not Roman Catholics but heretics belonging to a different sect.[154] A historian summarizes, "Christian opinion, in the later fourth century, was prepared neither to respect those who kept the barbarian outside the Empire, nor to tolerate and absorb the barbarian, once inside."[155]

Incompatible military, civilian, and religious attitudes opened major fault lines in the Roman government. The civilian bureaucracy controlled military provision, the inadequacy of which contributed much to the eventual disintegration of the western army, and with it, the Western Empire. Wealthy senators resisted taxes even as the army dwindled.[156] Not until 441–444 did the emperor demand that aristocrats and the Catholic Church should pay regular taxes. By then the state was so bankrupted by the loss of Africa it was unable to supply veteran troops, not to mention equip new recruits. Even so, much of the extra revenue went to compensate dignitaries who lost African estates.[157]

Gratian left another detrimental legacy. Illyricum in the Balkans was home to some of the best soldiers and military leaders in the Empire. It was hitherto under the jurisdiction of the western emperor. Gratian ceded it to the east when he appointed Theodosius to succeed Valens, although as the dominant emperor he had no reason to give up anything. The alienation of this military nursery reduced the number of martial competitors for government offices. It also created great recruitment difficulties for later generals who faced a critical shortage of soldiers to counter barbarian invaders.[158]

Sixteen when his father died, Gratian inaugurated the age of ineffective emperors. It was not preordained. An alternative came in the form of Maximus, a Spanish general to whom Gratian's disgruntled army deserted en masse. However, Theodosius intervened militarily to uphold the boy Valentinian II. When the boy was overthrown, Theodosius defeated the challenger in a bigger civil war that culminated in the 394 battle of Frigidus. Theodosius died a few months after the victory, but not before designating as western emperor his son Honorius and entrusting the ten-year-old boy to the care of his chief general, Stilicho.

For both civil wars, Theodosius mustered troops of the Visigoth émigré state. Up to 10,000 Visigoths fell at Frigidus. Aggrieved by Constantinople's callous treatment, the Visigoths revolted in 395, led by Alaric. Stilicho responded swiftly. Besides the western army, he also had with him the eastern army, which Theodosius had brought for civil war. The superiority of two imperial armies under united command against the Visigoths, who were weakened by casualties, offered a good chance for a decisive victory. The opportunity was forsaken. Constantinople ordered Stilicho to return the eastern army and withdraw from eastern territory. Stilicho obeyed. The Visigoths were free to despoil Macedonia and Greece. Unopposed, they walked through the narrow pass of Thermopylae, where once 300 Spartans had stood against the mighty Persian army. Many Greek cities fell.[159] Constantinople gave Alaric a regional command and access to imperial arsenals. Recuperated and better armed, the Visigoths turned west and twice invaded northern Italy between 401 and 403. Stilicho drove them back into the Balkans.[160]

The western Roman army, decimated in Frigidus and having suffered further casualties fighting the Visigoths, soon faced a string of crises. Toward the end of 405, Radagaisus invaded northern Italy with a large group of Goths from beyond the Danube. On the last day of 406, large bands of Vandals, Suevi, and Alans walked over the frozen Rhine near Mainz. Sometime between the two invasions, a series of usurpations began in Britain. The third usurper, Constantine III, abandoned Britain, crossed the Channel in 407, and won control of Roman troops in Gaul. Alaric smelled opportunity and returned to Italy around the same time. Stilicho decisively defeated Radagaisus. The cost of his victory was probably heavy; the western army lost 48 percent of its troops during the years 395 to 420. To counter subsequent troubles, he negotiated with Alaric and bought Visigothic assistance for 4,000 Roman pounds of gold. Infuriated wealthy senators fueled intrigues. Stilicho was falsely accused of treason and beheaded in 408.[161]

Stilicho was one of many Roman officers of German descent who rose to high positions through the army under soldier-emperors. None of these second-generation immigrants with a thorough Roman education was known to betray the interest of the Empire to his compatriots. Stilicho's preference of a dignified death to a ruinous civil war would put many pure-blooded Romans to shame. Nevertheless, the tide had turned against naturalized citizens with the ascendancy of aristocratic and theological ideologies. No one with a German name held supreme Roman command after Stilicho. The glass ceiling was nothing compared to the gory floor. Constantinople led the way in 400. In the coup against a powerful general of Gothic extraction, thousands of barbarians serving in the Roman army were burned to death in the church wherein they took asylum. If Alaric had been nudged by the event to stir in 401, he benefited much more in the aftermath of Stilicho's demise. The Romans slaughtered wholesale the families of more than 10,000 barbarian soldiers he enlisted, many formerly Radagaisus's Goths. The outraged husbands and fathers threw in their lots with Alaric.[162]

The master of office who plotted the downfall of the generalissimo and took control of the government neither honored Stilicho's agreement with Alaric nor prepared for Visigothic reaction. The imperial court was untouchable in Ravenna, protected by swamps and supplied from the sea. Rome was more vulnerable. The Visigoths started to blockade the city in the autumn of 408, their ranks swelled by slaves who poured out to reclaim freedom. Citizens prayed in vain for the imperial army. Frightened senators ponied up more than 5,000 Roman pounds of gold and agreed to mediate on the barbarian's behalf. Honorius sent for the Huns, scaring Alaric into reducing his demands to "extremely reasonable" terms, as a Roman historian commented. He asked for an annual supply of grain and land in a frontier province for settlement as a Roman ally—similar to what the Xiongnu got from the Han Dynasty. Nevertheless, antibarbarian ideology fanned by political faction fights precluded negotiation. Alaric returned to Rome for a second blockade and induced senatorial collaboration to erect a competing emperor. Honorius almost agreed to negotiate, but 4,000 troops from Constantinople stiffened his intransigence. Foiled again at Ravenna, Alaric returned to Rome; he had his own constituency to satisfy. The previous two blockades created such hardship that someone cried out in the circus, "set a price on human flesh." When the Visigoths came again in August 410, Rome opened its gate. For three days Alaric rewarded his men. They killed and plundered at will, but under strict orders to spare the clergy and churches. This was the first sack of Rome since the Gauls had violated it eight centuries ago. In 390 BCE, the whole city suffered except the Capitol Hill. In 410, the Senate House alone was torched. The difference underlines the significances of the two sacks, if the Senate House retained some symbolism for the Roman state.[163]

Loaded with loot from Rome, the Visigoths continued their grand tour of the Empire, from Italy to Gaul, then Spain. These countries were crowded with Rome's enemies. The Vandals, Suevi, and Alans, who crossed the Rhine in 406, made their way through Gaul and over the Pyrenees into Spain in 409, despite the Roman troops under the usurper Constantine III. Historians explain, "It was most likely only by winking at the presence of the invaders and at their doings that Constantine obtained possession, so far as Roman troops and Roman administration were concerned, of all Gaul from the Channel to the Alps."[164]

After almost five years of inaction, the imperial army awoke in 411; perhaps the Hunnic ally finally arrived, or perhaps a victor emerged from debilitating faction fights. Constantius eliminated Constantine III. A blockade starved the Visigoths into surrendering and they defeated the Vandals and Alans for Rome. Instead of pressing for a durable solution, however, Constantius recalled the Visigoths and settled them in southern Gaul in 418. Politics claimed his attention.[165]

Constantius married Honorius's sister Placidia and became Honorius's co-emperor in 421. He died within the year. Power struggles erupted immediately and turned white-hot when Honorius died sonless two years later.

A successor emerged at Ravenna. Constantinople sent a large expedition against him, battered the western army in a tough campaign, and erected in Rome Valentinian III, Constantius's six-year-old son. Placidia acted as regent but had to contend with several factions. Two civil wars followed, hacking down more Romans. Paralysis again afflicted the government until Aetius triumphed in 433 with the help of his Hunnic friends, to whom the Empire ceded territory in Pannonia.[166]

Barbarians prospered while Romans played political backstabbing. The Alans joined the Vandals in Spain. Led by Geiseric, they invaded Africa in 429. A single round trip across the Strait of Gibraltar normally took twenty-four hours, weather allowing. Assembling a flotilla and ferrying over 80,000 persons with their animals and baggage took months. The Roman navy, although deteriorated, still controlled the sea and could disrupt preparations, as the Vandals later did to a Roman staging. That the Vandals crossed unharassed revealed the dysfunction of the imperial government. The invaders trudged eastward some 2,000 kilometers along the Roman main road across the rugged North African coast, defeated the Roman army near Hippo, and blockaded the city while its bishop, Augustine, lay dying. However, bandit-like operations could carry the Vandals only so far. Like the Visigoths—or Shi Le in China—they needed a stable base with secure resources to settle and then expand as a state. The Romans gave it to them, not having learned from the behavior of the Visigoths whom they thrice settled. By the treaty of 435, the Vandals received land in relatively poor provinces, while the Romans kept the richest provinces around Carthage. Instead of using the truce to strengthen defense against a dangerous neighbor, the Romans cut the garrison at Carthage and were surprised when the Vandals walked in to take the city in 439.[167]

Africa was a major breadbasket for the Western Empire. Moreover, warships launched from Carthage threatened the whole Mediterranean. Finally cured of their strategic blindness, the two Roman Empires scrambled for a counterattack. Alas, their window of opportunity had closed. They had three decades to subdue the invaders of 406 with Hunnic help but squandered the time at each other's throat. The Huns turned from an ally to an enemy. Attila struck in 441 and absorbed Roman energy until his death in 453.

Shortly after the Hunnic Empire disintegrated, Valentinian III stabbed Aetius. He in turn was murdered. The mastermind of the two plots, Petronius Maximus, was among the most prominent of blue-blooded senators. As soon as he succeeded to the throne, he sought support from the Visigoths, thus elevating barbarian kings to top players of Roman politics. His reign lasted less than three months. While Roman attention was riveted on Attila, the Vandals honed their skill in sea raiding. In 455, an expedition landed on the outskirts of Rome. If 600 years earlier Scipio Aemilianus could have predicted the state of his beloved country to be seen by the avengers of Carthage, his tears would have been bitterer. The citizens of Rome surrendered. They had already opened their gates to the Visigoths and had chosen not to rebuild their capacity for defending their honor.[168]

When Alaric stormed through Greece, many cities yielded without resistance. Zosimus wrote, "Even Sparta herself was swept away in the common destruction of Hellas. She was no longer fortified by arms or by warriors owing to the exploitation of the Romans."[169] The Greeks blamed the Romans. Who could the conquerors of the world blame? During the high Empire, Tacitus wrote, "Passivity does not preserve great empires. There are things to be fought for."[170] Once there was a great people to whom "freedom" meant more than free bread and circuses.

The Visigoths who raped Rome raped Sparta first. The Huns despoiled the Balkans, a part of the East. Of the four great engagements with barbarians, the East lost disastrously at Hadrianople and Chersonesus, the West won marginally at the Catalaunian Plains and completely over Radagaisus's invasion. Despite its dismal military record with barbarians, the East unloaded intruders, not back into Germania, but into the West. The Visigoths eventually settled in Gaul, the Ostrogoths in Italy, ruining the West while sparing the East.[171]

Constantinople was not totally indifferent to Rome's plight. Its two coordinated efforts with the West to retake Africa were not merely to protect itself from sea raids. The first effort was frustrated by the Huns. The Vandal adventure at Rome prompted a final try. The Western Empire gathered its remaining troops. The Eastern Empire assembled an armada designed to land a large army on Africa. The Vandal fleet seized the opportunity of a favorable wind to launch fireships into the invading armada. The fireships in the 468 battle of Cape Bon burned away the last hope of the Western Roman Empire, just as the fireships of the 208 battle of Red Cliff blazed the way to a fragmented China for centuries.[172]

The Visigoths sensed the wind change and switched from playing Roman politics to military expansion, until they established an autonomous kingdom in Spain and southern Gaul. Other resident barbarians promptly followed suit. When all provinces with their tax revenues broke away, the Roman army in Italy demanded land to substitute for lost pay. With the consent of the Eastern Roman emperor, Zeno, the army commander Odovacar deposed the Western emperor, the boy Romulus Augustulus. Thus was the Western Roman Empire officially ended in 476. Thirteen years later, Zeno persuaded the Ostrogothic leader Theodoric, a warlord who had been threatening his own position, to leave the Eastern Empire and attack Odovacar. Theodoric joined Italy and the Danube region originally belonging to the Western Empire into the Ostrogothic kingdom (Map 18).[173]

8.10 Tomorrow Never Dies

Half of each empire survived. The continuous cultural and religious flourishing of Jianye and Constantinople, the capitals of southern China and the Eastern Roman Empire, attracts much scholarly attention.[174] Those concerned with politically significant changes, however, must examine the original imperial heartlands. Five hundred and thirty-seven years after Qin united the warring states in 221 BCE, north China disintegrated into kingdoms of ethnic minorities. Five hundred and ten years after Augustus founded the Roman Empire in 31 BCE, barbarian kingdoms partitioned the lands around the western Mediterranean. The knockout blows were brutal, but not necessarily lethal. The minorities and barbarians who wrought destruction also infused vigorous blood and culture. What did not kill an empire could make it stronger.

Minorities and barbarians were the ultimate winners, but external infections could not have toppled the empires without aid from internal cancers. Pragmatic Jin officers had warned of massive immigration and lax administration. The imperial government might have been able to assuage the problems if not for the fratricidal wars from 301 to 306. The Xiongnu émigré state took advantage of the chaos to rebel in 304 and annihilate the Jin field army in 311. Though swift, its conquest was not unopposed. The few imperial troops left in Luoyang fought twelve battles and died with the city. Local forces in Changan withstood the Xiongnu for four years. With the city's outer wall breached and cannibalism the only source of food, they would have kept their vow to hold the inner city until death were they not deserted by the emperor they erected.[175] Resistance was not localized. The most persistent armed movement came from the tough folks who once contributed to the defense-in-depth of the northern frontier. After evacuating into the interior in 306, they formed the Qihuo and played a significant role in eliminating Shi Le's kingdom. Their overt and covert organizations against minority occupation spread into many provinces and persevered for more than a century.[176]

Roman resistance was milder. The Visigothic émigré state first rebelled in 378, but not until 476 did it succeed in carving out an independent kingdom. In the interim, it pillaged through the length of the Empire with near impunity. Defeated, it was given generous settlement under the condition that it provided troops, often for civil wars. Fighting did occur, but major battles were rare and none of them decisive.[177] The legal ban on private arms had been lifted in 440. However, only a handful of Roman resistance efforts were known, mostly a magnate assembling a force to defend his own locality, as Valentinus did to fend off a Gothic assault on Selge.[178] Rome twice opened its gates to enemies incapable of siege. Some scholars see Romans and Germans accommodating each other to transform their world.[179] Others say, "The most depressing feature of the later empire is the apparent absence of public spirit."[180]

The sparseness of military engagement does not imply a peaceful transformation. Lack of hard protection may have made soft targets more vulnerable. "The whole of Gaul smoked on a single funeral pyre," lamented a Roman. "Floating bodies clogged rivers, bleached bones scattered across the earth," wrote a Chinese.[181] Famine and epidemic followed war and pillage. People abandoned their homes to survive. Dislocation was severe in China, where many peasants depended on large irrigational waterworks that, once damaged, could not be repaired by individual efforts. Texts recorded the largest migration out of north China. The refugees' homeland would have to endure more than a century of violent wars. *Hanren* would turn from "people of the Han Dynasty" to designate ethnicity, when the Han-Chinese got their name from the disparagement of their minority masters.[182] Mobility seemed less in the Mediterranean world; strong property rights tied down landlords and legal status bound tenants. Nevertheless, archeologists found that settlements in many areas thinned out drastically from the fifth to eighth centuries. Impoverishment in material culture is the general picture of the aftermath of empire.[183]

After Corinth yielded to the Visigoths, a youth in captivity transcribed Homer: "the most fortunate of the inhabitants were saved, by death, from beholding the slavery of their families, and the conflagration of their cities." A modern historian explained, "The female captives submitted to the laws of war."[184] Leo, the bishop of Rome increasingly called the pope, wrote regarding the nuns raped by the Vandals. These "handmaids of God who have lost the integrity of their honour through the oppression of the barbarians" had not sinned in mind, he decreed, but the violation of their bodies lowered their status: "They will be more praiseworthy in their humility and sense of shame, if they do not dare to compare themselves to uncontaminated virgins."[185]

In the mayhem that proceeded the fall of the Latter Han Dynasty, Cai Yan was abducted, sold to a Xiongnu king, kept for twelve years, and bore two sons. Daughter to a leading scholar, she was accomplished in music and literature. Several of her poems survived. Through her "Indignant Sorrow" we see Han armor shining on Hu warriors and men's heads hanging beside the horses on which women are bound. We hear warhorses neigh in accompaniment to the sad tune of the nomad's reed, and, back at her former home, jackals howl in the silence of human voices. When ransom comes, she is overcome with joy, then grief. Her sons cling to her bosom and cry: We are so young, why do you leave us, mother? Her fellow captives gather to bid farewell, congratulating her, mourning their own fate, and inducing tears from bystanders. Amid the chorus the poet stays her horse, torn between the calls of her Han parents and Xiongnu sons.[186]

More than sorrow pours from Cai's "Eighteen Variations on the *Hujia*." Arranging the tunes of the *hujia*, a nomadic reed instrument, for the *qin*, the traditional Chinese string instrument for meditation, she explains in the lyric: "*Hujia* originates among the Hu, but its transposed music also suits the *qin*."[187] Accommodation did occur, but amid horrendous conflict and suffering. Images of bloodless wars in sanitized histories or newscasts nurture not sensitivity but callousness. They encourage perpetrators of violence to ignore the misery of their victims.

The fall of the imperial government was only the first act of a long tragedy. Many more barbarians or nomads would enter the territories of the former empires. The original residents would have to suffer many violent changes in regional rulers, all of different ethnicities and cultures. As subjects, they had to accommodate. They were superior in number and knowledge, which could balance the superior military might of their rulers. The elites of both realms survived; their new masters needed their service in order to rule. With decadent high culture no longer affordable, they returned to their characteristic roots—Roman military organization and landed wealth, Chinese kin cohesion and administrative skill. Would the vaunted Greco-Roman or Han-Chinese character enable the captives to capture their conquerors and absorb them into their ways of life? Would the Eagle or the Dragon revive?

The evolutions of the two realms, hitherto convergent, began to diverge.[188] Perhaps the Roman Empire was unsustainable as a whole. However, the essence of Rome resided in the Western Empire, comprising Italy, Gaul, Spain, and Africa, which had been a political unit by itself. Its provinces were most thoroughly Romanized. Latin remained the common language and many Roman institutions persisted in the German kingdoms. Christianity, which the Romans and Germans shared, had an organized church wielding significant political power. Rome physically stood as the eternal city and the idea of its empire persisted. Yet these favorable conditions seemed unable to heal the wounds of invasion. The fragments did not coalesce to reconstitute an integral state as they did in north China. One millennium after the birth of Jesus in the Roman Empire and the registration of 60 million inhabitants in China, historians bemoaning the vicissitudes of fortune would wonder: Of the fall of two comparable empires, why was the fall of Rome alone terminal? Another millennium later, would they wonder at an international situation in which the United States, sometimes perceived as the American Empire akin to a New Rome, faces the rise of New China?[189]

Notes

1. Barnes 1981: 249.
2. Bury 1958: 15–16. Jones 1964: 83, 92, 97, 107–109. Heather 2005: 68.
3. Panegyric quoted in Mitchell 2007: 67.
4. Barnes 1981: 259.

5. *Houhanshu* 4: 165.
6. Ebrey 1986: 621.
7. *Houhanshu* 4: 195.
8. Beck 1986: 357–369. Lewis 2009.
9. Heather 2005: xii.
10. Ward-Perkins 2005: 32–33.
11. Brown 1971. Goffart 1989. Pohl 1997.
12. Millar 1981: 9.
13. Ebrey 1986: 611.
14. Heather 2005: 17. See also Brown 1971: 14, 118.
15. Ebrey 1986: 643–645. Qian 1940: 169–171, 176–177, 184–185.
16. Yü 2003: 252–253. Brown 1971: 116–117.
17. Jones 1964: 444. Cameron 1993: 116–117.
18. Ebrey 1986: 612–613. Scheidel 2009b: 154, 175–176.
19. Whittaker and Garnsey 1998: 279–284. Heather 2005: 114–115. MacMullen 1988: 36–37.
20. Hsu 1980: Chs. 4 and 5. Ebrey 1986: 609, 613–614, 622–624.
21. McNeill 1976: Ch. 3.
22. Bivar 1983b: 93–94.
23. Birley 1987: 149–151. Gibbon 1994: 2:302.
24. *Houhanshu*, Zhi 17, 3350–3351. *Sanguozhi* 2: 82; 3: 101. *Jinshu* 4: 92; 5: 124.
25. *Houhanshu*, Zhi 17, 3351. *Jinshu* 103: 2691, 2693. Wang Z. 2003: 21–26, 221, 235.
26. *Houhanshu* 71: 2299. *Sanguozhi* 54: 1262, 1265. Wang W. 2007: 102–106, 115–116.
27. Heather 2005: 182. Hopkins 1980: 117–118. Potter 2004: 17.
28. Jones 1964: 684. Heather 2005: 63–64. MacMullen 1988: 41, 174.
29. *Hanshu* 28b: 1640. *Houhanshu*, Zhi 23: 3533, 3534 annotation. *Sanguozhi* 22: 637 annotation.
30. *Sanguozhi* 22: 637. Wang Z. 2003: 170. Graff 2002: 35–36.
31. Luo 1989. De Crespigny 2009: 110–111.
32. *Hanshu* 16: 527. *Jinshu* 26: 791.
33. Graff 2002: 30–39. He and Wang 1997: 61–63, 86–87.
34. Jones 1964: 1031. Goldsworthy 2009: 272.
35. Thompson 1996: 56. See also Heather 2005: 328.
36. Thompson 1982: 15–19.
37. Heather 2005: 446. Bury 1958: 104–105.
38. Heather 2005: 63–64. Mitchell 2007: 167.
39. Ward-Perkins 2005: 68. Heather 2005: 198. Goldsworthy 2009: 43.
40. *Houhanshu* 89: 2953.
41. *Jinshu* 97: 2548–2549. Ma 2006a: 88–91. Weng 2001: 169–170.
42. Ma 2006b: 181, 191, 204, 231. Weng 2001: 178–180, 195–196.
43. Weng 2001: 134–135. Zhang C. 2008: 116.
44. *Jinshu* 56, 1531–1533. Wang Z. 2003: 186.
45. *Jinshu* 2: 40; 102: 2665.
46. *Hanshu* 28. *Houhanshu*, Zhi 19–23. *Jinshu* 15–16.
47. *Jinshu* 56: 1531–1533; 97: 2549. Weng 2001: 180–181.
48. *Houhanshu* 90: 2991; 84: 2801; 48: 1610. Barfield 1989: 93.
49. Thompson 1958: 3, 6.

50. Goldsworthy 2009: 220–221, 254, 311. Thompson 1958: 18–22.
51. *Houhanshu* 87: 2890. *Jinshu* 57: 1554–1555.
52. Ammianus 31.7.2, quoted in Whittaker 1994: 193.
53. Thompson 1958: 18–19. Heather 2005: 183–184.
54. Grant 1990: 22–23. Goldsworthy 2009: 415.
55. MacMullen 1988: 191.
56. Hanahan and Weinberg 2000.
57. MacMullen 1974: 38.
58. *Hanshu* 19a: 721, annotation. MacMullen 1974: 94.
59. Lin 2003: 829–830, 863–864, 925–927. Hsu 1980: 198–199, 201–206.
60. *Houhanshu* 42: 1431. Ebrey 1986: 624.
61. Wells 1992: 178–179. Brown 1971: 34. Jones 1964: 554–556, 784, 787. Starr 1982: 170–171. Bastomsky 1990: 41.
62. Jones 1964: 1045.
63. *Houhanshu* 54: 1772.
64. Jones 1964: 1046–1047. Goldsworthy 2009: 361.
65. Ebrey 1986: 643–645. Qian 1940: 169–171, 176–179, 184–185. *Houhanshu* 53: 1752.
66. Jones 1974: 116; 1964: 795–796, 1043. Ch'ü 1972: 110–111. *Hanshu* 24a, 1137.
67. Starr 1982: 171. Ebrey 1986: 625–626. Hsu 1980: 63–65.
68. Whittaker and Garnsey 1998: 293. Jones 1964: 795–797. Marcone 1998: 357.
69. *Sanguozhi* 46: 1105. He and Wang 1997: 61–63. Lü 2005b: 612–614.
70. Jones 1964: 614–617, 619–621, 683–684, 1042. Shaw 1999: 135. MacMullen 1966: 199.
71. *Sanguozhi* 35: 923. Wardman 1984: 224.
72. Shaw 1984: 9–16, 37–40. MacMullen 1966: 193–198, 200. Potter 2004: 120–122, 131, 281.
73. Hsu 1980: 142–145. Lin 2003: 963–966.
74. Goldsworthy 2009: 301–302.
75. *Jinshu* 4: 108.
76. *Houhanshu* 79a: 2547. De Crespigny 2009: 103–105, 109.
77. Heather 2005: 221, 312. Jones 1964: 527, 539, 555. Gibbon 1994: 2:172.
78. Brown 1971: 119.
79. Jones 1964: 371, 608.
80. Syme 1958: 62.
81. See also Jones 1964: 1066, 160, 177, 559–561.
82. Brown 1971: 120, 30.
83. Liu C. 2006: 136–138.
84. *Houhanshu* 46: 1548.
85. Xu Gan, quoted in Yü 2003: 255.
86. *Houhanshu* 8: 342; 52: 1731; 78: 2535–2536. Beck 1986: 331–333.
87. Jones 1964: 393–398.
88. Ammianus, in Jones 1964: 109.
89. MacMullen 1988: 151.
90. *Houhanshu* 56: 1826. Qian 1940: 186–190.
91. Jones 1964: 400. MacMullen 1988: 196.
92. Goldsworthy 2009: 310. MacMullen 1988: 172–177, 192.

93. Whittaker 1994: 263–264.
94. Jones 1964: 684.
95. Yu 2000: 430–431.
96. *Houhanshu* 74a: 2378. Tian and An 2008: 385–387.
97. Chen 1986: 789.
98. Ebrey 1983: 535–541. De Crespigny 1980: 52–53. Qian 1940: 175, 216–218.
99. Yü 2003: 359–360. Qian 1940: 217.
100. Hao and Johnston 2002: 594–595. Harris 2003: 66–67.
101. Grant 1990: 28–34. Gibbon 1994: 2: 618–621. Shaw 1999: 148.
102. Zosimus, quoted in Potter 2004: 448. Luttwak 1976: 188, 178–179.
103. Ammianus 21.16. Jones 1964: 653.
104. Ward-Perkins 2005: 44–46. Goldsworthy 2009: 22, 119, 203, 408.
105. Hobsbawm 1959. Blok 1972.
106. Escherick 1983: 276–277.
107. *Shiji* 8: 344; 7: 296.
108. *Shiji* 48: 1952.
109. *Shiji* 6: 277.
110. *Hanshi* 1a: 21.
111. *Sanguozhi* 6: 210, annotation. Chen 1975: 53.
112. *Mengzi* 1.15. Pines 2009a: 217.
113. *Lunyu* 19.20.
114. *Houhanshu* 71: 2303. *Sanguozhi* 1: 4. Beck 1986: 324.
115. De Crespigny 2009: 110.
116. *Zhouyi*, Hexagram 49.
117. Beck 1986: 317–325.
118. Beck 1986: 338–339.
119. *Houhanshu* 75: 2431–2432. Beck 1986: 339–340.
120. Beck 1986: 341–345. Liu C 2006: 6–7.
121. *Sanguozhi* 15: 467. Beck 1986: 345–350.
122. Beck 1986: 350–352. Chen C-Y. 1975: 44–47.
123. Beck 1986: 354–357. Lewis 2009: 35–36.
124. *Sanguozhi* 1: 24, 32; 35: 917, 928, 934.
125. Lewis 2009: 36, 61–62.
126. Dreyer 2009: 118–137.
127. *Sanguozhi* 15: 469; 22: 638. *Jinshu* 97: 2548. Barfield 1989: 95–96.
128. *Jinshu* 52: 1445.
129. Dreyer 2009: 141. Weng 2001: 169–170, 180–181.
130. Dreyer 2009: 130. Barfield 1989: 99, 101–103.
131. *Jinshu* 104: 2708–2711.
132. Dreyer 2009: 136.
133. Wang Z. 2003: 223–231.
134. Dreyer 2009: 136.
135. W. Henning, quoted in Vaissière 2004: 22.
136. Beckwith 2009: 72–73.
137. Ammianus 31.2.1; 23.6.67.
138. Sinor 1990a: 177–179. Yü 1986: 404–405. Gibbon 1994: 2:1035–1042.
139. Maenchen-Helfen 1973: Heather 2005: 148–149. Kelly 2008: 43–45.
140. Heather 2005: 324–333. Thompson 1996: 50–51, 230–231. Barfield 1989: 33, 36, 49–51.

141. Heather 2005: 150–154. 202–203. Thompson 1996: 35.
142. Thompson 1996: 52, 62–64. Kelly 2008: 54–55. Heather 2005: 330–332.
143. Thompson 1996: 71–72. Heather 2005: 281–282, 286–287. Kelly 2008: 113–115.
144. Thompson 1996: 90. Heather 2005: 300–304.
145. Heather 2005: 302–303. Goldsworthy 2009: 320–324.
146. Heather 2005: 312, 333–339. Thompson 1996: 213–214.
147. Lindner 1981. Beckwith 2009: 98.
148. Heather 2005: 340–341. Bury 1958: 295–296.
149. Thompson 1996: 45.
150. Bury 1958: 297–298. Wickham 2010: 84.
151. Heather 2005: 369, 372–373.
152. Gibbon 1994: 2:70.
153. Jones 1964: 160, 177, 207, 1066. Brown 1971: 36, 120.
154. Gibbon 1994: 2:20.
155. Brown 1967: 331–332.
156. Gibbon 1994: 2:99. Cameron 1993: 149–150. MacMullen 1988: 172–177, 192.
157. Heather 2005: 295–297. Bury 1958: 253–254.
158. Bury 1958: 110–111. Heather 2005: 219.
159. Heather 2005: 212–214. Gibbon 1994: 2:124.
160. Bury 1958: 109–112, 119–120, 160–163. MacMullen 1988: 185–186, 188–189.
161. Bury 1958: 160, 166–169. Heather 2005: 205–206, 221, 247.
162. Heather 2005: 214–217, 224. Jones 1964: 177, 1038.
163. Bury 1958: 182, 178–183. Heather 2005: 224–229.
164. Bury 1958: 189.
165. Heather 2005: 253–257.
166. Heather 2005: 258–262, 286–287.
167. Heather 2005: 265–272, 285–286, 288–289.
168. Heather 2005: 372–375, 378–379.
169. Zosimus, quoted in Thompson 1982: 240.
170. Tacitus, *Annals*, 15.1.
171. Goffart 1989: 13–14.
172. Heather 2005: 385, 388–389, 399–406. Goldsworthy 2009: 357–359.
173. Heather 2005: 416–418, 425–430. Wickham 2010: 89–98.
174. Holcombe 1994. Bowersock, Brown, and Grabar 1999.
175. *Zizhi Tongjian* 85: 2763, 2834–2835.
176. Zhou 1997: 15–26.
177. Goldsworthy 2009: 311.
178. MacMullen 1988: 52–53. Thompson 1982: 239.
179. For critical summaries of such views, see Ward-Perkins 2005: 3–10, 174. Wickham 2010: 8–10.
180. Jones 1964: 1058–1062.
181. Orientus, quoted in Ward-Perkins 2005: 23. *Jinshu* 26: 791.
182. Holcombe 1994: 26–28. Wang Z 2003: 320.
183. Ward-Perkins 2005: 117–124, 139–146.
184. Gibbon 1994: 2:124.
185. Leo, quoted in Ward-Perkins 2005: 11.
186. Frankel 1983: 135–137.

187. Frankel 1983: 142.
188. Scheidel 2009a: 20–23.
189. Goldsworthy 2009: 4–5. Mutschler and Mittag 2009: xiii–xiv.

APPENDICES

Appendix 1: Mutual Perceptions of Rome and Han China

In 97, Ban Chao, the Han's protector general of the Western Territory, dispatched Gan Ying in quest of Daqin, as the Roman Empire was called by the ancient Chinese. Gan reached Mesopotamia but was discouraged from crossing a great sea by sailors presumably Parthian.[1] Had he come eighteen years later, he might have met Trajan leading the invasion army. By then, however, Han power in the western regions had begun to contract. The Romans, too, abandoned Trajan's conquest, and in just three years. In their final expansive lurches, the empires at the two ends of Eurasia almost made contact—almost.

Ban Chao's pacification of the Western Territory reopened communication with the West. Visitors came from distant states previously unknown.[2] It is unclear whether the new visitor from Mengqi was related to the Macedonian merchant Maes Titianus, whose journey from Syria to the Pamir during Hadrian's reign was recorded by the Greek geographer Ptolemy. Maes sent agents further on to the capital of Serice, land of the Silk People.[3] If they brought back intelligence about China, however, it seemed to make no impression on Ammianus Marcellinus.

Here are a few prominent literary sources that reveal what the Roman and Han Empires thought about each other. Most scholars agree that "Seres" in Roman writings and "Sinae" in Ptolemy's *Geography* refer to the Chinese realm.[4] The Elder Pliny's encyclopedic *Natural History*, written in the mid-first century, mentioned the Seres under two topics:

> "But of all the varieties of Iron, the palm goes to the Seric, sent us by the Seres with their fabric and skins."

> "And by the lowest reckoning India, China (Seres) and the Arabian peninsula take from our empire 100 million sesterces every year—that is the sum

> which our luxuries and our women cost us." The amount was equivalent to 7 tons of gold. About half of it went to India for its spices.[5]

Pliny also collected two accounts of travelers:

> "They also told us . . . that when they arrived there the Chinese always hastened down to the beach to meet them. That people themselves are of more than normal height, and have flaxen hair and blue eyes, and they speak in harsh tones and use no language in dealing with travelers."
>
> "The first human occupants are the people called the Chinese, who are famous for the woolen substance obtained from their forests; after a soaking in water they comb off the white down of the leaves, and so supply our women with the double task of unraveling the threads and weaving them together again; so manifold is the labour employed, and so distant is the region of the globe drawn upon, to enable the Roman matron to flaunt transparent raiment in public. The Chinese, though mild in character, yet resemble wild animals, in that they also shun the company of the remainder of mankind, and wait for trade to come to them."[6]

Ammianus Marcellinus wrote in the 380s:

> The Seres themselves live a peaceful life, forever unacquainted with arms and warfare; and since to gentle and quiet folk ease is pleasurable, they are troublesome to none of their neighbours. Their climate is agreeable and healthful, the sky is clear, the winds gentle and very pleasant. There is an abundance of well-lighted woods, the trees of which produce a substance which they work with frequent sprinkling, like a kind of fleece; then from the wool-like material, mixed with water, they draw out very fine threads, spin the yarn, and make sericum, formerly for the use of the nobility, but nowadays available even to the lowest without any distinction. The Seres themselves are frugal beyond all others, live a quiet life, and avoid intercourse with the rest of mortals. And when strangers, in order to buy threads or anything else, cross the river, their wares are laid out and with no exchange of words their value is estimated by the eye alone; and they are so abstemious, that they hand over their own products without themselves getting any foreign ware in return.[7]

The Mediterranean realm appears first as Lijian in Chinese sources. After the Roman conquest of the eastern Mediterranean, the name was changed to Daqin.[8] The most substantial account occurs in the *Book of Latter Han* by Fan Ye, who started writing in the 420s. He put it in the chapter on the western regions and acknowledged his reliance on the notes of Ban Yong, son of Ban Chao.

> Daqin is located west of the sea, therefore is also called Haixiguo [State West of the Sea]. It has over four hundred cities and tens of subject states. Its stonewalled cities are connected by postal roads on white-earth foundations. Pine and all kinds of vegetation flourish there. Their people work hard in farming, plant many trees and mulberry. They crop their hair short, wear embroidered cloths, and travel in chariots with white canopies, preceded by drums and banners. Their main city is more than a hundred *li* [Chinese mile] in circumference. Within are five palaces, separated from each other by ten *li*. The pillars of their palaces are made of crystal, so are their tableware. Their king chooses a palace each day, holds court there for five days, and then changes location. When he goes out, an attendant follows the chariot with a bag, into which anyone with grievances can drop their petitions. The king reads them back in the palace and judges rights and wrongs. They have officers for various tasks and thirty-six generals, all meeting in conference on state matters. Their king is not a permanent figure, being chosen as the man most worthy. When the state encounters adversity or natural disaster, a new king is erected, and the disposed king is not embittered. The people are tall and regular featured. They resemble people of the Middle Kingdom and their country is called Daqin [Great Qin]. Theirs is a land rich in gold, silver, and precious stones, with fluorescent jewels . . . and everything precious that foreign countries produce. They use gold and silver for money, ten silver pieces for one gold piece. On the sea, they trade with Anshi [Parthia] and Tianzu [India] and make ten-fold profits. They are upright and honest, setting one price for goods and do not haggle. Their grain is cheap and state prosperous. Envoys from neighboring countries are escorted from the border by postal roads to the capital, where they receive gold money. Their kings often wish to contact the Han but are obstructed by Anshi, which wishes to sell Han silk to them. In the ninth year of the Yanxi period [166 CE], King Andun of Daqin sent an envoy to Rinan [now central Vietnam]and presented ivory, rhinoceros horn, and turtle shell, thus began contact. The insignia being ordinary and tribute lacking anything precious, the envoy was suspect.[9]

The list of products masked by the ellipsis in this quotation includes fifteen other items. Among them were glass, a famous Roman product; coral and pearl, found in the Mediterranean, and amber from the Baltic; gold-embroidered rugs, produced in Alexandria and Syria; and various fragrances, probably from Syria and Arabia. Other items, such as jade, were unknown to the Romans but found in the western mountains where the trade routes traversed.[10]

Conspicuously absent from this list of Daqin products are ivory, rhinoceros horn, and turtle shell, which were available in southeast Asia. The agent who presented them as gifts of King Andun of Daqin arrived five years after Marcus Aurelius Antoninus succeeded Antoninus Pius as Roman emperor. However, the Romans left no trace of sending emissaries to Serice. Modern scholars mostly agree that the fellow who visited Rinan and several like him later were not state representatives but adventurers who borrowed the name of an emperor too remote to know the offense.[11] The Han had similar experiences in other cases: "the envoys were mean merchants who, desiring profit, pretended to be tribute bearers."[12]

Appendix 2: The Silk-Routes Commerce

Coined by a German geographer in 1877 for a caravan road, the epithet "Silk Road" has been broadened to mean a patchwork of transcontinental trade routes.[13] At the times of the Han and Roman Empires, when the long-distance trade first emerged, these routes differed from the Silk Road of later ages in two ways. First, most trade combined land and sea legs. Second, residual power of the Xiongnu blocked the northern routes through the Ili Valley or across the steppe, where the availability of grass for pack animals would reduce transportation costs (Map 2).

Changan, the capital of the Former Han and Tang Dynasties and the eastern terminus of the Silk Road, acquired a cosmopolitan air in its heyday. From there, westward travelers soon entered the Hexi Corridor, a 1,000-kilometer long natural depression between the Qilian Range and the deserts. Dunhuang, its west-most city, would become a cultural center for the spread of Buddhism from India into China. Not far from Dunhuang, the Jade Gate and Sun Gate opened onto the Western Territory, now China's province of Xinjiang. There the route split to avoid the Taklimakan Desert at the heart of the Tarim Basin. The southern branch in the shadow of the Tibetan Plateau passed Shanshan around Lop Nor to Shule near today's Kashgar. The northern branch passed the Turfan depression, the doorway to the Mongolian plateau and the trophy of many Han-Xiongnu struggles. From there it trekked along the southern slope of the Tianshan to the headquarters of the Protectoral General of the Western Territory. The two routes converged at Shule just east of the Pamir, the roof of the world and the knot from which great mountain chains flow like ribbons.

Climbing up the Pamir, at 4,934 meters, the Khunjerab pass led to the Amu Darya flowing down to Bactra (Balkh) in Bactria, a trading hub in what is now northern Afghanistan until the Mongols destroyed it. To its north, a lower route led to the Ferghana Valley, home of superb horses, Sogdiana, home to many long-distance traders, and Bactria. These lands in today's Kyrgyzstan, Uzbekistan, and Tajikistan once belonged to the Persian Empire. From their peoples Alexander, who came in 329 BCE, met his fiercest resistance and found his queen, Roxane.

From Bactra, west-bound caravans proceeded to another trade hub, Merv in today's Turkmenistan. They passed the Caspian Gate southeast of today's Tehran to Parthia's summer capital Ecbatana on the Iranian plateau. There they picked up the Persian Royal Road to Ctesiphon near today's Baghdad, then up the Tigris to Zeugma and other north Syrian towns that handled busy trade between the Roman and Parthian Empires. Antioch on the Mediterranean coast was an anchor of transcontinental trade. This overland route, mostly in Parthian territory, undoubtedly carried some trade. However, evidence suggests that the bulk of trade took another route.[14]

In the first century, Bactra was a part of the Kushan Empire, which had its own ideas. (Map1). From Bactra, most goods from China were directed through Kushan territory, crossing the Hindu Kush to Begram, founded as Alexandria under the Caucasus, then into today's Pakistan and down the Indus River to the ports of the Arabian Sea. There they met the merchant fleet from the Roman realm. The *Book of Latter Han* tells how the Yuezhi, once the Han's neighbor, founded the kingdom of Kushan with its capital at the city of Lanshi. Later it took over India, land of Buddhism, elephant-riding warriors, and many precious products. More important for traders, India "has contact with Daqin in the west. Precious Daqin goods are available there."[15] The claim is bolstered by the royal storehouse uncovered in Begram, stuffed with Chinese, Roman, and other foreign products.[16]

Arabs and Egyptians had traded with Indians across the Arabian Sea since time immemorial. Commercial activities picked up under Roman prosperity. *The Periplus of the Erythraean Sea*, a first-century guidebook for travelers of the Red and Arabian Seas, directed those desiring a regular supply of silk and fur to the ports of the Indus Delta. "Beyond this country, now under the very north, the sea outside coming to an end somewhere, there lies a very great inland city called Thina, from which raw silk and silk yarn, and Chinese cloth, are brought overland to Barugaza through the Baktrians, and again to Limurikē by way of the river Gangēs. This Thina is not easy to reach. People seldom come from it, and not many go there."[17]

Two groups of traders serving Roman markets docked at Indian ports. Those from the Red Sea brought their cargos back to Alexandria, an emporium of the eastern Mediterranean. Those from the Persian Gulf brought their cargos up Parthian Mesopotamia, by caravan or by the Euphrates, to Roman Syria and Antioch.[18] Among the second group were perhaps the most famous of Roman merchants, seminomadic Arabs who founded the oasis city of Palmyra, known to the Chinese as Qiemo. Palmyrenes organized caravans, traded with neighboring Parthians, owned ships on the Persian Gulf for oceangoing trade, cut a route through the Syrian desert to connect the Euphrates and the Mediterranean, and made their city the center of a trading network. Inscriptions of Palmyrene merchant houses were found in Merv in northern Parthia and ports of northwestern India, both nodes on the Silk Routes.[19]

Besides the major routes via the Western Territory, two other trade routes existed between Chinese and Roman territories.[20] A trunk route across northern India linked thriving cities and the River Ganges. Through it Roman merchandise from Barugaza and Barbarikon could be shipped to northeastern India, where trails led through today's Myanmar to southwestern China. In 107, an alien state in this southwestern region sent tribute to the Han court, among which were magicians who claimed to hail from the Roman realm. This was at least the second time that such men appeared in Han records. Early in 113 BCE, when Parthia first established relations with the Han, it sent gifts of ostrich eggs and magicians from the eastern Mediterranean.[21]

Another possibility, the all-maritime route, emerged later. Roman and Palmyrene traders visited south India frequently, mainly for spices. From south Indian ports, sailors could round Malaysia via the Strait of Malacca into the South China Sea, where the Chinese had been active in commerce. A major Han port was Rinan in what is now central Vietnam.[22] The Han and India had established diplomatic relations via the Western Territory but broke contact when the Western Territory rebelled. Then, in 159 and 161, India sent embassies via Rinan. On their heels, in 166, a self-styled imperial envoy from Rome landed in Rinan carrying products of southeast Asia. Three more such "envoys" appear in Chinese records up to 284.[23]

The direct sea route between the Han Chinese and Roman realms, though possible for individual adventurers, seemed insignificant for quantity trade. Red coral, grown in the Red Sea and the western Mediterranean, was a major item shipped to India.[24] The Chinese valued coral and identified it as a Roman product, available through the western regions, not from Rinan and the south. None of the claimed Roman merchants who landed there was recorded to carry coral, glass, or any specifically Roman products.[25]

Arabian incense, Indian spices, and Chinese silk constituted the bulk of Rome's eastern trade. Silk came latest. Large-scale export commenced only after the Han pacified the Western Territory in the first century BCE. Archeological excavation in Palmyra confirmed the availability of silk in the first century CE. Very few Roman products have been recovered in China. Only a single gold coin appeared in Vietnam, and experts judge the low-quality glassware found elsewhere non-Roman. This indicates that the Han and Rome were not direct trading partners. The Kushan, Parthians, and nomads were not merely intermediaries but active participants offering their own products for trade.[26]

Multiple transactions also offer an explanation of Pliny's observation that the Romans had to unravel imported fabric and reweave the silk yarn. The Chinese themselves wove semitransparent gauze, as evident in a second-century BCE silk robe excavated in southern China, where fashionable women were said to be so delicate they could dance on a man's palm.[27] However, such light apparel was unsuitable for the cold and rough countries of the northwest where the trade routes began. One can surmise that the thick and sturdy silk fabric excavated in Xinjiang and Central Asia catered to local peoples, especially when exported for diplomatic rather than commercial reasons. If the remote Romans desired something else, the demand had not yet filtered back to the source of supply. Eventually it would. At least they could demand bundles of silk yarn, which for their uniformity, high value, and light weight served as a kind of currency in the Western Territory of the Latter Han.[28]

In contrast to modern imperialism where the flag followed commercial penetration, the Han and Roman Empires attended foremost to geopolitics, not commerce.[29] Roman peace and roads benefited trade, but Rome was indifferent to trade itself and never raised it as an issue in its many treaties with Parthia. Above all, Rome never allowed trade to interfere with its foreign policies. Although on the verge of bankruptcy when Palmyra rebelled in 273, Rome did not hesitate to sack the city that brought it enormous revenues from the 25 percent import duty it imposed. Palmyra's commercial network collapsed, pulling down with it much eastern trade.[30]

Like the Romans, the Han government facilitated trade but put it at a distant second to political and military concerns. Its venture into the western regions was originally a part of its strategy to isolate the Xiongnu by diplomacy. To suit its political purposes, the Han gifts of gold and colorful silk usually exceeded the value of foreign gifts that it received. Such diplomatic exchange functioned as a form of economic subsidy in return for frontier peace or interstate cooperation in maintaining a world order. Through these exchanges, large amounts of silk flowed out to foreign courts and nomadic tribes, whence redistribution could occur.[31] Perhaps it was not wholly absurd for the Romans to think that the Silk People gave out their products free or for Han literati to complain about the unprofitability of western trade.[32]

Appendix 3: Long Wall Building

Changcheng is a generic term literally meaning "long wall," applicable to Hadrian's wall across Britain. Long-wall construction under the First Emperor has become a paradigm of vicious exploitation that allegedly caused Qin's demise. Recent research has shown the horrendous accounts of wall building to be a myth and traced its evolution in centuries of propaganda.[33] The following are a few technical considerations.

Like other ancient Chinese constructions, the First Emperor's long wall was mostly made of earth stamped hard, layer by layer, between wooden forms that were dismantled upon completion. Stone facing was usually absent. It should not be confused with the now-standing Great Wall, a brick and stone structure built by the Ming Dynasty in the fifteenth and sixteenth century. Qin's long wall ran much further north and was much smaller in height and width.

Archeologists recently determined that the total length of the First Emperor's long wall, including all its loops and branches, was 7,860 kilometers, of which 6,650 kilometers were the old walls of Yan, Zhao, and Qin. Its base width varied between 3 and 4 meters.[34] Assuming that on the average, it was 3.5 meters wide and 3.5 meters high, then the 1,210 kilometers of wall built by the First Emperor had a total volume of 14,822,500 cubic meters.

I do not know any account of long-wall building in ancient texts, but some descriptions for city walls survive. Chu walled Xi in 598 BCE, and Jin coordinated several states to wall the Zhou capital Luo in 509 BCE. After designing the wall and moat, officials estimated the requisite labor, tools, materials, and the distances of transportation. Both walls were complete in thirty days. For Xi, the record adds, "It did not exceed the plan."[35] The sizes of the workforces were not on record for these cases, but that for another was. The Han Empire walled its capital Changan in two bouts. The intensive constructions in 192 BCE and 190 BCE each called up about 145,000 workers and each "ended in thirty days."[36] I think the four thirty-day work periods on record were not coincidental. Noninterference with agriculture was always paramount for scheduling, because corvée laborers were peasants, and one month of service per annum seemed to be the traditional norm, which Qin also adopted. Agriculture being seasonal, it was logical to squeeze construction into slack times by massive mobilization.[37] The Changan construction also involved 20,000 convicts, who could have worked continuously for up to twenty-seven months. In sum, it engaged 69,300 man-years of labor.

According to textual and archeological data, the Changan circuit was 25.7 kilometers in length, with a base width of 12 to 16 meters, a height exceeding 12 meters, and twelve city gates.[38] Assuming an average width of 14 meters, its total volume was 4,317,600 cubic meters.

According to these accounts, the volume of the First Emperor's new wall was 3.4 times that of the Changan circuit. With comparable work efficiency, it would have required 238,000 man-years of labor. This is probably an overestimate, because the numerous gates and towers of Changan, in addition to the fine finish of the capital wall, were all labor-intensive.

The long walls were in remote areas but not too inaccessible; otherwise, fortification would be superfluous. Soldiers routinely traversed rough terrains. The building material, earth, was available on site. Tools were relatively simple and the wooden planks reusable. Provision for workers was the largest item for long-distance transportation. For these, the finished portion of the long wall, hugging the crests of ranges, could serve as a highway facilitating its further construction, just as the railroad bears the rails for its own extension. If the above estimation is correct, then we can understand why Qin's long wall building has received so little coverage in *Records of the Historian* and other ancient texts.

Comparison with another ancient wonder is instructive. Recent researches have refuted traditional accounts that between 100,000 and 400,000 workers toiled for twenty to thirty years to build the Great Pyramid of Giza. Excavation of a workers' cemetery indicated a permanent crew of 4,000 to 5,000 skilled masons. Paid temporary laborers varied in number. Two independent projects, one directed by an archeologist and another by an engineer with the help of computer modeling and empirical data based on building a small pyramid using ancient methods, arrived at similar conclusions. They assumed the pyramid built in twelve years but posited different schedules. Both studies found that work intensity peaked during two years and then fell off rapidly. At the peak, a maximum workforce of 24,000 to 43,000 sufficed for all chores from quarry operation and harbor and ramp construction to transportation and pyramid building. Compared to the received picture, these constituted a small fraction of the traditionally described workforce engaged for a small fraction of the traditional time span. As remarkable as ancient structures were the ingenuity and prowess of ancient workers.[39]

Notes

1. *Houhanshu* 88: 2918. Yü 1967: 156.
2. *Houhanshu* 88: 2910.
3. Ptolemy 1.11–12, 1.17. Young 2001: 188–191.
4. Pulleyblank 1999: 71.
5. Pliny 34.41, 12.41, 4.26, 84.
6. Pliny 6.24, 6.20.
7. Ammianus 23.6.67–68.
8. Leslie and Gardiner 1996.
9. *Houhanshu* 88: 2918–2920.
10. Thorley 1971: 76–79. Yü 1967: 198–99.
11. Ball 2000: 400. Yü 1967: 159–160, 175.
12. *Hanshu* 96a: 3886.
13. Elisseeff 2000. Whitefield 2004. Hansen 2012.
14. Ptolemy 1.11–12, 1.17. Young 2001: 188–191.
15. *Houhanshu* 88: 2920–2922. *Hanshu* 96a: 3872.

16. Lu 1988: 9–10, 19, 26–27.
17. *Periplus* 64.
18. Ball 2000: 123–128. Young 2001: 28–31. Lu 1988: 19–27.
19. Ball 2000: 74–76. Young 2001: 136–140.
20. Lu 1988: 55–56.
21. *Houhanshu* 86: 2851. *Hanshu* 95: 3841, 96a: 3890.
22. Young 2001: 28–31. Yü 1967: 172–182.
23. Yü 1967: 152–155, 160–161. Young 2001: 33–34.
24. *Periplus* 28, 39, 49.
25. Lu 1988: 54–56. Yü 1967: 160–161.
26. Ball 2000: 74–76, 135–139. Lu 1988: 19–20.
27. Pirazzoli-t'Serstevens 1982: 46.
28. Yü 1967: 164. Lu 1988: 70.
29. Young 2001: 1–4, 195. Lattimore 1940: 173–176.
30. Young 2001: 193, 211–217. Dignas and Winter 2007: 203.
31. Yü 1967: 36–64, 151, 164, 195.
32. Ammianus 23.6.67–68. *Yantielün* 16.
33. Waldron 1990: 16–28, 194-203.
34. Jing 2002: 24–27, 158–181, 341–342, 33–42.
35. *Zuozhuan*, Xuan 11; Zhao 32, Ding 1.
36. *Hanshu* 2: 88, 89, 90, 91.
37. *Zuozhuan*, Zhuang 29.
38. Wang Z. 1982: 2.
39. Smith 2004: 130–131, 206–207, 230–231. Romer 2007: 458–460.

TIMELINE 1

CHINA AND ROME IN THE WORLD CONTEXT

The Mediterranean	BCE	中國 China
Destruction of the citadel of Mycenae	c. 1150	
	c. 1066–771	西周 West Zhou dynasty
Phoenician and Greek colonization	c. 775– c. 650	
	771–256	東周 East Zhou dynasty
	771	秦立國 State of Qin invested
Traditional date of the foundation of Rome	753	
	722–481	春秋 Spring and Autumn period
King Servius Tullius of Rome	c. 579–543	
	c. 566–486	釋迦 Siddhartha (Buddha, in India)
	551–479	孔丘 Confucius
Foundation of the Roman Republic	509	
Wars between Persia and the Greeks	490–449	
Socrates	470–399	
	453–221	戰國 Warring States period

Peloponnesian War between Athens and Sparta	431–404	
	359	商鞅變法 Qin starts political reform
Latin League dissolved; Rome controls central Italy	338	
Alexander the Great	356–323	
Rome begins overseas expansion	264	
	221–206	秦朝 Qin dynasty, beginning of imperial China
Second Punic War between Rome and Carthage	218–202	
	206–202	楚漢相爭 Civil war between Chu and Han
	202–1 CE	西漢 Western Han dynasty
	200	單于立 Maodun becomes chanyu of Xiongnu
Rome sacks Corinth and Carthage	146	
	138	始營西域 China begins westward expansion
Roman civil wars	49–27	
Augustus as princeps	27–14 CE	
	c. 2	佛學東漸 Buddhism enters China
Jesus	1–30	
	1–22	新朝 Xin Dynasty
	22–220	東漢 Eastern Han dynasty
	220–280	三國 Civil wars: three kingdoms
Sassanians (Persians) overthrow Parthia	226	
Military anarchy in Roman Empire	235–284	
	265–316	西晉 Western Jin dynasty
	316	洛陽淪陷 Fall of Luoyang
	316–589	東晉南北朝 China divides into North and South
Foundation of Constantinople	324	

The Mediterranean	CE	China
Sack of Rome by Alaric the Visigoth	410	
End of the Western Roman Empire	476	
Muhammad	571–632	
	589–618	隋朝 China reunites under Sui dynasty
	618–907	唐朝 Tang dynasty
Islam spreads to Egypt, Syria, and Iran	633–655	
Fall of Constantinople, end of the Byzantium Empire	1453	

TIMELINE 2

EVENTS IN CHINA

770 **BCE**	Zhou moves its capital east to Luo. Qin becomes a state	周平王東遷洛邑. 秦襄公始爲候
685–643	Lord Huan of Qi	齊桓公
677	Qin moves capital to Yong	秦遷都於雍
660	Red Di overruns Wey	赤狄攻衛，殺懿公
659–621	Lord Mu of Qin	秦穆公
636–628	Lord Wen of Jin	晉文公
632	Jin defeats Chu at Chengpu. Covenant at Jiantu	晉敗楚於城濮，踐土之盟
627	Jin defeats Qin at Xiao	晉敗秦師於崤
613–591	King Zhuang of Chu	楚莊王
597	Chu defeats Jin at Bi	楚敗晉於邲
594	Lu starts collecting land tax	魯初稅畝
546	Peace conference organized by Xiangxu	向戌弭兵
536	Code of laws published in Zheng	鄭子產鑄刑鼎
524	King Jing of Zhou casts "big" coins	周景王鑄大錢
513	Jin publishes a code of laws on an iron tripod	晉鑄刑鼎
506	Wu captures Chu's capital, Ying	吳敗楚、入郢
481	Tian family controls Qi. Spring and Autumn period ends	田氏專齊政。魯《春秋》絕筆

473	Yue annexes Wu	越滅吳
453	Hann, Zhao, and Wei extinguish Zhibo, become effective states	韓趙魏滅知伯、分其地
445–396	Lord Wen of Wei, initiates reforms under Li Kui	魏文侯，用李悝變法
403	Hann, Zhao, and Wei acquire official state status	韓、趙、魏爲侯
385–362	Lord Xian of Qin, starts household registration in 375	秦獻公，戶籍相伍
361	Wei moves its capital east to Daliang	魏遷都大梁
361–338	Lord Xiao of Qin	秦孝公
356	Qin starts reforms under Shang Yang	秦商鞅變法開始
350	Qin moves capital to Xianyang, reorganizes local districts	秦遷都咸陽，普遍設縣
342	Battle of Maling between Qi and Wei	齊魏馬陵之戰
337–311	King Huiwen of Qin (elevated to king in 325)	秦惠文王（325 稱王）
334	Rulers of Qi and Wei honor each other as king	齊魏徐州相王
329–311	Zhang Yi pursues divide-and-conquer diplomacy for Qin	張儀爲秦行連橫策略
328	Qin recovers all land west of the Yellow River from Wei	魏盡獻河西地、上郡於秦
316	Qin annexes Shu and Ba	秦伐蜀，蜀亡
314–312	Qi annexes Yan, and is driven out by a revolt	齊趁燕亂取燕，燕人叛
312	Qin defeats Chu and takes Hanzhong	秦敗楚於藍田, 取漢中
307	Zhao adopts Hu costumes to promote mounted archery	趙武靈王胡服騎射
306–251	King Zhaoxiang of Qin	秦昭襄王
296	Qi, Hann, Wei breach Qin's Hangu Pass. Zhao annexes Zhongshan.	齊、魏、韓攻入函谷關。趙滅中山，

295	Wei Ran becomes prime minister of Qin	魏冉相秦
293	Qin's Bo Qi defeats Wei and Han at Yique	秦白起敗韓, 魏於伊闕
284	Five states ally to attack Qi. Yan takes Qi's capital, Linzi.	五國合縱伐齊。燕樂毅破齊下臨淄
279	Qi repels Yan. Qin invades Chu. Chu expands into the southwest	田單復齊。白起伐楚。莊蹻入滇
266–255	Fan Ju is prime minister of Qin	范睢相秦
260	Qin defeats Zhao at Changping	.秦敗趙於長平
257	Wei and Chu rescue Zhao and raise the siege of Handan	魏信陵、楚春申救趙，解韓鄲圍
256	Qin annexes Zhou	秦滅西周
249–237	Lü Biwei is prime minister of Qin	呂不韋相秦
246	Accession of King Zheng of Qin (future First Emperor)	秦王政即位
241	The final alliance: Zhao leads Chu, Wei, Hann, and Yan against Qin	趙、楚、魏、韓、燕最後合縱伐秦
239	King Zheng assumes power upon reaching manhood	秦王政親政
230	Qin annexes Hann	秦滅韓
221	Qin unifies China. King Zheng becomes the First Emperor	秦一統中國。嬴政始稱皇帝。
209	Dazexiang uprising	大澤鄉起義
206	End of the Qin Dynasty, civil war between Han and Chu begins	秦亡。楚漢相爭起
202–9 **CE**	Former Han Dynasty	西漢
200	Xiongnu defeat Gaodì at Pingcheng	匈奴圍高祖於平城
154	Suppression of revolt of seven kingdoms by Jingdì	景帝平七國之亂
138–126	Zhang Qian's first mission to western territory	張騫通西域

136	Wudì extols Confucianism	武帝罷百家、尊儒學
129–119	War against the Xiongnu	漢擊匈奴
122	Initiation of diplomacy with states in western territory	漢始營西域
108	Start of campaigns in western territory	出兵西域
89	Wudì's Luntai edict stops imperial expansion	武帝輪台之詔止戰
81	Salt and Iron Conference	鹽鐵會議
60	Establishment of Protectorate of the Western Territory	漢始置西域都護
54	Xiongnu split; Chanyu Huhanye surrenders	匈奴分南北，呼韓邪單于降
22 **BCE**	Regency of Wang family	王氏執政
9 **CE**	Wang Mang replaces the Han with the Xin Dynasty	王莽新朝
23–220	Latter Han Dynasty	後漢
48	Xiongnu split, South Xiongnu surrenders	匈奴分裂，南單于降
73	War against Xiongnu, Ban Chao in Western Territory	竇固擊北匈奴，班超至西域
91	Final defeat of North Xiongnu, Ban Chao becomes Protectorate General of Western Territory	竇憲破北匈奴，班超爲西域都護
107–118	First Qiang rebellion	羌亂
139–145	Second Qinag rebellion	羌亂
159–168	Third Qiang rebellion	羌亂
166–184	Proscription against anti-eunuch partisans	禁錮清議黨人
184	Yellow Turban rebellion	黃巾之亂
189	Dong Zhuo seizes Luoyang	董卓入京，廢立獻帝
208	Battle of the Red Cliff, fragmentation inevitable	赤壁之戰，三分勢成
220	Abdication of the last Han emperor to the Wei	漢帝禪位于魏
220–280	Period of three kingdoms: Wei, Shu, and Wu	魏、蜀、吳鼎足三分
280	Reunification of China under the Western Jin Dynasty	西晉

301–306	Rebellion of eight Jin kings	八王之亂
304	Xiongnu declared the first of the sixteen Hu kingdoms	匈奴人劉淵稱漢王
316	Xiongnu sacks Changan. Period of disunity with the Eastern Jin Dynasty in southern China begins.	匈奴佔長安，東晉南渡

TIMELINE 3

EVENTS IN ROME

509 **BCE**	Foundation of the Roman Republic
c. 494	First secession of the plebs; first tribunes
451–450	Twelve Tables of laws
449	Lex Valeria Horatia: *provocatio*, citizen's right of appeal
396	Fall of Veii
387	Rome sacked by the Gauls
367	Licinio-Sextian laws: patrician-plebeian power sharing
343–341	First Samnite War
340–338	Latin Wars
326–304	Second Samnite War
298–290	Third Samnite War (Battle of Sentinum, 295)
289	Lax Hortensia: plebiscite binding on the whole people
282–275	War with Pyrrhus of Epirus
264	First gladiatorial show at Rome
264–241	First Punic War with Carthage (Battle of Aegates, 241)
238	Seizure of Sardinia from Carthage
228	The first province established in Sicily
219	Lex Claudia: commercial activities of senators curbed
218–201	Second Punic War with Carthage (Battles of Trasimene, 217; Cannae, 216; Ilipa, 206; Zama, 202)
202–191	Conquest of Cisalpine Gaul
200–197	Second Macedonian War with Philip V (Battle of Cynoscephalae, 197)
197–133	Wars in Spain (sack of Numantia, 133)
192–188	Syrian War with Antiochus (Battle of Magnesia, 189)
171–167	Third Macedonian War with Perseus (Battle of Pydna, 167)

167	Direct taxation of Roman citizens abolished
149–146	Third Punic War
146	Destruction of Corinth and Carthage
136–132	First Sicilian Slave War
133	Tiberius Grachus's tribunate, agrarian reforms. Sack of Numantia
123–122	Gaius Gracchus's tribunate
113–106	War against Jugurtha of Mauretania
107–100	Consulates of Marius; reformation of the army
105–101	Wars against the Cimbri and Teutones (Battles of Arausio, 105; Aquae Sextiae, 102; Vercellae, 101)
104–102	Second Sicilian Slave War
91–87	Social War with Italian allies
88–82	Wars against Mithridates of Pontus
82–80	Sulla's dictatorship, proscription, and reform
74–63	Third war against Mithridates
73–71	Slave revolt led by Spartacus
66–63	Pompey in the East
60	First triumvirate between Pompey, Crassus, and Caesar
58–49	Conquest of Gaul by Caesar
55–53	War against Parthia (Battle of Carrhae, 53)
49–48	Civil war between Caesar and Pompey (Battle of Pharsalus, 48)
47–44	Caesar's dictatorship
44	Assassination of Caesar
43	Second triumvirate between Antony, Lepidus, and Octavian. Proscription
42	Defeat of Republicans at Philippi
31	Battle of Actium
27 **BCE**	Constitutional settlement. Octavian becomes Augustus
9 **CE**	Battle of Teutoburg Forest; Roman frontier set at the Rhine
69	Civil war, year of four emperors
101–106	Trajan conquers Dacia
114–117	Trajan's Parthian war
162–166	Verus' Parthian war
168–175	German wars of Marcus Aurelius
193–197	Civil war after the death of Commodus
198	Septimius Severus annexes northern Mesopotamia
224	Persian Sassanid Dynasty replaces Parthia
235–284	Civil wars, military anarchy, fragmentation
270	Aurelian evacuates Dacia
273	Destruction of Palmyra
284–306	Diocletian reestablishes central power and founds the tetrarchy

312	Battle at Mulvian Bridge, Constantine fights under Christian sign
363	Julian dies in Persian campaign
378	Battle of Hadrianople with the Visigoths, Valen killed
394	Battle of Frigidus, civil war between Theodosius and Eugenius
395	Partition of Roman Empire into east and west halves
395–408	Stilicho dominates Western Empire
406	Breach of the Rhine frontier by Vandals, Alans, and Suevi
410	Rome sacked by Alaric the Visigoth; Rome evacuates Britain
411–421	Flavius Constantius dominates Western Empire
429	Vandals led by Geiseric cross from Spain to Africa
433–454	Aetius dominates Western Empire
440–453	Hunnic Empire under Attila
455	Rome sacked by Vandals from Carthage
468	Battle of Cape Bon, Vandals defeat Roman armada
476	Romulus Augustulus, the last Western Roman emperor, deposed

TIMELINE 4

EMPERORS OF THE QIN, HAN, AND JIN DYNASTIES 秦漢西晉

221 **BCE**	China unified under Qin Dynasty		秦一統中國
221–210	Qin Shinhuangdi, the First Emperor	Qin	秦始皇帝
210–207	The Second Emperor of Qin	Dynasty	秦二世
206–202	War between kings of Chu and Han		楚漢相爭
202–195	Han Gaodì		漢高祖
195–188	Han Huidì		漢惠帝
188–180	Regency of Empress Dowager Lü		呂后專政
180–157	Han Wendì		漢文帝
157–141	Han Jingdì	Former	漢景帝
140–87	Han Wudì	Han	漢武帝
87–74	Han Zhaodì	Dynasty	漢昭帝
74–49	Han Xuandì		漢宣帝
49–33	Han Yuandì		漢元帝
33–7	Han Chengdì		漢成帝
7–1	Han Aidì		漢哀帝
1 **BCE–5 CE**	Han Pingdì		漢平帝
9–23	Xin Dynasty under Wang Mang		王莽新朝
25–57	Han Guangwudì		漢光武帝
57–75	Han Mingdì		漢明帝
75–88	Han Zhangdì		漢章帝

88–106	Han Hedì		漢和帝
106–125	Han Andì	Latter	漢安帝
125–144	Han Shundì	Han	漢順帝
144–146	Han Chongdì, Zhidì	Dynasty	漢沖帝、漢質帝
146–168	Han Huandì		漢桓帝
168–189	Han Lingdì		漢靈帝
189–190	Han Shaodì		漢少帝
190–220	Han Xiandì		漢獻帝
220–280	Three Kingdoms: Wei, Shu, Wu		魏、蜀、吳三國鼎立
265–289	Jin Wudì		晉武帝
290–306	Jin Huidì	West Jin	晉惠帝
307–312	Jin Huaidì	Dynasty	晉懷帝
312–316	Jin Mindì		晉愍帝

TIMELINE 5

ROMAN EMPERORS

Sometimes an emperor erects a junior co-emperor to ensure the smooth transition of power, which is why some reigns overlap.*

27 **BCE**–14 **CE**	Augustus	
14–37	Tiberius	Julio-
37–41	Gaius (Caligula)	Claudian
41–54	Claudius	Dynasty
54–69	Nero	
69	Year of four emperors	
69–79	Vespasian	Flavian
78–81	Titus	Dynasty
81–96	Domitian	
96–98	Nerva	
98–117	Trajan	
118–138	Hadrian	the Antonines
138–161	Antoninus Pius	
161–180	Marcus Aurelius	
178–193	Commodus	
193–211	Septimius Severus	

198–217	Caracalla	Severan
218–222	Elagabalus	Dynasty
222–235	Severus Alexander	
235–284	military anarchy	24 emperors
284–305	Diocletian and colleagues	

	WEST		**EAST**		**NON-ROMAN**
305–306	Constantius I	305–311	Galerius		
		308–324	Licinius		
306–337	Constantine I	324–337	Constantine I		
337–340	Constantine II				
337–350	Constans				
350–361	Constantius II	337–361	Constantius II		
361–363	Julian	361–363	Julian		
363–364	Jovian	363–364	Jovian		
364–375	Valentinian I	364–378	Valens		
367–383	Gratian				
375–392	Valentinian II				
394–395	Theodosius I	379–395	Theodosius I		
394–423	Honorius	383–408	Arcadius	391–411	Alaric, Visigoth
425–455	Valentinian III	408–450	Theodosius II	427–477	Geiseric, Vandal
457–461	Marjorian	450–457	Marcian	440–453	Attila, Hun
467–472	Anthemius	457–474	Leo I		
475–476	Romulus Augustulus			474–526	Theodoric, Ostrogoth

*Incomplete list.

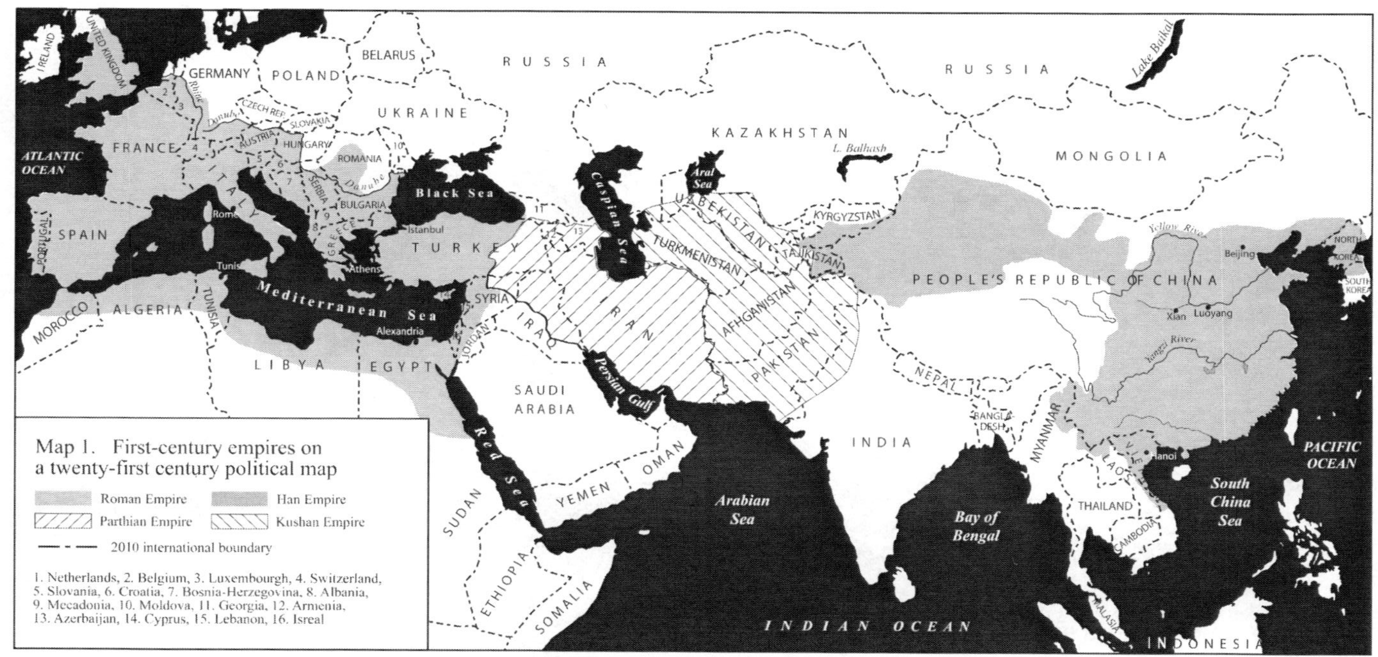

Map 1. First-century empires on a twenty-first century political map

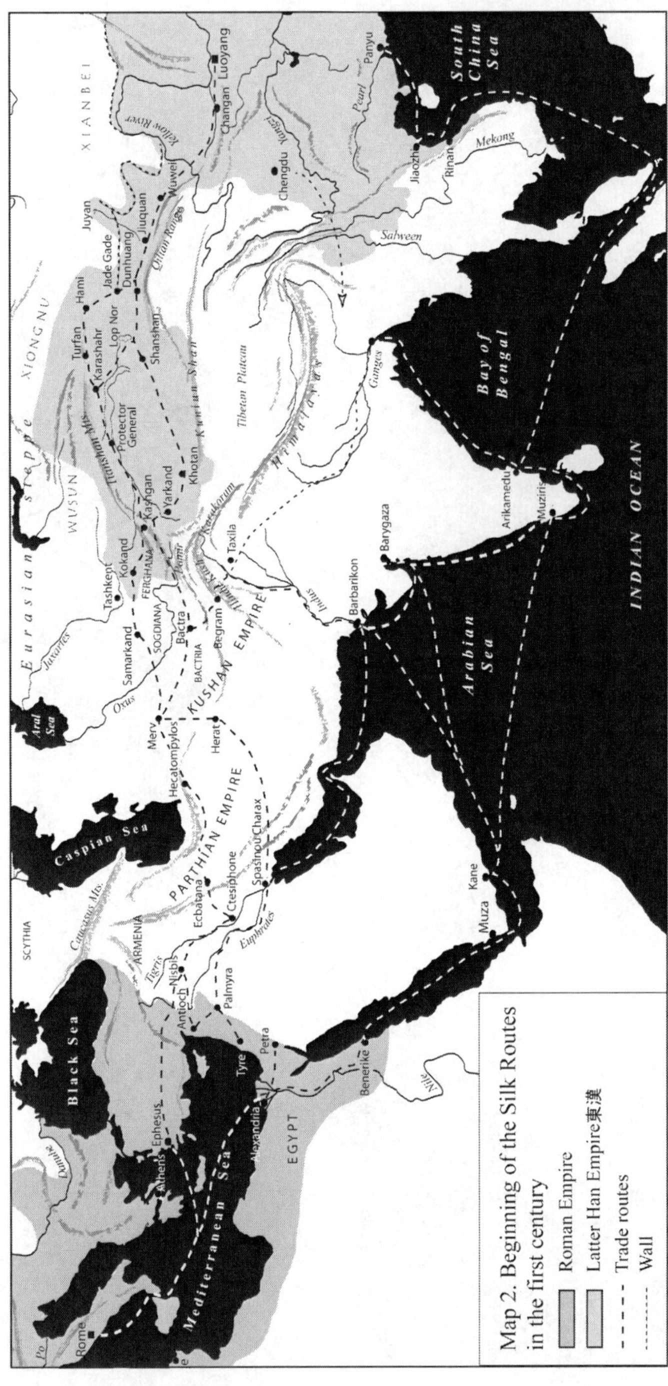

Map 2. Beginning of the Silk Routes in the first century

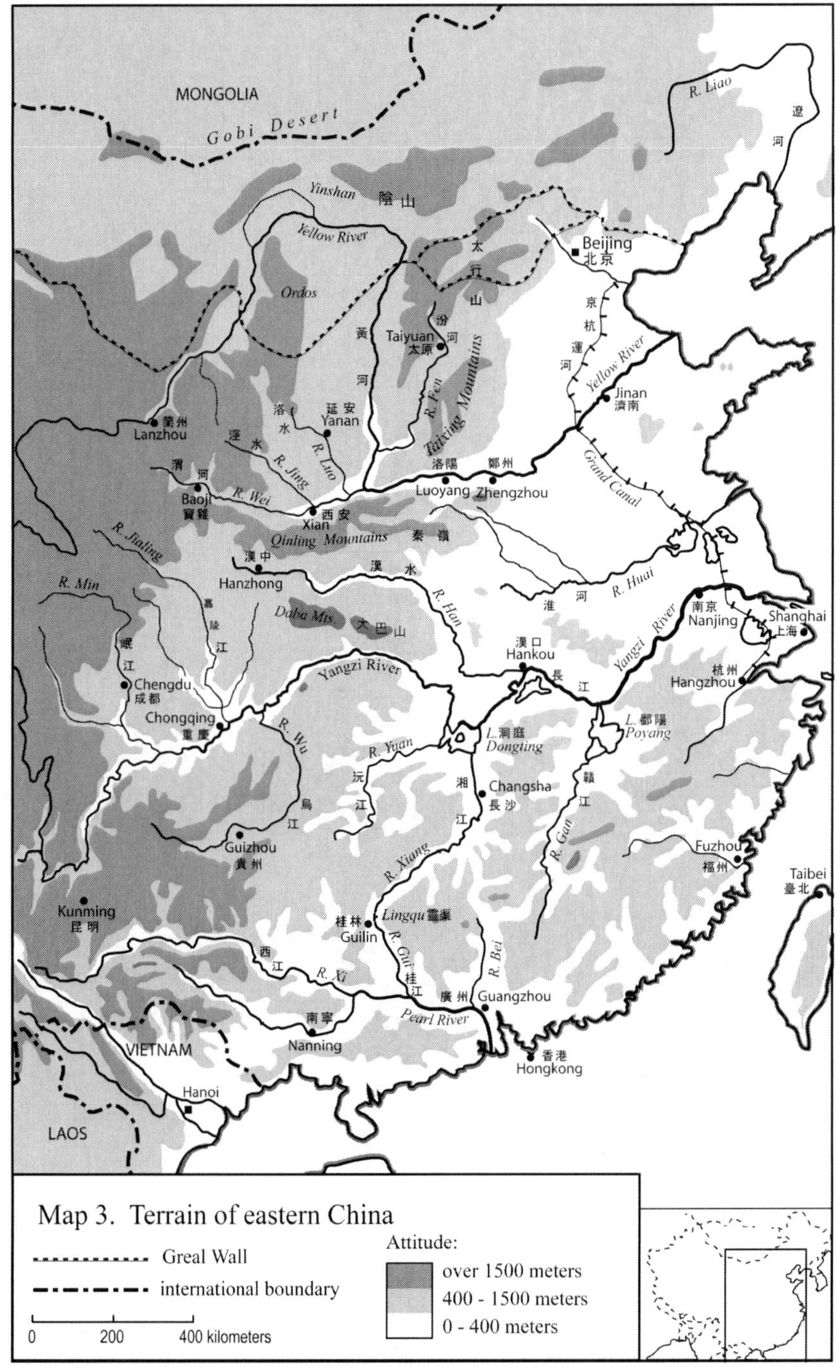

Map 3. Terrain of eastern China

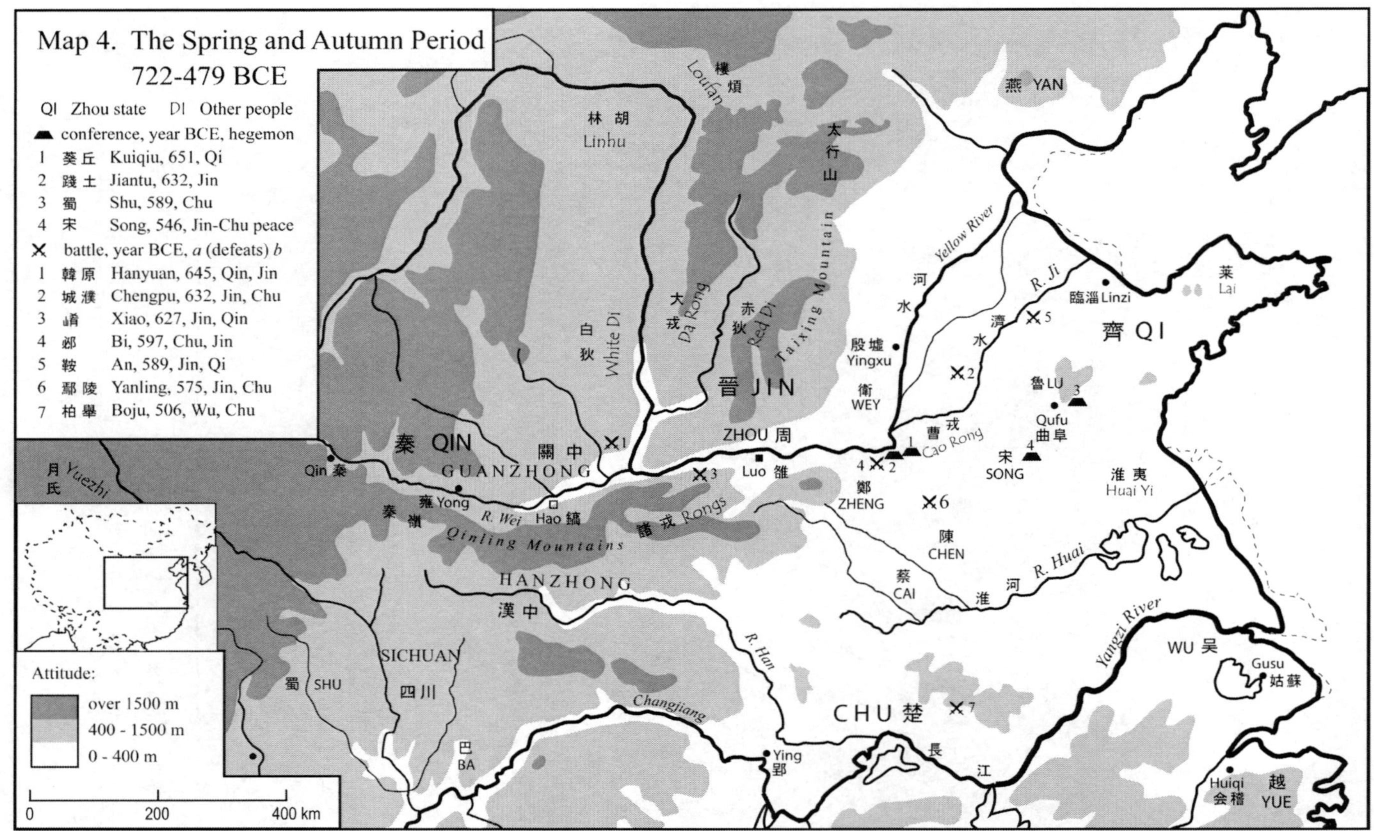

Map 4. The Spring and Autumn Period 722-479 BCE

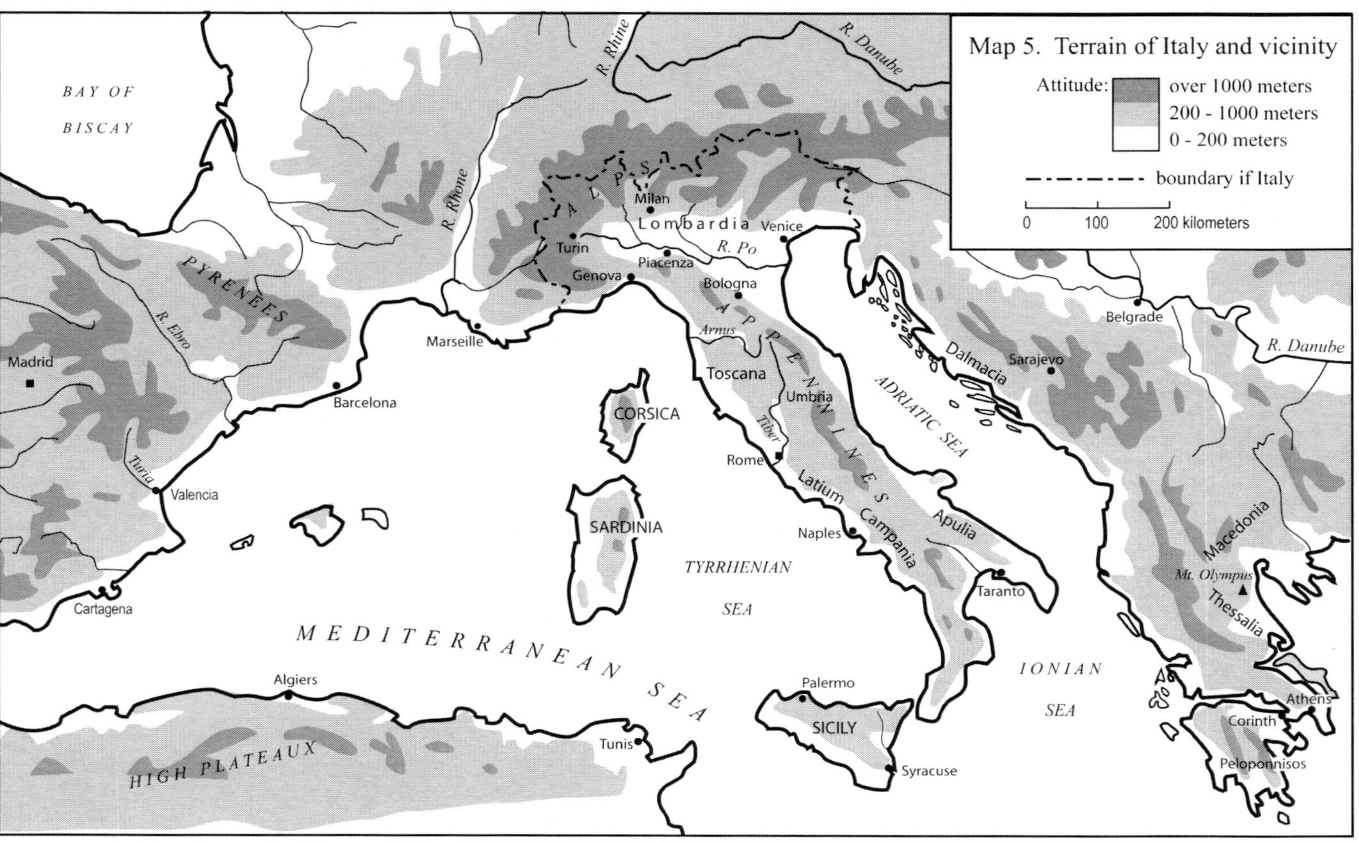

Map 5. Terrain of Italy and vicinity

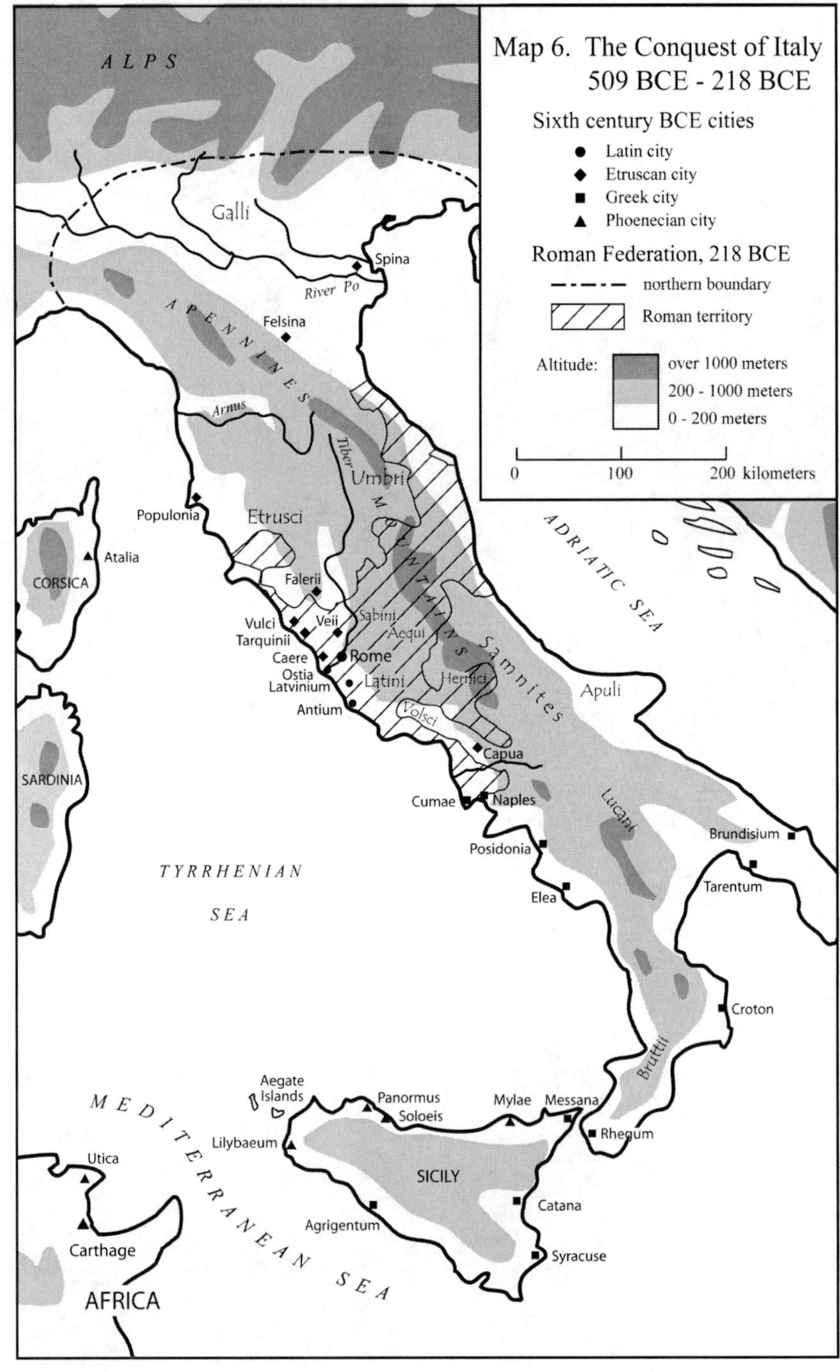
Map 6. The Conquest of Italy
509 BCE - 218 BCE
Sixth century BCE cities
Latin city
Etruscan city
Greek city
Phoenecian city
Roman Federation, 218 BCE
northern boundary
Roman territory
Altitude:
over 1000 meters
200 - 1000 meters
0 - 200 meters
0
100
200 kilometers
ALPS
Galli
Spina
River Po
APENNINES
Felsina
Arnus
Tiber
Umbri
MOUNTAINS
Etrusci
Populonia
Atalia
CORSICA
Falerii
Veii
Vulci
Tarquinii
Caere
Ostia
Latvinium
Antium
Rome
Sabini
Aequi
Latini
Hernici
Volsci
Samnites
Apuli
ADRIATIC SEA
Capua
Cumae
Naples
SARDINIA
Lucani
Posidonia
Brundisium
Tarentum
Elea
TYRRHENIAN
SEA
Croton
Bruttii
Aegate
Islands
Panormus
Soloeis
Mylae
Messana
Rhegum
Lilybaeum
MEDITERRANEAN SEA
Utica
SICILY
Catana
Agrigentum
Syracuse
Carthage
AFRICA

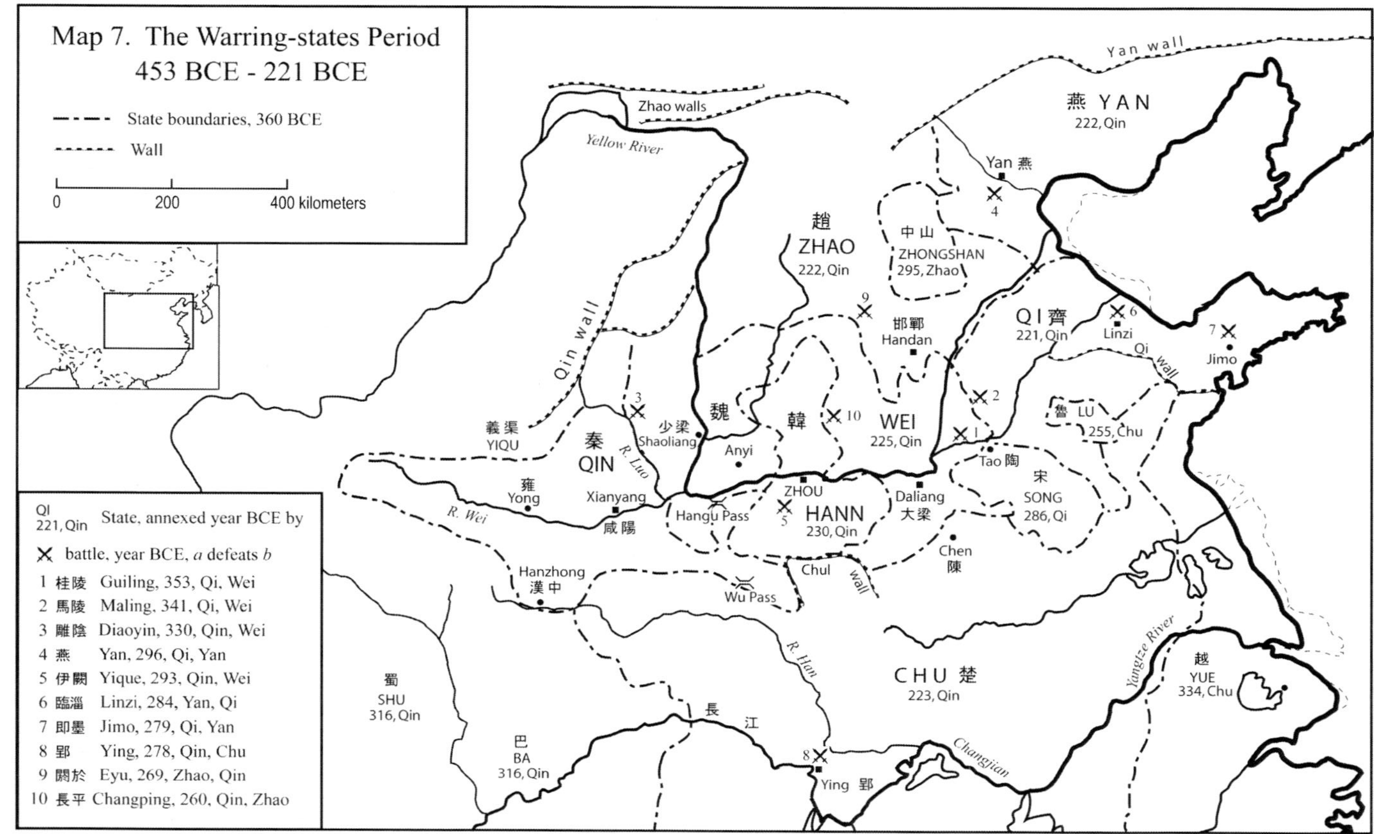
Map 7. The Warring-states Period
453 BCE - 221 BCE
State boundaries, 360 BCE
Wall
0
200
400 kilometers
QI
221, Qin
State, annexed year BCE by
battle, year BCE, *a* defeats *b*
1 桂陵 Guiling, 353, Qi, Wei
2 馬陵 Maling, 341, Qi, Wei
3 雕陰 Diaoyin, 330, Qin, Wei
4 燕 Yan, 296, Qi, Yan
5 伊闕 Yique, 293, Qin, Wei
6 臨淄 Linzi, 284, Yan, Qi
7 即墨 Jimo, 279, Qi, Yan
8 郢 Ying, 278, Qin, Chu
9 閼於 Eyu, 269, Zhao, Qin
10 長平 Changping, 260, Qin, Zhao
Yan wall
燕 YAN
222, Qin
Yan 燕
Zhao walls
Yellow River
趙
ZHAO
222, Qin
中山
ZHONGSHAN
295, Zhao
QI 齊
221, Qin
Linzi
Qi wall
Jimo
Qin wall
邯鄲
Handan
魏
韓
WEI
225, Qin
魯 LU
255, Chu
義渠
YIQU
少梁
Shaoliang
Anyi
秦
QIN
R. Luo
Tao 陶
宋
SONG
286, Qi
雍
Yong
Xianyang
咸陽
R. Wei
ZHOU
Hangu Pass
HANN
230, Qin
Daliang
大梁
Chen
陳
Hanzhong
漢中
Chul wall
Wu Pass
R. Han
蜀
SHU
316, Qin
CHU 楚
223, Qin
越
YUE
334, Chu
Yangtze River
長 江
巴
BA
316, Qin
Ying 郢
Changjian

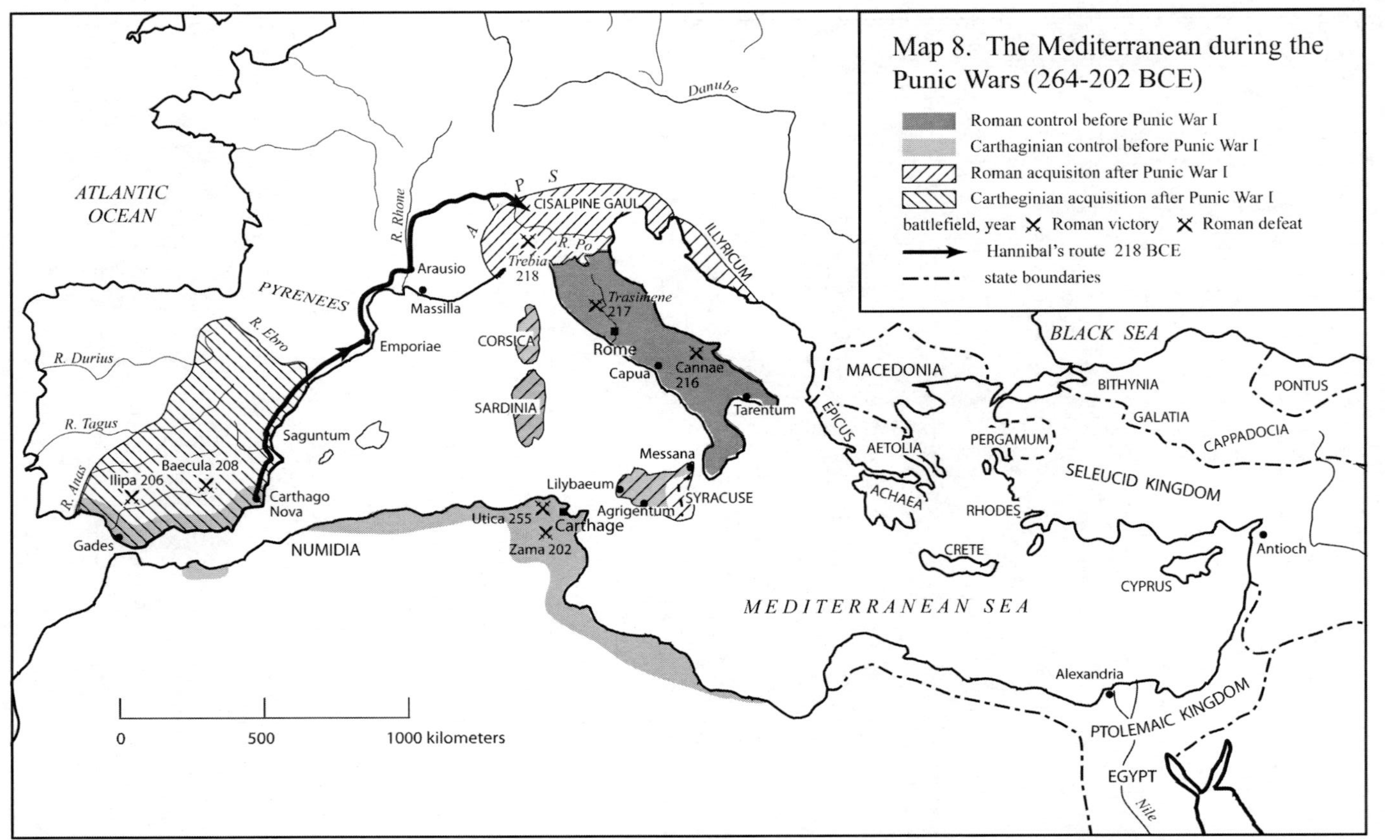

Map 8. The Mediterranean during the Punic Wars (264-202 BCE)

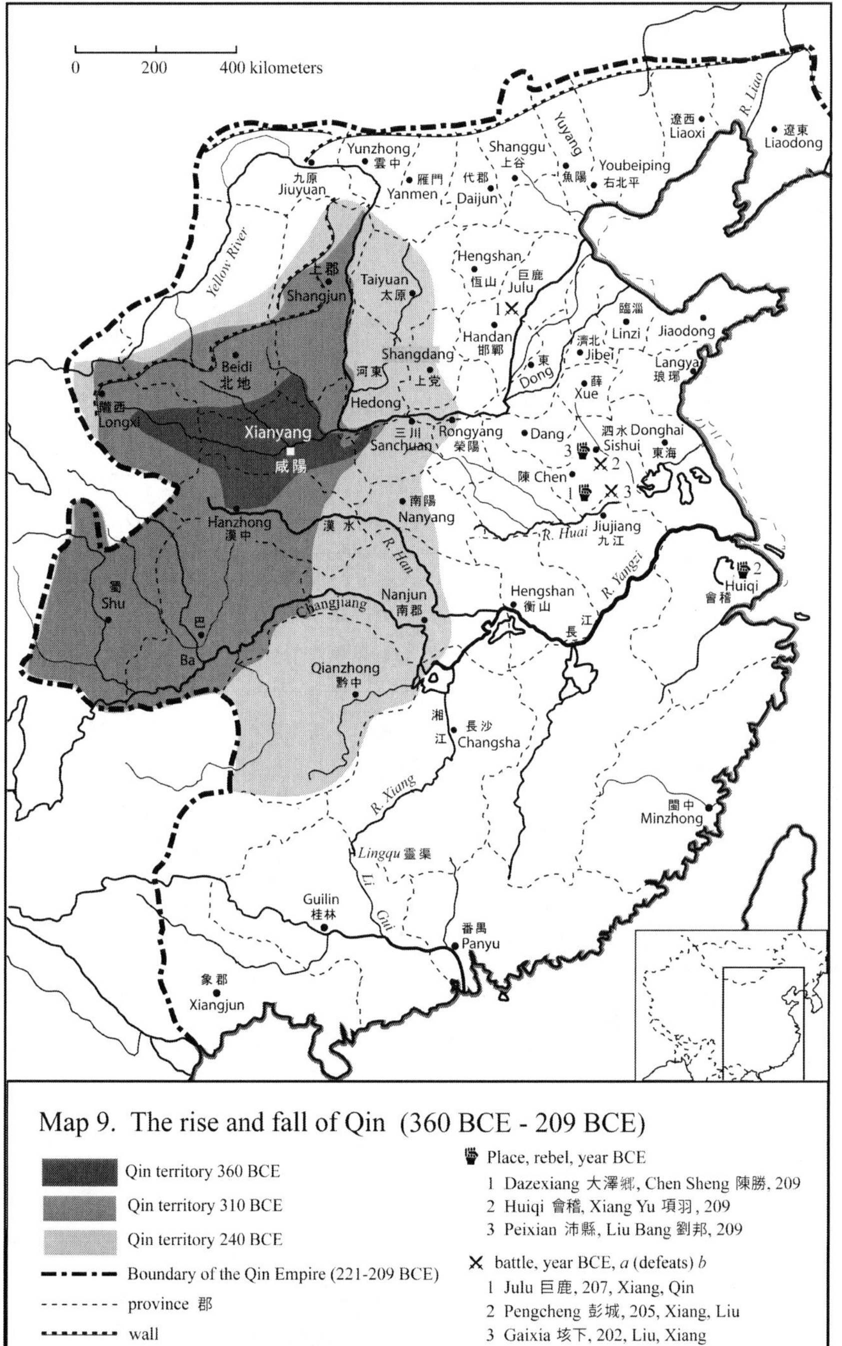

Map 9. The rise and fall of Qin (360 BCE - 209 BCE)

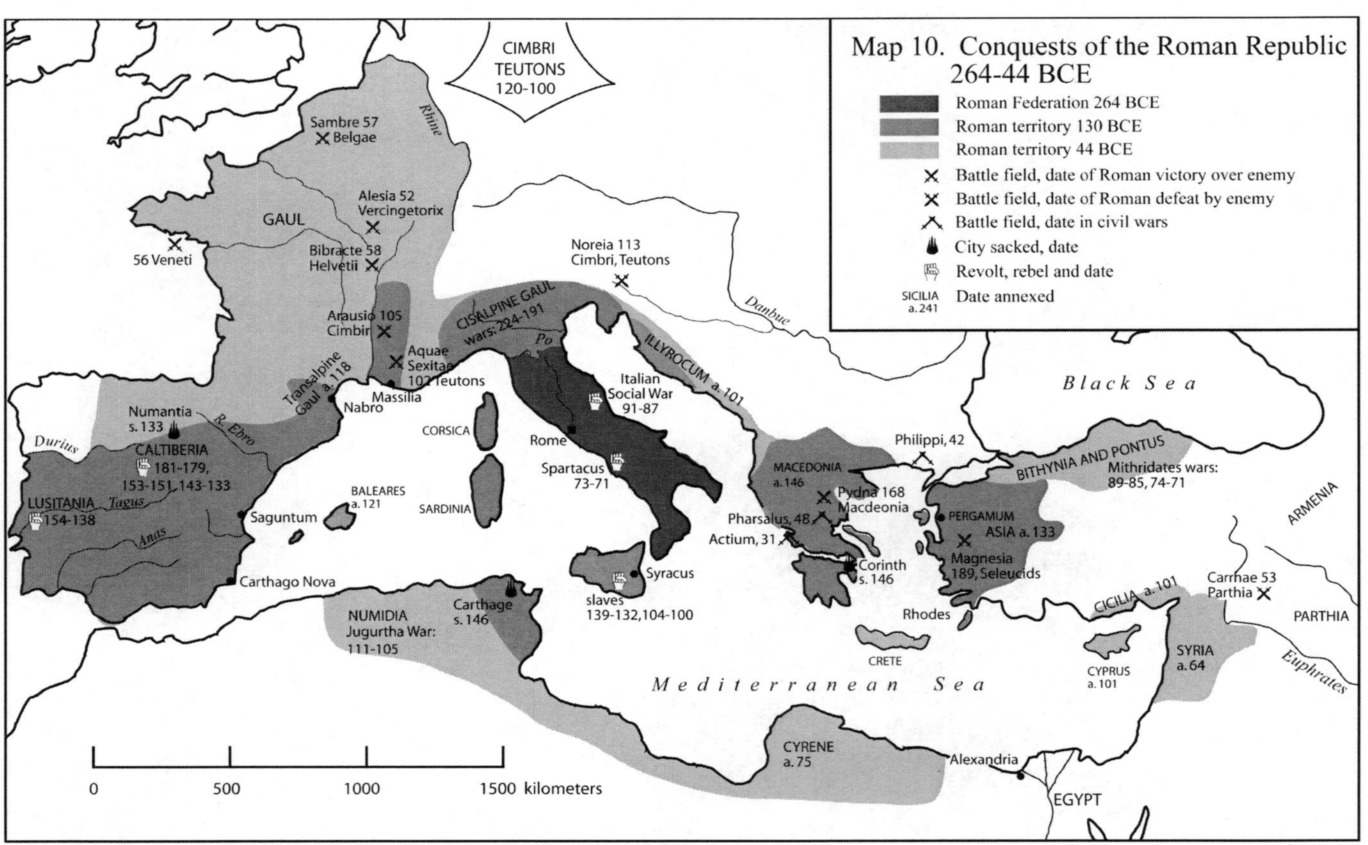
Map 10. Conquests of the Roman Republic 264-44 BCE
Roman Federation 264 BCE
Roman territory 130 BCE
Roman territory 44 BCE
Battle field, date of Roman victory over enemy
Battle field, date of Roman defeat by enemy
Battle field, date in civil wars
City sacked, date
Revolt, rebel and date
SICILIA a. 241 Date annexed
CIMBRI TEUTONS 120-100
Sambre 57 Belgae
Rhine
Alesia 52 Vercingetorix
GAUL
56 Veneti
Bibracte 58 Helvetii
Noreia 113 Cimbri, Teutons
Danbue
Arausio 105 Cimbri
CISALPINE GAUL wars: 224-191
Po
Aquae Sexitae 102 Teutons
Massilia
Nabro
Transalpine Gaul a. 118
ILLYROCUM a. 101
Italian Social War 91-87
Numantia s. 133
R. Ebro
Durius
CALTIBERIA 181-179, 153-151, 143-133
LUSITANIA 154-138
Tagus
Anas
Saguntum
Carthago Nova
CORSICA
SARDINIA
BALEARES a. 121
Rome
Spartacus 73-71
Syracus
slaves 139-132, 104-100
NUMIDIA Jugurtha War: 111-105
Carthage s. 146
Black Sea
MACEDONIA a. 146
Philippi, 42
Pydna 168 Macdeonia
Pharsalus, 48
Actium, 31
Corinth s. 146
BITHYNIA AND PONTUS
Mithridates wars: 89-85, 74-71
ARMENIA
PERGAMUM
ASIA a. 133
Magnesia 189, Seleucids
Rhodes
CRETE
CICILIA a. 101
Carrhae 53 Parthia
PARTHIA
SYRIA a. 64
CYPRUS a. 101
Euphrates
Mediterranean Sea
CYRENE a. 75
Alexandria
EGYPT
0 500 1000 1500 kilometers

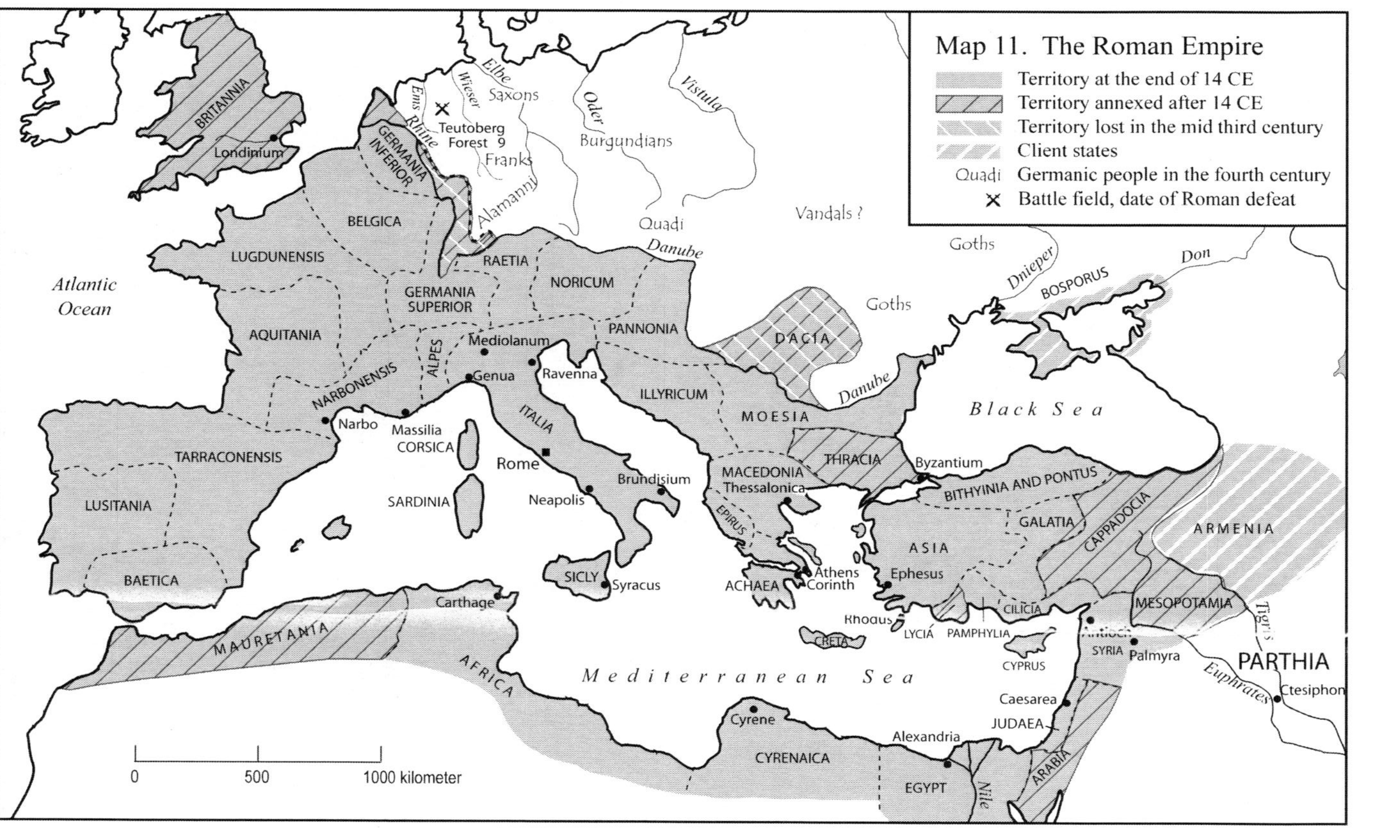
Map 11. The Roman Empire
Territory at the end of 14 CE
Territory annexed after 14 CE
Territory lost in the mid third century
Client states
Quadi Germanic people in the fourth century
Battle field, date of Roman defeat
Atlantic Ocean
BRITANNIA
Londinium
GERMANIA INFERIOR
Ems
Rhine
Wieser
Elbe
Saxons
Teutoberg Forest 9
Franks
Alamanni
Oder
Burgundians
Vistula
Quadi
Vandals ?
Danube
Goths
Dnieper
Don
BOSPORUS
BELGICA
LUGDUNENSIS
AQUITANIA
GERMANIA SUPERIOR
RAETIA
NORICUM
PANNONIA
DACIA
ALPES
Mediolanum
Genua
Ravenna
NARBONENSIS
Narbo
Massilia
CORSICA
SARDINIA
ITALIA
Rome
Neapolis
Brundisium
SICLY
Syracus
TARRACONENSIS
LUSITANIA
BAETICA
ILLYRICUM
MOESIA
THRACIA
MACEDONIA
Thessalonica
EPIRUS
ACHAEA
Athens
Corinth
Byzantium
Black Sea
BITHYINIA AND PONTUS
GALATIA
CAPPADOCIA
ARMENIA
ASIA
Ephesus
LYCIA
PAMPHYLIA
CILICIA
CRETA
CYPRUS
SYRIA
Palmyra
MESOPOTAMIA
Tigris
Euphrates
PARTHIA
Ctesiphon
Caesarea
JUDAEA
ARABIA
Alexandria
EGYPT
Nile
CYRENAICA
Cyrene
Mediterranean Sea
AFRICA
Carthage
MAURETANIA
0
500
1000 kilometer

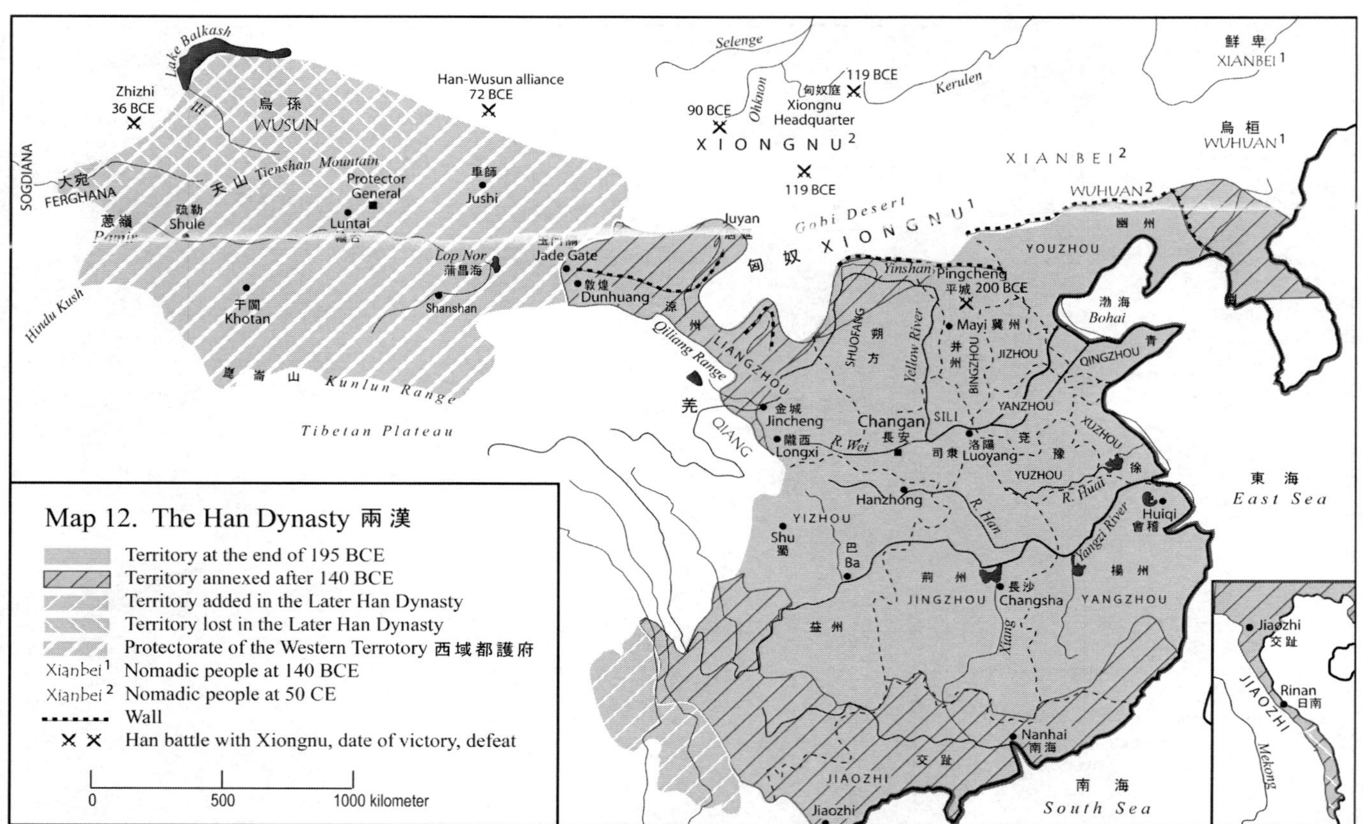
Map 12. The Han Dynasty 兩漢
Territory at the end of 195 BCE
Territory annexed after 140 BCE
Territory added in the Later Han Dynasty
Territory lost in the Later Han Dynasty
Protectorate of the Western Terrotory 西域都護府
Xianbei 1 Nomadic people at 140 BCE
Xianbei 2 Nomadic people at 50 CE
Wall
Han battle with Xiongnu, date of victory, defeat
0
500
1000 kilometer
Lake Balkash
Zhizhi 36 BCE
烏孫 WUSUN
Ili
Han-Wusun alliance 72 BCE
SOGDIANA
大宛 FERGHANA
天山 Tienshan Mountain
Protector General
車師 Jushi
疏勒 Shule
蔥嶺
Luntai
Lop Nor 蒲昌海
Shanshan
Jade Gate
敦煌 Dunhuang
Hindu Kush
于闐 Khotan
崑崙山 Kunlun Range
Tibetan Plateau
Selenge
Okhon
90 BCE
匈奴庭 Xiongnu Headquarter
119 BCE
Kerulen
XIONGNU 2
119 BCE
Juyan
Gobi Desert
匈奴 XIONGNU 1
鮮卑 XIANBEI 1
烏桓 WUHUAN 1
XIANBEI 2
WUHUAN 2
幽州 YOUZHOU
渤海 Bohai
Yinshan
Pingcheng 平城 200 BCE
Mayi 冀州
JIZHOU
并州 BINGZHOU
朔方 SHUOFANG
Yellow River
涼州 LIANGZHOU
Qiliang Range
羌 QIANG
金城 Jincheng
Changan 長安
SILI
隴西 Longxi
R. Wei
洛陽 Luoyang
司隸
YANZHOU
兗
QINGZHOU 青
XUZHOU 徐
豫 YUZHOU
R. Huai
Hanzhong
R. Han
東海 East Sea
Huiqi 會稽
Yangzi River
YIZHOU
Shu 蜀
巴 Ba
荊州 JINGZHOU
長沙 Changsha
揚州 YANGZHOU
益州
Xiang
Nanhai 南海
交趾 JIAOZHI
Jiaozhi
南海 South Sea
Jiaozhi 交趾
Rinan 日南
JIAOZHI
Mekong

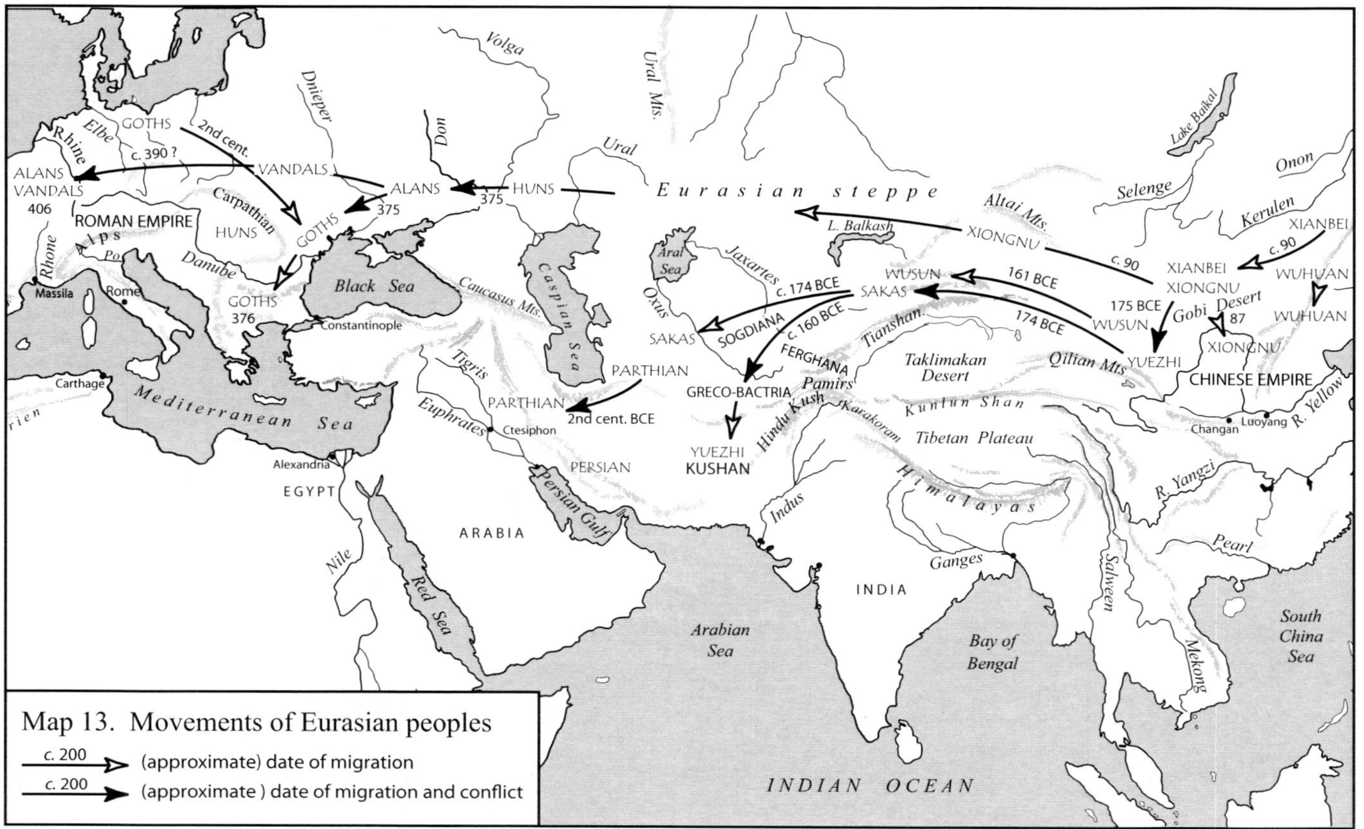

Map 13. Movements of Eurasian peoples

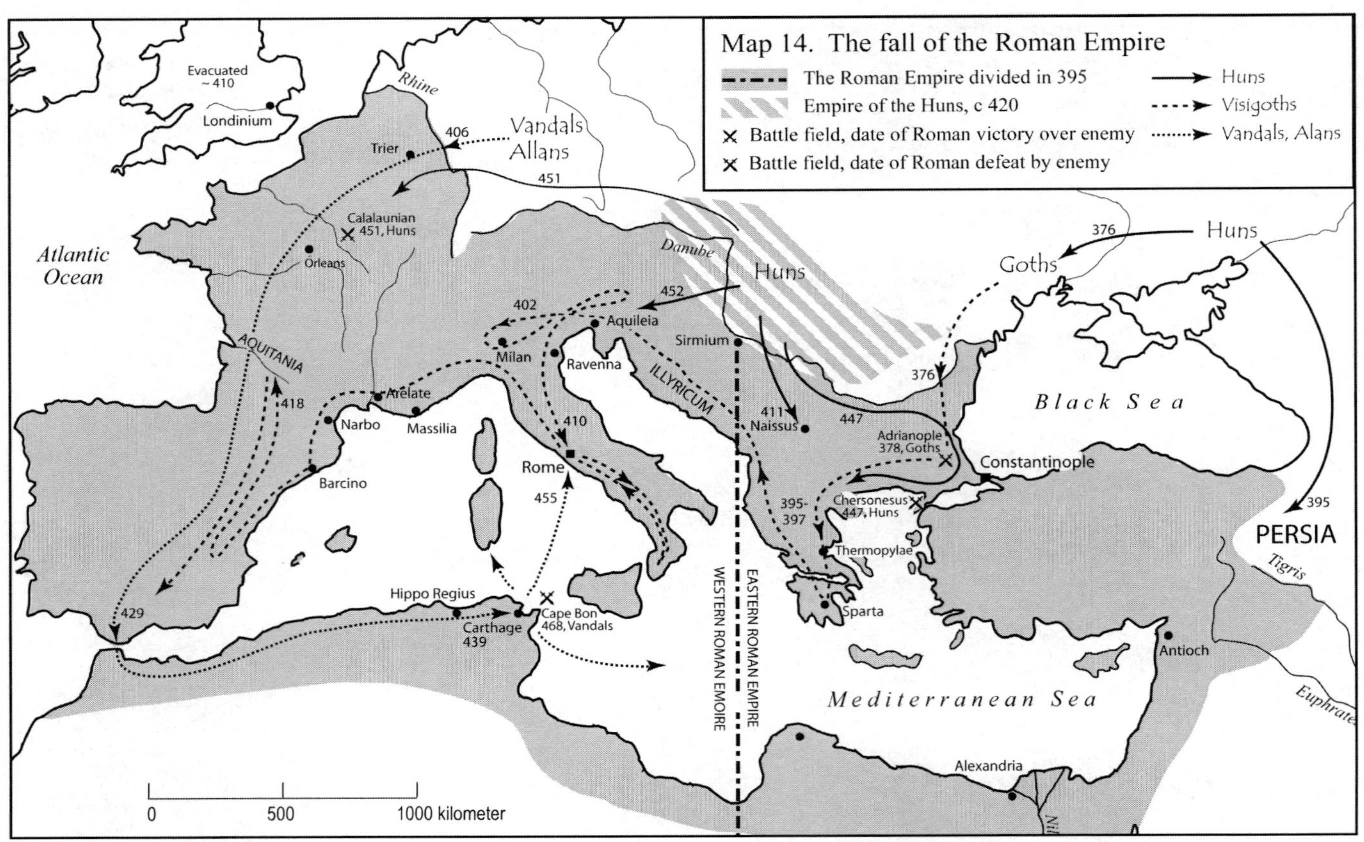
Map 14. The fall of the Roman Empire
The Roman Empire divided in 395
Empire of the Huns, c 420
Battle field, date of Roman victory over enemy
Battle field, date of Roman defeat by enemy
Huns
Visigoths
Vandals, Alans
Evacuated
~410
Londinium
Rhine
406
Vandals
Allans
Trier
451
Calalaunian
451, Huns
Orleans
Atlantic
Ocean
Danube
Huns
376
Huns
Goths
452
402
Aquileia
Sirmium
Milan
Ravenna
ILLYRICUM
AQUITANIA
376
418
Arelate
Narbo
Massilia
410
411
Naissus
447
Black Sea
Adrianople
378, Goths
Constantinople
Rome
Barcino
455
395-
397
Chersonesus
447, Huns
395
PERSIA
Thermopylae
Tigris
Hippo Regius
429
Cape Bon
468, Vandals
Carthage
439
Sparta
WESTERN ROMAN EMOIRE
EASTERN ROMAN EMPIRE
Antioch
Mediterranean Sea
Euphrates
Alexandria
0
500
1000 kilometer

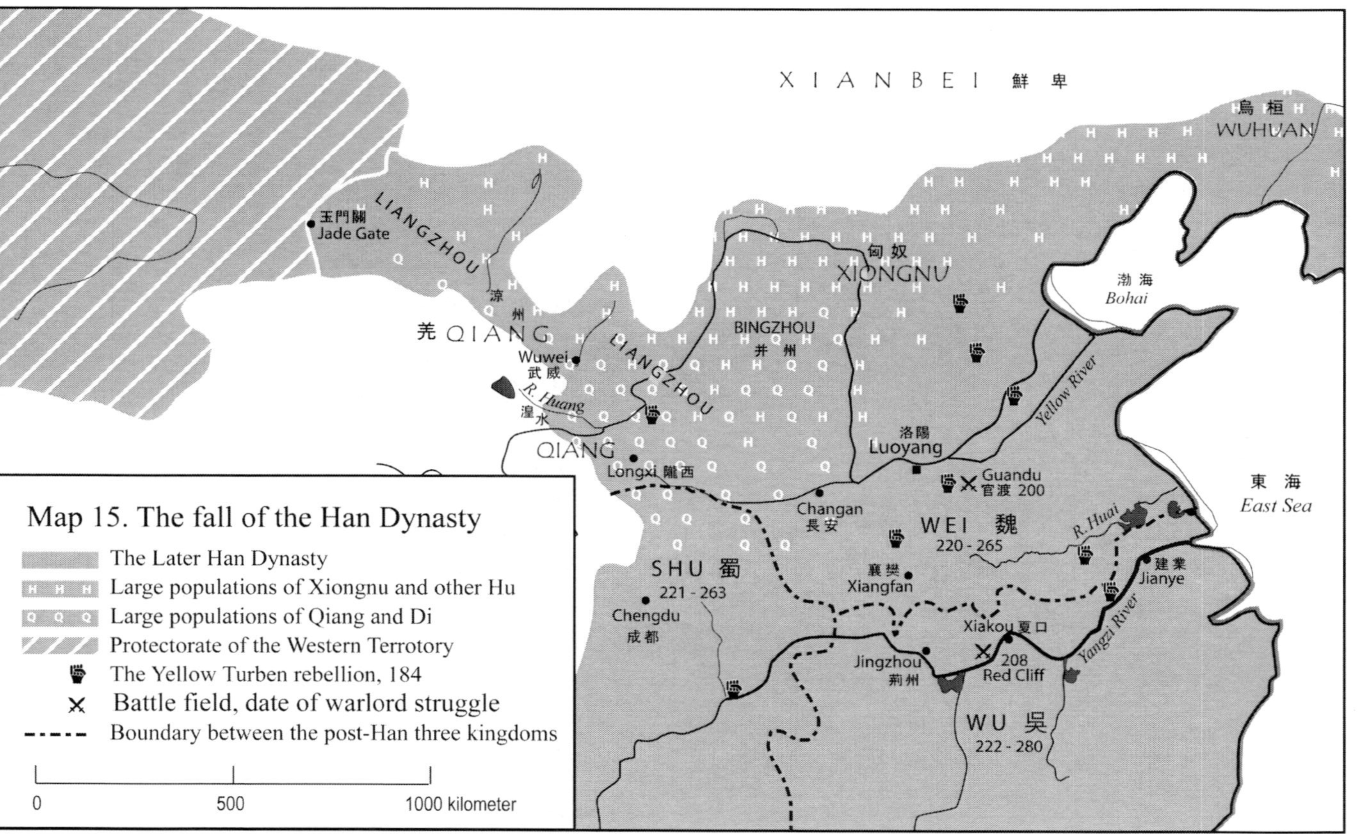

Map 15. The fall of the Han Dynasty

Map 16. Population distribution of China

(a) 2 CE. Total registered households: 12,233,062
Total registered population: 59,594,978 (*Book of Han* 28)

(b) 280 CE. Total registered households: 2,459,840
Total registered population: 16,163,863 (*Book of Jin* 14)

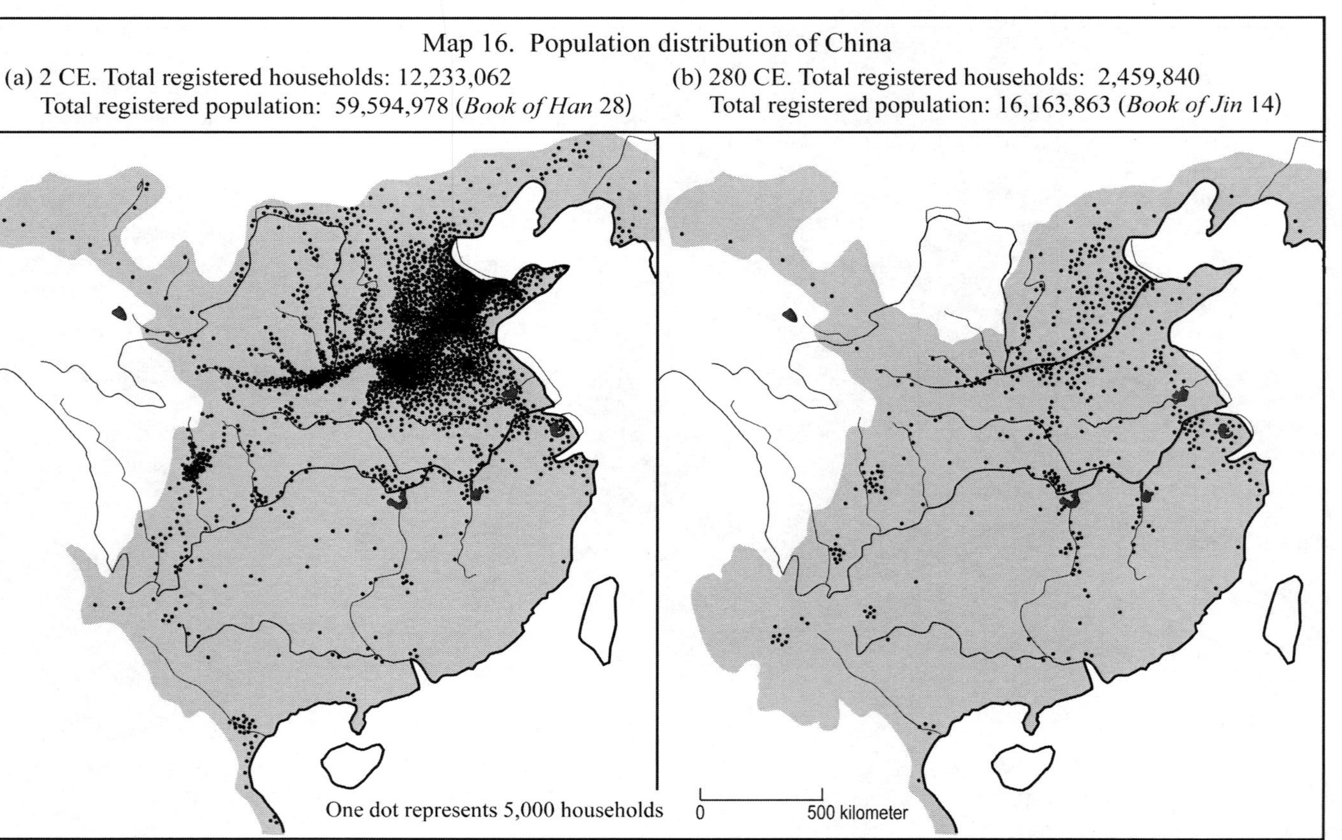

Map 17. Northern China in the early fourth century

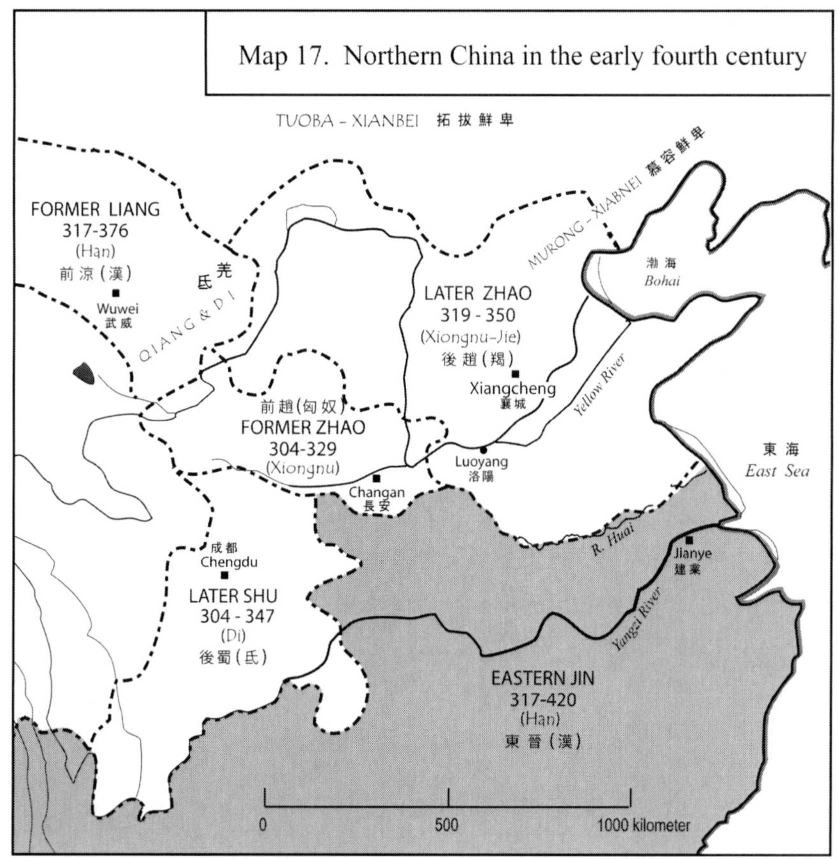

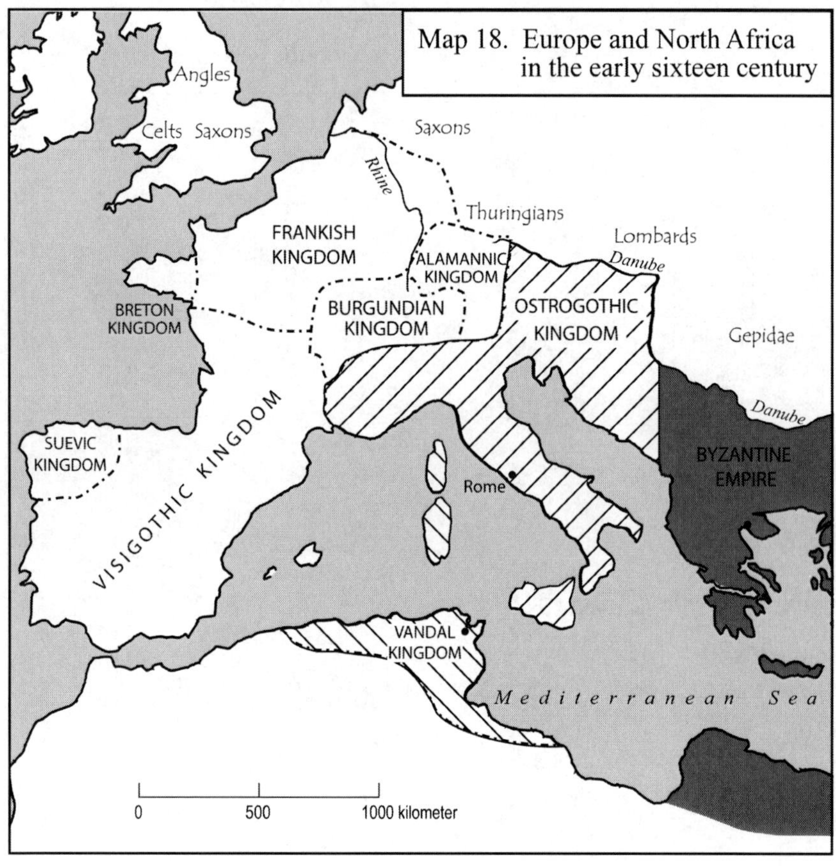
Map 18. Europe and North Africa
in the early sixteen century
Angles
Celts
Saxons
Saxons
Rhine
Thuringians
Lombards
Danube
FRANKISH
KINGDOM
ALAMANNIC
KINGDOM
BRETON
KINGDOM
BURGUNDIAN
KINGDOM
OSTROGOTHIC
KINGDOM
Gepidae
Danube
SUEVIC
KINGDOM
VISIGOTHIC KINGDOM
BYZANTINE
EMPIRE
Rome
VANDAL
KINGDOM
Mediterranean Sea
0
500
1000 kilometer

BIBLIOGRAPHY

Ancient Chinese sources are listed by book title according to the convention in Chinese-language literature. The exact author or date of many is unknown. Except those for which page numbers or paragraph numbers are cited in the notes, editions are not cited, since too many exist. Selected translations are provided in square brackets.

All other sources are listed by author. In primary sources, the author's name is followed by the book title; in secondary sources, by the date, either of initial publication or of the edition cited.

Abernethy, D.B. 2000. *The Dynamics of Global Dominance*. Yale University Press.

Adkins, L., and R.A. Adkins. 1994. *Handbook to Life in Ancient Rome*. Oxford University Press.

Alston, R. 1998. *Aspects of Roman History, AD 14–117*. Routledge.

Ammianus Marcellinus. *History*. Tr. J.C. Rolfe. Harvard (1948).

Anderson, P. 1974. *Lineages of the Absolutist State*. Verso.

Appian. *The Civil Wars*. Tr. J. Carter. Penguin (1996).

Aristides. To Rome. In *Complete Works*, Vol. 2. Tr. C.A. Behr. Leiden (1981).

Aristotle. *Ethics*. Tr. J.A.K. Thomson. Penguin (1955).

———. *Politics*. Tr. E. Barker. Oxford (1995).

Arjava, A. 1998. Paternal power in late antiquity. *Journal of Roman Studies* 88: 147–165.

Astin, A.E. 1967. *Scipio Aemilianus*. Oxford University Press.

———. 1978. *Cato the Censor*. Oxford University Press.

———. 1989. Roman government and politics. In Astin et al. 1989: 163–196.

Astin, A.E., F.W. Walbank, M.W. Fredericksen, and R.M. Ogilvie, eds. 1989. *The Cambridge Ancient History*, 2nd ed., vol. 8. Cambridge University Press.

Augustus. *The Achievements of the Deified Augustus*. Tr. R. Mellor. In Mellor 1998: 356–364.

Bagnall, N. 1990. *The Punic Wars*. Thomas Dunne Books.

Ball, W. 2000. *Rome in the East*. Routledge.

Bang, P.F. 2012. Predation. In Scheidel 2012a: 197–217.

Barfield, T.J. 1989. *The Perilous Frontier*. Basil Blackwell.

Barnes, T.D. 1981. *Constantine and Eusebius*. Harvard University Press.

Bastomsky, S.J. 1990. Rich and poor: The great divide in ancient Rome and Victorian England. *Greece and Rome* 37: 37–43.

Beard, M. 2007. Looking for the emperor. *New York Review of Books*, November 8, 53–55.

———. 2009. *The Roman Triumph*. Harvard University Press.

Beard, M., and M. Crawford. 1985. *Rome in the Late Republic*. Cornell University Press.

Beck, B.J.M. 1986. The fall of Han. In Twitchett and Loewe 1986: 317–76.

Beckwith, C.I. 2009. *Empires of the Silk Road*. Princeton University Press.

Bell, D.A. 2008. *China's New Confucianism*. Princeton University Press.

Bendix, R. 1977. *Max Weber*. University of California Press.

Benn, C. 2002. *China's Golden Age*. Oxford University Press.

Bennett, J. 1997. *Trajan, Optimus Princeps*. Indiana University Press.

Berlin, I. 1969. *Four Essays on Liberty*. Oxford University Press.

Bernstein, A.H. 1994. The strategy of a warrior-state: Rome and the wars against Carthage. In Murray, Knox, and Bernstein 1994: 56–84.

Bielenstein, H. 1986a. The institutions of Later Han. In Twitchett and Loewe 1986: 491–519.

———. 1986b. Wang Mang, the restoration of the Han dynasty, and Later Han. In Twitchett and Loewe 1986: 223–290.

Birley, A. 1987. *Marcus Aurelius*. Barnes & Noble.

———. 1997. *Hadrian*. Routledge.

Bivar, A.D.H. 1983a. The history of eastern Iran. In Yarshater 1983: 181–231.

———. 1983b. The political history of Iran under the Arsacids. In Yarshater 1983: 21–99.

Blok, A. 1972. The peasant and the brigand: Social banditry reconsidered. *Comparative Studies in Society and History* 14: 494–503.

Boardman, J., J. Griffin, and O. Murray, eds. 1991. *The Oxford History of the Roman World*. Oxford University Press.

Bodde, D. 1981. *Essays on Chinese Civilization*. Princeton University Press.

———. 1986. The state and empire in Ch'in. In Twitchett and Loewe 1986: 20–102.

Bodde, D., and C. Morris 1967. *Law in Imperial China*. Harvard University Press.

Boren, H.C. 1968. *The Gracchi*. Twayne.

Borkowski, A. 1997. *Roman Law*, 2nd ed. Oxford University Press.

Boulnois, L. 2005. *Silk Road: Monks, Warriors and Merchants*. Odyssey.

Bowersock, G.W., P. Brown, and O. Grabar, eds. 1999. *Late Antiquity*. Harvard University Press.

Bowman, A., P. Garnsey, and D. Rathbone, eds. 2000. *The Cambridge Ancient History*, 2nd ed., vol. 11. Cambridge University Press.

Boylan, E.S. 1982. The Chinese cultural style of warfare. *Comparative Strategy* 3: 341–346.

Bradley, A.C. 1962. Hegel's theory of tragedy. In *Hegel, On Tragedy*, ed. A. and H. Paolucci, 367–388. Harper.

Bradley, K., and P. Cartledge, eds. 2011. *The Cambridge World History of Slavery*, vol. 1. Cambridge University Press.

Braund, D.C. 1984. *Rome and the Friendly King*. St. Martin's Press.

Brennan, T.C. 2004. Power and process under the Republican "constitution." In Flower 2004: 31–65.

Brown, P. 1967. The Later Roman Empire. *Economic History Review* 20: 327–343.

———. 1971. *The World of Late Antiquity*. Norton.
Brunt, P.A. 1961. Charges of provincial maladministration under the early Principate. *Historia* 10: 189–227.
———. 1965. Reflections on Roman and British imperialism. *Comparative Studies in Society and History* 7: 267–288.
———. 1971. *Italian Manpower, 225 B.C.–A.D. 14*. Oxford University Press.
———. 1978. *Laus imperii*. In Garnsey and Whittaker 1978: 159–192.
———. 1981. The revenues of Rome. *Journal of Roman Studies* 71: 161–172.
———. 1982. Nobilitas and novitas. *Journal of Roman Studies* 72: 1–17.
———. 1988. *The Fall of the Roman Republic*. Oxford University Press.
Bu Xianqun 卜憲群. 2002. *Qinhan Guanliao Zhidu* 秦漢官僚制度 (Bureaucracy of the Qin and Han Dynasties). Shehui Kexue Wenxian Chubanshe.
Burbank, J., and F. Cooper. 2010. *Empires in World History*. Princeton University Press.
Bury, J.B. 1958. *History of the Later Roman Empire*. Dover.
Caesar. *The Civil War*. Tr. J.F. Mitchell. Penguin (1967).
———. *The Conquest of Gaul*. Tr. S.A. Handford. Penguin (1982).
Cai Feng 蔡鋒. 2004. *Chunqiu Shiqi Guizu Shehuai Shenghuo Yanjiu* 春秋時期貴族社會生活研究 (Research on Aristocratic Society and Living in the Spring and Autumn Period). Beijing Zhongguo Shehuai Kexue Chubanshe.
Cameron, A. 1993. *The Later Roman Empire*. Harvard University Press.
Cameron, A., and P. Garnsey, eds. 1998. *The Cambridge Ancient History*, vol. 13. Cambridge University Press.
Campbell, B. 2002. *War and Society in Imperial Rome, 31 BC–AD 284*. Routledge.
Cao Luning 曹旅寧. 2005. *Zhangjiashan Hanlu Yanjiu* 張家山漢律研究 (Research on Han Laws Excavated in Zhangjiashan). Zhonghua Shuju.
Champlin, E. 2003. *Nero*. Harvard University Press.
Chan, A. K.L., ed. 2002. *Mencius: Contexts and Interpretations*. University of Hawaii Press.
Chang, C-S. 2007. *The Rise of the Chinese Empire*. University of Michigan Press.
Chang, H. 1996. The intellectual heritage of the Confucian ideal of *ching-shih*. In Tu 1996: 72–91.
Chang, K-C., et al. 2005. *The Formation of Chinese Civilization: An Archeological Perspective*. Yale University Press.
Chen Xujing 陳序經. 2007. *Xiongnu Shigao* 匈奴史稿 (A Draft History of the Xiong nu). Zhongguo Renmin Daxue Chubanshe.
Chen, C-Y. 1975. *Hsün Yüeh*. Cambridge University Press.
———. 1984. Review: Han Dynasty China: Economy, society, and state power. *T'oung Pao* 70: 127–148.
———. 1986. Confucian, Legalist, and Taoist thought in the Later Han. In Twitchett and Loewe 1986: 766–807.
Ch'ü, T-T. 1965. *Law and Society in Traditional China*. Mouton.
———. 1972. *Han Social Structure*. University of Washington Press.
Chua, A. 2006. *Day of Empire*. Doubleday.
Cicero. *On Obligation*. Tr. P.G. Walsh. Oxford (2000).
———. On the command of Cnaeus Pompeius. In *Selected Political Speeches*, tr. M. Grant, 33–70. Penguin (1969).
———. *The Laws*. Tr. N. Rudd. Oxford (1998).
———. *The Republic*. Tr. N. Rudd. Oxford (1998).

Collins, J.T. 2003. The zeal of Phinhas: The Bible and the legitimation of violence. *Journal of Biblical Literature* 122: 3–21.

Collins, R. 1978. Some principles of long-term social change: The territorial power of states. *Research in Social Movements, Conflicts and Change* 1: 1–34.

Committee on Chinese Military History. 2006. *Zhongguo Lidai Junshi Zhiduo* 中國歷代軍事制度 (History of Chinese Military Systems). Jiefangjun Chubanse.

Connolly, P. 1981. *Greece and Rome at War*. Prentice-Hall.

Cook, C., and J.S. Major, eds. 1999. *Defining Chu: Image and Reality in Ancient China*. University of Hawaii Press.

Cook, S.A., F.E. Adcock, and M.P. Charlesworth, eds. 1930. *The Cambridge Ancient History*, 1st ed. Vol. VIII. Cambridge University Press.

———. 1954. *The Cambridge Ancient History*, 1st ed. Vol. XI. Cambridge University Press.

Cornell, T.J. 1989. Rome: The history of an anachronism. In Molho et al. 1989: 53–70.

———. 1995. *The Beginning of Rome*. Routledge.

Cornell, T.J., and J. Matthews. 1990. *The Cultural Atlas of the World: The Roman World*. Stonehenge Press.

Cotterell, A., ed. 1980. *The Encyclopedia of Ancient Civilizations*. Penguin.

———. 1981. *The First Emperor of China*. Holt, Rinehart and Winston.

———. 2004. *Chariot*. Overlook Press.

Crawford, M. 1976. Review: Hamlet without the prince. *Journal of Roman Studies* 66: 214–217.

———. 1991. Early Rome and Italy. In Boardman et al. 1991: 13–49.

———. 1993. *The Roman Republic*. Harvard University Press.

Creel, H.G. 1970. *The Origins of Statecraft in China*. Vol. 1: *The Western Chou Empire*. University of Chicago Press.

Creveld, M. van. 1999. *The Rise and Decline of the State*. Cambridge University Press.

Crook, J.A. 1967. *Law and Life of Rome, 90 B.C.–A.D. 212*. Cornell University Press.

Crook, J.A., A. Lintott, and E. Rawson. 1994a. Epilogue: The fall of the Roman Republic. In Crook et al. 1994b: 769–776.

———, eds. 1994b. *The Cambridge Ancient History*, 2nd ed., vol. 9. Cambridge University Press.

Crowell, W.G. 1983. Social unrest and rebellion in Jiangnan during the Six Dynasties. *Modern China* 9: 319–354.

Cunliffe, B. 1997. *The Ancient Celts*. Oxford University Press.

David, J-M. 1997. *The Roman Conquest of Italy*. Blackwell.

Davies, J.K. 1993. *Democracy and Classical Greece*. Harvard University Press.

———. 2004. Athenian citizenship: The descent group and the alternatives. In *Athenian Democracy*, ed. P.J. Rhodes, 18–39. Oxford University Press.

De Bary, W.T. 1991. *The Trouble with Confucianism*. Harvard University Press.

De Crespigny, R. 1980. Politics and philosophy under the government of Emperor Huan 159–168 AD. *T'oung Pao* 66: 41–83.

———. 2009. The military culture of Later Han. In Di Cosmo 2009: 90–111.

Dench, E. 1995. *From Barbarians to New Men*. Oxford University Press.

Derow, P.S. 1979. Polybius, Rome, and the East. *Journal of Roman Studies* 69: 1–15.

———. 1989. Rome, the fall of Macedon and the sack of Corinth. In Astin et al. 1989: 290–323.
Dettenhofer, M.H. 2009. Eunuchs, women, and imperial courts. In Scheidel 2009c: 83–99.
Di Cosmo, D. 1994. Ancient Asian nomads: Their economic basis and its significance in Chinese history. *Journal of Asian Studies* 53: 1092–1126.
———. 2002. *Ancient China and Its Enemies*. Cambridge University Press.
———, ed. 2009. *Military Culture in Imperial China*. Harvard University Press.
Dien, A.D. 1986. The stirrup and its effects on Chinese military history. *Ars Orientalis* 16: 33–56.
Dignas, B., and E. Winter. 2007. *Rome and Persia in Late Antiquity*. Cambridge University Press.
Dio Cassius. *The Roman History*. Tr. I. Scott-Kilvert. Penguin (1987).
Dio Chrysostom. *The Discourses*. Tr. J.W. Cohoon. Harvard (1951).
Dodds, E.R. 1951. *The Greeks and the Irrational*. University of California Press.
Downing, B.M. 1992. *The Military Revolution and Political Change*. Princeton University Press.
Doyle, M.W. 1986. *Empires*. Cornell University Press.
Drews, R. 1993. *The End of the Bronze Age*. Princeton University Press.
Dreyer, E.L. 2009. Military aspects of the War of the Eight Princes. In Di Cosmo 2009: 112–142.
Du Zhengsheng 杜正勝. 1979. *Zhoudai Chengbang* 周代城邦 (The Zhou City-States). Taibei Lianjing.
Dull, J.L. 1983. Anti-Qin rebels: No peasant leaders here. *Modern China* 9: 285–318.
Dunstan, H. 2004. Premodern Chinese political thought. In Gaus and Kukathas 2004: 320–337.
Dyson, S.L. 1971. Native revolts in the Roman Empire. *Historia* 20: 239–274.
Eadie, J.W. 1967. The development of Roman mailed cavalry. *Journal of Roman Studies* 57: 161–173.
Eastman, L.E. 1989. *Family, Fields, and Ancestors*. Oxford University Press.
Ebrey, P. 1983. Patron-client relations in the Later Han. *Journal of the American Oriental Society* 103: 533–542.
———. 1986. The economic and social history of Later Han. In Twitchett and Loewe 1986: 608–648.
———. 1990. Toward a better understanding of the Later Han upper class. In *State and Society in Early Medieval China*, ed. A.E. Dien, 49–72. Stanford University Press.
Eck, W. 2000a. The emperor and his advisers. In Bowman et al. 2000: 159–213.
———. 2000b. The growth of administrative posts. In Bowman et al. 2000: 238–265.
Edel, A. 1982. *Aristotle and His Philosophy*. University of North Carolina Press.
Eder, W. 1986. The political significance of the codification of law in archaic societies. In Raaflaub 1986b: 262–300.
———. 1990. Augustus and the power of transition: The Augustan principate as binding link between Republic and Empire. In Raaflaub and Toher 1990: 71–122.
Elisseeff, V., ed. 2000. *The Silk Roads: Highways of Culture and Commerce*. Berghahn Books.
Elvin, M. 1973. *The Pattern of the Chinese Past*. Stanford University Press.

Errington, R.M. 1989. Rome against Philip and Antiochus. In Astin et al. 1989: 244–289.

Ershiershi Zhaji 二十二史劄記 (Notes on the *Twenty-Two Histories*), by Zhao Yi 趙翼.

Ertman, T. 1997. *Birth of the Leviathan*. Cambridge University Press.

Escherick, J.W. 1983. Symposium on peasant rebellions: Some introductory comments. *Modern China* 9: 275–284.

Euripides, *Iphigenia in Aulis*. Tr. P. Vellacott. Penguin (1972).

Evans, P.R., D. Rueschemeyer, and T. Skocpol, eds. 1985. *Bringing the State Back In*. Cambridge University Press.

Fairbank, J.K. 1974. Varieties of the Chinese military experience. In *Chinese Wars in History*, ed. F.A. Kierman and J.K. Fairbank, 1–26. Harvard University Press.

———. 1987. *China Watch*. Harvard University Press.

———. 1992. *China: A New History*. Harvard University Press.

Falkenhauser, L. von. 1999. The waning of the Bronze Age: Material culture and social developments, 770–481 B.C. In Loewe and Shaughnessy 1999: 450–544.

Feng, H. 2007. *Chinese Strategic Culture and Foreign Policy Decision-Making*. Routledge.

Ferguson, N. 2004. *Colossus: The Rise and Fall of the American Empire*. Penguin.

Fine, J.V.A. 1983. *The Ancient Greeks*. Harvard University Press.

Finer, S.E. 1997. *The History of Government from the Earliest Times*, vol 1. Oxford University Press.

Finley, M.I. 1968. Slavery. *International Encyclopedia of the Social Sciences* 14: 307–313.

———. 1978. Empire in the Greco-Roman world. *Greece & Rome* 25: 1–15.

———. 1980. *Ancient Slavery and Modern Ideology*. Viking.

———. 1983. *Economy and Society in Ancient Greece*. Penguin.

Flower, H.I. 1996. *Ancestor Masks and Aristocratic Power in Roman Culture*. Oxford University Press.

———, ed. 2004. *The Cambridge Companion to the Roman Republic*. Cambridge University Press.

Fong, W., ed. 1980. *The Great Bronze Age of China*. Metropolitan Museum of Art.

Forsythe, G. 2005. *A Critical History of Early Rome*. University of California Press.

Frankel, H.H. 1983. Cai Yan and the poems attributed to her. *Chinese Literature: Essays, Articles, Reviews* 5: 133–156.

Freeman, P. 2008. *Julius Caesar*. Simon & Schuster.

Fu Lecheng 傅樂成. 2002. *Zhongguo Tongshi* 中國通史 (History of China). Taibei Dazhongguo Tushu.

Fu Zhengyuan. 1996. *China's Legalists: The Earliest Totalitarians and the Art of Ruling*. M.E. Sharpe.

Fukuyama, F. 1992. *The End of History and the Last Man*. Free Press.

———. 2011. *The Origins of Political Order*. Farrar, Straus and Giroux.

Fulford, M. 1992. Territorial expansion and the Roman Empire. *World Archeology* 23: 294–305.

Fuller, J.F.C. 1965. *Julius Caesar*. Da Capo Press.

Fung, Y-L. 1952. *A History of Chinese Philosophy*, tr. D. Bodde. Princeton University Press.

Gabba, E. 1976. *Republican Rome: The Army and the Allies*. University of California Press.
———. 1987. Rome and Italy in the second century B.C. In Astin et al. 1987: 197–243.
Galinsky, K., ed. 2005. *The Cambridge Companion to the Age of Augustus*. Cambridge University Press.
Gao Heng 高恆. 2008. *Qinhan Jiandu zhong Fazhi Wenshu Jikao* 秦漢簡牘中法制文書輯考 (Investigations into the Legal Documents among the Excavated Strips of Qin and Han). Shehui Kexue Wenxian Chubanshe.
Gao Min 高敏. 1998. *Qinhan Shi Tantao* 秦漢史探討 (Research in the History of Qin and Han). Zhongzhou Gushi.
Gardner, J.F. 2011. Slavery and Roman law. In Bradley and Cartledge 2011: 414–437.
Garlan, Y. 1975. *War in the Ancient World.* Chatto & Windus.
———. 1988. *Slavery in Ancient Greece*. Cornell University Press.
Garnsey, P., and R. Saller. 1987. *The Roman Empire: Economy, Society and Culture*. University of California Press.
Garnsey, P., and C.R. Whittaker, eds. 1978. *Imperialism in the Ancient World.* Cambridge University Press.
Gaus, G.F., and C. Kukathas, eds. 2004. *Handbook of Political Theory*. Sage.
Gelzer, M. 1968. *Caesar: Politician and Statesman*. Harvard University Press.
Giardina, A. 1993a. Roman man. In Giardina 1993b: 1–15.
———, ed. 1993b. *The Romans*. University of Chicago Press.
Gibbon, E. 1994. *The History of the Decline and Fall of the Roman Empire*. Penguin.
Gills, B.K., and A.G. Frank. 1993. World system cycles, crises, and hegemonic shifts, 1700 BCE to 1700 AD. In *The World System*, ed. A.G. Frank and B.K. Gills, 143–199. Routledge.
Goffart, W. 1980. *Barbarians and Romans*. Princeton University Press.
———. 1989. *Rome's Fall and After*. Hambledon Press.
Goldsworthy, A. 1996. *The Romany Army at War, 100 BC–AD 200*. Oxford University Press.
———. 2006. *Caesar*. Yale University Press.
———. 2009. *How Rome Fell*. Yale University Press.
Graff, D.A. 2002. *Medieval Chinese Warfare:* 300–900. Routledge.
Grant, M. 1978. *History of Rome*. Faber and Faber.
———. 1990. *The Fall of the Roman Empire*. Collier Books.
———. 1994. *The Antonines*. Routledge.
Greene, K. 1986. *The Archeology of the Roman Economy*. University of California Press.
———. 2000. Technology innovation and economic progress in the ancient world. *Economic History Review* 53: 29–59.
Gruen, E.S. 1973. Review: Roman imperialism and Greek resistance. *Journal of Interdisciplinary History* 4: 273–286.
———. 1974. *The Last Generation of the Roman Republic*. University of California Press.
———. 1984. *The Hellenistic World and the Coming of Rome*. University of California Press.
———. 1989. Exercise of power in the Roman Republic. In Molho et al. 1989: 251–268.

———. 1990. The imperial policy of Augustus. In Raaflaub and Toher 1990: 395–416.
———. 2005. Augustus and the making of the Principate. In Galinsky 2005: 33–54.
Gu Derong and Zhu Shunlong 顧德融, 朱順龍. 2003. *Chunqiu Shi* 春秋史 (History of the Spring and Autumn Period). Shanghai Remin Chubanshe.
Guanzi 管子 (*Master Guan*). [*Guanzi: Political, Economic, and Philosophical Essays from Early China*, tr. W.A. Rickett, Princeton University Press, 1985.]
Guoyu 國語. (*Sayings of the States*).
Hamilton, N. 2010. *American Caesars*. Yale University Press.
Hanahan, D., and R.A. Weinberg. 2000. The hallmarks of cancer. *Cell* 100: 57–70.
Handel, M.I. 2001. *Masters of War*, 3rd ed. Frank Cass.
Hannfeizi 韓非子 (*Master Hannfei*). [*Han Fei Tzu*, tr. B. Watson, Columbia University Press, 1964.]
Hansen, V. 2012. *The Silk Road: A New History*. Oxford University Press.
Hanshu 漢書 (*The Book of Han*), by Ban Gu 班固. Zhonghua Shuju (1962).
Hanson, V.D. 2005. The Roman way of war 250 BC–AD 300. In Parker 2005b: 46–60.
Hao, Y., and M. Johnston. 2002. Corruption and the future of economic reform in China. In *Political Corruption*, third ed., eds. A.J. Heidenheimer and M. Johnston, Transaction Publisher (2002): 583–604.
Harris, R. 2003. *Political Corruption*. Routledge.
Harris, W.V. 1979. *War and Imperialism in Republican Rome, 327–70 B.C.* Oxford University Press.
———. 1989. Roman expansion in the west. In Astin et al. 1989: 107–162.
———. 1990. On defining the political culture of the Roman Republic: Some comments on Rosenstein, Williamson, and North. *Classical Philology* 85: 288–294.
———. 2011. *Rome's Imperial Economy*. Oxford University Press.
Hart, H.L.A. 1961. *The Concept of Law*. Oxford University Press.
He Guangyue 何光岳. 1996. *Han Yuanliu Shi* 漢源流史 (Origins of Han). Jiangxi Jiaoyue.
He Zhiqing and Wang Xiaowei 赫治清, 王曉衛. 1997. *Zhongguo Bingzhi Shi* 中國兵制史 (History of Chinese Military Systems). Wenjing Chuban.
Heather, P. 1996. *The Goths*. Blackwell.
———. 1997. *Foedera* and *foederati* of the fourth century. In *Kingdoms of the Empire*, ed. E. Pohl, 57–75. Brill.
———. 2005. *The Fall of the Roman Empire*. Pan Books.
Hegel, G.W.F. 1965. *The Philosophy of History*. Dover.
Henderson, J.B. 1991. *Scripture, Canon and Commentary*. Princeton University Press.
Herodotus. *The Histories*. Tr. A. de Sélincourt. Penguin (1954).
Hingley, R. 2005. *Globalizing Roman Culture*. Routledge.
Hiromi Kinoshita. 2007. Qin palaces and architecture. In Portal 2007: 83–93.
Hobsbawm, E.J. 1959. *Primitive Rebels*. Norton.
Holcombe, C. 1994. *In the Shadow of the Han*. University of Hawaii Press.
Hölkeskamp, K-J. 2004. Under Roman roofs: Family, house and household. In Flower 2004: 113–138.
Holleaux, M. 1930. Rome and Antiochus. In Cook et al. 1930: 199–240.
Homer, *Iliad*. Tr. R. Lattimore. University of Chicago Press (1951).
Honoré, T. 1995. *About Law*. Oxford University Press.

Hopkins, K. 1978a. *Conquerors and Slaves*. Cambridge University Press.
———. 1978b. Economic growth and towns in classical antiquity. In *Towns in Society*, ed. P. Abrams and E.A. Wrigley, 35–78. Cambridge University Press.
———. 1980. Taxes and trades in the Roman Empire (200 B.C.–A.D. 400). *Journal of Roman Studies* 70: 101–125.
———. 1983a. *Death and Renewal*. Cambridge University Press.
———. 1983b. Models, ships and staples. *In Trade and Famine in Classical Antiquity*, ed. P. Garnsey and C.R. Whittaker, 84–109. Cambridge Philological Society.
Houhanshu 後漢書 (The Book of Latter Han), by Fan Ye 范曄. Zhonghua Shuju (1965).
Hsiao, K-C. 1979. *A History of Chinese Political Thought*. Princeton University Press.
Hsu, C-Y. 1965a. *Ancient China in Transition*. Stanford University Press.
———. 1965b. The changing relation between local society and the central political power in Former Han: 206 B.C.–8 A.D. *Comparative Studies in Society and History* 3: 358–370.
———. 1980. *Han Agriculture*. University of Washington Press.
———. 1999. The Spring and Autumn period. In Loewe and Shaughnessy 1999: 545–586.
Hsu, C-Y., and K.M. Linduff. 1988. *Western Chou Civilization*. Yale University Press.
Huang Jinyan 黃今言. 2005. *Qinhan Shangpin Jingji Yanjiu* 秦漢商品經濟研究 (*Research on the Commercial Economy of Qin and Han*). Renmin Chubanshe.
Huang Liuzhu 黃留珠. 2002. *Qinhan Lishi Wenhua Lüngao* 秦漢歷史文化論稿 (*Essays on the History and Culture of Qin and Han*). Sanqin Chubanshe.
Huang, P.C.C. 1996. *Civil Justice in China*. Stanford University Press.
Huang, R. 1990. *China: A Macro History*. M.E. Sharpe.
Huayang Guozhi 華陽國志 (Records of the kingdoms of Huayang [southwestern China]).
Hui, V.T. 2005. *War and State Formation in Ancient China and Early Modern Europe*. Cambridge University Press.
Hulsewé, A.F.P. 1978. The Ch'in documents discovered in Hupei in 1975. *T'oung Pao* 64: 175–217.
———. 1985. The influence of the "Legalist" government of Qin on the economy as reflected in the texts discovered in Yunmeng County. In *The Scope of State Power in China*, ed. S.R. Schram, 81–126. St. Martin's Press.
———. 1986. Ch'in and Han laws. In Twitchett and Loewe 1986: 520–544.
———. 1987. Han China: A proto "welfare state"? *T'song Pao* 73: 265–285.
———. 1989. Founding fathers and yet forgotten men: A closer look at the tables of the nobility in the "Shih Chi" and "Han Shu." *T'oung Pao* 75: 43–126.
Hunt, P. 2011. Slaves in Greek literary culture. In Bradley and Cartledge 2011: 22–47.
Huntington, S.P. 1968. *Political Order in Changing Societies*. Yale University Press.
Huzar, E.G. 1978. *Mark Antony*. University of Minnesota Press.
Isaac, B. 1992. *The Limits of Empire*, rev. ed. Oxford University Press.
Jacques, M. 2009. *When China Rules the World*. Penguin.
James, H. 2006. *The Roman Predicament*. Princeton University Press.
Jing Ai 景爱. 2002. *Zhongguo Changcheng Shi* 中國長城史 (A History of Chinese Long Walls). Shanghai Remin.

Jinshu 晉書 (The Book of Jin), by Fang Xuanning et al. 房玄齡. Zhonghua Shuju (1974).

Johnson, C. 2000. *Blowback: The Costs and Consequences of American Empire*. Basic Books.

———. 2004. *The Sorrows of Empire*. Metropolitan Books.

Johnston, A.I. 1995. *Cultural Realism, Strategic Culture, and Grand Strategy in Chinese History*. Princeton University Press.

Jones, A.H.M. 1940. *The Greek City*. Oxford University Press.

———. 1956. Slavery in the ancient world. *Economic History Review* 9: 185–199.

———. 1964. *The Later Roman Empire: 284–602*. Johns Hopkins University Press.

———. 1970. *Augustus*. Norton.

———. 1974. *The Roman Economy*. Basil Blackwell.

Jones, B.W. 1979. *Domitian and the Senatorial Order*. American Philosophical Society.

Kagen, K. 2006. Redefining Roman grand strategy. *Journal of Military History* 70: 333–362.

Kalinowski, M., D. Wenkuan, and M. Bujard, eds. 2009. *Rome-Han: Comparer l'Incomparable*. École française d'Extrême-Orient. Beijing.

Kallert-Marx, R.M. 1995. *Hegemony to Empire*. University of California Press.

Katouzian, H. 2009. *The Persians*. Yale University Press.

Kelly, C. 2004. *Ruling the Later Roman Empire*. Harvard University Press.

———. 2008. *The End of Empire*. Norton.

Kennedy, P., ed. 1983. *Grand Strategy in War and Peace*. Yale University Press.

Keppie, L. 1984. *The Making of the Roman Army*. University of Oklahoma Press.

Kern, M. 2000. *The Stele Inscriptions of Ch'in Shih'huang: Text and Ritual in Early Chinese Imperial Representation*. American Oriental Society.

———. 2007. Imperial tours and mountain inscriptions. In Portal 2007: 104–113.

Khazanov, A.M. 1994. *Nomads and the Outside World*, 2nd ed. Wisconsin University Press.

Kissinger, H. 1994. *Diplomacy*. Touchstone.

———. 2011. *On China*. Penguin.

Kolendo, J. 1993. The peasant. In Giardina 1993b: 199–213.

Kunkel, W. 1973. *An Introduction to Roman Legal and Constitutional History*, 2nd ed. Oxford University Press.

Lakoff, S. 1996. *Democracy, History, Theory, Practice*. Westview Press.

Lancel, S. 1998. *Hannibal*. Basil Blackwell.

Lao Gan 勞幹. 2006. *Gudai Zhongquo di Lishi yu Wenhua* 古代中國的歷史與文化 (History and Culture of Ancient China). Beijing Zhonghua.

Laozi 老子. [*Tao Te Ching*, tr. D.C. Lau, Penguin, 1963.]

Lary, D. 1980. Warlord studies. *Modern China* 6: 439–470.

Lattimore, O. 1940. *Inner Asian Frontiers of China*. Beacon Press.

Lawson, F.H. 1965. Roman law. In *The Romans*, ed. J.P.V.D. Balsdon, 102–128. Basic Books.

Lazenby, J.F. 2004. Rome and Carthage. In Flower 2004: 225–241.

Le Bohec, Y. 1989. *The Imperial Roman Army*. Hippocrene Books.

Le Glay, M., J. Voisin, and Y. Le Bohec. 2001. *A History of Rome*, 2nd ed. Basil Blackwell.

Leeming, F. 1980. Official landscape in traditional China. *Journal of the Economic and Social History of the Orient* 23: 153–204.

Lendon, J.E. 1997. *Empire of Honour*. Oxford University Press.

Leslie, D.D., and K.H.J. Gardiner. 1996. *The Roman Empire in Chinese Sources*. Bardi.

Lewis, M.E. 1990. *Sanctioned Violence in Early China*. State University of New York Press.

———. 1999. Warring States political history. In Loewe and Shaughnessy 1999: 589–650.

———. 2007. *The Early Chinese Empires: Qin and Han*. Harvard University Press.

———. 2009. *China Between Empires*. Harvard University Press.

Lewis, N., and M. Reinhold, eds. 1990. *Roman Civilization: Selected Readings*, 3rd ed. Columbia University Press.

Li Dalong 李大龍. 2006. *Hantang Fanshu Tizhi Yanjiu* 漢唐藩屬體制研究 (Research on the Client-State Systems of the Han and Tang). Zhongguo Shehui Kexiu.

Li Xueqin 李學勤. 2004. Chudu Liye Qinjian 初讀里耶秦簡 (The First Reading of Qin Strips Excavated at Liye). In *Gushi Wencun* 古史文存, 秦漢魏晉南北朝卷, 58–79. Shehui Kexue Wenxian Chubansh.

Li Yufu. 2002. 李玉福. *Qinhan Zhidu Shilün* 秦漢制度史論 (Essays on the Institutional History of Qin and Han). Shandong University Press.

Li, F. 2006. *Landscape and Power in Early China*. Cambridge University Press.

Li, J. 1996. *Chinese Civilization in the Making, 1766–221 BC*. St. Martin's Press.

Li, X. 1985. *Eastern Zhou and Qin Civilizations*. New Haven: Yale University Press.

Liang Qichao 梁啓超. 1996. *Xianqin Zhengzhi Sixiang Shi* 先秦政治思想史 (History of Pre-Qin Political Thinking). Beijing Dongfang Cubanshe.

Liao Baiyuan 廖伯源. 2003. *Qinhan Shi Lüncong* 秦漢史論叢 (Essays on the History of Qin and Han). Wunan.

Liddell Hart, B.H. 1926. *Scipio Africanus*. Da Capo Press.

Light, P.C. 2003. Fact sheet on the new true size of government. www.brookings.edu/articles/2003/0905politics_light.aspx.

Lightfoot, C.S. 1990. Trajan's Parthian War and the fourth century perspective. *Journal of Roman Studies* 80: 114–126.

Liji 禮記 (Rites). Shanghai Guju Chubanshe (2004).

Lin Ganquan林甘泉. 2007. *Zhongguo Jingji Tongshi, Qinhan Jingji Juan* 中國經濟通史, 秦漢經濟卷 (Economic History of China, Qin and Han Dynasties). Zhongguo Shehui Kexue Chubanshe.

Lin Jianming 林劍鳴. 1992. *Qin Shi* 秦史 (History of Qin). Taibei Wunang Tushu.

———. 2003. *Qinhan Shi* 秦漢史 (History of Qin and Han). Shanghai Renmin.

Lindner, R. 1981. Nomadism, Huns and horses. *Past and Present* 92: 1–19.

Lintott, A. 1981. What was the "Imperium Romanum"? *Greece and Rome* 28: 53–67.

———. 1999. *The Constitution of the Roman Republic*. Oxford University Press.

Liu Chunxin 柳春新. 2006. *Hanmo Jinchu Zhiji Zhengzhi Yanjiu* 漢末晉初之際政治研究 (Research on the Politics of Late Han and Early Jin). Yuelu Shushe.

Liu Hianian 劉海年. 2006. *Zhanguo Qindai Fazhi Guankui* 戰國秦代法制管窺 (A Brief Study of the Legal Institutions of the Warring States and the Qin Dynasty). Beijing Falü Chubanshe.

Liu Zehua 劉澤華. 2004. *Xianqin Shiren yu Shehui* 先秦士人與社會 (Pre-imperial *Shi* and Society). Tienjin Renmin Chubanshe.
Liu, S-H. 1998. *Understanding Confucian Philosophy*. Praeger.
Liu, X. 2001. Migration and settlement of the Yuezhi-Kushan. *Journal of World History* 12: 261–292.
Livy. *History*. Tr. A. de Sélincourt. Penguin (1965).
Lloyd, G.E.R. 2005. *The Delusion of Invulnerability*. Duckworth.
Loewe, M. 1986a. The conduct of government and the issues at stake. In Twitchett and Loewe 1986: 291–316.
———. 1986b. The former Han Dynasty. In Twitchett and Loewe 1986: 103–221.
———. 1999. The heritage left to the empires. In Loewe and Shaughnessy 1999: 967–1031.
———. 2005a. *Everyday Life in Early Imperial China*. Hackett.
———. 2005b. *Faith, Myth and Reason in Han China*. Hackett.
———. 2006. *The Government of the Qin and Han Empires, 221 BCE—220 CE*. Hackett.
———. 2007. The First Emperor and the Qin Empire. In Portal 2007: 58–79.
———. 2009. The Western Han army. In Di Cosmo 2009: 65–89.
Loewe, M., and E.L. Shaughnessy, eds. 1999. *The Cambridge History of Ancient China: From the Origin of Civilization to 221 B.C*. Cambridge University Press.
Longden, R.P. 1954. Nerva and Trajan. In Cook et al. 1954: 188–222.
Lü Simian 呂思勉. 2005a. *Xianqin Shi* 先秦史 (Pre-Qin History). Shanghai Guji Chubanshe.
———. 2005b. *Qinhan Shi* 秦漢史 (History of Qin and Han). Shanghai Guji Chubanshe.
Lu, X. 1988. *Ancient India and Ancient China.* Oxford University Press.
Lucas, J.R. 1985. *The Principles of Politics*. Oxford University Press.
Lunheng 論衡 (*On Measure*), by Wang Chong 王充.
Lunyu 論語. Shanghai Guji Chubanshe (2004). [*The Original Analects: Sayings of Confucius and His Successors*, tr. E.B. Brooks and A.T. Brooks, Columbia University Press, 1998.]
Luo Danhua 羅丹華. 1989. *Handai di Liumin Wenti* 漢代的流民問題 (The Drifters Problem in the Han Dynasty). Taiwan Shueseng Shuju.
Lüshi Chunqiu 呂氏春秋 [*The Annals of Lü Buwei*, tr. J. Knoblock and J. Riegel, Stanford University Press, 2000.]
Luttwak, W.N. 1976. *The Grand Strategy of the Roman Empire*. Johns Hopkins University Press.
Ma Changshou 馬長壽. 2006a. *Beidi yu Xiongnu* 北狄與匈奴 (The Beidi and the Xiongnu). Guangxi Shifan Daxue.
———. 2006b. *Wuhuan yu Xianbei* 烏桓與鮮卑 (The Wuhuan and the Xianbei). Guangxi Shifan Daxue.
MacMullen, R. 1966. *Enemies of the Roman Order*. Harvard University Press.
———. 1974. *Roman Social Relations*. Yale University Press.
———. 1986. Judicial savagery in the Roman Empire. *Chiron* 16: 147–166.
———. 1988. *Corruption and the Decline of Rome*. Yale University Press.
Madden, T.F. 2007. *Empires of Trust*. Dutton.
Maddison, A. 2007. *Contours of the World Economy, 1–2030 A.D*. Oxford University Press.
Maenchen-Helfen, J.O. 1973. *The World of the Huns*. University of California Press.

Maier, C.S. 2006. *Among Empires: American Ascendancy and Its Predecessors*. Harvard University Press.
Mann, J.C. 1979. Power, force and the frontier of the Empire. *Journal of Roman Studies* 69: 175–183.
Mann, M. 1986. *The Sources of Social Power*, vol. 1. Cambridge University Press.
———. 1988. *States, War, and Capitalism*. Basil Blackwell.
Marcone, A. 1998. Late Roman social relations. In Cameron and Garnsey 1998: 338–370.
Marcus Aurelius. *Meditations*. 2007. Tr. George Long. Skylight Paths Publishing.
Mattern, S.P. 1999. *Rome and the Enemy*. University of California Press.
Mattern-Parks, S.P. 2003. The defeat of Crassus and the just war. *Classical World* 96: 387–396.
McDonald, A.H. 1938. Scipio Africanus and Roman politics in the second century B.C. *Journal of Roman Studies*, 28: 153–164.
McLeod, K.C.D., and R.D.S. Yates. 1981. Forms of Ch'in law. *Harvard Journal of Asiatic Studies* 41: 111–163.
McNeill, W.H. 1963. *The Rise of the West*. University of Chicago Press.
———. 1976. *Plagues and Peoples*. Anchor Books.
———. 1982. *The Pursuit of Power*. University of Chicago Press.
Meier, C. 1990. The formation of the alternative in Rome. In Raaflaub and Toher 1990: 54–70.
Mellor, R., ed. 1998. *The Historians of Ancient Rome*. Routledge.
Mengzi 孟子. Shanghai Guji Chubanshe (2004). [*Mencius,* tr. D.C. Lau, Penguin, 1970.]
Millar, F. 1981. *The Roman Empire and Its Neighbours*, 2nd ed. Duckworth.
———. 1992. *The Emperor in the Roman World*, 2nd ed. Duckworth.
———. 1993. *The Roman Near East 31 BC–AD 337*. Harvard University Press.
———. 1998. *The Crowd in Rome in the Late Republic*. University of Michigan Press.
———. 2002a. *The Roman Republic and the Augustan Revolution*. University of North Carolina Press.
———. 2002b. *The Roman Republic in Political Thought*. Brandeis University Press.
———. 2004. *Government, Society, and Culture in the Roman Empire*. University of North Carolina Press.
Millward, J.A. 2007. *Eurasian Crossroads*. Columbia University Press.
Mitchell, S. 2007. *A History of the Later Roman Empire*. Basil Blackwell.
Mittag, A., and F. Mutschler. 2009. Epilogue. In Mutschler and Mittag 2009: 421–447.
Mokyr, J. 1990. *The Lever of Riches*. Oxford University Press.
Molho, A., K.A. Raaflaub, and J. Emlen, eds. 1989. *City States in Classical Antiquity and Medieval Italy*. University of Michigan Press.
Morris, I. 2010. *Why the West Rules—For Now*. Farrar, Straus and Giroux.
Mozi 墨子 [*Mo Tzu*, tr. B. Watson, Columbia University Press, 1963.]
Münkler, H. 2007. *Empires: The Logic of World Domination from Ancient Rome to the United States*. Polity.
Murphy, C. 2007. *Are We Rome?* Houghton Mifflin.
Murray, W., and M. Grimsley. 1994. On strategy. In Murray, Knox, and Bernstein 1994: 1–23.

Murray, W., M. Knox, and A. Bernstein, eds. 1994. *The Making of Strategy*. Cambridge University Press.
Mutschler, F., and A. Mittag, eds. 2009. *Conceiving the Empire: China and Rome Compared*. Oxford University Press.
Narain, A.K. 1990. Indo-Europeans in Inner Asia. In Sinor 1990b: 151–176.
Needham, J., G. Lu, and L. Wang. 1971. *Science and Civilization in China*, vol. 4 part 3, *Civil Engineering and Nautics*. Cambridge University Press.
Needham, J., and R.D.S. Yates. 1994. *Science and Civilization in China*, vol. 5 part 6, *Military Technology: Missiles and Sieges*. Cambridge University Press.
Nicolet, C. 1980. *The World of the Citizen in Republican Rome*. University of California Press.
———. 1993. The citizen: the political man. In Giardina 1993b: 16–54.
Nishijima, S. 1986. The economic and social history of former Han. In Twitchett and Loewe 1986: 551–607.
Nivison, D.S. 1996. *The Ways of Confucianism*. Open Court Press.
———. 1999. The classical philosophical writings. In Loewe and Shaughnessy 1999: 745–812.
North, J.A. 1981. The development of Roman imperialism. *Journal of Roman Studies*, 71: 1–9.
———. 1990. Democratic politics in Republican Rome. *Past and Present* 126: 3–21.
Nye, J. 2002. The New Rome meets the New Barbarians. *Economist*, March 23, 23–25.
———. 2005. *Soft Power: The Means to Succeed in World Politics*. Public Affairs.
Ober, J. 1982. Tiberius and the political testament of Augustus. *Historia* 31: 306–328.
Orend, B. 2006. *The Morality of War*. Broadview Press.
Osgood, J. 2006. *Caesar's Legacy*. Cambridge University Press.
Parker, G. 1996. *The Military Revolution*, 2nd ed. Cambridge University Press.
———. 2005a. The western way of war. In Parker 2005b: 1–14.
———, ed. 2005b. *The Cambridge History of Warfare*. Cambridge University Press.
Parsons, T.H. 2010. *The Rule of Empires*. Oxford University Press.
Patterson, O. 1991. *Freedom*, vol. 1: *Freedom in the Making of Western Culture*. Basic Books.
Peerenboom, R. 2002. *China's Long March Toward Rule of Law*. Cambridge University Press.
Peng Jianying 彭建英. 2004. *Zhongguo Gudai Jimi Zhengce de Yanbian* 中國古代羈縻政策的演變 (The Evolution of the Jimi Policy of Ancient China). Zhongguo Shehui Kexui Chubanshe.
Periplus of the Erythraean Sea. Tr. G.W.B. Huntingford. Hakluyt Society (1980).
Perry, E.J. 1992. Casting a Chinese "democracy" movement. In *Popular Protest and Political Culture in Modern China*, ed. J.N. Wasserstrom and E.J. Perry, 146–164. Westview Press.
Pines, Y. 2002. *Foundations of Confucian Thought*. University of Hawaii Press.
———. 2009a. *Envisioning Eternal Empire*. University of Hawaii Press.
———. 2009b. Imagining the Empire? Concepts of "primeval unity" in pre-imperial historiographic tradition. In Mutschler and Mittag 2009: 67–90.
Pirazzoli-t'Serstevens, M. 1982. *The Han Dynasty*. Rizzoli.

Pitts, J. 2005. *A Turn to Empire*. Princeton University Press.
Pitts, L.F. 1989. Relations between Rome and the German "kings" on the middle Danube in the first to the fourth centuries A.D. *Journal of Roman Studies* 79: 45–58.
Plato. *The Laws*. Tr. T.J. Saunders. Penguin (1970).
Pliny. *Natural History*. Harvard (1938).
Plutarch. *Lives*. Tr. B. Perrin. Harvard (1914).
Pohl E., ed. 1997. *Kingdoms of the Empire*. Brill.
Polybius. *Histories*. Tr. I. Scott-Kilvert. Penguin (1979).
Portal, J., ed. 2007. *The First Emperor*. Harvard University Press.
Potter, D.S. 2004. *The Roman Empire at Bay, A.D. 180–395*. Routledge.
Potter, T.W. 1987. *Roman Italy*. University of California Press.
Ptolemy. *Geography*. Tr. E.L. Stevenson. Dover (1991).
Pulleyblank, E.G. 1958. The origin and nature of chattel slavery in China. *Journal of the Economic and Social History of the Orient* 1: 185–220.
———. 1999. Review: The Roman Empire as known to Han China. *Journal of the American Oriental Society* 119: 71–79.
Purcell, N. 1991. The arts of government. In Boardman et al. 1991: 180–214.
Pye, L.W. 1985. *Asian Power and Politics*. Harvard University Press.
Qian Mu 錢穆. 1940. *Guoshi Dagang* 國史大綱 (An Essential History of China). Taiwan Commercial Press.
———. 1957. *Qinhan Shi* 秦漢史 (History of Qin and Han). Dongda Tushu.
———. 1989. *Guoshi Xinlün*, 國史新論 (New Essays on Chinese History). Dongda Tushu.
———. 2001. *Lianghan Jingxue Jingu Pingyi* 兩漢經學今古平議 (On the New-and-Old Controversy in the Canon Scholarship of the Two Han Dynasties). Taiwan Commercial Press.
Qianfulün 潛夫論 (Essays of a Recluse) by Wang Fu 王符.
Raaflaub, K.A. 1986a. From protection and defense to offense and participation: Stages in the conflict of orders. In Raaflaub 1986b: 198–243.
———, ed. 1986b. *Social Struggles in Archaic Rome*. University of California Press.
———. 2004. *The Discovery of Freedom in Ancient Greece*. University of Chicago Press.
Raaflaub, K.A., and N. Rosenstein, eds. 1999. *War and Society in the Ancient and Medieval Worlds*. Harvard University Press.
Raaflaub, K.A., and L.J. Samons. 1990. Opposition to Augustus. In Raaflaub and Toher 1990: 417–454.
Raaflaub, K.A., and M. Toher, eds. 1990. *Between Republic and Empire*. University of California Press.
Ramsey, J.T., and A.L. Licht. 1997. *The Comet of 44 B.C. and Caesar's Funeral Games*. Scholar Press.
Rathbone, D.W. 1981. The development of agriculture in the "Ager Cosanus" during the Roman Republic. *Journal of Roman Studies* 71: 10–23.
Rawson, E. 1975. *Cicero: A Portrait*. Basic Classical.
Rawson, J. 1999. Western Zhou archeology. In Loewe and Shaughnessy 1999: 352–449.
Reinhold, M. 2002. *Studies in Classical History and Society*. Oxford University Press.
Rhodes, P.J. 2007. Democracy and empire. In *The Cambridge Companion to the Age*

of Pericles, ed. L.J. Samons, 24–45. Cambridge University Press.

Richardson, J.S. 1991. Imperium Romanum: Empire and the language of power. *Journal of Roman Studies* 81: 1–9.

Riddle, J.M., ed. 1970. *Tiberius Gracchus*. Heath.

Romer, J. 2007. *The Great Pyramid: Ancient Egypt Revisited*. Cambridge University Press.

Ropp, P.S., ed. 1990. *Heritage of China*. University of California Press.

Rosenstein, N. 1999. Republican Rome. In Raaflaub and Rosenstein 1999: 193–216.

———. 2009. War, state formation, and the evolution of military institutions in ancient China and Rome. In Scheidel 2009c: 24–51.

Rostovtzeff, M. 1957. *Social and Economic History of the Roman Empire*, 2nd ed. Oxford University Press.

———. 1960. *Rome*. Oxford University Press.

Rüpke, J. 2004. Roman religion. In Flower 2004: 179–198.

Rutledge, S.H. 2001. *Imperial Inquisitions*. Routledge.

Sallust. *Conspiracy of Catiline.* Tr. S.A. Handford. Penguin (1963).

———. *Jugurthine War.* Tr. S.A. Handford. Penguin (1963).

Salmon, E.T. 1982. *The Making of Roman Italy*. Cornell University Press.

Sanguozhi 三國志 (Records of the Three Kingdoms), by Chen Shou 陳壽. Zhonghua Shuju (1959).

Sanguoyanyi 三國演義 (Romance of the Three Kingdoms), by Luo Guanzhong 羅貫中.

Sargent, C.B. 1944. Subsidized history: Pan Ku and the Historical Records of the former Han Dynasty. *Far East Quarterly* 3: 119–143.

Sawyer, R.D. 1993. *The Seven Military Classics of Ancient China*. Westview Press.

———. 2004. *Fire and Water*. Westview.

Scheffler, S., ed. 1988. *Consequentialism and Its Critics*. Oxford University Press.

Scheid, J. 1993. The priest. In Giardina 1993b: 85–99.

Scheidel, W. 2009a. Introduction and From the "great convergence" to the "first great divergence." In Scheidel 2009c: 3–23.

———. 2009b. The monetary systems of the Han and Roman Empires. In Scheidel 2009c: 137–208.

———, ed. 2009c. *Rome and China: Comparative Perspectives on Ancient World Empires*. Oxford University Press.

———. 2012a. Slavery. In Scheidel 2012b: 89–113.

———, ed. 2012b. *The Cambridge Companion to the Roman Economy*. Cambridge University Press.

Schiavone, A. 2000. *The End of the Past*. Harvard University Press.

Schirokauer, C., and R.P. Hymes. 1993. Introduction. In *Ordering the World*, ed. R.P. Hymes and C. Schirokauer, 1–58. University of California Press.

Schumann, R. 1992. *Italy in the Last Fifteen Hundred Years*, 2nd ed. University Press of America.

Schwartz, B.I. 1985. *The World of Thought in Ancient China*. Harvard University Press.

———. 1996. *China and Other Matters*. Harvard University Press.

Scullard, H.H. 1973. *Roman Politics 220–150 B.C.* Greenwood Press.

———. 1976. *From the Gracchi to Nero*. Methuen.

———. 1980. *A History of the Roman World: 753–146 BC*, 4th ed. Routledge.

———. 1989. Carthage and Rome. In Walbank et al. 1989: 486–569.

Seager, R. 1972. *Tiberius*. Basil Blackwell.

———. 2002. *Pompey the Great*. Basil Blackwell.

Sellers, M.N.S. 2004. The Roman Republic and the French and American Revolutions. In Flower 2004: 347–364.

Shangjunshu 商君書. [*The Book of Lord Shang*, tr. J.J.L. Duyvendak, Probsthain, 1928.]

Shangshu 尚書 (*The Book of Documents*). Shanghai Guji Chubanshe (2004).

Shaughnessy, E.L. 1999. Western Zhou history. In Loewe and Shaughnessy 1999: 292–351.

Shaw, B.D. 1984. Bandits in the Roman Empire. *Past and Present* 105: 3–52.

———. 1999. War and violence. In Bowersock et al. 1999: 130–169.

Sherwin-White, A.N. 1957. Caesar as an imperialist. *Greece & Rome* 4: 36–45.

———. 1980. Review: Rome the aggressor? *Journal of Roman Studies* 70: 177–181.

Shiji 史記, by Sima Qian 司馬遷. Zhonghua Shuju (1959). [*Records of the Historian*, tr. B. Watson, Columbia University Press, 1993.]

Shijing 詩經 (*The Odes*). Shanghai Guii Chubanshe (2004). [*The Book of Songs*, tr. A. Waley, Grove Press, 1996.]

Shryock, J.K. 1966. *The Origin and Development of the State Cult of Confucius*. Paragon Book Reprint Corp.

Sinor, D. 1981. The inner Asian warriors. *Journal of the American Oriental Society* 101: 133–141.

———. 1990a. The Hun period. In Sinor 1990b: 177–205.

———, ed. 1990b. *The Cambridge History of Early Inner Asia*. Cambridge University Press.

Skinner, G.W. 1977. Cities and the hierarchy of local systems. In *Studies in Chinese Society*, ed. A.P. Wolf, 1–78. Stanford University Press.

Skocpol, T. 1985. Bringing the state back in: Strategies of analysis in current research. In Evans et al. 1985: 3–43.

Smith, C.B. 2004. *How the Great Pyramid Was Built*. Smithsonian Books.

Song Hongbing 宋洪兵. 2010. *Hannfeizi Zhengzhi Sixiang Zaiyanjiu* 韓非子政治思想再研究 (The Political Thoughts of Hannfeizi Reconsidered). Zhongguo Renmin Daxue Chubanshe.

Southern, P. 1998. *Augustus*. Routledge.

———. 2001. *The Roman Empire from Severus to Constantine*. Routledge.

Starr, C.G. 1982. *The Roman Empire, 27 B.C.–A.D. 476*. Oxford University Press.

———. 1991. *A History of the Ancient World*, 4th ed. Oxford University Press.

Ste. Croix, G.E.M. de. 1981. *The Class Struggle in the Ancient Greek World*. Cornell University Press.

Steadman, L.B., C.T. Palmer, and C.F. Tilley. 1996. The universality of ancestor worship. *Ethnology* 35: 63–76.

Stockton, D. 1991. The founding of the Empire. In Boardman et al. 1991: 146–179.

Stone, L. 1965. *The Crisis of the Aristocracy: 1558–1641*. Abridged ed. Oxford University Press.

Strabo. *Geography*. Tr. H. Jones. Harvard (1948).

Strobe, J.A. 1998. Justification of war in ancient China. *Asian Philosophy* 8(3): 165–181.

Su Junliang 蘇俊良. 2001. *Hanchao Dianzhang Zhidu* 漢朝典章制度 (Institutions of the Han Dynasty). Jiling Wenshi Chubanshe.

Suetonius. *The Twelve Caesars*. Tr. R. Graves. Penguin (1957).

Sunzi Bingfa 孫子兵法 (Master Sun's Art of War). [*The Art of War*, tr. T. Cleary, Shambhala, 2003.]

Swaine, M.D., and A.J. Tellis. 2000. *Interpreting China's Grand Strategy*. RAND.

Swanson, J.A. 1992. *The Public and the Private in Aristotle's Political Philosophy*. Cornell.

Syme, R. 1939. *The Roman Revolution*. Oxford University Press.

———. 1958. *Tacitus*. Oxford University Press.

Taagepera, R. 1979. Size and duration of empires: Growth-decline curves, 600 B.C. to 600 A.D. *Social Science History* 3: 115–138.

Tacitus. *The Annals of Imperial Rome*. Tr. M. Grant. Penguin (1956).

———. *Germania*. Tr. H.W. Bernario. Aris & Phillips (1999).

———. *The Histories*. Tr. W.H. Fyfe. Oxford (1999).

———. *The Life of Agricola*. Tr. A.J. Church and W.J. Brodibb. In Mellor 1998: 394–416.

Taliaferro, J.W., S.E. Lobell, and N.M. Ripsman. 2009. Introduction. In *Neoclassical Realism, The State, and Foreign Policy*, ed. S.E. Lobell, N.M. Ripsman, and J.W. Taliaferro, 1–41. Cambridge University Press.

Tan, S-H. 2002. Between family and state. In Chan 2002: 169–188.

Tan Hong 譚紅. 2006. *Bashu Yimin Shi* 巴蜀移民史 (*A History of Migration in Ba and Shu*). Chengdu Sichuan Publisher.

Tanner, S. 2009. *Afghanistan*, rev. ed. Da Capo.

Taylor, L.R. 1962. Forerunners of the Gracchi. *Journal of Roman Studies* 52: 19–27.

Teggart, F.J. 1939. *China and Rome: A Study of Correlations in Historical Events*. University of California Press.

Temple, R. 1986. *The Genius of China: 3000 Years of Science, Discovery and Invention*. Simon & Schuster.

Thompson, E.A. 1952. Peasant revolts in late Roman Gaul and Spain. *Past and Present* 2: 11–23.

———. 1958. Early Germanic Warfare. *Past and Present* 14: 2–29.

———. 1982. *Romans and Barbarians*. University of Wisconsin Press.

———. 1996. *The Huns*. Basil Blackwell.

Thorley, J. 1971. The silk trade between China and the Roman Empire at its height, circa A.D. 90–130. *Greece & Rome* 18: 71–80.

———. 1981. When was Jesus born? *Greece and Rome* 28: 81–89.

Thucydides. *The Peloponnesian War*. Tr. R. Warner. Penguin (1954).

Tian Changwu and An Zuozhang 田昌五, 安作璋. 2008. *Qinhan Shi* 秦漢史 (History of Qin and Han). Renmin Chubanshe.

Tillman, H.C. 1981. The development of tension between virtue and achievement in early Confucianism. *Philosophy East and West* 31: 17–28.

Tilly, C. 1975. Reflections on the history of European state-making. In *The Formation of National States in Western Europe*, ed. C. Tilly, 3–83. Princeton University Press.

———. 1985. War making and state making as organized crime. In Evans et al. 1985: 169–191.

———. 1990. *Coercion, Capital, and European States*. Basil Blackwell.

Todd, M. 1992. *The Early Germans*. Basil Blackwell.

Tong Shuye 童書業. 2006a. *Chunqiu Shi* 春秋史 (History of the Spring and Autumn Period). Beijing Zhonghua.

———. 2006b. *Chunqiu Zuozhuan Yanjiu* 春秋左傳研究 (Researches on the Zuo Commentary of the Spring and Autumn Annal). Beijing Zhonghua.

Toynbee, A.J. 1957. *A Study of History* (abridged). Dell.

———. 1965. *Hannibal's Legacy.* Oxford University Press.

Tu, W-M, ed. 1996. *Confucian Traditions in East Asian Modernity.* Harvard University Press.

Turner, K. 1990. Sage kings and laws in the Chinese and Greek traditions. In Ropp 1990: 86–111.

———. 1993. War, punishment, and the law of nature in early Chinese concepts of the state. *Harvard Journal of Asiatic Studies* 53: 285–324.

———. 2009. Law and punishment in the formation of empire. In Scheidel 2009c: 52–82.

Twitchett, D., and M. Loewe, eds. 1986. *The Cambridge History of China*, vol. 1, *The Ch'in and Han Empires, 221 B.C.–A.D. 220*. Cambridge University Press.

Ungern-Sternberg, J. von. 1986. The end of the Conflict of the Orders. In Raaflaub 1986b: 353–378.

Vaissière, E. de la. 2004. The rise of Sogdian merchants and the role of the Huns. In *The Silk Road*, ed. S. Whitefield, 19–23. Serindia.

Veyne, P. 1993. *Humanitas: Romans and non-Romans*. In Giardina 1993b: 342–370.

Virgil. *The Aeneid*. Tr. R. Fitzgerald. Vintage (1981).

———. *Georgics.* Tr. P. Fallon. Gallery Books (2004).

Wagner, D.B. 1993. *Iron and Steel in Ancient China*. Brill.

Walbank, F.W. 1970. *Historical Commentary on Polybius*. Oxford University Press.

———. 1981. *The Hellenistic World*. Harvard University Press.

Walbank, F.W., A.E. Astin, M.W. Frederiksen, and R.M. Ogilvie, eds. 1989. *Cambridge Ancient History*, 2nd ed., vol. 7, pt. 2. Cambridge University Press.

Waldron, A. 1990. *The Great Wall of China*. Cambridge University Press.

Walzer, M. 2006. *Just and Unjust Wars*. Basic Books.

Wang Rihua. 2011. Political hegemony in ancient China. In Yan 2011: 181–195.

Wang Ronghai 汪榮海. 2010. *Zhongguo Zhengzhi Sixiangshi Jiujiang* 中國政治思想史九講 (Nine Lectures on the History of Chinese Thoughts). Beijingdaxue Chubanshe.

Wang Xingshan 王興尚. 2011. *Qinguo Zerenlunli Yanjiu* 秦國責任倫理研究 (Research on Qin's Ethics of Responsibility). Renmin Chubanshe.

Wang Wentao 王文濤. 2007. *Qinhan Shehui Baozhang Yanjiu* 秦漢社會保障研究 (Research on Social Security in the Qin and Han). Zhonghua Shuju.

Wang, Z. 1982. *Han Civilization*. Yale University Press.

Wang Zhihuan 王之渙. Liangzhou 涼州詞. In *Tangshi Sanbaishou* 唐詩三百首 (Three Hundred Tang Poems).

Wang Zhonghun 王仲葷. 2003. *Weijin Nanbeichao Shi* 魏晉南北朝史 (History of the Wei, Jin, and North-South Dynasties). Shanghai Renmin.

Wang Zijin王子今. 2006. *Qinhan Shehuishi Lunkao* 秦漢社會史論考 (Essays on the Social History of Qin and Han). Shangwu Yingshuguan.

Ward, A. M. 1977. *Marcus Crassus*. University of Missouri Press.

Ward-Perkins, B. 2005. *The Fall of Rome and the End of Civilization*. Oxford University Press.

Wardman, A.E. 1984. Usurpers and internal conflicts in the 4th century A.D. *Historia* 33: 220–237.

Wellesley, K. 1975. *The Long Year A.D. 69*. Westview Press.

Wells, C. 1992. *The Roman Empire*, 2nd ed. Harvard University Press.

Weng Dujian 翁獨健. 2001. *Zhongguo Minzu Guanxi Shi Gangyao* 中國民族關系史綱要 (Essentials of the History of Chinese National Relations). Zhongguo Shehui Kexue Chubanshe.

Wheeler, E. 1993. Methodological limits and the mirage of Roman strategy. *Journal of Military History* 57: 7–41, 215–240.

Whitefield, S. ed. 2004. *The Silk Road: trade, travel, war and faith*. Serindia.

Whitehead, D. 1989. Norms of citizenship in ancient Greece. In Molho et al. 1989: 135–154.

Whittaker, C.R. 1978. Carthaginian imperialism in the fifth and fourth centuries. In Garnsey and Whittaker 1978: 59–90.

———. 1994. *Frontiers of the Roman Empire*. Johns Hopkins University Press.

Whittaker, C.R., and P. Garnsey. 1998. Rural life in the Later Roman Empire. In Cameron and Garnsey 1998: 277–311.

Wickersham, J. 1994. *Hegemony and Greek Historians*. Rowman and Littlefield.

Wickham, C. 2010. *The Inheritance of Rome*. Penguin.

Wiedemann, T. 1981. *Greek and Roman Slavery*. Johns Hopkins University Press.

———. 2000. Reflections of Roman political thought in Latin historical writing. In *The Cambridge History of Greek and Roman Political Thought*, ed. C. Rowe and M. Schofield, 517–531. Cambridge University Press.

Wilbur, C.M. 1943. *Slavery in China during the Former Han Dynasty*. University of Chicago Press.

Wilkinson, E. 1998. *Chinese History: A Manual*. Harvard University Asia Center.

Wirszubski, C. 1960. *Libertas as a Political Idea at Rome During the Late Republic and Early Principate*. Cambridge University Press.

Wong, R.B. 1997. *China Transformed*. Cornell University Press.

Wood, N. 1988. *Cicero's Social and Political Thought*. University of California Press.

Wuzi Bingfa 吳子兵法 (*Master Wu's Art of War*). [Translation in Chapter 4 of Sawyer 1993.]

Xu Fuguan 徐復觀. 1985. *Lianghan Sixiangshi* 兩漢思想史 (History of Thought for the Two Hans), 3rd ed. Xuesheng Shuju.

Xu Xiangmin and Hu Shikai 徐祥民 , 胡世凱. 2000. *Zhongguo Fazhishi* 中國法制史 (History of Chinese Legal Systems). Shangdong Renmin Chubanshe.

Xu, J. 2011. The two poles of Confucianism. In Yan 2011: 161–180.

Xunzi 荀子 (*Master Xun*). [*Xunzi*, tr. J. Knoblock, Stanford University Press, 1994.]

Yan Buke 閻步克. 1996. *Shidafu Zhengzhi Yansheng Shigao* 士大夫政治演生史稿 (Toward a History of the Political Life of Shidafu). Beijing Dawue Chubanshe.

Yan, X. 2011. *Ancient Chinese Thought, Modern Chinese Power*. Princeton University Press.

Yang Hongnian and Ouyang Xin楊鴻年, 歐陽鑫. 2005. *Zhongguo Zhengzhishi* 中國政制史 (History of Chinese Political Systems), rev. ed. Wuhan Dixue Chubanshe.

Yang Kuan 楊寬. 2003a. *Xizhou Shi* 西周史 (History of Western Zhou). Shanghai Renmin.

———. 2003b. *Zhanguo Shi* 戰國史 (History of the Warring States). Shanghai Renmin.

———. 2006. *Zhongguo Gudai Ducheng Zhidushi* 中國古代都城制度史 (A History of Ancient Chinese City Systems). Shanghai Renmin.

Yang, H., and F. Mutschler. 2009. The emergence of empire: Rome and the surrounding world in historical narratives from the late third century BC to the early first century AD. In Mutschler and Mittag 2009: 91–114.

Yang, L-S. 1968. Historical notes on the Chinese world order. In *The Chinese World Order*, ed. J.K. Fairbank, Harvard University Press. 20–33.

Yantielun 鹽鐵論 (*Discourse on Salt and Iron*), ed. Huan Kuan 桓寬.

Yates, R.D.S. 1987. Social Status in the Ch'in. *Harvard Journal of Asiatic Studies* 47: 197–237.

———. 1999. Early China. In Raaflaub and Rosenstein 1999: 7–46.

Ye Zhiheng 葉志衡. 2007. *Zhanguo Xueshu Wenhua Biannian* 戰國學術文化編年 (Chronology of Warring States Learning and Culture). Zhejiang University Press.

Young, G.K. 2001. *Rome's Eastern Trade*. Routledge.

Yu Yingchun 于迎春. 2000. *Qinhan Shishi* 秦漢士史 (History of the *Shi* in the Qin and Han). Beijing Daxue Chubanshe.

Yü Yingshi 余英時. 2003. *Shi yu Zhongguo Wenhua* 士與中國文化 (*Shi* and the Chinese Civilization). Shanghai Renmin.

Yu, J. 2007. *The Ethics of Confucius and Aristotle*. Routledge.

Yü, Y-S. 1967. *Trade and Expansion in Han China*. University of California Press.

———. 1986. Han foreign relations. In Twitchett and Loewe 1986: 377–462.

———. 1990. The Hsiung-nu. In Sinor 1990b: 118–146.

Zhang Canhui 張燦輝. 2008. *Lianghan Weijin Liangzhou Zhengzhishi Yanjiu* 兩漢魏晉涼州政治史研究 (Research on the Political History of Liangzhou during the Han, Wei, and Jin Dynasties). Yuelushushe.

Zhang Fengtian 張分田. 2003. *Qinshihuang Zhuan* 秦始皇傳 (The First Emperor). Taiwan Shangwu Yinshuguan.

Zhang Xiaofeng 張小鋒. 2007. *Xihan Zhonghouqi Zhengju Yanbian Tanwei* 西漢中後期政局演變探微 (Inquiry into Political Changes in Middle and Late Western Han.) Tianjin Gushi.

Zhanguoce 戰國策 (Stratagems of the Warring States). [*Chan-kuo Ts'e*, tr. J.I. Crump, University of Michigan Press, 1996.]

Zhao Gang 趙岡. 2006. *Zhongguo Chengshi Fazhanshi Lunji* 中國城市發展史論集 (Essays on the History of Chinese Urban Development). Beijing: New Star Press.

Zhongyong 中庸 (The Mean).

Zhou Yiliang 周一良. 1997. *Weijin Nanbeichao Shilunji* 魏晉南北朝史論合集 (Essays on the History of the Wei, Jin, and North-South Dynasties). Beijing Daxue Chubanshe.

Zhouyi 周易 (The Book of Change). Shanghai Guji Chubanshe (2004). [*I Ching: The Book of Change*, tr. J. Blofeld. Dutton, 1965.]

Zhu Zhongxi 祝中熹. 2004. *Zaoqi Qinshi* 早期秦史 (History of Early Qin). Dunhuang Wenyi Chubanshe.

Zhuangzi 莊子. [*Chuang-tzü*, tr. A.C. Graham, George Allen and Unwin 1981.]

Zizhi Tongjian 資治通鑑 (General Mirrors for Aid in Government), by Sima Guang 司馬光. Zhonghua Shuju (1956).

Zuozhuan 左傳 (Zuo Commentaries to the Spring and Autumn Annals). Shanghai Guji Chubanshe (2004).

INDEX

Note: Page numbers in italics indicate illustrations.

Many Chinese logograms are homophonic. To avoid major confusion, I have varied a few transliterations from the standard Pinyin. In such cases, the standard transliteration is provided in parenthesis.

Q

S

ABOUT THE AUTHOR

Sunny Auyang 歐陽瑩之 was born in China and came to the United States to attend college and received her PhD in physics from Massachusetts Institute of Technology, where she worked for twenty years. After retirement, she turned to research in the history and philosophy of science, from economics to cognitive science, on which she has published four books. A profuse reader, she works alone to maintain her independence of mind and pursue cross-disciplinary topics. For the past ten years, she has devoted her energy to studying world history.